Applied Missing Data Analysis

# Methodology in the Social Sciences
David A. Kenny, Founding Editor
Todd D. Little, Series Editor

This series provides applied researchers and students with analysis and research design books that emphasize the use of methods to answer research questions. Rather than emphasizing statistical theory, each volume in the series illustrates when a technique should (and should not) be used and how the output from available software programs should (and should not) be interpreted. Common pitfalls as well as areas of further development are clearly articulated.

SPECTRAL ANALYSIS OF TIME-SERIES DATA
  *Rebecca M. Warner*

A PRIMER ON REGRESSION ARTIFACTS
  *Donald T. Campbell and David A. Kenny*

REGRESSION ANALYSIS FOR CATEGORICAL MODERATORS
  *Herman Aguinis*

HOW TO CONDUCT BEHAVIORAL RESEARCH OVER THE INTERNET:
A Beginner's Guide to HTML and CGI/Perl
  *R. Chris Fraley*

CONFIRMATORY FACTOR ANALYSIS FOR APPLIED RESEARCH
  *Timothy A. Brown*

DYADIC DATA ANALYSIS
  *David A. Kenny, Deborah A. Kashy, and William L. Cook*

MISSING DATA: A Gentle Introduction
  *Patrick E. McKnight, Katherine M. McKnight, Souraya Sidani, and Aurelio José Figueredo*

MULTILEVEL ANALYSIS FOR APPLIED RESEARCH: It's Just Regression!
  *Robert Bickel*

THE THEORY AND PRACTICE OF ITEM RESPONSE THEORY
  *R. J. de Ayala*

THEORY CONSTRUCTION AND MODEL-BUILDING SKILLS:
A Practical Guide for Social Scientists
  *James Jaccard and Jacob Jacoby*

DIAGNOSTIC MEASUREMENT: Theory, Methods, and Applications
  *André A. Rupp, Jonathan Templin, and Robert A. Henson*

APPLIED MISSING DATA ANALYSIS
  *Craig K. Enders*

# APPLIED MISSING DATA ANALYSIS

Craig K. Enders

*Series Editor's Note by Todd D. Little*

## THE GUILFORD PRESS
New York   London

© 2010 The Guilford Press
A Division of Guilford Publications, Inc.
72 Spring Street, New York, NY 10012
www.guilford.com

Printed in the United States of America

This book is printed on acid-free paper.

Last digit is print number:   9   8   7   6   5   4   3   2   1

**Library of Congress Cataloging-in-Publication Data**

Enders, Craig K.
   Applied missing data analysis / Craig K. Enders.
      p.  cm. — (Methodology in the social sciences)
   Includes bibliographical references and index.
   ISBN 978-1-60623-639-0 (hardcover : alk. paper)
   1. Social sciences—Statistical methods. 2. Missing observations (Statistics) 3. Social
sciences—Research—Methodology.  I. Title.
   HA29.E497   2010
   300.1′5195—dc22                                                  2010008465

# Series Editor's Note

Missing data are a real bane to researchers across all social science disciplines. For most of our scientific history, we have approached missing data much like a doctor from the ancient world might use bloodletting to cure disease or amputation to stem infection (e.g, removing the infected parts of one's data by using list-wise or pair-wise deletion). My metaphor should make you feel a bit squeamish, just as you should feel if you deal with missing data using the antediluvian and ill-advised approaches of old. Fortunately, Craig Enders is a gifted quantitative specialist who can clearly explain missing data procedures to diverse readers from beginners to seasoned veterans. He brings us into the age of modern missing data treatments by demystifying the arcane discussions of missing data mechanisms and their labels (e.g., MNAR) and the esoteric acronyms of the various techniques used to address them (e.g., FIML, MCMC, and the like).

Enders's approachable treatise provides a comprehensive treatment of the causes of missing data and how best to address them. He clarifies the principles by which various mechanisms of missing data can be recovered, and he provides expert guidance on which method to implement and how to execute it, and what to report about the modern approach you have chosen. Enders's deft balancing of practical guidance with expert insight is refreshing and enlightening. It is rare to find a book on quantitative methods that you can read for its stated purpose (educating the reader about modern missing data procedures) and find that it treats you to a level of insight on a topic that whole books dedicated to the topic cannot match. For example, Enders's discussions of maximum likelihood and Bayesian estimation procedures are the clearest, most understandable, and instructive discussions I have read—your inner geek will be delighted, really.

Enders successfully translates the state-of-the art technical missing data literature into an accessible reference that you can readily rely on and use. Among the treasures of Enders's work are the pointed simulations that he has developed to show you exactly what the technical literature obtusely presents. Because he provides such careful guidance of the foundations and the step-by-step processes involved, you will quickly master the concepts and issues of this critical literature. Another treasure is his use of a common running example that he builds upon as more complex issues are presented. And if these features are not enough, you can also visit the accompanying website (*www.appliedmissingdata.com*), where you will find up-to-date program files for the examples presented, as well as additional examples of the different software programs available for handling missing data.

What you will learn from this book is that missing data imputation is not cheating. In fact, you will learn why the egregious scientific error would be the business-as-usual approaches that still permeate our journals. You will learn that modern missing data procedures are so effective that intentionally missing data designs often can provide more valid and generalizable results than traditional data collection protocols. In addition, you will learn to rethink how you collect data to maximize your ability to recover any missing data mechanisms and that many quandaries of design and analysis become resolvable when recast as a missing data problem. Bottom line—after you read this book you will have learned how to go forth and impute with impunity!

TODD D. LITTLE
*University of Kansas*
*Lawrence, Kansas*

# Preface

Methodologists have been studying missing data problems for the better part of a century, and the number of published articles on this topic has increased dramatically in recent years. A great deal of recent methodological research has focused on two "state-of-the-art" missing data methods: maximum likelihood and multiple imputation. Accordingly, this book is devoted largely to these techniques. Quoted in the American Psychological Association's *Monitor on Psychology*, Stephen G. West, former editor of *Psychological Methods,* stated that "routine implementation of these new methods of addressing missing data will be one of the major changes in research over the next decade" (Azar, 2002). Although researchers are using maximum likelihood and multiple imputation with greater frequency, reviews of published articles in substantive journals suggest that a gap still exists between the procedures that the methodological literature recommends and those that are actually used in the applied research studies (Bodner, 2006; Peugh & Enders, 2004; Wood, White, & Thompson, 2004).

It is understandable that researchers routinely employ missing data handling techniques that are objectionable to methodologists. Software packages make old standby techniques (e.g., eliminating incomplete cases) very convenient to implement. The fact that software programs routinely implement default procedures that are prone to substantial bias, however, is troubling because such routines implicitly send the wrong message to researchers interested in using statistics without having to keep up with the latest advances in the missing data literature. The technical nature of the missing data literature is also a significant barrier to the widespread adoption of maximum likelihood and multiple imputation. While many of the flawed missing data handling techniques (e.g., excluding cases, replacing missing values with the mean) are very easy to understand, the newer approaches can seem like voodoo. For example, researchers often appear perplexed by the possibility of conducting an analysis without discarding cases and without filling in the missing values—and rightfully so. The seminal books on missing data analyses (Little & Rubin, 2002; Schafer, 1997) are rich sources of technical information, but these books can be a daunting read for substantive researchers and methodologists alike. In large part, the purpose of this book is to "translate" the technical missing data literature into an accessible reference text.

Because missing data are a pervasive problem in virtually any discipline that employs quantitative research methods, my goal was to write a book that would be relevant and accessible to researchers from a wide range of disciplines, including psychology, education, sociology, business, and medicine. For me, it is important for the book to serve as an accessible reference for substantive researchers who use quantitative methods in their work but do not consider themselves quantitative specialists. At the same time, many quantitative methodologists are unfamiliar with the nuances of modern missing data handling techniques. Therefore, it was also important to provide a level of detail that could serve as a springboard for accessing technically oriented missing data books such as Little and Rubin (2002) and Schafer (1997). Most of the information in this book assumes that readers have taken graduate-level courses in analysis of variance (ANOVA) and multiple regression. Some basic understanding of structural equation modeling (e.g., the interpretation of path diagrams) is also useful, as is cursory knowledge of matrix algebra and calculus. However, it is vitally important to me that this book be accessible to a broad range of readers, so I constantly strove to translate key mathematical concepts into plain English.

The chapters in this book roughly break down into four sections. The first two chapters provide a backdrop for modern missing data handling methods by describing missing data theory and traditional analysis approaches. Given the emphasis that maximum likelihood estimation and multiple imputation have received in the methodological literature, the majority of the book is devoted to these topics; Chapters 3 through 5 address maximum likelihood, and Chapters 6 through 9 cover multiple imputation. Finally, Chapter 10 describes models for an especially problematic type of missingness known as "missing not at random data." Throughout the book, I use small data sets to illustrate the underlying mechanics of the missing data handling procedures, and the chapters typically conclude with a number of analysis examples.

The level with which to integrate specific software programs was an issue that presented me with a dilemma throughout the writing process. In the end, I chose to make the analysis examples independent of any program. In the 2 years that it took to write this book, software programs have undergone dramatic improvements in the number of and type of missing data analyses they can perform. For example, structural equation modeling programs have greatly expanded their missing data handling options, and one of the major general-use statistical software programs—SPSS—implemented a multiple imputation routine. Because software programs are likely to evolve at a rapid pace in the coming years, I decided to use a website to maintain an up-to-date set of program files for the analysis examples that I present in the book at *www.appliedmissingdata.com*. Although I relegate a portion of the final chapter to a brief description of software programs, I tend to make generic references to "software packages" throughout much of the book and do not mention specific programs by name.

Finally, I have a long list of people to thank. First, I would like to thank the baristas at the Coffee Plantation in North Scottsdale for allowing me to spend countless hours in their coffee shop working on the book. Second, I would like to thank the students in my 2008 missing data course at Arizona State University for providing valuable feedback on draft chapters, including Krista Adams, Margarita Olivera Aguilar, Amanda Baraldi, Iris Beltran, Matt DiDonato, Priscilla Goble, Amanda Gottschall, Caitlin O'Brien, Vanessa Ohlrich, Kassondra

Silva, Michael Sulik, Jodi Swanson, Ian Villalta, Katie Zeiders, and Argero Zerr. Third, I am also grateful to a number of other individuals who provided feedback on draft chapters, including Carol Barry, Sara Finney, Megan France, Jeanne Horst, Mary Johnston, Abigail Lau, Levi Littvay, and James Peugh; and the Guilford reviewers: Julia McQuillan, Sociology, University of Nebraska, Lincoln; Ke-Hai Yuan, Psychology, University of Notre Dame; Alan Acock, Family Science, Oregon State University; David R. Johnson, Sociology, Pennsylvania State University; Kristopher J. Preacher, Psychology, University of Kansas; Zhiyong Johnny Zhang, University of Notre Dame; Hakan Demirtas, Biostatistics, University of Illinois, Chicago; Stephen DuToit, Scientific Software; and Scott Hofer, Psychology, University of Victoria. In particular, Roy Levy's input on the Bayesian estimation chapter was a godsend. Thanks also to Tihomir Asparouhov, Bengt Muthén, and Linda Muthén for their feedback and assistance with Mplus. Fourth, I would like to thank my quantitative colleagues in the Psychology Department at Arizona State University. Collectively, Leona Aiken, Sanford Braver, Dave MacKinnon, Roger Millsap, and Steve West are the best group of colleagues anyone could ask for, and their support and guidance has meant a great deal to me. Fifth, I want to express gratitude to Todd Little and C. Deborah Laughton for their guidance throughout the writing process. Todd's expertise as a methodologist and as an editor was invaluable, and I am convinced that C. Deborah is unmatched in her expertise. Sixth, I would like to thank all of my mentors from the University of Nebraska, including Cal Garbin, Jim Impara, Barbara Plake, Ellen Weissinger, and Steve Wise. I learned a great deal from each of these individuals, and their influences flow through this book. In particular, I owe an enormous debt of gratitude to my advisor, Deborah Bandalos. Debbi has had an enormous impact on my academic career, and her continued friendship and support mean a great deal to me. Finally, I would like to thank my mother, Billie Enders. Simply put, without her guidance, none of this would have been possible.

# Contents

**1 • An Introduction to Missing Data**                                        1

1.1   Introduction      1
1.2   Chapter Overview      2
1.3   Missing Data Patterns      2
1.4   A Conceptual Overview of Missing Data Theory      5
1.5   A More Formal Description of Missing Data Theory      9
1.6   Why Is the Missing Data Mechanism Important?      13
1.7   How Plausible Is the Missing at Random Mechanism?      14
1.8   An Inclusive Analysis Strategy      16
1.9   Testing the Missing Completely at Random Mechanism      17
1.10  Planned Missing Data Designs      21
1.11  The Three-Form Design      23
1.12  Planned Missing Data for Longitudinal Designs      28
1.13  Conducting Power Analyses for Planned Missing Data Designs      30
1.14  Data Analysis Example      32
1.15  Summary      35
1.16  Recommended Readings      36

**2 • Traditional Methods for Dealing with Missing Data**                      37

2.1   Chapter Overview      37
2.2   An Overview of Deletion Methods      39
2.3   Listwise Deletion      39
2.4   Pairwise Deletion      40
2.5   An Overview of Single Imputation Methods      42
2.6   Arithmetic Mean Imputation      42
2.7   Regression Imputation      44
2.8   Stochastic Regression Imputation      46
2.9   Hot-Deck Imputation      49
2.10  Similar Response Pattern Imputation      49
2.11  Averaging the Available Items      50
2.12  Last Observation Carried Forward      51
2.13  An Illustrative Computer Simulation Study      52

2.14  Summary     54
2.15  Recommended Readings     55

## 3 • An Introduction to Maximum Likelihood Estimation     56

3.1   Chapter Overview     56
3.2   The Univariate Normal Distribution     56
3.3   The Sample Likelihood     59
3.4   The Log-Likelihood     60
3.5   Estimating Unknown Parameters     60
3.6   The Role of First Derivatives     63
3.7   Estimating Standard Errors     65
3.8   Maximum Likelihood Estimation with Multivariate Normal Data     69
3.9   A Bivariate Analysis Example     73
3.10  Iterative Optimization Algorithms     75
3.11  Significance Testing Using the Wald Statistic     77
3.12  The Likelihood Ratio Test Statistic     78
3.13  Should I Use the Wald Test or the Likelihood Ratio Statistic?     79
3.14  Data Analysis Example 1     80
3.15  Data Analysis Example 2     81
3.16  Summary     83
3.17  Recommended Readings     85

## 4 • Maximum Likelihood Missing Data Handling     86

4.1   Chapter Overview     86
4.2   The Missing Data Log-Likelihood     88
4.3   How Do the Incomplete Data Records Improve Estimation?     92
4.4   An Illustrative Computer Simulation Study     95
4.5   Estimating Standard Errors with Missing Data     97
4.6   Observed versus Expected Information     98
4.7   A Bivariate Analysis Example     99
4.8   An Illustrative Computer Simulation Study     102
4.9   An Overview of the EM Algorithm     103
4.10  A Detailed Description of the EM Algorithm     105
4.11  A Bivariate Analysis Example     106
4.12  Extending EM to Multivariate Data     110
4.13  Maximum Likelihood Estimation Software Options     112
4.14  Data Analysis Example 1     113
4.15  Data Analysis Example 2     115
4.16  Data Analysis Example 3     118
4.17  Data Analysis Example 4     119
4.18  Data Analysis Example 5     122
4.19  Summary     125
4.20  Recommended Readings     126

## 5 • Improving the Accuracy of
## Maximum Likelihood Analyses     127

5.1   Chapter Overview     127
5.2   The Rationale for an Inclusive Analysis Strategy     127
5.3   An Illustrative Computer Simulation Study     129
5.4   Identifying a Set of Auxiliary Variables     131

5.5    Incorporating Auxiliary Variables into a Maximum Likelihood Analysis    133
5.6    The Saturated Correlates Model    134
5.7    The Impact of Non-Normal Data    140
5.8    Robust Standard Errors    141
5.9    Bootstrap Standard Errors    145
5.10   The Rescaled Likelihood Ratio Test    148
5.11   Bootstrapping the Likelihood Ratio Statistic    150
5.12   Data Analysis Example 1    154
5.13   Data Analysis Example 2    155
5.14   Data Analysis Example 3    157
5.15   Summary    161
5.16   Recommended Readings    163

## 6 • An Introduction to Bayesian Estimation

6.1    Chapter Overview    164
6.2    What Makes Bayesian Statistics Different?    165
6.3    A Conceptual Overview of Bayesian Estimation    165
6.4    Bayes' Theorem    170
6.5    An Analysis Example    171
6.6    How Does Bayesian Estimation Apply to Multiple Imputation?    175
6.7    The Posterior Distribution of the Mean    176
6.8    The Posterior Distribution of the Variance    179
6.9    The Posterior Distribution of a Covariance Matrix    183
6.10   Summary    185
6.11   Recommended Readings    186

## 7 • The Imputation Phase of Multiple Imputation

7.1    Chapter Overview    187
7.2    A Conceptual Description of the Imputation Phase    190
7.3    A Bayesian Description of the Imputation Phase    191
7.4    A Bivariate Analysis Example    194
7.5    Data Augmentation with Multivariate Data    199
7.6    Selecting Variables for Imputation    201
7.7    The Meaning of Convergence    202
7.8    Convergence Diagnostics    203
7.9    Time-Series Plots    204
7.10   Autocorrelation Function Plots    207
7.11   Assessing Convergence from Alternate Starting Values    209
7.12   Convergence Problems    210
7.13   Generating the Final Set of Imputations    211
7.14   How Many Data Sets Are Needed?    212
7.15   Summary    214
7.16   Recommended Readings    216

## 8 • The Analysis and Pooling Phases of Multiple Imputation

8.1    Chapter Overview    217
8.2    The Analysis Phase    218
8.3    Combining Parameter Estimates in the Pooling Phase    219
8.4    Transforming Parameter Estimates Prior to Combining    220

8.5    Pooling Standard Errors    221
8.6    The Fraction of Missing Information and the Relative Increase in Variance    224
8.7    When Is Multiple Imputation Comparable to Maximum Likelihood?    227
8.8    An Illustrative Computer Simulation Study    229
8.9    Significance Testing Using the $t$ Statistic    230
8.10    An Overview of Multiparameter Significance Tests    233
8.11    Testing Multiple Parameters Using the $D_1$ Statistic    233
8.12    Testing Multiple Parameters by Combining Wald Tests    239
8.13    Testing Multiple Parameters by Combining Likelihood Ratio Statistics    240
8.14    Data Analysis Example 1    242
8.15    Data Analysis Example 2    245
8.16    Data Analysis Example 3    247
8.17    Summary    252
8.18    Recommended Readings    252

## 9 • Practical Issues in Multiple Imputation    254

9.1    Chapter Overview    254
9.2    Dealing with Convergence Problems    254
9.3    Dealing with Non-Normal Data    259
9.4    To Round or Not to Round?    261
9.5    Preserving Interaction Effects    265
9.6    Imputing Multiple-Item Questionnaires    269
9.7    Alternate Imputation Algorithms    272
9.8    Multiple-Imputation Software Options    278
9.9    Data Analysis Example 1    279
9.10    Data Analysis Example 2    281
9.11    Summary    283
9.12    Recommended Readings    286

## 10 • Models for Missing Not at Random Data    287

10.1    Chapter Overview    287
10.2    An Ad Hoc Approach to Dealing with MNAR Data    289
10.3    The Theoretical Rationale for MNAR Models    290
10.4    The Classic Selection Model    291
10.5    Estimating the Selection Model    295
10.6    Limitations of the Selection Model    296
10.7    An Illustrative Analysis    297
10.8    The Pattern Mixture Model    298
10.9    Limitations of the Pattern Mixture Model    300
10.10    An Overview of the Longitudinal Growth Model    301
10.11    A Longitudinal Selection Model    303
10.12    Random Coefficient Selection Models    305
10.13    Pattern Mixture Models for Longitudinal Analyses    306
10.14    Identification Strategies for Longitudinal Pattern Mixture Models    307
10.15    Delta Method Standard Errors    309
10.16    Overview of the Data Analysis Examples    312
10.17    Data Analysis Example 1    314
10.18    Data Analysis Example 2    315
10.19    Data Analysis Example 3    317
10.20    Data Analysis Example 4    321
10.21    Summary    326
10.22    Recommended Readings    328

## 11 • Wrapping Things Up: Some Final Practical Considerations    329

11.1  Chapter Overview    329
11.2  Maximum Likelihood Software Options    329
11.3  Multiple-Imputation Software Options    333
11.4  Choosing between Maximum Likelihood and Multiple Imputation    336
11.5  Reporting the Results from a Missing Data Analysis    340
11.6  Final Thoughts    343
11.7  Recommended Readings    344

**References**    347
**Author Index**    359
**Subject Index**    365
**About the Author**    377

The companion website (*www.appliedmissingdata.com*) includes data files and syntax for the examples in the book, as well as up-to-date information on software.

# Applied Missing Data Analysis

# 1

# An Introduction to Missing Data

## 1.1 INTRODUCTION

Missing data are ubiquitous throughout the social, behavioral, and medical sciences. For decades, researchers have relied on a variety of ad hoc techniques that attempt to "fix" the data by discarding incomplete cases or by filling in the missing values. Unfortunately, most of these techniques require a relatively strict assumption about the cause of missing data and are prone to substantial bias. These methods have increasingly fallen out of favor in the methodological literature (Little & Rubin, 2002; Wilkinson & Task Force on Statistical Inference, 1999), but they continue to enjoy widespread use in published research articles (Bodner, 2006; Peugh & Enders, 2004).

Methodologists have been studying missing data problems for nearly a century, but the major breakthroughs came in the 1970s with the advent of maximum likelihood estimation routines and multiple imputation (Beale & Little, 1975; Dempster, Laird, & Rubin, 1977; Rubin, 1978b; Rubin, 1987). At about the same time, Rubin (1976) outlined a theoretical framework for missing data problems that remains in widespread use today. Maximum likelihood and multiple imputation have received considerable attention in the methodological literature during the past 30 years, and researchers generally regard these approaches as the current "state of the art" (Schafer & Graham, 2002). Relative to traditional approaches, maximum likelihood and multiple imputation are theoretically appealing because they require weaker assumptions about the cause of missing data. From a practical standpoint, this means that these techniques will produce parameter estimates with less bias and greater power.

Researchers have been relatively slow to adopt maximum likelihood and multiple imputation and still rely heavily on traditional missing data handling techniques (Bodner, 2006; Peugh & Enders, 2004). In part, this hesitancy may be due to a lack of software options, as maximum likelihood and multiple imputation did not become widely available in statistical packages until the late 1990s. However, the technical nature of the missing data literature probably represents another significant barrier to the widespread adoption of these techniques. Consequently, the primary goal of this book is to provide an accessible and user-friendly introduction to missing data analyses, with a special emphasis on maximum likelihood and

1

multiple imputation. It is my hope that this book will help address the gap that currently exists between the analytic approaches that methodologists recommend and those that appear in published research articles.

## 1.2 CHAPTER OVERVIEW

This chapter describes some of the fundamental concepts that appear repeatedly throughout the book. In particular, the first half of the chapter is devoted to missing data theory, as described by Rubin (1976) and colleagues (Little & Rubin, 2002). Rubin is responsible for establishing a nearly universal classification system for missing data problems. These so-called missing data mechanisms describe relationships between measured variables and the probability of missing data and essentially function as assumptions for missing data analyses. Rubin's mechanisms serve as a vital foundation for the remainder of the book because they provide a basis for understanding why different missing data techniques succeed or fail.

The second half of this chapter introduces the idea of planned missing data. Researchers tend to believe that missing data are a nuisance to be avoided whenever possible. It is true that unplanned missing data are potentially damaging to the validity of a statistical analysis. However, Rubin's (1976) theory describes situations where missing data are relatively benign. Researchers have exploited this fact and have developed research designs that produce missing data as an intentional by-product of data collection. The idea of intentional missing data might seem odd at first, but these research designs actually solve a number of practical problems (e.g., reducing respondent burden and reducing the cost of data collection). When used in conjunction with maximum likelihood and multiple imputation, these planned missing data designs provide a powerful tool for streamlining and reducing the cost of data collection.

I use the small data set in Table 1.1 to illustrate ideas throughout this chapter. I designed these data to mimic an employee selection scenario in which prospective employees complete an IQ test and a psychological well-being questionnaire during their interview. The company subsequently hires the applicants who score in the upper half of the IQ distribution, and a supervisor rates their job performance following a 6-month probationary period. Note that the job performance scores are systematically missing as a function of IQ scores (i.e., individuals in the lower half of the IQ distribution were never hired, and thus have no performance rating). In addition, I randomly deleted three of the well-being scores in order to mimic a situation where the applicant's well-being questionnaire is inadvertently lost.

## 1.3 MISSING DATA PATTERNS

As a starting point, it is useful to distinguish between missing data patterns and missing data mechanisms. These terms actually have very different meanings, but researchers sometimes use them interchangeably. A **missing data pattern** refers to the configuration of observed and missing values in a data set, whereas **missing data mechanisms** describe possible relationships between measured variables and the probability of missing data. Note that a missing

**TABLE 1.1. Employee Selection Data Set**

| IQ | Psychological well-being | Job performance |
|---|---|---|
| 78 | 13 | — |
| 84 | 9 | — |
| 84 | 10 | — |
| 85 | 10 | — |
| 87 | — | — |
| 91 | 3 | — |
| 92 | 12 | — |
| 94 | 3 | — |
| 94 | 13 | — |
| 96 | — | — |
| 99 | 6 | 7 |
| 105 | 12 | 10 |
| 105 | 14 | 11 |
| 106 | 10 | 15 |
| 108 | — | 10 |
| 112 | 10 | 10 |
| 113 | 14 | 12 |
| 115 | 14 | 14 |
| 118 | 12 | 16 |
| 134 | 11 | 12 |

data pattern simply describes the location of the "holes" in the data and does not explain why the data are missing. Although the missing data mechanisms do not offer a causal explanation for the missing data, they do represent generic mathematical relationships between the data and missingness (e.g., in a survey design, there may be a systematic relationship between education level and the propensity for missing data). Missing data mechanisms play a vital role in Rubin's missing data theory.

Figure 1.1 shows six prototypical missing data patterns that you may encounter in the missing data literature, with the shaded areas representing the location of the missing values in the data set. The **univariate pattern** in panel A has missing values isolated to a single variable. A univariate pattern is relatively rare in some disciplines but can arise in experimental studies. For example, suppose that $Y_1$ through $Y_3$ are manipulated variables (e.g., between-subjects factors in an ANOVA design) and $Y_4$ is the incomplete outcome variable. The univariate pattern is one of the earliest missing data problems to receive attention in the statistics literature, and a number of classic articles are devoted to this topic.

Panel B shows a configuration of missing values known as a **unit nonresponse pattern**. This pattern often occurs in survey research, where $Y_1$ and $Y_2$ are characteristics that are available for every member of the sampling frame (e.g., census tract data), and $Y_3$ and $Y_4$ are surveys that some respondents refuse to answer. Later in the book I describe a planned missing data design that yields a similar pattern of missing data. In the context of planned missingness, this pattern can arise when a researcher administers two inexpensive measures to the entire sample (e.g., $Y_1$ and $Y_2$) and collects two expensive measures (e.g., $Y_3$ and $Y_4$) from a subset of cases.

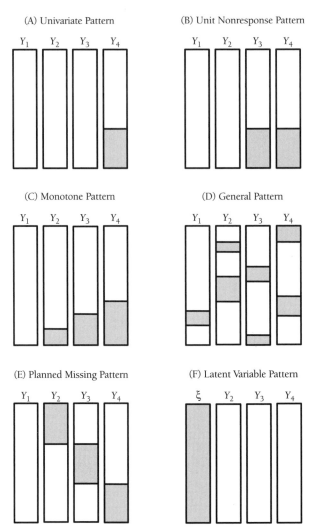

**FIGURE 1.1.** Six prototypical missing data patterns. The shaded areas represent the location of the missing values in the data set with four variables.

A **monotone missing data pattern** in panel C is typically associated with a longitudinal study where participants drop out and never return (the literature sometimes refers to this as **attrition**). For example, consider a clinical trial for a new medication in which participants quit the study because they are having adverse reactions to the drug. Visually, the monotone pattern resembles a staircase, such that the cases with missing data on a particular assessment are always missing subsequent measurements. Monotone missing data patterns have received attention in the missing data literature because they greatly reduce the mathematical complexity of maximum likelihood and multiple imputation and can eliminate the need for iterative estimation algorithms (Schafer, 1997, pp. 218–238).

A **general missing data pattern** is perhaps the most common configuration of missing values. As seen in panel D, a general pattern has missing values dispersed throughout the data matrix in a haphazard fashion. The seemingly random pattern is deceptive because the values can still be systematically missing (e.g., there may be a relationship between $Y_1$ values and the propensity for missing data on $Y_2$). Again, it is important to remember that the missing data pattern describes the location of the missing values and not the reasons for missingness. The data set in Table 1.1 is another example of a general missing data pattern, and you can further separate this general pattern into four unique missing data patterns: cases with only IQ scores ($n = 2$), cases with IQ and well-being scores ($n = 8$), cases with IQ and job performance scores ($n = 1$), and cases with complete data on all three variables ($n = 9$).

Later in the chapter, I outline a number of designs that produce intentional missing data. The **planned missing data pattern** in panel E corresponds to the three-form questionnaire design outlined by Graham, Hofer, and MacKinnon (1996). The basic idea behind the three-form design is to distribute questionnaires across different forms and administer a subset of the forms to each respondent. For example, the design in panel E distributes the four questionnaires across three forms, such that each form includes $Y_1$ but is missing $Y_2$, $Y_3$, or $Y_4$. Planned missing data patterns are useful for collecting a large number of questionnaire items while simultaneously reducing respondent burden.

Finally, the **latent variable pattern** in panel F is unique to latent variable analyses such as structural equation models. This pattern is interesting because the values of the latent variables are missing for the entire sample. For example, a confirmatory factor analysis model uses a latent factor to explain the associations among a set of manifest indicator variables (e.g., $Y_1$ through $Y_3$), but the factor scores themselves are completely missing. Although it is not necessary to view latent variable models as missing data problems, researchers have adapted missing data algorithms to estimate these models (e.g., multilevel models; Raudenbush & Bryk, 2002, pp. 440–444).

Historically, researchers have developed analytic techniques that address a particular missing data pattern. For example, Little and Rubin (2002) devote an entire chapter to older methods that were developed specifically for experimental studies with a univariate missing data pattern. Similarly, survey researchers have developed so-called hot-deck approaches to deal with unit nonresponse (Scheuren, 2005). From a practical standpoint, distinguishing among missing data patterns is no longer that important because maximum likelihood estimation and multiple imputation are well suited for virtually any missing data pattern. This book focuses primarily on techniques that are applicable to general missing data patterns because these methods also work well with less complicated patterns.

## 1.4 A CONCEPTUAL OVERVIEW OF MISSING DATA THEORY

Rubin (1976) and colleagues introduced a classification system for missing data problems that is widely used in the literature today. This work has generated three so-called missing data mechanisms that describe how the probability of a missing value relates to the data, if at all. Unfortunately, Rubin's now-standard terminology is somewhat confusing, and researchers often misuse his vernacular. This section gives a conceptual overview of missing data theory that uses hypothetical research examples to illustrate Rubin's missing data mechanisms. In the next section, I delve into more detail and provide a more precise mathematical definition of the missing data mechanisms. Methodologists have proposed additions to

Rubin's classification scheme (e.g., Diggle & Kenward, 1994; Little, 1995), but I focus strictly on the three missing data mechanisms that are common in the literature. As an aside, I try to use a minimal number of acronyms throughout the book, but I nearly always refer to the missing data mechanisms by their abbreviation (MAR, MCAR, MNAR). You will encounter these acronyms repeatedly throughout the book, so it is worth committing them to memory.

## Missing at Random Data

Data are **missing at random** (MAR) when the probability of missing data on a variable $Y$ is related to some other measured variable (or variables) in the analysis model but not to the values of $Y$ itself. Said differently, there is no relationship between the propensity for missing data on $Y$ and the values of $Y$ after partialling out other variables. The term *missing at random* is somewhat misleading because it implies that the data are missing in a haphazard fashion that resembles a coin toss. However, MAR actually means that a systematic relationship exists between one or more measured variables and the probability of missing data. To illustrate, consider the small data set in Table 1.2. I designed these data to mimic an employee selection scenario in which prospective employees complete an IQ test during their job interview and a supervisor subsequently evaluates their job performance following a 6-month probationary period. Suppose that the company used IQ scores as a selection measure and did not hire applicants that scored in the lower quartile of the IQ distribution. You can see that the job performance ratings in the MAR column of Table 1.2 are missing for the applicants with the lowest IQ scores. Consequently, the probability of a missing job performance rating is solely a function of IQ scores and is unrelated to an individual's job performance.

There are many real-life situations in which a selection measure such as IQ determines whether data are missing, but it is easy to generate additional examples where the propensity for missing data is less deterministic. For example, suppose that an educational researcher is studying reading achievement and finds that Hispanic students have a higher rate of missing data than Caucasian students. As a second example, suppose that a psychologist is studying quality of life in a group of cancer patients and finds that elderly patients and patients with less education have a higher propensity to refuse the quality of life questionnaire. These examples qualify as MAR as long as there is no residual relationship between the propensity for missing data and the incomplete outcome variable (e.g., after partialling out age and education, the probability of missingness is unrelated to quality of life).

The practical problem with the MAR mechanism is that there is no way to confirm that the probability of missing data on $Y$ is solely a function of other measured variables. Returning to the education example, suppose that Hispanic children with poor reading skills have higher rates of missingness on the reading achievement test. This situation is inconsistent with an MAR mechanism because there is a relationship between reading achievement and missingness, even after controlling for ethnicity. However, the researcher would have no way of verifying the presence or absence of this relationship without knowing the values of the missing achievement scores. Consequently, there is no way to test the MAR mechanism or to verify that scores are MAR. This represents an important practical problem for missing data analyses because maximum likelihood estimation and multiple imputation (the two techniques that methodologists currently recommend) assume an MAR mechanism.

**TABLE 1.2. Job Performance Ratings with MCAR, MAR, and MNAR Missing Values**

| IQ | Job performance ratings | | | |
| --- | --- | --- | --- | --- |
| | Complete | MCAR | MAR | MNAR |
| 78 | 9 | — | — | 9 |
| 84 | 13 | 13 | — | 13 |
| 84 | 10 | — | — | 10 |
| 85 | 8 | 8 | — | — |
| 87 | 7 | 7 | — | — |
| 91 | 7 | 7 | 7 | — |
| 92 | 9 | 9 | 9 | 9 |
| 94 | 9 | 9 | 9 | 9 |
| 94 | 11 | 11 | 11 | 11 |
| 96 | 7 | — | 7 | — |
| 99 | 7 | 7 | 7 | — |
| 105 | 10 | 10 | 10 | 10 |
| 105 | 11 | 11 | 11 | 11 |
| 106 | 15 | 15 | 15 | 15 |
| 108 | 10 | 10 | 10 | 10 |
| 112 | 10 | — | 10 | 10 |
| 113 | 12 | 12 | 12 | 12 |
| 115 | 14 | 14 | 14 | 14 |
| 118 | 16 | 16 | 16 | 16 |
| 134 | 12 | — | 12 | 12 |

## Missing Completely at Random Data

The **missing completely at random** (MCAR) mechanism is what researchers think of as purely haphazard missingness. The formal definition of MCAR requires that the probability of missing data on a variable $Y$ is unrelated to other measured variables and is unrelated to the values of $Y$ itself. Put differently, the observed data points are a simple random sample of the scores you would have analyzed had the data been complete. Notice that MCAR is a more restrictive condition than MAR because it assumes that missingness is completely unrelated to the data.

With regard to the job performance data in Table 1.2, I created the MCAR column by deleting scores based on the value of a random number. The random numbers were uncorrelated with IQ and job performance, so missingness is unrelated to the data. You can see that the missing values are not isolated to a particular location in the IQ and job performance distributions; thus the 15 complete cases are relatively representative of the entire applicant pool. It is easy to think of real-world situations where job performance ratings could be missing in a haphazard fashion. For example, an employee might take maternity leave prior to her 6-month evaluation, the supervisor responsible for assigning the rating could be promoted to another division within the company, or an employee might quit because his spouse accepted a job in another state. Returning to the previous education example, note that children could have MCAR achievement scores because of unexpected personal events (e.g., an illness, a funeral, family vacation, relocation to another school district), scheduling difficulties (e.g., the class was away at a field trip when the researchers visited the school), or administrative snafus (e.g., the researchers inadvertently misplaced the tests before the data could be entered). Similar types of issues could produce MCAR data in the quality of life study.

In principle, it is possible to verify that a set of scores are MCAR. I outline two MCAR tests in detail later in the chapter, but the basic logic behind these tests will be introduced here. For example, reconsider the data in Table 1.2. The definition of MCAR requires that the observed data are a simple random sample of the hypothetically complete data set. This implies that the cases with observed job performance ratings should be no different from the cases that are missing their performance evaluations, on average. To test this idea, you can separate the missing and complete cases and examine group mean differences on the IQ variable. If the missing data patterns are randomly equivalent (i.e., the data are MCAR), then the IQ means should be the same, within sampling error. To illustrate, I classified the scores in the MCAR column as observed or missing and compared the IQ means for the two groups. The complete cases have an IQ mean of 99.73, and the missing cases have a mean of 100.80. This rather small mean difference suggests that the two groups are randomly equivalent, and it provides evidence that the job performance scores are MCAR. As a contrast, I used the performance ratings in the MAR column to form missing data groups. The complete cases now have an IQ mean of 105.47, and the missing cases have a mean of 83.60. This large disparity suggests that the two groups are systematically different on the IQ variable, so there is evidence against the MCAR mechanism. Comparing the missing and complete cases is a strategy that is common to the MCAR tests that I describe later in the chapter.

## Missing Not at Random Data

Finally, data are **missing not at random** (MNAR) when the probability of missing data on a variable Y is related to the values of Y itself, even after controlling for other variables. To illustrate, reconsider the job performance data in Table 1.2. Suppose that the company hired all 20 applicants and subsequently terminated a number of individuals for poor performance prior to their 6-month evaluation. You can see that the job performance ratings in the MNAR column are missing for the applicants with the lowest job performance ratings. Consequently, the probability of a missing job performance rating is dependent on one's job performance, even after controlling for IQ.

It is relatively easy to generate additional examples where MNAR data could occur. Returning to the previous education example, suppose that students with poor reading skills have missing test scores because they experienced reading comprehension difficulties during the exam. Similarly, suppose that a number of patients in the cancer trial become so ill (e.g., their quality of life becomes so poor) that they can no longer participate in the study. In both examples, the data are MNAR because the probability of a missing value depends on the variable that is missing. Like the MAR mechanism, there is no way to verify that scores are MNAR without knowing the values of the missing variables.

## 1.5 A MORE FORMAL DESCRIPTION OF MISSING DATA THEORY

The previous section is conceptual in nature and omits the mathematical details behind Rubin's missing data theory. This section expands the previous ideas and gives a more precise description of the missing data mechanisms. As an aside, the notation and the terminology that I use in this section are somewhat different from Rubin's original work, but they are consistent with the contemporary missing data literature (Little & Rubin, 2002; Schafer, 1997; Schafer & Graham, 2002).

### Preliminary Notation

Understanding Rubin's (1976) missing data theory requires some basic notation and terminology. The **complete data** consist of the scores that you would have obtained had there been no missing values. The complete data is partially a hypothetical entity because some of its values are missing. However, in principle, each case has a score on every variable. This idea is intuitive in some situations (e.g., a student's reading comprehension score is missing because she was unexpectedly absent from school) but is somewhat unnatural in others (e.g., a cancer patient's quality of life score is missing because he died). Nevertheless, you have to assume that a complete set of scores does exist, at least hypothetically. I denote the complete data as $Y_{com}$ throughout the rest of this section.

In practice, some portion of the hypothetically complete data set is often missing. Consequently, you can think of the complete data as consisting of two components, the **observed data** and the **missing data** ($Y_{obs}$ and $Y_{mis}$, respectively). As the names imply, $Y_{obs}$ contains the observed scores, and $Y_{mis}$ contains the hypothetical scores that are missing. To illustrate, reconsider the data set in Table 1.2. Suppose that the company used IQ scores as a selection measure and did not hire applicants that scored in the lower quartile of the IQ distribution. The first two columns of the table contain the hypothetically complete data (i.e., $Y_{com}$), and the MAR column shows the job performance scores that the human resources office actually collected. For a given individual with incomplete data, $Y_{obs}$ corresponds to the IQ variable and $Y_{mis}$ is the hypothetical job performance rating. As you will see in the next section, partitioning the hypothetically complete data set into its observed and missing components plays an integral role in missing data theory.

### The Distribution of Missing Data

The key idea behind Rubin's (1976) theory is that missingness is a variable that has a probability distribution. Specifically, Rubin defines a binary variable $R$ that denotes whether a score on a particular variable is observed or missing (i.e., $r = 1$ if a score is observed, and $r = 0$ if a value is missing). For example, Table 1.3 shows the MAR job performance ratings and the corresponding missing data indicator. A single indicator can summarize the distribution of missing data in this example because the IQ variable is complete. However, multivariate data sets tend to have a number of missing variables, in which case $R$ becomes a matrix of missing data indicators. When every variable has missing values, this **R** matrix has the same number of rows and columns as the data matrix.

**TABLE 1.3. Missing Data Indicator
for MAR Job Performance Ratings**

| Job performance | | Indicator |
|---|---|---|
| Complete | MAR | |
| 9 | — | 0 |
| 13 | — | 0 |
| 10 | — | 0 |
| 8 | — | 0 |
| 7 | — | 0 |
| 7 | 7 | 1 |
| 9 | 9 | 1 |
| 9 | 9 | 1 |
| 11 | 11 | 1 |
| 7 | 7 | 1 |
| 7 | 7 | 1 |
| 10 | 10 | 1 |
| 11 | 11 | 1 |
| 15 | 15 | 1 |
| 10 | 10 | 1 |
| 10 | 10 | 1 |
| 12 | 12 | 1 |
| 14 | 14 | 1 |
| 16 | 16 | 1 |
| 12 | 12 | 1 |

Rubin's (1976) theory essentially views individuals as having a pair of observations on each variable: a score value that may or may not be observed (i.e., $Y_{obs}$ or $Y_{mis}$) and a corresponding code on the missing data indicator, R. Defining the missing data as a variable implies that there is a probability distribution that governs whether R takes on a value of zero or one (i.e., there is a function or equation that describes the probability of missingness). For example, reconsider the cancer study that I described earlier in the chapter. If the quality of life scores are missing as a function of other variables such as age or education, then the coefficients from a logistic regression equation might describe the distribution of R. In practice, we rarely know why the data are missing, so it is impossible to describe the distribution of R with any certainty. Nevertheless, the important point is that R has a probability distribution, and the probability of missing data may or may not be related to other variables in the data set. As you will see, the nature of the relationship between R and the data is what differentiates the missing data mechanisms.

## A More Precise Definition of the Missing Data Mechanisms

Having established some basic terminology, we can now revisit the missing data mechanisms in more detail. The formal definitions of the missing data mechanisms involve different probability distributions for the missing data indicator, R. These distributions essentially describe different relationships between R and the data. In practice, there is generally no way to specify the parameters of these distributions with any certainty. However, these details are not important because it is the presence or absence of certain associations that differentiates the missing data mechanisms.

The probability distribution for MNAR data is a useful starting point because it includes all possible associations between the data and missingness. You can write this distribution as

$$p(R \mid Y_{\text{obs}}, Y_{\text{mis}}, \phi) \tag{1.1}$$

where $p$ is a generic symbol for a probability distribution, $R$ is the missing data indicator, $Y_{\text{obs}}$ and $Y_{\text{mis}}$ are the observed and missing parts of the data, respectively, and $\phi$ is a parameter (or set of parameters) that describes the relationship between $R$ and the data. In words, Equation 1.1 says that the probability that $R$ takes on a value of zero or one can depend on both $Y_{\text{obs}}$ and $Y_{\text{mis}}$. Said differently, the probability of missing data on $Y$ can depend on other variables (i.e., $Y_{\text{obs}}$) as well as on the underlying values of $Y$ itself (i.e., $Y_{\text{mis}}$).

To put Equation 1.1 into context, reconsider the data set in Table 1.2. Equation 1.1 implies that the probability of missing data is related to an individual's IQ or job performance score (or both). Panel A of Figure 1.2 is a graphical depiction of these relationships that I adapted from a similar figure in Schafer and Graham (2002). Consistent with Equation 1.1, the figure contains all possible associations (i.e., arrows) between $R$ and the data. The box labeled $Z$ represents a collection of unmeasured variables (e.g., motivation, health problems, turnover intentions, and job satisfaction) that may relate to the probability of missing data and to IQ and job performance. Rubin's (1976) missing data mechanisms are only concerned with relationships between $R$ and the data, so there is no need to include $Z$ in Equation 1.1. However, correlations between measured and unmeasured variables can induce spurious associations between $R$ and $Y$, which underscores the point that Rubin's mechanisms are not real-world causal descriptions of the missing data.

An MAR mechanism occurs when the probability of missing data on a variable $Y$ is related to another measured variable in the analysis model but not to the values of $Y$ itself. This implies that $R$ is dependent on $Y_{\text{obs}}$ but not on $Y_{\text{mis}}$. Consequently, the distribution of missing data simplifies to

$$p(R \mid Y_{\text{obs}}, \phi) \tag{1.2}$$

Equation 1.2 says that the probability of missingness depends on the observed portion of data via some parameter $\phi$ that relates $Y_{\text{obs}}$ to $R$. Returning to the small job performance data set, observe that Equation 1.2 implies that an individual's propensity for missing data depends only on his or her IQ score. Panel B of Figure 1.2 depicts an MAR mechanism. Notice that there is no longer an arrow between $R$ and the job performance scores, but a linkage remains between $R$ and IQ. The arrow between $R$ and IQ could represent a direct relationship between these variables (e.g., the company uses IQ as a selection measure), or it could be a spurious relationship that occurs when $R$ and IQ are mutually correlated with one of the unmeasured variables in $Z$. Both explanations satisfy Rubin's (1976) definition of MAR, so the underlying causal process is unimportant.

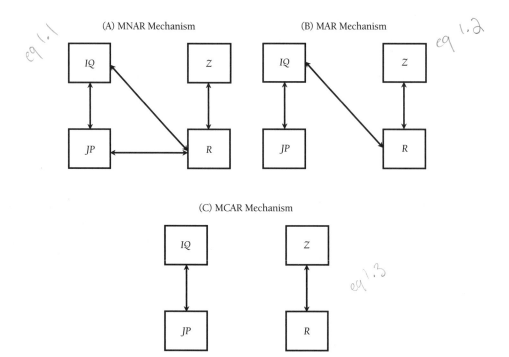

**FIGURE 1.2.** A graphical representation of Rubin's missing data mechanisms. The figure depicts a bivariate scenario in which IQ scores are completely observed and the job performance scores (JP) are missing for some individuals. The double-headed arrows represent generic statistical associations and $\phi$ is a parameter that governs the probability of scoring a 0 or 1 on the missing data indicator, R. The box labeled Z represents a collection of unmeasured variables.

Finally, the MCAR mechanism requires that missingness is completely unrelated to the data. Consequently, both $Y_{obs}$ and $Y_{mis}$ are unrelated to R, and the distribution of missing data simplifies even further to

$$p(R \,|\, \phi) \tag{1.3}$$

Equation 1.3 says that some parameter still governs the probability that R takes on a value of zero or one, but missingness is no longer related to the data. Returning to the job performance data set, note that Equation 1.3 implies that the missing data indicator is unrelated to both IQ and job performance. Panel C of Figure 1.2 depicts an MCAR mechanism. In this situation, the $\phi$ parameter describes possible associations between R and unmeasured variables, but there are no linkages between R and the data. Although it is not immediately obvious, panel C implies that the unmeasured variables in Z are uncorrelated with IQ and job performance because the presence of such a correlation could induce a spurious association between R and Y.

## 1.6 WHY IS THE MISSING DATA MECHANISM IMPORTANT?

Rubin's (1976) missing data theory involves two sets of parameters: the parameters that address the substantive research questions (i.e., the parameters that you would have estimated had there been no missing data) and the parameters that describe the probability of missing data (i.e., $\phi$). Researchers rarely know why the data are missing, so it is impossible to describe $\phi$ with any certainty. For example, reconsider the cancer study described in the previous section. Quality of life scores could be missing as an additive function of age and education, as an interactive function of treatment group membership and baseline health status, or as a direct function of quality of life itself. The important point is that there is generally no way to determine or estimate the parameters that describe the propensity for missing data.

The parameters that describe the probability of missing data are a nuisance and have no substantive value (e.g., had the data been complete, there would be reason to worry about $\phi$). However, in some situations these parameters may influence the estimation of the substantive parameters. For example, suppose that the goal of the cancer study is to estimate the mean quality of life score. Furthermore, imagine that a number of patients become so ill (i.e., their quality of life becomes so poor) that they can no longer participate in the study. In this scenario, $\phi$ is a set of parameters (e.g., logistic regression coefficients) that relates the probability of missing data to an individual's quality of life score. At an intuitive level, it would be difficult to obtain an accurate mean estimate because scores are disproportionately missing from the lower tail of the distribution. However, if the researchers happened to know the parameter values in $\phi$, it would be possible to correct for the positive bias in the mean. Of course, the problem with this scenario is that there is no way to estimate $\phi$.

Rubin's (1976) work is important because he clarified the conditions that need to exist in order to accurately estimate the substantive parameters without also knowing the parameters of the missing data distribution (i.e., $\phi$). It ends up that these conditions depend on how you analyze the data. Rubin showed that likelihood-based analyses such as maximum likelihood estimation and multiple imputation do not require information about $\phi$ if the data are MCAR or MAR. For this reason, the missing data literature often describes the MAR mechanism as **ignorable missingness** because there is no need to estimate the parameters of the missing data distribution when performing analyses. In contrast, Rubin showed that analysis techniques that rely on a sampling distribution are valid only when the data are MCAR. This latter set of procedures includes most of the ad hoc missing data techniques that researchers have been using for decades (e.g., discarding cases with missing data).

From a practical standpoint, Rubin's (1976) missing data mechanisms are essentially assumptions that govern the performance of different analytic techniques. Chapter 2 outlines a number of missing data handling methods that have been mainstays in published research articles for many years. With few exceptions, these techniques assume an MCAR mechanism and will yield biased parameter estimates when the data are MAR or MNAR. Because these traditional methods require a restrictive assumption that is unlikely to hold in practice, they have increasingly fallen out of favor in recent years (Wilkinson & Task Force on Statistical Inference, 1999). In contrast, maximum likelihood estimation and multiple imputation yield unbiased parameter estimates with MCAR or MAR data. In some sense, maximum likelihood and multiple imputation are robust missing data handling procedures because they require less stringent assumptions about the missing data mechanism. However, these methods are not a perfect solution because they too will produce bias with MNAR data. Methodologists have developed analysis methods for MNAR data, but these approaches require strict assumptions that limit their practical utility. Chapter 10 outlines models for MNAR data and shows how to use these models to conduct sensitivity analyses.

## 1.7 HOW PLAUSIBLE IS THE MISSING AT RANDOM MECHANISM?

The methodological literature recommends maximum likelihood and multiple imputation because these approaches require the less stringent MAR assumption. It is reasonable to question whether this assumption is plausible, given that there is no way to test it. Later in the chapter, I describe a number of planned missing data designs that automatically produce MAR or MCAR data, but these situations are unique because missingness is under the researcher's control. In the vast majority of studies, missing values are an unintentional byproduct of data collection, so the MAR mechanism becomes an unverifiable assumption that influences the accuracy of the maximum likelihood and multiple imputation analyses.

As is true for most statistical assumptions, it seems safe to assume that the MAR assumption will not be completely satisfied. The important question is whether routine violations are actually problematic. The answer to this question is situation-dependent because not all violations of MAR are equally damaging. To illustrate, reconsider the job performance scenario I introduced earlier in the chapter. The definition of MNAR states that a relationship exists between the probability of missing data on $Y$ and the values of $Y$ itself. This association can occur for two reasons. First, it is possible that the probability of missing data is directly related to the incomplete outcome variable. For example, if the company terminates a number of individuals for poor performance prior to their 6-month evaluation, then there is a direct relationship between job performance and the propensity for missing data. However, an association between job performance and missingness can also occur because these variables are mutually correlated with an unmeasured variable. For example, suppose that individuals with low autonomy (an unmeasured variable) become frustrated and quit prior to their six-month evaluation. If low autonomy is also associated with poor job performance, then this unmeasured variable can induce a correlation between performance and missingness, such that individuals with poor job performance have a higher probability of missing their six-month evaluation.

Figure 1.3 is a graphical depiction of the previous scenarios. Note that I use a straight arrow to specify a causal influence and a double-headed arrow to denote a generic association. Although both diagrams are consistent with Rubin's (1976) definition of MNAR, they are not equally capable of introducing bias. Collins, Schafer, and Kam (2001) showed that a direct relationship between the outcome and missingness (i.e., panel A) can introduce substantial bias, whereas MNAR data that results from an unmeasured variable is problematic only when correlation between the unmeasured variable and the missing outcome is relatively strong (e.g., greater than .40). The situation in panel B seems even less severe when you consider that the IQ variable probably captures some of the variation that autonomy would have explained, had it been a measured variable that was included in the statistical

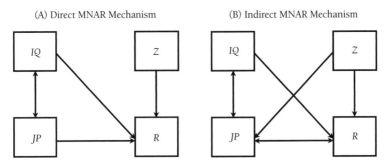

**FIGURE 1.3.** A graphical representation of two causal processes that produce MNAR data. The figure depicts a bivariate scenario in which IQ scores are completely observed and the job performance scores (*JP*) are missing for some individuals. The double-headed arrows represent generic statistical associations, and the straight arrows specify a causal influences. Panel A corresponds to a situation in which the probability of missing data is directly related to the missing outcome variable (i.e., the straight arrow between *JP* and *R*). Panel B depicts a scenario in which the probability of missing data is indirectly related to the missing outcome variable via the unmeasured cause of missingness in box *Z*.

analysis. This means that an unmeasured cause of missingness is problematic only if it has a strong relationship with the missing outcome after partialling out other measured variables. Schafer and Graham (2002, p. 173) argue that this is unlikely in most situations.

Notice that the MNAR mechanism in Panel B of Figure 1.3 becomes an MAR mechanism if autonomy is a measured variable that is included in the statistical analysis (i.e., the spurious correlation between job performance and *R* disappears once autonomy is partialled out). This suggests that you should be proactive about satisfying the MAR assumption by measuring variables that might explain missingness. For example, Graham, Taylor, Olchowski, and Cumsille (2006) suggest that variables such as reading speed and conscientiousness might explain why some respondents leave questionnaire items blank. In a longitudinal study, Schafer and Graham (2002) recommend using a survey question that asks respondents to report their likelihood of dropping out of the study prior to the next measurement occasion. As noted by Schafer and Graham (2002, p. 173), collecting data on the potential causes of missingness "may effectively convert an MNAR situation to MAR," so you should strongly consider this strategy when designing a study.

Of course, not all MNAR data are a result of unmeasured variables. In truth, the likelihood of the two scenarios in Figure 1.3 probably varies across research contexts. There is often a tendency to assume that data are missing for rather sinister reasons (e.g., a participant in a drug cessation study drops out, presumably because she started using again), and this presumption may be warranted in certain situations. For example, Hedeker and Gibbons (1997) describe data from a psychiatric clinical trial in which dropout was likely a function of response to treatment (e.g., participants in the placebo group were likely to leave the study because their symptoms were not improving, whereas dropouts in a drug condition experienced rapid improvement prior to dropping out). Similarly, Foster and Fang (2004) describe an evaluation of a conduct disorder intervention in which highly aggressive boys were less likely to continue participating in the study. However, you should not discount the possibility that a substantial proportion of the missing observations are MAR or even MCAR. For example, Graham, Hofer, Donaldson, MacKinnon, and Schafer (1997) and Enders, Dietz, Montague, and Dixon (2006) describe longitudinal studies that made systematic attempts to document the reasons for missing data. These studies had a substantial proportion of un-planned missing data, yet intensive follow-up analyses suggested that the missing data were largely benign (e.g., the most common reason for missing data was that students moved out of the school where the study took place).

Some researchers have argued that serious violations of MAR are relatively rare (Graham et al., 1997, p. 354; Schafer & Graham, 2002, p. 152), but the only way to evaluate the MAR assumption is to collect follow-up data from the missing respondents. Of course, this is dif-ficult or impossible in many situations. Sensitivity analyses are also useful for assessing the potential impact of MNAR data. Graham et al. (1997, pp. 354–358) provide a good illustra-tion of a sensitivity analysis; I discuss these procedures in Chapter 10.

## 1.8 AN INCLUSIVE ANALYSIS STRATEGY

The preceding section is overly simplistic because it suggests that the MAR assumption is automatically satisfied when the "cause" of missingness is a measured variable. In truth, the MAR mechanism is a characteristic of a specific analysis rather than a global characteristic of a data set. That is, some analyses from a given data set may satisfy the MAR assumption, whereas others are consistent with an MCAR or MNAR mechanism. To illustrate the subtle-ties of the MAR mechanism, consider a study that examines a number of health-related be-haviors (e.g., smoking, drinking, and sexual activity) in a teenage population. Because of its sensitive nature, researchers decide to administer the sexual behavior questionnaire to partici-pants who are above the age of 15. At first glance, this study may appear to satisfy the MAR assumption because a measured variable determines whether data are missing. However, this is not necessarily true.

Technically, MAR is satisfied only if the researchers incorporate age into the missing data handling procedure. For example, suppose that the researchers use a simple regression model to examine the influence of self-esteem on risky sexual behavior. Many software packages that implement maximum likelihood missing data handling methods can estimate a regression model with missing data, so this is a relatively straightforward analysis. However, the regres-sion analysis is actually consistent with the MNAR mechanism and may produce biased pa-rameter estimates, particularly if age and sexual activity are correlated. To understand the problem, consider Figure 1.4. This figure depicts an indirect MNAR mechanism that is simi-lar to the one in Panel B of Figure 1.3. Age is not part of the regression model, so it effectively operates an unmeasured variable and induces an association between missingness and the sexual behavior scores; the figure denotes this spurious correlation as a dashed line. The bias that results from omitting age from the regression model may not be problematic and de-pends on the correlation between age and sexual activity. Nevertheless, the regression analy-sis violates the MAR assumption.

The challenge of satisfying the MAR assumption has prompted methodologists to rec-ommend a so-called **inclusive analysis strategy** that incorporates a number of **auxiliary variables** into the analysis model or into the imputation process (Collins, Schafer, & Kam,

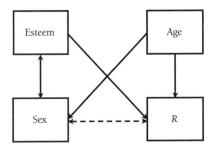

**FIGURE 1.4.** A graphical representation of an indirect MNAR mechanism. The figure depicts a bivariate scenario in which self-esteem scores are completely observed and sexual behavior questionnaire items are missing for respondents who are less than 15 years of age. If age (the "cause" of missingness) is excluded from the analysis model, it effectively acts as an unmeasured variable and induces an association between the probability of missing data and the unobserved sexual activity scores. The dashed line represents this spurious correlation. Including age in the analysis model (e.g., as an auxiliary variable) converts an MNAR analysis into an MAR analysis.

2001; Rubin, 1996; Schafer, 1997; Schafer & Graham, 2002). Auxiliary variables are variables you include in an analysis because they are either correlates of missingness or correlates of an incomplete variable. Auxiliary variables are not necessarily of substantive interest (i.e., you would not have included these variables in the analysis, had the data been complete), so their primary purpose is to fine-tune the missing data analysis by increasing power or reducing nonresponse bias. In the health study, age is an important auxiliary variable because it is a determinant of missingness, but other auxiliary variables may be correlates of the missing sexual behavior scores. For example, a survey question that asks teenagers to report whether they have a steady boyfriend or girlfriend is a good auxiliary variable because of its correlation with sexual activity. Theory and past research can help identify auxiliary variables, as can the MCAR tests described later in the chapter. Incorporating auxiliary variables into the missing data handling procedure does not guarantee that you will satisfy the MAR assumption, but it certainly improves the chances of doing so. I discuss auxiliary variables in detail in Chapter 5.

## 1.9 TESTING THE MISSING COMPLETELY AT RANDOM MECHANISM

MCAR is the only missing data mechanism that yields testable propositions. You might question the utility of testing this mechanism given that the majority of this book is devoted to techniques that require the less stringent MAR assumption. In truth, testing whether an entire collection of variables is consistent with MCAR is probably not that useful because some of the variables in a data set are likely to be missing in a systematic fashion. Furthermore, finding evidence for or against MCAR does not change the recommendation to use maximum likelihood or multiple imputation. However, identifying individual variables that are not MCAR is potentially useful because there may be a relationship between these variables and the probability of missingness. As I explained previously, methodologists recommend incorporating correlates of missingness into the missing data handling procedure because doing so can mitigate bias and improve the chances of satisfying the MAR assumption (Collins et al., 2001; Rubin, 1996; Schafer, 1997; Schafer & Graham, 2002).

To illustrate how you might use the information from an MCAR test, suppose that a psychologist is studying quality of life in a group of cancer patients and finds that patients who refused the quality of life questionnaire have a higher average age and a lower average education than the patients who completed the survey. These mean differences provide compelling evidence that the data are not MCAR and suggest a possible relationship between the demographic variables and the probability of missing data. Incorporating the demographic characteristics into the missing data handling procedure (e.g., using the auxiliary variable procedures in Chapter 5) adjusts for age- and education-related bias in the quality of life scores and increases the chances of satisfying the MAR assumption. Consequently, using MCAR tests to identify potential correlates of missingness is often a useful starting point, even if you have no interest in assessing whether an entire set of variables is MCAR.

Rubin's (1976) definition of MCAR requires that the observed data are a simple random sample of the hypothetically complete data set. This implies that the cases with missing data belong to the same population (and thus share the same mean vector and covariance matrix) as the cases with complete data. Kim and Bentler (2002) refer to this condition as **homogeneity of means and covariances**. One way to test for homogeneity of means is to separate the missing and the complete cases on a particular variable and examine group mean differences on other variables in the data set. Testing for homogeneity of covariances follows a similar logic and examines whether the missing data subgroups have different variances and covariances. Finding that the missing data patterns share a common mean vector and a common covariance matrix provides evidence that the data are MCAR, whereas group differences in the means or the covariances provide evidence that the data are not MCAR.

Methodologists have proposed a number of methods for testing the MCAR mechanism (Chen & Little, 1999; Diggle, 1989; Dixon, 1988; Kim & Bentler, 2002; Little, 1988; Muthén, Kaplan, & Hollis, 1987; Park & Lee, 1997; Thoemmes & Enders, 2007). This section describes two procedures that evaluate mean differences across missing data patterns. I omit procedures that assess homogeneity of covariances because it seems unlikely that covariance differences would exist in the absence of mean differences. In addition, simulation studies offer conflicting evidence about the performance of covariance-based tests (Kim & Bentler, 2002; Thoemmes & Enders, 2007). It therefore seems safe to view these procedures with caution until further research accumulates. Interested readers can consult Kim and Bentler (2002) for an overview of covariance-based tests.

## Univariate *t*-Test Comparisons

The simplest method for assessing MCAR is to use a series of independent *t* tests to compare missing data subgroups (Dixon, 1988). This approach separates the missing and the complete cases on a particular variable and uses a *t* test to examine group mean differences on other variables in the data set. The MCAR mechanism implies that the cases with observed data should be the same as the cases with missing values, on average. Consequently, a nonsignificant *t* test provides evidence that the data are MCAR, whereas a significant *t* statistic (or alternatively, a large mean difference) suggests that the data are MAR or MNAR.

To illustrate the *t*-test approach, reconsider the data in Table 1.1. To begin, I used the job performance scores to create a binary missing data indicator and subsequently used independent $t$ tests to assess group mean differences on IQ and psychological well-being. The missing and complete cases have IQ means of 88.50 and 111.50, respectively, and Welch's $t$ test indicated that this mean difference is statistically significant, $t(14.68) = 6.43, p < .001$. Considering psychological well-being, the means for the missing and complete cases are 9.13 and 11.44, respectively, and the $t$ test was not significant, $t(11.70) = 1.39, p = .19$. Collectively, these tests suggest that the job performance ratings are not MCAR because the missing and observed cases systematically differ with respect to IQ. This conclusion is correct because I deleted job performance scores for the cases in the lower half of the IQ distribution. Next, I repeated this procedure by forming a missing data indicator from the psychological well-being scores and by testing whether the resulting groups had different IQ means (it was impossible to compare the job performance means because only one case from the missing data group had a job performance score). The $t$ test indicated that the group means are equivalent, $t(3.60) = .50, p = .65$, which correctly provides support for the MCAR mechanism.

The $t$-test approach has a number of potential problems to consider. First, generating the test statistics can be very cumbersome unless you have a software package that automates the process (e.g., the SPSS Missing Values Analysis module). Second, the tests do not take the correlations among the variables into account, so it is possible for a missing data indicator to produce mean differences on a number of variables, even if there is only a single cause of missingness in the data. Related to the previous points, the potential for a large number of statistical tests and the possibility of spurious associations seem to warrant some form of type I error control. The main reason for implementing the $t$-test approach is to identify auxiliary variables that you can later adjust for in the missing data handling procedure. I would argue against any type of error control procedure because there is ultimately no harm in using auxiliary variables that are unrelated to missingness (Collins et al., 2001). Another problem with the $t$-test approach is the possibility of very small group sizes (e.g., there are only three cases in Table 1.1 with missing well-being scores). This can decrease power and make it impossible to perform certain comparisons. To offset a potential loss of power, it might be useful to augment the $t$ tests with a measure of effect size such as Cohen's (1988) standardized mean difference. Finally, it is important to note that mean comparisons do not provide a conclusive test of MCAR because MAR and MNAR mechanisms can produce missing data subgroups with equal means.

## Little's MCAR Test

Little (1988) proposed a multivariate extension of the $t$-test approach that simultaneously evaluates mean differences on every variable in the data set. Unlike univariate $t$ tests, Little's procedure is a global test of MCAR that applies to the entire data set. Omnibus tests of the MCAR mechanism are probably not that useful because they provide no way to identify potential correlates of missingness (i.e., auxiliary variables). Nevertheless, Little's test is available in some statistical software packages (e.g., the SPSS Missing Values Analysis module), so the procedure warrants a description.

Like the $t$-test approach, Little's test evaluates mean differences across subgroups of cases that share the same missing data pattern. The test statistic is a weighted sum of the standardized differences between the subgroup means and the grand means, as follows:

$$d^2 = \sum_{j=1}^{J} n_j \left( \hat{\boldsymbol{\mu}}_j - \hat{\boldsymbol{\mu}}_j^{(ML)} \right)^T \hat{\boldsymbol{\Sigma}}_j^{-1} \left( \hat{\boldsymbol{\mu}}_j - \hat{\boldsymbol{\mu}}_j^{(ML)} \right) \tag{1.4}$$

where $n_j$ is the number of cases in missing data pattern $j$, $\hat{\boldsymbol{\mu}}_j$ contains the variable means for the cases in missing data pattern $j$, $\hat{\boldsymbol{\mu}}_j^{(ML)}$ contains maximum likelihood estimates of the grand means, and $\hat{\boldsymbol{\Sigma}}_j$ is the maximum likelihood estimate of the covariance matrix. The $j$ subscript indicates that the number of elements in the parameter matrices vary across missing data patterns. The $d^2$ statistic is essentially a weighted sum of $J$ squared $z$ scores. Specifically, the parentheses contain deviation scores that capture differences between pattern $j$'s means and the corresponding grand means. With MCAR data, the subgroup means should be within sampling error of the grand means, so small deviations are consistent with an MCAR mechanism. In matrix algebra, multiplying by the matrix inverse is analogous to division, so the $\hat{\boldsymbol{\Sigma}}_j^{-1}$ term functions like the denominator of the $z$ score formula by converting the raw deviation values to a standardized metric. Finally, multiplying the squared $z$ values by $n_j$ weights each pattern's contribution to the test statistic. When the null hypothesis is true (i.e., the data are MCAR), $d^2$ is approximately distributed as a chi-square statistic with $\Sigma k_j - k$ degrees of freedom, where $k_j$ is the number of complete variables for pattern $j$, and $k$ is the total number of variables. Consistent with the univariate $t$-test approach, a significant $d^2$ statistic provides evidence against MCAR.

To illustrate Little's MCAR test, reconsider the small data set in Table 1.1. The data contain four missing data patterns: cases with only IQ scores ($n_j = 2$), cases with IQ and well-being scores ($n_j = 8$), cases with IQ and job performance scores ($n_j = 1$), and cases with complete data on all three variables ($n_j = 9$). The test statistic in Equation 1.4 compares the subgroup means to the maximum likelihood estimates of the grand means. I outline maximum likelihood missing data handling in Chapter 4, but for now, the necessary parameter estimates are as follows:

$$\hat{\boldsymbol{\mu}} = \begin{bmatrix} \hat{\mu}_{IQ} \\ \hat{\mu}_{JP} \\ \hat{\mu}_{WB} \end{bmatrix} = \begin{bmatrix} 100.00 \\ 10.23 \\ 10.27 \end{bmatrix}$$

$$\hat{\boldsymbol{\Sigma}} = \begin{bmatrix} \hat{\sigma}_{IQ}^2 & \hat{\sigma}_{IQ,JP} & \hat{\sigma}_{IQ,WB} \\ \hat{\sigma}_{JP,IQ} & \hat{\sigma}_{JP}^2 & \hat{\sigma}_{JP,WB} \\ \hat{\sigma}_{WB,IQ} & \hat{\sigma}_{WB,JP} & \hat{\sigma}_{WB}^2 \end{bmatrix} = \begin{bmatrix} 189.60 & 22.31 & 12.21 \\ 22.31 & 8.68 & 5.61 \\ 12.21 & 6.50 & 11.04 \end{bmatrix}$$

To begin, consider the group of cases with data on only IQ ($n_j = 2$). This pattern has an IQ mean of 91.50, so its contribution to the $d^2$ statistic is as follows:

$$d_j^2 = 2(91.50 - 100.00)(189.60^{-1})(91.50 - 100.00) = 0.762$$

Next, consider the subgroup of cases with complete data on IQ and well-being ($n_j = 8$). The IQ and well-being means for this pattern are 87.75 and 9.13, respectively, and the contribution to the $d^2$ statistic is

$$d_j^2 = 8 \left( \begin{bmatrix} 87.75 \\ 9.13 \end{bmatrix} - \begin{bmatrix} 100.00 \\ 10.27 \end{bmatrix} \right)^T \begin{bmatrix} 189.60 & 12.21 \\ 12.21 & 11.04 \end{bmatrix}^{-1} \left( \begin{bmatrix} 87.75 \\ 9.13 \end{bmatrix} - \begin{bmatrix} 100.00 \\ 10.27 \end{bmatrix} \right) = 6.432$$

In both of the previous examples, notice that $\hat{\boldsymbol{\mu}}_j$ and $\hat{\boldsymbol{\Sigma}}_j$ contain the maximum likelihood estimates that correspond to the observed variables for a particular pattern (i.e., the estimates that correspond to the missing variables do not appear in the matrices). Repeating the computations for the remaining missing data patterns and summing the resulting $d_j^2$ values yields $d^2 = 14.63$, and referencing the test statistic to a chi-square distribution with 5 degrees of freedom returns a probability value of $p = .01$. The null hypothesis for Little's test states that the data are MCAR, so a statistically significant test statistic provides evidence against the MCAR mechanism.

Like the $t$-test approach, Little's test has a number of problems to consider. First, the test does not identify the specific variables that violate MCAR, so it is only useful for testing an omnibus hypothesis that is unlikely to hold in the first place. Second, the version of the test outlined above assumes that the missing data patterns share a common covariance matrix. MAR and MNAR mechanisms can produce missing data patterns with different variances and covariances, and the test statistic in Equation 1.4 would not necessarily detect covariance-based deviations from MCAR. Third, simulation studies suggest that Little's test suffers from low power, particularly when the number of variables that violate MCAR is small, the relationship between the data and missingness is weak, or the data are MNAR (Thoemmes & Enders, 2007). Consequently, the test has a propensity to produce Type II errors and can lead to a false sense of security about the missing data mechanism. Finally, mean comparisons do not provide a conclusive test of MCAR because MAR and MNAR mechanisms can produce missing data subgroups with equal means.

## 1.10 PLANNED MISSING DATA DESIGNS

The next few sections outline research designs that produce MCAR or MAR data as an intentional by-product of data collection. The idea of intentional missing data might seem odd at first, but you may already be familiar with a number of these designs. For example, in a randomized study with two treatment conditions, each individual has a hypothetical score from both conditions, but participants only provide a response to their assigned treatment condition. The unobserved response to the other condition (i.e., the potential outcome or counterfactual) is MCAR. Viewing randomized experiments as a missing data problem is popular in the statistics literature and is a key component of Rubin's Causal Model (Rubin, 1974, 1978a; West & Thoemmes, in press). A fractional factorial design (Montgomery, 1997) is another research design that yields MCAR missing data. In a fractional factorial, you purposefully select a subset of experimental conditions from a full factorial design and randomly assign participants to these conditions. A classic example of intentional MAR data occurs in selection designs where scores on one variable determine whether respondents provide data on a second variable. For example, universities frequently use the Graduate Record Exam (GRE) as a selection tool for graduate school admissions, so first-year grade point averages are subsequently missing for students who score below some GRE threshold. A related issue arises in survey designs where the answer to a screener question dictates a particular skip pattern. Selection problems such as this have received considerable attention in the methodological literature (Sackett & Yang, 2000) and date back to Pearson's (1903) work on range restriction.

The previous designs are classic examples of intentional missing data that do not necessarily require missing data techniques. The advent of maximum likelihood estimation and multiple imputation has prompted methodologists to develop specialized **planned missing data designs** that address a number of practical problems (Graham et al., 2006). For example, researchers often face constraints on the number of questionnaire items that they can reasonably expect respondents to answer, and this problem becomes more acute in longitudinal studies where respondents fill out questionnaire batteries on multiple occasions. Limiting the number of variables is one obvious solution to this problem, but introducing planned missing data is another possibility. In a planned missing data design, you distribute the questionnaire items across different forms and administer a subset of the forms to each respondent. This strategy allows you to collect data on the full set of questionnaire items while simultaneously reducing respondent burden.

Planned missingness is not limited to questionnaire data and has a number of other interesting applications. For example, suppose that a researcher wants to use two data collection methods, one of which is very expensive. To illustrate, imagine a study in which a researcher is collecting brain image data. Ideally, she would like to collect her data using magnetic resonance imaging (MRI), but the MRI is very expensive and she has difficulty accessing it for extended periods. However, she can readily collect data using the less expensive computed tomography (CT) scan. Planned missingness is ideally suited for this situation because the researcher can collect CT data from every participant and restrict the MRI data to a subset of her sample. A similar example occurs with body fat measurements from an exercise physiology study. A researcher can readily use a set of calipers to take skinfold measurements from all of his subjects but might use a more expensive technique (e.g., air displacement in a BOD POD) on a subset of the participants. Importantly, maximum likelihood and multiple imputation allow researchers to analyze data from planned missingness designs without having to discard the incomplete cases. For example, the exercise physiologist can use the entire sample to estimate the associations between the expensive measure and other study variables, even though a subset of the cases has missing data on the expensive measure.

Planned missing data strategies have been available for many years and have a number of interesting applications (Johnson, 1992; Lord, 1962; Raghunathan & Grizzle, 1995; Shoemaker, 1973). I focus primarily on the planned missing data designs outlined by John Graham and his colleagues (Graham et al., 1996; Graham, Taylor, & Cumsille, 2001; Graham et al., 2006). In particular, the subsequent sections describe a three-form design that is widely applicable to questionnaire data collection and planned missingness designs for longitudinal studies. Readers interested in additional details on planned missingness designs can consult Graham et al. (2006).

As an aside, my experience suggests that researchers tend to view the idea of planned missing data with some skepticism and are often reluctant to implement this strategy. This skepticism probably stems from a presumption that missing data can bias the analysis results. However, the planned data designs in this section produce MCAR data, so the only potential downside is a loss of statistical power. Planned missingness designs are very flexible and allow you to address power concerns by restricting the missing data to certain variables. Every research study involves compromises, so you have to decide whether collecting additional variables offsets the resulting loss of power. Of course, increasing the sample size will always improve power, but this may not be feasible. In any case, planned missing data designs are highly useful and underutilized tools that will undoubtedly increase in popularity as researchers become familiar with their benefits.

## 1.11 THE THREE-FORM DESIGN

Researchers in many disciplines use multiple-item questionnaires to measure complex constructs. For example, psychologists routinely use several questionnaire items to measure depression, each of which taps into a different depressive symptom (e.g., sadness, lack of energy, sleep difficulties, feelings of hopelessness). Using multiple-item questionnaires to measure even a relatively small number of variables can introduce a substantial respondent burden. Graham et al. (1996) addressed this problem with a **three-form design** that distributes a subset of questionnaire items to each respondent. The design divides the item pool into four sets (X, A, B, and C) and allocates these sets across three questionnaire forms, such that each form includes X and is missing A, B, or C. Table 1.4 shows the distribution of the item sets across the three questionnaire forms. Note that each item set can include multiple questionnaires or combinations of items from multiple questionnaires (e.g., item set X can include a depression questionnaire and a self-esteem questionnaire).

To illustrate the three-form design, suppose that a researcher plans to use eight questionnaires, each of which has 10 items. Concerned that her study participants will not have time to complete all 80 questions, she uses a three-form design to reduce respondent burden. Table 1.5 shows what the three-form design would look like if the researcher equally distributed her questionnaires across the four item sets (i.e., she assigns two questionnaires to set X, A, B, and C). Notice that the 3-form design allows the researcher to collect data on 80 questionnaire items, even though any given respondent only answers 60 items. Importantly, maximum likelihood estimation and multiple imputation allow the researcher to analyze the data without discarding incomplete cases.

The three-form design is flexible and does not require an equal number of questionnaire items in each item set. For example, the researcher could use the three-form design in Table 1.6 if she wanted to increase the number of variables in the X set, although this would require each participant to answer 70 items. In addition, there is no need to group questionnaire items together in the same set (e.g., assign all $Q_1$ items to set X), and it is possible to distribute questionnaire items across more than one item set (e.g., assign five of the $Q_1$ items to set

### TABLE 1.4. Missing Data Pattern for a Three-Form Design

|      | Item sets |     |     |     |
| ---- | --------- | --- | --- | --- |
| Form | X         | A   | B   | C   |
| 1    | ✓         | —   | ✓   | ✓   |
| 2    | ✓         | ✓   | —   | ✓   |
| 3    | ✓         | ✓   | ✓   | —   |

*Note.* A check mark denotes complete data.

**TABLE 1.5. Missing Data Pattern for a Three-Form Design with Eight Questionnaires**

| | Item Sets | | | | | | | |
| | X | | A | | B | | C | |
| Form | $Q_1$ | $Q_2$ | $Q_3$ | $Q_4$ | $Q_5$ | $Q_6$ | $Q_7$ | $Q_8$ |
|---|---|---|---|---|---|---|---|---|
| 1 | ✓ | ✓ | ✓ | ✓ | ✓ | ✓ | — | — |
| 2 | ✓ | ✓ | ✓ | ✓ | — | — | ✓ | ✓ |
| 3 | ✓ | ✓ | — | — | ✓ | ✓ | ✓ | ✓ |
| Items | 10 | 10 | 10 | 10 | 10 | 10 | 10 | 10 |

*Note*. A check mark denotes complete data.

X and the remaining five items to set A). Graham et al. (1996) used a computer simulation study to investigate this issue and found that splitting the questionnaire across multiple item sets reduced the standard errors from a regression analysis. Despite this slight power advantage, Graham et al. (2006) recommend grouping the questionnaire items together in the same item set because this strategy facilitates the statistical analyses, particularly with a large number of variables.

## How Does the Three-Form Design Impact Power?

The main downside of planned data designs is a potential loss of statistical power. Fortunately, you can mitigate this power loss by carefully aligning the questionnaire forms to your substantive goals. However, doing so requires an understanding of some of the subtleties of the three-form design and its influence on statistical power. This section describes a number of these subtleties and illustrates the influence of planned missing data on statistical power. For simplicity, I restrict the subsequent discussion to correlations, but the basic ideas generalize to other analyses. Interested readers can find a more thorough discussion of power in Graham et al. (2006).

There are essentially three tiers of power in the three-form design, and the power of a given statistical test depends on the particular combination of item sets that are involved. To illustrate, reconsider the three-form design in Table 1.5. Table 1.7 shows a **covariance coverage matrix** that gives the percentage of respondents with complete data on a given question-

**TABLE 1.6. Missing Data Pattern for a Three-Form Design with Unequal Item Sets**

| | Item sets | | | | | | | |
| | X | | | | | A | B | C |
| Form | $Q_1$ | $Q_2$ | $Q_3$ | $Q_4$ | $Q_5$ | $Q_6$ | $Q_7$ | $Q_8$ |
|---|---|---|---|---|---|---|---|---|
| 1 | ✓ | ✓ | ✓ | ✓ | ✓ | ✓ | ✓ | — |
| 2 | ✓ | ✓ | ✓ | ✓ | ✓ | ✓ | — | ✓ |
| 3 | ✓ | ✓ | ✓ | ✓ | ✓ | — | ✓ | ✓ |
| Items | 10 | 10 | 10 | 10 | 10 | 10 | 10 | 10 |

*Note*. A check mark denotes complete data.

**TABLE 1.7. Covariance Coverage Matrix for a Three-Form Design**

| | | Item set | | | | | | | |
| --- | --- | --- | --- | --- | --- | --- | --- | --- | --- |
| | | X | | A | | B | | C | |
| Set | Scale | $Q_1$ | $Q_2$ | $Q_3$ | $Q_4$ | $Q_5$ | $Q_6$ | $Q_7$ | $Q_8$ |
| X | $Q_1$ | 100% | | | | | | | |
| | $Q_2$ | 100% | 100% | | | | | | |
| A | $Q_3$ | 66% | 66% | 66% | | | | | |
| | $Q_4$ | 66% | 66% | 66% | 66% | | | | |
| B | $Q_5$ | 66% | 66% | 33% | 33% | 66% | | | |
| | $Q_6$ | 66% | 66% | 33% | 33% | 66% | 66% | | |
| C | $Q_7$ | 66% | 66% | 33% | 33% | 33% | 33% | 66% | |
| | $Q_8$ | 66% | 66% | 33% | 33% | 33% | 33% | 66% | 66% |

*Note.* The percentages represent the amount of complete data for a variable or variable pair.

naire (the diagonal elements) or pair of questionnaires (the off-diagonal elements). The entire sample has complete data on a single pair of questionnaires (i.e., $Q_1$ and $Q_2$), 15 of the questionnaire pairs have a 33% missing data rate (e.g., $Q_1$ and $Q_3$), and 12 pairs have 66% missing data (e.g., $Q_3$ and $Q_5$). Not surprisingly, the percentages in Table 1.7 have an impact on statistical power. Analyses that involve two variables from the X set (e.g., the correlation between $Q_1$ and $Q_2$) have the highest power because these variables have no missing data. A second tier of associations has somewhat less power and includes correlations between an X variable and a variable from item set A, B, or C (e.g., the correlation between $Q_1$ and $Q_3$) and relationships between variables within set A, B, or C (e.g., the correlation between $Q_3$ and $Q_4$). Finally, any correlations between A, B, or C variables (e.g., the correlation between $Q_3$ and $Q_5$) will have the lowest power.

With such a large proportion of missing data, you might expect certain associations to produce abysmal power. However, this is not necessarily true. To illustrate, I performed two computer simulation studies that examined the influence of the three-form design on power. To mimic the previous research scenario, I generated 5,000 samples of $N = 300$, each with eight normally distributed variables. The first simulation generated variables with a population correlation of $\rho = .30$, and the second simulation generated data from a population with $\rho = .10$. These population correlations correspond to Cohen's (1988) benchmarks for a medium and a small effect size, respectively. I subsequently deleted data according to the three-form design in Table 1.5 and then used maximum likelihood missing data handling to estimate the sample correlation matrix for each of the 5,000 replicates. Because I generated the data from a population with a nonzero correlation, the proportion of the 5,000 replications that produced a statistically significant correlation is an estimate of power.

Table 1.8 gives the power estimates from the simulation studies. To begin, consider the power values from the $\rho = .30$ simulation. Notice that the correlation between $Q_1$ and $Q_3$ (the two X set variables) had a power of 1.00. These variables had complete data, so this power estimate serves as a useful benchmark for assessing the impact of planned missingness. It may be somewhat surprising and counterintuitive to find that the decrease in power was not

**TABLE 1.8. Correlation Power Estimates from a Three-Form Design**

| | | | Item set | | | | | | | |
|---|---|---|---|---|---|---|---|---|---|---|
| | | | X | | A | | B | | C | |
| $\rho$ | Set | Scale | $Q_1$ | $Q_2$ | $Q_3$ | $Q_4$ | $Q_5$ | $Q_6$ | $Q_7$ | $Q_8$ |
| 0.3 | X | $Q_1$ | — | | | | | | | |
| | | $Q_2$ | 1.00 | — | | | | | | |
| | A | $Q_3$ | .99 | .99 | — | | | | | |
| | | $Q_4$ | .99 | .99 | .99 | — | | | | |
| | B | $Q_5$ | .99 | .99 | .90 | .90 | — | | | |
| | | $Q_6$ | .99 | .99 | .90 | .90 | .99 | — | | |
| | C | $Q_7$ | .99 | .99 | .91 | .91 | .90 | .91 | — | |
| | | $Q_8$ | .99 | .99 | .90 | .91 | .91 | .90 | .99 | — |
| 0.1 | X | $Q_1$ | — | | | | | | | |
| | | $Q_2$ | .41 | — | | | | | | |
| | A | $Q_3$ | .29 | .30 | — | | | | | |
| | | $Q_4$ | .30 | .30 | .28 | — | | | | |
| | B | $Q_5$ | .30 | .30 | .18 | .18 | — | | | |
| | | $Q_6$ | .30 | .30 | .19 | .18 | .29 | — | | |
| | C | $Q_7$ | .30 | .31 | .20 | .19 | .19 | .18 | — | |
| | | $Q_8$ | .29 | .29 | .18 | .18 | .18 | .19 | .29 | — |

commensurate with overall reduction in sample size. For example, consider the correlation between $Q_1$ and $Q_3$. A 33% missing data rate on $Q_3$ produced a 1% drop in power. The correlation between $Q_3$ and $Q_5$ is even more remarkable because one-third of the sample had complete data on this variable pair, yet power decreased by only 10%. The fact that power did not decrease dramatically is largely a by-product of maximum likelihood estimation. As you will see in Chapter 4, maximum likelihood uses the entire sample to estimate the parameters, so estimation effectively borrows information from the observed data to estimate the parameters of the incomplete variables (e.g., cases with missing $Q_3$ scores have $Q_1$ data that can help estimate the correlation between $Q_1$ and $Q_3$). Consequently, the loss of power from a planned missing data design is not necessarily as extreme as you might expect.

Next, consider the power estimates from the $\rho = .10$ simulation. In this situation, the correlation between the two complete variables (i.e., $Q_1$ and $Q_2$) had a power value of .41. Again, this power estimate serves as a useful benchmark for assessing the impact of planned missingness. Consistent with the previous simulation results, the decrease in power was not commensurate with overall reduction in sample size, although it was more nearly so. For example, the variable pairs with 33% missing data had an average power decrease of approximately 28%, while power dropped by roughly 55% for the variable pairs with a 66% missing data rate. In this simulation, relatively weak correlations limited the amount of information that maximum likelihood could borrow from the observed data, so the drop in power more closely approximates the missing data rate. As a rule, the impact of missing data on power will diminish as the correlations among the variables increase in magnitude.

Increasing the number of variables in the X set is one way to improve the power of a planned missingness design because it will increase the number of hypotheses that you can test with the full sample. Fortunately, the three-form design is flexible and does not require an equal distribution of questionnaire items across the four item sets. For example, the three-form design in Table 1.6 assigns five questionnaires to the X set and one questionnaire to each of the remaining sets. This design dramatically increases the number of variable pairs with complete data and decreases the number of tests with low power. Effect size is another factor that you can use to manipulate the power of a planned missing data design. For example, variables that you expect to produce a large effect size are good candidates for the A, B, or C set because they have lower sample size requirements. Conversely, you should consider placing a variable in the X set if you expect it to produce a small effect size because doing so will maximize power. Implementing a planned missingness design clearly requires some careful preparation, but these designs are very flexible and allow you to balance substantive and power concerns. Graham et al. (2006) provide additional details on the power of a three-form design.

## Estimating Interaction Effects from a Three-Form Design

There are a number of nuances to consider when deciding how to distribute questionnaires across the four item sets. The previous section clearly suggests that the placement of a questionnaire influences statistical power. Questionnaire placement becomes even more critical when the goal is to estimate interaction effects. Unlike some planned missing data designs, the three-form design allows you to estimate every zero-order association in the data. However, the design does have limitations for testing higher-order effects.

Returning to the three-form design in Table 1.5, suppose that the researcher wants to examine whether $Q_5$ moderates the relationship between $Q_3$ and $Q_7$ (i.e., a B variable moderates the association between an A variable and a C variable). One way to address this question is to estimate a regression model with $Q_3$, $Q_5$, and the $Q_3Q_5$ product term as predictors of $Q_7$ (Aiken & West, 1991). However, it is impossible to estimate this regression model from the three-form design in Table 1.5. To illustrate the problem, Table 1.9 shows the missing data patterns that result when you form a product term between an A variable and a B variable (e.g., the $Q_3Q_5$ product term). Notice that one-third of the sample has complete data on both A and B (and thus the AB product term), but this subset of cases does not have data on the criterion variable from the C set. Consequently, there is no way to estimate the association between the outcome variable and the product term.

The three-form design does allow for two-way interactions, but one or more of the analysis variables must be from the X set (it does not matter whether this variable is a predictor or the criterion). To illustrate, suppose that an X variable moderates the association between a B variable and a C variable (e.g., a regression model with X, B, and the XB product term as predictors of C). Table 1.9 shows the missing data patterns for this new configuration of variables. Notice that every bivariate relationship among the regression model variables appears

**TABLE 1.9. Missing Data Pattern for a Three-Form Design with Interaction Terms**

| | Item sets | | | | Interaction terms | |
|---|---|---|---|---|---|---|
| Form | X | A | B | C | AB | XB |
| 1 | ✓ | — | ✓ | ✓ | — | ✓ |
| 2 | ✓ | ✓ | — | ✓ | — | — |
| 3 | ✓ | ✓ | ✓ | — | ✓ | ✓ |

*Note.* A check mark denotes complete data.

in at least one questionnaire form, so it is now possible to estimate the model. Not surprisingly, questionnaire placement becomes more complex with three-way interactions. The three-form design does allow you to estimate certain three-way interactions, but the X set must include the criterion variable and at least one of the predictor variables.

## 1.12 PLANNED MISSING DATA FOR LONGITUDINAL DESIGNS

The problem of respondent burden can be particularly acute in longitudinal studies where participants fill out questionnaire batteries on multiple occasions. Graham et al. (2001) applied the logic of the three-form design to longitudinal data and investigated the power of several planned missingness designs. The basic idea behind these designs is to split the sample into a number of random subgroups and impose planned missing data patterns on each subgroup. Table 1.10 is an example of one such design where the random subgroups have missing data at a single wave.

Graham et al. (2001) outlined a number of planned missing data designs and examined each design's power to detect an intervention effect in a longitudinal analysis. The design in Table 1.10 was 94% as powerful as a complete-data analysis, but there were other designs that produced comparable power with fewer data points. For example, Table 1.11 shows a design that was 91% as powerful as a complete-data analysis but eliminated 44% of the total data points. (By data points, I mean the total number of observations in the data matrix.) The interesting thing about these results is that the planned missing data designs were actually

**TABLE 1.10. Planned Missing Data Pattern 1 for a Longitudinal Design**

| | Data collection wave | | | | | |
|---|---|---|---|---|---|---|
| Group | 1 | 2 | 3 | 4 | 5 | % of N |
| 1 | ✓ | ✓ | ✓ | ✓ | ✓ | 16.7 |
| 2 | ✓ | ✓ | ✓ | ✓ | — | 16.7 |
| 3 | ✓ | ✓ | ✓ | — | ✓ | 16.7 |
| 4 | ✓ | ✓ | — | ✓ | ✓ | 16.7 |
| 5 | ✓ | — | ✓ | ✓ | ✓ | 16.7 |
| 6 | — | ✓ | ✓ | ✓ | ✓ | 16.7 |

*Note.* A check mark denotes complete data.

**TABLE 1.11. Planned Missing Data Pattern 2 for a Longitudinal Design**

| Group | Data collection wave 1 | 2 | 3 | 4 | 5 | % of N |
|-------|-----|-----|-----|-----|-----|--------|
| 1 | ✓ | ✓ | ✓ | ✓ | ✓ | 9.1 |
| 2 | ✓ | ✓ | ✓ | — | — | 10.1 |
| 3 | ✓ | ✓ | — | ✓ | — | 10.1 |
| 4 | ✓ | — | ✓ | ✓ | — | 10.1 |
| 5 | ✓ | ✓ | — | — | ✓ | 20.2 |
| 6 | ✓ | — | ✓ | — | ✓ | 20.2 |
| 7 | ✓ | — | — | ✓ | ✓ | 20.2 |

*Note.* A check mark denotes complete data.

more powerful than a complete-data design that used the same number of data points. This has important implications for designing a longitudinal study. For example, suppose that each assessment (i.e., data point) costs $50 to administer and your grant budget allows you to collect 1,000 assessments. Graham et al.'s simulation results suggest that collecting complete data from N participants will actually yield less power than collecting incomplete data from a larger number of respondents.

The Graham et al. (2001) designs are particularly useful for studies that examine change following an intervention or a treatment. However, many researchers are interested in developmental processes that involve age-related change (e.g., the development of reading skills in early elementary school, the development of religiousness throughout the life span, the development of behavioral problems during the teenage years). The so-called **cohort-sequential design** (Duncan, Duncan, & Hops, 1996; Nesselroade & Baltes, 1979) is a common planned missing data design that is ideally suited for this type of research question.

The basic idea behind the cohort-sequential design is to combine a number of short-term longitudinal studies into a single longitudinal data analysis. You do this by sampling different age cohorts at the initial data collection wave and following each cohort over the same period. Table 1.12 shows the cohort-sequential design from a 3-year study of teenage alcohol use (Duncan et al., 1996). Notice that each age cohort has three waves of intentional missing data (e.g., the 12-year-olds have missing data at ages 15, 16, and 17, the 13-year-olds have missing data at ages 12, 16, and 17, and so on). Maximum likelihood missing data handling allows you to combine data from multiple cohorts into a single data analysis, so you can examine change over a developmental span that exceeds the data collection period. For example, Duncan et al. (1996) used the design in Table 1.12 to examine the change in alcohol use over the 5-year period between ages 12 and 17. Like other planned missingness designs, the cohort-sequential design yields MCAR data.

The cohort-sequential design is extremely useful for developmental research but has an important limitation. Unlike the other designs in this section, the cohort-sequential design includes variable pairs that are completely missing. For example, the design in Table 1.12 yields missing data for six variable pairs: ages 12 and 15, 12 and 16, 12 and 17, 13 and 16, 13 and 17, and 14 and 17. These missing data patterns pose no problem for a longitudinal growth curve analysis, but they limit your ability to estimate zero-order correlations. The only way to eliminate this problem is to collect data across the entire developmental span, but this

**TABLE 1.12. Missing Data Pattern for a Cohort-Sequential Design**

| Cohort | Yearly data collection points | | | | | |
|--------|------|------|------|------|------|------|
|        | 12   | 13   | 14   | 15   | 16   | 17   |
| 12     | ✓    | ✓    | ✓    | —    | —    | —    |
| 13     | —    | ✓    | ✓    | ✓    | —    | —    |
| 14     | —    | —    | ✓    | ✓    | ✓    | —    |
| 15     | —    | —    | —    | ✓    | ✓    | ✓    |

*Note.* A check mark denotes complete data.

defeats the purpose of the design. Despite this important limitation, the cohort-sequential design is a useful tool for examining age-related change that is quite common, particularly in psychological research. As an aside, the fact that certain correlations are inestimable rules out multiple imputation as a missing data handling technique for this design (the sample covariance matrix plays an integral role in the imputation process). This problem is not a concern when using maximum likelihood to estimate a growth curve model.

## 1.13 CONDUCTING POWER ANALYSES FOR PLANNED MISSING DATA DESIGNS

Estimating power is one of the difficulties associated with implementing a planned missing data design. The power loss in these designs is generally not proportional to the decrease in the sample size and depends on the magnitude of the correlations among the methods. This makes it very difficult to get accurate power estimates from standard analysis techniques. Researchers have outlined power analysis techniques that account for missing data, but these approaches are limited in scope (Hedeker, Gibbons, & Waternaux, 1999; Tu et al., 2007). Monte Carlo computer simulations are a useful alternative that you can use to estimate power for virtually any analysis. This section describes how to use computer simulations to estimate power for the three-form design, but the basic approach generalizes to any number of power analyses, with or without missing data. Paxton, Curran, Bollen, Kirby, and Chen (2001) give a more detailed overview of Monte Carlo methodology, and Muthén and Muthén (2002) illustrate Monte Carlo power simulations.

A Monte Carlo simulation generates a large number of samples from a population with a hypothesized set of parameter values. Estimating a statistical model on each artificial sample and saving the resulting parameter estimates yield an empirical sampling distribution for each model parameter. The ultimate goal of a power simulation is to determine the proportion of statistically significant parameter estimates in this distribution. Many statistical software packages have built-in data generation routines that do not require much programming, so it is relatively straightforward to perform power simulations. Structural equation modeling packages are particularly useful because they offer a variety of different data generation and analysis options. Some of these packages also have a number of built-in routines for simulating missing data.*

---

*Analysis syntax is available on the companion website, *www.appliedmissingdata.com.*

The first step of a computer simulation is to specify the population parameters. In my previous power simulations, I specified eight standardized variables from a normally distributed population with correlations of $\rho = .10$ and .30. This is a very straightforward data generation model, but specifying the population parameters is typically the most difficult aspect of a computer simulation. For example, a Monte Carlo power analysis for a regression model requires population values for all model parameters (i.e., the regression coefficients, correlations among predictors, and residual variance). This is not unique to Monte Carlo power simulations, and standard power analyses effectively require the same information expressed in the form of an effect size. For example, Cohen's (1988) approach converts the regression model parameters into an $f^2$ effect size metric. The population correlations that I used are convenient because they align with Cohen's small and medium effect size benchmarks, but deriving parameter values from published research studies or meta-analyses is a much better approach.

The next step of the simulation process is to generate a large number of samples from the specified population model. For example, my previous simulations generated 5,000 samples of $N = 300$ cases each. Software packages with built-in Monte Carlo routines typically require only a couple of key words or commands to specify the number of samples and the size of each sample. Simulating missing values can be a difficult aspect of a power simulation. Some software packages have built-in routines for generating missing data, whereas others do not. Again, structural equation modeling packages are particularly useful because some programs offer a number of options for simulating missing data. The availability of such a routine may be a factor to consider when choosing a software package.

The next step of the simulation is to estimate a statistical model on each artificial data set. In my previous power simulations, I used maximum likelihood missing data handling to estimate the correlation matrix for each of the 5,000 samples. As you will see in Chapter 4, maximum likelihood estimation is very easy to implement and typically requires only a single additional key word or line of code. Maximum likelihood missing data handling is implemented in virtually every structural equation modeling program, and I rely heavily on these packages throughout the book.

Describing the empirical sampling distribution of the parameter estimates is the final step of a computer simulation. For the purpose of a power analysis, you would always generate the data from a population where the null hypothesis is false (e.g., the population correlation is nonzero). Consequently, power is the proportion of samples that produce a statistically significant parameter estimate. Programs that have built-in Monte Carlo facilities often report the proportion of significant replications as part of their standard output, so obtaining the power estimates often requires no additional programming.

Using Monte Carlo simulations to estimate power sounds tedious, but software packages tend to automate the process. Generating the power estimates in Table 1.8 was actually quite easy and took just a few lines of code. Specifying reasonable values for the population parameters is by far the most time-consuming part of the process. Once you write the program, the software package automatically generates the data, estimates the model, and summarizes the simulation results. For many common statistical models, this entire process takes just a few minutes to complete.

As an aside, you can also use standard analysis techniques to estimate the power for planned missingness designs (Graham et al., 2006, p. 340), but this is a less accurate approach. As an illustration, reconsider the three-form design in Table 1.5. Suppose that you were considering a total sample size of $N = 300$ and wanted to estimate power for the correlation between $Q_3$ and $Q_5$ (an A variable and a B variable). This portion of the design has 66% missing data, so you could simply use $N = 100$ to estimate power. The power of a two-tailed significance test with $\alpha = .05$ and $\rho = .30$ is approximately .86 (Cohen, 1988, p. 93). Standard power analyses do not account for the fact that maximum likelihood estimation borrows strength from other analysis variables, so they underestimate the true power (e.g., the Monte Carlo power estimate in Table 1.8 is slightly higher at .90). Nevertheless, standard power analysis methods are a viable option for generating conservative power estimates.

## 1.14 DATA ANALYSIS EXAMPLE

This section presents a data analysis example that illustrates how to use MCAR tests to identify potential correlates of missingness.* The analyses use artificial data from a questionnaire on eating disorder risk. Briefly, the data contain the responses from 400 college-aged women on 10 questions from the Eating Attitudes Test (EAT; Garner, Olmsted, Bohr, & Garfinkel, 1982), a widely used measure of eating disorder risk. The 10 questions measure two constructs, Drive for Thinness (e.g., "I avoid eating when I'm hungry") and Food Preoccupation (e.g., "I find myself preoccupied with food"), and mimic the two-factor structure proposed by Doninger, Enders, and Burnett (2005). Figure 4.3 shows a graphic of the EAT factor structure and abbreviated descriptions of the item stems. The data set also contains an anxiety scale score, a variable that measures beliefs about Western standards of beauty (e.g., high scores indicate that respondents internalize a thin ideal of beauty), and body mass index (BMI) values.

Variables in the EAT data set are missing for a variety of reasons. I simulated MCAR data by randomly deleting scores from the anxiety variable, the Western standards of beauty scale, and two of the EAT questions ($EAT_2$ and $EAT_{21}$). It seems reasonable to expect a relationship between body weight and missingness, so I created MAR data on five variables ($EAT_1$, $EAT_{10}$, $EAT_{12}$, $EAT_{18}$, and $EAT_{24}$) by deleting the EAT scores for a subset of cases in both tails of the BMI distribution. These same EAT questions were also missing for individuals with elevated anxiety scores. Finally, I introduced a small amount of MNAR data by deleting a number of the high body mass index scores (e.g., to mimic a situation where females with high BMI values refuse to be weighed). The deletion process typically produced a missing data rate of 5 to 10% on each variable.

I began the analysis by computing Little's (1988) MCAR test. The test was statistically significant, $\chi^2(489) = 643.32, p < .001$, which indicates that the missing data patterns produced mean differences that are inconsistent with the MCAR mechanism. This is an appropriate conclusion given that a number of variables in the data set are either MAR or MNAR. Little's procedure is essentially an omnibus test that evaluates whether all of the missing data patterns in a data set are mutually consistent with the MCAR mechanism. Consequently, the test is not particularly useful for identifying individual variables that are potential correlates of missingness.

---

*Analysis syntax and data are available on the companion website, *www.appliedmissingdata.com*.

A more focused approach for testing MCAR is to classify individuals as observed or missing on a particular variable and then test for group mean differences on other measured variables (Dixon, 1988). To illustrate, I created a missing data indicator for each of the seven incomplete EAT questionnaire items, such that $r = 1$ if an individual's score was observed and $r = 0$ if the value was missing. I then used each indicator as the grouping variable in a series of independent $t$ tests that compared the means of the remaining variables. Table 1.13 shows the $t$ statistics and the standardized mean difference values for these comparisons. The table lists the grouping variables (i.e., the missing data indicators) in the rows and uses bold typeface to denote the $t$ statistics that exceed an approximate critical value of plus or minus two. I computed the standardized mean difference values by dividing the raw mean difference by the maximum likelihood estimate of the standard deviation. Cohen (1988) suggested values of .20, .50, and .80 as thresholds for a small, medium, and large standardized mean difference, respectively.

Table 1.13 illustrates several important points. To begin, 20 of the 91 $t$ statistics are statistically significant, and several others are very nearly so. You would expect a collection of tests this large to produce about five type I errors, so the sheer number of significant comparisons provides compelling evidence that the EAT variables are not MCAR. Again, this is an appropriate conclusion given that five of the questionnaire items are MAR. Although the $t$ tests correctly rule out the MCAR mechanism, they do a poor job of identifying the cause of missing data. For example, notice that several pairs of EAT variables produced significant $t$ tests. In reality, the probability of missing data is solely a function of body mass index and anxiety, so these results are a spurious by-product of the mutual associations among the variables. Finally, notice that the $t$ tests fail to identify body mass index as a cause of missingness on the five EAT variables with MAR data. Deleting the EAT scores for cases in both tails of body mass index distribution produced missing data groups with roughly equal BMI means. It is therefore not surprising that the $t$ tests fail to identify the relationship between body mass index and missingness. Any test that evaluates homogeneity of means would fail to detect BMI as a correlate of missingness, so this underscores the fact that these procedures are not definitive tests of MCAR.

The primary benefit of performing MCAR tests is to identify potential correlates of missingness (i.e., auxiliary variables) that you can subsequently incorporate into the missing data handling procedure. The $t$ tests are useful in this regard because they identify specific variables that are not MCAR. To illustrate, suppose that the ultimate analysis goal is to fit a confirmatory factor analysis model to the EAT questionnaire data. The MAR assumption is automatically satisfied if missingness on an EAT variable is related to another questionnaire item in the factor model. Consequently, you can ignore any $t$ test that has an EAT question as the outcome because these correlates of missingness are already in the analysis. The bigger concern is whether probability of missing data relates to variables outside of the analysis model because excluding these correlates of missingness violates the MAR assumption and can produce biased parameter estimates. For example, the $t$ test results in the three rightmost columns of Table 1.13 suggest that body mass index, anxiety, and beliefs about Western standards of beauty are potential correlates of missingness because each variable is significantly related to at least one of the EAT indicators. In truth, the Western standards of beauty variable is unrelated to missingness, but Collins et al. (2001) showed that mistakenly using an auxiliary variable that is unrelated to missingness has no negative impact on the subsequent

**TABLE 1.13. Comparison of Missing and Complete Cases from the Data Analysis Example**

| Indicator | Statistic | EAT₁ | EAT₂ | EAT₁₀ | EAT₁₁ | EAT₁₂ | EAT₁₄ | EAT₂₄ | EAT₃ | EAT₁₈ | EAT₂₁ | BMI | WSB | ANX |
|---|---|---|---|---|---|---|---|---|---|---|---|---|---|---|
| | | | | | | | Comparison variable | | | | | | | |
| $EAT_1$ | $t$ | — | -1.17 | -0.28 | -0.35 | -1.64 | -1.93 | -1.31 | -2.13 | -2.50 | -1.56 | -0.09 | -0.49 | -2.38 |
| | $d$ | — | -0.29 | -0.07 | -0.07 | -0.43 | -0.39 | -0.4 | -0.47 | -0.58 | -0.34 | -0.02 | -0.11 | -0.53 |
| $EAT_2$ | $t$ | 1.28 | — | 0.22 | 0.51 | 0.02 | 1.14 | 0.08 | 1.49 | 0.74 | 1.15 | -0.66 | 0.11 | 0.24 |
| | $d$ | 0.31 | — | 0.04 | 0.09 | 0.00 | 0.16 | 0.01 | 0.27 | 0.14 | 0.20 | -0.15 | 0.03 | 0.05 |
| $EAT_{10}$ | $t$ | -2.32 | -1.27 | — | -1.19 | 0.98 | -1.40 | -0.63 | -1.37 | -1.79 | -1.87 | -1.06 | -0.92 | -3.66 |
| | $d$ | -0.57 | -0.21 | — | -0.22 | 0.20 | -0.25 | -0.14 | -0.25 | -0.39 | -0.36 | -0.22 | -0.20 | -0.47 |
| $EAT_{12}$ | $t$ | -2.38 | -1.62 | -0.88 | -1.97 | — | -1.84 | -1.55 | -1.98 | -1.32 | -1.57 | 0.80 | 0.06 | -5.39 |
| | $d$ | -0.47 | -0.28 | -0.18 | -0.42 | — | -0.33 | -0.25 | -0.43 | -0.28 | -0.32 | 0.16 | 0.01 | -0.85 |
| $EAT_{24}$ | $t$ | -2.41 | -3.19 | -1.96 | -3.03 | -1.95 | -2.28 | — | -1.37 | -1.20 | -0.60 | -0.89 | -2.03 | -4.16 |
| | $d$ | -0.42 | -0.71 | -0.38 | -0.60 | -0.39 | -0.46 | — | -0.30 | -0.31 | -0.12 | -0.19 | -0.33 | -0.70 |
| $EAT_{18}$ | $t$ | -1.45 | -2.89 | -2.02 | -2.48 | -0.71 | -1.62 | -2.73 | -1.98 | — | -1.76 | -1.69 | -3.03 | -4.65 |
| | $d$ | -0.28 | -0.60 | -0.39 | -0.47 | -0.10 | -0.31 | -0.54 | -0.37 | — | -0.35 | -0.34 | -0.51 | -0.79 |
| $EAT_{21}$ | $t$ | 1.77 | 0.38 | 0.20 | -0.72 | 0.72 | 1.31 | -1.09 | 0.30 | 0.04 | — | -2.10 | -0.33 | -0.01 |
| | $d$ | 0.31 | 0.10 | 0.06 | -0.19 | 0.18 | 0.29 | -0.30 | 0.08 | 0.01 | — | -0.53 | -0.09 | 0.00 |

*Note.* $d$ = standardized mean difference; BMI = body mass index; WSB = Western standards of beauty; ANX = anxiety. Positive values of $d$ indicate that the observed cases had a higher mean, and negative $d$ values indicate that the missing cases had a higher mean. **Bold** typeface denotes statistically significant comparisons.

analysis results. This suggests that you can be liberal when using the *t* tests to identify potential correlates of missingness because there is ultimately no harm in committing a type I error. However, my experience suggests that there is little benefit to using a large number of auxiliary variables. Consequently, you may want to identify a small set of variables that produce the largest standardized mean difference values.

## 1.15 SUMMARY

This chapter described some of the fundamental concepts that you will encounter repeatedly throughout the book. In particular, the first half of the chapter outlined missing data theory. Rubin (1976) and colleagues (Little & Rubin, 2002) introduced a classification system for missing data problems that is widely used in the literature today. This work has generated three so-called missing data mechanisms that describe how the probability of a missing value relates to the data, if at all. First, data are MAR when the probability of missing data on a variable Y is related to some other measured variable (or variables) but not to the values of Y itself. Second, the MCAR mechanism is stricter because it requires that the probability of missing data on a variable Y is unrelated to other measured variables and to the values of Y itself (i.e., the observed scores are a random sample of the hypothetically complete data set). Finally, the data are MNAR when the probability of missing data on a variable Y is related to the values of Y itself, even after controlling for other variables.

Rubin's missing data mechanisms are important because they essentially operate as assumptions that govern the performance of different missing data handling methods. For example, most of the ad hoc missing data techniques that researchers have been using for decades (e.g., discarding cases with incomplete data) require MCAR data. In contrast, the two state-of-the-art techniques—maximum likelihood estimation and multiple imputation—require the less stringent MAR assumption. Rubin's mechanisms are of great practical importance because all missing data techniques produce biased parameter estimates when their requisite assumptions do not hold.

The second half of the chapter introduced the idea of planned missing data. Researchers have proposed a number of designs that produce MCAR or MAR data as an intentional by-product of data collection. These so-called planned missingness designs use benign missing data to solve a number of practical problems. Among other things, planned missing data can reduce respondent burden in questionnaire designs, lower the cost associated with data collection, and diminish the data collection burden in longitudinal designs. Maximum likelihood and multiple imputation allow researchers to analyze data from planned missingness designs without having to discard the incomplete cases, and the power loss from the missing data is generally not proportional to the missing data rate. Planned missing data designs are highly useful and underutilized tools that will undoubtedly increase in popularity in the future.

Having established the basic theory behind missing data analyses, in the next chapter I describe a number of traditional missing data techniques that are still common in published research articles. These approaches typically assume an MCAR mechanism and yield biased parameter estimates with MAR and MNAR data. The methods in Chapter 2 have increasingly fallen out of favor in recent years, but the widespread availability and use of these techniques make it important to understand when and why they fail.

## 1.16 RECOMMENDED READINGS

Graham, J. W., Taylor, B. J., Olchowski, A. E., & Cumsille, P. E. (2006). Planned missing data designs in psychological research. *Psychological Methods, 11,* 323–343.

Little, R. J. A., & Rubin, D. B. (2002). *Statistical analysis with missing data* (2nd ed.). Hoboken, NJ: Wiley.

Rubin, D. B. (1976). Inference and missing data. *Biometrika, 63,* 581–592.

Schafer, J. L., & Graham, J. W. (2002). Missing data: Our view of the state of the art. *Psychological Methods, 7,* 147–177.

# 2

# Traditional Methods for Dealing with Missing Data

## 2.1 CHAPTER OVERVIEW

Methodologists have been studying missing data for decades and have proposed dozens of techniques to address the problem. Many of these approaches have enjoyed widespread use, while others are now little more than a historical footnote. This chapter describes a few of the more common "traditional" missing data handling methods that you are likely to encounter in published research articles or in statistical software packages. Despite their widespread use, these traditional approaches have increasingly fallen out of favor in the methodological literature (Little & Rubin, 2002; Wilkinson & Task Force on Statistical Inference, 1999), so it is important to understand when and why they fail.

The methods in this chapter deal with missing data by removing the cases with incomplete data or by filling in the missing values (i.e., imputation). Deleting the missing data is a strategy that is firmly entrenched in statistical software packages and is exceedingly common in disciplines such as psychology and education (Peugh & Enders, 2004). Eliminating the missing cases requires the missing completely at random (MCAR) mechanism (i.e., missingness is unrelated to any measured variables) and will produce biased parameter estimates when this assumption does not hold. The imputation methods are diverse in their approach and generally perform poorly, even when the data are MCAR. Only one of the methods in this chapter—stochastic regression imputation—gives unbiased parameter estimates with missing at random (MAR) data (i.e., missingness is related to other measured variables). Despite its more relaxed assumption, stochastic regression has problems that make it inferior to maximum likelihood and multiple imputation, the MAR-based approaches that I describe in subsequent chapters.

I use the small bivariate data set in Table 2.1 to illustrate ideas throughout this chapter. I designed these data to mimic an employee selection scenario in which prospective employees complete an IQ test and a psychological well-being questionnaire during their interview. The company subsequently hires the applicants that score in the upper half of the IQ

**TABLE 2.1. Employee Selection Data Set**

| Complete data | | Missing data |
|---|---|---|
| IQ | Job performance | Job Performance |
| 78 | 9 | — |
| 84 | 13 | — |
| 84 | 10 | — |
| 85 | 8 | — |
| 87 | 7 | — |
| 91 | 7 | — |
| 92 | 9 | — |
| 94 | 9 | — |
| 94 | 11 | — |
| 96 | 7 | — |
| 99 | 7 | 7 |
| 105 | 10 | 10 |
| 105 | 11 | 11 |
| 106 | 15 | 15 |
| 108 | 10 | 10 |
| 112 | 10 | 10 |
| 113 | 12 | 12 |
| 115 | 14 | 14 |
| 118 | 16 | 16 |
| 134 | 12 | 12 |

distribution, and a supervisor rates their job performance following a 6-month probationary period. Note that the job performance scores are missing at random (MAR) because they are systematically missing as a function of IQ (i.e., individuals in the lower half of the IQ distribution were never hired, and thus have no performance rating). Figure 2.1 shows a scatterplot of the hypothetically complete data set. I use the complete-data scatterplot throughout

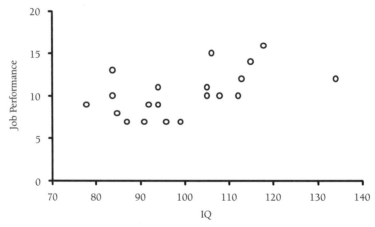

**FIGURE 2.1.** Complete-data scatterplot of the IQ and job performance scores from Table 2.1.

the chapter to visually illustrate the impact of applying certain traditional missing data handling techniques.

## 2.2 AN OVERVIEW OF DELETION METHODS

Listwise and pairwise deletion are by far the most common missing data handling approaches in many areas of the social and behavioral sciences (Peugh & Enders, 2004). The primary advantage of these methods is that they are convenient to implement and are standard options in statistical software packages. However, deletion methods have serious limitations that preclude their use in most situations. Most importantly, these approaches assume MCAR data and can produce distorted parameter estimates when this assumption does not hold. Even if the MCAR assumption is plausible, eliminating data is wasteful and can dramatically reduce power. Consequently, there is little to recommend these techniques unless the proportion of missing data is trivially small. A report by the American Psychological Association Task Force on Statistical Inference (Wilkinson & Task Force on Statistical Inference, 1999, p. 598) echoed this sentiment, stating that "The two popular methods for dealing with missing data that are found in basic statistical packages—listwise and pairwise deletion of missing values—are among the worst methods available for practical applications." A relatively large number of empirical studies support the Task Force's conclusion (Arbuckle, 1996; Azen, Van Guilder, & Hill, 1989; Brown, 1994; Enders, 2001; Enders & Bandalos, 2001; Haitovsky, 1968; Kim & Curry, 1977; Kromrey & Hines, 1994; Wothke, 2000).

## 2.3 LISTWISE DELETION

**Listwise deletion** (also known as **complete-case analysis**) discards the data for any case that has one or more missing values. The primary benefit of listwise deletion is convenience. Restricting the analyses to the complete cases eliminates the need for specialized software and complex missing data handling techniques (in truth, some of the procedures in subsequent chapters are quite easy to implement). Relative to pairwise deletion, listwise deletion also has the advantage of producing a common set of cases for all analyses.

In most situations, the disadvantages of listwise deletion far outweigh its advantages. The primary problem with listwise deletion is that it requires MCAR data and can produce distorted parameter estimates when this assumption does not hold. To illustrate this propensity for bias, Figure 2.2 shows the listwise deletion scatterplot of the data in Table 2.1. Recall that the data are MAR because the applicants in the lower half of the IQ distribution have missing job performance ratings. By virtue of this selection process, listwise deletion discards the entire lower half of the IQ distribution. Because IQ scores and job performance ratings are positively correlated, listwise deletion also excludes cases from the lower tail of the job performance distribution (i.e., the cases with low IQ scores). Not surprisingly, the remaining cases are unrepresentative of the hypothetically complete data set because they have systematically higher scores on both variables. Consequently, the listwise deletion mean estimates are too high. In addition, the restriction of range that results from discarding the lower tails

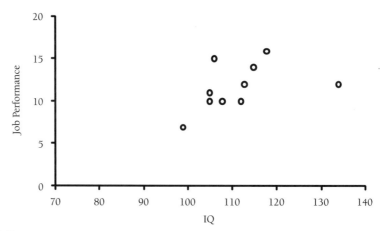

**FIGURE 2.2.** Listwise deletion scatterplot of the IQ and job performance data from Table 2.1. Because the variables are positively correlated, listwise deletion systematically discards cases from the lower tails of both distributions. This overestimates the means and attenuates the variability and the correlation.

of the distributions restricts the variability of the data and reduces the magnitude of the correlation. The scatterplot in Figure 2.2 clearly illustrates these biases.

Bias aside, listwise deletion is potentially very wasteful, particularly when the discarded cases have data on a large number of variables. Deleting the incomplete data records can produce a dramatic reduction in the total sample size, the magnitude of which increases as the missing data rate or number of variables increases. For example, consider a data set with 10 variables, each of which has 2% of its observations missing in a completely random fashion. Although the proportion of missing data on any single variable is relatively small, listwise deletion should eliminate approximately 18% of the data records, on average. With 20 variables, the expected percentage of complete cases drops to about 67%. Not surprisingly, this sample size reduction can dramatically reduce statistical power, especially with small to moderate samples. This reduction in power is always a problem, even in the best case scenario where the data are MCAR.

Interestingly, listwise deletion can produce unbiased estimates of regression slopes under any missing data mechanism, provided that missingness is a function of a predictor variable and not the outcome variable (Little, 1992). This relatively esoteric scenario is the only situation in which listwise deletion is likely to outperform maximum likelihood estimation and multiple imputation with missing not at random (MNAR) data.

## 2.4 PAIRWISE DELETION

**Pairwise deletion** (also known as **available-case analysis**) attempts to mitigate the loss of data by eliminating cases on an analysis-by-analysis basis. The prototypical application of pairwise deletion occurs when a researcher uses a different subset of cases to compute each element in a correlation matrix. However, pairwise deletion is not limited to correlations, and it is common to find published research articles that report varying sample sizes across a set of ANOVA or regression analyses (Peugh & Enders, 2004). Using as much of the data as possible is certainly a good idea, and it is true that pairwise deletion tends to be more powerful than listwise deletion, particularly when the variables in a data set have low to moderate correlations (Glasser, 1964). However, the disadvantages of pairwise deletion limit its utility.

Consistent with listwise deletion, the primary problem with pairwise deletion is that it requires MCAR data and can produce distorted parameter estimates when this assumption does not hold. However, pairwise deletion also has a number of unique problems. For example, using different subsets of cases poses subtle problems with measures of association. To illustrate, consider the following formula for the sample covariance.

$$\hat{\sigma}_{XY} = \frac{\Sigma(x_i - \hat{\mu}_X)(y_i - \hat{\mu}_Y)}{N - 1} \tag{2.1}$$

Pairwise deletion uses the subset of cases with complete data on both $X$ and $Y$ to compute the covariance. Most software packages use the same subsample to compute the variable means, but it is also possible to compute $\hat{\mu}_X$ from the cases that have data on $X$ and compute $\hat{\mu}_Y$ from the cases that have data on $Y$. A similar issue arises when computing the denominator of the correlation coefficient.

$$r = \frac{\hat{\sigma}_{XY}}{\sqrt{\hat{\sigma}_X^2 \hat{\sigma}_Y^2}} \tag{2.2}$$

Software packages typically use the subset of cases with complete data on both $X$ and $Y$ to compute the variances, but another option is to compute $\hat{\sigma}_X^2$ and $\hat{\sigma}_Y^2$ from separate subsamples (e.g., compute $\hat{\sigma}_X^2$ from the cases that have data on $X$ alone). The latter approach is problematic because it can produce correlation values that exceed plus or minus 1.

A correlation that exceeds 1 is an example of a more general problem in which the elements within a correlation or covariance matrix are mutually inconsistent with one another. In the context of missing data, these so-called **nonpositive definite matrices** occur when the correlation or covariance matrix contains combinations of estimates that would have been mathematically impossible, had the data been complete. These matrices cause estimation problems for multivariate analyses that use a covariance matrix as input data (e.g., regression models and structural equation models). Although there are numerous causes of nonpositive definitive matrices, methodologists often associate pairwise deletion with this problem (Little, 1992; Marsh, 1998; Wothke, 1993).

The lack of a consistent sample base also leads to problems in computing standard errors. For example, consider a regression analysis that uses a pairwise deletion covariance matrix as input data. The sample size is a key component of any standard error, but no single value of $N$ is applicable to the entire covariance matrix. Consequently, there is no straightforward way to compute standard errors. Some software packages use the average sample size per variable for these computations, but this approach is likely to underestimate the standard errors for some variables and overestimate the standard errors for others (Little, 1992). This sample size issue becomes even more complex when using a pairwise deletion covariance matrix to estimate a structural equation model because no single value of $N$ simultaneously maximizes the accuracy of standard errors and tests of model fit (Marsh, 1998).

## 2.5 AN OVERVIEW OF SINGLE IMPUTATION METHODS

The rest of this chapter is devoted to so-called **single imputation** methods that impute (i.e., fill in) the data prior to analysis. The term *single imputation* stems from the fact that these approaches generate a single replacement value for each missing data point. This is in contrast to multiple imputation, which creates several copies of the data set and imputes each copy with different plausible estimates of the missing values.

Imputation is an attractive strategy because it yields a complete data set. Consequently, convenience is a major benefit of any single imputation technique. At first glance, imputation is also advantageous because it makes use of data that deletion approaches would otherwise discard. Despite these apparent advantages, single imputation techniques have potentially serious drawbacks. Most of the approaches in this chapter produce biased parameter estimates, even in an ideal situation where the data are MCAR. Stochastic regression imputation is the sole exception because it is the only approach that produces unbiased parameter estimates with MAR data. In addition, single imputation techniques attenuate standard errors. At an intuitive level, missing values should increase standard errors because they add another layer of noise to the parameter estimates. However, analyzing a single imputed data set effectively treats the filled-in values as real data, so even the best single imputation technique (e.g., stochastic regression imputation) will underestimate sampling error. As you will see in Chapter 8, multiple imputation does not suffer from this problem because it appropriately adjusts the standard errors for missing data. Given their important drawbacks, there is very little to recommend the single imputation techniques.

## 2.6 ARITHMETIC MEAN IMPUTATION

**Arithmetic mean imputation** (also referred to as **mean substitution** and **unconditional mean imputation**) takes the seemingly appealing tack of filling in the missing values with the arithmetic mean of the available cases. The idea of replacing missing values with the mean is an old one that methodologists often attribute to Wilks (1932). Like other imputation techniques, mean imputation is convenient because it produces a complete data set. However, convenience is not a compelling advantage because this approach severely distorts the resulting parameter estimates, even when the data are MCAR.

At an intuitive level, imputing values at the center of the distribution reduces the variability of the data. It therefore makes sense that mean imputation will attenuate the standard deviation and the variance. Restricting the variability of the data also attenuates the magnitude of covariances and correlations. To illustrate, reconsider the covariance formula in Equation 2.1. Cases with missing values on either $X$ or $Y$ attenuate the magnitude of the covariance

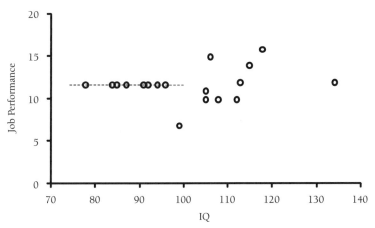

**FIGURE 2.3.** Mean imputation scatterplot of the IQ and job performance data from Table 2.1. The imputed values fall on the dashed line. Because mean imputation imputes a constant value for the missing job performance scores, it effectively infuses the data with uncorrelated observations. This attenuates the variability and the correlation.

because they contribute a value of zero to the numerator of the formula. The covariance is a key component of Pearson's *r* formula (see Equation 2.2), so the same is true for correlation coefficients. Little and Rubin (2002, pp. 61–62) give adjustment terms that produce unbiased estimates of variances and covariances with MCAR data, but these corrections end up producing estimates that are identical to those of pairwise deletion.

To illustrate mean imputation, I replaced the missing job performance scores in Table 2.1 with the average performance rating from the 10 complete cases. Figure 2.3 shows a scatterplot of the filled-in data. To begin, notice that the variability (i.e., the vertical spread) of the job performance scores is smaller than that of the complete-data scatterplot in Figure 2.1. Again, this is a consequence of imputing values at the center of the distribution. Second, notice that the imputed values fall directly on a horizontal line, which implies that the correlation between IQ and job performance is zero for the subset of cases with imputed performance ratings. Mean imputation attenuates measures of association (e.g., correlations and covariances) because it essentially infuses the data with scores that are uncorrelated with other variables in the data set. The biases in Figure 2.3 are present under any missing data mechanism, including MCAR. Not surprisingly, the bias increases as the missing data rate increases.

The biases in Figure 2.3 are consistent with the findings from empirical research studies (Brown, 1994; Enders & Bandalos, 2001; Gleason & Staelin, 1975; Kim & Curry, 1975; Kromrey & Hines, 1994; Olinsky, Chen, & Harlow, 2003; Raymond & Roberts, 1987; Timm, 1970; Wothke, 2000). In fact, simulation studies suggest that mean imputation is possibly the worst missing data handling method available. Consequently, in no situation is mean imputation defensible, and you should absolutely avoid this approach.

## 2.7 REGRESSION IMPUTATION

**Regression imputation** (also known as **conditional mean imputation**) replaces missing values with predicted scores from a regression equation. Like arithmetic mean imputation, regression imputation has a long history that dates back nearly 50 years (Buck, 1960). The basic idea behind this approach is intuitively appealing: use information from the complete variables to fill in the incomplete variables. Variables tend to be correlated, so it makes good sense to generate imputations that borrow information from the observed data. In fact, borrowing information from the observed data is a strategy that regression imputation shares with maximum likelihood and multiple imputation, although the latter approaches do so in a more sophisticated manner.

The first step of the imputation process is to estimate a set of regression equations that predict the incomplete variables from the complete variables. A complete-case analysis usually generates these estimates. The second step is to generate predicted values for the incomplete variables. These predicted scores fill in the missing values and produce a complete data set. To illustrate the imputation process, reconsider the bivariate data set in Table 2.1. I used the 10 complete cases to estimate the regression of job performance ratings on IQ. The resulting regression equation is

$$JP_i^* = \hat{\beta}_0 + \hat{\beta}_1(IQ_i) = -2.065 + 0.123(IQ_i) \tag{2.3}$$

where $JP_i^*$ is the predicted job performance score for case $i$. The applicants that were never hired have no job performance ratings, so this equation generates predicted scores (i.e., imputed values) for these cases. For example, substituting the appropriate IQ scores into the equation yields the values in the Predicted Score column of Table 2.2. These predicted scores fill in the missing job performance ratings and serve as data for all subsequent analyses.

Regression imputation is largely the same with multivariate data sets but is somewhat more complicated to implement. To illustrate, consider a hypothetical data set with three variables, $Y_1$, $Y_2$, and $Y_3$, all of which have missing data. Not including the complete cases, there are six possible missing data patterns: cases with missing data on (1) only $Y_1$, (2) only $Y_2$, (3) only $Y_3$, (4) $Y_1$ and $Y_2$, (5) $Y_1$ and $Y_3$, and (6) $Y_2$ and $Y_3$. The presence of multiple missing data patterns complicates the imputation process somewhat because each missing data pattern requires a unique regression equation. To illustrate, Table 2.3 shows the regression equations for the six missing data patterns. An easy way to construct the equations is to start with an estimate of the mean vector and the covariance matrix because the elements in these matrices define all of the necessary regression coefficients. Again, a complete-case analysis usually generates $\hat{\mu}$ and $\hat{\Sigma}$. Substituting the observed scores into the relevant regression equations generates predicted values for the incomplete variables, and these predicted scores fill in the missing values and produce a complete data set. Although it sounds tedious to construct a unique regression equation for each missing data pattern, a computational algorithm called the sweep operator can automate this process (Dempster, 1969; Goodnight, 1979; Little & Rubin, 2002).

Regression imputation is superior to mean imputation, but it too has predictable biases. To illustrate, I replaced the missing job performance scores in Table 2.1 with the predicted

**TABLE 2.2. Regression Imputation of the Employee Selection Data**

| IQ | Job performance | Predicted score | Random residual | Stochastic imputation |
|---|---|---|---|---|
| 78 | — | 7.53 | −0.35 | 7.18 |
| 84 | — | 8.27 | 2.70 | 10.97 |
| 84 | — | 8.27 | −0.59 | 7.68 |
| 85 | — | 8.39 | 2.39 | 10.78 |
| 87 | — | 8.64 | 1.64 | 10.28 |
| 91 | — | 9.13 | 5.77 | 14.90 |
| 92 | — | 9.25 | 2.47 | 11.72 |
| 94 | — | 9.50 | −1.04 | 8.46 |
| 94 | — | 9.50 | 1.69 | 11.19 |
| 96 | — | 9.74 | −3.58 | 6.16 |
| 99 | 7 | — | — | — |
| 105 | 10 | — | — | — |
| 105 | 11 | — | — | — |
| 106 | 15 | — | — | — |
| 108 | 10 | — | — | — |
| 112 | 10 | — | — | — |
| 113 | 12 | — | — | — |
| 115 | 14 | — | — | — |
| 118 | 16 | — | — | — |
| 134 | 12 | — | — | — |

*Note.* The following regression equation generated the predicted scores: $JP_i = -2.025 + .123(IQ_i)$.

scores from Table 2.2. Figure 2.4 shows a scatterplot of the filled-in data. First, notice that the imputed values fall directly on a regression line with a nonzero slope. This implies that the correlation between IQ and job performance is 1.00 in the subset of cases with imputed values. Regression imputation effectively suffers from the exact opposite problem as mean imputation because it imputes the data with perfectly correlated scores. In multivariate data sets, the imputed values will not have perfect correlations with other variables, but the correlations will still be high. Consequently, regression imputation overestimates correlations and $R^2$ statistics, even when the data are MCAR. The fact that the imputed values fall directly on a straight line (or a flat surface, in the case of multiple regression) implies that the filled-in data lack variability that would have been present had the data been complete. Not

**TABLE 2.3. Missing Data Patterns and Equations Used by Regression Imputation**

| Missing variables | Regression equations |
|---|---|
| $Y_1$ | $\hat{y}_1 = B_0 + B_1 y_2 + B_2 y_3$ |
| $Y_2$ | $\hat{y}_2 = B_0 + B_1 y_2 + B_2 y_3$ |
| $Y_3$ | $\hat{y}_3 = B_0 + B_1 y_2 + B_2 y_2$ |
| $Y_1$ and $Y_2$ | $\hat{y}_1 = B_0 + B_1 y_3$    $\hat{y}_2 = B_0 + B_1 y_3$ |
| $Y_1$ and $Y_3$ | $\hat{y}_1 = B_0 + B_1 y_2$    $\hat{y}_2 = B_0 + B_1 y_2$ |
| $Y_2$ and $Y_3$ | $\hat{y}_2 = B_0 + B_1 y_1$    $\hat{y}_2 = B_0 + B_1 y_1$ |

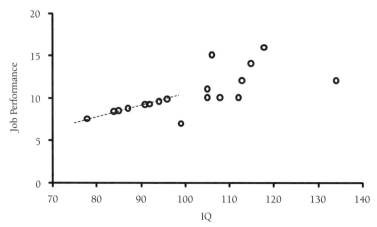

**FIGURE 2.4.** Regression imputation scatterplot of the IQ and job performance data from Table 2.1. The imputed values fall on the dashed line. Because the imputed values fall directly on a regression line, regression imputation effectively infuses the data with perfectly correlated observations. This attenuates the variability but overestimates the correlation and the $R^2$ value.

surprisingly, this attenuates variances and covariances, although not to the same extent as mean imputation.

A number of empirical studies have reported biases that are consistent with those in Figure 2.4 (Beale & Little, 1975; Gleason & Staelin, 1975; Kromrey & Hines, 1994; Olinsky et al., 2003; Raymond & Roberts, 1987; Timm, 1970). The magnitude of the bias in the variances and covariances is predictable, and methodologists have outlined corrective adjustments for these parameters (Beale & Little, 1975; Buck, 1960). Under an MCAR mechanism, these corrections yield consistent estimates of the covariance matrix, meaning that the estimates get closer to their true population values as the sample size increases. Despite the intuitive appeal of regression imputation, there is no reason to go to the additional effort of applying these corrections because more sophisticated missing data techniques are readily available.

## 2.8 STOCHASTIC REGRESSION IMPUTATION

Despite its intuitive appeal, regression imputation can lead to substantial biases. **Stochastic regression imputation** also uses regression equations to predict the incomplete variables from the complete variables, but it takes the extra step of augmenting each predicted score with a normally distributed residual term. Adding residuals to the imputed values restores lost variability to the data and effectively eliminates the biases associated with standard regression imputation schemes. In fact, stochastic regression imputation is the only procedure in this chapter that gives unbiased parameter estimates under an MAR missing data mechanism. Consequently, this is the sole traditional method that arguably has some merit.

Consistent with standard regression imputation, stochastic regression begins by using a complete-case analysis to estimate a set of regression equations that predict the incomplete variables from the complete variables. Substituting the observed scores into these regression equations yields predicted values for the missing data. As a final step, the procedure restores lost variability to the data by adding a normally distributed residual term to each predicted score. To illustrate the imputation process, reconsider the bivariate data set in Table 2.1. The imputation regression equation is as follows:

$$JP_i^* = \hat{\beta}_0 + \hat{\beta}_1(IQ_i) = -2.065 + 0.123(IQ_i) + z_i \tag{2.4}$$

Stochastic regression uses the same basic procedure as standard regression imputation, so the regression coefficients in Equation 2.4 are identical to those in Equation 2.3. However, the equation above has an additional $z_i$ term. This residual term is a random value from a normal distribution with a mean of zero and a variance equal to the residual variance from the regression of job performance on IQ. The complete-case regression analysis produced a residual variance estimate of $\hat{\sigma}^2_{JP|IQ} = 6.650$. Consequently, I used Monte Carlo simulation techniques to generate 10 scores from a normal distribution with a mean of zero and a variance equal to 6.650. The Random Residual column of Table 2.2 shows these values. Adding the residuals to the predicted scores gives the values in the Stochastic Imputation column of Table 2.2. These scores fill in the missing job performance ratings and produce a complete data set.

Figure 2.5 shows a scatterplot of the filled-in data from the stochastic regression procedure. The dashed line in the figure represents the regression of job performance on IQ (i.e., the predicted job performance scores), and the arrows denote random residuals. Comparing Figure 2.5 to the complete-data scatterplot in Figure 2.1 illustrates that stochastic regression imputation preserves the variability of the data in a manner that other single imputation techniques do not. Furthermore, the close correspondence between the two figures suggests that stochastic regression yields unbiased parameter estimates with MAR data. Although a single small data set does not provide convincing evidence that the procedure is unbiased, other authors have used analytic methods to demonstrate that this is the case (Little & Rubin, 2002). Furthermore, computer simulation studies suggest that stochastic regression produces parameter estimates that are similar to those of maximum likelihood and multiple imputation (Gold & Bentler, 2000; Newman, 2003). The fact that stochastic regression yields comparable estimates to other MAR-based missing data handling techniques is not a surprise because stochastic regression and multiple imputation actually share the same imputation routine. Conceptually, multiple imputation is just an iterative version of stochastic regression imputation. I describe the linkages between the two approaches in Chapter 7.

Extending stochastic regression imputation to multivariate data sets with several missing data patterns is typically more complex because each missing data pattern requires a unique regression equation (or set of equations). The process of constructing the regression equations is identical to standard regression imputation, so there is no need to revisit these steps. With multivariate data, the additional nuance is that each regression equation requires its own residual distribution. Each residual distribution is still a normal curve with a mean of zero, but the variances differ across missing data patterns. In patterns that have two or more variables that are missing, the residual distribution is multivariate normal with a mean vector of zero and a covariance matrix equal to the residual covariance matrix from the multivariate regression of the incomplete variables on the complete variables. For example, reconsider the

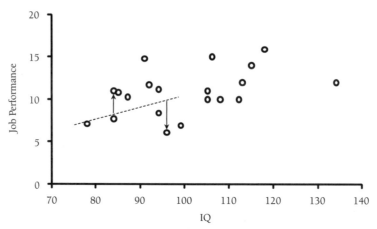

**FIGURE 2.5.** Stochastic regression imputation scatterplot of the IQ and job performance data from Table 2.1. The dashed line denotes predicted values and the arrows depict residuals. Stochastic regression generates predicted values from a regression equation and augments each predicted score with a normally distributed residual term. This preserves the distributions of the variables and produces a scatterplot that closely resembles that of the complete data.

missing data pattern in Table 2.3 where both $Y_1$ and $Y_2$ are missing. This pattern requires residuals from a multivariate normal distribution with a covariance matrix equal to the residual covariance matrix from the multivariate regression of $Y_1$ and $Y_2$ on $Y_3$.

At first glance, stochastic regression may appear to be a viable alternative to maximum likelihood and multiple imputation because it produces unbiased parameter estimates with MAR data. However, like every single imputation technique, stochastic regression attenuates standard errors, leading to an increased risk of type I errors. It makes intuitive sense that a missing data analysis should produce larger standard errors than a hypothetical complete-data analysis. However, standard analysis techniques treat the filled-in values as real data and effectively ignore the additional sampling error from the missing data. Consequently, the standard errors from a singly imputed data set will be inappropriately small. The bootstrap resampling approach that I describe in Chapter 5 can correct the bias in the stochastic regression standard errors, but implementing the bootstrap usually requires more effort than a maximum likelihood or multiple imputation analysis.

As an aside, there has been some discussion in the missing data literature regarding the imputation of missing independent variables. To illustrate, consider a small data set with three variables, $Y_1$, $Y_2$, and $Y_3$. Suppose that a researcher wants to perform a regression analysis where $Y_1$ and $Y_2$ predict $Y_3$. If either $Y_1$ or $Y_2$ has missing values, it may seem incorrect and somewhat circular to impute the missing explanatory variables using a regression equation that includes the dependent variable as a predictor. Standard regression imputation would not be appropriate in this situation because it would bias the estimates from the subsequent regression analysis (Little, 1992). However, this is not a concern with stochastic regression imputation because the random residual terms eliminate this source of bias. Consequently, there is no need to consider a variable's role in the subsequent statistical analysis when specifying an imputation model. This conclusion also applies to the multiple imputation procedure that I describe later in the book.

## 2.9 HOT-DECK IMPUTATION

Hot-deck imputation is a collection of techniques that impute the missing values with scores from "similar" respondents. Statisticians at the Census Bureau originally developed the hot-deck to deal with missing data in public-use data sets, and the procedure has a long history in survey applications (Scheuren, 2005). Researchers in the behavioral and social sciences rarely use hot-deck imputation, but the procedure has received a good deal of attention in the survey literature. This section gives a brief overview of hot-deck imputation; detailed descriptions of the technique are available in other sources (Ford, 1983; Little & Rubin, 2002; Rubin, 1987).

Methodologists have proposed several variations of hot-deck imputation. The basic premise is to impute missing values with the scores of other respondents. In its simplest incarnation, a random draw from the observed data replaces each missing value. The more typical application of hot-deck imputation replaces each missing value with a random draw from a subsample of respondents that scored similarly on a set of matching variables. For example, consider a general population survey in which some respondents refuse to disclose their income. The hot-deck procedure classifies respondents into cells based on demographic characteristics such as gender, age, race, and marital status. It then replaces the missing values with a random draw from the income distribution of respondents that shared the same constellation of demographic characteristics as the individual with missing data. Note that the background variables need not be categorical, and some hot-deck algorithms match individuals on continuous variables (e.g., nearest neighbor hot deck).

Hot-deck imputation generally preserves the univariate distributions of the data and does not attenuate the variability of the filled-in data to the same extent as other imputation methods. However, hot-deck approaches are not well suited for estimating measures of association and can produce substantially biased estimates of correlations and regression coefficients (Brown, 1994; Schafer & Graham, 2002). Like other imputation procedures, hot deck underestimates standard errors, although researchers have proposed corrective procedures (e.g., the jackknife) for estimating sampling error.

## 2.10 SIMILAR RESPONSE PATTERN IMPUTATION

Similar response pattern imputation is a technique that is available in the structural equation modeling software package LISREL (Jöreskog & Sörbom, 1993). The basic idea behind similar response pattern imputation is to impute each missing value with the score from another individual (i.e., a "donor" case) who has a similar score profile on a set of matching variables. The similar response pattern approach closely resembles a variant of hot-deck imputation known as nearest neighbor hot deck. Researchers in the social and the behavioral sciences do not use this approach very frequently, but its availability in a popular software package makes it worthy of discussion. This section gives a brief description of similar response pattern imputation, and Jöreskog and Sörbom (1993) describe the procedure in more detail.

Similar response pattern imputation requires the user to specify a set of matching variables and a set of incomplete variables. I denote these variable sets as $\mathbf{Z}$ and $\mathbf{Y}$, respectively.

Ideally, the variables in the matching set are complete and do not belong to the **Y** set, but this need not be the case. The imputation process begins by selecting a "recipient" case with missing values in **Y** and complete data in **Z**. The pool of potential donor cases has complete data on both **Y** and **Z**, and the goal is to locate the single donor whose response profile on **Z** most closely resembles that of the recipient. The matching process standardizes the variables in **Z** and computes a distance measure for each potential donor that quantifies the similarity between the donor's response profile and the recipient's response profile, as follows:

$$D = \sum_{j=1}^{k} (z_{Dj} - z_{Rj})^2 \qquad (2.5)$$

where $k$ is the number of matching variables, $z_{Dj}$ is the donor's score on matching variable $j$, and $z_{Rj}$ is the recipient's score on matching variable $j$. If a single donor minimizes $D$, that donor's **Y** scores replace the recipient's missing values. If multiple donors produce the same distance measure, the algorithm imputes each missing value with the average donor score.

Similar response pattern imputation does not necessarily produce a complete data set, and there are a number of nuances to implementing this approach. For example, identifying a set of matching variables with complete data may be a significant obstacle in and of itself. Although it is possible for incomplete variables to serve as matching variables, imputation will fail if there are no donor cases with complete data on the matching variables. Consequently, using incomplete variables as matching variables can reduce the pool of donors to the point where imputation becomes impossible, at least for a subset of cases. In addition, the similar response pattern approach sequentially imputes the missing variables, so properly ordering the variables in the **Y** set can influence the success of imputation. For example, suppose that the set of matching variables includes a number of complete variables as well as two incomplete variables, $Y_1$ and $Y_2$. Specifying $Y_1$ as the first variable in the imputation list allows $Y_1$ to function as a complete matching variable for $Y_2$. If the goal is to maximize the number of successful imputations, the variables with the highest missing data rates should be the first variables on the imputation list because this will maximize the size of the donor pool. Finally, Jöreskog and Sörbom (1993) suggest that the matching variables should not be part of the subsequent statistical analysis because this may negatively affect the resulting parameter estimates. No empirical studies have investigated this issue.

Similar response pattern imputation has no theoretical foundation, so it is difficult to predict the procedure's performance. Computer simulation studies suggest that this approach can produce relatively accurate parameter estimates with MCAR data, but it is prone to substantial biases when the data are MAR (Brown, 1994; Enders, 2001; Enders & Bandalos, 2001; Gold & Bentler, 2000). Given the widespread availability of MAR-based analysis methods, there appears to be little to recommend the use of similar response pattern imputation, particularly if the goal is to estimate the associations among a set of variables.

## 2.11 AVERAGING THE AVAILABLE ITEMS

Researchers in many disciplines use multiple-item questionnaires to measure complex constructs. For example, psychologists routinely use several questionnaire items to measure depression, each of which taps into a different depressive symptom (e.g., sadness, lack of energy, sleep difficulties, feelings of hopelessness). Rather than analyzing the individual item responses, researchers typically compute a **scale score** by summing or averaging the items that measure a common theme. The resulting scale score reflects each respondent's overall standing on the construct of interest (e.g., a higher numeric value indicates more depressive symptoms).

It is often the case that respondents answer some, but not all, of the items on a questionnaire. Rather than discard the incomplete questionnaires, researchers frequently compute scale scores by **averaging the available items**. For example, if a respondent answered 8 out of 10 items on a depression questionnaire, his scale score would be the average of those 8 items. Multiplying the resulting average by the total number of items (e.g., 10) expresses the scale score as a sum, but the choice between an average and a sum is completely arbitrary. The missing data literature sometimes describes this procedure as **person mean imputation**, but researchers in other disciplines sometimes refer to it as a **prorated scale score** (Keel, Mitchell, Davis, & Crow, 2002; Share, McCrady, & Epstein, 2002). It may not be immediately obvious, but averaging the available items is equivalent to imputing the missing values with the mean of a respondent's complete items—thus the name "person mean imputation."

Very few empirical studies have examined person mean imputation, so it is difficult to predict the procedure's performance. Schafer and Graham (2002) point out a number of potential problems with the approach (e.g., the meaning of the scale scores varies across respondents) and speculate that it might produce biased parameter estimates with MCAR data. To date, empirical studies have only investigated person mean imputation in the context of internal consistency reliability analyses (Downey & King, 1998; Enders, 2003). Coefficient alpha estimates are generally inaccurate, particularly when compared to those of maximum likelihood and deletion methods (Enders, 2003). Because coefficient alpha is largely a function of the item variances and covariances, biases may also be present in measures of variation and association. One factor that is likely to influence the performance of person mean imputation is the variability in item means and correlations. For example, averaging the available items might be reasonable when the item means are similar, but it could be problematic when the missing items have different means than the complete items. In a similar vein, the procedure probably works best when the item correlations are relatively uniform in magnitude (Graham, 2009; Schafer & Graham, 2002).

Averaging the available items is probably the most common approach for dealing with item-level missing data on questionnaires. Test manuals often give instructions for computing prorated scale scores with missing data, yet they offer no cautionary statements about the biases that can result from this procedure. Until more research accumulates, you should use person mean imputation with caution and should perhaps avoid it altogether, particularly if there are high rates of item nonresponse. Multiple imputation is a much better solution for imputing item-level missing data, and maximum likelihood can also address this problem for certain analyses.

## 2.12 LAST OBSERVATION CARRIED FORWARD

**Last observation carried forward** is a missing data technique that is specific to longitudinal designs. As its name implies, the procedure imputes missing repeated measures variables with

**TABLE 2.4. Longitudinal Data Set Imputed with Last Observation Carried Forward**

| | Observed data | | | | Last observation carried forward | | | |
|---|---|---|---|---|---|---|---|---|
| ID | Wave 1 | Wave 2 | Wave 3 | Wave 4 | Wave 1 | Wave 2 | Wave 3 | Wave 4 |
| 1 | 50 | 53 | — | — | 50 | 53 | **53** | **53** |
| 2 | 47 | 46 | 49 | 51 | 47 | 46 | 49 | 51 |
| 3 | 43 | — | — | — | 43 | **43** | **43** | **43** |
| 4 | 55 | — | 56 | 59 | 55 | **55** | 56 | 59 |
| 5 | 45 | 45 | 47 | 46 | 45 | 45 | 47 | 46 |

*Note.* **Bold** typeface denotes imputed values.

the observation that immediately precedes dropout. For example, if a participant drops out after the fifth week of an 8-week study, his week five score fills in the remaining waves of data. To illustrate, Table 2.4 shows four waves of longitudinal data for a small sample of cases. Notice that the last complete observation for each case "carries forward" to subsequent missing data points. This strategy applies to the cases that permanently drop out as well as to the cases with intermittent missing data. Like other imputation approaches, the primary benefit of last observation carried forward is convenience because it generates a complete data set.

Last observation carried forward is relatively rare in the behavioral and the social sciences, but researchers routinely use this method in medical studies and clinical trials (Wood, White, & Thompson, 2004). This technique effectively assumes that scores do not change after the last observed measurement or during the intermittent period where scores are missing. The conventional wisdom is that last observation imputation yields a conservative estimate of treatment group differences at the end of a study because it infuses the data with scores that do not change over time. However, empirical research has shown that this is not necessarily true. In fact, the imputation scheme can actually exaggerate group differences at the end of a study (Cook, Zeng, & Yi, 2004; Liu & Gould, 2002; Mallinckrodt, Clark, & David, 2001; Molenberghs et al., 2004). The direction and the magnitude of the bias are difficult to predict and depend on specific characteristics of the data, but last observation carried forward is likely to produce distorted parameter estimates, even when the data are MCAR (Molenberghs et al., 2004). Despite its frequent use in medical studies and clinical trials, a growing number of empirical studies suggest that this approach is poor strategy for dealing with longitudinal missing data (Cook et al., 2004; Liu & Gould, 2002; Mallinckrodt et al., 2001; Molenberghs et al., 2004; Shao & Zhong, 2004). These same studies generally recommend maximum likelihood or multiple imputation.

## 2.13 AN ILLUSTRATIVE COMPUTER SIMULATION STUDY

Throughout this chapter, I used scatterplots to demonstrate some of the popular traditional missing data techniques. Although these scatterplots are useful for illustration purposes, they do not offer compelling evidence about the performance of these methods. To better illustrate the properties of the traditional missing data techniques, I conducted a series of Monte Carlo computer simulations. A Monte Carlo simulation generates a large number of samples from a population with a specified set of parameter values. Estimating a statistical model on each sample and saving the resulting parameter estimates create an empirical sampling distribution for each model parameter. The difference between the average parameter estimate and the true population parameter is particularly important because it quantifies bias.

The simulation programs generated 1,000 samples of $N = 250$ from a population model that mimicked the IQ and job performance data in Table 2.1. The first simulation created MCAR data by randomly deleting 50% of the job performance ratings. The second simulation modeled MAR data and eliminated job performance scores for the cases in the lower half of the IQ distribution. The final simulation generated missing not at random (MNAR) by deleting the job performance scores for the cases in the lower half of the job performance distribution. After generating the artificial data sets, I used four different missing data techniques to estimate the mean vector and the covariance matrix from each sample: listwise deletion, arithmetic mean imputation, regression imputation, and stochastic regression imputation. Table 2.5 shows the average parameter estimates for each technique and uses **bold** typeface to highlight severely biased estimates.

As seen in the table, arithmetic mean imputation produced biased parameter estimates in all three simulations (i.e., the average estimate differed from the true population value) and was the least accurate missing data technique. Regression imputation produced biased estimates of the variance and the correlation in all three simulations, but its estimates of the mean and the covariance were relatively accurate in the MCAR and MAR simulations. Listwise deletion parameter estimates were unbiased in the MCAR simulation but were severely distorted in the MAR and MNAR simulations. Finally, the stochastic regression produced unbiased parameter estimates in the MCAR and MAR simulations, but its estimates were biased in the MNAR simulation.

Although these simulations were limited in scope, the results are consistent with missing data theory (Little & Rubin, 2002; Rubin, 1976) and with previous simulation studies. Among the procedures that I examined, stochastic regression imputation is clearly the best option because it produced unbiased estimates under MCAR and MAR mechanisms. In fact, the performance of stochastic regression is on a par with the maximum likelihood and multiple imputation approaches that I describe in subsequent chapters. The accuracy of this approach is even more remarkable when you consider that 50% of the scores were missing.

Although stochastic regression imputation appears to have some merit, it can severely attenuate standard errors. To illustrate, I computed the confidence interval coverage rates from the MAR simulation. Confidence interval coverage quantifies the percentage of samples where the 95% confidence interval contains the true population parameter. If standard errors are accurate, confidence interval coverage should equal 95%. In contrast, if the standard errors are too low, confidence intervals will not capture the population parameter as frequently as they should, and coverage rates will drop below 95%. Confidence interval coverage rates are a useful indicator of standard error bias because they directly relate to type I error rates (e.g., a confidence interval coverage value of 90% suggests a twofold increase in type I errors).

Stochastic regression produced coverage rates that ranged between 60 and 70%. These low values suggest that the standard errors were far too small. For example, the average standard error for the job performance mean underestimated the true standard error by approximately 50%. From a practical standpoint, confidence interval coverage values of 70% are

**TABLE 2.5. Average Parameter Estimates from the Illustrative Computer Simulation**

| Estimate | Population parameter | Missing data technique | | | |
|---|---|---|---|---|---|
| | | LD | AMI | RI | SRI |
| | | MCAR simulation | | | |
| IQ Mean | 100.00 | 99.98 | 99.99 | 99.99 | 99.99 |
| JP Mean | 12.00 | 12.00 | 12.00 | 12.01 | 12.00 |
| IQ Variance | 169.00 | 170.29 | 169.64 | 169.64 | 169.64 |
| JP Variance | 9.00 | 8.99 | 4.47 | 5.62 | 8.99 |
| IQ-JP Covariance | 19.50 | 19.53 | 9.72 | 19.45 | 19.42 |
| IQ-JP Correlation | 0.50 | 0.50 | 0.35 | 0.63 | 0.50 |
| | | MAR simulation | | | |
| IQ Mean | 100.00 | 110.35 | 100.04 | 100.04 | 100.04 |
| JP Mean | 12.00 | 13.21 | 13.21 | 12.00 | 12.01 |
| IQ Variance | 169.00 | 61.79 | 168.17 | 168.17 | 168.17 |
| JP Variance | 9.00 | 7.61 | 3.79 | 5.79 | 9.14 |
| IQ-JP Covariance | 19.50 | 7.22 | 3.60 | 19.64 | 19.60 |
| IQ-JP Correlation | 0.50 | 0.33 | 0.14 | 0.62 | 0.50 |
| | | MNAR simulation | | | |
| IQ Mean | 100.00 | 105.15 | 100.02 | 100.02 | 100.02 |
| JP Mean | 12.00 | 14.40 | 14.40 | 14.14 | 14.14 |
| IQ Variance | 169.00 | 141.69 | 168.30 | 168.30 | 168.30 |
| JP Variance | 9.00 | 3.27 | 1.63 | 1.88 | 3.33 |
| IQ-JP Covariance | 19.50 | 6.97 | 3.47 | 8.29 | 8.27 |
| IQ-JP Correlation | 0.50 | 0.32 | 0.21 | 0.46 | 0.35 |

*Note.* JP = job performance; LD = listwise deletion; AMI = arithmetic mean imputation; RI = regression imputation, SRI = stochastic regression imputation.

problematic because they represent a sixfold increase in the type I error rate (i.e., a type I error rate of approximately 30%). This simulation had a rather large proportion of missing data, but the confidence interval coverage values clearly suggest that stochastic regression standard errors are prone to severe bias. This limits the utility of this method, particularly given the ease of implementing maximum likelihood estimation and multiple imputation.

## 2.14 SUMMARY

Methodologists have been studying missing data for decades and have proposed dozens of techniques to address the problem. Many of these approaches have enjoyed widespread use, while others are now little more than a historical footnote. This chapter described a few of the more common "traditional" missing data handling methods that you are likely to encounter in published research articles or in statistical software packages. The methods in this chapter address missing data by removing the incomplete cases or by imputing the missing values. In general, neither of these strategies works well in a wide range of situations.

Listwise and pairwise deletion are by far the most common missing data handling approaches in many areas of the social and behavioral sciences and are often the default missing data handling options in statistical software packages. These methods require an MCAR mechanism and produce biased parameter estimates with MAR and MNAR data. Even when the data are MCAR, eliminating incomplete cases can dramatically reduce power. The methodological literature has been critical of deletion methods, so you should consider using these approaches only if the proportion of missing data is trivially small.

Single imputation methods generate a single replacement value for each missing data point. Imputation is an attractive idea because it produces a complete data set and makes use of data that deletion approaches would otherwise discard. Unfortunately, most single imputation methods produce biased parameter estimates, even with MCAR data. Stochastic regression imputation is the one exception and is the only traditional approach that yields unbiased estimates under an MAR mechanism. Unfortunately, stochastic regression underestimates standard errors, potentially by a substantial amount.

The next chapter takes a hiatus from missing data issues and describes the mechanics of maximum likelihood estimation with complete data. Missing data introduce relatively few unique nuances to the estimation process, so it is useful to gain some familiarity with maximum likelihood estimation in the context of a complete-data analysis. As you will see, maximum likelihood estimation plays a central role in missing data analyses and is one of two approaches that methodologists currently regard as state-of-the-art (Schafer & Graham, 2002).

## 2.15 RECOMMENDED READINGS

Brown, R. L. (1994). Efficacy of the indirect approach for estimating structural equation models with missing data: A comparison of five methods. *Structural Equation Modeling: A Multidisciplinary Journal, 1,* 287–316.

Enders, C. K., & Bandalos, D. L. (2001). The relative performance of full information maximum likelihood estimation for missing data in structural equation models. *Structural Equation Modeling: A Multidisciplinary Journal, 8,* 430–457.

Little, R. J. A., & Rubin, D. B. (2002). *Statistical analysis with missing data* (2nd ed.). Hoboken, NJ: Wiley.

Peugh, J. L., & Enders, C. K. (2004). Missing data in educational research: A review of reporting. practices and suggestions for improvement. *Review of Educational Research, 74,* 525–556.

Wood, A. M., White, I. R., & Thompson, S. G. (2004). Are missing outcome data adequately handled? A review of published randomized controlled trials in major medical journals. *Clinical Trials, 1,* 368–376.

# 3

# An Introduction to Maximum Likelihood Estimation

## 3.1 CHAPTER OVERVIEW

Many modern statistical procedures in widespread use today rely on maximum likelihood estimation. Maximum likelihood also plays a central role in missing data analyses and is one of two approaches that methodologists currently regard as state of the art (Schafer & Graham, 2002). This chapter introduces the mechanics of maximum likelihood estimation in the context of a complete-data analysis. Although the basic estimation process is largely the same with missing data, understanding the basic estimation principles is made easier without this additional complication.

The starting point for a maximum likelihood analysis is to specify a distribution for the population data. Researchers in the social and the behavioral sciences routinely assume that their variables are normally distributed in the population, so I describe maximum likelihood in the context of multivariate normal data. The normal distribution provides a familiar platform for illustrating estimation principles, but it also offers the basis for the missing data handling procedure that I outline in Chapters 4 and 5. Although the normal distribution plays an integral role throughout the entire estimation process, the basic mechanics of estimation are largely the same with other population distributions. For example, Chapter 6 describes a maximum likelihood analysis that uses the binomial distribution for a binary outcome, and many of the key ideas from this chapter resurface in that example.

## 3.2 THE UNIVARIATE NORMAL DISTRIBUTION

Most applications of maximum likelihood estimation rely on the multivariate normal distribution. However, a univariate example is a useful starting point for illustrating basic estimation principles. As you will see, the estimation process is largely the same with multivariate data. The mathematical machinery behind maximum likelihood relies heavily on a **probability**

**density function** that describes the distribution of the population data. The density function for the univariate normal distribution is

$$L_i = \frac{1}{\sqrt{2\pi\sigma^2}} e^{\frac{-.5(y_i - \mu)^2}{\sigma^2}} \tag{3.1}$$

where $y_i$ is a score value, $\mu$ is the population mean, $\sigma^2$ is the population variance, and $L_i$ is a likelihood value that describes the height of the normal curve at a particular score value. In words, the density function describes the relative probability of obtaining a score value from a normally distributed population with a particular mean and variance. Although the density function is complex, the driving force behind the equation is simply a squared $z$ score, $(y_i - \mu)^2 / \sigma^2$. This **Mahalanobis distance** term quantifies the standardized distance between a score and the mean and largely determines the result of the equation. Density functions typically contain a collection of scaling terms that make the area under the distribution sum (i.e., integrate) to one, and the portion of the equation to the left of the exponent symbol serves this purpose for the normal curve. These terms are not vital for understanding the estimation process.

To illustrate the probability density function, consider the IQ scores in Table 3.1. I designed this small data set to mimic an employee selection scenario in which prospective employees complete an IQ test during their interview and a supervisor subsequently rates their job performance following a 6-month probationary period. Ultimately, maximum likelihood uses the density function in Equation 3.1 to estimate the population parameters, but

**TABLE 3.1. IQ and Job Performance Data**

| IQ | Job performance |
|----|-----------------|
| 78 | 9 |
| 84 | 13 |
| 84 | 10 |
| 85 | 8 |
| 87 | 7 |
| 91 | 7 |
| 92 | 9 |
| 94 | 9 |
| 94 | 11 |
| 96 | 7 |
| 99 | 7 |
| 105 | 10 |
| 105 | 11 |
| 106 | 15 |
| 108 | 10 |
| 112 | 10 |
| 113 | 12 |
| 115 | 14 |
| 118 | 16 |
| 134 | 12 |

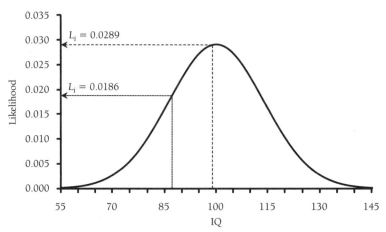

**FIGURE 3.1.** Univariate normal distribution with $\mu = 100$ and $\sigma^2 = 189.60$. The likelihood values represent the height of the distribution at score values of 99 and 87.

understanding the basic estimation principles is easier when the parameter values are known. Consequently, I temporarily assume that the population mean is $\mu = 100$ and the population variance is $\sigma^2 = 189.60$.

The density function in Equation 3.1 describes the relative probability of obtaining a score value from a normally distributed population with a particular mean and variance. For example, consider two IQ scores, 99 and 87. Substituting $y_i = 99$, $\mu = 100$, and $\sigma^2 = 189.60$ into the density function yields a **likelihood** value of $L_i = .0289$. Similarly, substituting an IQ score of 87 into Equation 3.1 returns a likelihood of $L_i = .0186$. Although they resemble probabilities, it is more accurate to think of a likelihood value as the relative probability of drawing a particular IQ score from a normal distribution with a mean of 100 and a variance of 189.60. Consequently, it is incorrect to say that an IQ score of 99 has a probability of .0289, but it is true that an IQ score of 99 is more probable than a score of 87. (With a continuous score distribution, there are an infinite number of $y_i$ values, so the probability of any single score is effectively zero.) Visually, the likelihood represents the height of the normal curve at a particular score value. To illustrate, Figure 3.1 presents a graphical depiction of the previous likelihood values. Notice that the elevation of the normal curve is higher at an IQ score of 99, which is consistent with the relative magnitude of the two likelihood values.

It is also useful to view the likelihood as a measure of "fit" between a score and the population parameters. In Figure 3.1, the largest possible likelihood value (i.e., the highest point on the distribution) corresponds to the score that is exactly equal to the population mean, and the likelihood values decrease in magnitude as the distance from the mean increases. Returning to Equation 3.1, this implies that smaller Mahalanobis distance values (i.e., smaller squared $z$ scores) produce larger likelihood values, whereas larger Mahalanobis distance values yield smaller likelihoods. Consequently, a score that yields a high likelihood value also has a good fit because it falls close to the population mean. As you will see, interpreting the likelihood as a measure of fit becomes useful when the population parameters are unknown.

## 3.3 THE SAMPLE LIKELIHOOD

The goal of maximum likelihood estimation is to identify the population parameter values that have the highest probability of producing a particular *sample* of data. Identifying the most likely parameter values requires a summary fit measure for the entire sample, not just a single score. In probability theory, the joint probability for a set of independent events is the product of individual probabilities. For example, the probability of flipping a fair coin twice and getting two heads is $.50 \times .50 = .25$. Although they are not exactly probabilities, the same rule applies to likelihood values. Consequently, the likelihood for a sample of cases is the product of $N$ individual likelihood values.

More formally, the sample likelihood is

$$L = \prod_{i=1}^{N} \left\{ \frac{1}{\sqrt{2\pi\sigma^2}} e^{\frac{-.5(y_i - \mu)^2}{\sigma^2}} \right\} \tag{3.2}$$

where the braces contain the likelihood of a single score (i.e., Equation 3.1), and $\prod$ is the multiplication operator. In words, Equation 3.2 says to compute the likelihood for each member of a sample and multiply the resulting values. For example, Table 3.2 shows the likelihood values for the IQ scores in Table 3.1. Multiplying the 20 values gives the likelihood for the entire sample, $L = 7.89E-36$ (in scientific notation, $E-36$ means to move the decimal to the left by 36 places). The sample likelihood quantifies the joint probability of drawing this

### TABLE 3.2. Individual Likelihood and Log-Likelihood Values

| IQ | $L_i$ | $\log L_i$ |
|---|---|---|
| 78 | .008 | −4.818 |
| 84 | .015 | −4.217 |
| 84 | .015 | −4.217 |
| 85 | .016 | −4.135 |
| 87 | .019 | −3.987 |
| 91 | .023 | −3.755 |
| 92 | .024 | −3.710 |
| 94 | .026 | −3.636 |
| 94 | .026 | −3.636 |
| 96 | .028 | −3.584 |
| 99 | .029 | −3.544 |
| 105 | .027 | −3.607 |
| 105 | .027 | −3.607 |
| 106 | .026 | −3.636 |
| 108 | .024 | −3.710 |
| 112 | .020 | −3.921 |
| 113 | .019 | −3.987 |
| 115 | .016 | −4.135 |
| 118 | .012 | −4.396 |
| 134 | .001 | −6.590 |

collection of 20 scores from a normal distribution with a mean of 100 and a variance of 189.60.

Because a number of factors influence the value of the sample likelihood (e.g., the sample size, the number of variables), there is no cutoff that determines good or bad fit. Consistent with the interpretation of the individual likelihood values, it is best to view the sample likelihood as a measure of relative fit. Ultimately, the likelihood (or more accurately, the log-likelihood) will provide a basis for choosing among a set of plausible population parameter values.

## 3.4 THE LOG-LIKELIHOOD

Because the sample likelihood is such a small number, it is difficult to work with and is prone to rounding error. Computing the natural logarithm of the individual likelihood values solves this problem and converts the likelihood to a more tractable metric. To illustrate, the rightmost column of Table 3.2 shows the **log-likelihood** value for each IQ score. Taking the natural logarithm of a number between zero and one yields a negative number, but the log-likelihood values serve the same role and have the same meaning as the individual likelihoods. For example, reconsider the IQ scores of 99 and 87, the likelihood values for which are .0289 and .0186, respectively. The corresponding log-likelihood values are −3.544 versus −3.987, respectively. Again, the IQ score of 99 has a higher likelihood than a score of 87 because it is closer to the mean. An IQ score of 99 also has a higher (i.e., "less negative") log-likelihood value than a score of 87. The log-likelihood values still quantify relative probability, but they simply do so using a different metric. Consequently, values that are closer to zero reflect a higher relative probability and a closer proximity to the population mean.

Working with logarithms simplifies the computation of the sample log-likelihood. One of the basic logarithm rules states that log(AB) is equal to log(A) + log(B). Consequently, the **sample log-likelihood** is the *sum* of the individual log-likelihood values, as follows:

$$\log L = \sum_{i=1}^{N} \log \left\{ \frac{1}{\sqrt{2\pi\sigma^2}} e^{\frac{.5(y_i - \mu)^2}{\sigma^2}} \right\} \tag{3.3}$$

Returning to the data in Table 3.2, note that summing the log-likelihood values yields logL = −80.828. Consistent with the sample likelihood, the sample log-likelihood is a summary measure that quantifies the joint probability of drawing the sample of 20 scores from a normal distribution with a mean of 100 and a variance of 189.60.

## 3.5 ESTIMATING UNKNOWN PARAMETERS

Thus far, I have assumed that the population parameters (i.e., $\mu$ and $\sigma^2$) are known. These parameters typically need to be estimated from the data. Fortunately, switching to a situation where the parameter values are unknown does change the previous computations. Conceptually, the estimation procedure is an iterative process that repeatedly "auditions" different values for $\mu$ and $\sigma^2$ until it finds the estimates that are most likely to have produced the data. It does this by repeating the log-likelihood computations many times, each time with different values of the population parameters. The sample log-likelihood gauges the relative fit of the prospective estimates and provides a basis for choosing among a set of plausible parameter values. The ultimate goal of estimation is to identify the unique combination of estimates that maximize the log-likelihood and thus produce the best fit to the data (i.e., the estimates that minimize the standardized distances between the scores and the mean).

To illustrate the estimation process, reconsider the IQ data in Table 3.1. Suppose that the company wants to use maximum likelihood to estimate the IQ mean. One way to identify the most likely value of the population mean is to substitute different values of $\mu$ into Equation 3.3 and compute the sample log-likelihood for each estimate. Table 3.3 gives the log-likelihood values for five different estimates of the population mean. (Substituting any non-zero value of the variance into Equation 3.3 leads to the same estimate of the mean, so I continue to fix $\sigma^2$ at 189.60.) To begin, notice that each mean estimate yields a different set of individual log-likelihood values. For example, when $\mu = 98$, an IQ score of 96 is close to the mean and has a higher log-likelihood (i.e., better fit) than a score of 105. In contrast,

**TABLE 3.3. Individual and Sample Log-Likelihood Values for Five Different Estimates of the Population Mean**

| IQ | Population mean | | | | |
|---|---|---|---|---|---|
| | $\mu = 98$ | $\mu = 99$ | $\mu = 100$ | $\mu = 101$ | $\mu = 102$ |
| 78 | −4.596 | −4.704 | −4.818 | −4.936 | −5.060 |
| 84 | −4.058 | −4.135 | −4.217 | −4.304 | −4.396 |
| 84 | −4.058 | −4.135 | −4.217 | −4.304 | −4.396 |
| 85 | −3.987 | −4.058 | −4.135 | −4.217 | −4.304 |
| 87 | −3.860 | −3.921 | −3.987 | −4.058 | −4.135 |
| 91 | −3.671 | −3.710 | −3.755 | −3.805 | −3.860 |
| 92 | −3.636 | −3.671 | −3.710 | −3.755 | −3.805 |
| 94 | −3.584 | −3.607 | −3.636 | −3.671 | −3.710 |
| 94 | −3.584 | −3.607 | −3.636 | −3.671 | −3.710 |
| 96 | −3.552 | −3.565 | −3.584 | −3.607 | −3.636 |
| 99 | −3.544 | −3.541 | −3.544 | −3.552 | −3.565 |
| 105 | −3.671 | −3.636 | −3.607 | −3.584 | −3.565 |
| 105 | −3.671 | −3.636 | −3.607 | −3.584 | −3.565 |
| 106 | −3.710 | −3.671 | −3.636 | −3.607 | −3.584 |
| 108 | −3.805 | −3.755 | −3.710 | −3.671 | −3.636 |
| 112 | −4.058 | −3.987 | −3.921 | −3.860 | −3.805 |
| 113 | −4.135 | −4.058 | −3.987 | −3.921 | −3.860 |
| 115 | −4.304 | −4.217 | −4.135 | −4.058 | −3.987 |
| 118 | −4.596 | −4.493 | −4.396 | −4.304 | −4.217 |
| 134 | −6.959 | −6.772 | −6.590 | −6.413 | −6.242 |
| log$L$ = | −81.039 | −80.881 | −80.828 | −80.881 | −81.039 |

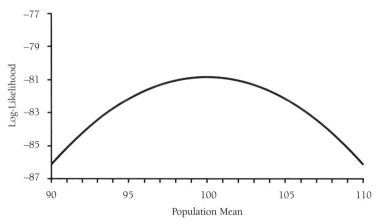

**FIGURE 3.2.** The log-likelihood function for the mean. The figure shows how the sample log-likelihood values vary across a range of plausible values for the population mean. The maximum of the function occurs at $\mu = 100$.

substituting a value of $\mu = 102$ into the equation reverses the relative fit of these two data points because the IQ score of 105 is closer to the mean. The sample log-likelihood is the sum of the individual log-likelihood values, so changing the population mean affects its value as well. Comparing the relative fit of the five mean estimates, $\mu = 100$ yields the highest log-likelihood and thus provides the best fit to the data.

The sample log-likelihood values in the bottom row of Table 3.3 suggest that $\mu = 100$ is the best estimate of the mean, but thus far I have only considered five possible values. I conducted a more comprehensive search by computing the sample log-likelihood for mean values between 90 and 110. Figure 3.2 is a **log-likelihood function** that plots the resulting log-likelihood values against the corresponding estimates of the mean on the horizontal axis. The log-likelihood function resembles a hill, with the most likely parameter value located at its peak. Conceptually, the estimation process is akin to hiking to the top of the hill. Consistent with Table 3.3, the peak of the log-likelihood function is located at $\mu = 100$, and the sample log-likelihood values decrease as $\mu$ gets farther away from 100 in either direction. After thoroughly auditioning a range of plausible parameter values, the data provide the most evidence in support of $\mu = 100$. Consequently, $\hat{\mu} = 100$ is the **maximum likelihood estimate** of the mean, or the population parameter with the highest probability of producing this sample of IQ scores.

Next, I applied the same iterative search procedure to the population variance. Specifically, I fixed the value of $\mu$ at 100 in Equation 3.3 and computed the sample log-likelihood for variance values between 50 and 450. Figure 3.3 shows a log-likelihood function that plots the resulting log-likelihood values against the corresponding estimates of $\sigma^2$ on the horizontal axis. The log-likelihood function of the variance looks very different from that of the mean, but it works in exactly the same way. Although it is difficult to determine graphically, the peak of the log-likelihood function is located at $\sigma^2 = 189.60$. Consequently, $\hat{\sigma}^2 = 189.60$ is the maximum likelihood estimate of the variance (i.e., the population variance that has the highest probability of producing the sample of IQ scores in Table 3.1).

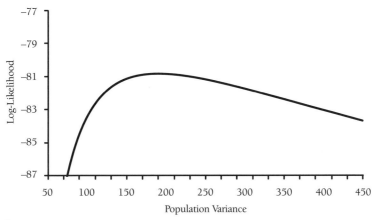

**FIGURE 3.3.** The log-likelihood function for the variance. The figure shows how the sample log-likelihood values vary across a range of plausible values for the population variance. The maximum of the function occurs at $\sigma^2 = 189.60$.

## 3.6 THE ROLE OF FIRST DERIVATIVES

The random search process in the previous examples would become exceedingly tedious in most real-world estimation problems. In practice, software packages use calculus derivatives to identify the maximum of the log-likelihood function (i.e., the peak of the hill). Returning to Figure 3.2, the **first derivative** is the slope of the log-likelihood function at a particular value of the population mean (or more accurately, the slope of a line that is tangent to a certain point on the function). To illustrate, imagine using a magnifying glass to zoom in on a very small section of the log-likelihood function located directly above $\mu = 95$. Although the entire function has substantial curvature, the log-likelihood would begin to resemble a positively sloping straight line as the magnifying glass comes into sharper focus. The slope of this minute section of the log-likelihood function is the first derivative (or more accurately, the first derivative of the log-likelihood function with respect to the mean). Now imagine focusing the magnifying glass on the highest point of the log-likelihood function, directly above $\mu = 100$. Again, with a sharp enough focus, the log-likelihood would appear as a straight line, this time with a slope of zero. Figure 3.4 shows a tangent line at the maximum of the log-likelihood function. The slope of this line is the first derivative.

Obtaining the first derivatives of the log-likelihood equation is tedious and involves a process known as differentiation. Illustrating the mechanics of differential calculus is beyond the scope of this chapter, but most introductory calculus texts contain the differentiation rules. The important point is that first derivatives are equations that give the slope of each parameter's log-likelihood at any given point along the function. More importantly, Figure 3.4 suggests that substituting the maximum likelihood estimate into the derivative equation returns a slope of zero. This implies a relatively straightforward strategy: set the result of the derivative formula to zero and solve for the unknown parameter value.

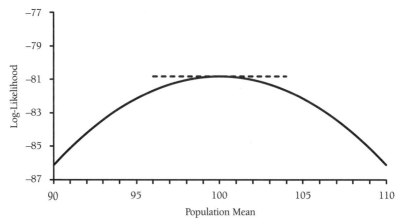

**FIGURE 3.4.** The log-likelihood function with a tangent line imposed at its maximum. The slope of this line is the first derivative of the log-likelihood function at $\mu = 100$.

To illustrate how derivatives simplify the estimation process, I used differential calculus to obtain the first derivative of the log-likelihood function with respect to $\mu$. The first derivative equation for the population mean is as follows:

$$\frac{\partial \log L}{\partial \mu} = \frac{1}{\sigma^2}\left(-N\mu + \sum_{i=1}^{N} y_i\right)$$

(3.4)

In words, the terms to the left of the equal sign read "the first derivative of the log-likelihood function with respect to the population mean" (the $\partial$ symbol denotes a derivative), and the equation to the right of the equal sign defines the slope of the log-likelihood function at a particular value of $\mu$. Substituting the maximum likelihood estimate of the mean into the equation returns a slope of zero, so the first step is to set the slope equation equal zero. Next, multiplying both sides of the resulting equation by $\sigma^2$ eliminates the variance from the formula and leaves the collection of terms in parentheses equal to zero. Finally, using algebra to solve for $\mu$ gives the maximum likelihood estimate of the mean.

$$\hat{\mu} = \sum_{i=1}^{N} y_i / N$$

(3.5)

Notice that Equation 3.5 is the usual formula for the sample mean.

The same differentiation process applies to the population variance. Applying differential calculus rules to the log-likelihood equation gives the derivative equation for the variance.

$$\frac{\partial \log L}{\partial \sigma^2} = -\frac{N}{2\sigma^2} + \sum_{i=1}^{N}(y_i - \mu)^2 / 2\sigma^4$$

(3.6)

Setting the right side of the equal to zero and solving for $\sigma^2$ gives the maximum likelihood estimate of the variance, as follows:

$$\hat{\sigma}^2 = \sum_{i=1}^{N}(y_i - \mu)^2 / N$$

(3.7)

Notice that Equation 3.7 has $N$ rather than $N - 1$ in the denominator, so it is identical to the usual formula for the population variance. The use of $N$ in the denominator of the variance formula implies that maximum likelihood estimation yields negatively biased estimates of variances (and covariances). This is a well-known property of maximum likelihood that extends to more complex analyses (e.g., structural equation models, multilevel models). However, this bias is only a concern in small samples because it quickly becomes negligible as the sample size increases.

The previous examples are straightforward because familiar equations define the maximum likelihood estimates. This is true in a limited number of situations (e.g., means, variances, covariances, regression coefficients), but more complex applications of maximum likelihood estimation (e.g., structural equation models, multilevel models, missing data estimation) generally require iterative optimization algorithms to identify the most likely set of parameter values. The expectation maximization (EM) algorithm is one such method that I discuss in the next chapter. Nevertheless, estimating the mean and the variance is a useful exercise because it provides a familiar platform from which to explore maximum likelihood.

## 3.7 ESTIMATING STANDARD ERRORS

The primary goal of a statistical analysis is to estimate a set of unknown model parameters, but obtaining standard errors for the resulting point estimates is an important secondary goal. The log-likelihood function provides a mechanism for estimating standard errors, and this too relies heavily on calculus derivatives. To illustrate, Figure 3.5 shows the log-likelihood functions for two data sets, both of which have a mean of 100. I used the data in Table 3.1 to generate the top function, and the bottom function corresponds to a set of IQ scores with a variance that is exactly two and a half times larger than that of the data in Table 3.1.

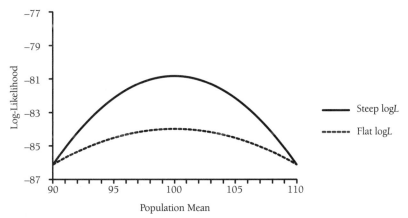

**FIGURE 3.5.** Two log-likelihood functions for the mean. The steep function is from a sample of 20 IQ scores with $\mu = 100$ and $\sigma^2 = 189.60$, and the flat function corresponds to a data set with $\mu = 100$ and $\sigma^2 = 474.00$. The two functions produce the same estimate of the mean (i.e., the maxima are located at $\mu = 100$), but they have very different curvatures. The steep function has a larger second derivative (i.e., is more peaked) and a smaller standard error.

Throughout this section, I refer to the top function as the "steep" log-likelihood and to the bottom function as the "flat" log-likelihood. Although the two log-likelihood functions produce the same estimate of the mean (i.e., the maxima are located at $\mu = 100$), they have a very different curvature. As you will see, the magnitude of this curvature largely determines the maximum likelihood standard error.

At an intuitive level, the curvature of the log-likelihood function provides important information about the uncertainty of an estimate. A flat function makes it difficult to discriminate among competing estimates because the log-likelihood values are relatively similar across a range of plausible parameter estimates. In contrast, a steep log-likelihood function more clearly differentiates the maximum likelihood estimate from other possible parameter values. To illustrate, consider the log-likelihood functions in Figure 3.5. The flat function yields log-likelihood values of $-84.518$ and $-83.991$ at $\mu = 95$ and $\mu = 100$, respectively, which is a difference of 0.527. In contrast, the corresponding log-likelihood values for the steep function are $-82.147$ and $-80.828$, which is a difference of 1.319. Both functions yield the same estimate of the population mean, but the log-likelihood values from the steep function decrease more rapidly as $\mu$ gets farther away from 100. Consequently, the steep function better differentiates $\mu = 100$ from other plausible parameter estimates. Not coincidentally, the steep function decreases at a rate that is two and a half times larger than that of the flat function (i.e., $1.319 / 0.527 = 2.5$). Recall that this is the same factor by which the variances differed.

## The Role of Second Derivatives

Mathematically, the **second derivative** quantifies the curvature of the log-likelihood function. Technically, a second derivative measures the rate at which the first derivatives change across a function. For example, a steep log-likelihood function has rapidly changing first derivatives (i.e., slopes), so its second derivative is large. In contrast, a flat log-likelihood function has a small second derivative because its first derivatives change slowly (i.e., the slopes are relatively flat across the entire range of the function). To make this idea more concrete, Table 3.4 shows the first derivatives of the two functions in Figure 3.5 (I obtained the derivatives by substitut-

**TABLE 3.4. First Derivative Values for the Steep and Flat Log-Likelihood Functions**

| $\mu$ | Steep function | Flat Function |
|---|---|---|
| 95 | 0.527 | 0.211 |
| 96 | 0.422 | 0.169 |
| 97 | 0.316 | 0.127 |
| 98 | 0.211 | 0.084 |
| 99 | 0.105 | 0.042 |
| 100 | 0.000 | 0.000 |
| 101 | −0.105 | −0.042 |
| 102 | −0.211 | −0.084 |
| 103 | −0.316 | −0.127 |
| 104 | −0.422 | −0.169 |
| 105 | −0.527 | −0.211 |

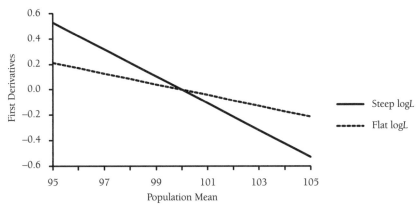

**FIGURE 3.6.** First from two log-likelihood functions. The solid line plots the first derivatives of the steep log-likelihood function in Figure 3.4, and the dashed line depicts the first derivatives for the flat log-likelihood function in Figure 3.4.

ing the appropriate values of $\mu$ and $\sigma^2$ into Equation 3.4). Beginning at $\mu = 95$, the first derivatives are positive (i.e., the slope of the log-likelihood function is positive) and decrease in magnitude until $\mu = 100$, after which they become increasingly negative (i.e., the log-likelihood has a negative slope when $\mu$ is greater than 100). This trend is true for both functions, but the steep function's derivatives change at a faster rate. Figure 3.6 shows these first derivatives plotted against the values of the population mean on the horizontal axis. The two lines depict the rate of change in the first derivatives, and the slopes of these lines are the second derivatives. Again, the values of the second derivatives determine the magnitude of standard errors, such that larger second derivatives (i.e., more peaked functions) translate into smaller standard errors.

### An Example: The Standard Error of the Mean

Having established some important background information, I now show how the second derivatives translate into standard errors. Computing a maximum likelihood standard involves four steps: (1) calculate the value of the second derivative, (2) multiply the second derivative by negative 1, (3) compute the inverse (i.e., reciprocal) of the previous product, and (4) take the square root of the resulting inverse. To keep things simple, I outline the computational steps for the standard error of the mean, but the process is identical for other parameters.

The first step of the standard error computations requires the second derivative equations. Applying differential calculus rules to the first derivative equations (e.g., Equation 3.4) produces the necessary formulas. As an example, differentiating Equation 3.4 yields the second derivative equation for the mean, which is simply $-N^2/\sigma$. As I explain later, the second derivative should always be a negative number, which it is in this case. The next step is to multiply the second derivative by negative 1. This operation yields a quantity called **information**. Information quantifies the curvature of the log-likelihood function, such that steeper functions produce larger (i.e., more positive) information values. The third step is to compute the inverse (i.e., the reciprocal ) of the information. Taking the inverse of the information gives the **sampling variance** (i.e., squared standard error) of the mean. Equation 3.8 summarizes the first three steps

$$\mathrm{var}(\hat{\mu}) = -\left[\frac{\partial^2 \mathrm{LogL}}{\partial^2 \mu}\right]^{-1} = -\left[\frac{-N}{\sigma^2}\right]^{-1} = \frac{\sigma^2}{N} \tag{3.8}$$

where $\mathrm{var}(\hat{\mu})$ denotes the sampling variance, and $\partial^2$ symbolizes a second derivative. The rightmost term in Equation 3.8 may look familiar because it is the square of the standard error of the mean. Researchers typically report sampling error on the standard deviation metric rather than the variance metric, so the final step is to take the square root of the sampling variance. Doing so yields $\sigma/\sqrt{N}$, which is the usual formula for the standard error of the mean.

To illustrate the computation of maximum likelihood standard errors, reconsider the log-likelihood functions in Figure 3.5. The steep function is from a sample of 20 IQ scores with $\mu = 100$ and $\sigma^2 = 189.60$, and the flat function corresponds to a data set with $\mu = 100$ and $\sigma^2 = 474.00$. Substituting the sample size and the variance into the second derivative formula yields derivative values of $-0.105$ and $-0.042$ for the steep and flat functions, respectively. Visually, these values are the slopes of the two lines in Figure 3.6. Multiplying the second derivative values by negative 1 gives the information. Again, peaked log-likelihood functions produce larger information values, so the relative magnitude of the two information values (0.105 versus 0.042) reflects the fact that the two functions have different curvature. Computing the inverse of the information yields the sampling variance of the mean (i.e., squared standard error), the values of which are 9.48 and 23.70 for the steep and flat functions, respectively. Notice that the sampling variances differ by a ratio of 2.5, which is the same factor that differentiates the second derivatives and the score variances. Finally, taking the square root of the sampling variance yields the standard error. Not surprisingly, the steep function has a smaller standard error than the flat function (3.08 versus 4.87, respectively), owing to the fact that its second derivative value is larger in absolute value.

## Why Is the Second Derivative Value Negative?

It may not be immediately obvious, but the fact that the second derivative takes on a negative value is important. To understand why this is the case, imagine a U-shaped log-likelihood function that is a mirror image of the function in Figure 3.2. With a U-shaped log-likelihood, the first derivative takes on a value of zero at the *lowest* point on the function (i.e., the bottom of the valley). Consequently, setting the first derivative formula to zero and solving for the unknown parameter value yields an estimate with the lowest possible log-likelihood value. The fact that the peak and the valley of a function both have first derivative values of zero is problematic because there is no way to differentiate the "best" and "worst" parameter values based on first derivatives alone. From the perspective of the first derivative formula, the top of the hill and the bottom of the valley look identical because both points on the function have a zero slope.

Fortunately, the sign of the second derivative provides a mechanism for differentiating the minimum and the maximum of a function. To illustrate, imagine climbing to the top of the log-likelihood function in Figure 3.2 beginning at a value of $\mu = 95$. The first derivatives are positive during the ascent to the top of the function and become negative on the descent past $\mu = 100$. This sequence of positive to negative derivatives produces the negative sloping line (i.e., negative second derivative) in Figure 3.6. In contrast, imagine traversing a U-shaped function beginning at a value of $\mu = 95$. In this case, the first derivatives are negative during the descent to the minimum of the function and turn positive during the ascent back up the hill. Unlike Figure 3.6, this sequence of negative to positive values yields a line with a positive slope (i.e., a positive second derivative). Consequently, a negative second derivative indicates that the parameter estimate is located at the maximum, rather than the minimum, of the log-likelihood function.

## 3.8 MAXIMUM LIKELIHOOD ESTIMATION WITH MULTIVARIATE NORMAL DATA

A univariate example is useful for illustrating the mathematics behind maximum likelihood estimation, but most realistic applications of maximum likelihood (including maximum likelihood missing data handling) rely on the multivariate normal distribution. Applying maximum likelihood to multivariate data is typically more complex because the search process involves several parameters. In the subsequent sections, I use the IQ and job performance scores from Table 3.1 to extend the previous estimation principles to two variables. A bivariate analysis is still relatively straightforward, but the underlying logic generalizes to data sets with any number of variables.

As its name implies, the multivariate normal distribution generalizes the normal curve to multiple variables. For example, Figure 3.7 shows a multivariate normal distribution with two variables. This **bivariate normal distribution** retains the familiar shape of the normal curve and looks like a bell-shaped mound in three-dimensional space. Consistent with the univariate normal curve, a probability density function defines the shape of the multivariate normal distribution:

$$L_i = \frac{1}{(2\pi)^{k/2} |\Sigma|^{1/2}} e^{-.5(Y_i - \mu)^T \Sigma^{-1}(Y_i - \mu)} \tag{3.9}$$

The univariate density function has three primary components: a score value, the population mean, and the population variance. These quantities now appear as matrices in Equation 3.9. Specifically, each individual now has a set of $k$ scores that are contained in the score vector $Y_i$. Similarly, the equation replaces the mean and the variance with a mean vector and a covariance matrix (i.e., $\mu$ and $\Sigma$, respectively). The key portion of the formula is the Mahalanobis distance value to the right of the exponent, $(Y_i - \mu)^T \Sigma^{-1}(Y_i - \mu)$. Despite the shift to matrices, this portion of the formula is still a squared $z$ score that quantifies the standardized distance between an individual's data points and the center of the multivariate normal distribution. Consistent with the univariate normal density, small deviations between the score vector and the mean vector produce large likelihood (i.e., relative probability) values, whereas large deviations yield small likelihoods. Finally, the collection of terms to the left of the exponent symbol is a scaling factor that makes the area under the distribution sum (i.e., integrate) to 1.

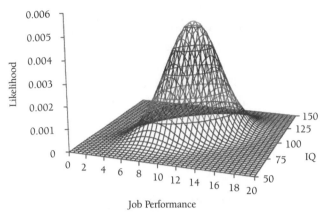

Job Performance

**FIGURE 3.7.** A bivariate normal distribution. The population mean and variance of the IQ variable are 100 and 189.60, respectively, and the mean and variance of the job performance variable are 10.35 and 6.83, respectively. The correlation between the variables is .55.

## Computing Individual Likelihoods

The multivariate normal density describes the relative probability of drawing a *set* of scores from a multivariate normal distribution with a particular mean vector and covariance matrix. To illustrate the computations, consider the IQ and job performance scores in Table 3.1. For the sake of demonstration, assume that the population parameter values are as follows:

$$\boldsymbol{\mu} = \begin{bmatrix} \mu_{IQ} \\ \mu_{JP} \end{bmatrix} = \begin{bmatrix} 100.00 \\ 10.35 \end{bmatrix}$$

$$\boldsymbol{\Sigma} = \begin{bmatrix} \sigma_{IQ}^2 & \sigma_{IQJP} \\ \sigma_{JP,IQ} & \sigma_{JP}^2 \end{bmatrix} = \begin{bmatrix} 189.60 & 19.50 \\ 19.50 & 6.83 \end{bmatrix}$$

To begin, consider the individual who has an IQ score of 99 and a job performance rating of 7. Substituting these scores into Equation 3.9 yields a likelihood value of .0018, as follows:

$$L_i = \frac{1}{(2\pi)^{2/2} \begin{vmatrix} 189.60 & 19.50 \\ 19.50 & 6.83 \end{vmatrix}^{1/2}} e^{-.5\left(\begin{bmatrix} 99 \\ 7 \end{bmatrix} - \begin{bmatrix} 100.00 \\ 10.35 \end{bmatrix}\right)^T \begin{bmatrix} 189.60 & 19.50 \\ 19.50 & 6.83 \end{bmatrix}^{-1} \left(\begin{bmatrix} 99 \\ 7 \end{bmatrix} - \begin{bmatrix} 100.00 \\ 10.35 \end{bmatrix}\right)} = .0018$$

In the context of a bivariate analysis, the likelihood is the relative probability of drawing scores of 99 and 7 from a bivariate normal distribution with the previous mean vector and covariance matrix. Visually, the likelihood is the height of the bivariate normal distribution at the point where scores of 99 and 7 intersect. Next, consider the case with IQ and job performance scores of 87 and 7, respectively. Substituting these scores into the density function returns a likelihood value of 0.0022.

At first glance, the previous likelihood values might seem counterintuitive because the pair of scores with the largest deviations from the mean (i.e., 87 and 7) produces the higher

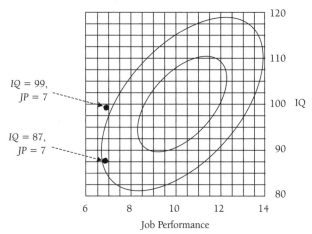

**FIGURE 3.8.** The bivariate normal distribution shown from an overhead perspective. The center of the distribution ($\mu$ = 100, 10.35) is located in the middle of the ellipse. The location of two pairs of scores is marked by a •. The angle of the ellipse indicates a positive correlation between IQ and job performance. Because of the positive correlation, the intersection of 87 and 7 is actually at a slightly higher elevation (i.e., closer to the center of the distribution) than the intersection of 99 and 7.

likelihood value (i.e., better fit). To illustrate why this is the case, Figure 3.8 shows the bivariate normal distribution from an overhead perspective with contour rings that denote the elevation of the surface. The diagonal orientation of the contour rings follows from the fact that the two variables are positively correlated. This, in turn, puts the intersection of 87 and 7 at a slightly higher elevation (i.e., closer to the center of the distribution) than the intersection of 99 and 7. The Mahalanobis distance measure that quantifies the standardized distance between the score vector and the mean vector accounts for the positive correlation, so the seemingly counterintuitive likelihood values are accurate. Interested readers can consult any number of multivariate statistics textbooks for additional details on Mahalanobis distance (e.g., Johnson & Wichern, 2007; Tabachnick & Fidell, 2007).

## The Multivariate Normal Log-Likelihood

As I explained earlier in the chapter, computing the natural logarithm of the individual likelihood values simplifies the mathematics of maximum likelihood. The individual log-likelihood for multivariate normal data is

$$\log L_i = \log\left\{ \frac{1}{(2\pi)^{k/2}|\mathbf{\Sigma}|^{1/2}} e^{-.5(Y_i-\mathbf{\mu})^T\mathbf{\Sigma}^{-1}(Y_i-\mathbf{\mu})} \right\} \tag{3.10}$$

where the terms in the braces produce the likelihood value for case $i$. After distributing the logarithm, the individual log-likelihood becomes

$$\log L_i = -\frac{k}{2}\log(2\pi) - \frac{1}{2}\log|\mathbf{\Sigma}| - \frac{1}{2}(Y_i-\mathbf{\mu})^T\mathbf{\Sigma}^{-1}(Y_i-\mathbf{\mu}) \tag{3.11}$$

Although Equations 3.10 and 3.11 are equivalent, the missing data literature often uses Equation 3.11 to express an individual's contribution to the sample log-likelihood. This formula will resurface in the next chapter, so it is worth mentioning at this point.

The log-likelihood values serve the same role and have the same meaning as the individual likelihoods. For example, reconsider the individual with an IQ score of 99 and a job performance rating of 7. The likelihood for this case is 0.0018, and the corresponding log-likelihood is –6.343. Next, the case with IQ and job performance scores of 87 and 7, respectively, has a likelihood value of 0.0022 and a log-likelihood of –6.113. Notice that the case with the highest likelihood value also has the highest (i.e., least negative) log-likelihood. Again, the log-likelihood values still quantify relative probability, but they do so using a different metric. Consequently, the score values of 87 and 7 have a better relative fit to the parameter values because they are closer to the center of the distribution.

Consistent with the univariate context, the sample log-likelihood is the sum of the individual log-likelihood values, as follows:

$$\log L = \sum_{i=1}^{N} \log L_i \qquad (3.12)$$

As before, the sample log-likelihood is a summary measure that quantifies the fit of the sample data to the parameter estimates, such that higher values (i.e., values closer to zero) are indicative of better fit. Again, the sample log-likelihood provides a basis for choosing among a set of plausible parameter values.

## Identifying the Maximum Likelihood Estimates

Estimating the parameters of the multivariate normal distribution (i.e., the mean vector and the covariance matrix) follows the same logic as univariate estimation. Conceptually, the estimation routine repeats the log-likelihood computations many times, each time with different estimates of $\mu$ and $\Sigma$. Each unique combination of parameter estimates yields a different log-likelihood value, and the goal of estimation is to identify the particular constellation of estimates that produce the highest log-likelihood and thus the best fit to the data. Again, model fitting programs tend to use calculus derivatives to facilitate the estimation process.

Although the logic of estimation does not change much with multivariate data, identifying the maximum likelihood estimates is more complex because the search process involves multiple parameters. As an illustration, consider a simple bivariate analysis where the goal is to estimate the IQ and job performance means from the data in Table 3.1. The log-likelihood equation now depends on five parameters (i.e., two means and three unique covariance matrix elements), but fixing the covariance matrix elements to their sample estimates simplifies the illustration and has no impact on the mean estimates. Fixing the covariance matrix elements leaves the variable means as the only unknown quantities in Equation 3.11. I conducted a comprehensive search by computing the sample log-likelihood for many different combinations of the IQ and job performance means. Figure 3.9 shows the resulting log-likelihood values plotted against the values of $\mu_{IQ}$ and $\mu_{JP}$. The log-likelihood function is now a three-dimensional surface with the pair of maximum likelihood estimates located at its peak. The orientation of the graph makes it difficult to precisely determine the parameter values,

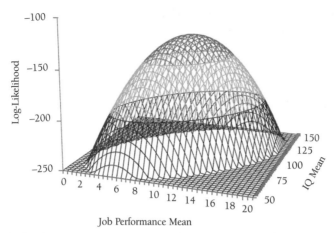

**FIGURE 3.9.** The log-likelihood function for a bivariate estimation problem. The figure shows the log-likelihood values plotted against different estimates of the IQ and job performance means. The maximum likelihood estimates are located at the peak of the function, which is roughly located at the intersection of $\mu_{IQ} = 100$ and $\mu_{JP} = 10$.

but the maximum of the function is approximately located at the intersection of $\mu_{IQ} = 100$ and $\mu_{JP} = 10$.

## 3.9 A BIVARIATE ANALYSIS EXAMPLE

Figure 3.9 provides a rough estimate of the variable means, but a more precise solution requires differential calculus. I described the role of first derivatives earlier in the chapter, so there is no need to delve deeper into the calculus details. Instead, I use the analysis results from a statistical software package to illustrate the details of a bivariate analysis. The maximum likelihood estimates of the mean vector and covariance matrix from the data in Table 3.1 are as follows:

$$\hat{\boldsymbol{\mu}} = \begin{bmatrix} \hat{\mu}_{IQ} \\ \hat{\mu}_{JP} \end{bmatrix} = \begin{bmatrix} 100.00 \\ 10.35 \end{bmatrix}$$

$$\hat{\boldsymbol{\Sigma}} = \begin{bmatrix} \hat{\sigma}_{IQ}^2 & \hat{\sigma}_{IQ,JP} \\ \hat{\sigma}_{JP,IQ} & \hat{\sigma}_{JP}^2 \end{bmatrix} = \begin{bmatrix} 189.60 & 19.50 \\ 19.50 & 6.83 \end{bmatrix}$$

The maximum likelihood means are identical to the usual sample means, but the variances and covariances are somewhat different because they use $N$ in the denominator rather than $N - 1$. For example, the standard formula for the sample variance yields $\hat{\sigma}_{IQ}^2 = 199.58$ and $\hat{\sigma}_{JP}^2 = 7.19$. The negative bias in the maximum likelihood estimates is particularly evident in this example because of the small sample size. However, the bias quickly becomes negligible as the sample size increases, so it is usually not a major concern.

Recall from a previous section that maximum likelihood standard errors involve four computational steps: (1) calculate the value of the second derivative, (2) multiply the second

**TABLE 3.5. Hessian, Information, and Parameter Covariance Matrices from the Bivariate Analysis Example**

| Parameter | 1 | 2 | 3 | 4 | 5 |
|---|---|---|---|---|---|
| | | | Hessian matrix | | |
| 1: $\mu_{IQ}$ | −0.149358 | | | | |
| 2: $\mu_{JP}$ | 0.426582 | −4.147689 | | | |
| 3: $\mu_{IQ}^2$ | 0 | 0 | −0.000558 | | |
| 4: $\mu_{IQ,JP}$ | 0 | 0 | 0.003186 | −0.040073 | |
| 5: $\mu_{JP}^2$ | 0 | 0 | −0.004549 | 0.088466 | −0.430083 |
| | | | Information matrix | | |
| 1: $\mu_{IQ}$ | 0.149358 | | | | |
| 2: $\mu_{JP}$ | −0.426582 | 4.147689 | | | |
| 3: $\mu_{IQ}^2$ | 0 | 0 | 0.000558 | | |
| 4: $\mu_{IQ,JP}$ | 0 | 0 | −0.003186 | 0.040073 | |
| 5: $\mu_{JP}^2$ | 0 | 0 | 0.004549 | −0.088466 | 0.430083 |
| | | | Parameter covariance matrix | | |
| 1: $\mu_{IQ}$ | 9.480000 | | | | |
| 2: $\mu_{jp}$ | 0.975000 | 0.341375 | | | |
| 3: $\mu_{IQ}^2$ | 0 | 0 | 3594.816100 | | |
| 4: $\mu_{IQ,JP}$ | 0 | 0 | 369.719890 | 83.737176 | |
| 5: $\mu_{JP}^2$ | 0 | 0 | 38.024977 | 13.313618 | 4.661474 |

*Note.* **Bold** typeface denotes the sampling variance (i.e., squared standard error) of each parameter estimate.

derivative by negative one, (3) compute the inverse (i.e., reciprocal) of the previous product, and (4) take the square root of the resulting inverse. With multivariate analyses, the basic steps remain the same, but the computations involve matrices. Because each parameter has a unique derivative formula, the standard error computations start with a matrix of second derivatives. This so-called **Hessian matrix** is a symmetric matrix that has the same number of rows and columns as the number of parameters. The top panel of Table 3.5 shows the Hessian matrix for the bivariate analysis example. As seen in the table, the Hessian is a 5 by 5 symmetric matrix where each row and column corresponds to one of the estimated parameters. The diagonal elements contain the second derivatives, and the off-diagonal elements quantify the extent to which the log-likelihood functions for two parameters share similar curvature. Notice that the diagonal elements of the matrix are negative, which verifies that the parameter estimates are located at the maximum of the log-likelihood function.

The elements of the Hessian have a visual interpretation that is similar to that of the previous univariate example. To illustrate, consider the block of derivative values that correspond to the variable means (i.e., the elements in the upper left corner of the matrix). Returning to Figure 3.9, imagine standing midway along the IQ axis at the base of the log-likelihood surface. From this perspective, the log-likelihood would appear as a two-dimensional hill, and the derivative value of –0.149 quantifies the curvature of that hill. Similarly, imagine viewing the log-likelihood surface from the midway point of the job performance axis. The derivative value of –4.148 quantifies the curvature of the two-dimensional hill from this angle. Finally, the off-diagonal element of 0.427 essentially quantifies the extent to which the two estimates have similar curvature (i.e., whether their first derivatives are changing at a similar rate across the function).

The second computational step multiplies the second derivatives by negative 1. In the univariate example, this operation produced a quantity known as information. In a multivariate analysis, multiplying the Hessian matrix by negative 1 yields the so-called **information matrix** (also known as **Fisher's information matrix**). As seen in the middle panel of Table 3.5, this step simply reverses the sign of each element in the Hessian. The main diagonal of the information matrix contains the information for each parameter estimate. These values quantify the curvature of each parameter's log-likelihood function, holding the other parameters constant.

With a single parameter, taking the reciprocal of information gives the sampling variance (i.e., squared standard error). There is no division in matrix algebra, but the inverse of a matrix is analogous to the reciprocal of a single number. Illustrating how to compute the inverse of a matrix is beyond the scope of this book, and there is typically no need to perform these computations by hand. The important point is that the inverse of the information matrix is another symmetric matrix known as the **parameter covariance matrix**. The bottom panel of Table 3.5 shows the parameter covariance matrix for the bivariate analysis example. The diagonal elements of the parameter covariance matrix contain sampling variances (i.e., squared standard errors), and the off-diagonals contain covariances between pairs of estimates. These covariances quantify the extent to which two estimates are dependent on one another. The diagonal elements of the parameter covariance matrix are particularly important because the square roots of these values are the maximum likelihood standard errors. For example, the standard error of the IQ mean is $\sqrt{9.480} = 3.079$, and the standard error of the covariance between IQ and job performance is $\sqrt{83.737} = 9.151$. As an aside, the block of zeros in the parameter covariance matrix follow from the fact that the mean and the covariance structure of the data are independent (e.g., recall from the earlier univariate example that I was able to estimate the mean without worrying about the variance). This is a well-established characteristic of maximum likelihood estimation with complete data.

## 3.10 ITERATIVE OPTIMIZATION ALGORITHMS

Estimating a mean vector and a covariance matrix is relatively straightforward because the first derivatives of the log-likelihood function produce familiar equations that define the maximum likelihood estimates. Maximum likelihood estimation is actually far more flexible than my previous examples imply because the mean vector and the covariance matrix can be functions of other model parameters. For example, a multiple regression analysis expresses the mean vector and the covariance matrix as a function of the regression coefficients and a residual variance estimate. Similarly, a confirmatory factor analysis model defines $\Sigma$ as a model-implied covariance matrix that depends on factor loadings, residual variances, and the latent variable covariance matrix, and it defines $\boldsymbol{\mu}$ as a model-implied mean vector, the values of which depend on factor means, factor loadings, and measurement intercepts (Bollen, 1989). Estimating one of these more complex models typically involves a collection of equations, each of which contains one or more unknown parameter values. Because solving for the unknown parameter values in a set of equations can be complex, advanced applications of maximum likelihood estimation generally require iterative optimization algorithms. A detailed overview of optimization algorithms could easily fill an entire chapter, so I give a brief conceptual explanation of the process. Eliason (1993) provides an accessible overview of a few common algorithms.

To understand how iterative algorithms work, imagine climbing to the top of the log-likelihood surface in Figure 3.9. The first step is to choose the starting coordinates for the hike. Starting the climb from a position that is close to the peak is advantageous because it reduces the number of steps required to get to the top. Iterative algorithms also require some initial coordinates, and these coordinates take the form of a set of **starting values** that provide an initial guess about the parameter estimates. Model fitting programs generally default to a set of starting values that do not closely resemble the true parameter values (e.g., correlation values of zero). However, many programs allow the user to specify starting values, and there are good reasons for doing so. For one, good starting values can reduce the number of steps to the peak of the log-likelihood function. In addition, some log-likelihood surfaces are difficult to climb because they are comprised of a number of smaller peaks and valleys. A good set of initial coordinates can improve the chances of locating the maximum of the function as opposed to the top of one of the smaller peaks (i.e., a local maximum).

After determining the initial coordinates, the rest of the climb consists of a series of steps toward the peak of the log-likelihood surface. Each step corresponds to a single iteration of the optimization process. Getting to the top requires a positioning device that keeps the climb going in a vertical direction, and the sample log-likelihood essentially serves as the algorithm's altimeter. At the first step, the algorithm substitutes the starting values into the density function and computes the log-likelihood. The goal of each subsequent step is to adjust the parameter values in a direction that increases the log-likelihood value. Algorithms differ in the numerical methods that they use to make these sequential improvements. For example, the EM algorithm I described in Chapter 4 uses a regression-based procedure, whereas other optimization routines (e.g., the scoring algorithm) use derivatives to adjust the parameters and improve the log-likelihood.

The log-likelihood keeps the algorithm climbing in a vertical direction, but it also determines when the climb is finished. The first few steps toward the peak often produce the largest changes in the log-likelihood (and thus the parameters), whereas the latter steps yield much smaller changes. In effect, the optimization algorithm traverses the steepest portion of the ascent at the beginning of the hike, and the climb becomes more gradual near the plateau. As the algorithm nears the peak of the function, each additional step produces a very small improvement in the log-likelihood value (i.e., a small change in altitude). Near the end of the climb, the adjustments to the parameter estimates are so small that the log-likelihood effectively remains the same between successive steps. At this point, the climb is over, and the algorithm has converged on the maximum likelihood estimates.

## 3.11 SIGNIFICANCE TESTING USING THE WALD STATISTIC

Testing whether a parameter estimate is within sampling error of some hypothesized value is an important part of a statistical analysis. Maximum likelihood estimation provides two significance testing mechanisms: the Wald statistic and the likelihood ratio test. This section outlines univariate and multivariate versions of the Wald statistic, and the next section describes the likelihood ratio test. The univariate Wald test is analogous to the $t$ statistic from an ordinary least squares analysis, and its multivariate counterpart is akin to an omnibus $F$ statistic.

### The Univariate Wald Test

The univariate Wald statistic compares the difference between a point estimate and a hypothesized value to the standard error, as follows:

$$\omega = \frac{\hat{\theta} - \theta_0}{SE} \tag{3.13}$$

where $\hat{\theta}$ is a maximum likelihood parameter estimate, and $\theta_0$ is some hypothesized value. Researchers typically want to determine whether a parameter is significantly different from zero, in which case the Wald test reduces to the ratio of the point estimate to its standard error. Maximum likelihood estimates are asymptotically (i.e., in very large samples) normally distributed, so the standard normal distribution generates a probability value for the Wald test. For this reason, the methodology literature sometimes refers to the test as the Wald $z$ statistic.

Squaring Equation 3.13 gives an alternate formulation of the Wald test. This version of the test is

$$\omega = \frac{(\hat{\theta} - \theta_0)^2}{\text{var}(\hat{\theta})} \tag{3.14}$$

where $\text{var}(\hat{\theta})$ is the sampling variance (i.e., squared standard error) of the parameter. Squaring a standard normal $z$ score yields a chi-square variable, so a central chi-square distribution with one degree of freedom generates a probability value for this version of the test. The chi-square formulation of the Wald test is arguably more flexible because it can accommodate multiple parameters.

To illustrate the Wald test, consider the covariance between IQ scores and job performance ratings. The previous bivariate analysis produced a parameter estimate of $\hat{\sigma}_{JPIQ} = 19.50$ and a standard error of $SE = 9.15$. Using the Wald $z$ test to determine whether the estimate is significantly different from zero gives $\omega = (19.50—0) / 9.15 = 2.13$, and referencing the test statistic to a unit normal table returns a two-tailed probability value of $p = .03$. Alternatively, Equation 3.14 yields a Wald test of $\omega = (19.50—0)^2 / 9.15^2 = 4.54$. Referencing this value against a chi-square distribution with one degree of freedom also yields $p = .03$, so the choice of test statistic makes no difference.

## The Multivariate Wald Test

In many situations it is of interest to determine whether a set of parameters is significantly different from zero. For example, in a multiple regression analysis, researchers are often interested in testing whether two or more regression slopes are mutually different from zero. In an ordinary least squares analysis with complete data, it is standard practice to use an omnibus $F$ test for this purpose. In the context of maximum likelihood estimation, the multivariate Wald test is an analogous procedure.

The multivariate Wald test is

$$\omega = (\hat{\boldsymbol{\theta}} - \boldsymbol{\theta}_0)^T \text{var}(\hat{\boldsymbol{\theta}})^{-1}(\hat{\boldsymbol{\theta}} - \boldsymbol{\theta}_0) \tag{3.15}$$

where $\hat{\boldsymbol{\theta}}$ is a vector of parameter estimates, $\boldsymbol{\theta}_0$ is a vector of hypothesized values (typically zeros), and $\text{var}(\hat{\boldsymbol{\theta}})$ contains the elements from the parameter covariance matrix that correspond to the estimates in $\hat{\boldsymbol{\theta}}$. Equation 3.15 is fundamentally the same as its univariate counterpart, but it replaces each term in Equation 3.14 with a matrix (with a single parameter, Equation 3.15 reduces to Equation 3.14). If the null hypothesis is true, the multivariate Wald test follows a central chi-square distribution with degrees of freedom equal to the number of parameters in $\hat{\boldsymbol{\theta}}$. I illustrate this test in one of the data analysis examples later in the chapter.

## 3.12 THE LIKELIHOOD RATIO TEST STATISTIC

The likelihood ratio test is a common alternative to the Wald statistic. Like the Wald statistic, the likelihood ratio test is flexible and can accommodate a single estimate or multiple estimates. However, the likelihood ratio test takes the very different tack of comparing the relative fit of two **nested models**. Nested models can take on a variety of different forms, but a common example occurs when the parameters from one model are a subset of the parameters from a second model. For example, consider a multiple regression analysis in which a researcher is interested in testing whether two regression slopes are significantly different from zero. In this situation, the regression analysis that includes both predictor variables serves as the **full model**, and a second regression analysis that constrains the regression slopes to zero during estimation is the **restricted model**. The difference between the log-likelihood values from the two analyses provides the basis for a significance test. The restricted model can also differ from the full model by a set of complex parameter constraints. For example, in a confirmatory factor analysis, the full model is a saturated model (e.g., a model that estimates the sample covariance matrix), and the restricted model is the factor model that expresses the population covariance matrix as a function of the factor model parameters. The so-called chi-square test of model fit is a likelihood ratio test that compares the relative fit of these two models.

The likelihood ratio test is

$$\text{LR} = -2(\log L_{\text{Restricted}} - \log L_{\text{Full}}) \tag{3.16}$$

where $logL_{Restricted}$ and $logL_{Full}$ are the log-likelihood values from the restricted and the full models, respectively. The restricted model always has fewer parameters than the full model, so its log-likelihood must be less than or equal to that of the full model (i.e., because it uses fewer parameters to explain the data, the restricted model must have worse fit than the full model). The question is whether the log-likelihood difference exceeds random chance. If the null hypothesis is true (i.e., the full and restricted models have the same fit), the likelihood ratio follows a central chi-square distribution with degrees of freedom equal to the difference in the number of estimated parameters between the two models. A significant likelihood ratio test indicates that the restricted model does not fit the data as well as the full model (e.g., the estimates in question are significantly different from zero).

To illustrate the likelihood ratio test, reconsider the covariance between IQ scores and job performance ratings. To begin, I estimated the mean vector and the covariance matrix from the data in Table 3.1. This initial analysis estimated five parameters (two means and three unique covariance matrix elements) and served as the full model for the likelihood ratio test. Next, I estimated a restricted model by constraining the covariance to a value of zero during estimation (statistical software packages routinely allow users to specify parameter constraints such as this). The two models produced log-likelihood values of $logL_{Full} = -124.939$ and $logL_{Restricted} = -128.416$. Notice that the log-likelihood for the restricted model is somewhat lower than that of the full model, which suggests that the restricted model has worse fit to the data. Substituting the log-likelihood values into Equation 3.16 gives a likelihood ratio statistic of $LR = 6.96$. The two models differ by a single parameter, so a chi-square distribution with one degree of freedom generates a probability value for the test, $p = .008$. The fact that the restricted model is significantly worse than that of the full model suggests that the covariance between IQ and job performance is statistically different from zero (i.e., constraining the covariance to zero during estimation significantly degrades model fit).

## 3.13 SHOULD I USE THE WALD TEST OR THE LIKELIHOOD RATIO STATISTIC?

The Wald test and the likelihood ratio statistic can address identical hypotheses, so the natural question is, "Which test should I use?" The answer to this question largely depends on the sample size and the parameters that you are testing. The two tests are asymptotically (i.e., in very large samples) equivalent but can give markedly different answers in small to moderate samples (Buse, 1982). The potential for different test results stems from the fact that some parameter estimates (e.g., variances, covariances, correlations) have skewed sampling distributions. These sampling distributions eventually normalize as the sample size gets very large, but they can be markedly nonnormal in small and moderate samples. This is a problem for the Wald test because it uses the normal distribution to generate probability values (Fears, Benichou, & Gail, 1996; Pawitan, 2000). The likelihood ratio test makes no assumptions about the shape of the sampling distribution, so it is generally superior to the Wald test in small samples.

Statistical issues aside, there are practical considerations to examine when choosing between the Wald and likelihood ratio tests. First, Wald tests are easy to implement because most software packages produce these tests as part of their standard output. The likelihood ratio test is somewhat less convenient because it requires two analyses. In addition, it is often necessary to compute the likelihood ratio test by hand, although this is not a compelling disadvantage. Second, the Wald test is not invariant to changes in model parameterization (Fears, Benichou, & Gail, 1996). For example, researchers frequently estimate confirmatory factor analysis models by fixing either the factor variance or a factor loading to 1. These parameterizations are statistically equivalent (i.e., have the same degrees of freedom and produce the same model fit) but are likely to produce different Wald statistics (Gonzalez & Griffin, 2001). In contrast, the likelihood ratio statistic is invariant to model parameterization, so its value is unaffected by the choice of model specification.

As a final word of caution, non-normal data (particularly excessive kurtosis) can distort the values of the Wald test and the likelihood ratio statistic (e.g., Finney & DiStefano, 2006; West, Finch, & Curran, 1995). Methodological studies have repeatedly demonstrated that non-normal data can inflate type I error rates, so you should interpret these tests with some caution. Fortunately, methodologists have developed corrective procedures for non-normal data, so it is relatively easy to obtain accurate inferences. I outline some of these corrective procedures in Chapter 5.

## 3.14 DATA ANALYSIS EXAMPLE 1

In the remainder of the chapter, I use two data analysis examples to illustrate maximum likelihood estimation. The first analysis example uses maximum likelihood to estimate a mean vector, covariance matrix, and a correlation matrix.* The data for this analysis are comprised of scores from 480 employees on eight work-related variables: gender, age, job tenure, IQ, psychological well-being, job satisfaction, job performance, and turnover intentions. I generated these data to mimic the correlation structure of published research articles in the management and psychology literature (e.g., Wright & Bonett, 2007; Wright, Cropanzano, & Bonett, 2007).

Table 3.6 shows the maximum likelihood estimates along with the estimates from the usual sample formulas. Notice that the two sets of means are identical, but the maximum likelihood estimates of variances and covariances are slightly smaller in value. I previously explained that maximum likelihood estimates of variances and covariances are negatively biased because they use $N$ rather than $N - 1$ in the denominator. However, with a sample size of 480, the difference in the two sets of estimates is essentially trivial. As an aside, some software packages implement a **restricted maximum likelihood** estimator that effectively uses $N - 1$ to compute variance components (e.g., see Raudenbush & Bryk, 2002, pp. 52–53).

---

*Analysis syntax and data are available on the companion website, *www.appliedmissingdata.com.*

**TABLE 3.6. Mean, Covariance, and Correlation Estimates from Data Analysis Example 1**

| Variable | 1. | 2. | 3. | 4. | 5. | 6. | 7. | 8. |
|---|---|---|---|---|---|---|---|---|
| | | | | Maximum likelihood | | | | |
| 1. Age | 28.908 | 0.504 | −0.010 | 0.182 | 0.111 | −0.049 | −0.150 | 0.015 |
| 2. Tenure | 8.459 | 9.735 | −0.034 | 0.173 | 0.157 | 0.016 | 0.011 | 0.001 |
| 3. Female | −0.028 | −0.052 | 0.248 | 0.097 | 0.038 | −0.015 | 0.005 | 0.068 |
| 4. Well-being | 1.208 | 0.667 | 0.060 | 1.518 | 0.348 | 0.447 | −0.296 | 0.306 |
| 5. Satisfaction | 0.697 | 0.576 | 0.022 | 0.503 | 1.377 | 0.176 | −0.222 | 0.378 |
| 6. Performance | −0.330 | 0.061 | −0.009 | 0.690 | 0.259 | 1.570 | −0.346 | 0.426 |
| 7. Turnover | −0.377 | 0.016 | 0.001 | −0.170 | −0.122 | −0.203 | 0.218 | −0.180 |
| 8. IQ | 0.674 | 0.026 | 0.284 | 3.172 | 3.730 | 4.496 | −0.706 | 70.892 |
| Means | 37.948 | 10.054 | 0.542 | 6.271 | 5.990 | 6.021 | 0.321 | 100.102 |
| | | | | Sample formulas | | | | |
| 1. Age | 28.968 | 0.504 | −0.010 | 0.182 | 0.111 | −0.049 | −0.150 | 0.015 |
| 2. Tenure | 8.477 | 9.755 | −0.034 | 0.173 | 0.157 | 0.016 | 0.011 | 0.001 |
| 3. Female | −0.028 | −0.052 | 0.249 | 0.097 | 0.038 | −0.015 | 0.005 | 0.068 |
| 4. Well-being | 1.210 | 0.668 | 0.060 | 1.521 | 0.348 | 0.447 | −0.296 | 0.306 |
| 5. Satisfaction | 0.699 | 0.577 | 0.022 | 0.504 | 1.380 | 0.176 | −0.222 | 0.378 |
| 6. Performance | −0.331 | 0.062 | −0.009 | 0.692 | 0.259 | 1.574 | −0.346 | 0.426 |
| 7. Turnover | −0.378 | 0.016 | 0.001 | −0.171 | −0.122 | −0.203 | 0.218 | −0.180 |
| 8. IQ | 0.676 | 0.026 | 0.285 | 3.179 | 3.738 | 4.505 | −0.707 | 71.040 |
| Means | 37.948 | 10.054 | 0.542 | 6.271 | 5.990 | 6.021 | 0.321 | 100.102 |

*Note.* Correlations are in the upper diagonal in **bold** typeface.

## 3.15 DATA ANALYSIS EXAMPLE 2

The second analysis example applies maximum likelihood estimation to a multiple regression model.[*] The analysis uses the employee data set from the first example to estimate the regression of job performance ratings on psychological well-being and job satisfaction, as follows:

$$JP_i = \beta_0 + \beta_1(WB_i) + \beta_2(SAT_i) + \varepsilon$$

Structural equation modeling software programs are a convenient platform for implementing maximum likelihood estimation, with or without missing data. Figure 3.10 shows the path diagram of the regression model. Path diagrams use single-headed straight arrows to denote regression coefficients and double-headed curved arrows to represent correlations. In addition, the diagrams differentiate manifest variables and latent variables using rectangles and ellipses, respectively (Bollen, 1989; Kline, 2005). In Figure 3.10, the predictor variables and the outcome variable are manifest variables (e.g., scores from a questionnaire), and the

---

[*] Analysis syntax and data are available on the companion website, *www.appliedmissingdata.com*.

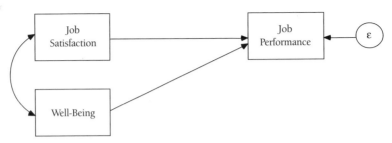

**FIGURE 3.10.** A path diagram for a multiple regression model. The single-headed straight lines represent regression coefficients, the double-headed curved arrow is a correlation, the rectangles are manifest variables, and the ellipse is a latent variable.

residual term is a latent variable that captures a collection of unobserved influences on the outcome variable.

Researchers typically begin a regression analysis by examining the omnibus $F$ test. As a baseline for comparison, a least squares analysis produced a significant omnibus test, $F(2, 247) = 60.87, p < .001$. The likelihood ratio statistic and the multivariate Wald test are analogous procedures in a maximum likelihood analysis. To begin, consider the likelihood ratio test. The full model corresponds to the regression in Figure 3.10, and the restricted model is one that constrains both regression slopes to zero during estimation (the regression intercept is not part of the usual omnibus $F$ test, so it appears in both models). Estimating the two models produced log-likelihood values of $\log L_{\text{Full}} = -1130.977$ and $\log L_{\text{Restricted}} = -1181.065$, respectively. Notice that log-likelihood for the restricted model is quite a bit lower than that of the full model, which suggests that fixing the slopes to zero deteriorates model fit. Substituting the log-likelihood values into Equation 3.16 yields a likelihood ratio statistic of $LR = 100.18$. The two models differ by two parameters (i.e., the restricted model constrains two coefficients two zero); therefore, referencing the test statistic to a chi-square distribution with two degrees of freedom returns a probability value of $p < .001$. The significant likelihood ratio test indicates that the fit of the restricted model is significantly worse than that of the full model. Consistent with the interpretation of the $F$ statistic, this suggests that at least one of the regression coefficients is significantly different from zero.

For the purpose of illustration, I also used the multivariate Wald statistic to construct an omnibus test. Recall from Equation 3.15 that the Wald test requires elements from the parameter covariance matrix. Software packages that implement maximum likelihood estimation typically offer the option to print this matrix, although it may not be part of the standard output. The regression model has four parameter estimates (i.e., the regression intercept, two slope coefficients, and a residual variance), so the full parameter covariance matrix has four rows and four columns. However, the Wald test only requires the covariance matrix elements for the two slope coefficients (i.e., the 2 by 2 submatrix that contains the sampling variance of each coefficient and the covariance between the two estimates). Substituting the regression coefficients ($\hat{\beta} = 0.025$ and $0.446$) and the appropriate elements from the parameter covariance matrix into Equation 3.15 gives a Wald statistic of $\omega = 119.25$, as follows:

$$\omega = \begin{bmatrix} .025 \\ .446 \end{bmatrix}^T \begin{bmatrix} .002175 & -.000720 \\ -.000720 & .001973 \end{bmatrix}^{-1} \begin{bmatrix} .025 \\ .446 \end{bmatrix} = 119.25$$

**TABLE 3.7. Regression Model Estimates from Data Analysis Example 2**

| Parameter | Est. | SE | $z$ |
|---|---|---|---|
| Maximum likelihood | | | |
| $\beta_0$ (Intercept) | 6.021 | 0.051 | 117.705 |
| $\beta_1$ (Well-being) | 0.446 | 0.044 | 10.083 |
| $\beta_2$ (Satisfaction) | 0.025 | 0.046 | 0.533 |
| $\sigma_e^2$ (Residual) | 1.256 | | |
| $R^2$ | .200 | | |
| | | | |
| Ordinary least squares | | | |
| $\beta_0$ (Intercept) | 6.021 | 0.051 | 117.337 |
| $\beta_1$ (Well-being) | 0.446 | 0.044 | 10.050 |
| $\beta_2$ (Satisfaction) | 0.025 | 0.047 | 0.531 |
| $\sigma_e^2$ (Residual) | 1.262 | | |
| $R^2$ | .200 | | |

*Note.* Ordinary least squares uses a *t* statistic.

Comparing the Wald test to a chi-square distribution with two degrees of freedom (i.e., there are two parameters under consideration) returns a probability value of $p < .001$. Consistent with the *F* test and the likelihood ratio statistic, the Wald test suggests that at least one of the regression slopes is different from zero.

Researchers typically follow up a significant omnibus test by examining partial regression coefficients. Table 3.7 gives the maximum likelihood estimates along with those from an ordinary least squares analysis. As seen in the table, psychological well-being was a significant predictor of job performance, $\hat{\beta}_1 = 0.446$, $z = 10.08$, $p < .001$, but job satisfaction was not, $\hat{\beta}_2 = 0.025$, $z = 0.53$, $p = .59$. The interpretation of the estimates is the same for both estimators. For example, holding job satisfaction constant, a one-point increase in psychological well-being yields a .446 increase in job performance ratings, on average. Notice that maximum likelihood and ordinary least squares produced identical regression coefficients but slightly different residual variance estimates. The two estimators share the same equations for the regression coefficients, so it makes sense that these estimates are identical. The slight difference between the residual variances owes to the fact that maximum likelihood variance estimates are negatively biased. Again, the discrepancy in this example is trivial, but the bias would be more apparent in small samples.

## 3.16 SUMMARY

Many modern statistical procedures that are in widespread use today rely on maximum likelihood estimation. Maximum likelihood also plays a central role in missing data analyses and is one of two approaches that methodologists currently regard as the state of the art (Schafer & Graham, 2002). The purpose of this chapter was to introduce the mechanics of maximum likelihood estimation in the context of a complete-data analysis. Researchers in the social and the behavioral sciences routinely assume that their variables are normally distributed in the population, so I described maximum likelihood in the context of multivariate normal data. The normal distribution supplies a familiar platform for illustrating estimation principles, but it also provides the basis for the missing data handling procedure outlined in subsequent chapters.

The goal of maximum likelihood estimation is to identify the population parameters that have the highest probability of producing the sample data. The sample log-likelihood is central to this process because it quantifies the relative probability of drawing a sample of scores from a normal distribution with a particular mean vector and covariance matrix. Substituting a score value (or a set of scores) into a probability density function returns the log-likelihood value for a single case, and the sample log-likelihood is the sum of the individual log-likelihood values. The sample log-likelihood quantifies the fit between the data and the parameter estimates and provides a basis for choosing among a set of plausible parameter values.

Conceptually, estimation is an iterative process that repeatedly auditions different parameter values until it finds the estimates that are most likely to have produced the data. The estimation procedure essentially repeats the log-likelihood calculations many times, each time substituting different values of the population parameters into the log-likelihood equation. Each unique combination of parameter estimates yields a different log-likelihood value, and the goal of estimation is to identify the particular constellation of estimates that produce the highest log-likelihood and thus the best fit to the data. In some situations, the first derivatives of the log-likelihood function produce familiar equations that define the maximum likelihood estimates, but more complex applications of maximum likelihood estimation (including missing data handling) require iterative optimization algorithms to identify the most likely parameter values.

The curvature of the log-likelihood function provides important information about the uncertainty of an estimate. A flat log-likelihood function makes it difficult to discriminate among competing estimates because the log-likelihood values are relatively similar across a range of parameter estimates. In contrast, a steep log-likelihood function more clearly differentiates the maximum likelihood estimate from other possible parameter values. Mathematically, the second derivative quantifies the curvature of the log-likelihood function. Second derivatives largely determine the maximum likelihood standard errors, such that larger second derivatives (i.e., more peaked functions) translate into smaller standard errors and smaller second derivatives (i.e., flatter functions) translate into larger standard errors.

Maximum likelihood analyses provide two significance testing mechanisms, the Wald statistic and the likelihood ratio test. The univariate Wald test is the ratio of the point estimate to its standard error. The multivariate Wald test is similar to its univariate counterpart but uses matrices to determine whether a set of estimates is significantly different from zero. The likelihood ratio test is procedurally different from the Wald statistic because it requires two analysis models: a full model that includes the parameters of substantive interest, and a restricted model (i.e., nested model) that constrains one or more of the parameter values to zero during estimation. The difference between the log-likelihood values from the two models provides the basis for a significance test. Like the Wald statistic, the likelihood ratio test is flexible and can accommodate a single estimate or multiple estimates. The two test statistics are asymptotically equivalent, but the likelihood ratio test is generally superior in small samples.

Chapter 4 extends maximum likelihood estimation to missing data analyses. Conceptually, maximum likelihood estimation works the same way with or without missing data. Consistent with a complete-data analysis, the ultimate goal is to identify the parameter estimates that maximize the log-likelihood and produce the best fit to the data. However, the incomplete data records require a slight alteration to the individual log-likelihood equation. Missing data also introduce some nuances to the standard error computations. I describe these changes in detail in the next chapter.

## 3.17 RECOMMENDED READINGS

Buse, A. (1982). The likelihood ratio, Wald, and Lagrange multiplier tests: An expository note. *The American Statistician, 36*, 153–157.

Eliason, S. R. (1993). *Maximum likelihood estimation: Logic and practice*. Newbury Park, CA: Sage.

Enders, C. K. (2005). Estimation by maximum likelihood. In B. Everitt & D.C. Howell (Eds.), *Encyclopedia of behavioral statistics* (pp. 1164–1170). West Sussex, UK: Wiley.

# Maximum Likelihood Missing Data Handling

## 4.1 CHAPTER OVERVIEW

Having established some basic estimation principles with complete data, this chapter describes maximum likelihood missing data handling (the literature sometimes refers to this procedure as **full information maximum likelihood** and **direct maximum likelihood**). The idea of using maximum likelihood to deal with missing data is an old one that dates back more than 50 years (Anderson, 1957; Edgett, 1956; Hartley, 1958; Lord, 1955). These early maximum likelihood solutions were limited in scope and had relatively few practical applications (e.g., bivariate normal data with a single incomplete variable). Many of the important breakthroughs came in the 1970s when methodologists developed the underpinnings of modern missing data handling techniques (Beale & Little, 1975; Finkbeiner, 1979; Dempster, Laird, & Rubin, 1977; Hartley & Hocking, 1971; Orchard & Woodbury, 1972). However, maximum likelihood routines have only recently become widely available in statistical software packages.

Recall from Chapter 3 that maximum likelihood estimation repeatedly auditions different combinations of population parameter values until it identifies the particular constellation of values that produces the highest log-likelihood value (i.e., the best fit to the data). Conceptually, the estimation process is the same with or without missing data. However, missing data introduce some additional nuances that are not relevant for complete-data analyses. For one, incomplete data records require a slight alteration to the individual log-likelihood computations to accommodate the fact that individuals no longer have the same number of observed data points. Missing data also necessitate a subtle, but important, adjustment to the standard error computations. Finally, with few exceptions, missing data analyses require iterative optimization algorithms, even for very simple estimation problems. This chapter describes one such algorithm that is particularly important for missing data analyses, the expectation maximization (EM) algorithm.

Methodologists currently regard maximum likelihood as a state-of-the-art missing data technique (Schafer & Graham, 2002) because it yields unbiased parameter estimates under a missing at random (MAR) mechanism. From a practical standpoint, this means that maximum likelihood will produce accurate parameter estimates in situations where traditional approaches fail. Even when the data are missing completely at random (MCAR), maximum likelihood will still be superior to traditional techniques (e.g., deletion methods) because it maximizes statistical power by borrowing information from the observed data. Despite these desirable properties, maximum likelihood estimation is not a perfect solution and will yield biased parameter estimates under a missing not at random (MNAR) mechanism. However, this bias tends to be isolated to a subset of the analysis model parameters, whereas traditional techniques are more apt to propagate bias throughout the entire model. Consequently, maximum likelihood estimation is virtually always a better option than the traditional methods from Chapter 2. The fact that maximum likelihood is easy to implement and is widely available in statistical software packages makes it all the more attractive.

I use the small data set in Table 4.1 to illustrate ideas throughout this chapter. I designed these data to mimic an employee selection scenario in which prospective employees complete an IQ test and a psychological well-being questionnaire during their interview. The company subsequently hires the applicants who score in the upper half of the IQ distribution, and a supervisor rates their job performance following a 6-month probationary period. Note that the job performance scores are MAR because they are systematically missing as a function of IQ scores (i.e., individuals in the lower half of the IQ distribution were never

**TABLE 4.1. Employee Selection Data Set**

| IQ | Psychological well-being | Job performance |
|---|---|---|
| 78 | 13 | — |
| 84 | 9 | — |
| 84 | 10 | — |
| 85 | 10 | — |
| 87 | — | — |
| 91 | 3 | — |
| 92 | 12 | — |
| 94 | 3 | — |
| 94 | 13 | — |
| 96 | — | — |
| 99 | 6 | 7 |
| 105 | 12 | 10 |
| 105 | 14 | 11 |
| 106 | 10 | 15 |
| 108 | — | 10 |
| 112 | 10 | 10 |
| 113 | 14 | 12 |
| 115 | 14 | 14 |
| 118 | 12 | 16 |
| 134 | 11 | 12 |

hired and thus have no performance rating). In addition, I randomly deleted three of the well-being scores in order to mimic an MCAR mechanism (e.g., the human resources department inadvertently loses an applicant's well-being questionnaire). This data set is too small for a serious application of maximum likelihood estimation, but it is useful for illustrating the basic mechanics of the procedure.

## 4.2 THE MISSING DATA LOG-LIKELIHOOD

Recall from Chapter 3 that the starting point for a maximum likelihood analysis is to specify a distribution for the population data. To be consistent with the previous chapter, I describe maximum likelihood missing data handling in the context of multivariate normal data. The mathematical machinery behind maximum likelihood relies on a probability density function that describes the shape of the multivariate normal distribution. Substituting a score vector and a set of population parameter values into the density function returns a likelihood value that quantifies the relative probability of drawing the scores from a normally distributed population. Because likelihood values tend to be very small numbers that are prone to rounding error, it is more typical to work with the natural logarithm of the likelihood values (i.e., the log-likelihood). Rather than rehash the computational details of the likelihood values, I use the individual log-likelihood as the starting point for this chapter. Readers who are interested in more information on the likelihood can review Chapter 3.

Assuming a multivariate normal distribution for the population, note that the complete-data log-likelihood for a single case is

$$\log L_i = -\frac{k}{2}\log(2\pi) - \frac{1}{2}\log|\Sigma| - \frac{1}{2}(Y_i-\mu)^T\Sigma^{-1}(Y_i-\mu) \tag{4.1}$$

where $k$ is the number of variables, $Y_i$ is the score vector for case $i$, and $\mu$ and $\Sigma$ are the population mean vector and covariance matrix, respectively. The key portion of the formula is the Mahalanobis distance value, $(Y_i-\mu)^T\Sigma^{-1}(Y_i-\mu)$. Mahalanobis distance is a squared $z$ score that quantifies the standardized distance between an individual's data points and the center of the multivariate normal distribution. This value largely determines the magnitude of the log-likelihood, such that small deviations between the score vector and the mean vector produce large (i.e., less negative) log-likelihood values, whereas large deviations yield small likelihoods. In simple terms, Equation 4.1 quantifies the relative probability that an individual's scores originate from a multivariate normal population with a particular mean vector and covariance matrix.

With missing data, the log-likelihood for case $i$ is

$$\log L_i = -\frac{k_i}{2}\log(2\pi) - \frac{1}{2}\log|\Sigma_i| - \frac{1}{2}(Y_i-\mu_i)^T\Sigma_i^{-1}(Y_i-\mu_i) \tag{4.2}$$

where $k_i$ is the number of complete data points for that case and the remaining terms have the same meaning as they did in Equation 4.1. At first glance, the two log-likelihood formulas look identical, except for the fact that the missing data log-likelihood has an $i$ subscript next to the parameter matrices. This subscript is important and denotes the possibility that the size and the contents of the matrices can vary across individuals, such that the log-likelihood computations for case $i$ depend only on the variables and the parameters for which that case has complete data.

To illustrate the missing data log-likelihood, suppose that the company wants to use the data in Table 4.1 to estimate the mean vector and the covariance matrix. Estimating these parameters is relatively straightforward with complete data but requires an iterative optimization algorithm when some of the data are missing. For the sake of demonstration, suppose that the population parameters at a particular iteration are as follows:

$$\hat{\boldsymbol{\mu}} = \begin{bmatrix} \hat{\mu}_{IQ} \\ \hat{\mu}_{JP} \\ \hat{\mu}_{WB} \end{bmatrix} = \begin{bmatrix} 100.00 \\ 10.23 \\ 10.27 \end{bmatrix}$$

$$\hat{\boldsymbol{\Sigma}} = \begin{bmatrix} \hat{\sigma}_{IQ}^2 & \hat{\sigma}_{IQ,JP} & \hat{\sigma}_{IQ,WB} \\ \hat{\sigma}_{JP,IQ} & \hat{\sigma}_{JP}^2 & \hat{\sigma}_{JP,WB} \\ \hat{\sigma}_{WB,IQ} & \hat{\sigma}_{WB,JP} & \hat{\sigma}_{WB}^2 \end{bmatrix} = \begin{bmatrix} 189.60 & 22.31 & 12.21 \\ 22.31 & 8.68 & 5.61 \\ 12.21 & 5.60 & 11.04 \end{bmatrix}$$

The log-likelihood computations for each individual depend only on the variables and the parameters for which a case has complete data. This implies that the log-likelihood formula looks slightly different for each missing data pattern. Returning to the data set in Table 4.1, observe four unique missing data patterns: (1) cases with only IQ scores, (2) cases with IQ and well-being scores, (3) cases with IQ and job performance scores, and (4) cases with complete data on all three variables. To begin, consider the employee with an IQ score of 105, a job performance rating of 10, and a well-being score of 12. Because this individual has complete data, the log-likelihood computations involve every element in the mean vector and the covariance matrix, as follows:

$$\log L_i = -\frac{k_i}{2}\log(2\pi) - \frac{1}{2}\log \begin{vmatrix} \hat{\sigma}_{IQ}^2 & \hat{\sigma}_{IQ,JP} & \hat{\sigma}_{IQ,WB} \\ \hat{\sigma}_{JP,IQ} & \hat{\sigma}_{JP}^2 & \hat{\sigma}_{JP,WB} \\ \hat{\sigma}_{WB,IQ} & \hat{\sigma}_{WB,JP} & \hat{\sigma}_{WB}^2 \end{vmatrix}$$

$$-\frac{1}{2}\left(\begin{bmatrix} IQ_i \\ JP_i \\ WB_i \end{bmatrix} - \begin{bmatrix} \hat{\mu}_{IQ} \\ \hat{\mu}_{JP} \\ \hat{\mu}_{WB} \end{bmatrix}\right)^T \begin{bmatrix} \hat{\sigma}_{IQ}^2 & \hat{\sigma}_{IQ,JP} & \hat{\sigma}_{IQ,WB} \\ \hat{\sigma}_{JP,IQ} & \hat{\sigma}_{JP}^2 & \hat{\sigma}_{JP,WB} \\ \hat{\sigma}_{WB,IQ} & \hat{\sigma}_{WB,JP} & \hat{\sigma}_{WB}^2 \end{bmatrix}^{-1} \left(\begin{bmatrix} IQ_i \\ JP_i \\ WB_i \end{bmatrix} - \begin{bmatrix} \hat{\mu}_{IQ} \\ \hat{\mu}_{JP} \\ \hat{\mu}_{WB} \end{bmatrix}\right)$$

$$= -\frac{3}{2}\log(2\pi) - \frac{1}{2}\log \begin{vmatrix} 189.60 & 22.31 & 12.21 \\ 22.31 & 8.68 & 5.61 \\ 12.21 & 5.60 & 11.04 \end{vmatrix}$$

$$-\frac{1}{2}\left(\begin{bmatrix} 105 \\ 10 \\ 12 \end{bmatrix} - \begin{bmatrix} 100.00 \\ 10.23 \\ 10.27 \end{bmatrix}\right)^T \begin{bmatrix} 189.60 & 22.31 & 12.21 \\ 22.31 & 8.68 & 5.61 \\ 12.21 & 5.60 & 11.04 \end{bmatrix}^{-1} \left(\begin{bmatrix} 105 \\ 10 \\ 12 \end{bmatrix} - \begin{bmatrix} 100.00 \\ 10.23 \\ 10.27 \end{bmatrix}\right) = -7.66$$

Consistent with complete-data maximum likelihood estimation, −7.66 is the relative probability of drawing this set of three scores from a multivariate normal distribution with the previous parameter values. The log-likelihood computations for the remaining complete cases follow the same procedure, but use different score values.

Next, consider the subsample of cases with IQ and well-being scores. These individuals have missing job performance ratings, so it is no longer possible to use all three variables to compute the log-likelihood. The missing data log-likelihood accommodates this situation by ignoring the parameters that correspond to the missing job performance ratings. For example, consider the individual with IQ and well-being scores of 94 and 3, respectively. Eliminating the job performance parameters from the mean vector and the covariance matrix leaves the following subset of parameter estimates.

$$\hat{\boldsymbol{\mu}}_i = \begin{bmatrix} \hat{\mu}_{IQ} \\ \hat{\mu}_{WB} \end{bmatrix} = \begin{bmatrix} 100.00 \\ 10.27 \end{bmatrix}$$

$$\hat{\boldsymbol{\Sigma}}_i = \begin{bmatrix} \hat{\sigma}_{IQ}^2 & \hat{\sigma}_{IQ,WB} \\ \hat{\sigma}_{WB,IQ} & \hat{\sigma}_{WB}^2 \end{bmatrix} = \begin{bmatrix} 189.60 & 12.21 \\ 12.21 & 11.04 \end{bmatrix}$$

The log-likelihood computations use only these parameter values, as follows:

$$\begin{aligned}
logL_i = & -\frac{k_i}{2}\log(2\pi) - \frac{1}{2}\log\begin{vmatrix} \hat{\sigma}_{IQ}^2 & \hat{\sigma}_{IQ,WB} \\ \hat{\sigma}_{WB,IQ} & \hat{\sigma}_{WB}^2 \end{vmatrix} \\
& -\frac{1}{2}\left(\begin{bmatrix} IQ_i \\ WB_i \end{bmatrix} - \begin{bmatrix} \hat{\mu}_{IQ} \\ \hat{\mu}_{WB} \end{bmatrix}\right)^T \begin{bmatrix} \hat{\sigma}_{IQ}^2 & \hat{\sigma}_{IQ,WB} \\ \hat{\sigma}_{WB,IQ} & \hat{\sigma}_{WB}^2 \end{bmatrix}^{-1} \left(\begin{bmatrix} IQ_i \\ WB_i \end{bmatrix} - \begin{bmatrix} \hat{\mu}_{IQ} \\ \hat{\mu}_{WB} \end{bmatrix}\right) \\
= & -\frac{2}{2}\log(2\pi) - \frac{1}{2}\log\begin{vmatrix} 189.60 & 12.21 \\ 12.21 & 11.04 \end{vmatrix} \\
& -\frac{1}{2}\left(\begin{bmatrix} 94 \\ 3 \end{bmatrix} - \begin{bmatrix} 100.00 \\ 10.27 \end{bmatrix}\right)^T \begin{bmatrix} 189.60 & 12.21 \\ 12.21 & 11.04 \end{bmatrix}^{-1} \left(\begin{bmatrix} 94 \\ 3 \end{bmatrix} - \begin{bmatrix} 100.00 \\ 10.27 \end{bmatrix}\right) = -8.03
\end{aligned}$$

Notice that the log-likelihood equation no longer contains any reference to the job performance variable. Thus, the resulting log-likelihood value is the relative probability of drawing the two scores from a bivariate normal distribution with a mean vector and covariance matrix equal to $\hat{\boldsymbol{\mu}}_i$ and $\hat{\boldsymbol{\Sigma}}_i$, respectively. Again, the log-likelihood computations for the remaining cases that share this missing data pattern follow the same approach.

As a final example, consider the subsample of cases that have data on the IQ variable only. Consistent with the previous example, the log-likelihood computations ignore the parameters that correspond to the missing variables, leaving only the IQ parameters.

$$\hat{\boldsymbol{\mu}}_i = [\hat{\mu}_{IQ}] = [100.00]$$

$$\hat{\boldsymbol{\Sigma}}_i = [\hat{\sigma}_{IQ}^2] = [189.60]$$

To illustrate, the log-likelihood for the employee with an IQ score of 87 is as follows:

$$logL_i = -\frac{k_i}{2}\log(2\pi) - \frac{1}{2}\log|\hat{\sigma}^2_{IQ}| - \frac{1}{2}(IQ_i - \hat{\mu}_{IQ})^T(\hat{\sigma}^2_{IQ})^{-1}(IQ_i - \hat{\mu}_{IQ})$$

$$= -\frac{1}{2}\log(2\pi) - \frac{1}{2}\log|189.60| - \frac{1}{2}(87 - 100)^T(189.60)^{-1}(87 - 100)$$

$$= -3.99$$

The log-likelihood value is now the relative probability of drawing an IQ score of 87 from a univariate normal distribution with a mean of 100 and a variance of 189.60.

Table 4.2 shows the log-likelihood values for all 20 employees. Consistent with complete-data estimation, the sample log-likelihood is the sum of the individual log-likelihood values. For example, summing the log-likelihood values in Table 4.2 gives $logL = -146.443$. Despite the missing values, the sample log-likelihood is still a summary measure that quantifies the joint probability of drawing the observed data from a normally distributed population with a particular mean vector and covariance matrix (e.g., the previous estimates of $\mu$ and $\Sigma$). Furthermore, the estimation process follows the same logic as Chapter 3. Conceptually, an iterative optimization algorithm repeats the log-likelihood computations many times, each time with different estimates of the population parameters. Each unique combination of parameter estimates yields a different log-likelihood value. The goal of estimation is to identify

**TABLE 4.2. Individual Log-Likelihood Values**

| IQ | Psychological well-being | Job performance | $logL_i$ |
|----|----|----|----|
| 78 | 13 | — | −7.73904 |
| 84 | 9 | — | −6.30206 |
| 84 | 10 | — | −6.32745 |
| 85 | 10 | — | −6.24113 |
| 87 | — | — | −3.98707 |
| 91 | 3 | — | −8.02047 |
| 92 | 12 | — | −6.03874 |
| 94 | 3 | — | −8.02968 |
| 94 | 13 | — | −6.19267 |
| 96 | — | — | −3.58359 |
| 99 | 6 | 7 | −8.37010 |
| 105 | 12 | 10 | −7.66375 |
| 105 | 14 | 11 | −8.07781 |
| 106 | 10 | 15 | −9.54606 |
| 108 | — | 10 | −5.64284 |
| 112 | 10 | 10 | −7.88229 |
| 113 | 14 | 12 | −8.23350 |
| 115 | 14 | 14 | −8.33434 |
| 118 | 12 | 16 | −9.49084 |
| 134 | 11 | 12 | −10.73921 |

the particular constellation of estimates that produce the highest log-likelihood and thus the best fit to the data. Importantly, the estimation algorithm does not need to impute or replace the missing values. Rather, it uses all of the available data to estimate the parameters and the standard errors.

As an aside, maximum likelihood missing data handling is far more flexible than my previous examples imply because the mean vector and the covariance matrix can be functions of other model parameters. For example, a multiple regression analysis expresses the mean vector and the covariance matrix as a function of the regression coefficients and a residual variance estimate. Similarly, a confirmatory factor analysis model defines $\Sigma$ as a model-implied covariance matrix that depends on factor loadings, residual variances, and the latent variable covariance matrix. It defines $\mu$ as a model-implied mean vector, the values of which depend on factor means, factor loadings, and measurement intercepts (Bollen, 1989). I illustrate some of these more advanced applications of maximum likelihood estimation later in the chapter.

## 4.3 HOW DO THE INCOMPLETE DATA RECORDS IMPROVE ESTIMATION?

Using all of the available data to estimate the parameters is an intuitively appealing approach, but it is not necessarily obvious why including the incomplete data records improves the accuracy of the resulting parameter estimates. A bivariate analysis in which one of the variables has missing data may provide deeper insight into the estimation process. Returning to the data in Table 4.1, suppose that the company wants to estimate the IQ and job performance means. Table 4.3 shows the maximum likelihood estimates along with those of listwise deletion. By virtue of the selection process, listwise deletion discards the entire lower half of the IQ distribution (the company only hires applicants with high IQ scores, so low-scoring applicants do not contribute to the analysis). Because IQ scores and job performance ratings are positively correlated, listwise deletion also excludes cases from the lower tail of the job performance distribution. Not surprisingly, the remaining cases are unrepresentative of the hypothetically complete data set because they have systematically higher scores on both variables. Consequently, the listwise deletion mean estimates are too high. In contrast, the maximum likelihood estimates are relatively similar to those of the complete data. An analysis based on a sample size of 20 does not provide compelling evidence in favor of maximum

**TABLE 4.3. IQ and Job Performance Means from the Employee Selection Data**

| Estimator | $\hat{\mu}_{IP}$ | $\hat{\mu}_{JP}$ |
|---|---|---|
| Complete data | 100.00 | 10.35 |
| Maximum likelihood | 100.00 | 10.28 |
| Listwise deletion | 111.50 | 11.70 |

*Note.* The complete data estimates are from the data in Table 3.1.

likelihood estimation, but the estimates in Table 4.3 are consistent with Rubin's (1976) theoretical predictions for an MAR mechanism.

The log-likelihood equation can provide some insight into the differences between the maximum likelihood and listwise deletion parameter estimates. With missing data, the individual log-likelihood computations depend only on the variables and the parameter estimates for which a case has data. Because the bivariate analysis has just two missing data patterns (i.e., cases with complete data and cases with data on IQ only), there are two log-likelihood formulas. The individual log-likelihood equation for the subsample of employees with complete data is

$$
\log L_i = -\frac{k_i}{2}\log(2\pi) - \frac{1}{2}\log \begin{vmatrix} \sigma_{IQ}^2 & \sigma_{JP,IQ} \\ \sigma_{JP,IQ} & \sigma_{JP}^2 \end{vmatrix}
$$

$$
- \frac{1}{2}\left( \begin{bmatrix} IQ_i \\ JP_i \end{bmatrix} - \begin{bmatrix} \mu_{IQ} \\ \mu_{JP} \end{bmatrix} \right)^T \begin{bmatrix} \sigma_{IQ}^2 & \sigma_{JP,IQ} \\ \sigma_{JP,IQ} & \sigma_{JP}^2 \end{bmatrix}^{-1} \left( \begin{bmatrix} IQ_i \\ WB_i \end{bmatrix} - \begin{bmatrix} \mu_{IQ} \\ \mu_{JP} \end{bmatrix} \right)
$$

(4.3)

and eliminating the job performance parameters gives the individual log-likelihood equation for the applicants with incomplete data, as follows:

$$
\log L_i = -\frac{k_i}{2}\log(2\pi) - \frac{1}{2}\log|\sigma_{IQ}^2| - \frac{(IQ_i - \mu_{IQ})^2}{2\sigma_{IQ}^2}
$$

(4.4)

Finally, summing the previous equations across the entire sample gives the sample log-likelihood

$$
\log L = \left\{ -n_C\left( \frac{k_i}{2}\log[2\pi] - \frac{1}{2}\log|\Sigma| \right) - \frac{1}{2}\sum_{i=1}^{n_C}(Y_i - \mu)\Sigma^{-1}(Y_i - \mu) \right\}
$$

$$
- n_M\left( \frac{k_i}{2}\log[2\pi] - \frac{1}{2}\log|\sigma_{IQ}^2| \right) - \frac{1}{2\sigma_{IQ}^2}\sum_{i=1}^{n_M}(IQ_i - \mu_{IQ})^2
$$

(4.5)

$$
= \{\log L_{\text{Complete}}\} + \log L_{\text{Incomplete}}
$$

where $n_C$ is the number of complete cases, and $n_M$ is the number of incomplete cases. To make the equation more compact, I do not display the individual matrix elements from Equation 4.3 (e.g., $\mu$ replaces the vector in Equation 4.3 that contains $\mu_{IQ}$ and $\mu_{JP}$).

Equation 4.5 is useful because it partitions the sample log-likelihood into two components. The bracketed terms reflect the contribution of the complete cases to the sample log-likelihood, and remaining terms contain the additional information from the incomplete data records. A maximum likelihood analysis based on the 10 complete cases (i.e., an analysis that uses only the bracketed terms) would produce the listwise estimates in Table 4.3. This implies that the incomplete data records are solely responsible for differences between the listwise deletion and maximum likelihood parameter estimates. In some sense, the portion of the log-likelihood equation for the incomplete cases serves as a correction factor that steers the estimator to a more accurate set of parameter estimates.

The fact that maximum likelihood better estimates the IQ mean should come as no surprise because the variable is complete. The accuracy of the job performance mean is less intuitive when you consider that the incomplete cases have no job performance ratings. To illustrate how the incomplete data records affect estimation, Table 4.4 shows the sample log-likelihood for different combinations of the IQ and job performance means. For simplicity, I limited the IQ estimates to values of 100.00 and 111.50 (these are the maximum likelihood and listwise deletion estimates, respectively). The column labeled $logL_{Complete}$ contains the sample log-likelihood values from a listwise deletion analysis (i.e., maximum likelihood estimation based only on the bracketed terms in Equation 4.5); the column labeled $logL_{Incomplete}$ shows the log-likelihood contribution for the incomplete data records; and the $logL$ column gives the sample log-likelihood values for maximum likelihood missing data handling (i.e., the sum of $logL_{Complete}$ and $logL_{Incomplete}$).

Recall that the goal of estimation is to identify the constellation of parameter values that produces the highest log-likelihood and thus the best fit to the data. As seen in the $logL_{Complete}$ column, a listwise deletion analysis would produce estimates of $\hat{\mu}_{IQ} = 111.50$ and $\hat{\mu}_{JP} = 11.75$ because this combination of parameter values has the highest (i.e., least negative) log-likelihood value. (Had I used smaller increments for the job performance mean, these estimates would exactly match the listwise estimates in Table 4.3.) Next, the $logL_{Incomplete}$ column gives the contribution of the 10 incomplete cases to the sample log-likelihood. Because these applicants do not have job performance ratings, the log-likelihood values are constant across different estimates of the job performance mean (i.e., Equation 4.4 depends only on the IQ parameters). However, the incomplete data records do carry information about the IQ mean, and the log-likelihood values suggest that $\mu_{IQ} = 100.00$ is more plausible than $\mu_{IQ} = 111.50$ (i.e., the log-likelihood for $\mu_{IQ} = 100.00$ is higher than that of $\mu_{IQ} = 111.50$). Finally, the $logL$ column gives the sample log-likelihood values for maximum likelihood missing data handling. As you can see, $\mu_{IQ} = 100.00$ and $\mu_{JP} = 10.25$ provide the best fit to the data because this combination of parameter values has the highest log-likelihood.

Mathematically, the goal of maximum likelihood estimation is to identify the parameter values that minimize the standardized distances between the data points and the center of a multivariate normal distribution. Whenever the estimation process involves a set of model parameters, fine-tuning one estimate can lead to changes in the other estimates. This is precisely what happened in the bivariate analysis example. Specifically, the log-likelihood values in the $logL_{Incomplete}$ column of Table 4.4 strongly favor a lower value for the IQ mean. Including these incomplete data records in the analysis therefore pulls the IQ mean down to a value that is identical to that of the complete data. Higher values for the job performance mean (e.g., $\mu_{JP} = 11.75$) are an unlikely match for an IQ mean of 100, so the downward adjustment to the IQ average effectively steers the estimator toward a job performance mean that more closely matches that of the complete data. In effect, maximum likelihood estimation improves the accuracy of the parameter estimates by "borrowing" information from the observed data (e.g., the IQ scores), some of which is contained in the incomplete data records. Although it is difficult to illustrate with equations, the same process applies to complex multivariate analyses with general missing data patterns.

**TABLE 4.4. Sample Log-Likelihood Values for Different Combinations of the IQ and Job Performance Means**

| $\mu_{IQ}$ | $\mu_{JP}$ | Log-likelihood | | |
|---|---|---|---|---|
| | | $logL_{Complete}$ | $logL_{Incomplete}$ | $logL$ |
| 100.00 | 10.00 | −63.754 | −39.694 | −103.449 |
| | 10.25 | −63.681 | −39.694 | −103.376 |
| | 10.50 | −63.726 | −39.694 | −103.420 |
| | 10.75 | −63.888 | −39.694 | −103.582 |
| | 11.00 | −64.167 | −39.694 | −103.861 |
| | 11.25 | −64.564 | −39.694 | −104.258 |
| | 11.50 | −65.079 | −39.694 | −104.773 |
| | 11.75 | −65.711 | −39.694 | −105.405 |
| | 12.00 | −66.460 | −39.694 | −106.154 |
| 111.50 | 10.00 | −62.909 | −50.157 | −113.066 |
| | 10.25 | −62.169 | −50.157 | −112.326 |
| | 10.50 | −61.547 | −50.157 | −111.703 |
| | 10.75 | −61.041 | −50.157 | −111.198 |
| | 11.00 | −60.654 | −50.157 | −110.810 |
| | 11.25 | −60.383 | −50.157 | −110.540 |
| | 11.50 | −60.231 | −50.157 | −110.387 |
| | 11.75 | −60.195 | −50.157 | −110.352 |
| | 12.00 | −60.278 | −50.157 | −110.434 |

## 4.4 AN ILLUSTRATIVE COMPUTER SIMULATION STUDY

The preceding bivariate analysis is useful for illustration purposes, but it does not offer compelling evidence about the performance of maximum likelihood missing data handling. To better illustrate the properties of maximum likelihood estimation, I conducted a series of Monte Carlo computer simulations. The simulation programs generated 1,000 samples of $N = 250$ from a population model that mimicked the IQ and job performance data in Table 4.1. The first simulation created MCAR data by randomly deleting 50% of the job performance ratings. The second simulation modeled MAR data and eliminated job performance scores for the cases in the lower half of the IQ distribution. The final simulation generated MNAR data by deleting the job performance scores for the cases in the lower half of the job performance distribution. After generating each data set, the simulation programs used maximum likelihood missing data handling to estimate the mean vector and the covariance matrix.

Table 4.5 shows the average parameter estimates from the simulations and uses bold typeface to highlight severely biased estimates. For comparison purposes, the table also shows the corresponding estimates from listwise deletion. As seen in the table, maximum likelihood and listwise deletion produced unbiased estimates in the MCAR simulation, and both sets of estimates were virtually identical. Although not shown in the table, the listwise deletion standard errors were generally 7 to 40% larger than those of maximum likelihood estimation. Not surprisingly, this translates into a substantial power advantage for maximum likelihood. The MAR simulation produced dramatic differences between the two missing data techniques,

**TABLE 4.5. Average Parameter Estimates from the Illustrative Computer Simulation**

| Parameter | Population value | Maximum likelihood | Listwise deletion |
|---|---|---|---|
| | MCAR simulation | | |
| $\mu_{IQ}$ | 100.00 | 100.02 | 100.00 |
| $\mu_{JP}$ | 12.00 | 11.99 | 11.99 |
| $\sigma^2_{IQ}$ | 169.00 | 168.25 | 166.94 |
| $\sigma^2_{JP}$ | 9.00 | 8.96 | 8.94 |
| $\sigma_{IQ,JP}$ | 19.50 | 19.48 | 19.31 |
| | MAR simulation | | |
| $\mu_{IQ}$ | 100.00 | 100.01 | 110.35 |
| $\mu_{JP}$ | 12.00 | 12.01 | 13.18 |
| $\sigma^2_{IQ}$ | 169.00 | 168.50 | 61.37 |
| $\sigma^2_{JP}$ | 9.00 | 8.96 | 7.49 |
| $\sigma_{IQ,JP}$ | 19.50 | 19.15 | 6.99 |
| | MNAR simulation | | |
| $\mu_{IQ}$ | 100.00 | 100.00 | 105.19 |
| $\mu_{JP}$ | 12.00 | 14.12 | 14.38 |
| $\sigma^2_{IQ}$ | 169.00 | 169.11 | 141.41 |
| $\sigma^2_{JP}$ | 9.00 | 3.33 | 3.25 |
| $\sigma_{IQ,JP}$ | 19.50 | 8.55 | 7.14 |

such that listwise deletion produced substantial bias, and the maximum likelihood estimates were quite accurate. Finally, both maximum likelihood and listwise deletion produced biased estimates in the MNAR simulation, although the bias in the maximum likelihood estimates was restricted to a subset of the parameter estimates. These simulation studies are limited in scope, but the results in Table 4.5 are predictable based on Rubin's (1976) missing data theory and are consistent with a number of published computer simulation studies (e.g., Arbuckle, 1996; Enders, 2001; Enders & Bandalos, 2001; Gold & Bentler, 2000; Muthén et al., 1987; Olinsky, Chen, & Harlow, 2003; Wothke, 2000).

You might recall from Chapter 2 that stochastic regression imputation is the only traditional missing data handling technique that also produces unbiased parameter estimates under an MCAR or MAR mechanism (see Table 2.5). The downside of stochastic regression is that it underestimates standard errors, potentially by a substantial amount. If its assumptions (multivariate normality and an MAR mechanism) are met, maximum likelihood estimation does not suffer from this same problem. To illustrate, I computed the confidence interval coverage rates from the MAR simulation. Confidence interval coverage quantifies the percentage of samples where the 95% confidence interval contains the true population parameter. If standard errors are accurate, confidence interval coverage should equal 95%. In contrast, if the standard errors are too low, confidence intervals will not capture the population parameter as frequently as they should, and coverage rates will drop below 95%. Confidence interval coverage rates are a useful indicator of standard error bias because they directly relate to type I error rates (e.g., a confidence interval coverage value of 90% suggests a twofold increase in type I errors). The confidence interval coverage values from the MAR simulation were quite close to the optimal 95% rate, which implies that the standard errors were relatively free of bias. In contrast, using stochastic regression imputation to analyze the same simulation data produced coverage rates between 60 and 70% (i.e., on average, standard errors were far too small). All things considered, the simulation results clearly favor maximum likelihood estimation, despite the fact that stochastic regression imputation requires identical assumptions.

## 4.5 ESTIMATING STANDARD ERRORS WITH MISSING DATA

Chapter 3 described the important role that second derivatives play in the computation of standard errors. Recall that the standard error computations begin with the matrix of second derivatives, the so-called Hessian matrix. Multiplying the Hessian by negative 1 yields the information matrix, and computing the inverse of the information gives the parameter covariance matrix. The diagonal elements of the parameter covariance matrix contain the sampling variances of the parameter estimates, and taking the square root of these elements gives the standard errors. The computational steps are identical with missing data, except that it is necessary to distinguish between standard errors based on the observed information matrix versus those based on the expected information matrix.

Recall that the information matrix contains values that quantify the curvature of the log-likelihood function. The magnitude of the curvature directly influences standard errors, such that peaked functions produce large information values and small standard errors, whereas flat functions produce small information values and large standard errors. In a missing data analysis, two approaches can be used to convert second derivatives into information values, and thus two approaches have developed for computing standard errors (with complete data, the observed and the expected information matrices tend to yield the same standard errors). The distinction between the two computational approaches is important because the expected information matrix yields standard errors that require the MCAR assumption, whereas the observed information matrix gives standard errors that are appropriate with MAR data (Kenward & Molenberghs, 1998; Little & Rubin, 2002; Molenberghs & Kenward, 2007). The next few sections describe the differences between these two procedures in more detail.

As an aside, some of the subsequent information is relatively technical in nature. For readers who are not interested in the mathematical details behind the two computational approaches, there is a simple take-home message: whenever possible, use the observed information matrix to compute standard errors. Many (but not all) software packages implement this method, although it may not be the default analysis option. Later in the chapter I present some simulation results that strongly favor standard errors based on the observed information matrix. It is therefore a good idea to consider this computational option when choosing a software package.

## 4.6 OBSERVED VERSUS EXPECTED INFORMATION

The **expected information** matrix replaces certain terms in the second derivative formulas with their expected values (i.e., long-run averages), whereas the **observed information** uses the realized data values to compute these terms. Before describing how this process applies to missing data, it is useful to demonstrate the computational approaches in the context of a complete-data scenario. Efron and Hinkley (1978) use an intuitive example that involves the weighted mean to illustrate the distinction between the observed and the expected information. In their example, one of two different measurement instruments generates a score for each case, and a coin toss determines which device generates each score. Because a coin toss dictates the use of each measurement instrument, the two instruments should generate the same number of scores over the long run, even though the observed frequency is likely to deviate from a 50/50 split in any given sample.

The standard error of the weighted mean relies on the score variance from each measurement instrument (i.e., $\sigma_1^2$ and $\sigma_2^2$) as well as on the number of observations that each device generates (i.e., $n_1$ and $n_2$). There are two options for computing the standard error of the weighted mean. Because the two instruments should generate the same number of observations over the long run, one approach is to weight the variances equally in the standard error computations. Weighting the variances by the realized values of $n_1$ and $n_2$ is also appropriate because the observed frequencies are unlikely to be exactly equal in any given sample. These two strategies are consistent with the notion of expected and observed information, respectively.

Computing the information (and thus the standard error) requires the second derivative of the log-likelihood function. The second derivative formula for the weighted mean is $-n_1/\sigma_1^2 - n_2/\sigma_2^2$. Because a random process with a probability of .50 dictates the values of $n_1$ and $n_2$, the expectation (i.e., long-run average) of these two values is $(n_1 + n_2)/2 = N/2$. Substituting this expectation into the second derivative formula in place of $n_1$ and $n_2$ and multiplying the derivative by negative 1 yields the following equation for the expected information

$$I_E = -E\left\{\frac{\partial^2 \log L}{\partial^2 \mu}\right\} = -E\left\{-\frac{n_1}{\sigma_1^2} - \frac{n_2}{\sigma_2^2}\right\} = -\left(-\frac{N/2}{\sigma_1^2} - \frac{N/2}{\sigma_2^2}\right) = \frac{N/2}{\sigma_1^2} + \frac{N/2}{\sigma_2^2} \qquad (4.6)$$

where $\partial^2$ denotes the second derivative, and E is the expectation symbol. In contrast, the observed information relies on the realized values of $n_1$ and $n_2$, as follows:

$$I_O = -\left\{\frac{\partial^2 \log L}{\partial^2 \mu}\right\} = -\left\{-\frac{n_1}{\sigma_1^2} - \frac{n_2}{\sigma_2^2}\right\} = \frac{n_1}{\sigma_1^2} + \frac{n_2}{\sigma_2^2} \qquad (4.7)$$

Following the procedures from Chapter 3, computing the inverse (i.e., reciprocal) of the information gives the sampling variance of the mean, and taking the square root of the sampling variance returns the standard error. As you can see, the two information equations will yield the same standard error only if the observed data (i.e., the values of $n_1$ and $n_2$) match the long-run expectation (i.e., $N/2$).

## How Does the Observed and Expected Information Apply to Missing Data?

The previous example is useful for understanding the conceptual difference between the observed and the expected information, but it does not illustrate how these concepts apply to missing data analyses. Applying the previous ideas to missing data, we find that the realized values of $n_1$ are $n_2$ are roughly analogous to the observed missing data pattern. In the weighted mean example, the expected information yields standard errors that do not depend on the values of $n_1$ and $n_2$, whereas the observed information uses the values of $n_1$ and $n_2$ to compute standard errors. In the context of a missing data analysis, the expected information produces standard errors that effectively ignore the pattern of missing values, whereas standard errors based on the observed information depend on the missing data pattern. This distinction has important practical implications because the two computational approaches make different assumptions about the missing data mechanism.

The missing data literature refers to the MAR mechanism as ignorable missingness because the distribution of missing data carries no information about the analysis model parameters. Interestingly, the realized missing data pattern does contain information that influences the information matrix, and thus the standard errors (Kenward & Molenberghs, 1998; Little, 1976). Specifically, the expected information matrix yields standard errors that require the MCAR assumption, whereas the observed information matrix produces standard errors that are appropriate with MCAR and MAR data (Kenward & Molenberghs, 1998; Little & Rubin, 2002; Molenberghs & Kenward, 2007). Kenward and Molenberghs (1998) provide a detailed discussion of this issue, and I summarize their main points in the next section.

## 4.7 A BIVARIATE ANALYSIS EXAMPLE

To illustrate the difference between the observed and expected information, suppose that it is of interest to use the IQ scores and job performance ratings from Table 4.1 to estimate the mean vector and the covariance matrix. The matrix of second derivatives (i.e., the Hessian) for this analysis is a 5 by 5 symmetric matrix in which each row and column corresponds to one of the estimated parameters (there are two means and three unique covariance matrix elements). Furthermore, the diagonal elements of the Hessian matrix contain the second derivatives for each parameter, and the off-diagonal elements quantify the extent to which the log-likelihood functions for two parameters share similar curvature. Collectively, the elements in the Hessian matrix are the building blocks of maximum likelihood standard errors.

The observed and the expected information matrices differ in how they treat the deviation scores (i.e., $y_i - \mu$) that appear in certain second derivative formulas. In particular, the two computational approaches produce different values for the off-diagonal elements of the Hessian that involve a mean parameter and a covariance matrix parameter. To illustrate, consider the second derivative formula for the off-diagonal element that involves the mean and the variance of the IQ scores (i.e., $\mu_{IQ}$ and $\sigma^2_{IQ}$, respectively). The second derivative formula is

$$\frac{\partial^2 \log L}{\partial \mu_{IQ} \partial \sigma^2_{IQ}} = \left\{ -\begin{bmatrix} 1 & 0 \end{bmatrix} \Sigma^{-1} \begin{bmatrix} 1 & 0 \\ 0 & 0 \end{bmatrix} \Sigma^{-1} \sum_{i=1}^{n_C} \left( \begin{bmatrix} IQ_i \\ JP_i \end{bmatrix} - \begin{bmatrix} \mu_{IQ} \\ \mu_{JP} \end{bmatrix} \right) \right\} - \frac{1}{(\sigma^2_{IQ})^2} \sum_{i=1}^{n_M} (IQ_i - \mu_{IQ}) \quad (4.8)$$

where $\partial^2$ denotes a second derivative, $n_C$ is the number of complete cases, and $n_M$ is the number of incomplete cases. Note that the bracketed terms reflect the contribution of the complete cases to the second derivative value, and the remaining terms contain the additional information from the incomplete cases. Although the derivative formula is relatively complex, the deviation scores and their sums are the key to understanding the distinction between the observed and the expected information.

Consider what happens to Equation 4.8 when the data are complete. In this situation, the bracketed terms alone generate the second derivative and the remaining terms vanish. The observed information uses the realized data values (i.e., $IQ_i$ and $JP_i$) to compute the second derivative. By definition, the sum of the deviation scores equals zero, so the entire second derivative equation returns a value of zero. In contrast, the expected information replaces the observed scores with their expected values (i.e., long-run averages). The expected value of a random variable is the mean, and so the data values in Equation 4.8 get replaced by their respective averages. In this situation, the sum of the deviation scores also equals zero, as does the value of the second derivative. With complete data, all of the second derivative equations that involve a mean parameter and a covariance matrix parameter work in the same fashion and return a value of zero (i.e., the mean parameters are independent of the covariance matrix parameters).

Thus far, using the observed data or the expected values to compute the second derivative formulas leads to the same answer. However, the two computational approaches diverge with missing data, and the second derivative values depend on the missing data mechanism. Consider what happens to Equation 4.8 when the job performance ratings are MCAR. If the values are missing in a purely random fashion, the observed job performance scores should be equally dispersed above and below the mean. Using the realized data values to compute the sums should therefore still produce a value of zero, on average. Consistent with the complete-data scenario, the expected information replaces the observed data values with their respective averages; thus, the deviation terms vanish and the entire equation returns a value of zero. Consequently, the observed and the expected information should produce the same second derivative value (and thus the same standard error), on average. Again, this result holds for any off-diagonal element of the Hessian that involves a mean parameter and a covariance matrix parameter.

The situation changes with MAR data. By virtue of the employee selection process, the job performance ratings in Table 4.1 are primarily missing from the lower tail of the score distribution. This implies that the observed data points are not equally dispersed above and below the mean. For example, a quick inspection of the data in Table 4.1 shows that the majority of the observed job performance ratings are above the maximum likelihood estimate of the mean, which is $\hat{\mu}_{JP} = 10.28$. Consequently, the sum of the deviation scores (and thus the value of the second derivative) no longer equals zero. In contrast, because the expected information replaces the observed data values with their respective averages, the second derivative formula will always return a value of zero, regardless of the missing data mechanism.

To numerically illustrate the differences between the observed and the expected information, Table 4.6 shows the information matrices and the parameter covariance matrices from the bivariate analysis. First, notice that the expected information matrix contains values of zero for the off-diagonal elements that involve a mean parameter and a covariance matrix

**TABLE 4.6. Information and Parameter Covariance Matrices from the Bivariate Analysis Example**

| Parameter | 1 | 2 | 3 | 4 | 5 |
|---|---|---|---|---|---|
| | | | Information matrix (observed) | | |
| 1: $\mu_{IQ}$ | 0.134132 | | | | |
| 2: $\mu_{JP}$ | −0.232050 | 1.879713 | | | |
| 3: $\sigma^2_{IQ}$ | 0.001738 | −0.014075 | 0.000492 | | |
| 4: $\sigma_{IQ,JP}$ | −0.014075 | 0.114012 | −0.002065 | 0.022111 | |
| 5: $\sigma^2_{JP}$ | 0.000000 | 0.000001 | 0.002692 | −0.043618 | 0.176666 |
| | | | | | |
| | | | Parameter covariance matrix (observed) | | |
| 1: $\mu_{IQ}$ | 9.479986 | | | | |
| 2: $\mu_{JP}$ | 1.170302 | **1.507618** | | | |
| 3: $\sigma^2_{IQ}$ | −0.000020 | 0.000059 | **3594.794000** | | |
| 4: $\sigma_{IQ,JP}$ | −0.000044 | −13.703090 | 443.774440 | **280.705520** | |
| 5: $\sigma^2_{JP}$ | −0.000011 | −3.383282 | 54.783599 | 62.542877 | **20.267296** |
| | | | | | |
| | | | Information matrix (expected) | | |
| 1: $\mu_{IQ}$ | 0.134132 | | | | |
| 2: $\mu_{JP}$ | −0.232050 | 1.879713 | | | |
| 3: $\sigma^2_{IQ}$ | 0 | 0 | 0.000470 | | |
| 4: $\sigma_{IQ,JP}$ | 0 | 0 | −0.001889 | 0.020684 | |
| 5: $\sigma^2_{JP}$ | 0 | 0 | 0.002692 | −0.043619 | 0.176666 |
| | | | | | |
| | | | Parameter covariance matrix (expected) | | |
| 1: $\mu_{IQ}$ | 9.479986 | | | | |
| 2: $\mu_{JP}$ | 1.170299 | **0.676469** | | | |
| 3: $\sigma^2_{IQ}$ | 0 | 0 | 3594.805000 | | |
| 4: $\sigma_{IQ,JP}$ | 0 | 0 | 443.776810 | 155.650330 | |
| 5: $\sigma^2_{JP}$ | 0 | 0 | 54.784017 | 31.666846 | **12.644013** |

*Note.* **Bold** typeface denotes the sampling variance (i.e., squared standard error) of each parameter estimate.

parameter. Again, this is a consequence of replacing the observed data values with their expectations. In contrast, the observed information matrix has nonzero off-diagonal elements, which suggests that the mean parameters and the covariance matrix parameters are no longer independent. Computing the inverse of the information matrix gives the parameter covariance matrix, the diagonal elements of which contain sampling variances (i.e., squared standard errors). Notice that the expected information matrix produces smaller sampling variances for the parameters affected by missing data. Considering the job performance mean, the observed information matrix gives a sampling variance of 1.508, whereas the expected information matrix produces an estimate of .676. Not surprisingly, the disparity between these two values translates into a marked difference in the standard errors. For example, the observed information matrix yields a standard error of 1.228, whereas the expected information matrix yields a standard error of 0.822.

The sampling variances in Table 4.6 illustrate that the two computational approaches can produce very different standard errors, particularly with MAR data. At an intuitive level, using the observed information is desirable because the standard errors take into account the realized missing data pattern. The methodological literature clearly favors this approach because the resulting standard errors are accurate with MAR data. Referring to the observed information matrix, Kenward and Molenberghs (1998, p. 238) stated that "its use in missing data problems should be the rule rather than the exception." Other authors have echoed this sentiment (Laird, 1988; Little & Rubin, 2002; Molenberghs & Kenward, 2007). Fortunately, many software packages can compute standard errors from the observed information matrix, although this may not be the default analysis option.

## 4.8 AN ILLUSTRATIVE COMPUTER SIMULATION STUDY

The results in Table 4.6 are useful for illustration purposes, but they do not provide strong evidence about the differences that can result from using the observed versus the expected information to compute standard errors. To better illustrate the performance of these computational approaches, I conducted a series of Monte Carlo computer simulations. The simulation programs generated 1,000 samples of $N = 250$ from a population model that mimicked the IQ and job performance data in Table 4.1. The first simulation created MCAR data by randomly deleting 50% of the job performance ratings, and the second simulation mimicked an MAR mechanism by eliminating the job performance scores for the cases in the lower half of the IQ distribution. After generating each data set, the simulation programs used maximum likelihood missing data handling to estimate the mean vector and the covariance matrix. They subsequently computed standard errors using both the observed and the expected information matrix.

Table 4.7 shows the average standard error for each parameter estimate. To gauge the accuracy of the standard errors, the table also gives the standard deviation of the parameter estimates across the 1,000 samples, along with the confidence interval coverage values. The standard deviations quantify the actual sampling fluctuation of the estimates and provide a benchmark for assessing the average standard errors. Confidence interval coverage quantifies the percentage of samples where the 95% confidence interval contains the true population parameter. If standard errors are accurate, confidence interval coverage should equal 95%. In contrast, if the standard errors are too low, confidence intervals will not capture the population parameter as frequently as they should, and coverage rates will drop below 95%. Confidence interval coverage rates are a useful indicator of standard error bias because they directly relate to type I error rates (e.g., a confidence interval coverage value of 90% suggests a twofold increase in type I errors).

As seen in the table, the two computational approaches produced nearly identical results in the MCAR simulation, and the standard errors from both methods were quite accurate (i.e., the average standard errors were quite close to the standard deviations, and the coverage values were roughly 95%). In the MAR simulation, the observed information matrix produced standard errors that closely resembled the standard deviation values (i.e., the true standard errors), and the corresponding confidence interval coverage values were quite close

**TABLE 4.7. Simulation Results Comparing Observed and Expected Standard Errors**

| Parameter | SD | Observed information | | Expected information | |
|---|---|---|---|---|---|
| | | Average *SE* | Coverage | Average *SE* | Coverage |
| | | MCAR simulation | | | |
| $\mu_{IQ}$ | 0.791 | 0.820 | 0.963 | 0.820 | 0.963 |
| $\mu_{JP}$ | 0.247 | 0.250 | 0.951 | 0.250 | 0.951 |
| $\sigma^2_{IQ}$ | 14.777 | 15.049 | 0.948 | 15.049 | 0.948 |
| $\sigma^2_{JP}$ | 1.105 | 1.117 | 0.939 | 1.114 | 0.937 |
| $\sigma_{IQ,JP}$ | 3.434 | 3.484 | 0.949 | 3.465 | 0.946 |
| | | MAR simulation | | | |
| $\mu_{IQ}$ | 0.806 | 0.820 | 0.947 | 0.820 | 0.947 |
| $\mu_{JP}$ | 0.394 | 0.395 | 0.953 | 0.249 | 0.804 |
| $\sigma^2_{IQ}$ | 15.074 | 15.071 | 0.949 | 15.071 | 0.949 |
| $\sigma^2_{JP}$ | 1.490 | 1.439 | 0.920 | 1.112 | 0.851 |
| $\sigma_{IQ,JP}$ | 5.275 | 5.283 | 0.959 | 3.463 | 0.795 |

to the optimal 95% rate. In contrast, the expected information matrix produced inaccurate standard errors for the parameters affected by missing data. For example, the standard error of the job performance mean was too small, on average, and had a coverage value of approximately 80%. From a practical standpoint, a confidence interval coverage value of 80% represents a type I error rate of approximately 20%, which is a fourfold increase over the nominal 5% type I error rate.

It is difficult to say whether the simulation results in Table 4.7 are representative of real-world analysis examples, but they clearly suggest that standard errors based on the expected information matrix are prone to severe bias and are only valid with MCAR data. Many (but not all) software programs can compute standard errors from the observed information matrix, so you should consider this option when choosing a software package. If you do not have access to software that computes the observed information matrix, you can always use the likelihood ratio statistic to perform significance tests (e.g., by fitting two models, one of which constrains the parameter of interest to zero during estimation) because the likelihood ratio is unaffected by the choice of information matrix.

## 4.9 AN OVERVIEW OF THE EM ALGORITHM

Certain complete-data applications of maximum likelihood estimation (e.g., the estimation of means, variances, covariances, and regression coefficients) are straightforward because familiar equations define the maximum likelihood parameter estimates. With few exceptions, missing data analyses require iterative optimization algorithms, even for very simple estimation problems. The **EM algorithm** is one such procedure that is particularly important for missing data analyses. The origins of EM date back to the 1970s (Beale & Little, 1975; Dempster et al., 1977; Orchard & Woodbury, 1972), with Dempster et al. (1977) playing a

key role in developing the algorithm. The early applications of EM primarily focused on estimating a mean vector and a covariance matrix with missing data, but methodologists have
since extended the algorithm to address a variety of difficult complete-data estimation problems, including multilevel models, finite mixtures, and structural equation models, to name
a few (Jamshidian & Bentler, 1999; Liang & Bentler, 2004; McLachlan & Krishnan, 1997;
Muthén & Shedden, 1999; Raudenbush & Bryk, 2002). To keep things simple, I describe
the estimation process for a mean vector and a covariance matrix, but the EM algorithm is
readily suited for more complex missing data problems (e.g., structural equation models with
missing data; Jamshidian & Bentler, 1999).

The EM algorithm is a two-step iterative procedure that consists of an E-step and an
M-step (E and M stand for expectation and maximization, respectively). The iterative process
starts with an initial estimate of the mean vector and the covariance matrix (e.g., a listwise
deletion estimate of $\mu$ and $\Sigma$). The **E-step** uses the elements in the mean vector and the covariance matrix to build a set of regression equations that predict the incomplete variables
from the observed variables. The purpose of the E-step is to fill in the missing values in a
manner that resembles stochastic regression imputation (I use the words "fill in" loosely
here, because the algorithm does not actually impute the missing values). The **M-step** subsequently applies standard complete-data formulas to the filled-in data to generate updated
estimates of the mean vector and the covariance matrix. The algorithm carries the updated
parameter estimates forward to the next E-step, where it builds a new set of regression equations to predict the missing values. The subsequent M-step then re-estimates the mean vector
and the covariance matrix. EM repeats these two steps until the elements in $\hat{\mu}$ and $\hat{\Sigma}$ no longer change between consecutive M-steps, at which point the algorithm has converged on the
maximum likelihood estimates. These estimates might be of substantive interest in and of
themselves, or they can serve as input data for other multivariate statistical procedures
(Enders, 2003; Enders & Peugh, 2004; Yuan & Bentler, 2000). It is important to reiterate
that the algorithm does not impute or replace the missing values. Rather, it uses all of the
available data to estimate the mean vector and the covariance matrix.

In Chapter 3, I used a hill-climbing analogy to introduce iterative optimization algorithms. In this analogy, the goal of estimation is to locate the peak of the log-likelihood function (i.e., climb to the top of a hill) where the maximum likelihood estimates are located. In
an EM analysis, the initial estimates of the mean vector and the covariance matrix effectively
serve as the starting coordinates for the climb, and a single iteration (i.e., one E- and one
M-step) represents a step toward the top of the hill. Numerically, the goal of each iteration
is to adjust the parameter values in a direction that increases the log-likelihood value (i.e., the
algorithm should climb in a vertical direction). The regression-based procedure at each
E-step does just that, and the updated parameter estimates at each M-step will produce a
higher log-likelihood value than the estimates from the preceding M-step. As the climb nears
the plateau, the adjustments to the parameter estimates are very small and the log-likelihood
effectively remains the same across successive M-steps. When the difference between successive estimates of $\mu$ and $\Sigma$ falls below some very small threshold (software programs often
refer to this threshold as the **convergence criterion**), the iterative process stops. At this
point, the algorithm has located the peak of the log-likelihood function, and the values of the

mean vector and the covariance matrix from the final M-step serve as the maximum likelihood estimates.

## 4.10 A DETAILED DESCRIPTION OF THE EM ALGORITHM

The previous description of EM is conceptual in nature and omits many of the mathematical
details of the procedure. This section expands the previous ideas and gives a more precise
explanation of the E-step and the M-step. To illustrate the mechanics of EM, I use a bivariate
analysis example where one of the variables is incomplete. Throughout this section, I use $X$
to denote the complete variable (e.g., IQ scores) and $Y$ to represent the incomplete variable
(e.g., job performance ratings). This is a relatively simple estimation problem, but the basic
ideas readily extend to multivariate analyses with general patterns of missing data.

With complete data, the following formulas generate the maximum likelihood estimates
of the mean, the variance, and the covariance.

$$\hat{\mu}_Y = \frac{1}{N}\sum Y \tag{4.9}$$

$$\hat{\sigma}_Y^2 = \frac{1}{N}\left(\sum Y^2 - \frac{(\sum Y)^2}{N}\right) \tag{4.10}$$

$$\hat{\sigma}_{X,Y} = \frac{1}{N}\left(\sum XY - \frac{\sum X \sum Y}{N}\right) \tag{4.11}$$

Notice that the sum of the scores (i.e., $\sum X$ and $\sum Y$), the sum of the squared scores (i.e., $\sum X^2$
and $\sum Y^2$), and the sum of the cross product terms (i.e., $\sum XY$) are the basic building blocks
of the previous equations. Collectively, these quantities are known as **sufficient statistics**
because they contain all of the necessary information to estimate the mean vector and the
covariance matrix. As you will see, these sufficient statistics play an important role in the
E-step.

The purpose of the E-step is to "fill in" the missing values so that the M-step can use
Equations 4.9 through 4.11 to generate parameter estimates. More accurately, the E-step fills
in each case's contribution to the sufficient statistics (Dempster et al., 1977). The E-step uses
the elements in the mean vector and the covariance matrix to build a set of regression equations that predict the incomplete variables from the observed variables. In a bivariate data set
with missing value on $Y$, the necessary equations are

$$\hat{\beta}_1 = \frac{\hat{\sigma}_{X,Y}}{\hat{\sigma}_X^2} \tag{4.12}$$

$$\hat{\beta}_0 = \hat{\mu}_Y - \hat{\beta}_1\hat{\mu}_X \tag{4.13}$$

$$\hat{\sigma}^2_{Y|X} = \hat{\sigma}^2_Y - \hat{\beta}^2_1 \hat{\sigma}^2_X \qquad (4.14)$$

$$\hat{Y}_i = \hat{\beta}_0 + \hat{\beta}_1 X_i \qquad (4.15)$$

where $\hat{\beta}_0$ and $\hat{\beta}_1$ are the intercept and slope coefficients, respectively, $\hat{\sigma}^2_{Y|X}$ is the residual variance from the regression of $Y$ on $X$, and $\hat{Y}_i$ is the predicted $Y$ score for a given value of $X$. The means, variances, and covariances that appear on the right side of the equations are elements from the mean vector and the covariance matrix.

The missing data complicate an otherwise straightforward analysis because the incomplete cases have nothing to contribute to $\Sigma Y$, $\Sigma Y^2$, and $\Sigma XY$. The E-step replaces the missing components of these sufficient statistics with their expected values (i.e., long-run averages). EM borrows information from other variables, so the algorithm actually uses so-called **conditional expectations** to replace the missing components of the formulas. To illustrate, consider the sum of the scores and the sum of the cross product terms (i.e., $\Sigma Y$ and $\Sigma XY$, respectively). The expected value of $Y$ is the predicted score from Equation 4.15, so the E-step replaces the missing components of $\Sigma Y$ and $\Sigma XY$ with $\hat{Y}_i$. Next, consider the sum of the squared scores, $\Sigma Y^2$. The expected value of a squared variable is $\hat{Y}_i^2 + \hat{\sigma}^2_{Y|X}$, where $\hat{Y}_i^2$ is the squared predicted score, and $\hat{\sigma}^2_{Y|X}$ is the residual variance from the regression of $Y$ on $X$. The E-step replaces the missing components of $\Sigma Y^2$ with this expectation.

Notice that the E-step does not actually impute the raw data. Rather, it fills in the computational building blocks for the mean, the variance, and the covariance (i.e., the sufficient statistics). Once this process is complete, the M-step becomes a straightforward estimation problem that uses the filled-in sufficient statistics to compute Equations 4.9 through 4.11. The resulting parameter estimates carry forward to the next E-step, where the process begins anew.

## 4.11 A BIVARIATE ANALYSIS EXAMPLE

Having outlined the necessary mathematical details, I use the IQ and job performance scores in Table 4.1 to illustrate a worked analysis example. Software programs that implement the EM algorithm fully automate the estimation procedure, so there is no need to perform the computational steps manually. Nevertheless, examining what happens at each step of the process is instructive and gives some insight into the inner workings of the algorithm.

EM requires an initial estimate of the mean vector and the covariance matrix. A number of traditional missing data techniques can generate these starting values, including deletion methods and single imputation (Little & Rubin, 2002, p. 225). To be consistent with statistical software packages (e.g., the SAS MI procedure), I use pairwise deletion estimates of the means and the variances and set the covariance to zero, as follows:

$$\hat{\boldsymbol{\mu}}_0 = \begin{bmatrix} \hat{\mu}_{IQ} \\ \hat{\mu}_{JP} \end{bmatrix} = \begin{bmatrix} \hat{\mu}_X \\ \hat{\mu}_Y \end{bmatrix} = \begin{bmatrix} 100.000 \\ 11.700 \end{bmatrix}$$

$$\hat{\boldsymbol{\Sigma}}_0 = \begin{bmatrix} \hat{\sigma}^2_{IQ} & \hat{\sigma}_{IQ,JP} \\ \hat{\sigma}_{JP,IQ} & \hat{\sigma}^2_{JP} \end{bmatrix} = \begin{bmatrix} \hat{\sigma}^2_X & \hat{\sigma}_{X,Y} \\ \hat{\sigma}_{Y,X} & \hat{\sigma}^2_Y \end{bmatrix} = \begin{bmatrix} 199.579 & 0 \\ 0 & 7.344 \end{bmatrix}$$

Throughout the example, I use a numeric subscript to index each EM cycle, and a value of zero denotes the fact that these parameter values precede the first E-step. Finally, to maintain consistency with the previous notation, I use $X$ and $Y$ to denote the IQ and job performance scores, respectively.

The first E-step uses the elements in the mean vector and the covariance matrix to build a regression equation that predicts the incomplete variable (e.g., job performance) from the complete variable (e.g., IQ). Substituting the appropriate elements from $\hat{\boldsymbol{\mu}}_0$ and $\hat{\boldsymbol{\Sigma}}_0$ into Equations 4.12 through 4.14 yields the following estimates: $\hat{\beta}_0 = 11.700$, $\hat{\beta}_1 = 0$, and $\hat{\sigma}^2_{Y|X} = 7.344$. Because the regression slope is zero, all of the predicted values happen to be the same, $\hat{Y}_1 = 11.700$. The ultimate goal of the E-step is to fill in the missing components of $\sum Y$, $\sum Y^2$, and $\sum XY$. Specifically, the predicted values fill in the missing components of $\sum Y$ and $\sum XY$, and $\hat{Y}_i^2 + \hat{\sigma}^2_{Y|X} = 11.700^2 + 7.344 = 144.234$ replaces the missing parts of $\sum Y^2$. Table 4.8 shows the computations for the first E-step, and the resulting sufficient statistics appear in the bottom row of the table.

Having dealt with the missing values in the E-step, the M-step uses standard complete-data formulas to update the mean vector and the covariance matrix. Substituting the sufficient statistics from Table 4.8 into Equations 4.9 through 4.11 updates the parameter estimates, as follows.

$$\hat{\boldsymbol{\mu}}_1 = \begin{bmatrix} \hat{\mu}_{IQ} \\ \hat{\mu}_{JP} \end{bmatrix} = \begin{bmatrix} \hat{\mu}_X \\ \hat{\mu}_Y \end{bmatrix} = \begin{bmatrix} 100.000 \\ 11.700 \end{bmatrix}$$

$$\hat{\boldsymbol{\Sigma}}_1 = \begin{bmatrix} \hat{\sigma}^2_{IQ} & \hat{\sigma}_{IQ,JP} \\ \hat{\sigma}_{JP,IQ} & \hat{\sigma}^2_{JP} \end{bmatrix} = \begin{bmatrix} \hat{\sigma}^2_X & \hat{\sigma}_{X,Y} \\ \hat{\sigma}_{Y,X} & \hat{\sigma}^2_Y \end{bmatrix} = \begin{bmatrix} 189.600 & 5.200 \\ 5.200 & 6.977 \end{bmatrix}$$

Notice that the job performance mean did not change, even though this variable has missing values. Because the initial regression slope is zero, the intercept (i.e., the mean job performance rating) replaces the missing $Y$ values. Consequently, the mean does not change in the first step, although it will in subsequent steps. In addition, notice that the IQ variance changed, even though this variable is complete. This change occurred because the maximum likelihood estimate uses $N$ rather than $N - 1$ in the denominator (the usual formula for the sample variance generated the initial estimate).

With the first cycle completed, the updated parameter estimates carry forward to the next E-step, where EM builds a new regression equation. Substituting the appropriate elements from $\hat{\boldsymbol{\mu}}_1$ and $\hat{\boldsymbol{\Sigma}}_1$ into Equations 4.12 through 4.14 yields the following estimates: $\hat{\beta}_0 = 8.957$, $\hat{\beta}_1 = 0.027$, and $\hat{\sigma}^2_{Y|X} = 6.834$. Consistent with the previous E-step, expected values replace the missing components of the sufficient statistics. For example, the individual with an IQ score of 78 contributes a predicted job performance rating of $\hat{Y}_i = 8.975 + 0.027(78) = 11.063$ to the computation of $\sum Y$ and $\sum XY$. Similarly, this case's contribution to $\sum Y^2$ is $11.063^2 + 6.834 = 129.224$. Table 4.9 shows the computations for the second E-step, with the sufficient statistics in the bottom row of the table.

As before, the M-step uses the sufficient statistics from the preceding E-step to update the mean vector and the covariance matrix. The sufficient statistics in Table 4.9 produce the following estimates.

**TABLE 4.8. Computation of the Sufficient Statistics for the First E-Step**

| X | $X^2$ | Y | $Y^2$ | XY |
|---|---|---|---|---|
| 78 | 6084 | 11.700 | $11.700^2 + 7.344$ | 912.600 |
| 84 | 7056 | 11.700 | $11.700^2 + 7.344$ | 982.800 |
| 84 | 7056 | 11.700 | $11.700^2 + 7.344$ | 982.800 |
| 85 | 7225 | 11.700 | $11.700^2 + 7.344$ | 994.500 |
| 87 | 7569 | 11.700 | $11.700^2 + 7.344$ | 1017.900 |
| 91 | 8281 | 11.700 | $11.700^2 + 7.344$ | 1064.700 |
| 92 | 8464 | 11.700 | $11.700^2 + 7.344$ | 1076.400 |
| 94 | 8836 | 11.700 | $11.700^2 + 7.344$ | 1099.800 |
| 94 | 8836 | 11.700 | $11.700^2 + 7.344$ | 1099.800 |
| 96 | 9216 | 11.700 | $11.700^2 + 7.344$ | 1123.200 |
| 99 | 9801 | 7 | 49 | 693 |
| 105 | 11025 | 10 | 100 | 1050 |
| 105 | 11025 | 11 | 121 | 1155 |
| 106 | 11236 | 15 | 225 | 1590 |
| 108 | 11664 | 10 | 100 | 1080 |
| 112 | 12544 | 10 | 100 | 1120 |
| 113 | 12769 | 12 | 144 | 1356 |
| 115 | 13225 | 14 | 196 | 1610 |
| 118 | 13924 | 16 | 256 | 1888 |
| 134 | 17956 | 12 | 144 | 1608 |
| $\sum X =$ 2000.000 | $\sum X^2 =$ 203792.000 | $\sum Y =$ 234.000 | $\sum Y^2 =$ 2877.340 | $\sum XY =$ 23504.500 |

*Note.* X = IQ and Y = job performance. **Bold** typeface denotes imputed values.

$$\hat{\pmb{\mu}}_2 = \begin{bmatrix} \hat{\mu}_{IQ} \\ \hat{\mu}_{JP} \end{bmatrix} = \begin{bmatrix} \hat{\mu}_X \\ \hat{\mu}_Y \end{bmatrix} = \begin{bmatrix} 100.000 \\ 11.523 \end{bmatrix}$$

$$\hat{\pmb{\Sigma}}_2 = \begin{bmatrix} \hat{\sigma}_{IQ}^2 & \hat{\sigma}_{IQ,JP} \\ \hat{\sigma}_{JP,IQ} & \hat{\sigma}_{JP}^2 \end{bmatrix} = \begin{bmatrix} \hat{\sigma}_X^2 & \hat{\sigma}_{X,Y} \\ \hat{\sigma}_{Y,X} & \hat{\sigma}_Y^2 \end{bmatrix} = \begin{bmatrix} 189.600 & 7.663 \\ 7.663 & 6.764 \end{bmatrix}$$

Notice that the IQ mean and variance do not change because these parameters immediately converge to the maximum likelihood estimates in the first EM cycle. However, the parameters affected by missing data do change, and they continue to do so from one M-step to the next.

As you might have guessed, $\hat{\pmb{\mu}}_2$ and $\hat{\pmb{\Sigma}}_2$ carry forward to the next E-step, where the algorithm generates a new set of regression estimates that fill in the missing components of the sufficient statistics. The following M-step then uses the sufficient statistics to update the parameter values. EM repeats these two steps until the elements in the mean vector and the covariance matrix no longer change (or change by a trivially small amount) between consecutive M-steps, at which point the algorithm has converged on the maximum likelihood estimates. This example requires 59 cycles to converge and yields the following parameter estimates.

$$\hat{\pmb{\mu}} = \begin{bmatrix} \hat{\mu}_{IQ} \\ \hat{\mu}_{JP} \end{bmatrix} = \begin{bmatrix} 100.000 \\ 10.281 \end{bmatrix}$$

$$\hat{\pmb{\Sigma}} = \begin{bmatrix} \hat{\sigma}_{IQ}^2 & \hat{\sigma}_{IQ,JP} \\ \hat{\sigma}_{JP,IQ} & \hat{\sigma}_{JP}^2 \end{bmatrix} = \begin{bmatrix} 189.600 & 23.393 \\ 23.393 & 8.206 \end{bmatrix}$$

**TABLE 4.9. Computation of the Sufficient Statistics for the Second E-Step**

| X | $X^2$ | Y | $Y^2$ | XY |
|---|---|---|---|---|
| 78 | 6084 | 11.063 | $11.063^2 + 6.834$ | 862.914 |
| 84 | 7056 | 11.225 | $11.225^2 + 6.834$ | 942.900 |
| 84 | 7056 | 11.225 | $11.225^2 + 6.834$ | 942.900 |
| 85 | 7225 | 11.252 | $11.252^2 + 6.834$ | 956.420 |
| 87 | 7569 | 11.306 | $11.306^2 + 6.834$ | 983.622 |
| 91 | 8281 | 11.414 | $11.414^2 + 6.834$ | 1038.674 |
| 92 | 8464 | 11.441 | $11.441^2 + 6.834$ | 1052.572 |
| 94 | 8836 | 11.495 | $11.495^2 + 6.834$ | 1080.530 |
| 94 | 8836 | 11.495 | $11.495^2 + 6.834$ | 1080.530 |
| 96 | 9216 | 11.549 | $11.549^2 + 6.834$ | 1108.704 |
| 99 | 9801 | 7 | 49 | 693 |
| 105 | 11025 | 10 | 100 | 1050 |
| 105 | 11025 | 11 | 121 | 1155 |
| 106 | 11236 | 15 | 225 | 1590 |
| 108 | 11664 | 10 | 100 | 1080 |
| 112 | 12544 | 10 | 100 | 1120 |
| 113 | 12769 | 12 | 144 | 1356 |
| 115 | 13225 | 14 | 196 | 1610 |
| 118 | 13924 | 16 | 256 | 1888 |
| 134 | 17956 | 12 | 144 | 1608 |
| $\sum X =$ 2000.000 | $\sum X^2 =$ 203792.000 | $\sum Y =$ 230.465 | $\sum Y^2 =$ 2790.990 | $\sum XY =$ 23199.766 |

*Note.* X = IQ; Y = job performance. **Bold** typeface denotes imputed values.

The regression-based procedure that EM uses to update the parameters largely ob-
scures the fact that the estimates are incrementally improving from one step to the next. To
illustrate how EM "climbs" to the top of the log-likelihood function, I used the parameter
estimates from each iteration to compute the sample log-likelihood values. (EM does not
actually manipulate the log-likelihood equation, so the log-likelihood values are not an automatic by-product of the analysis.) For example, substituting the starting values (i.e., $\hat{\mu}_0$ and
$\hat{\Sigma}_0$) and the observed data into Equation 4.2 yields an initial log-likelihood value of logL =
–76.9318195. Similarly, substituting $\hat{\mu}_1$ and $\hat{\Sigma}_1$ into Equation 4.2 gives the log-likelihood
for the first EM cycle, and so on. Table 4.10 shows the log-likelihood values and the job performance parameters from selected cycles of the bivariate EM analysis. As you can see, the
first few EM cycles produce the largest changes in the log-likelihood, whereas the latter
steps yield much smaller changes. The same is also true for the parameter estimates. In effect, the optimization algorithm traverses the steepest portion of the ascent at the beginning of the hike, and the climb becomes more gradual near the plateau. As the algorithm
nears the peak of the log-likelihood function, each additional cycle produces a very small
improvement in the log-likelihood value, and the adjustments to the parameters are so small
that the estimates effectively remain the same between successive M-steps. For example, in
the final three EM cycles, the changes to the job performance mean occur in the fourth decimal, and the changes to the sample log-likelihood occur past the seventh decimal. At this
point, the hill climb is effectively over, and the algorithm has converged on the maximum likelihood estimates.

**TABLE 4.10. Sample Log-Likelihood Values across EM Cycles**

| EM cycle | Log-likelihood | $\hat{\mu}_{JP}$ | $\hat{\sigma}^2_{JP}$ | $\hat{\sigma}_{IQ,JP}$ |
|---|---|---|---|---|
| 0 | −76.9318195 | 11.7000000 | 7.3440000 | 0.0000000 |
| 1 | −76.5939005 | 11.7000000 | 6.9772220 | 5.2002527 |
| 2 | −76.4254785 | 11.5225410 | 6.7641355 | 7.6631331 |
| 3 | −76.2929150 | 11.3944910 | 6.6538592 | 9.3296347 |
| 4 | −76.1883350 | 11.2643060 | 6.6285983 | 10.9748205 |
| 5 | −76.1059020 | 11.1493190 | 6.6552569 | 12.4275358 |
| 6 | −76.0410225 | 11.0477700 | 6.7152964 | 13.7104777 |
| 7 | −75.9900400 | 10.9580870 | 6.7959299 | 14.8434952 |
| 8 | −75.9500360 | 10.8788850 | 6.8882473 | 15.8441088 |
| 9 | −75.9186850 | 10.8089380 | 6.9860245 | 16.7277910 |
| 10 | −75.8941405 | 10.7471650 | 7.0849410 | 17.5082066 |
| … | … | … | … | … |
| 50 | −75.8064920 | 10.2835690 | 8.1993288 | 23.3651099 |
| 51 | −75.8064915 | 10.2831910 | 8.2005058 | 23.3698912 |
| 52 | −75.8064905 | 10.2828570 | 8.2015456 | 23.3741137 |
| 53 | −75.8064900 | 10.2825610 | 8.2024642 | 23.3778428 |
| 54 | −75.8064895 | 10.2823010 | 8.2032757 | 23.3811362 |
| 55 | −75.8064890 | 10.2820710 | 8.2039925 | 23.3840446 |
| 56 | −75.8064890 | 10.2818670 | 8.2046257 | 23.3866132 |
| 57 | −75.8064885 | 10.2816880 | 8.2051849 | 23.3888817 |
| 58 | −75.8064885 | 10.2815290 | 8.2056789 | 23.3908850 |
| 59 | −75.8064885 | 10.2813890 | 8.2061153 | 23.3926542 |

As an aside, the EM differs from other optimization algorithms (e.g., the scoring algorithm; Hartley & Hocking, 1971; Trawinski & Bargmann, 1964) because it does not require the computation of first or second derivatives. Consequently, the EM algorithm does not automatically produce the basic building blocks of maximum likelihood standard errors. Methodologists have outlined approaches for generating standard errors in an EM analysis (Little & Rubin, 2002; Meng & Rubin, 1991), but these methods require additional computational steps that are not implemented in all software packages. Bootstrap resampling is a simulation-based approach that is particularly useful for estimating standard errors with non-normal data, but it is also applicable to an EM analysis. I give a detailed description of bootstrap in Chapter 5.

## 4.12 EXTENDING EM TO MULTIVARIATE DATA

The preceding bivariate analysis is relatively straightforward because the missing values are isolated to a single variable. Applying EM to multivariate data is typically more complex because the E-step requires a unique regression equation (or set of equations) for each missing data pattern. Despite this complication, the basic logic of EM remains the same and requires just a few additional details. To illustrate the changes to the E-step, I use the full data set in Table 4.1. EM with three variables is still relatively straightforward, but the logic of this example generalizes to data sets with any number of variables. Finally, note that the procedural details of the M-step do not change because this step always uses the standard complete-data formulas in Equations 4.9 through 4.11 to update the parameter estimates. Consequently, the following discussion focuses solely on the E-step. To maintain consistent notation, $X$ denotes the IQ scores, $Y$ represents the job performance ratings, and $Z$ corresponds to the well-being scores.

Applying the E-step to the data in Table 4.1 requires the following set of sufficient statistics: $\Sigma X$, $\Sigma X^2$, $\Sigma Y$, $\Sigma Y^2$, $\Sigma Z$, $\Sigma Z^2$, $\Sigma XY$, $\Sigma XZ$, and $\Sigma YZ$. Notice that these quantities are the same as those from the previous bivariate example (i.e., the sum of the scores, the sum of the squared scores, and the sum of the cross product terms). As before, the purpose of the E-step is to replace the missing components of the sufficient statistics with expectations, but this now requires a unique set of regression equations for missing data pattern. Returning to the data in Table 4.1, note that there are four missing data patterns: (1) cases with only IQ scores, (2) cases with IQ and well-being scores, (3) cases with IQ and job performance scores, and (4) cases with complete data on all three variables. The complete cases are not a concern, so the E-step only deals with the three patterns that have missing data. Table 4.11 shows the missing sufficient statistics and the relevant expectation terms for each missing data pattern.

Consider the subsample of cases with missing job performance ratings (i.e., missing $Y$ values). These individuals have complete data on the IQ and psychological well-being variables (i.e., $X$ and $Z$, respectively), so the problematic sufficient statistics are $\Sigma Y$, $\Sigma XY$, $\Sigma YZ$, and $\Sigma Y^2$. Following the logic from the bivariate example, predicted scores replace the missing components of the variable sums and sums of products. This missing data pattern has two complete variables, so a multiple regression equation generates the predicted scores, as follows:

$$\hat{Y}_{i|X,Z} = \hat{\beta}_0 + \hat{\beta}_1 X_i + \hat{\beta}_2 Z_i \tag{4.16}$$

where $\hat{Y}_{i|X,Z}$ is the predicted $Y$ value for case $i$ (the vertical bar denotes the fact that the predicted score is conditional on both $X$ and $Z$). Consistent with the bivariate analysis, the expectation for $\Sigma Y^2$ involves a squared predicted score and a residual variance estimate.

**TABLE 4.11. Expectations for a Multivariate Application of the EM Algorithm**

| Missing variable | Missing sufficient statistics | Imputed expectations |
|---|---|---|
| $Y$ (job performance) | $\Sigma Y$, $\Sigma XY$, $\Sigma YZ$ <br> $\Sigma Y^2$ | $\hat{Y}_{i|X,Z}$ <br> $\hat{Y}_{i|X,Z}^2 + \hat{\sigma}_{Y|X,Z}^2$ |
| $Z$ (well-being) | $\Sigma Z$, $\Sigma XZ$, $\Sigma YZ$ <br> $\Sigma Z^2$ | $\hat{Z}_{i|X,Y}$ <br> $\hat{Z}_{i|X,Y}^2 + \hat{\sigma}_{Z|X,Y}^2$ |
| $Y$ and $Z$ (job performance and well-being) | $\Sigma Y$, $\Sigma XY$, $\Sigma YZ$ <br> $\Sigma Y^2$ <br> $\Sigma Z$, $\Sigma XY$, $\Sigma YZ$ <br> $\Sigma Z^2$ <br> $\Sigma YZ$ | $\hat{Y}_{i|X}$ <br> $\hat{Y}_{i|X}^2 + \hat{\sigma}_{Y|X}^2$ <br> $\hat{Z}_{i|X}$ <br> $\hat{Z}_{i|X}^2 + \hat{\sigma}_{Z|X}^2$ <br> $(\hat{Y}_{i|X})(\hat{Z}_{i|X}) + \hat{\sigma}_{Y,Z|X}$ |

Consequently, $\hat{Y}^2_{i|X,Z} + \hat{\sigma}^2_{Y|X,Z}$ replaces the missing components of $\Sigma Y^2$, where $\hat{\sigma}^2_{Y|X,Z}$ is the residual variance from the regression of $Y$ on $X$ and $Z$.

Next, consider the individual with a missing well-being score (i.e., missing $Z$ value). Again, a multiple regression equation generates the predicted score

$$\hat{Z}_{i|X,Y} = \hat{\beta}_0 + \hat{\beta}_1 X_i + \hat{\beta}_2 Y_i, \tag{4.17}$$

and this predicted value replaces the missing components of $\Sigma Z$, $\Sigma XZ$, and $\Sigma YZ$. As seen in Table 4.11, the expectation for the missing $Z^2$ value is similar to the previous missing data pattern and equals the squared predicted score plus the residual variance from the regression of $Z$ on $X$ and $Y$.

Thus far, the E-step has not changed very much. Each missing data pattern requires a unique set of regression equations and expectations, but the underlying logic is the same as it was in the bivariate example. The only additional nuance occurs with patterns that have two or more missing variables. For example, consider the subsample of cases with missing job performance ratings and well-being scores (i.e., $Y$ and $Z$, respectively). As before, regression equations generate predicted scores for each missing variable, as follows:

$$\hat{Y}_{i|X} = \hat{\beta}_0 + \hat{\beta}_1 X_i \tag{4.18}$$

$$\hat{Z}_{i|X} = \hat{\beta}_2 + \hat{\beta}_3 X_i \tag{4.19}$$

As seen in Table 4.11, the predicted scores and corresponding residual variances fill in all but one of the sufficient statistics. The cross product term for the two missing variables (i.e., $\Sigma YZ$) involves a new expectation, $(\hat{Y}_{i|X})(\hat{Z}_{i|X}) + \hat{\sigma}_{Y,Z|X}$, where the terms in parentheses are the predicted values from previous regression equations, and $\sigma_{Y,Z|X}$ is the residual covariance between job performance and well-being, which is $\hat{\sigma}_{Y,Z|X} = \hat{\sigma}_{Y,Z} - \hat{\beta}_1\hat{\beta}_3\hat{\sigma}^2_X$.

Extending the E-step computations to complex multivariate analyses with general missing data patterns is straightforward because the relevant expectations are identical to those in Table 4.11. The main procedural difficulty is the computation of regression equations for each missing data pattern. Not surprisingly, the number of missing data patterns (and thus the number of regression equations) can get quite large as the number of variables increases. Although it sounds tedious to construct a set of regressions for each missing data pattern, a computational algorithm called the sweep operator can automate this process. The sweep operator combines the mean vector and the covariance matrix into a single augmented matrix and applies a series of transformations that produce the desired regression coefficients and residual variances. A number of sources give detailed descriptions of the sweep operator (Dempster, 1969; Goodnight, 1979; Little & Rubin, 2002).

## 4.13 MAXIMUM LIKELIHOOD ESTIMATION SOFTWARE OPTIONS

Although the mathematical foundations of maximum likelihood missing data handling have been in the literature for many years, estimation routines have only recently become widely available in statistical software packages. In the late 1980s, methodologists outlined techniques that effectively tricked complete-data software packages into implementing maximum likelihood missing data handling by treating each missing data pattern as a subpopulation in a multiple group structural equation model (Allison, 1987; Muthén, Kaplan, and Hollis, 1987). However, these approaches did not enjoy widespread use because they were complicated to program and were unwieldy to implement with more than a small handful of missing data patterns. Fortunately, this approach is no longer necessary.

Many of the recent software innovations have occurred within the latent variable modeling framework, and virtually every structural equation modeling software package now implements maximum likelihood missing data handling. (This approach is often referred to as full information maximum likelihood estimation, or simply FIML.) The latent variable modeling framework encompasses a vast number of analytic methods that researchers use on a routine basis (e.g., correlation, regression, factor analysis, path analysis, structural equation models, mixture models, multilevel models). Structural equation modeling software is therefore an ideal tool for many missing data problems. Structural equation modeling programs have undergone dramatic improvements in the number of and type of missing data analyses that they are capable of performing, and these packages continue to evolve at a rapid pace. Because of their flexibility and breadth, I rely heavily on structural equation programs to generate the analysis examples throughout the book. I discuss the capabilities of specific packages in more detail in Chapter 11.

As an aside, a word of caution is warranted concerning software programs that implement the EM algorithm. Some popular packages (e.g., LISREL and SPSS) offer the option of imputing the raw data after the final EM cycle. This is somewhat unfortunate because it gives the impression that a maximum likelihood approach has properly handled the missing values. In reality, this imputation scheme is nothing more than regression imputation. The only difference between EM imputation and regression imputation is that the EM approach uses a maximum likelihood estimate of the mean vector and the covariance matrix to generate the regression equations, whereas standard regression imputation schemes tend to use listwise deletion estimates of $\mu$ and $\Sigma$ to build the regressions. Although it may sound appealing to base the imputation process on maximum likelihood estimates, doing so leads to the same negative outcomes described in Chapter 2, namely, biased parameter estimates and attenuated standard errors (von Hippel, 2004). Consequently, it is a good idea to avoid EM-based single imputation routines. In situations that necessitate a filled-in data set, multiple imputation is a much better option.

## 4.14 DATA ANALYSIS EXAMPLE 1

This section describes a data analysis that uses the EM algorithm to generate maximum likelihood estimates of a mean vector, covariance matrix, and correlation matrix.* The data for this analysis consist of scores from 480 employees on eight work-related variables: gender, age, job tenure, IQ, psychological well-being, job satisfaction, job performance, and turnover

---

*Analysis syntax and data are available on the companion website, *www.appliedmissingdata.com*.

**TABLE 4.12. Mean, Covariance, and Correlation Estimates from Data Analysis Example 1**

| Variable | 1 | 2 | 3 | 4 | 5 | 6 | 7 | 8 |
|---|---|---|---|---|---|---|---|---|
| *Missing data maximum likelihood* | | | | | | | | |
| 1: Age | 28.908 | 0.504 | –0.010 | 0.182 | 0.136 | –0.049 | –0.150 | 0.015 |
| 2: Tenure | 8.459 | 9.735 | –0.034 | 0.155 | 0.154 | 0.016 | 0.011 | 0.001 |
| 3: Female | –0.028 | –0.052 | 0.248 | 0.115 | 0.047 | –0.015 | 0.005 | 0.068 |
| 4: Well-being | 1.148 | 0.569 | 0.067 | 1.382 | 0.322 | 0.456 | –0.257 | 0.291 |
| 5: Satisfaction | 0.861 | 0.565 | 0.028 | 0.446 | 1.386 | 0.184 | –0.234 | 0.411 |
| 6: Performance | –0.330 | 0.061 | –0.009 | 0.671 | 0.271 | 1.570 | –0.346 | 0.426 |
| 7: Turnover | –0.377 | 0.016 | 0.001 | –0.141 | –0.129 | –0.203 | 0.218 | –0.180 |
| 8: IQ | 0.674 | 0.026 | 0.284 | 2.876 | 4.074 | 4.496 | –0.706 | 70.892 |
| Means | 37.948 | 10.054 | 0.542 | 6.288 | 5.950 | 6.021 | 0.321 | 100.102 |
| *Complete data maximum likelihood* | | | | | | | | |
| 1: Age | 28.908 | 0.504 | –0.010 | 0.182 | 0.111 | –0.049 | –0.150 | 0.015 |
| 2: Tenure | 8.459 | 9.735 | –0.034 | 0.173 | 0.157 | 0.016 | 0.011 | 0.001 |
| 3: Female | –0.028 | –0.052 | 0.248 | 0.097 | 0.038 | –0.015 | 0.005 | 0.068 |
| 4: Well-being | 1.208 | 0.667 | 0.060 | 1.518 | 0.348 | 0.447 | –0.296 | 0.306 |
| 5: Satisfaction | 0.697 | 0.576 | 0.022 | 0.503 | 1.377 | 0.176 | –0.222 | 0.378 |
| 6: Performance | –0.330 | 0.061 | –0.009 | 0.690 | 0.259 | 1.570 | –0.346 | 0.426 |
| 7: Turnover | –0.377 | 0.016 | 0.001 | –0.170 | –0.122 | –0.203 | 0.218 | –0.180 |
| 8: IQ | 0.674 | 0.026 | 0.284 | 3.172 | 3.730 | 4.496 | –0.706 | 70.892 |
| Means | 37.948 | 10.054 | 0.542 | 6.271 | 5.990 | 6.021 | 0.321 | 100.102 |

*Note.* Correlations are shown in the upper diagonal in **bold** typeface. Elements affected by missing data are enclosed in the shaded box.

intentions. I generated these data to mimic the correlation structure of published research articles in the management and psychology literature (e.g., Wright & Bonett, 2007; Wright, Cropanzano, & Bonett, 2007). The data have three missing data patterns, each of which contains one-third of the sample. The first pattern consists of cases with complete data, and the remaining two patterns have missing data on either well-being or job satisfaction. These patterns mimic a situation in which the data are missing by design (e.g., to reduce the cost of data collection).

Table 4.12 shows the maximum likelihood estimates, along with the corresponding estimates from the complete data. To facilitate comparison, a shaded box encloses the parameter estimates affected by the missing data. As seen in the table, the missing data estimates are quite similar to those of the complete data. For example, the two sets of correlation values typically differ by approximately .02, and the largest difference is .04 (the correlation between well-being and turnover intentions). The similarity of the two sets of estimates might seem somewhat remarkable given that 33% of the satisfaction and well-being scores are missing.

## 4.15 DATA ANALYSIS EXAMPLE 2

The second analysis example uses maximum likelihood to estimate a multiple regression model. The analysis uses the same employee data set as the first example and involves the regression of job performance ratings on psychological well-being and job satisfaction, as follows:

$$JP_i = \beta_0 + \beta_1(WB_i) + \beta_2(SAT_i) + \varepsilon$$

The top panel of Figure 4.1 shows the path diagram of the regression model. I used a structural equation modeling program to estimate the regression model because these packages offer a convenient platform for implementing maximum likelihood estimation with missing data.* Finally, note that I requested standard errors based on the observed information matrix.

Researchers typically begin a regression analysis by examining the omnibus $F$ test. The likelihood ratio statistic and the multivariate Wald test are analogous procedures in a maximum likelihood analysis. The procedural details of both tests are identical with or without missing data. Recall from Chapter 3 that the likelihood ratio test involves a pair of nested models. The full model corresponds to the multiple regression in the top panel of Figure 4.1, and the restricted model is one that constrains both regression slopes to zero during estimation. (The regression intercept is not part of the usual omnibus $F$ test, so it appears in both models.) Estimating the two models produced log-likelihood values of $logL_{Full} = -1753.093$ and $logL_{Restricted} = -1793.181$, respectively. Notice that log-likelihood for the restricted model is quite a bit lower than that of the full model, which suggests that fixing the slopes to zero deteriorates model fit. Using the log-likelihood values to compute the likelihood ratio test (see Equation 3.16) yields $LR = 80.18$. The models differ by two parameters (i.e., the restricted model constrains two coefficients two zero), so referencing the test statistic to a chi-square distribution with two degrees of freedom returns a probability value of $p < .001$. The significant likelihood ratio test indicates that the fit of the restricted model is significantly worse than that of the full model. Consistent with the interpretation of an $F$ statistic, this suggests that at least one of the regression coefficients is significantly different from zero.

Researchers typically follow up a significant omnibus test by examining partial regression coefficients. Table 4.13 gives the regression model estimates along with those of the corresponding complete-data analysis from Chapter 3. As seen in the table, psychological well-being was a significant predictor of job performance, $\hat{\beta}_1 = 0.476$, $z = 8.66$, $p < .001$, but job satisfaction was not, $\hat{\beta}_2 = 0.027$, $z = 0.45$, $p = 0.66$. Notice that the missing data estimates are quite similar to those of the complete data, despite the fact that each predictor variable has a missing data rate of 33%. The missing data analysis produced somewhat larger standard errors, but this is to be expected. Finally, note that the interpretation of the regression coefficients is the same as it is in a complete-data regression analysis. For example, holding job satisfaction constant, a one-point increase in psychological well-being yields a .476 increase in job satisfaction, on average.

---

*Analysis syntax and data are available on the companion website, *www.appliedmissingdata.com*.

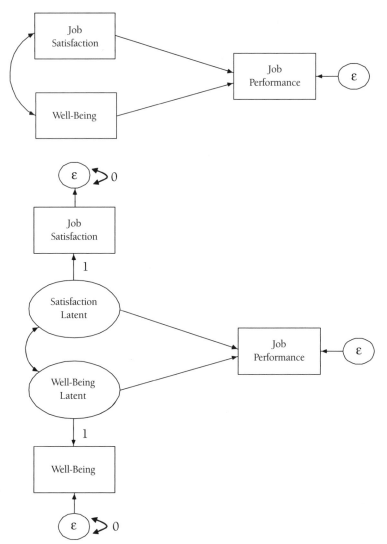

**FIGURE 4.1.** A path diagram for the multiple regression model. The single-headed straight lines represent regression coefficients, the double-headed curved arrow is a correlation, the rectangles are manifest variables, and the ellipse is a latent variable. The top panel of the figure shows the manifest variable regression model. The bottom panel of the figure shows the regression model recast as a latent variable model, where the two latent variables have a single manifest indicator. The factor loadings are fixed at values of one, and the residual variances (the doubled-headed curved arrows the manifest variable residual terms to themselves) are constrained to zero.

## A Note on Missing Explanatory Variables

Before proceeding to the next analysis example, it is important to note that software packages are not uniform in their treatment of missing explanatory variables. Specifically, some software programs exclude cases that have incomplete data on explanatory variables, while others do not. To understand why this is the case, reconsider the log-likelihood formula in Equation 4.2.

**TABLE 4.13. Regression Model Estimates from Data Analysis Example 2**

| Parameter | Estimate | SE | $z$ |
|---|---|---|---|
| | Missing data maximum likelihood | | |
| $\beta_0$ (intercept) | 6.021 | 0.053 | 113.123 |
| $\beta_1$ (well-being) | 0.476 | 0.055 | 8.664 |
| $\beta_2$ (satisfaction) | 0.027 | 0.060 | 0.445 |
| $\hat{\sigma}_e^2$ (residual) | 1.243 | 0.087 | 14.356 |
| $R^2$ | 0.208 | | |
| | Complete data maximum likelihood | | |
| $\beta_0$ (intercept) | 6.021 | 0.051 | 117.705 |
| $\beta_1$ (well-being) | 0.446 | 0.044 | 10.083 |
| $\beta_2$ (satisfaction) | 0.025 | 0.046 | 0.533 |
| $\hat{\sigma}_e^2$ (residual) | 1.256 | 0.081 | 15.492 |
| $R^2$ | 0.200 | | |

*Note.* Predictors were centered at the maximum likelihood estimates of the mean.

The log-likelihood quantifies the standardized distance between the outcome variables (i.e., the **Y** vector) and the population mean. Depending on the software package and the underlying statistical model, the explanatory variables may not be included in the score vector. For example, in a regression analysis, some software platforms specify the explanatory variables as part of the population mean vector, such that $\beta_0 + \beta_1(X_1) + \beta_2(X_2)$ replaces the $\mathbf{\mu}$ term in Equation 4.2. In these situations, the software program is likely to exclude the cases with the missing explanatory variables. To further complicate matters, a given software program may not be consistent in its treatment of missing explanatory variables across different analyses. For example, a package might include the incomplete cases in a regression model but exclude those data records in more complex models.

Structural equation modeling programs incorporate some flexibility for dealing with incomplete explanatory variables. Specifically, recasting an incomplete predictor variable as the sole manifest indicator of a latent variable effectively tricks the software program into treating the explanatory variable as an outcome, while still maintaining the variable's exogenous status in the model. For example, the bottom panel of Figure 4.1 shows the previous regression analysis as a latent variable model. In the latent variable specification, the factor loadings are constrained to one (this equates the latent variable's metric to the manifest variable's metric) and the residual variances are constrained to zero (this equates the latent variable's variance to the manifest variable's variance). Because the latent variables predict the explanatory variables, the incomplete predictors become part of the **Y** vector in Equation 4.2. Importantly, this programming trick does not change the interpretation of the model parameters (e.g., the arrow that connects the latent job satisfaction variable to the job performance variable is still a partial regression coefficient). Readers interested in more details on single-indicator latent variables can consult any number of structural equation modeling textbooks (e.g., see Kline, 2005, pp. 229–231).

As an important aside, the single-indicator latent variable approach can have a bearing on the likelihood ratio test. As an illustration, reconsider the likelihood ratio test from the multiple regression analysis. I specified the restricted model by constraining both regression slopes to zero during estimation. Had the data been complete, I could have specified an equivalent restricted model by simply excluding the explanatory variables from the analysis. However, this approach would not produce a nested model if the manifest explanatory variables are both indicators of a latent variable, because the two models will have different sets of variables that contribute to the **Y** vector in the log-likelihood equation. Consequently, the only correct way to specify a nested model is to constrain parameters from the full model to zero. Returning to the latent variable model in the bottom panel of Figure 4.1, note that constraining the arrows that connect the latent variables to the job performance variable to zero during estimation produces an appropriate nested model, whereas excluding job satisfaction and well-being from the model does not.

## 4.16 DATA ANALYSIS EXAMPLE 3

The third analysis example uses maximum likelihood to estimate a multiple regression model with an interaction term. The analysis uses the employee data set from the previous examples and involves the regression of job performance on well-being, gender, and the interaction between well-being and gender. The goal of the analysis is to determine whether gender moderates the association between psychological well-being and job performance. The multiple regression equation is as follows:

$$JP_i = \beta_0 + \beta_1(WB_i) + \beta_2(FEMALE_i) + \beta_3(WB_i)(FEMALE_i) + \varepsilon$$

and Figure 4.2 shows the corresponding path diagram of the model. Notice that the interaction term (i.e., the product of gender and well-being) simply serves as an additional explanatory variable in the model. Using maximum likelihood to estimate a model with an interaction term is straightforward and follows the same procedure as any multiple regression analysis. I include this example as a point of contrast with multiple imputation. As you will see in Chapter 9, multiple imputation requires special procedures to deal with interactive effects such as this. Consistent with the previous analysis example, I used structural equation software to estimate the regression model and requested standard errors based on the observed information matrix.*

Prior to conducting the analysis, I centered the psychological well-being scores at the maximum likelihood estimate of the grand mean from Table 4.12. Next, I created a product term by multiplying gender (0 = male, 1 = female) and the centered well-being scores. The resulting product term is missing for any case with a missing well-being score. Because males have a gender code of zero, their product terms should always equal zero, regardless of whether the well-being variable is complete. Consequently, I recoded the missing product terms to have a value of zero within the male subsample.

---

* Analysis syntax and data are available on the companion website, *www.appliedmissingdata.com*.

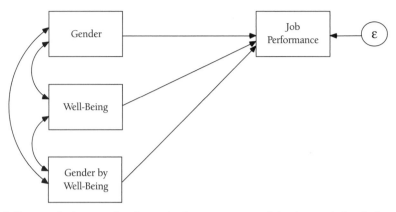

**FIGURE 4.2.** A path diagram for the multiple regression model. The single-headed straight lines represent regression coefficients, the double-headed curved arrow is a correlation, the rectangles are manifest variables, and the ellipse is a latent variable.

Because the previous analysis illustrates the use of the likelihood ratio test, there is no need to demonstrate the procedure further. Table 4.14 gives the regression model estimates along with those of the corresponding complete-data analysis. The analysis results suggest that males and females do not differ with respect to their mean job performance ratings, $\hat{\beta}_2 = -0.167$, $z = -1.59$, $p = .11$, but the significant interaction term indicates that the association between well-being and performance is different for males and females, $\hat{\beta}_3 = 0.362$, $z = 3.43$, $p < .001$. Because the gender variable is coded such that female = 1 and male = 0, the sign of the interaction coefficient indicates that the relationship is stronger for females. Notice that the interpretation of the regression coefficients is identical to what it would have been had the data been complete. In addition, the computation of simple slopes is identical to that of a complete-data analysis. For example, the regression equation for the subsample of males (the group coded 0) is $\hat{Y}_M = \hat{\beta}_0 + \hat{\beta}_1(WB)$, and the corresponding equation for females (the group coded 1) is $\hat{Y}_F = (\hat{\beta}_0 + \hat{\beta}_2) + (\hat{\beta}_1 + \hat{\beta}_3)(WB)$. Finally, notice that the missing data estimates are quite similar to those of the complete data, but they have larger standard errors. The increase in the standard errors is not surprising given that the well-being variable and the interaction term have a substantial proportion of missing values.

## 4.17 DATA ANALYSIS EXAMPLE 4

This section presents a data analysis example that illustrates how to use an EM covariance matrix to conduct an exploratory factor analysis and an internal consistency reliability analysis.* The analyses use artificial data from a questionnaire on eating disorder risk. Briefly, the data contain the responses from 400 college-aged women on 10 questions from the Eating Attitudes Test (EAT; Garner, Olmsted, Bohr, & Garfinkel, 1982), a widely used measure of eating disorder risk. The 10 questions measure two constructs: Drive for Thinness (e.g., "I avoid

---

\* Analysis syntax and data are available on the companion website, *www.appliedmissingdata.com*.

**TABLE 4.14. Regression Model Estimates from Data Analysis Example 3**

| Parameter | Estimate | SE | $z$ |
|---|---|---|---|
| Missing data maximum likelihood | | | |
| $\beta_0$ (intercept) | 6.091 | 0.076 | 79.755 |
| $\beta_1$ (well-being) | 0.337 | 0.071 | 4.723 |
| $\beta_2$ (gender) | −0.167 | 0.105 | −1.587 |
| $\beta_3$ (interaction) | 0.362 | 0.106 | 3.426 |
| $\hat{\sigma}_e^2$ (residual) | 1.234 | 0.084 | 14.650 |
| $R^2$ | .214 | | |
| Complete data maximum likelihood | | | |
| $\beta_0$ (intercept) | 6.080 | 0.075 | 81.536 |
| $\beta_1$ (well-being) | 0.304 | 0.057 | 5.339 |
| $\beta_2$ (gender) | −0.146 | 0.101 | −1.438 |
| $\beta_3$ (interaction) | 0.326 | 0.082 | 3.975 |
| $\hat{\sigma}_e^2$ (residual) | 1.211 | 0.078 | 15.492 |
| $R^2$ | .229 | | |

*Note.* Predictors were centered at the maximum likelihood estimates of the mean.

eating when I'm hungry") and Food Preoccupation (e.g., "I find myself preoccupied with food"), and they mimic the two-factor structure proposed by Doninger, Enders, and Burnett (2005). Figure 4.3 shows a graphic of the EAT factor structure and abbreviated descriptions of the item stems. The data set also contains an anxiety scale score, a variable that measures beliefs about Western standards of beauty (e.g., high scores indicate that respondents internalize a thin ideal of beauty), and body mass index (BMI) values.

Variables in the EAT data set are missing for a variety of reasons. I simulated MCAR data by randomly deleting scores from the anxiety variable, the Western standards of beauty scale, and two of the EAT questions ($EAT_2$ and $EAT_{21}$). It seems reasonable to expect a relationship between body weight and missingness, so I created MAR data on five variables ($EAT_1$, $EAT_{10}$, $EAT_{12}$, $EAT_{18}$, and $EAT_{24}$) by deleting the EAT scores for a subset of cases in both tails of the BMI distribution. These same EAT questions were also missing for individuals with elevated anxiety scores. Finally, I introduced a small amount of MNAR data by deleting a number of the high body mass index scores (e.g., to mimic a situation in which females with high BMI values refuse to be weighed). The deletion process typically produced a missing data rate of 5 to 10% on each variable.

Most software packages use deletion methods to handle missing data in factor analyses and reliability analyses. The same software programs can usually accommodate a covariance matrix as input data, so you can effectively implement maximum likelihood by estimating the mean vector and the covariance matrix (e.g., using the EM algorithm) and using the resulting estimates as input data for the analysis. The problem with using an EM covariance matrix as input data is that no single value of $N$ is applicable to the entire matrix (Enders & Peugh, 2004). This poses a problem for standard error computations and requires corrective proce-

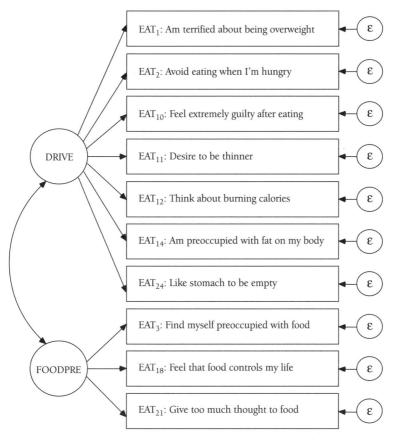

**FIGURE 4.3.** A path diagram for the two-factor confirmatory factor analysis model. The single-headed straight lines represent regression coefficients, the double-headed curved arrow is a correlation, the rectangles are manifest variables, and the ellipses are latent variables.

dures such as bootstrap resampling. However, software programs typically do not report standard errors for exploratory factor analyses and reliability analyses. Therefore, specifying a sample size is not a concern for the analyses in this section.

Table 4.15 shows the maximum likelihood estimates of the variable means, covariances, and correlations for the EAT questionnaire items. Although the factor analysis and the reliability analysis rely only on the 10 questionnaire items, I included all 13 variables in the initial EM analysis. Chapter 1 introduced the idea of an inclusive analysis strategy that utilizes auxiliary variables that are correlates of missingness or correlates of the analysis variables (Collins, Schafer, & Kam, 2001). The three additional variables effectively served as auxiliary variables in the initial EM analysis. Excluding these variables from the EM analysis would have been detrimental to the accuracy of the parameter estimates because body mass index and anxiety scores determine missingness. Adopting an inclusive analysis strategy is nearly always beneficial because it can improve the chances of satisfying the MAR assumption and can fine-tune the resulting parameter estimates by decreasing bias or increasing power.

I used the correlations in Table 4.15 as input data for an exploratory factor analysis. The principal axis factor analysis produced two factors with eigenvalues greater than one, which

**TABLE 4.15. Mean, Covariance, and Correlation Estimates from Data Analysis Example 4**

| Variable | 1 | 2 | 3 | 4 | 5 | 6 | 7 | 8 | 9 | 10 |
|---|---|---|---|---|---|---|---|---|---|---|
| 1: $EAT_1$ | 1.158 | 0.508 | 0.548 | 0.553 | 0.512 | 0.593 | 0.435 | 0.362 | 0.268 | 0.365 |
| 2: $EAT_2$ | 0.536 | 0.960 | 0.521 | 0.554 | 0.479 | 0.576 | 0.387 | 0.288 | 0.260 | 0.374 |
| 3: $EAT_{10}$ | 0.585 | 0.506 | 0.983 | 0.648 | 0.539 | 0.727 | 0.506 | 0.430 | 0.449 | 0.502 |
| 4: $EAT_{11}$ | 0.560 | 0.511 | 0.604 | 0.886 | 0.569 | 0.720 | 0.529 | 0.352 | 0.334 | 0.404 |
| 5: $EAT_{12}$ | 0.545 | 0.465 | 0.529 | 0.531 | 0.981 | 0.562 | 0.435 | 0.255 | 0.264 | 0.345 |
| 6: $EAT_{14}$ | 0.654 | 0.578 | 0.738 | 0.694 | 0.570 | 1.049 | 0.563 | 0.439 | 0.412 | 0.495 |
| 7: $EAT_{24}$ | 0.467 | 0.378 | 0.500 | 0.496 | 0.430 | 0.575 | 0.994 | 0.190 | 0.241 | 0.264 |
| 8: $EAT_3$ | 0.392 | 0.285 | 0.429 | 0.334 | 0.254 | 0.452 | 0.191 | 1.014 | 0.583 | 0.656 |
| 9: $EAT_{18}$ | 0.291 | 0.257 | 0.449 | 0.317 | 0.264 | 0.426 | 0.242 | 0.593 | 1.020 | 0.637 |
| 10: $EAT_{21}$ | 0.395 | 0.368 | 0.500 | 0.382 | 0.344 | 0.510 | 0.265 | 0.664 | 0.647 | 1.011 |
| Means | 4.010 | 3.940 | 3.950 | 3.940 | 3.930 | 3.960 | 3.990 | 3.970 | 3.980 | 3.950 |

*Note.* Correlations are shown in the upper diagonal and are in **bold** typeface.

suggests the presence of two underlying dimensions. I subsequently used direct oblimin rotation to examine the relationships between the factors and the questionnaire items; Table 4.16 shows the resulting pattern weights and structure coefficients. The structure coefficients are correlations between the questionnaire items and the factors, whereas the pattern weights are partial regression coefficients that quantify the influence of a factor on an item after partialling out the influence of the other factor. Both the pattern weights and structure coefficients suggest a two-factor solution, although the structure coefficients are less clear owing to the strong correlation between the factors ($r = .55$). The first factor consists of seven questions that measure a construct that the eating disorder literature refers to as Drive for Thinness, and the remaining three items form a Food Preoccupation factor. Finally, I used the EM correlations as input data for an internal consistency reliability analysis and computed the coefficient alpha for the two EAT subscales (Enders, 2003, 2004). The coefficient alpha reliability estimates for the Drive for Thinness and Food Preoccupation subscale scores are .893 and .834, respectively.

## 4.18 DATA ANALYSIS EXAMPLE 5

The final data analysis example illustrates a confirmatory factor analysis. I used structural equation modeling software to fit the two-factor model in Figure 4.3 to the EAT questionnaire data set.* Estimating a confirmatory factor analysis model with missing data is largely the same as it is with complete data, and software packages typically invoke maximum likelihood missing data handling with a single additional keyword or line of code. Consistent with the previous analyses, I requested standard errors based on the observed information matrix.

Researchers have traditionally used a covariance matrix as input data for structural equation modeling analyses. A complete data set simplifies the estimation process because the

---

* Analysis syntax and data are available on the companion website, *www.appliedmissingdata.com.*

**TABLE 4.16. Factor Analysis Estimates from Data Analysis Example 4**

| Variable | Pattern weights | | Structure coefficients | |
|---|---|---|---|---|
|  | DT | FP | DT | FP |
| $EAT_1$ | 0.684 | 0.030 | 0.701 | 0.409 |
| $EAT_2$ | 0.664 | 0.014 | 0.671 | 0.381 |
| $EAT_{10}$ | 0.691 | 0.190 | 0.796 | 0.572 |
| $EAT_{11}$ | 0.825 | −0.008 | 0.820 | 0.448 |
| $EAT_{12}$ | 0.714 | −0.042 | 0.690 | 0.353 |
| $EAT_{14}$ | 0.803 | 0.114 | 0.866 | 0.558 |
| $EAT_{24}$ | 0.686 | −0.093 | 0.634 | 0.286 |
| $EAT_3$ | −0.008 | 0.785 | 0.426 | 0.780 |
| $EAT_{18}$ | −0.010 | 0.758 | 0.410 | 0.753 |
| $EAT_{21}$ | 0.061 | 0.807 | 0.508 | 0.841 |

*Note.* DT = drive for thinness; FP = food preoccupation.

sample log-likelihood is less complex and does not require raw data (Kaplan, 2000, pp. 25–27). The missing data log-likelihood in Equation 4.2 necessitates the use of raw data, adding a mean structure that is not usually present in standard structural equation models. The key part of the missing data log-likelihood is the collection of terms that form Mahalanobis distance, $(\mathbf{Y}_i - \boldsymbol{\mu}_i)^T \boldsymbol{\Sigma}_i^{-1}(\mathbf{Y}_i - \boldsymbol{\mu}_i)$. A confirmatory factor analysis expresses $\boldsymbol{\mu}_i$ as a model-implied mean vector that depends on the measurement intercepts, factor loadings, and latent variable means (i.e., $\boldsymbol{\mu} = \boldsymbol{\upsilon} + \boldsymbol{\Lambda}\boldsymbol{\kappa}$, where $\boldsymbol{\upsilon}$ is the vector of measurement intercepts, $\boldsymbol{\Lambda}$ is the factor loading matrix, and $\boldsymbol{\kappa}$ is the vector of latent variable means). The measurement intercepts and the latent variable means are parameter estimates that you may not be accustomed to seeing on a confirmatory factor analysis printout. These additional parameters are a technical nuance associated with the missing data handling procedure; they may or may not be of substantive interest. However, the mean structure does require its own identification constraint, and constraining the latent variable means to zero during estimation is a straightforward way to achieve model identification. Consistent with a complete-data analysis, fixing the latent factor variance to unity or setting one of the factor loadings to one identifies the covariance structure portion of the model (Bollen, 1989; Kline, 2005).

Table 4.17 shows the confirmatory factor analysis parameter estimates along with those from a corresponding complete-data analysis. The factor loadings quantify the expected change in the questionnaire items for a one-standard-deviation increase in the latent construct, and the measurement intercepts are the expected scores for a case that has a value of zero on the latent factor (i.e., is at the mean of the latent variable). Because the factor means equal zero, the measurement intercepts estimate the item means. A complete-data confirmatory factor analysis model would not ordinarily include the measurement intercepts, but I estimated these parameters for comparability.

The two-factor model fits the data well according to conventional standards (Hu & Bentler, 1998, 1999), $\chi^2(34) = 47.10$, $p = .07$, CFI = 0.993, RMSEA = 0.031, SRMR = 0.029, and all of the factor loadings are statistically significant at $p < .001$. The missing data estimates are quite similar to those of the complete data (the $EAT_{18}$ loading is a notable exception)

**TABLE 4.17. Confirmatory Factor Analysis Estimates from Data Analysis Example 5**

| Variable | Loadings | | Intercepts | | Residuals | |
|---|---|---|---|---|---|---|
| | Estimate | SE | Estimate | SE | Estimate | SE |
| | | | Missing data maximum likelihood | | | |
| $EAT_1$ | 0.741 | 0.050 | 4.002 | 0.055 | 0.602 | 0.048 |
| $EAT_2$ | 0.650 | 0.045 | 3.934 | 0.050 | 0.534 | 0.042 |
| $EAT_{10}$ | 0.807 | 0.043 | 3.955 | 0.050 | 0.329 | 0.030 |
| $EAT_{11}$ | 0.764 | 0.040 | 3.937 | 0.047 | 0.300 | 0.026 |
| $EAT_{12}$ | 0.662 | 0.047 | 3.926 | 0.051 | 0.538 | 0.043 |
| $EAT_{14}$ | 0.901 | 0.041 | 3.962 | 0.051 | 0.235 | 0.025 |
| $EAT_{24}$ | 0.623 | 0.048 | 3.980 | 0.051 | 0.597 | 0.047 |
| $EAT_3$ | 0.772 | 0.046 | 3.967 | 0.050 | 0.416 | 0.041 |
| $EAT_{18}$ | 0.749 | 0.048 | 3.974 | 0.052 | 0.453 | 0.044 |
| $EAT_{21}$ | 0.862 | 0.045 | 3.950 | 0.051 | 0.262 | 0.039 |
| | | | Complete data maximum likelihood | | | |
| $EAT_1$ | 0.731 | 0.048 | 3.995 | 0.053 | 0.600 | 0.046 |
| $EAT_2$ | 0.638 | 0.045 | 3.940 | 0.049 | 0.534 | 0.041 |
| $EAT_{10}$ | 0.797 | 0.042 | 3.943 | 0.049 | 0.344 | 0.029 |
| $EAT_{11}$ | 0.763 | 0.040 | 3.938 | 0.047 | 0.302 | 0.026 |
| $EAT_{12}$ | 0.692 | 0.047 | 3.965 | 0.051 | 0.570 | 0.044 |
| $EAT_{14}$ | 0.901 | 0.041 | 3.963 | 0.051 | 0.235 | 0.025 |
| $EAT_{24}$ | 0.630 | 0.046 | 3.995 | 0.050 | 0.603 | 0.045 |
| $EAT_3$ | 0.780 | 0.046 | 3.967 | 0.050 | 0.404 | 0.041 |
| $EAT_{18}$ | 0.700 | 0.047 | 3.970 | 0.050 | 0.494 | 0.043 |
| $EAT_{21}$ | 0.855 | 0.045 | 3.953 | 0.050 | 0.275 | 0.039 |

but have larger standard errors. It is important to point out that this analysis does not satisfy the MAR assumption because the "causes" of missing data (i.e., body mass index and anxiety) do not appear in the model. Collins et al. (2001) show that omitting a cause of missingness tends to be problematic if the correlation between the omitted variable and the analysis variables is relatively strong (e.g., $r > .40$) or if the missing data rate is greater than 25%. The body mass index and anxiety variables are not that highly correlated with the EAT questionnaire items, which probably explains why the missing data estimates are similar to those of the complete data. Chapter 5 illustrates how to incorporate correlates of missingness into a maximum likelihood analysis, and doing so would satisfy the MAR assumption for this analysis.

As a final note, the model fit statistics and the standard errors from this analysis are not entirely trustworthy because the data do not satisfy the multivariate normality assumption. (The EAT questionnaire items use a discrete Likert-type scale and are a somewhat positively skewed and kurtotic.) Methodological studies have repeatedly shown that normality violations can distort model fit statistics and standard errors, with or without missing data (Enders, 2001; Finney & DiStefano, 2006; West, Finch, & Curran, 1995). The next chapter describes corrective techniques that remedy these problems.

## 4.19 SUMMARY

This chapter describes how maximum likelihood estimation applies to missing data problems. The methodological literature regards maximum likelihood estimation as a state-of-the-art missing data technique because it yields unbiased parameter estimates with MAR data. From a practical standpoint, this means that maximum likelihood will produce accurate parameter estimates when traditional approaches fail. Even if the data are MCAR, maximum likelihood is still superior to traditional techniques because it maximizes statistical power by borrowing information from the observed data. Despite these desirable properties, maximum likelihood estimation is not a perfect solution and will yield biased parameter estimates when the data are MNAR. However, this bias tends to be isolated to a subset of the analysis model parameters, whereas traditional techniques are more apt to propagate bias throughout the entire model.

Maximum likelihood estimation repeatedly auditions different combinations of population parameter values until it identifies the particular constellation of values that produce the highest log-likelihood value (i.e., the best fit to the data). Conceptually, the estimation process is the same with or without missing data. However, the incomplete data records require a slight alteration to the individual log-likelihood equation. The missing data log-likelihood does not require each case to have the same number of observed data points, and the computation of the individual log-likelihood uses only the variables and parameters for which a case has complete data. Although the log-likelihood formula looks slightly different for each missing data pattern, the individual log-likelihood still quantifies the relative probability that an individual's scores originate from a multivariate normal distribution with a particular mean vector and covariance matrix. Consistent with a complete-data analysis, the sample log-likelihood is the sum of the individual log-likelihoods, and the goal of estimation is to identify the parameter estimates that maximize the sample log-likelihood.

The process of computing maximum likelihood standard errors does not change much with missing data, except that it is necessary to distinguish between standard errors that are based on the observed information matrix and the expected information matrix. The expected information matrix replaces certain terms in the second derivative formulas with their expected values (i.e., long-run averages), whereas the observed information uses the realized data values to compute these terms. This is an important distinction because the expected information matrix yields standard errors that require the MCAR assumption, whereas the observed information matrix gives standard errors that are appropriate with MAR data. Because they make less stringent assumptions, the missing data literature clearly favors standard errors based on the observed information matrix.

With few exceptions, missing data analyses require iterative optimization algorithms, even for very simple estimation problems. This chapter described one such algorithm that is particularly important for missing data analyses, the EM algorithm. The EM algorithm is a two-step iterative procedure that consists of an E-step and an M-step. The E-step uses the elements from the mean vector and the covariance matrix to derive regression equations that predict the incomplete variables from the complete variables, and the M-step subsequently uses standard complete-data formulas to generate updated estimates of the mean vector and the covariance matrix. The algorithm carries these updated parameter values forward to the next E-step, where the process begins anew. EM repeats these two steps until the elements in the mean vector and the covariance matrix no longer change between consecutive M-steps, at which point the algorithm has converged on the maximum likelihood estimates.

With the basic principles of maximum likelihood estimation established in this chapter, the next chapter describes procedures useful for fine-tuning a maximum likelihood analysis. Specifically, the chapter outlines auxiliary variable models that incorporate correlates of missingness into a maximum likelihood analysis. Adopting this so-called inclusive analysis strategy can decrease bias, increase power, and improve the chances of satisfying the MAR assumption. The chapter also outlines corrective procedures that remedy the negative effects of nonnormal data.

## 4.20 RECOMMENDED READINGS

Arbuckle, J. L. (1996). Full information estimation in the presence of incomplete data. In G. A. Marcoulides & R. E. Schumacker (Eds.), *Advanced structural equation modeling* (pp. 243–277). Mahwah, NJ: Erlbaum.

Dempster, A. P., Laird, N. M., & Rubin, D. B. (1977). Maximum likelihood from incomplete data via the EM algorithm. *Journal of the Royal Statistical Society, Series B, 39*, 1–38.

Enders, C. K., & Bandalos, D. L. (2001). The relative performance of full information maximum likelihood estimation for missing data in structural equation models. *Structural Equation Modeling: An Interdisciplinary Journal, 8*, 430–457.

Kenward, M. G., & Molenberghs, G. (1998). Likelihood based frequentist inference when data are missing at random. Statistical Science, 13, 236–247.

# Improving the Accuracy of Maximum Likelihood Analyses

## 5.1 CHAPTER OVERVIEW

Now that the basic mechanics of maximum likelihood estimation have been established, this chapter outlines a collection of procedures that can improve the accuracy of a maximum likelihood analysis. The first half of the chapter focuses on the use of auxiliary variables— potential correlates of missingness or correlates of the incomplete analysis model variables. These variables are not of substantive interest; the sole purpose of including them in an analysis is to increase power or reduce bias. The chapter describes a number of issues related to the use of auxiliary variables, including their potential benefits, the process of identifying auxiliary variables, and approaches to incorporating these variables into a maximum likelihood analysis. Much of this discussion is very general and also applies to the use of auxiliary variables in multiple imputation analyses. However, the procedures for including auxiliary variables in a maximum likelihood analysis are unique and require a special model setup.

The second half of the chapter addresses problems related to non-normal data. Chapters 3 and 4 described the important role of normal distribution in a maximum likelihood analysis, but they did not discuss the ramifications of violating the normality assumption. The methodological literature shows that non-normal data tend to have a minimal impact on the parameter estimates themselves but can bias standard errors and distort the likelihood ratio test. Fortunately, methodologists have developed a number of corrective procedures for non-normal data (e.g., rescaled test statistics, the bootstrap, and robust standard errors), several of which are available for missing data analyses. The limited research to date suggests that these methods work quite well.

## 5.2 THE RATIONALE FOR AN INCLUSIVE ANALYSIS STRATEGY

Methodologists regard maximum likelihood estimation as a state-of-the-art missing data technique (Schafer & Graham, 2002) because it yields unbiased parameter estimates under the missing at random (MAR) mechanism. The MAR mechanism holds when the probability of missing data on a variable Y relates to some other measured variable (or variables) but not to the values of Y itself. This definition seems to imply that MAR is automatically satisfied when a correlate of missingness is a variable in the data set, but it is the variables in the analysis model that dictate whether the MAR assumption is met.

To illustrate the subtleties of the MAR mechanism, consider a study that examines a number of health-related behaviors (e.g., smoking, drinking, and sexual activity) in a teenage population. Because of its sensitive nature, researchers decide to administer the sexual behavior questionnaire to participants who are above the age of 15. At first glance, this example appears to satisfy the MAR assumption because a measured variable (i.e., age) determines whether data are missing. However, this is not necessarily true because the MAR assumption is only satisfied if the researchers incorporate age into their analysis model. For example, suppose that the researchers use maximum likelihood missing data handling to estimate a simple regression model where self-esteem predicts risky sexual behavior. Because the age variable is not in the model, this analysis is actually consistent with the missing not at random (MNAR) mechanism and is likely to produce biased parameter estimates, particularly if age and sexual activity are correlated.

Understanding why the regression model is biased requires a brief review of Rubin's (1976) missing data theory. In Rubin's theory, a binary variable R denotes whether a variable is observed or missing (e.g., $r = 1$ if the sexual activity score is observed and $r = 0$ if it is missing). The MAR mechanism allows for an association between R and other measured variables such as age, but it stipulates that R is unrelated to sexual activity. Omitting age from the regression model is likely to introduce bias because it induces a spurious association between R and the missing sexual activity scores. The magnitude of the bias may not be problematic and depends on the correlation between age and sexual activity, but the analysis is nevertheless consistent with an MNAR mechanism. Had the researchers incorporated age into the regression model, the spurious association between R and the sexual activity scores would disappear because the age variable fully explains the relationship (i.e., after controlling for age, there is no residual association between R and sexual activity).

The previous scenario illustrates that the variables in the analysis model dictate whether the MAR assumption is met. For this reason, methodologists recommend a so-called **inclusive analysis strategy** that incorporates a number of auxiliary variables into the missing data handling procedure (Collins, Schafer, & Kam, 2001; Graham, 2003; Rubin, 1996; Schafer & Graham, 2002). An **auxiliary variable** is one that is ancillary to the substantive research questions but is a potential correlate of missingness or a correlate of the missing variable. Incorporating these variables into the missing data handling procedure can mitigate (or eliminate) bias and can improve power. For example, had the researchers in the health study included age in their model, they would have converted the analysis from MNAR to MAR and would have completely eliminated bias. Omitting an important correlate of missingness from an analysis can produce an MNAR mechanism, but MNAR data can also result from a direct relationship between missingness and the scores on the incomplete variable (e.g., teenagers who are engaging in risky sexual behavior skip the questionnaire items that address this topic). In this situation, auxiliary variables can still reduce bias, but they cannot completely eliminate it. Finally, even if the analyses are consistent with an MCAR or MAR mechanism, auxiliary variables can improve power by recapturing some of the lost information in the missing variable. Consequently, it is nearly always beneficial to include auxiliary variables in the missing data handling procedure, and there appears to be no downside to an inclusive analysis strategy (Collins et al., 2001).

## 5.3 AN ILLUSTRATIVE COMPUTER SIMULATION STUDY

To illustrate the impact of auxiliary variables, I conducted a series of Monte Carlo computer simulations. The simulations mimicked a simple research scenario in which the goal is to estimate the mean vector and the covariance matrix for two variables, $X$ and $Y$. The artificial data sets also included a third variable, $A$, that served as an auxiliary variable. The first simulation program generated 1,000 samples of $N = 100$ and subsequently produced a 30% missing data rate by deleting $Y$ values for cases in the lower tail of an auxiliary variable's distribution. This simulation mimics the previous health study example because a measured variable completely determines missingness. The impact of omitting a correlate of missingness from an analysis depends on its association with the incomplete variables, so the population correlation between $Y$ and the auxiliary variable varied between 0.10 and 0.80. For simplicity, the population correlation between the two analysis variables was always $\rho = .30$, as was the correlation between $X$ and the auxiliary variable. After generating each data set, the simulation program used maximum likelihood to estimate the mean vector and the covariance matrix for $X$ and $Y$, but it did so by omitting the auxiliary variable (i.e., the "cause" of missingness) from the analysis.

The top panel of Table 5.1 shows the average parameter estimates across the 1,000 replications. The purpose of this simulation is to illustrate the impact of excluding a correlate of missingness from an analysis (i.e., performing an MNAR analysis when it would have been possible to perform an MAR analysis). The left-most column gives the population correlation between the auxiliary variable (i.e., the omitted cause of missingness) and the incomplete analysis model variable, $Y$. As you can see, omitting a correlate of missingness was not that detrimental when the correlation was weak (e.g., $r \leq .30$), but the estimates became increasingly biased as the correlation between the auxiliary variable and the incomplete analysis variable increased in magnitude. Because the auxiliary variable completely determined missingness, incorporating this variable into the maximum likelihood analysis would eliminate bias, regardless of the magnitude of the correlation between the auxiliary variable and $Y$.

An MNAR mechanism can also result from a direct relationship between missingness and the scores on the incomplete variable (e.g., teenagers who are engaging in risky sexual behavior skip the questionnaire items that address this topic). In this situation, auxiliary variables can reduce, but not eliminate, bias. To illustrate the impact of auxiliary variables in this context, I performed a second simulation study that produced a 30% missing data rate by deleting $Y$ values for cases in the lower tail of the $Y$ distribution. As before, I varied the magnitude of the correlation between $Y$ and the auxiliary variable, but this time I included the auxiliary variable in the analysis.

The bottom panel of Table 5.1 shows the average parameter estimates from the second simulation. As you can see, the overall magnitude of the bias was greater than in the first

**TABLE 5.1. Simulation Results Showing the Impact of an Auxiliary Variable on Parameter Estimate Bias**

| | Average parameter estimates | | |
|---|---|---|---|
| $\rho_{A,Y}$ | $\rho_{X,Y}$ | $\mu_Y$ | $\sigma_Y^2$ |
| MNAR due to omitted auxiliary variable | | | |
| 0.10 | 0.300 | 0.002 | 0.990 |
| 0.20 | 0.296 | 0.026 | 0.985 |
| 0.30 | 0.291 | 0.054 | 0.977 |
| 0.40 | 0.286 | 0.079 | 0.967 |
| 0.50 | 0.281 | 0.106 | 0.951 |
| 0.60 | 0.276 | 0.132 | 0.934 |
| 0.70 | 0.271 | 0.160 | 0.913 |
| 0.80 | 0.266 | 0.187 | 0.889 |
| MNAR due to Y | | | |
| 0.10 | 0.257 | 0.243 | 0.835 |
| 0.20 | 0.258 | 0.240 | 0.835 |
| 0.30 | 0.259 | 0.232 | 0.837 |
| 0.40 | 0.262 | 0.219 | 0.840 |
| 0.50 | 0.265 | 0.200 | 0.845 |
| 0.60 | 0.270 | 0.175 | 0.854 |
| 0.70 | 0.275 | 0.144 | 0.869 |
| 0.80 | 0.282 | 0.106 | 0.893 |
| True values | 0.300 | 0 | 1.000 |

*Note.* $\rho_{A,Y}$ is the population correlation between the auxiliary variable and the missing analysis variable, *Y*.

simulation, and the auxiliary variable did not eliminate bias. Although the average parameter estimates did get closer to the true population values as the correlation increased, the bias was still noticeable, even when the correlation between the auxiliary variable and the missing analysis variable was 0.80. Finally, the table shows that the largest reductions in bias occurred when the auxiliary variable's correlation with *Y* exceeded .50.

Auxiliary variables can also improve the power of maximum likelihood significance tests, regardless of their impact on bias (Collins et al., 2001). For example, I performed a third simulation study in which 30% of the *Y* values were MCAR. With MCAR data, an auxiliary variable has no impact on bias, but it can improve power. Consistent with the previous simulation, I varied the magnitude of the correlation between *Y* and the auxiliary variable and included the auxiliary variable in the analysis model. Because I generated the data from a population with a nonzero correlation, the proportion of the 1,000 replications that produced a statistically significant parameter estimate serves as an empirical estimate of statistical power.

Figure 5.1 shows the power estimates for the correlation between *X* and *Y* expressed relative to the power values from a maximum likelihood analysis that omits the auxiliary variable.

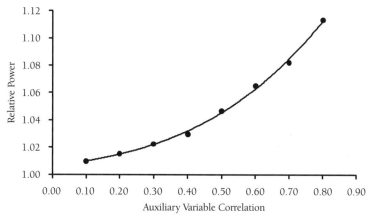

**FIGURE 5.1.** The figure shows how the correlation between an auxiliary variable and a missing analysis variable affects power. The largest gains in power occur after the auxiliary variable's correlation exceeds 0.40.

For example, a correlation of 0.30 between $Y$ and the auxiliary variable produced a relative power value of 1.023, which means that the auxiliary variable increased power by approximately 2.3%. As you can see, there is a nonlinear relationship between the auxiliary variable correlation and power, such that the largest gains occur when the correlation exceeds 0.40. Incorporating an auxiliary variable always produces some benefit, but stronger correlations are clearly desirable.

Taken as a whole, the simulation results suggest that an auxiliary variable is most useful when it has a relatively strong correlation (e.g., $r > .40$) with the missing analysis variable. Conversely, omitting a correlate of missingness from the analysis has a minimal impact when the correlation is low (e.g., $r < .40$). Although there is no harm in using auxiliary variables with weak (or even zero) correlations (Collins et al., 2001), the benefits of an inclusive analysis strategy become more evident as the correlations become greater. This suggests that selecting auxiliary variables based on their correlation with the missing analysis variables is a useful strategy. The next section outlines additional strategies for selecting auxiliary variables.

## 5.4 IDENTIFYING A SET OF AUXILIARY VARIABLES

Given the benefits of incorporating auxiliary variables into a maximum likelihood analysis, it is useful to consider how to go about choosing these variables. As a rule, a useful auxiliary variable is a potential cause or correlate of missingness or a correlate of the incomplete variables in the analysis model (Collins et al., 2001; Schafer, 1997). For example, age is an important auxiliary variable in the health study because it directly influences missingness (i.e., researchers only administer the sexual behavior questionnaire to participants who are above the age of 15). Other useful auxiliary variables are correlates of the analysis model variables, regardless of whether they are also related to missingness. For example, a survey question that asks teenagers to report whether they have a steady boyfriend or girlfriend is a good auxiliary variable because it is likely correlated with the missing sexual activity scores.

The health example is straightforward because the researchers know why the data are missing. In most situations, identifying correlates of missingness involves some educated guesswork. To illustrate the process, consider an educational study that examines the development of self-report behavioral problems throughout the course of middle school and high school. Student mobility is a common cause of attrition in school-based research studies (Enders, Dietz, Montague, & Dixon, 2006; Graham, Hofer, Donaldson, MacKinnon, & Schafer, 1997), so the researchers could administer a survey question that asks parents to report how likely they are to move during the course of the study. Socioeconomic status is another factor that can influence attrition in school- and community-based samples, so it would be useful to collect a measure of socioeconomic status or a suitable proxy (e.g., participation in a lunch assistance program). Finally, in states where students are required to pass a statewide assessment in order to matriculate, students who fail to achieve the minimum passing score are at risk for dropping out of school. Consequently, the scores from a standardized achievement test might relate to subsequent attrition.

Identifying auxiliary variables that are correlates of the missing behavior reports is relatively straightforward, and a literature review can facilitate this process, if necessary. For example, objective measures of behavior such as disciplinary referrals, absenteeism, and incidents with the juvenile justice system are variables that should be readily available from the school district's database. In addition, measures of parental supervision and stability of the home environment might also serve as useful auxiliary variables because the educational literature suggests that these factors influence problem behavior. The previous examples are just a few ideas for auxiliary variables in an educational study, and it is easy to generate additional examples.

In the absence of (or perhaps in addition to) other information, the MCAR tests from Chapter 1 can also identify potential auxiliary variables. Univariate $t$ tests are particularly useful in this regard because they can identify variables that are inconsistent with the MCAR mechanism. Recall that the $t$-test procedure separates the missing and complete cases on a variable and examines group mean differences on other variables in the data set. Variables that yield large mean differences are inconsistent with an MCAR mechanism and are potential correlates of missingness. The problem with $t$ tests is that they do a poor job of pinpointing the true cause of missingness and can produce a number of spurious associations. Although there is ultimately no harm in choosing the wrong auxiliary variable, focusing on the $t$ tests that produce the largest mean differences can help limit the pool of candidate variables.

Finally, it is a good idea to be proactive about satisfying the MAR assumption by collecting variables that are correlates of the analysis variables or correlates of missingness. For example, Graham, Taylor, Olchowski, and Cumsille (2006) suggest that variables such as reading speed and conscientiousness might explain why some respondents leave questionnaire items blank. In a longitudinal study, Schafer and Graham (2002) recommend a survey question that asks respondents to report their likelihood of dropping out of the study prior to the next measurement occasion. Schafer and Graham (2002, p. 173) suggest that collecting data on potential causes of missingness "may effectively convert an MNAR situation to MAR." You should therefore strongly consider this strategy when designing a study.

## Practical Considerations

In the context of a multiple imputation analysis, methodologists generally recommend using an extensive set of auxiliary variables. For example, Rubin (1996, p. 479) stated that "the advice has always been to include as many variables as possible when doing multiple imputation." This suggestion is more difficult to implement in a maximum likelihood analysis because the auxiliary variables require a slightly awkward model specification. From a practical standpoint, this means that you may have to limit the number of auxiliary variables in an analysis. It is difficult to establish a rule of thumb for the number of auxiliary variables, but the previous simulation results clearly show that the correlation between an auxiliary variable and the incomplete analysis model variables largely determines the influence of an auxiliary variable. Consequently, a reasonable goal is to maximize the squared multiple correlation between the auxiliary variables and the analysis model variables using as few auxiliary variables as possible. Although there is no harm in using auxiliary variables with low (or zero) correlations (Collins et al., 2001), the most useful auxiliary variables are those that have correlations greater than $\pm 0.40$ with the incomplete analysis variables.

## 5.5 INCORPORATING AUXILIARY VARIABLES INTO A MAXIMUM LIKELIHOOD ANALYSIS

Returning to the previous health study example, suppose that the researchers want to include age as an auxiliary variable in their regression model. One option is to add age as an additional predictor variable, but this is a bad solution because it accommodates the auxiliary variable by changing the substantive interpretation of the parameter estimates (i.e., the effect of self-esteem becomes a partial regression coefficient if age is a predictor in the model). Instead, the researchers need to incorporate the auxiliary variables in such a way that the interpretation of the parameter estimates is the same as it would have been had the data been complete. They can do this using a structural equation model (Graham, 2003) or a two-stage analysis approach (Savalei & Bentler, 2007; Yuan & Bentler, 2000).

Graham (2003) outlined two structural equation modeling strategies for incorporating auxiliary variables into a maximum likelihood analysis, the **extra dependent variable model** and the **saturated correlates model**. The basic goal of both approaches is to use a series of correlations to work the auxiliary variables into the analysis without altering the substantive interpretation of the parameters. Graham's simulation results favored the saturated correlates model, and this approach is generally easier to implement than the extra dependent variable model. Consequently, I focus on the saturated correlates model in the next section. Interested readers can consult Graham (2003) for details on the extra dependent variable model.

The **two-stage approach** is an alternative method for incorporating auxiliary variables into a maximum likelihood analysis (Savalei & Bentler, 2007; Yuan & Bentler, 2000). As its name implies, the two-stage approach deals with missing data in two steps: the first stage uses maximum likelihood missing data handling to estimate the mean vector and the covariance matrix, and the second stage uses the resulting estimates as input data for a subsequent analysis (an approach I used to perform an exploratory factor analysis in Chapter 4). The advantage of the two-stage approach is that it can readily incorporate any number of auxiliary variables into the first step of the procedure. Because the mean vector and the covariance matrix reflect the information from the auxiliary variables, there is no need to include the extra variables in the subsequent analysis stage.

Unfortunately, the two-stage approach has a serious drawback that limits its use. Using summary statistics as input data requires a sample size value. However, no single value of $N$ accurately describes the precision of the estimates in the mean vector and the covariance matrix. Therefore, specifying a particular sample size value is likely to bias the standard errors from the analysis stage (Enders & Peugh, 2004). Yuan and Bentler (2000) and Savalei and Bentler (2007) describe a corrective procedure that combines the information matrices from both stages of the analysis, but software programs have yet to implement their approach. Because the two-stage standard errors currently require custom computer programming, I do not discuss the technique in this chapter. However, the two-stage method may become a viable alternative to Graham's (2003) structural equation approach in the near future.

## 5.6 THE SATURATED CORRELATES MODEL

The saturated correlates model incorporates auxiliary variables via a series of correlations between the auxiliary variables and the analysis model variables (or their residual terms). As you will see, the name "saturated correlates" follows from the fact that the model includes all possible associations among the auxiliary variables as well as all possible associations between the auxiliary variables and the manifest analysis model variables (i.e., the auxiliary variable portion of the model is saturated). Because the rules for incorporating auxiliary variables vary slightly depending on whether the analysis model includes latent variables, I describe these two situations separately.

### Manifest Variable Models

To begin, consider an analysis that involves a set of manifest variables (i.e., a statistical model with no latent variables). Graham's (2003) rules for specifying a saturated correlates model are as follows: correlate an auxiliary variable with (1) explanatory variables, (2) other auxiliary variables, and (3) the residual terms of the outcome variables. As an example, consider a multiple regression analysis in which $X_1$ and $X_2$ predict $Y$. Furthermore, suppose that it was of interest to incorporate two auxiliary variables, $AV_1$ and $AV_2$, into the regression model. Figure 5.2 shows a path model diagram of the saturated correlates model. Path diagrams use single-headed straight arrows to denote regression coefficients and double-headed curved arrows to represent correlations, and they differentiate manifest variables and latent variables using rectangles and ellipses, respectively (Bollen, 1989; Kline, 2005). The model in Figure 5.2 illustrates all three of Graham's (2003) rules. Specifically, the curved arrows that connect the $AV$s and the $X$s are correlations between the auxiliary variables and the predictors, the curved arrow between $AV_1$ and $AV_2$ is the correlation between the auxiliary variables; and the

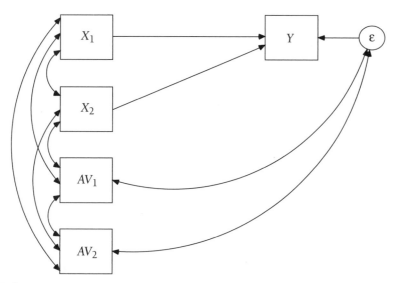

**FIGURE 5.2.** The saturated correlates version of a manifest variable regression model. The saturated correlates model requires that the auxiliary variables (i.e., $AV_1$ and $AV_2$) correlate with (1) one another, (2) the predictor variables, and (3) the residual term.

curved arrows that connect the $AV$s to the ellipse labeled $\varepsilon$ are the correlations between the auxiliary variables and the residual term.

The important aspect of the saturated correlates model is that it transmits the information from the auxiliary variables to the analysis model variables without affecting the interpretation of the parameter estimates. Consequently, the interpretation of the regression coefficients is the same as it would have been had the data been complete. For example, the straight arrow that connects $X_1$ to $Y$ is a partial regression coefficient that quantifies the expected change in $Y$ for a unit increase in $X_1$ after holding $X_2$ constant. Adding the auxiliary variables to the model can change the estimated value of this coefficient (e.g., by removing bias or reducing random error), but the interpretation of the slope is unaffected because $X_2$ is still the only variable being partialled out of $Y$.

## Latent Variable Models

The rules for specifying a latent variable model with auxiliary variables are as follows: correlate an auxiliary variable with (1) manifest predictor variables, (2) other auxiliary variables, and (3) the residual terms of the manifest indicator variables. Note that Graham's (2003) rules describe the linkages between the auxiliary variables and the manifest variables in the model, so that the auxiliary variables never correlate with latent variables or with latent disturbance (i.e., residual) terms. This means that rule 1 applies strictly to models with manifest predictor variables (e.g., so-called multiple indicators and multiple causes, or MIMIC models), and rule 3 applies only to manifest indicators of the latent variables.

To illustrate Graham's (2003) rules, consider a latent variable regression analysis in which $LX_1$ and $LX_2$ predict $LY$. Furthermore, assume that the latent variables each have two

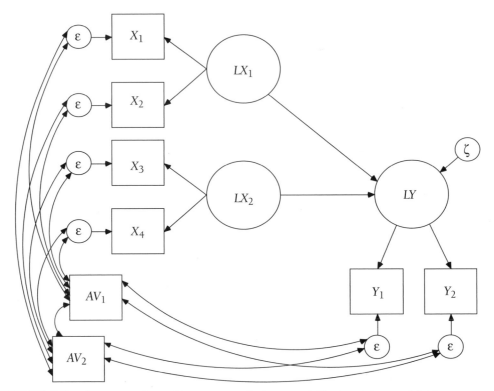

**FIGURE 5.3.** The saturated correlates version of a latent variable regression model. The saturated correlates model requires that the auxiliary variables (i.e., $AV_1$ and $AV_2$) correlate with (1) one another, (2) manifest predictor variables, and (3) the residual terms of the manifest variables. The auxiliary variables never correlate with a latent variable or with a latent variable residual term.

manifest indicators (e.g., $LY$ is measured by $Y_1$ and $Y_2$) and it is of interest to incorporate two auxiliary variables, $AV_1$ and $AV_2$, into the model. Figure 5.3 shows a path model diagram of the saturated correlates model for this analysis. To begin, notice that there are no associations (i.e., curved arrows) between the auxiliary variables and the latent factors. Instead, the curved arrows link the auxiliary variables to the residuals of the six manifest indicators. Like the manifest variable model in Figure 5.2, the curved arrow between $AV_1$ and $AV_2$ denotes the correlation between the auxiliary variables. Finally, because there are no manifest predictor variables, rule 1 does not apply to this analysis.

Two additional points are worth noting about the latent variable saturated correlates model. First, like its manifest variable counterpart, the inclusion of the auxiliary variables does not alter the interpretation of the latent variable model parameters. For example, the straight arrow that connects $LX_1$ with $LY$ is a partial regression coefficient that quantifies the expected change in $LY$ for a unit increase in $LX_1$ after holding $LX_2$ constant. Although the auxiliary variables can change the estimated value of this coefficient, the substantive interpretation of the path is the same as it would have been in a complete-data analysis with no auxiliary variables. Second, the auxiliary variable portion of the path model includes all possible associations between the auxiliary variables and the manifest variables as well as all possible associations among the auxiliary variables (i.e., the auxiliary variable portion of the model is saturated). This means that the auxiliary variables do not affect the degrees of freedom or the fit of the model.

## What If the Auxiliary Variables Have Missing Data?

Including auxiliary variables in an analysis can improve the missing data handling procedure, either by reducing bias (i.e., better approximating the MAR assumption) or by increasing power (i.e., recapturing some of the missing information). Ideally, the auxiliary variables have no missing values, but this need not be the case. From a procedural standpoint, there is nothing special about applying Graham's (2003) specification rules to incomplete auxiliary variables. However, it is reasonable to ask whether it is beneficial to include these variables in the analysis. Although little research has been done on this topic, but the answer appears to be yes.

Enders (2008) used Monte Carlo simulations to examine the impact of including an incomplete auxiliary variable in regression models similar to those in Figures 5.2 and 5.3. Because the auxiliary variable in this study determined missingness and had a strong correlation with the incomplete outcome variable, excluding it from the model produced biased estimates. The simulation results indicated that including the auxiliary variable in the analysis dramatically reduced bias, even when 50% of its scores were missing. Interestingly, the reduction in bias was virtually the same when the missing auxiliary variable was MCAR or MNAR. When the auxiliary variable was MNAR, the auxiliary variable portion of the model (e.g., the correlation between an auxiliary variable and a predictor) was severely biased, but the regression model parameter estimates were quite accurate. Fortunately, bias in the auxiliary variable portion of the model is no problem because these parameters are not of substantive interest.

When deciding whether to use an incomplete auxiliary variable, it is important to examine the proportion of cases that have missing data on both the auxiliary variable and the analysis model variables. When this proportion is high, the amount of information that the auxiliary variable can contribute to the estimation process becomes limited. Establishing definitive guidelines is difficult, but including an auxiliary variable appears to be of little benefit when more than 10% of its observations are concurrently missing with one of the analysis model variables (Enders, 2008).

## Computing Incremental Fit Indices

Assessing model fit is an important part of a structural equation modeling analysis. The fact that the saturated correlates model does not change the degrees of freedom implies that the likelihood ratio statistic (i.e., the chi-square test of model fit) and the RMSEA are unaffected by the auxiliary variables. However, the same is not true for incremental (i.e., comparative) fit indices, and it is currently necessary to compute these indices by hand. The idea behind an **incremental fit index** is to compare the relative fit of a hypothesized model (e.g., the latent variable regression model in Figure 5.3) to that of a baseline model. The most common choice of baseline model is a so-called **null model** or **independence model** that estimates the means and the variances of the manifest variables (Bollen, 1989; Kline, 2005).

To illustrate how auxiliary variables affect incremental fit indices, consider the Comparative Fit Index (CFI; Bentler, 1990). The CFI is

$$\text{CFI} = \frac{(\text{LR}_\text{I} - df_\text{I}) - (\text{LR}_\text{M} - df_\text{M})}{(\text{LR}_\text{I} - df_\text{I})} \tag{5.1}$$

where $\text{LR}_\text{M}$ and $\text{LR}_\text{I}$ are the likelihood ratio tests from the hypothesized model and the independence model, respectively, and $df_\text{M}$ and $df_\text{I}$ are the degrees of freedom for these two models. As I explained previously, the saturated correlates approach does not affect the likelihood ratio test for the hypothesized model because the degrees of freedom are the same with or without the auxiliary variables. However, the standard independence model constrains the auxiliary variable correlations to zero during estimation, which increases the values of the likelihood ratio test and its degrees of freedom. This effectively penalizes the independence model by making its fit worse than it would have been without the auxiliary variables. Consequently, the saturated correlates model artificially inflates the CFI and makes the hypothesized model appear to fit better than it actually does (the same is true for other incremental fit indices).

Fortunately, it is straightforward to compute the correct CFI value after fitting a special independence model that estimates the auxiliary variable correlations and constrains the correlations among the analysis model variables to zero. To illustrate, reconsider the saturated correlates model in Figure 5.3. The top panel of Figure 5.4 shows the standard independence model, and the bottom panel of the figure shows the correct independence model for this analysis. Notice that the correct independence model includes the same number of auxiliary variable correlations as the latent variable model in Figure 5.3, so the auxiliary variables exert a constant influence on the fit of both models. Substituting the likelihood ratio test and the degrees of freedom from the modified independence model into Equation 5.1 yields the correct CFI value. Structural equation modeling programs provide these quantities as part of their standard output; these computations are illustrated in an analysis example later in the chapter.

In general, applying the following steps to the manifest variables in the analysis yields an appropriate independence model: (1) estimate the variance of all variables, (2) estimate the correlations among the manifest predictors, (3) fix the correlations between manifest predictors and the outcomes to zero, (4) fix the correlations among the outcome variables to zero, (5) estimate the correlations between the auxiliary variables and all other variables, and (6) estimate the correlations among the auxiliary variables. These rules are applicable to situations in which the standard independence model would have been appropriate, had there been no auxiliary variables. However, the standard independence model is not appropriate for all circumstances (Widaman & Thompson, 2003), so you may need to modify these rules accordingly.

## Limitations of the Saturated Correlates Model

The saturated correlates model has a number of practical limitations. In my experience, using a large set of auxiliary variables can lead to estimation problems and convergence failures.

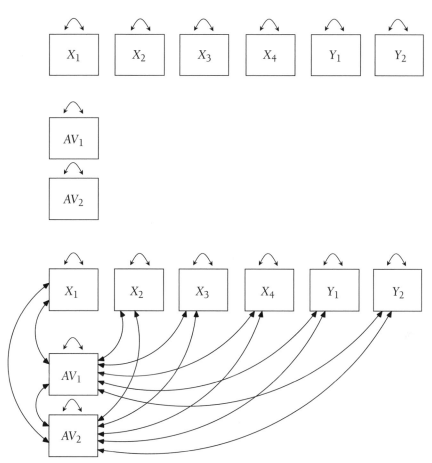

**FIGURE 5.4.** The top panel of the figure shows the standard independence model where all of the variables are uncorrelated. A double-headed curved arrow that connects a variable to itself denotes a variance. The bottom panel of the figure shows the modified independence model that adds covariances between the auxiliary variables and the analysis model variables.

Although it is not necessary for the auxiliary variables to have complete data, incomplete auxiliary variables can exacerbate these problems. Savalei and Bentler (2007) note that convergence problems are also related to small residual variance terms. In some situations, rescaling the variables to have a similar metric (e.g., by multiplying or dividing a variable by a constant) can alleviate these estimation problems, but reducing the number of auxiliary variables is often the best option. When you do have to reduce the number of auxiliary variables, it is a good idea to retain the variables that have the highest correlations with the incomplete variables in the analysis model.

Even when the saturated correlates model converges to a proper solution, some software programs issue a warning message indicating that the solution is invalid. Structural equation modeling programs use a set of parameter matrices to represent the analysis model, and the pattern of associations required by the saturated correlates approach can produce nonpositive definite matrices. In particular, the correlations between the auxiliary variables and the residual terms often lead to dire warning messages about the residual covariance matrix (i.e., the so-called psi matrix). Although computer programs tend to issue warning messages when a solution produces a nonpositive definite matrix, these messages are usually benign when they are caused by an auxiliary variable. If the model produces valid parameter estimates (e.g., parameter estimates that seem reasonable, no negative variance estimates) and converges properly without the auxiliary variables, then you can generally ignore these warning messages and interpret your results.

## 5.7 THE IMPACT OF NON-NORMAL DATA

The multivariate normal distribution plays an integral role in every phase of a maximum likelihood analysis (e.g., the log-likelihood provides a basis for identifying the most likely population parameter values, and the second derivatives of the normal distribution are the building blocks for standard errors). In practice, non-normal data are relatively common, and some authors argue that normality is the exception rather than the rule (Micceri, 1989). Given the important role that the normal distribution plays in the estimation process, it is reasonable to ask whether normality violations are problematic for maximum likelihood analyses.

A good deal of research has examined the impact of non-normality on complete-data estimation (Chou, Benter, & Satorra, 1991; Curran, West, & Finch, 1996; Finch, West, & MacKinnon, 1997; Hu, Bentler, & Kano, 1992; Yuan, Bentler, & Zhang, 2005), and an increasing number of studies have investigated the issue of non-normal missing data (Enders, 2001, 2002; Gold & Bentler, 2000; Graham, Hofer, & MacKinnon, 1996; Savalei, 2008; Savalei & Bentler, 2005, 2007; Yuan, 2007; Yuan & Bentler, 2000). This literature suggests that non-normal data tend to have a minimal impact on the parameter estimates themselves but can bias standard errors and distort the likelihood ratio test. Yuan et al. (2005) showed that kurtosis largely dictates this bias, whereby leptokurtic data can attenuate standard errors and inflate the likelihood ratio test, and platykurtic data can inflate standard errors and reduce the magnitude of the likelihood ratio statistic. Simulation studies suggest that skewness can also exert a negative impact, particularly with sample sizes that are common in the behavioral and the social sciences. Interested readers can consult Finney and DiStefano (2006) and West, Finch, and Curran (1995) for a detailed review of the non-normality literature.

Corrective procedures for complete data have been available for some time (Bentler, 1983; Bollen & Stine, 1992; Browne, 1984; Satorra & Bentler, 1988, 1994, 2001), and methodologists have extended many of these procedures to missing data analyses (Arminger & Sobel, 1990; Enders, 2002; Savalei & Bentler, 2007; Yuan & Bentler, 2000). The subsequent sections illustrate some of these corrective procedures. In particular, I describe two approaches for estimating standard errors ("robust" standard errors and bootstrap resampling) and two methods for correcting the bias in the likelihood ratio test (rescaling and bootstrap resampling). I chose these procedures because they are readily available in software packages, but other techniques will likely become available in the near future (e.g., distribution-free test statistics that do not rely on the multivariate normality assumption; Yuan & Bentler, 2000; Savalei & Bentler, 2007).

## 5.8 ROBUST STANDARD ERRORS

Recall from Chapter 3 that the curvature of the log-likelihood function dictates the magnitude of the maximum likelihood standard errors. In particular, the matrix of second derivatives (i.e., the Hessian matrix) plays an important role in the standard error computations. The second derivative formulas from the normal distribution are missing terms that depend on the skewness and the kurtosis of the population distribution. The absence of these terms can overestimate or underestimate the standard errors, depending on whether the population data are leptokurtic or platykurtic. The robust standard error formula combines information from the first and the second derivatives into a single estimate of sampling error, such that the information from the first derivatives effectively serves as an adjustment term that corrects for normality violations.

To illustrate robust standard errors, I use a univariate example that involves the standard error of the mean. This is not an ideal example because normality violations only affect the standard errors for variance and covariance parameters (White, 1982; Yuan et al., 2005). However, an algebraic relationship between the first and second derivative formulas plays an important role in the formulation of the robust standard errors, and illustrating this relationship is more tedious with covariance matrix parameters. Nevertheless, the computations in the subsequent sections readily extend to covariance matrix parameters as well as to multivariate estimation problems. For simplicity, I use complete-data formulas throughout this section, but the underlying logic is the same with missing data. Some of the information in the subsequent sections is relatively technical, so readers who are not interested in the mathematical underpinnings of robust standard errors may want to skim this section.

### First and Second Derivatives Revisited

Understanding the robust standard error computations requires some additional background information on derivatives. From Chapter 3, the equations for the first and second derivatives of the sample log-likelihood function with respect to the mean are as follows:

$$\frac{\partial \log L}{\partial \mu} = \frac{1}{\sigma^2}\left(-N\mu + \sum_{i=1}^{N} y_i\right) \tag{5.2}$$

$$\frac{\partial^2 \log L}{\partial^2 \mu} = \frac{-N}{\sigma^2} \tag{5.3}$$

The first derivative equation was useful for identifying the maximum of the log-likelihood function (e.g., by setting the formula to zero and solving for the population mean), and the second derivative equation quantified the curvature of the function.

Recall from Chapters 3 and 4 that the sample log-likelihood is the sum of $N$ individual log-likelihood equations. The individual log-likelihood equation (e.g., Equation 4.1) also has first and second derivatives, and Equations 5.2 and 5.3 are actually sums of these casewise derivative equations. Rewriting the previous equations as sums shows each case's contribution to the derivative formulas, as follows:

$$\frac{\partial \log L}{\partial \mu} = \frac{1}{\sigma^2}\left(-N\mu + \sum_{i=1}^{N} y_i\right) = \sum_{i=1}^{N}\left[\frac{1}{\sigma^2}(y_i - \mu)\right] = \sum_{i=1}^{N}\left[\frac{\partial \log L_i}{\partial \mu}\right] \tag{5.4}$$

$$\frac{\partial^2 \log L}{\partial^2 \mu} = \frac{-N}{\sigma^2} = \sum_{i=1}^{N}\left[\frac{-1}{\sigma^2}\right] = \sum_{i=1}^{N}\left[\frac{\partial^2 \log L_i}{\partial^2 \mu}\right] \tag{5.5}$$

where the bracketed terms contain the derivative formulas for the individual log-likelihood equation. In words, the right-most terms in the equations say that the derivatives of the sample log-likelihood function equal the sum of the derivatives of the individual log-likelihood equations. (In calculus, the derivative of a sum equals the sum of the derivatives.) The individual contributions to the derivative equations play an important role in the formulation of robust standard errors.

## Two Formulations of Information

Recall that the information matrix contains values that quantify the curvature of the log-likelihood function (e.g., peaked functions produce large information values and small standard errors, whereas flat functions produce small information values and large standard errors). When the population data are multivariate normal, there are two equivalent methods for computing information. The method from previous chapters is based on second derivatives, whereas the alternate approach uses first derivatives. As an illustration, consider each case's contribution to the first derivative equation, $(y_i - \mu)/\sigma^2$. This collection of terms is itself a variable, the value of which varies across cases. Applying expectation rules for variables, note that the variance of the casewise first derivative is as follows.

$$\text{var}\left(\frac{\partial \log L_i}{\partial \mu}\right) = \text{var}\left[\frac{1}{\sigma^2}(y_i - \mu)\right] = \left(\frac{1}{\sigma^2}\right)^2 \text{var}(y_i - \mu) = \frac{1}{\sigma^4}(\sigma^2) = \frac{1}{\sigma^2} \tag{5.6}$$

Notice that the result of Equation 5.6 is virtually identical to the second derivative of the individual log-likelihood equation (i.e., the bracketed terms in Equation 5.5), but differs by a multiplicative constant of negative 1. Stated differently, computing the variance of the individual first derivatives gives each case's contribution to the second derivative equation, as follows:

$$\text{var}\left(\frac{\partial \log L_i}{\partial \mu}\right) = -\left(\frac{\partial^2 \log L_i}{\partial^2 \mu}\right) \tag{5.7}$$

The equality in Equation 5.7 leads to two equivalent expressions for information, one of which is based on first derivatives (i.e., $I_F$) and the other on second derivatives (i.e., $I_S$).

$$I_F = N\left[\text{var}\left(\frac{\partial \log L_i}{\partial \mu}\right)\right] = N\left(\frac{1}{\sigma^2}\right) \tag{5.8}$$

$$I_S = -N\left[\frac{\partial^2 \log L_i}{\partial^2 \mu}\right] = -\frac{\partial^2 \log L}{\partial^2 \mu} = \frac{N}{\sigma^2} \tag{5.9}$$

The information values provide the building blocks for maximum likelihood standard errors, such that the inverse (i.e., reciprocal) of information is the sampling variance, and the square root of the sampling variance is the standard error. When the population data are normally distributed, the two formulations of information are equivalent and should produce very similar standard errors.

## The Sandwich Estimator

When the population data are non-normal, Equations 5.8 and 5.9 are no longer equivalent, and both formulas yield inaccurate standard errors. The problem is that the density function for the normal distribution generates the derivative equations, when some other non-normal distribution should have generated these formulas. From a practical standpoint, the derivative formulas are missing terms that depend on the skewness and kurtosis of the population distribution (White, 1982; Yuan et al., 2005). The absence of these terms can overestimate or underestimate the standard errors, depending on whether the population data are leptokurtic or platykurtic (Yuan et al., 2005).

The robust standard error combines the two information equations into a single estimate of sampling error (Freedman, 2006; Huber, 1967; White, 1982). This so-called **sandwich estimator** of the sampling variance is

$$\text{var}(\hat{\theta}) = I_S^{-1} I_F I_S^{-1} \tag{5.10}$$

where $I_F$ and $I_S$ are information estimates based on the first and second derivatives, respectively, and $\text{var}(\hat{\theta})$ is the sampling variance. The methodological literature refers to Equation 5.10 as the sandwich estimator because it resembles a piece of meat (i.e., $I_F$) sitting between two slices of bread (i.e., $I_S$). Consistent with previous chapters, taking the square root of the sampling variance gives the standard error.

## How Does the Robust Standard Error Work?

The "meat" of the sandwich estimator is important because it effectively serves as a correction factor that increases or decreases the standard error, depending on the kurtosis of the data. Returning to Equation 5.4, notice that the first derivative of the individual log-likelihood equation involves the deviation between a score and the mean (i.e., $y_i - \mu$). Because a leptokurtic distribution has thicker tails (i.e., a higher proportion of large deviation values) than a normal curve, the presence of outliers increases the value of $I_F$ relative to that of a normal distribution. Consequently, multiplying by $I_F$ increases the magnitude of the standard error and counteracts the negative bias that results from leptokurtic data. In contrast, a platykurtic distribution has fewer extreme scores than a normal curve and thus produces a smaller value of $I_F$. In this situation, using $I_F$ as multiplier produces a downward adjustment that decreases the inflation in the normal-theory standard errors. Finally, when the data are normally distributed, the sandwich estimator reduces to the usual maximum likelihood standard error because the first two terms of Equation 5.10 cancel out when $I_F = I_S$. Although the first derivative formulas for the covariance matrix parameters are more complex than those of the mean parameters, they too contain deviation scores. Consequently, the basic operation of the sandwich estimator is the same for any parameter. Finally, note that the basic form of Equation 5.10 is the same in multivariate estimation problems. In the multivariate context, $I_F$ and $I_S$ are information matrices and $var(\hat{\theta})$ is the parameter covariance matrix, the diagonal of which contains the squared standard errors.

## A Bivariate Example

To further illustrate the robust standard errors, I generated a single artificial data set with two variables and $N = 500$ cases. The purpose of this example is to illustrate the impact of non-normal data, so I generated $X$ to have a platykurtic distribution with kurtosis of $-1.00$ and $Y$ to have a leptokurtic distribution with kurtosis of $4.00$ (a normal distribution has kurtosis of zero). I used maximum likelihood to estimate the mean vector and the covariance matrix and obtained the normal-theory and robust standard errors for each parameter estimate.

Table 5.2 shows the parameter covariance matrices from the bivariate analysis. The parameter covariance matrix is a 5 by 5 symmetric matrix, where each row and column corresponds to one of the estimated parameters (there are two means and three unique covariance matrix elements). The diagonals of the two matrices are particularly important because they contain the sampling variances (i.e., squared standard errors). The mean parameters are un-

**TABLE 5.2. Parameter Covariance Matrices for the Kurtotic Data Analysis Example**

| Parameter | 1 | 2 | 3 | 4 | 5 |
|---|---|---|---|---|---|
| | | Parameter covariance matrix (normality assumed) | | | |
| 1: $\mu_X$ | 0.002119 | | | | |
| 2: $\mu_Y$ | 0.000928 | 0.001864 | | | |
| 3: $\sigma^2_X$ | 0 | 0 | 0.004490 | | |
| 4: $\sigma_{X,Y}$ | 0 | 0 | 0.001967 | 0.002406 | |
| 5: $\sigma^2_Y$ | 0 | 0 | 0.000862 | 0.001730 | 0.003474 |
| | | Parameter covariance matrix (robust) | | | |
| 1: $\mu_X$ | 0.002119 | | | | |
| 2: $\mu_Y$ | 0.000928 | 0.001864 | | | |
| 3: $\sigma^2_X$ | 0.000036 | −0.000096 | 0.002117 | | |
| 4: $\sigma_{X,Y}$ | −0.000096 | −0.000091 | 0.001094 | 0.002388 | |
| 5: $\sigma^2_Y$ | −0.000091 | −0.000111 | 0.000841 | 0.003494 | 0.010259 |

*Note.* $X$ has a platykurtic distribution ($K = 2$) and $Y$ has a leptokurtic distribution ($K = 7$). **Bold** typeface denotes the sampling variance (i.e., squared standard error) of each parameter estimate.

affected by nonnormal data (White, 1982; Yuan et al., 2005), so these elements are identical in both matrices. However, the covariance matrix elements are quite different. For example, notice that the normal-theory standard error for $\sigma_X^2$ is larger than the corresponding robust standard error (i.e., $\sqrt{.004490} = 0.067$ versus $\sqrt{.002117} = 0.046$, respectively), whereas the standard error for $\sigma_Y^2$ is smaller than that of the robust estimator (i.e., $\sqrt{.003474} = 0.059$ versus $\sqrt{.010259} = 0.101$, respectively). This pattern of differences is consistent with the notion that leptokurtic data can attenuate standard errors and platykurtic data can inflate standard errors (Yuan et al., 1995). Of course, analyzing a single sample provides very little evidence about the relative accuracy of the two estimators, but published computer simulation studies clearly favor robust standard errors (Chou & Bentler, 1995; Chou et al., 1991; DiStefano, 2002; Yuan & Bentler, 1997).

## Robust Standard Errors for Missing Data

The formulation of the sandwich estimator is identical with missing data (Arminger & Sobel, 1990; Yuan & Bentler, 2000). However, missing data introduce one small nuance that is not necessarily an issue with complete data. You might recall from Chapter 4 that the observed information matrix produces standard errors that are valid with MAR data (Kenward & Molenberghs, 1998), whereas the expected information matrix requires MCAR data. This implies that the observed information matrix is the appropriate "bread" for the sandwich estimator in Equation 5.10. At the time of this writing, most software programs that implement robust standard errors for missing data use the observed information matrix for this purpose, and simulation studies suggest that this approach provides a substantial improvement over normal-theory standard errors (Enders, 2001).

## 5.9 BOOTSTRAP STANDARD ERRORS

Bootstrap resampling is a second approach to generating standard errors with nonnormal data. The bootstrap is quite different from the sandwich estimator because it uses Monte Carlo simulation techniques to generate an empirical sampling distribution for each parameter, the standard deviation of which is the standard error. Because the bootstrap makes no distributional assumptions, the accuracy of the procedure is unaffected by normality violations. This section describes a so-called **naïve bootstrap** that is strictly limited to estimating standard errors. Later in the chapter, I describe an alternate bootstrap procedure (the Bollen-Stine bootstrap) that can correct for bias in the likelihood ratio test. A number of detailed overviews of the bootstrap are available in the literature for readers interested in more details (e.g., Bollen & Stine, 1992; Efron & Tibshirani, 1993; Enders, 2002; Stine, 1989). The vast majority of the bootstrap literature deals with complete-data applications, but the procedural details are essentially the same with or without missing data.

The basic idea behind **bootstrap resampling** is to repeatedly draw samples of size N *with replacement* from a data set. In effect, the sample data serve as a miniature population for the Monte Carlo sampling procedure. Because the samples are drawn with replacement, some data records will appear more than once in a given sample, whereas others will not appear at

**TABLE 5.3. Bootstrap Sample from an Employee Selection Data Set**

| | Sample data | | | | Bootstrap sample | | |
|---|---|---|---|---|---|---|---|
| ID | IQ | JP | WB | ID | IQ | JP | WB |
| 1 | 78 | — | 13 | 18 | 115 | 14 | 14 |
| 2 | 84 | — | 9 | 14 | 106 | 15 | 10 |
| 3 | 84 | — | 10 | 17 | 113 | 12 | 14 |
| 4 | 85 | — | 10 | 3 | 84 | — | 10 |
| 5 | 87 | — | — | 16 | 112 | 10 | 10 |
| 6 | 91 | — | 3 | 7 | 92 | — | 12 |
| 7 | 92 | — | 12 | 3 | 84 | — | 10 |
| 8 | 94 | — | 3 | 15 | 108 | 10 | — |
| 9 | 94 | — | 13 | 14 | 106 | 15 | 10 |
| 10 | 96 | — | — | 10 | 96 | — | — |
| 11 | 99 | 7 | 6 | 8 | 94 | — | 3 |
| 12 | 105 | 10 | 12 | 16 | 112 | 10 | 10 |
| 13 | 105 | 11 | 14 | 14 | 106 | 15 | 10 |
| 14 | 106 | 15 | 10 | 10 | 96 | — | — |
| 15 | 108 | 10 | — | 9 | 94 | — | 13 |
| 16 | 112 | 10 | 10 | 1 | 78 | — | 13 |
| 17 | 113 | 12 | 14 | 4 | 85 | — | 10 |
| 18 | 115 | 14 | 14 | 16 | 112 | 10 | 10 |
| 19 | 118 | 16 | 12 | 10 | 96 | — | — |
| 20 | 134 | 12 | 11 | 18 | 115 | 14 | 14 |

*Note.* JP = job performance; WB = well-being.

all. Table 5.3 shows a single bootstrap sample from the small employee selection data set that I have been using throughout the book. Notice that case 14 appears three times in the bootstrap sample, whereas case 2 does not appear at all.

The ultimate goal of the bootstrap is to construct an empirical sampling distribution for each parameter estimate. Drawing a large number of bootstrap samples (e.g., $B = 2000$) and fitting the analysis model to each sample yields a set of estimates for each parameter. The collection of $B$ parameter estimates forms an empirical sampling distribution, the standard deviation of which is the bootstrap standard error

$$SE_{\text{Bootstrap}} = \sqrt{\frac{1}{B-1}\sum_{b=1}^{B}(\hat{\theta}_b - \bar{\theta})^2} \tag{5.11}$$

where $B$ is the number of bootstrap samples, $\hat{\theta}_b$ is the parameter estimate from one of the bootstrap samples, and $\bar{\theta}$ is the mean of the $B$ parameter estimates. Notice that Equation 5.11 is the usual formula for the sample standard deviation, where the $B$ parameter estimates serve as data points. Although the process of repeatedly drawing samples and analyzing the data sounds tedious, software packages that implement the bootstrap completely automate the procedure. It is also relatively straightforward to implement the bootstrap in software packages that do not have built-in routines (Enders, 2005).

## A Bivariate Analysis Example

To illustrate the bootstrap, reconsider the artificial bivariate data set from the previous section. Recall that $X$ has platykurtic distribution with kurtosis equal to $-1.00$ and $Y$ has a leptokurtic distribution with kurtosis of 4.00. To begin, I drew 2,000 samples of $N = 500$ (the size of the original sample) with replacement from the data and subsequently used maximum likelihood to estimate the mean vector and the covariance matrix from each sample. This procedure produced 2,000 estimates of each mean and covariance parameter. Next, I generated standard errors by computing the standard deviation of each parameter across the 2,000 bootstrap samples. The bootstrap produced standard errors that are nearly identical to those of the sandwich estimator. For example, the bootstrap standard errors for $\sigma_X^2$ and $\sigma_Y^2$ are 0.046 and 0.099, respectively, and the corresponding robust standard errors are 0.046 and 0.101. It is not unusual for the two procedures to produce similar estimates, particularly when the sample size is relatively large. Consequently, convenience is often the only reason to prefer one approach to another.

## Bootstrap Confidence Intervals

There are two methods for constructing bootstrap confidence intervals. Following the usual complete-data procedure, the first approach is to multiply the bootstrap standard error by the appropriate critical value from the unit normal table:

$$CI_{Bootstrap} = \hat{\theta} + (z_{1-\alpha/2})(SE_{Bootstrap}) \qquad (5.12)$$

where $\hat{\theta}$ is the parameter estimate from the initial maximum likelihood analysis, and $z_{1-\alpha/2}$ is the two-tailed critical value (e.g., $z = 1.96$ for an alpha level of .05). Alternatively, the parameter estimates that correspond to the 95th and the 5th percentiles of the bootstrap sampling distribution can define the upper and lower confidence interval limits, respectively. Little and Rubin (2002) suggest that the former approach is appropriate when the empirical sampling distribution is approximately normal, but they prefer the second method when the distribution is non-normal. You can readily ascertain the shape of the empirical sampling distribution and determine the appropriate percentiles by examining a frequency distribution of the $B$ parameter estimates.

## How Many Bootstrap Samples Should I Use?

It is difficult to establish a good rule of thumb for the number of bootstrap samples because any such recommendation is a bit arbitrary. In part, this decision depends on the shape of the empirical sampling distribution. When the sampling distribution approximates a normal curve, Little and Rubin (2002, p. 197) suggest that a relatively small number of bootstrap samples will suffice. In contrast, they recommend using a large number of samples (e.g., $B >$ 2000) when the empirical sampling distribution is non-normal. Of course, the problem with these recommendations is that you cannot determine the shape of the empirical sampling distribution without first running the bootstrap procedure. With many analysis models, implementing the bootstrap takes very little time, so there is often no practical reason to avoid using a very large number of bootstrap samples.

## Limitations of the Bootstrap

The bootstrap procedure is advantageous because it requires no distributional assumptions. However, treating the sample data as a miniature population effectively assumes that the sample is a representative surrogate for the entire population. This assumption is tenuous in its own right, particularly in small samples. Another issue to be aware of is that a subset of the bootstrap samples may produce analyses that fail to converge. Small samples and misspecified models are common causes of convergence failures, and missing data only exacerbate the problem. Discarding the failed replicates is a common way to deal with convergence failures (Yung & Bentler, 1996), but methodologists have proposed other options (Yuan & Hayashi, 2003).

## 5.10 THE RESCALED LIKELIHOOD RATIO TEST

When the multivariate normality assumption is violated, the sampling distribution of the likelihood ratio test no longer follows the appropriate central chi-square distribution. With univariate population data, the likelihood ratio test is proportional to kurtosis, such that leptokurtic data inflate the test statistic, and platykurtic data attenuate its value (Yuan et al., 2005). Consequently, the likelihood ratio test can yield excessive type I or type II error rates, depending on the population kurtosis. The nature of the bias becomes more complex in multivariate analyses, but the underlying problem remains the same—the likelihood ratio test does not follow its theoretical sampling distribution. One solution to this problem is to rescale the likelihood ratio test so that it more closely approximates the appropriate chi-square distribution. This correction has been available for some time (Satorra & Bentler, 1988, 1994), although its application to missing data analyses is more recent (Yuan & Bentler, 2000). The limited research to date suggests that the rescaling procedure for missing data effectively controls the error rates of the likelihood ratio test (Enders, 2001; Savalei & Bentler, 2005). Because the logic of the rescaling process is the same with or without missing data, this section gives a generic description of the procedure. Yuan and Bentler (2000) give additional technical details on the rescaling procedure for missing data.

## The Satorra–Bentler Chi-Square

Readers who use structural equation modeling techniques may already be familiar with the rescaled likelihood ratio statistic. In this context, the so-called **Satorra–Bentler chi-square** (Satorra & Bentler, 1988, 1994) uses a correction factor to rescale the likelihood ratio test, as follows:

$$\text{LR}_{\text{RS}} = c\text{LR} \tag{5.13}$$

In a structural equation modeling analysis, $LR_{RS}$ is the rescaled (i.e., Satorra–Bentler) test statistic, LR is a likelihood ratio test that compares the relative fit of the hypothesized model (e.g., a confirmatory factor analysis model) to that of a saturated model (e.g., a model that estimates the sample covariance matrix), and $c$ is a scaling factor that depends on the distribution shape. With univariate data, Yuan et al. (2005) show that the scaling factor is related to kurtosis, such that $c$ decreases the value of LR when the distribution is leptokurtic and increases the test statistic when the distribution is platykurtic. When the population data are normally distributed, the scaling factor equals one, and the rescaled statistic is identical to the usual likelihood ratio test.

## A General Rescaling Procedure

Structural equation modeling applications of the rescaled test statistic are particularly straightforward to implement because software packages automatically perform the rescaling. The rescaling procedure is applicable to any likelihood ratio test, but implementing it requires special procedures (Satorra & Bentler, 2001). Recall from Chapter 3 that the likelihood ratio test is

$$LR = -2(\log L_{\text{Restricted}} - \log L_{\text{Full}}) \qquad (5.14)$$

where $\log L_{\text{Full}}$ and $\log L_{\text{Restricted}}$ are the log-likelihood values from the full and restricted models, respectively. The scaling factor for the likelihood ratio test incorporates information from both models, as follows:

$$c_{\text{LR}} = \frac{(q_{\text{Restricted}})(c_{\text{Restricted}}) - (q_{\text{Full}})(c_{\text{Full}})}{(q_{\text{Restricted}} - q_{\text{Full}})} \qquad (5.15)$$

where $q_{\text{Restricted}}$ is the number of parameter estimates from the restricted model, $c_{\text{Restricted}}$ is the scaling factor for the restricted model, $q_{\text{Full}}$ is the number of estimated parameters in the full model, and $c_{\text{Full}}$ is the scaling factor for the full model. Computing $c_{\text{LR}}$ is straightforward because software packages that implement the rescaling procedure report all of the necessary terms. Finally, the rescaled test statistic divides the likelihood ratio test by the scaling factor, as follows:

$$LR_{RS} = \frac{-2(\log L_{\text{Restricted}} - \log L_{\text{Full}})}{c_{\text{LR}}} = \frac{LR}{c_{\text{LR}}} \qquad (5.16)$$

I illustrate the rescaled likelihood ratio test in one of the analysis examples presented later in the chapter.

## 5.11 BOOTSTRAPPING THE LIKELIHOOD RATIO STATISTIC

Bootstrap resampling is a second option for correcting bias in the likelihood ratio test statistic. Whereas the rescaling procedure attempts to adjust the value of the likelihood ratio test so that it more closely approximates its theoretical sampling distribution, the bootstrap leaves the test statistic intact and uses Monte Carlo simulation techniques to generate a new sampling distribution. Rather than correcting the test statistic itself, the bootstrap corrects the probability value for the test by referencing the likelihood ratio statistic to the empirical sampling distribution. Although the actual resampling procedure is identical to that of the naïve bootstrap, obtaining the correct empirical distribution requires a transformation of the data prior to drawing the samples.

### The Problem with the Naïve Bootstrap

Using the naïve bootstrap to construct a sampling distribution for the likelihood ratio test is inappropriate because the resulting samples are inconsistent with the null hypothesis. For example, suppose that it was of interest to use the likelihood ratio to test the slope coefficient from a simple regression model. This test involves a comparison of the regression model (i.e., the full model) to a restricted model that constrains the regression coefficient to zero during estimation. The null hypothesis for this test states that the population regression coefficient is equal to zero (i.e., the restricted model is true), and the $p$-value quantifies the probability of observing a likelihood ratio test that is equal to or greater than that of the sample data, given that the null hypothesis is true.

Fitting the two regression models to a large number of bootstrap samples and computing the likelihood ratio test for each sample would not produce an appropriate sampling distribution because the collection of test statistics is inconsistent with the null hypothesis. Even if the regression slope is truly zero in the population, the sample estimate is unlikely to exactly equal zero. Consequently, drawing bootstrap samples from data yields a distribution that reflects natural sampling fluctuation as well as model misfit (i.e., the discrepancy between the data and the null hypothesis). The appropriate sampling distribution should reflect sampling fluctuation only.

### The Bollen–Stine Bootstrap

Beran and Srivastava (1985) and Bollen and Stine (1992) modified the bootstrap procedure by applying an algebraic transformation to the data prior to drawing samples. This transformation aligns the mean and the covariance structure of the data to the null hypothesis and produces a distribution that reflects only the sampling fluctuation of the likelihood ratio statistic. Because the transformation does not affect distribution shape, the bootstrap procedure effectively incorporates the influence of nonnormal data. Consequently, referencing the likelihood ratio test to the empirical sampling distribution of likelihood ratio statistics can generate an accurate probability value, even when the data are nonnormal. I refer to the modified bootstrap procedure as the **Bollen–Stine bootstrap** throughout the remainder of the chapter because the Bollen and Stine (1992) manuscript was largely responsible for popularizing the technique, particularly in structural equation modeling applications.

To align the data with the null hypotheses, Bollen and Stine transform the sample data to have the same mean and covariance structure as the restricted model. This transformation requires the mean vector and the covariance matrix from the sample data as well as the mean vector and the covariance matrix that would result if the null hypothesis were true (i.e., the model-implied mean vector and covariance matrix from the restricted model). Both sets of estimates are readily available from structural equation modeling programs.

The Bollen–Stine transformation is as follows:

$$\mathbf{Z}_i = (\mathbf{Y}_i - \hat{\boldsymbol{\mu}}_S)^T \hat{\boldsymbol{\Sigma}}_S^{-1/2} \hat{\boldsymbol{\Sigma}}_R^{1/2} + \hat{\boldsymbol{\mu}}_R^T \tag{5.17}$$

where $\mathbf{Z}_i$ is the transformed data vector for case $i$, $\mathbf{Y}_i$ is the raw data vector for case $i$, $\hat{\boldsymbol{\mu}}_S$ is the sample mean vector, $\hat{\boldsymbol{\Sigma}}_S$ is the sample covariance matrix, $\hat{\boldsymbol{\Sigma}}_R$ is the implied covariance matrix from the restricted model, and $\hat{\boldsymbol{\mu}}_R$ is the implied mean vector from restricted model. In words, the $(\mathbf{Y}_i - \hat{\boldsymbol{\mu}}_S)^T \hat{\boldsymbol{\Sigma}}_S^{-1/2}$ portion of the formula essentially "erases" the mean and the covariance structure of the sample data and converts the variables to uncorrelated $z$ scores. Next, multiplying the $z$ scores by $\hat{\boldsymbol{\Sigma}}_R^{1/2}$ transforms the data to have the same covariance matrix as the restricted model. Finally, adding $\hat{\boldsymbol{\mu}}_R$ equates the sample means to the predicted means from the restricted model.

The Bollen–Stine transformation produces a data set that is exactly consistent with the null hypothesis. After applying the transformation, the bootstrap procedure is the same as before. The specific steps are as follows: (1) draw $B$ bootstrap samples with replacement from the transformed data set, (2) fit the full model and the restricted model to each bootstrap sample, (3) compute the likelihood ratio statistic for each bootstrap sample, and (4) construct a frequency distribution of the $B$ likelihood ratio statistics. The proportion of bootstrap test statistics that exceed the value of the original likelihood ratio test serves as the corrected probability value.

## A Bivariate Example

To illustrate the Bollen–Stine bootstrap, reconsider the bivariate data set from the previous sections. Recall that $X$ has platykurtic distribution with kurtosis of $-1.00$ and $Y$ has a leptokurtic distribution with kurtosis of $4.00$. Furthermore, suppose that it is of interest to use the likelihood ratio statistic to test the slope from the regression of $Y$ on $X$. As I explained previously, this test involves a comparison of the regression model (i.e., the full model) to a restricted model that constrains the regression coefficient to zero during estimation. The first step is to estimate the two regression models and compute the likelihood ratio test. Doing so yields a likelihood ratio statistic of LR = 123.05. Normally, a central chi-square distribution with one degree of freedom would generate the probability value for the test. However, the theoretical chi-square distribution is likely to produce an inaccurate probability value because the data are nonnormal. The purpose of the bootstrap is to generate an empirical sampling distribution that reflects the influence of the nonnormal data.

**TABLE 5.4. Mean Vectors and Covariance Matrices for the Bollen–Stine Transformation**

| Variable | 1 | 2 | 1 | 2 | 1 | 2 |
|---|---|---|---|---|---|---|
| | Sample data | | Restricted model | | Transformed data | |
| 1: X | 1.060 | | 1.060 | | 1.060 | |
| 2: Y | 0.464 | 0.932 | 0 | 0.932 | 0 | 0.931 |
| Means | −0.030 | 0.045 | −0.030 | 0.045 | −0.030 | 0.046 |

The null hypothesis for the likelihood ratio test states that the population regression coefficient is equal to zero (i.e., the restricted model is true). The left-most section of Table 5.4 shows the mean vector and the covariance matrix for the sample data (i.e., $\hat{\boldsymbol{\mu}}_S$ and $\hat{\boldsymbol{\Sigma}}_S$, respectively). Notice that the two variables have a positive covariance, so the data are not perfectly consistent with the null hypothesis. (If the population regression coefficient is zero, this covariance should also equal zero.) Transforming the data to have a perfect fit to the null hypothesis requires the predicted mean vector and the predicted covariance matrix from the restricted model. I used a structural equation program to estimate the restricted model, and the middle section of Table 5.4 shows model-implied parameter estimates, $\hat{\boldsymbol{\mu}}_R$ and $\hat{\boldsymbol{\Sigma}}_R$. Notice that the covariance is zero because the restricted model implies that there is no association between the variables. Next, I transformed the sample data by substituting the parameter estimates from the table into Equation 5.17. After applying the transformation, I estimated the mean vector and the covariance matrix of the transformed data, and the right-most section of Table 5.4 shows the resulting estimates. As you can see, the transformed data have the same mean and covariance structure as the restricted model (within sampling error), so it is now appropriate to draw bootstrap samples from the data.

Having applied the Bollen–Stine transformation, I drew 2,000 bootstrap samples with replacement from the transformed data and subsequently fit the two regression models to each bootstrap sample. Next, I computed the likelihood ratio test from each bootstrap sample and constructed a frequency distribution of the test statistics. Figure 5.5 shows the empirical sampling distribution of the likelihood ratio statistic as well as the theoretical chi-square distribution with one degree of freedom. For illustration purposes, I also drew 2,000 naïve bootstrap samples from the untransformed data and computed the likelihood ratio test from each of those samples. I previously explained that the naïve bootstrap is inappropriate because it yields a distribution that reflects natural sampling fluctuation as well as model misfit. The fact that the naïve sampling distribution is shifted far to the right clearly illustrates this effect. In contrast, the Bollen–Stine sampling distribution is similar in shape to the theoretical chi-square distribution, but has a thicker tail. Leptokurtic data tend to inflate the likelihood ratio test, so the larger-than-expected proportion of statistics in the tail of the distribution makes intuitive sense.

Finally, I performed a significance test by referencing the likelihood ratio statistic to the empirical sampling distribution rather than to the theoretical chi-square distribution. Recall that the initial analysis produced a likelihood ratio statistic of LR = 123.05. The bootstrap sampling distribution did not include any values that were this large, so it is impossible to

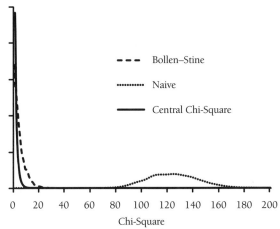

**FIGURE 5.5.** The theoretical central chi-square distribution and empirical sampling distributions of the likelihood ratio test generated from the Bollen–Stine bootstrap and naïve bootstrap. The naïve sampling distribution is centered on an inappropriately large chi-square value because it reflects natural sampling fluctuation as well as model misfit. In contrast, the Bollen–Stine sampling distribution is unaffected by model misfit and reflects the sampling fluctuation of the likelihood ratio test with nonnormal data. The Bollen–Stine distribution has a slightly thicker tail than the theoretical chi-square distribution, which is a result of the leptokurtic data.

compute an exact probability. However, the 99th percentile of the distribution corresponds to a test statistic of 17.97, so it is conservative to describe the probability value as $p < .01$.

## Applying the Bollen–Stine Bootstrap to Missing Data

The matrix computations in Equation 5.17 require complete data, but Enders (2002) proposed the following transformation for missing data:

$$Z_i = (Y_i - \hat{\boldsymbol{\mu}}_{Si})^T (\hat{\boldsymbol{\Sigma}}_{Si})^{-1/2} (\hat{\boldsymbol{\Sigma}}_{Ri})^{1/2} + \hat{\boldsymbol{\mu}}_{Ri}^T \tag{5.18}$$

The missing data transformation is nearly identical to that of the complete data, but the parameter matrices now have an $i$ subscript. The basic idea behind Equation 5.18 is to apply the transformation using only those estimates for which a case has complete data. Consequently, the $i$ subscript denotes the fact that the size and the contents of the matrices can vary across individuals.

To illustrate the missing data transformation, reconsider the previous simple regression example. Furthermore, suppose that a subset of cases has missing $Y$ values. Transforming the data effectively requires a unique transformation formula for each missing data pattern. For example, the transformation for the complete cases is

$$\mathbf{Z}_i = \left( \begin{bmatrix} X_i \\ Y_i \end{bmatrix} - \begin{bmatrix} \hat{\mu}_{X_S} \\ \hat{\mu}_{Y_S} \end{bmatrix} \right)^T \begin{bmatrix} \hat{\sigma}^2_{X_S} & \hat{\sigma}_{XY_S} \\ \hat{\sigma}_{YX_S} & \hat{\sigma}^2_{Y_S} \end{bmatrix}^{-1/2} \begin{bmatrix} \hat{\sigma}^2_{X_R} & \hat{\sigma}_{XY_R} \\ \hat{\sigma}_{YX_R} & \hat{\sigma}^2_{Y_R} \end{bmatrix}^{1/2} + \begin{bmatrix} \hat{\mu}_{X_R} \\ \hat{\mu}_{Y_R} \end{bmatrix}^T$$

For the cases with missing $Y$ values, the transformation eliminates the parameters that correspond to $Y$ and uses only those estimates that correspond to the complete variable, $X$. This transformation is as follows:

$$Z_i = (X_i - \hat{\mu}_{X_S})^T [\hat{\sigma}^2_{X_S}]^{-\frac{1}{2}} [\hat{\sigma}^2_{X_R}]^{\frac{1}{2}} + [\hat{\mu}_{X_R}]^T$$

Applying the transformation to each case's observed data yields a transformed data matrix that has the same missing data patterns as the sample data. At that point, the bootstrap procedure follows the same steps as before: (1) draw a large number of samples with replacement from the transformed data, (2) use maximum likelihood missing data handling to estimate the full model and the restricted model, (3) compute the likelihood ratio statistic for each bootstrap sample, and (4) generate a probability value by computing the proportion of bootstrap test statistics that exceed the value of the likelihood ratio test from the original analysis.

Some structural equation modeling programs (e.g., Mplus and EQS) implement the missing data bootstrap, and it is also relatively straightforward to implement the bootstrap in software packages that do not have built-in routines (Enders, 2005). The limited research to date suggests that the bootstrap yields relatively accurate type I error rates (Enders, 2001, 2002). For example, computer simulation studies report type I error rates between .05 and .07, even with kurtosis values as high as $K = 20$. The bootstrap appears to yield conservative error rates in small samples (e.g., type I error rates of 1% with $N = 100$), which suggests that the likelihood ratio test may lack power. However, studies have yet to examine this issue.

## 5.12 DATA ANALYSIS EXAMPLE 1

Recall from Chapter 4 that the EM algorithm does not require the computation of first or second derivatives, so many software packages do not report standard errors from an EM analysis. The first analysis example illustrates how to use bootstrap resampling to generate standard errors for EM estimates of a mean vector, covariance matrix, and a correlation matrix.* The data for this analysis are comprised of scores from 480 employees on eight work-related variables: gender, age, job tenure, IQ, psychological well-being, job satisfaction, job performance, and turnover intentions. I generated these data to mimic the correlation structure of published research articles in the management and psychology literature (e.g., Wright & Bonett, 2007; Wright, Cropanzano, & Bonett, 2007). The data have three missing data patterns, each of which is consists of one-third of the sample. The first pattern comprises cases with complete data, and the remaining two patterns have missing data on either well-being or job satisfaction. These patterns mimic a situation in which the data are missing by design (e.g., to reduce the cost of data collection).

I previously reported the EM parameter estimates in Table 4.12. I implemented the bootstrap procedure by drawing 2,000 samples of $N = 480$ with replacement from the job performance data set. Next, I performed an EM analysis on each bootstrap sample and saved the parameter estimates to a data file for further analysis. Finally, I generated standard errors

---

*Analysis syntax and data are available on the companion website, *www.appliedmissingdata.com*.

**TABLE 5.5. EM Covariance Matrix and Bootstrap Standard Errors from Data Analysis Example 1**

| Variable | 1 | 2 | 3 | 4 | 5 | 6 | 7 | 8 |
|---|---|---|---|---|---|---|---|---|
| | | | | EM covariance matrix | | | | |
| 1: Age | 28.908 | | | | | | | |
| 2: Tenure | 8.459 | 9.735 | | | | | | |
| 3: Female | −0.028 | −0.052 | 0.248 | | | | | |
| 4: Well-being | 1.148 | 0.569 | 0.067 | 1.382 | | | | |
| 5: Satisfaction | 0.861 | 0.565 | 0.028 | 0.446 | 1.386 | | | |
| 6: Performance | −0.330 | 0.061 | −0.009 | 0.671 | 0.271 | 1.570 | | |
| 7: Turnover | −0.377 | 0.016 | 0.001 | −0.141 | −0.129 | −0.203 | 0.218 | |
| 8: IQ | 0.674 | 0.026 | 0.284 | 2.876 | 4.074 | 4.496 | −0.706 | 70.892 |
| | | | | Bootstrap standard errors | | | | |
| 1: Age | 1.828 | | | | | | | |
| 2: Tenure | 0.823 | 0.630 | | | | | | |
| 3: Female | 0.121 | 0.070 | 0.002 | | | | | |
| 4: Well-being | 0.320 | 0.192 | 0.032 | 0.108 | | | | |
| 5: Satisfaction | 0.307 | 0.198 | 0.032 | 0.092 | 0.099 | | | |
| 6: Performance | 0.302 | 0.170 | 0.028 | 0.084 | 0.079 | 0.100 | | |
| 7: Turnover | 0.113 | 0.068 | 0.011 | 0.029 | 0.028 | 0.026 | 0.008 | |
| 8: IQ | 2.166 | 1.278 | 0.195 | 0.565 | 0.597 | 0.534 | 0.177 | 5.255 |

*Note.* Elements in **bold** typeface are statistically significant at the .05 level because the estimated divided by its standard error exceeds ± 1.96.

by computing the standard deviation of each parameter estimate across the 2,000 samples. This process sounds tedious and time consuming, but it took less than two minutes on a laptop computer. Table 5.5 shows the EM covariance matrix estimates from Chapter 4 along with the bootstrap standard errors. I computed test statistics for each covariance term by dividing the parameter estimate by its bootstrap standard error. If the empirical sampling distributions are relatively normal, it is reasonable to compare these tests to a critical $z$ value from the unit normal table. The table denotes the statistically significant estimates (i.e., the estimates for which the $z$ test exceeded the two-tailed critical value of ± 1.96) in **bold** typeface.

## 5.13 DATA ANALYSIS EXAMPLE 2

The second analysis example uses maximum likelihood to estimate a multiple regression model with auxiliary variables.* The analysis uses the same employee data set as the first example and involves the regression of job performance ratings on psychological well-being and job satisfaction, as follows:

$$JP_i = \hat{\beta}_0 + \hat{\beta}_1(WB_i) + \hat{\beta}_2(SAT_i) + \varepsilon$$

*Analysis syntax and data are available on the companion website, *www.appliedmissingdata.com*.

**TABLE 5.6. Regression Model Estimates from Data Analysis Example 2**

| Parameter | Estimate | SE | $z$ |
|---|---|---|---|
| Maximum likelihood (auxiliary variables) | | | |
| $\beta_0$ (Intercept) | 6.020 | 0.053 | 114.642 |
| $\beta_1$ (Well-being) | 0.475 | 0.054 | 8.798 |
| $\beta_2$ (Satisfaction) | 0.035 | 0.058 | 0.605 |
| $\hat{\sigma}_e^2$ (Residual) | 1.241 | 0.086 | 14.369 |
| $R^2$ | .210 | | |
| Maximum likelihood (no auxiliary variables) | | | |
| $\beta_0$ (Intercept) | 6.021 | 0.053 | 113.123 |
| $\beta_1$ (Well-being) | 0.476 | 0.055 | 8.664 |
| $\beta_2$ (Satisfaction) | 0.027 | 0.060 | 0.445 |
| $\hat{\sigma}_e^2$ (Residual) | 1.243 | 0.087 | 14.356 |
| $R^2$ | .208 | | |

*Note.* Predictors were centered at the maximum likelihood estimates of the mean.

I used Graham's (2003) saturated correlates approach to incorporate IQ and turnover intentions (a binary variable) as auxiliary variables in the regression model. The path diagram for this analysis is identical to that in Figure 5.2. I chose IQ and turnover intentions as auxiliary variables because they had the strongest correlations with the regression model variables (correlations ranged between 0.30 and 0.40). In practice, stronger correlations would be better, but these were the strongest associations in the data. Because the data are MCAR, the auxiliary variables should have minimal impact on the parameter estimates, but they can provide a slight increase in power.

Researchers typically begin a regression analysis by examining the omnibus $F$ test. In Chapter 4, I illustrated how to use the likelihood ratio statistic to perform a test of the regression coefficients. Because the addition of auxiliary variables does not affect this procedure, there is no need to illustrate the test here. Table 5.6 gives the regression model parameter estimates along with those from a maximum likelihood analysis with no auxiliary variables. I omit the estimates from the auxiliary variable portion of the model (e.g., the correlations between the auxiliary variables and the predictors) because they are not of substantive interest. As seen in the table, the parameter estimates from the saturated correlates model are virtually identical to those from Chapter 4. The analysis results suggest that psychological well-being was a significant predictor of job performance, $\hat{\beta}_1 = 0.475$, $z = 8.798$, $p < .001$, but job satisfaction was not, $\hat{\beta}_2 = 0.035$, $z = 0.605$, $p = .55$. Although the effect is subtle, the estimates from the saturated correlates model have slightly smaller standard errors and slightly larger $z$ statistics, indicating that the auxiliary variables produced a slight increase in power. Auxiliary variables with stronger correlations would have produced more noticeable gains.

## 5.14 DATA ANALYSIS EXAMPLE 3

The final example is a confirmatory factor analysis that illustrates the use of auxiliary variables and the corrective procedures for nonnormal data.* The analyses use artificial data from a questionnaire on eating disorder risk. Briefly, the data contain the responses from 400 college-aged women on 10 questions from the Eating Attitudes Test (EAT; Garner, Olmsted, Bohr, & Garfinkel, 1982), a widely used measure of eating disorder risk. The 10 questions measure two constructs, Drive for Thinness (e.g., "I avoid eating when I'm hungry") and Food Preoccupation (e.g., "I find myself preoccupied with food"), and mimic the two-factor structure proposed by Doninger, Enders, and Burnett (2005). The data set also contains an anxiety scale score, a variable that measures beliefs about Western standards of beauty (e.g., high scores indicate that respondents internalize a thin ideal of beauty), and body mass index (BMI) values. I generated the EAT questionnaire items to have discrete 7-point scales with positive skewness and kurtosis (e.g., skewness values typically ranged between 0.50 and 1.00, and kurtosis values of 1.00 were the norm). Inasmuch as the methodological literature has established that nonnormal data can bias standard errors and distort the likelihood ratio test, one of the goals of this analysis example is to illustrate how to correct for these problems.

Variables in the EAT data set are missing for a variety of reasons. I simulated MCAR data by randomly deleting scores from the anxiety variable, the Western standards of beauty scale, and two of the EAT questions ($EAT_2$ and $EAT_{21}$). It seems reasonable to expect a relationship between body weight and missingness, so I created MAR data on five variables ($EAT_1$, $EAT_{10}$, $EAT_{12}$, $EAT_{18}$, and $EAT_{24}$) by deleting the EAT scores for a subset of cases in both tails of the BMI distribution. These same EAT questions were also missing for individuals with elevated anxiety scores. Finally, I introduced a small amount of MNAR data by deleting a number of the high body mass index scores (e.g., to mimic a situation where females with high BMI values refuse to be weighed). The deletion process typically produced a missing data rate of 5 to 10% on each variable.

This analysis used the same two-factor model as the example in Chapter 4, but it included three auxiliary variables: body mass index, anxiety, and beliefs about Western standards of beauty. Figure 5.6 shows a path diagram of the model. Notice that the saturated correlates model includes all possible correlations among the auxiliary variables as well as all possible correlations between the auxiliary variables and the manifest variable residuals (the auxiliary variables do not correlate with the latent factors). The two-factor model fit the data reasonably well according to conventional standards (Hu & Bentler, 1998, 1999), $\chi^2(34) = 49.044$, $p = .046$, RMSEA = 0.033, SRMR = 0.026. It is worth reiterating that the auxiliary variables do not affect the degrees of freedom for the model fit statistic because the auxiliary variable portion of the model includes all possible associations between the auxiliary variables and the manifest indicators (i.e., the auxiliary variable portion of the model is saturated).

One consequence of non-normal data is that the likelihood ratio test no longer follows the appropriate central chi-square distribution. I used the rescaling procedure and the

---

*Analysis syntax and data are available on the companion website, *www.appliedmissingdata.com.*

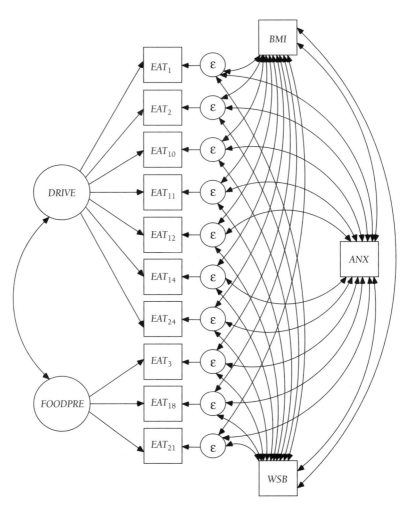

**FIGURE 5.6.** The Eating Attitudes Test CFA model with three auxiliary variables. Note that DRIVE = drive for thinness; FOODPRE = food preoccupation; BMI = body mass index; ANX = anxiety; WSB = Western standards of beauty. The saturated correlates model specifies correlations among the auxiliary variables and correlations between the auxiliary variables and the residual terms of the manifest indicators.

Bollen–Stine bootstrap to correct for bias in the likelihood ratio test (i.e., the chi-square test of model fit). In practice, there is no reason to implement both procedures, but I do so here for illustration purposes. To begin, the rescaled likelihood ratio test requires a scaling factor that pools information from the factor analysis model (i.e., the restricted model) and a saturated model that specifies all possible associations among the manifest variables (i.e., the full model). The two-factor model with 70 parameters produced a log-likelihood value and a scaling factor of $\log L_{\text{Restricted}} = -6957.674$ and $c_{\text{Restricted}} = 1.084$, respectively. The corresponding values from the saturated model with 104 parameters were $\log L_{\text{Full}} = -6933.152$ and $c_{\text{Full}} = 1.088$, respectively. Substituting these values into Equation 5.15 yields a scaling factor of $c_{\text{LR}} = 1.095$. Finally, dividing the likelihood ratio test by its scaling factor gives the rescaled test statistic, $\text{LR}_{\text{RS}} = 44.796$, and referencing this test to a central chi-square distribution with

34 degrees of freedom produces a probability value of $p = .102$. Notice that the rescaled test statistic is somewhat smaller than the original likelihood ratio test (LR = 49.044, $p = .046$) and is no longer statistically significant. Because the data are slightly leptokurtic, the downward adjustment in the test statistic makes intuitive sense.

The rescaling procedure transforms the likelihood test to more closely approximate the appropriate theoretical chi-square distribution. In contrast, the Bollen–Stine bootstrap leaves the likelihood ratio statistic intact and constructs a new empirical reference distribution. The null hypothesis for the likelihood ratio test states that the restricted model (i.e., the factor model) is true in the population, so the Bollen–Stine procedure transforms the sample data to have a perfect fit to the two-factor model. This transformation requires the mean vector and the covariance matrix from the sample data as well as the model-implied mean vector and covariance matrix from the factor analysis. These quantities are standard output in structural equation modeling packages. After applying the Bollen–Stine transformation, I drew 2,000 samples of N = 400 (the original sample size) with replacement from the transformed data set. Next, I used maximum likelihood missing data handling to estimate both models and saved the likelihood ratio statistic from each bootstrap sample.

Figure 5.7 shows the empirical sampling distribution of the likelihood ratio test along with the theoretical sampling distribution of a chi-square statistic with 34 degrees of freedom. For comparison purposes, the figure also shows the empirical sampling distribution for 2,000 naïve bootstrap samples. I previously explained that the naïve bootstrap is inappropriate because it yields a distribution that reflects natural sampling fluctuation as well as model misfit. The fact that the naïve sampling distribution is centered on an inappropriately large chi-square value illustrates this point. In contrast, the Bollen–Stine sampling distribution is unaffected by model misfit and reflects the sampling fluctuation of the likelihood ratio test

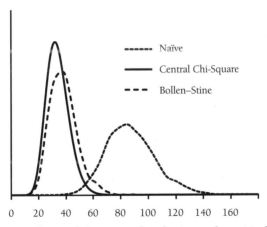

**FIGURE 5.7.** The theoretical central chi-square distribution and empirical sampling distributions of the likelihood ratio test generated from the Bollen–Stine bootstrap and naïve bootstrap. The naïve sampling distribution is centered on an inappropriately large chi-square value because it reflects natural sampling fluctuation as well as model misfit. In contrast, the Bollen–Stine sampling distribution is unaffected by model misfit and reflects the sampling fluctuation of the likelihood ratio test with nonnormal data. The Bollen–Stine distribution has a slightly thicker tail than the theoretical chi-square distribution, which is a result of the leptokurtic data.

with nonnormal data. The Bollen–Stine distribution has a slightly thicker tail than the theoretical chi-square distribution, which makes sense given that the data are slightly leptokurtic.

Next, I obtained an adjusted probability value for the likelihood ratio test by computing the proportion of test statistics from the Bollen–Stine sampling distribution that were equal to or greater than the value of the original likelihood ratio statistic. The Bollen–Stine probability value is $p = .208$, which means that 416 of the 2,000 bootstrap samples produced a test statistic that was equal to or greater than LR = 49.044. Visually, this probability value is the area under the Bollen–Stine sampling distribution that falls to the right of 49.044. You can see that this area is larger than that of the central chi-square distribution, which explains why the probability value increased from $p = .046$ to $p = .208$.

Incorporating auxiliary variables into a structural equation model yields invalid incremental (i.e., comparative) fit indices because the auxiliary variables inappropriately penalize the fit of the independence model. Earlier in the chapter, I illustrated how to remedy this problem by estimating a special independence model. The correct independence model for this analysis estimates the variances of the manifest variables, constrains the covariances among the manifest variables to zero, estimates the covariances between the auxiliary variables and the manifest variables, and estimates the covariances among the auxiliary variables. Estimating the modified independence model yields a likelihood ratio test of $LR_I = 1956.345$ with $df_I = 45$. Substituting these values into Equation 5.1 gives corrected CFI value of 0.993, as follows:

$$CFI = \frac{(1956.345 - 45) - (49.044 - 34)}{(1956.345 - 45)} = 0.993$$

The new CFI value is virtually identical to the incorrect value from the original analysis, but this will not always be the case. Although I only illustrate the correction to the CFI, the same corrective procedure applies to other incremental fit indices (e.g., the TLI, NFI).

Turning to the parameter estimates, note that Table 5.7 gives the factor loadings from the saturated correlates model along with those from a corresponding analysis with no auxiliary variables. I constrained the factor variances to unity in order to identify the model, so that the loadings reflect the expected change in the EAT item for a one-standard-deviation increase in the latent factor. Unlike the factor analysis from Chapter 4, this analysis satisfies the MAR assumption because the "causes" of missing data (i.e., body mass index and anxiety) appear as auxiliary variables in the model. Interestingly, the two sets of factor loadings in Table 5.7 are quite similar, so the addition of the auxiliary variables did little to change these estimates. Although not shown in the table, the auxiliary variable model did produce measurement intercepts (i.e., item means) that more closely resembled those of the complete data. The body mass index and anxiety variables have relatively modest correlations with the EAT questionnaire items. The impact of these auxiliary variables would therefore have been more pronounced had these correlations been stronger in magnitude.

The standard errors are of particular interest because non-normal data can distort these values. Table 5.7 shows the normal-theory standard errors along with those of the sandwich estimator and the naïve bootstrap. As seen in the table, the normal-theory standard errors were generally lower than the robust standard errors and the bootstrap standard errors. Lep-

**TABLE 5.7. Confirmatory Factor Analysis Loading Estimates from Data Analysis Example 3**

| EAT Item | No auxiliary | | Saturated correlates model | | | |
|---|---|---|---|---|---|---|
| | Estimate | SE | Estimate | SE | $SE_R$ | $SE_{BS}$ |
| $EAT_1$ | 0.741 | 0.050 | 0.741 | 0.050 | 0.049 | 0.048 |
| $EAT_2$ | 0.650 | 0.045 | 0.649 | 0.045 | 0.050 | 0.050 |
| $EAT_{10}$ | 0.807 | 0.043 | 0.808 | 0.043 | 0.052 | 0.053 |
| $EAT_{11}$ | 0.764 | 0.040 | 0.764 | 0.040 | 0.049 | 0.049 |
| $EAT_{12}$ | 0.662 | 0.047 | 0.662 | 0.047 | 0.055 | 0.056 |
| $EAT_{14}$ | 0.901 | 0.041 | 0.901 | 0.041 | 0.047 | 0.048 |
| $EAT_{24}$ | 0.623 | 0.048 | 0.622 | 0.048 | 0.053 | 0.053 |
| $EAT_3$ | 0.772 | 0.046 | 0.772 | 0.046 | 0.052 | 0.052 |
| $EAT_{18}$ | 0.749 | 0.048 | 0.751 | 0.048 | 0.056 | 0.056 |
| $EAT_{21}$ | 0.862 | 0.045 | 0.862 | 0.046 | 0.053 | 0.053 |

*Note. $SE_R$ = robust standard errors; $SE_{BS}$ = bootstrap standard errors.*

tokurtic data tend to attenuate standard errors, so these differences make sense. The limited research to date suggests that significance tests based on robust standard errors may be slightly conservative (i.e., standard errors are a bit too large), whereas bootstrap significance tests may be slightly liberal (i.e., standard errors are a bit too small). However, the difference between the two procedures is often trivial, and both approaches provide a rather dramatic improvement over standard errors that assume normality (Enders, 2001).

## 5.15 SUMMARY

This chapter describes techniques that can improve the accuracy of maximum likelihood missing data handling. The first half of the chapter is devoted to the use of auxiliary variables. The definition of MAR states that the probability of missing data on a variable $Y$ can relate to some other measured variable (or variables) but not to the values of $Y$ itself. Although this definition seems to be satisfied when a correlate of missingness is a variable in the data set, the variables in the analysis dictate the missing data mechanism. For this reason, methodologists recommend an inclusive analysis strategy that incorporates a number of auxiliary variables. An auxiliary variable is one that is ancillary to the substantive research questions but is a potential correlate of missingness or a correlate of the missing variable. Including auxiliary variables in a maximum likelihood analysis can reduce or eliminate bias (e.g., by making the MAR assumption more plausible) and can increase in power (e.g., by recapturing some of the lost information in the missing variable).

Two strategies can be used for implementing an inclusive analysis strategy: the saturated correlates model and the two-stage analysis procedure. The saturated correlates model uses structural equation modeling software to incorporate auxiliary variables as correlates of the analysis variables. A set of rules guide the specification of the model, and the basic idea behind these rules is to transmit the information from the auxiliary variables to the analysis model without affecting the interpretation of the parameters. The two-stage approach is an alternative to the saturated correlates model that deals with missing data in two steps: the first stage uses maximum likelihood missing data handling to estimate the mean vector and covariance matrix, and the second stage uses the resulting estimates as input data for subsequent analyses. The advantage of the two-stage approach is that it can readily incorporate any number of auxiliary variables into the first step of the procedure, so there is no need to include the auxiliary variables in the subsequent analysis step. The problem with the two-stage approach is that it requires complex standard error computations that have not yet been implemented in computer software programs. However, given the ease with which the two-stage approach incorporates auxiliary variables, it will likely become a viable alternative to the saturated correlates model in the near future.

The second half of the chapter is devoted to corrective procedures for nonnormal data. Maximum likelihood estimation relies heavily on the multivariate normality assumption, both for identifying the most likely parameter values and for computing standard errors. The methodological literature shows that non-normal data tend to have a minimal impact on the parameter estimates themselves but can bias standard errors and distort the likelihood ratio test. This chapter outlined two strategies for correcting the bias in standard errors, the so-called sandwich estimator (i.e., "robust" standard errors) and bootstrap resampling. With non-normal data, the second derivative formulas from the normal distribution are missing terms that depend on the skewness and kurtosis of the population distribution. The absence of these terms can overestimate or underestimate the standard errors, depending on whether the data are leptokurtic or platykurtic. Robust standard errors correct this problem by using a "sandwich" of terms that involve first and second derivatives. In contrast, bootstrap resampling uses Monte Carlo simulations to generate standard errors. The basic idea behind the bootstrap is to treat the sample data as a miniature population and draw repeated samples of size $N$ from the sample data set. Estimating the analysis model from the bootstrap samples yields an empirical sampling distribution for each parameter, the standard deviation of which estimates the standard error.

Non-normal data can also distort the likelihood ratio test. The basic problem with the test is that its sampling distribution no longer follows the appropriate central chi-square distribution. One solution is to rescale the test statistic so that it more closely approximates its theoretical chi-square distribution. This rescaling procedure divides the normal-theory likelihood ratio test by a correction factor that depends on the kurtosis of the data. The scaling factor can increase or decrease the value of the likelihood ratio test, depending on the distribution shape of the data. The Bollen–Stine bootstrap is a second method that can correct the bias in the likelihood ratio test. Whereas the rescaling procedure attempts to adjust the value of the likelihood ratio test so that it more closely approximates its theoretical sampling distribution, the bootstrap leaves the test statistic intact and uses Monte Carlo simulation to generate a new sampling distribution. The bootstrap corrects the probability value for the test by referencing the likelihood ratio statistic to the empirical sampling distribution rather than to the theoretical chi-square distribution. Although the Bollen–Stine bootstrap follows the same procedure as the naïve bootstrap, it applies an algebraic transformation to the sample data prior to drawing the samples. This transformation aligns the mean and covariance structure of the data to the null hypothesis and produces an empirical distribution that reflects only the sampling fluctuation of the likelihood ratio test.

The next chapter takes a break from missing data issues and provides an introduction to Bayesian estimation. Chapters 7 through 9 focus on a second "modern" missing data technique, multiple imputation. The mathematical machinery behind multiple imputation is heavily entrenched in Bayesian methodology. At one level, you can effectively implement multiple imputation in your own research without fully understanding its Bayesian underpinnings. However, understanding multiple imputation at a deeper level requires a background in Bayesian statistics; accessing the seminal missing data work can be difficult without this knowledge. The purpose of Chapter 6 is to provide a user-friendly introduction to Bayesian statistics, while still providing a level of detail that will serve as a springboard for accessing the technically oriented missing data literature.

## 5.16 RECOMMENDED READINGS

Bollen, K. A. & Stine, R. A. (1992). Bootstrapping goodness-of-fit measures in structural equation models. *Sociological Methods and Research*, *21*, 205–229.

Collins, L. M., Schafer, J. L, & Kam, C-M. (2001). A comparison of inclusive and restrictive strategies in modern missing data procedures. *Psychological Methods*, *6*, 330–351.

Finney, S. J., & DiStefano, C. (2006). Nonnormal and categorical data in structural equation models. In G. R. Hancock & R. O. Mueller (Eds.), *A second course in structural equation modeling* (pp. 269–314). Greenwich, CT: Information Age.

Freedman, D. A. (2006). On the so-called "Huber sandwich estimator" and "robust standard errors." *The American Statistician*, *60*, 299–302.

Graham, J. W. (2003). Adding missing-data relevant variables to FIML-based structural equation models. *Structural Equation Modeling: A Multidisciplinary Journal*, *10*, 80–100.

Yuan, K-H., Bentler, P. M., & Zhang, W. (2005). The effect of skewness and kurtosis on mean and covariance structure analysis: The univariate case and its multivariate implication. *Sociological Methods and Research*, *24*, 240–258.

# 6

# An Introduction to Bayesian Estimation

## 6.1 CHAPTER OVERVIEW

Chapter 7 introduces a second "modern" missing data approach, multiple imputation. Multiple imputation generates several copies of the data set and fills in (i.e., imputes) each copy with different estimates of the missing values. The imputation process is conceptually straightforward because it closely resembles the stochastic regression procedure from Chapter 2 (i.e., impute missing values with predicted scores and add a random residual to each imputed value). However, the mathematical machinery behind multiple imputation is heavily entrenched in Bayesian methodology. At one level, it is possible to effectively implement multiple imputation in a research study without fully understanding its Bayesian underpinnings. For example, multiple imputation software packages employ default settings that make Bayesian aspects of the analysis transparent to the user, and many multiple imputation primers make little to no reference to Bayesian methodology (Allison, 2002; Enders, 2006; Schafer & Graham, 2001; Schafer & Olsen, 1998; Sinharay, Stern, & Russell, 2001). However, understanding multiple imputation at a deeper level requires a background in Bayesian statistics, and accessing the seminal missing data work (Little & Rubin, 2002; Rubin, 1987; Schafer, 1997) can be difficult without this knowledge.

This chapter takes a hiatus from missing data issues to focus on Bayesian estimation. The goal of the chapter is to provide a user-friendly introduction to Bayesian statistics, while still providing a level of detail that will serve as a springboard for accessing the technically oriented missing data literature. The chapter is far from comprehensive, and I focus on aspects of Bayesian estimation that are particularly relevant to a multiple imputation analysis. A number of comprehensive resources are available in the literature (e.g., Bolstad, 2007; Gelman, Carlin, Stern, & Rubin, 1995), as are additional primer articles (e.g., Lee & Wagenmakers, 2005; Pruzek, 1997; Rupp, Dey, & Zumbo, 2004; Stephenson & Stern, 1998).

## 6.2 WHAT MAKES BAYESIAN STATISTICS DIFFERENT?

The definition of a parameter is a key distinction between Bayesian estimation and the so-called **frequentist paradigm** that is the predominant approach to estimation and significance testing in many disciplines (e.g., psychology, education, business). The frequentist approach defines a parameter as a fixed characteristic of the population. The goal of a frequentist analysis is to estimate *the* true value of the parameter and establish a confidence interval around that estimate. The standard error is integral to this process and estimates the variability of the estimate across repeated samples. Defining a parameter as a fixed quantity leads to some important subtleties. For example, consider the interpretation of a 95% confidence interval. It is incorrect to say that there is a 95% probability that the parameter falls between values of A and B because the confidence interval from any single sample contains the parameter or it does not. Instead, the confidence interval describes the expected performance of the interval across repeated samples. For example, if you drew 100 samples from a population and constructed a 95% confidence interval around the parameter estimate from each sample, you would expect 95 of the intervals to include the population parameter. In a similar vein, the probability value from a frequentist significance test describes the proportion of repeated samples that would yield a test statistic equal to or greater than that of the data. In both situations, the probability statement applies to the *data*, not to the parameter.

In contrast, the **Bayesian paradigm** views a parameter as a random variable that has a distribution. One of the goals of a Bayesian analysis is to describe the shape of this distribution. For example, the mean and the standard deviation describe the distribution's center and spread, respectively. The mean quantifies the parameter's most likely value (assuming that the distribution is symmetric) and is similar to a frequentist point estimate. The standard deviation (or alternatively, the variance) is analogous to a frequentist standard error, but it describes the degree of uncertainty about the parameter after observing the data. The Bayesian notion of uncertainty does not involve repeated sampling. Viewing the parameter as a random variable contrasts the frequentist approach in other ways. For example, a Bayesian **credible interval** (the analog to a frequentist confidence interval) allows you to say that there is a 95% probability that the parameter falls between values of A and B. This interpretation is very different from that of the frequentist approach because it attaches the probability statement to the *parameter*, not to the data.

## 6.3 A CONCEPTUAL OVERVIEW OF BAYESIAN ESTIMATION

A Bayesian analysis consists of three major steps: (1) specify a prior distribution for the parameter of interest, (2) use a likelihood function to summarize the data's evidence about different parameter values, and (3) combine information from the prior distribution and the likelihood to generate a posterior distribution that describes the relative probability of different parameter values. Describing the shape of the posterior distribution is a key goal of a Bayesian analysis, and familiar statistics such as the mean and the variance summarize the location (i.e., the center of) and the spread of the posterior, respectively. This section gives a conceptual description of these three steps. Because the goal is to introduce the underlying

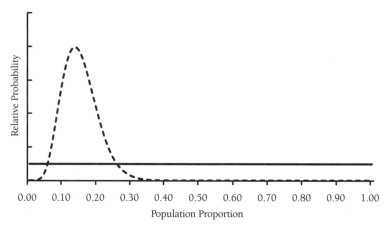

**FIGURE 6.1.** The prior distributions from the depression example. Researcher A's prior is the dashed curve that assigns higher probabilities to population proportions between 0.10 and 0.15. Researcher B's prior distribution is the solid line that assigns an equal weight to every parameter value.

logic behind Bayesian estimation, I am purposefully vague about many of the mathematical details. For now, I use a straightforward univariate analysis example where the goal is to estimate the proportion of clinically depressed individuals in a population. Subsequent sections, however, give a more thorough description of the mathematics and illustrate the application of Bayesian estimation to a mean vector and a covariance matrix (the key parameters in a multiple imputation analysis). As you will see, multivariate analyses use the same three-step procedure described in this section.

## The Prior Distribution

The first step in a Bayesian analysis is to specify a prior distribution for the parameter of interest. The **prior distribution** describes your subjective beliefs about the relative probability of different parameter values before collecting any data. To illustrate, suppose that two researchers want to use Bayesian methodology to estimate the proportion of clinically depressed individuals in a population, $\pi$. The prior distribution specifies the relative probability of every possible population proportion. After conducting a literature review, Researcher A believes that depression rates between 0.10 and 0.15 are very likely, and she feels that the relative probability rapidly decreases as the proportion approaches zero or one. The dashed curve in Figure 6.1 depicts this researcher's prior beliefs. Notice that the highest point of the distribution is located at $\pi = 0.13$, and the relative probability (i.e., the height of the curve) quickly decreases as $\pi$ approaches zero or one. In contrast, Researcher B is uncomfortable speculating about different parameter values, so he assigns an equal weight to every proportion between zero and one. The flat line in Figure 6.1 depicts this researcher's prior beliefs. The Bayesian literature often refers to Researcher B's prior distribution as a **noninformative prior** because it represents a lack of knowledge about the population parameter.

## The Likelihood Function

The second step of a Bayesian analysis is to collect data and use a **likelihood function** to summarize the data's evidence about different parameter values. This step applies the maximum

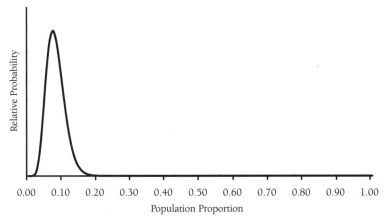

**FIGURE 6.2.** The binomial likelihood function from the depression example. The height of the likelihood function gives the relative probability that the population on the horizontal axis would produce a sample where 7 out of 100 individuals are diagnosed with depression. The maximum of the function (i.e., the maximum likelihood estimate) corresponds with $\pi = 0.07$, which is the sample proportion.

likelihood principles that I outlined in Chapter 3, but uses the likelihood rather than the log-likelihood. Recall from Chapter 3 that substituting the data and a parameter value into a probability density function (e.g., the equation that defines the normal curve) returns the likelihood (i.e., relative probability) of the data, given that particular parameter value. Repeating this process for different parameter values yields a likelihood function that describes the relative probability of the data across a range of parameter values.

For example, suppose that the two researchers drew a sample and found that 7 out of the 100 individuals whom they assessed met their criteria for clinical depression. The binomial density function is the appropriate likelihood for a binary outcome variable. The binomial density function is quite different from that of the normal curve in Chapter 3, but it works in the same way. Specifically, you substitute the data (e.g., 7 out of 100 diagnosed cases) and a population proportion (e.g., $\pi = 0.15$) into the density function, and the equation returns the likelihood of observing the sample data from a population with that particular prevalence rate. Repeating the computations using different population proportions yields a likelihood function that shows how the probability of the data varies as a function of $\pi$. For example, Figure 6.2 shows the binomial likelihood function for the depression data. Notice that the maximum likelihood estimate (i.e., the highest point on the function) is the sample proportion, $\hat{\pi} = .07$.

## The Posterior Distribution

The final step of a Bayesian analysis is to define the posterior distribution of the parameter. The **posterior distribution** is a composite distribution that combines information from the prior and the likelihood to generate an updated set of relative probabilities. I describe the posterior in more detail later in the chapter, but the basic idea is to weight each point on the likelihood function by the magnitude of your prior beliefs. For example, if you attached a high prior probability to a particular parameter value, the posterior would increase the height of the likelihood function at that point on the horizontal axis. Conversely, if you assigned a low prior probability to a particular parameter value, the posterior would decrease the height of the likelihood function at that point.

To illustrate, reconsider the depression scenario. Prior to collecting data, Researcher A assigned a high probability to depression rates between 0.10 and 0.15. The data supported somewhat lower values and indicated that $\pi = 0.07$ is the most likely population proportion. Figure 6.3 shows Researcher A's posterior distribution as a dashed line. The effect is subtle, but her posterior distribution is a blend of her prior and the likelihood function. For reasons that I explain later, the solid line in Figure 6.3 (Researcher B's posterior distribution) is identical to the likelihood function. Comparing the relative height of the two curves at $\pi = 0.05$, you can see that Researcher A's posterior distribution is less elevated than the likelihood function. Researcher A assigned a very low prior probability to $\pi = 0.05$, which effectively downweights the likelihood function at that point. Next, compare the relative height of the two distributions at $\pi = .15$. Researcher A assigned a high prior probability to this parameter value, so her posterior distribution is slightly elevated relative to the likelihood function (i.e., the prior probability boosts this point on the likelihood function). In contrast, Researcher B specified a prior distribution where every parameter value has the same probability. Consequently, his posterior distribution weights every point on the likelihood function by the same amount and is identical to the likelihood function in Figure 6.2.

Summarizing the shape of the posterior distribution is an important part of a Bayesian analysis. Without delving into any equations, Researcher A's posterior distribution has a mean of 0.095, a mode of 0.090, and a standard deviation of 0.024. In contrast, Researcher B's posterior has a mean of 0.078, a mode of 0.070, and a standard deviation of 0.026. The fact that Researcher A's distribution has somewhat higher measures of central tendency follows from the fact that she assigned high prior probabilities to proportions between 0.10 and

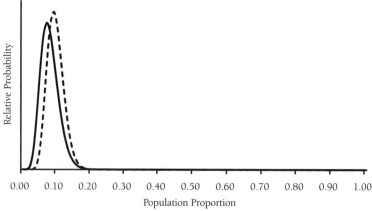

**FIGURE 6.3.** The posterior distributions from the depression example. Researcher A's posterior distribution is the dashed curve. She specified a prior distribution that assigns higher weights to population proportions between 0.10 and 0.15. Consequently, her posterior distribution has shifted slightly to the right of the likelihood function in Figure 6.2. Researcher B's posterior distribution is the solid curve. He specified a prior distribution where every parameter value has the same probability, so his posterior distribution is identical to the likelihood.

0.15. Nevertheless, the relative similarity of the two sets of summary statistics is noteworthy, particularly given that the researchers adopted radically different prior distributions.

For comparison purposes, a frequentist analysis of the depression data yields a point estimate and standard error of $\hat{\pi} = 0.07$ and $SE = 0.026$, respectively. Notice that these estimates are identical to Researcher B's posterior mode and posterior standard deviation. Although the Bayesian and frequentist analyses give the same numeric results, they have very different interpretations. For example, $\hat{\pi}$ estimates *the* true population proportion, and the standard error quantifies the variability of the point estimate across repeated samples. In contrast, the posterior mode is the most likely value from a distribution of proportions, and the posterior standard deviation quantifies the spread of the parameter distribution.

## More on the Prior Distribution

A Bayesian analysis uses the prior distribution to incorporate subjective beliefs as a data source. This may be troublesome to researchers who are accustomed to the frequentist paradigm, but the idea of using prior information actually makes good intuitive sense. For example, suppose that a researcher had access to a meta-analysis prior to designing a study. Meta-analyses estimate the average effect size in a body of research and often summarize the variability of the effect across different design characteristics (e.g., Ioannidis et al., 2001; Lipsey & Wilson, 1993; Rubin, 1992). The Bayesian approach provides a mechanism for incorporating prior knowledge into an analysis (e.g., by using the meta-analysis to formulate a prior distribution), whereas frequentist estimation essentially ignores the fact that previous studies even exist. In the frequentist paradigm, the benefit of having a meta-analysis is limited to estimating power, determining sample size, and formulating a directional hypothesis.

If the notion of using prior information as a data source still feels uncomfortable, there is one final consideration. The depression example did not illustrate this point, but it ends up that you can specify the amount of influence that the prior exerts on the analysis results. Specifying a prior distribution generally requires three pieces of information: the location of the distribution (e.g., its mean), the spread of the distribution (e.g., its standard deviation), and the number of "hypothetical data points" associated with the prior. Collectively, Bayesian texts sometimes refer to these characteristics as the distribution's **hyperparameters**. Importantly, you can use the sample size metric to quantify the prior distribution's influence. For example, if you have relatively little confidence in the prior distribution, you can assign a small number of imaginary data points to the prior. In contrast, you can assign a large number of data points to the distribution if you are very confident in your prior beliefs.

Returning to the depression example, note that the researchers' prior distributions have very different hyperparameters. The two distributions in Figure 6.1 are shaped quite differently, which implies that they differ with respect to their location and spread. However, the fact that the prior distributions imply different sample sizes is not so obvious. Without going into the mathematical details, Researcher A's prior distribution (i.e., the dashed curve) assigns a weight that is equivalent to approximately 45 imaginary data points. Because the prior is contributing roughly half as much information as the data, the resulting posterior distribution is a blend of the prior and the likelihood function. In contrast, Researcher B's noninformative prior distribution contributes nothing to the estimation process, so his posterior distribution has the same shape as the likelihood function, and his posterior mode is identical to the sample proportion. In general, adopting a noninformative prior yields a posterior distribution that is defined solely by the data. This is an important point that will be revisited in this chapter and the next.

## 6.4 BAYES' THEOREM

This section fills in some of the mathematical details omitted from the previous depression example. As you will see, Bayes' theorem is the mathematical machinery behind a Bayesian analysis and plays a key role in defining the shape of the posterior distribution. In fact, the three steps in a Bayesian analysis (i.e., specify a prior, estimate the likelihood, define the posterior) are terms in the theorem equation.

Bayes' theorem describes the relationship between two conditional probabilities. For two random events, $A$ and $B$, the theorem is

$$p(B|A) = \frac{p(B)p(A|B)}{p(A)} \tag{6.1}$$

where $p(B|A)$ is the conditional probability of observing event $B$, given that event $A$ has already occurred, $p(A|B)$ is the conditional probability of $A$ given $B$, $p(B)$ is the probability of $B$ alone, and $p(A)$ is the marginal probability of $A$.

The generic notation in Equation 6.1 offers little insight into the application of Bayes' theorem to statistics, but the linkage becomes slightly clearer if you replace $A$ with the sample data and $B$ with a parameter, as follows.

$$p(\theta|Y) = \frac{p(\theta)p(Y|\theta)}{p(Y)} \tag{6.2}$$

The terms in Equation 6.2 now align with the concepts that I introduced in the previous section. Specifically, $\theta$ is the parameter of interest (e.g., the proportion of clinically depressed individuals), $Y$ is the sample data, $p(\theta)$ is the parameter's prior distribution, $p(Y|\theta)$ is the likelihood (i.e., the conditional probability of the data, given some assumed value of $\theta$), $p(Y)$ is the marginal distribution of the data, and $p(\theta|Y)$ is the posterior distribution (i.e., the conditional probability of the parameter, given the data).

In words, Bayes' theorem is

$$\text{Posterior} = \frac{\text{Prior} \times \text{Likelihood}}{\text{Scaling factor}} \tag{6.3}$$

I previously described the posterior distribution as a weighted likelihood function, where the basic idea is to adjust each point on the likelihood function by the magnitude of the corresponding prior probability. This is accomplished in the numerator of Bayes' theorem by multiplying the likelihood function by the corresponding prior probabilities. As I explain later, the denominator of the theorem is simply a scaling constant that makes the area under the posterior distribution sum (i.e., integrate) to one. Dividing by a constant does not change the basic shape of the posterior distribution, so ignoring the denominator yields the following simplified expression.

$$\text{Posterior} \propto \text{Prior} \times \text{Likelihood} \tag{6.4}$$

Equation 6.4 says that *the posterior distribution is proportional to the prior distribution times the likelihood*. This is the fundamental idea behind Bayesian estimation and is a point that will resurface throughout the rest of the chapter.

## 6.5 AN ANALYSIS EXAMPLE

Having filled in some of the mathematical details, I return to the depression example and illustrate how Bayes' theorem applies to a statistical analysis. Again, the basic procedure that I describe in this section generalizes to multivariate estimation problems and to a multiple imputation analysis.

### The Prior Distribution

The first step of a Bayesian analysis is to specify a prior distribution. The prior distributions in Figure 6.1 belong to the **beta distribution** family (by family of distributions, I mean a collection of distributions that share the same basic shape or function, much like the *t*-distribution family). Like the normal curve, a probability density function defines the shape of the beta distribution. The beta density function is

$$p(\pi) \propto \pi^{a-1}(1-\pi)^{b-1} \tag{6.5}$$

where $p(\pi)$ is the height of the curve at a particular value of $\pi$, and $a$ and $b$ are constants that define the shape of the distribution (e.g., larger values of $a$ and $b$ produce a distribution with greater spread, and the distribution becomes asymmetric when $a \neq b$). Density functions typically contain a collection of scaling terms that make the area under the distribution sum to one. Excluding these terms has no bearing on the distribution's shape, so I omit the scaling factor from Equation 6.5 and use the "proportional to" symbol (i.e., $\propto$) to indicate that the two sides of the equation differ by a multiplicative constant. To simplify things, I use this convention throughout the chapter.

Returning to the depression example, note that Table 6.1 gives the height of the prior distributions at integer values of $\pi$ between 0.05 and 0.20. To begin, consider the height of Researcher A's prior distribution at $\pi = 0.05$ and $\pi = 0.10$. Her prior is a beta distribution with $a = 7$ and $b = 40$, so substituting $\pi = 0.05$ and $\pi = 0.10$ into the beta density function yields values of 0.792 and 6.153, respectively (note that I used the previously omitted scaling constant in these calculations). Visually, 0.792 and 6.153 represent the height of the prior distribution at parameter values of $\pi = 0.05$ and $\pi = 0.10$, respectively. Similar to the likelihood values from Chapter 3, you can think of these quantities as relative probabilities. The relative magnitude of the prior probabilities reflects Researcher A's belief that $\pi = 0.10$ was a more

**TABLE 6.1. Prior Distributions, Likelihood, and Posterior Distributions from the Depression Example**

| $\pi$ | Researcher A | | | | Researcher B | | | |
|---|---|---|---|---|---|---|---|---|
| | Prior | Likelihood | Prior × Likelihood | Scaled posterior | Prior | Likelihood | Prior × Likelihood | Scaled posterior |
| 0.05 | 0.7919 | 0.1060 | 0.0840 | 0.0036 | 1.0000 | 0.1060 | 0.1060 | 0.1169 |
| 0.06 | 1.5651 | 0.1420 | 0.2222 | 0.0190 | 1.0000 | 0.1420 | 0.1420 | 0.1565 |
| 0.07 | 2.6006 | 0.1545 | 0.4018 | 0.0570 | 1.0000 | 0.1545 | 0.1545 | 0.1703 |
| 0.08 | 3.8012 | 0.1440 | 0.5472 | 0.1134 | 1.0000 | 0.1440 | 0.1440 | 0.1587 |
| 0.09 | 5.0318 | 0.1188 | 0.5979 | 0.1640 | 1.0000 | 0.1188 | 0.1188 | 0.1310 |
| 0.10 | 6.1533 | 0.0889 | 0.5470 | 0.1835 | 1.0000 | 0.0889 | 0.0889 | 0.0980 |
| 0.11 | 7.0505 | 0.0613 | 0.4321 | 0.1661 | 1.0000 | 0.0613 | 0.0613 | 0.0675 |
| 0.12 | 7.6483 | 0.0394 | 0.3013 | 0.1257 | 1.0000 | 0.0394 | 0.0394 | 0.0434 |
| 0.13 | 7.9170 | 0.0238 | 0.1887 | 0.0815 | 1.0000 | 0.0238 | 0.0238 | 0.0263 |
| 0.14 | 7.8679 | 0.0137 | 0.1075 | 0.0461 | 1.0000 | 0.0137 | 0.0137 | 0.0151 |
| 0.15 | 7.5429 | 0.0075 | 0.0563 | 0.0232 | 1.0000 | 0.0075 | 0.0075 | 0.0082 |
| 0.16 | 7.0027 | 0.0039 | 0.0273 | 0.0104 | 1.0000 | 0.0039 | 0.0039 | 0.0043 |
| 0.17 | 6.3153 | 0.0020 | 0.0124 | 0.0043 | 1.0000 | 0.0020 | 0.0020 | 0.0022 |
| 0.18 | 5.5466 | 0.0009 | 0.0052 | 0.0016 | 1.0000 | 0.0009 | 0.0009 | 0.0010 |
| 0.19 | 4.7543 | 0.0004 | 0.0021 | 0.0005 | 1.0000 | 0.0004 | 0.0004 | 0.0005 |
| 0.20 | 3.9842 | 0.0002 | 0.0008 | 0.0002 | 1.0000 | 0.0002 | 0.0002 | 0.0002 |
| | | Sums = | 3.5338 | 1.0000 | | | 0.9073 | 1.0000 |

plausible parameter value than $\pi = 0.05$. Next, consider Researcher B's prior, which is a beta distribution with $a = 1$ and $b = 1$. In this situation, the beta density function in Equation 6.5 always returns a value of 1.00, so Researcher B is assigning the same weight to every possible value of $\pi$.

## The Likelihood Function

The second step of a Bayesian analysis is to collect data and use a likelihood function to summarize the data's evidence about different parameter values. This step applies the maximum likelihood principles outlined in Chapter 3. Specifically, substituting the sample data and a parameter value (i.e., $\pi$) into a density function yields the likelihood (i.e., relative probability) of the data, given that parameter value. Repeating this process for different parameter values yields a likelihood function that describes the relative probability of the data across a range of parameter values. The **binomial density function** is the appropriate likelihood for a binary outcome variable (i.e., each individual is classified as depressed or not depressed). The binomial density function is

$$p(y \mid \pi) \propto \pi^y (1 - \pi)^{N-y} \tag{6.6}$$

where $p(y \mid \pi)$ is the height of the curve at a particular value of $\pi$, $y$ is the number of "successes" (e.g., the number of depressed individuals), and $N$ is the total number of "trials" (e.g., the sample size). Again, I omit the scaling constant from the equation to simplify things.

Returning to the depression example, the researchers assessed a sample of 100 individuals and found that seven people met their criteria for clinical depression. Substituting $y = 7$ and $N = 100$ into Equation 6.6 yields the binomial likelihood function in Figure 6.2. The height of the likelihood function gives the relative probability of observing 7 depressed cases in a sample of 100 individuals, given the population parameter value on the horizontal axis (i.e., the conditional probability of the data, given some assumed value of $\pi$). Table 6.1 gives the numeric value of the likelihood for parameter values between $\pi = 0.05$ and 0.20 (again, I used the previously omitted scaling constant for these calculations in order to avoid excessive decimals). Consider the likelihood associated with $\pi = 0.05$ and $\pi = 0.10$, the values of which are 0.106 and 0.089, respectively. Consistent with the interpretation of the likelihood in Chapter 3, 0.106 and 0.089 are the relative probabilities of observing the data (i.e., 7 out of 100 diagnosed individuals) from a population with $\pi = 0.05$ and $\pi = 0.10$, respectively. Visually, these numeric values correspond with the height of the curve at $\pi = 0.05$ and $\pi = 0.10$. Because $\pi = 0.05$ returns a higher relative probability than $\pi = 0.10$, the data provide slightly more evidence in favor of $\pi = 0.05$.

Before proceeding, you may have noticed that Equations 6.5 and 6.6 are identical with the exception of their exponents. Specifically, the beta distribution has exponents of $a - 1$ and $b - 1$, whereas the binomial distribution has corresponding exponents of $y$ (i.e., the number of successes) and $N - y$ (i.e., the number of nonsuccesses). This similarity is not coincidental, because the binomial and beta densities actually belong to the same distribution family (i.e., the same function describes the shape of the distributions). Specifically, the binomial distribution is a beta distribution in which $a = y + 1$ and $b = N - y + 1$. Researchers frequently adopt priors that belong to the same distribution family as the likelihood function, and this is true of the depression example. These so-called **conjugate distributions** are advantageous because they produce a posterior distribution that also belongs to the same family.

In a previous section, I explained that assigning a number of imaginary data points to the prior determines its influence on the analysis results (the hypothetical sample size is one of the prior distribution's hyperparameters). The equivalence of the beta and the binomial distributions illustrates this point. For example, Researcher A's prior is a beta distribution with $a = 7$ and $b = 40$. A beta distribution with $a = 7$ equates to a binomial distribution with a hypothetical sample of six depressed cases (i.e., $a = y + 1$, so $y = a - 1 = 6$). Similarly, $b = 40$ corresponds to a binomial distribution with 45 imaginary data points (i.e., $b = N - y + 1$, so $N = b - 1 + y = 45$). In contrast, Researcher B's flat prior is a beta distribution with $a = 1$ and $b = 1$. This equates to a binomial distribution with an imaginary sample size of zero (i.e., $y = a - 1 = 0$ and $N = b - 1 + y = 0$). Note that I use the words "hypothetical" and "imaginary" to describe the sample size because the researchers specified their prior distributions before collecting data.

## The Posterior Distribution

The final step of a Bayesian analysis is to define the posterior distribution. Ignoring the denominator of Bayes' theorem for the moment, note that Equation 6.4 says that the height of the posterior distribution at each value of $\pi$ is proportional to the product of the prior times the likelihood. Conceptually, multiplying the likelihood by the prior weights each point on the likelihood function by its prior probability. To illustrate, return to the relative probabilities in Table 6.1. To begin, consider the height of Researcher A's prior distribution at $\pi = 0.05$ and $\pi = 0.10$, the values of which are 0.792 and 6.153, respectively. Multiplying each quantity by its corresponding likelihood gives $0.792 \times 0.106 = 0.084$ and $6.153 \times 0.089 = 0.547$. Visually, 0.084 and 0.547 represent the height of Researcher A's posterior distribution at $\pi = 0.05$ and $\pi = 0.10$, respectively. Consequently, after updating her prior beliefs with information from the data, Researcher A would claim that $\pi = 0.10$ is a more plausible parameter value than $\pi = 0.05$. Turning to Researcher B, the height of his prior distribution was 1.00 at every value of $\pi$. Multiplying the prior by the likelihood gives values of $1.00 \times 0.106 = 0.106$ and $1.00 \times .089 = 0.089$. Again, 0.106 and 0.089 represent the height of Researcher B's posterior distribution at $\pi = 0.05$ and $\pi = 0.10$, respectively. Unlike Researcher A, Researcher B would claim that $\pi = 0.05$ is somewhat more plausible than $\pi = 0.10$. However, notice that Researcher B's conclusion is based solely on the data because the shape of his posterior distribution is identical to that of the likelihood function. Again, this is an important consequence of adopting a noninformative prior distribution.

## The Role of the Marginal Distribution

Until now, I have ignored the marginal distribution that appears in the denominator of Bayes' theorem. As I explained previously, the **marginal distribution** is a scaling constant that does not influence the shape of the posterior. To understand how the marginal distribution works, consider a simple probability example. Suppose that you wanted to know the probability of flipping a coin three times and getting two heads. Three possible sequences produce this outcome: (1) heads, heads, tails, (2) heads, tails, heads, and (3) tails, heads, heads. By itself, the fact that the three different sequences produce two heads does not provide an accurate gauge of the probability because there is no way of knowing whether three sequences is a large number or a small number. Judging the probability becomes easier after dividing by the total number of possible sequences (there are eight). Now, it becomes clear that 37.5% of the sequences produce two heads. Notice that dividing by the total number of possible outcomes does not change the number of sequences that produce two heads, but it does standardize things in a way that makes the probabilities sum to one.

Using only the numerator of Bayes' theorem is akin to expressing the posterior probabilities on an unstandardized metric (e.g., three sequences produce two heads), and dividing by the marginal distribution standardizes the probabilities (e.g., 37.5% of the sequences produce two heads) such that the area under the posterior distribution sums to one. Conceptually, the marginal distribution works as follows. Suppose that you computed the height of the posterior distribution at every possible value of $\pi$ by multiplying the prior probabilities by their corresponding likelihood values. Summing these products yields a quantity that is analogous to the total number of possible outcomes from the coin toss example. To illustrate, the bottom row of Table 6.1 sums the product of the prior times the likelihood for integer values of $\pi$ between 0.05 and 0.20. The value of 3.5338 represents Researcher A's marginal distribution, and 0.9073 is the corresponding value for Researcher B. The Scaled Posterior columns of Table 6.1 divide the posterior probabilities by the appropriate marginal distribution.

Doing so effectively standardizes the height of the posterior distribution such that posterior probabilities sum to one.

In reality, the population proportion can take on an infinite number of values between zero and one, so the example in Table 6.1 is not mathematically accurate. That is, the correct marginal distributions sum the product over every possible value of $\pi$, not just integer values between 0.05 and 0.20. With a continuous density function such as the beta distribution, the summation of the prior times the likelihood involves a calculus integral. Nevertheless, whether you think about it as a sum or an integral, the marginal distribution is a constant value that standardizes the height of the posterior distribution such that the total area under the curve sums (i.e., integrates) to one.

## 6.6 HOW DOES BAYESIAN ESTIMATION APPLY TO MULTIPLE IMPUTATION?

Multiple imputation generates several copies of the data and fills in (i.e., imputes) each copy with different estimates of the missing values. This process uses an iterative algorithm that repeatedly cycles between an imputation step and a posterior step (an I-step and a P-step, respectively). The I-step uses the stochastic regression procedure from Chapter 2 to impute the missing values, and the P-step uses the filled-in data to generate new estimates of the mean vector and the covariance matrix. Virtually every aspect of multiple imputation is rooted in Bayesian methodology, but the ideas from the previous sections are particularly relevant to the P-step because it is essentially a standalone Bayesian analysis that describes the posterior distribution of a mean vector and a covariance matrix.

Generating multiple sets of imputed values requires different estimates of the mean vector and the covariance matrix at each I-step (recall from Chapter 2 that the stochastic regression procedure uses $\hat{\mu}$ and $\hat{\Sigma}$ to construct a set of imputation regression equations), and the purpose of the P-step is to generate these parameter values. At each P-step, the iterative algorithm uses the filled-in data from the preceding I-step to define the posterior distributions of $\mu$ and $\Sigma$. It then uses Monte Carlo simulation to "draw" new estimates of the mean vector and the covariance matrix from their respective posteriors. The subsequent I-step uses these updated parameter values to construct a new set of regression equations that are slightly different from those at the previous I-step. Repeating the two-step procedure a number of times generates several copies of the data, each of which contains unique estimates of the missing values.

Given the important role that the mean vector and the covariance matrix play in a multiple imputation analysis, the rest of the chapter is devoted to defining the posterior distributions of these parameters. As you will see, the estimation steps remain the same (i.e., specify a prior, estimate the likelihood, define the posterior), but the distribution families are different. Because each P-step uses a filled-in data set, the complete-data procedures described in this chapter are identical to those in a multiple imputation analysis. Finally, it is worth noting that the selection of prior distributions has received considerable attention in the Bayesian literature (e.g., see Kass & Wasserman, 1996). Because the majority of multiple imputation analyses rely on a standard set of noninformative priors, I limit the subsequent discussion to the prior distributions that you are likely to encounter in multiple imputation software packages.

## 6.7 THE POSTERIOR DISTRIBUTION OF THE MEAN

This section illustrates how to apply Bayesian estimation principles to the mean. I start by applying the three analysis steps to a univariate example and later extend the ideas to multivariate data. To simplify things, I assume that the population variance is known, but this does not affect the underlying logic of the estimation process, nor does it affect the shape of the posterior distribution.

### The Prior Distribution

The first step of a Bayesian analysis is to specify a prior distribution. Consistent with the previous depression example, you could specify a prior distribution that assigns a higher weight to mean values that you think are more probable, or you could use a noninformative prior that equally weights every value of the mean. The standard noninformative prior is a flat distribution that assigns an equal weight to every possible value of the mean. The Bayesian literature often refers to this as a **Jeffreys' prior**, after a Bayesian theoretician who proposed a set of principles for developing noninformative priors (Jeffreys, 1946, 1961). Using my previous notation, note that the Jeffreys' prior for the mean is $p(\mu) = 1.00$. In words, the prior states that every possible value of the population mean has the same a priori weight of 1.00. Visually, this prior is identical to the solid line in Figure 6.1.

### The Likelihood Function

The second step of a Bayesian analysis is to collect data and use the likelihood function to summarize the data's evidence about different parameter values. Assuming a normal distribution for the population data, the sample likelihood is

$$p(Y|\mu, \sigma^2) = \prod_{i=1}^{N}\left\{\frac{1}{\sqrt{2\pi\sigma^2}}\, e^{-.5(y_i-\mu)^2/\sigma^2}\right\} \tag{6.7}$$

where braces contain the probability density function for the normal distribution (i.e., the likelihood for a single score), $\prod$ is the multiplication operator, and $p(Y|\mu, \sigma^2)$ is the likelihood of the sample data, given the values of $\mu$ and $\sigma^2$. (In previous chapters, I used the generic symbol $L$ to denote the likelihood.) Recall from Chapter 3 that substituting a score value and the population parameters into the density function returns the likelihood for an individual score (i.e., the height of the normal curve at $y_i$), and multiplying the individual likelihood values gives the sample likelihood. Repeating these computations with different values of $\mu$ produces a likelihood function that describes the relative probability of the data across a range of population means.

**TABLE 6.2. IQ and Job Performance Data**

| IQ | Job performance |
|----|-----------------|
| 78 | 9 |
| 84 | 13 |
| 84 | 10 |
| 85 | 8 |
| 87 | 7 |
| 91 | 7 |
| 92 | 9 |
| 94 | 9 |
| 94 | 11 |
| 96 | 7 |
| 99 | 7 |
| 105 | 10 |
| 105 | 11 |
| 106 | 15 |
| 108 | 10 |
| 112 | 10 |
| 113 | 12 |
| 115 | 14 |
| 118 | 16 |
| 134 | 12 |

To illustrate the likelihood step, consider the IQ scores in Table 6.2. I designed these data to mimic an employee selection scenario in which prospective employees complete an IQ test during their interview and a supervisor subsequently rates their job performance following a 6-month probationary period. These are the same data that I used in Chapter 3 to illustrate maximum likelihood estimation. I used Equation 6.7 to compute the sample likelihood for population mean values between 80 and 120, and Figure 6.4 shows the resulting likelihood function (for simplicity, I fixed $\sigma^2$ at its sample estimate of 199.58). The height of the curve is the relative probability that the sample of IQ scores in Table 6.2 originate from a normally distributed population with a mean equal to the value of $\mu$ on the horizontal axis and a variance equal to $\sigma^2 = 199.58$. As seen in the figure, the maximum likelihood estimate of the mean is $\hat{\mu} = 100$, which is the same estimate that I derived from the log-likelihood function in Chapter 3.

## The Posterior Distribution

The final step of a Bayesian analysis is to define the posterior distribution. The numerator of Bayes' theorem states that the height of the posterior is proportional to the product of the prior times the likelihood. Consistent with the previous depression example, the height of the posterior distribution at any given value of $\mu$ is the product of the prior probability and the likelihood. In this situation, obtaining the posterior distribution is simply a matter of multiplying each point on the likelihood function by a value of 1.00. Consequently, the shape

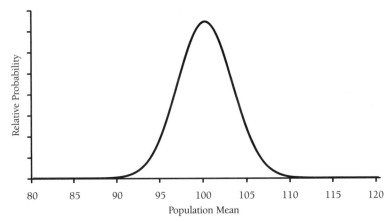

**FIGURE 6.4.** The likelihood function for the mean. The height of the curve is the relative probability that the IQ scores in Table 6.2 originated from a normally distributed population with a mean equal to the value of $\mu$ on the horizontal axis. The maximum of the function (i.e., the maximum likelihood estimate) corresponds with $\mu = 100$, which is the sample mean.

of the posterior distribution is identical to that of the likelihood function in Figure 6.4. More formally, the shape of the posterior distribution is

$$p(\mu \mid Y, \sigma^2) \sim N\left(\hat{\mu}, \frac{\sigma^2}{N}\right) \tag{6.8}$$

where $p(\mu \mid Y, \sigma^2)$ is the posterior distribution, ~$N$ denotes a normal curve (the ~ symbol means "distributed as"), $\hat{\mu}$ is the sample mean, and $\sigma^2/N$ is the variance of the posterior. In words, Equation 6.8 says that the posterior distribution is a normal curve that is centered at the sample mean and has a variance of $\sigma^2/N$. Notice that the data alone define the shape of the posterior (i.e., the distribution is centered at the maximum likelihood estimate), which is a consequence of adopting a noninformative prior distribution. In addition, the shape of the posterior is identical to the frequentist sampling distribution (e.g., the posterior variance is the square of the usual formula for the standard error of the mean).

## The Posterior Distribution of a Mean Vector

A univariate example is useful for understanding the mechanics of Bayesian estimation, but multiple imputation relies on the posterior distribution of a mean vector. Fortunately, the previous ideas readily extend to multivariate data. For example, the standard noninformative prior for a mean vector is a multidimensional flat surface that assigns an equal weight to every combination of mean values. Similarly, the likelihood function is a multivariate, rather than univariate, normal distribution. Finally, the posterior is a multivariate normal distribution that has the same shape as the likelihood function. More formally, the shape of the posterior is

$$p(\boldsymbol{\mu} \mid Y, \boldsymbol{\Sigma}) \sim MN(\hat{\boldsymbol{\mu}}, N^{-1}\boldsymbol{\Sigma}) \tag{6.9}$$

where $p(\boldsymbol{\mu}\,|\,Y, \boldsymbol{\Sigma})$ is the posterior distribution, ~$MN$ denotes the multivariate normal distribution, $\hat{\boldsymbol{\mu}}$ is the vector of sample means, and $\boldsymbol{\Sigma}$ is the population covariance matrix. Again, the fact that the posterior is centered at the sample means indicates that the prior has no influence on the distribution. Consistent with the univariate example, Equation 6.9 assumes that the population covariance matrix is known, but the equation remains the same when $\hat{\boldsymbol{\Sigma}}$ replaces $\boldsymbol{\Sigma}$.

## 6.8 THE POSTERIOR DISTRIBUTION OF THE VARIANCE

The covariance matrix plays an important role in a multiple imputation analysis, so it is important to understand its posterior distribution. However, this distribution is more complex than that of a mean vector, and it belongs to a distribution family that is less familiar. Consequently, starting with a univariate example that involves a single variance makes it easier to understand how Bayesian estimation applies to a covariance matrix. As you will see, the ideas in this section readily generalize to a full covariance matrix. For simplicity, I temporarily assume that the population mean is known, but I later describe how the posterior distribution changes when the mean is also a random variable.

### The Likelihood Function

The first step of a Bayesian analysis is to specify a prior distribution. Bayesian texts recommend a noninformative prior distribution that looks somewhat different from the flat prior described in previous sections. This new prior will make more sense if you first understand the shape of the likelihood function; I will therefore present things out of order in this section, beginning with the likelihood. Reconsider the normal likelihood in Equation 6.7. Multiplying the collection of bracketed terms by itself $N$ times gives the sample likelihood. After performing this operation, the sample likelihood becomes

$$p(Y\,|\,\mu, \sigma^2) \propto \frac{1}{(\sigma^2)^{\frac{N}{2}}}e^{\frac{-.5}{\sigma^2}\Sigma(y_i-\mu)^2} \tag{6.10}$$

The right-most term of Equation 6.10 is the sum of the squared deviations around the population mean. Thus, the likelihood further reduces to

$$p(Y\,|\,\mu, \sigma^2) \propto \frac{1}{(\sigma^2)^{\frac{N}{2}}}e^{-.5\left(\frac{SS}{\sigma^2}\right)} \tag{6.11}$$

where $SS$ is the sum of squares. The "proportional to" symbol (i.e., $\propto$) indicates that I omitted the scaling constant (i.e., $2\pi$) from the equation.

Equation 6.11 is useful because it shows how the relative probability of the data (i.e., the sum of squares) varies across different values of the population variance. To illustrate, reconsider the IQ scores in Table 6.2. Assuming a population mean of $\mu_{IQ} = 100$ yields a sum

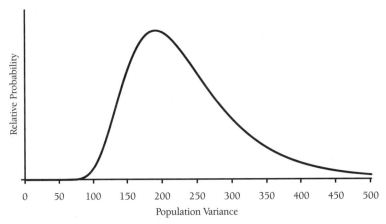

**FIGURE 6.5.** The likelihood function for the variance. The height of the likelihood function is the relative probability that a sample variance of 189.60 (the variance of the IQ data in Table 6.2) originated from a normally distributed population with a variance equal to the value of $\sigma^2$ on the horizontal axis. The likelihood function for the variance belongs to the family of inverse chi-square distributions.

of squares value of $SS = 3792$. I used Equation 6.11 to compute the sample likelihood across a range of population variances, and Figure 6.5 shows the resulting likelihood function. The likelihood function is a positively skewed distribution, but it works in the same manner as before. Specifically, the height of the curve is the relative probability of the data, given the population variance on the horizontal axis. Visually, the maximum of the likelihood function corresponds to a population variance that is slightly less than 200. You may recall from Chapter 3 that the maximum likelihood estimate of the IQ variance was $\hat{\sigma}^2_{IQ} = 189.60$, so Figure 6.5 agrees with this previous analysis.

The likelihood function in Figure 6.5 is an **inverse chi-square distribution**. More accurately, the likelihood is a scaled inverse chi-square distribution, but I simply refer to it as an inverse chi-square throughout the remainder of the chapter. Using generic notation, note that the shape of an inverse chi-square distribution with $\nu$ degrees of freedom is

$$\text{Inv-}\chi^2 \propto \frac{1}{x^{\frac{\nu}{2}+1}}e^{-.5\left(\frac{S}{x}\right)} \tag{6.12}$$

where $x$ is a variable, and $S$ is a scale parameter that dictates the spread of the distribution (e.g., larger values of $S$ produce a wider distribution). As before, the "proportional to" symbol (i.e., $\propto$) denotes an omitted scaling constant. Like the chi-square distribution, the inverse chi-square is a family of distributions where the exact shape of the curve is determined by the degrees of freedom (and in the case of a scaled inverse chi-square, the scale parameter).

Relabeling the terms in Equation 6.12 better illustrates the linkage between the likelihood and the inverse chi-square distribution. Specifically, replacing $x$ with $\sigma^2$, $\nu$ with $N$, and $S$ with $SS$ gives

$$\text{Inv-}\chi^2 \propto \frac{1}{(\sigma^2)^{\frac{N}{2}+1}}e^{-.5\left(\frac{SS}{\sigma^2}\right)} \tag{6.13}$$

Notice that Equation 6.13 is nearly identical to the likelihood, but $\sigma^2$ has an exponent of $(N/2) + 1$ rather than $N/2$. This disparity reflects a difference of two degrees of freedom, so the likelihood is actually an inverse chi-square distribution with $v = N - 2$ degrees of freedom.

## The Prior Distribution

Having gained some familiarity with the inverse chi-square distribution, I now return to the first step of a Bayesian analysis, which is to specify a prior distribution. Researchers frequently adopt conjugate priors that belong to the same distribution family as the likelihood, so the inverse chi-square distribution is a reasonable prior for $\sigma^2$. However, using the inverse chi-square as a prior distribution requires a sum of squares value and an imaginary sample size (i.e., the hyperparameters). Substituting $N = 0$ and $SS = 0$ into Equation 6.13 is akin to saying that you have no prior information about the variance. Doing so yields the Jeffreys' prior as follows:

$$p(\sigma^2) \propto \frac{1}{\sigma^2} \tag{6.14}$$

Equation 6.14 is different from the Jeffreys' prior for the mean because it assigns relative probabilities that increase as the population variance approaches zero. To illustrate, Figure 6.6 shows a graphic of the prior distribution, where the height of the curve represents the a priori relative probability for a particular value of $\sigma^2$.

## The Posterior Distribution

Having established the prior distribution and the likelihood function, the third step of a Bayesian analysis is to define the posterior distribution. As before, the posterior is propor-

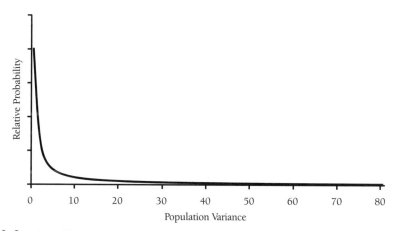

**FIGURE 6.6.** The Jeffreys' prior for the variance. The height of the curve represents each parameter value's a priori weight. Unlike the Jeffreys' prior for the mean, the prior probabilities increase as the population variance approaches zero.

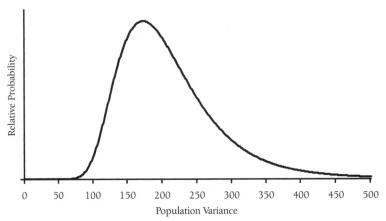

**FIGURE 6.7.** The posterior distribution of the variance. The posterior is very similar to the likelihood in Figure 6.5, but its left tail is slightly thicker than that of the likelihood. This subtle difference results from using a noninformative prior distribution that assigns higher weights to lower values of $\sigma^2$. The posterior distribution belongs to the family of inverse chi-square distributions.

tional to the prior times the likelihood, so the posterior distribution for the variance is as follows:

$$p(\sigma^2 \mid Y, \mu) \propto \frac{1}{\sigma^2} \times \frac{1}{(\sigma^2)^{\frac{N}{2}}} e^{-.5\left(\frac{SS}{\sigma^2}\right)} = \frac{1}{(\sigma^2)^{\frac{N}{2}+1}} e^{-.5\left(\frac{SS}{\sigma^2}\right)} \tag{6.15}$$

Notice that the posterior distribution is an inverse chi-square distribution with $N$ degrees of freedom and is identical to Equation 6.12. Substituting $SS = 3792$ into Equation 6.15 yields the posterior distribution in Figure 6.7. The effect is subtle, but you can see that left tail of the posterior distribution is slightly thicker than that of the likelihood function, which follows from the fact that the prior assigns higher weights to lower values of the population variance.

### Estimation with an Unknown Mean

Throughout this section, I have effectively assumed that the population mean is known. Treating the mean as an unknown random variable changes the shape of the posterior in a way that is analogous to using the sample, rather than the population, formula to compute the variance. Bayesian texts give the mathematical details behind this change (e.g., see Gelman et al., 1995, pp. 67–68), but the result is a marginal posterior distribution with $N - 1$ degrees of freedom (i.e., the exponent of $\sigma^2$ changes from $(N/2) + 1$ to $(N+1)/2$). More formally, the shape of the posterior distribution is

$$p(\sigma^2 \mid \hat{\mu}, Y) \sim \text{Inv-}\chi^2(N - 1, SS) \tag{6.16}$$

where $p(\sigma^2 \mid Y, \mu)$ is the posterior distribution, $\sim\text{Inv-}\chi^2$ denotes an inverse chi-square distribution, $N - 1$ is the degrees of freedom, and $SS$ is the sum of squares. The degrees of freedom and sum of squares values are known as the location and scale parameters, respectively, because they determine the expected value and the spread of the posterior distribution (the mean and the variance play a similar role in defining the posterior distribution of the mean). As an aside, the sampling distribution of the variance is also an inverse chi-square distribution with $N - 1$ degrees of freedom; thus, adopting the Jeffreys' prior in Equation 6.14 brings the Bayesian and frequentist paradigms into alignment.

## 6.9 THE POSTERIOR DISTRIBUTION OF A COVARIANCE MATRIX

This section extends Bayesian estimation to an entire covariance matrix. The basic procedure is similar to estimating a variance, and the distributions are multivariate extensions of the inverse chi-square. By now, you are probably familiar with the three steps of a Bayesian analysis, so I give an abbreviated outline of the process. Consistent with the previous section, I present things out of order, beginning with the likelihood. For simplicity, I temporarily assume that the population means are known, but this does not affect the logic of the estimation process.

### The Likelihood Function

Equation 6.11 describes how the likelihood of the sample data varies across different values of the population variance. The corresponding likelihood function for a covariance matrix is

$$p(Y \mid \boldsymbol{\mu}, \boldsymbol{\Sigma}) \propto |\boldsymbol{\Sigma}|^{-N/2} e^{-.5(\text{tr}[\boldsymbol{\Sigma}^{-1}\boldsymbol{\Lambda}])} \tag{6.17}$$

where $\boldsymbol{\mu}$ is the population mean vector, $\boldsymbol{\Sigma}$ is the population covariance matrix, and $\boldsymbol{\Lambda}$ is the sum of squares and cross products matrix. Equation 6.17 replaces the terms in Equation 6.11 with their matrix analogs, but the likelihood still gives the relative probability of the data (in this case, the sum of squares and cross products matrix represents the data) across different values of the population parameters. To illustrate, Figure 6.8 shows the likelihood surface for a bivariate covariance matrix. I based the likelihood on a sample of 20 cases that I generated from a multivariate normal distribution with means of zero, variances equal to three, and a covariance equal to zero. Notice that the likelihood function is now a three-dimensional positively skewed distribution, but its shape resembles that of the univariate likelihood function in Figure 6.5. Consistent with its univariate counterpart, the height of the likelihood surface at any given point is the relative probability of the data, given the combination of population variances on the horizontal and depth axes.

The likelihood function in Figure 6.8 is a member of the **inverse Wishart distribution** family. The inverse Wishart density function is

$$W^{-1} \propto |\boldsymbol{\Sigma}|^{-(v+k+1)/2} e^{-.5(\text{tr}[\boldsymbol{\Sigma}^{-1}\boldsymbol{\Lambda}])} \tag{6.18}$$

where $W^{-1}$ denotes the inverse Wishart distribution, $v$ is the degrees of freedom, $\boldsymbol{\Lambda}$ is the sum of squares and cross products matrix, $\boldsymbol{\Sigma}$ is the population covariance matrix, and $k$ is the number of variables. As before, the "proportional to" symbol (i.e., $\propto$) indicates that I

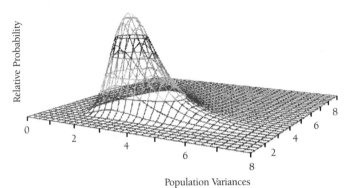

**FIGURE 6.8.** The likelihood surface for a bivariate covariance matrix. This likelihood is based on a sample of 20 cases from a multivariate normal population with means of zero, variances equal to three, and a covariance equal to zero. The likelihood surface is a three-dimensional positively skewed distribution, but its shape resembles that of the univariate likelihood in Figure 6.5. The height of the likelihood surface at any given point quantifies the relative probability of the sample covariance matrix, given the population variances on the horizontal and depth axes. The likelihood function belongs to the family of inverse Wishart distributions.

excluded a scaling constant from the equation. Notice that the likelihood function and the inverse Wishart distribution are nearly identical, but have different exponents. This is not coincidental, because the likelihood function is an inverse Wishart distribution where $v$ equals $N - k - 1$. Finally, note that Equation 6.18 reduces to the inverse chi-square distribution in Equation 6.13 when $k = 1$.

## The Prior Distribution

Having gained some familiarity with the inverse Wishart distribution, I now return to the first step of a Bayesian analysis, which is to specify a prior distribution. Researchers often choose conjugate priors that belong to the same distribution family as the likelihood, so the inverse Wishart is a reasonable prior distribution for the covariance matrix. Substituting $v = 0$ (i.e., zero imaginary data points) and $\Lambda = 0$ into Equation 6.18 is akin to saying that you have no prior information about the population covariance matrix. Doing so yields the multivariate version of the Jeffreys' prior.

$$p(\Sigma) \propto |\Sigma|^{-\frac{k+1}{2}} \tag{6.19}$$

The determinant $|\Sigma|$ is a scalar value that quantifies the total variation in the population covariance matrix. Because the value of the determinant decreases as variability decreases, the prior probabilities increase as the elements in the population covariance matrix approach zero. This was also true of the Jeffreys' prior for the variance, and Equation 6.19 reduces to Equation 6.14 when $k = 1$.

## The Posterior Distribution

The final step of a Bayesian analysis is to define the posterior distribution. Consistent with the previous examples, the height of the posterior distribution is proportional to the product of the prior distribution times the likelihood. Multiplying the prior and the likelihood yields an inverse Wishart distribution with $N$ degrees of freedom. This distribution is identical to Equation 6.18 but replaces $v$ with $N$. Like its univariate counterpart, the posterior distribution changes slightly when the means are unknown and becomes an inverse Wishart distribution with $N - 1$ degrees of freedom. More formally, the posterior is

$$p(\mathbf{\Sigma} \,|\, \hat{\mathbf{\mu}}, \mathbf{Y}) \sim W^{-1}(N - 1, \hat{\mathbf{\Lambda}}) \tag{6.20}$$

where $p(\mathbf{\Sigma} \,|\, \hat{\mathbf{\mu}}, \mathbf{Y})$ is the posterior distribution, $W^{-1}$ denotes the inverse Wishart distribution, $N - 1$ is the degrees of freedom, and $\hat{\mathbf{\Lambda}}$ is the sample sum of squares and cross products matrix. In words, Equation 6.20 says that the posterior distribution of a covariance matrix is an inverse Wishart distribution with $N - 1$ degrees of freedom and scale parameter equal to the sum of squares and cross products matrix. The degrees of freedom and sum of squares and cross products matrix determine the expected value and the spread of the distribution, respectively. Importantly, the data (i.e., the sample size and $\mathbf{\Lambda}$) define the shape of the posterior, and the prior effectively plays no role. This has been a consistent theme throughout this chapter and is a result of adopting a noninformative prior distribution. The sampling distribution of $\hat{\mathbf{\Sigma}}$ is also an inverse Wishart distribution with $N - 1$ degrees of freedom, so the Jeffreys' prior in Equation 6.19 brings the Bayesian and frequentist paradigms into alignment.

## 6.10 SUMMARY

Chapter 7 introduces a second "modern" missing technique, multiple imputation. Rubin (1987) developed multiple imputation within the Bayesian framework, so understanding the nuances of imputation requires a basic working knowledge of Bayesian statistics. The goal of this chapter was to provide a user-friendly account of Bayesian statistics, while still providing interested readers with the technical information necessary to understand the seminal missing data literature (e.g., Little & Rubin, 2002; Rubin, 1987; Schafer, 1997).

Understanding Bayesian statistics requires a shift in thinking about the population parameter. Unlike the frequentist paradigm, Bayesian methodology defines a parameter as a random variable that has a distribution. An important analysis goal is to describe this distribution's shape, and doing so requires three steps. The first step is to specify a prior distribution that describes your subjective beliefs about the relative probability of different parameter values before collecting data. In general, you can specify an informative prior that assigns a higher weight to parameter values that you feel are more probable, or you can specify a noninformative prior that uniformly weights different values—multiple imputation analyses generally use the latter approach. The second step of a Bayesian analysis is to use a likelihood function to summarize the data's evidence about different parameter values. The final step of a Bayesian analysis is to define the parameter's posterior distribution. Multiplying the likelihood by the prior distribution adjusts the height of the likelihood function up or down according to the magnitude of the prior probabilities and yields a new composite distribution that describes the relative probability of different parameter values.

Because the mean vector and the covariance matrix play an important role in a multiple-imputation analysis, a key goal of this chapter was to define the posterior distributions of these parameters. The posterior distribution of a mean vector is a multivariate normal distribution, whereas the posterior distribution of a covariance matrix is an inverse Wishart distribution. The majority of multiple imputation analyses rely on a standard set of noninformative prior distributions (i.e., so-called Jeffreys' priors). Adopting a Jeffreys' prior effectively eliminates the influence of the prior distribution and yields a posterior distribution that is defined solely by the data. The Jeffreys' priors also bring the Bayesian and the frequentist paradigms into alignment because the posterior distributions of the mean vector and the covariance matrix are identical to the frequentist sampling distributions.

The next chapter introduces multiple imputation. Multiple imputation is actually a broad term that encompasses a collection of different techniques, but I focus on a data augmentation algorithm that assumes a multivariate normal distribution (Schafer, 1997; Tanner & Wong, 1987). Data augmentation is an iterative algorithm that repeatedly cycles between an I-step and a P-step (i.e., an imputation and a posterior step, respectively). The I-step uses the stochastic regression procedure from Chapter 2 to impute the missing values, and the P-step defines the shape of the posterior distributions and uses Monte Carlo simulation to "draw" new estimates of $\mu$ and $\Sigma$ from their respective posteriors. Repeating this two-step procedure a number of times generates several copies of the data, each of which contains unique estimates of the missing values. The posterior step is essentially a standalone Bayesian analysis of $\mu$ and $\Sigma$, so the ideas in this chapter play an important role throughout Chapter 7.

## 6.11 RECOMMENDED READINGS

Bolstad, W. M. (2007). *Introduction to Bayesian statistics* (2nd ed.). New York: Wiley.

Gelman, A., Carlin, J. B., Stern, H. S., & Rubin, D. B. (1995). *Bayesian data analysis*. Boca Raton, FL: Chapman & Hall.

Lee, M. D., & Wagenmakers, E-J. (2005). Bayesian statistical inference in psychology: Comment on Trafimow (2003). *Psychological Review, 112,* 662–668.

Pruzek, R. M. (1997). An introduction to Bayesian inference and its applications. In L. L. Harlow, S. A. Mulaik, & J. H. Steiger (Eds.), *What if there were no significance tests?* (pp. 287–318). Mahwah, NJ: Erlbaum.

Rupp, A. A., Dey, D. K., & Zumbo, B. D. (2004). To Bayes or not to Bayes, from whether to when: Applications of Bayesian methodology to modeling. *Structural Equation Modeling: An Interdisciplinary Journal, 11,* 424–451.

# 7

# The Imputation Phase of Multiple Imputation

## 7.1 CHAPTER OVERVIEW

Recall from previous chapters that maximum likelihood estimation uses a log-likelihood function to identify the population parameter values that are most likely to have produced the observed data. The estimation process essentially auditions different parameter values until it identifies the estimates that minimize the standardized distance to the observed data. This process does not involve imputation. Rather, maximum likelihood estimates the parameters directly from the available data, and it does so in a way that does not require individuals to have complete data records. Multiple imputation is an alternative to maximum likelihood estimation and is the other state-of-the-art missing data technique that methodologists currently recommend (Schafer & Graham, 2002). The imputation approach outlined in this chapter makes the same assumptions as maximum likelihood estimation—missing at random (MAR) data and multivariate normality—but takes the very different tack of filling in the missing values prior to analysis.

A multiple imputation analysis consists of three distinct steps: the imputation phase, the analysis phase, and the pooling phase. Figure 7.1 shows a graphical depiction of the process. The **imputation phase** creates multiple copies of the data set (e.g., $m = 20$), each of which contains different estimates of the missing values. Conceptually, this step is an iterative version of stochastic regression imputation, although its mathematical underpinnings rely heavily on Bayesian estimation principles. As its name implies, the goal of the **analysis phase** is to analyze the filled-in data sets. This step applies the same statistical procedures that you would have used had the data been complete. Procedurally, the only difference is that you perform each analysis $m$ times, once for each imputed data set. The analysis phase yields $m$ sets of parameter estimates and standard errors, so the purpose of the **pooling phase** is to combine everything into a single set of results. Rubin (1987) outlined relatively straightforward formulas for pooling parameter estimates and standard errors. For example, the pooled parameter estimate is simply the arithmetic average of the $m$ estimates from the

187

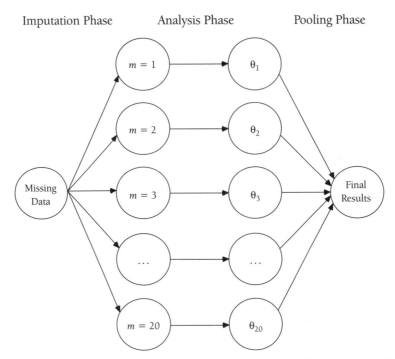

**FIGURE 7.1.** Graphical depiction of a multiple imputation analysis. The imputation phase creates multiple copies of the data set (i.e., $m = 20$) and imputes each with different missing values. The analysis phase estimates the model parameters using each of the complete data sets. The pooling phase combines the parameter estimates and standard errors into a single set of of results.

analysis phase. Combining the standard errors is slightly more complex but follows the same logic. The process of analyzing multiple data sets and pooling the results sounds very tedious, but multiple imputation software packages completely automate the procedure. The imputation phase is arguably the most difficult aspect of a multiple imputation analysis, so I devote Chapter 7 to this topic and outline the analysis and pooling phases in Chapter 8.

Multiple imputation is actually a broad term that encompasses a collection of techniques. The three-step process (i.e., imputation, analysis, pooling) is common to all multiple imputation procedures, but methodologists have proposed a variety of algorithms for the imputation phase (King, Honaker, Joseph, & Scheve, 2001; Lavori, Dawson, & Shera, 1995; Raghunathan, Lepkowski, Van Hoewyk, & Solenberger, 2001; Royston, 2005; Schafer, 1997, 2001; van Buuren, 2007). These algorithms address different types of problems (e.g., categorical versus continuous data, longitudinal versus cross-sectional data, monotone missing data patterns versus general patterns), so no single procedure works best in every situation. Because the normal distribution is arguably one of the most widely used data models in the social and behavioral sciences, I devote this chapter to an imputation approach that assumes multivariate normality. This so-called data augmentation algorithm (Schafer, 1997; Tanner & Wong, 1987) is perhaps the most widely used imputation approach and is readily available in a number of commercial and freeware software packages. I briefly outline a few alternative imputation algorithms in Chapter 9.

As an important aside, researchers often object to imputation on grounds that the procedure is somehow cheating by "making up data." This concern is ungrounded for at least three reasons. First, it is important to remember that the primary goal of a statistical analysis is to estimate the population parameters. In truth, multiple imputation is nothing more than a mathematical tool that facilitates that task, so imputation itself is ancillary to the end goal. Second, multiple imputation and maximum likelihood estimation are asymptotically (i.e., in very large samples) equivalent and tend to produce the same results. The fact that the two procedures—only one of which fills in the data—are effectively interchangeable underscores the point that imputation is not inherently problematic. Finally, unlike other imputation routines, multiple imputation explicitly accounts for the uncertainty associated with the missing data. By repeatedly filling in the data, multiple imputation yields parameter estimates that average over a number of plausible replacement values, so the process never places faith in a single set of imputations. This is in stark contrast to imputation techniques that treat a single set of filled-in values as real data (e.g., the single imputation methods from Chapter 2).

I use the small data set in Table 7.1 to illustrate ideas throughout this chapter. I designed these data to mimic an employee selection scenario where prospective employees complete an IQ test and a psychological well-being questionnaire during their interview. The company subsequently hires the applicants that score in the upper half of the IQ distribution, and a supervisor rates their job performance following a 6-month probationary period. Note that the job performance scores are missing at random (MAR) because they are systematically missing as a function of IQ scores (i.e., individuals in the lower half of the IQ distribution were never hired and thus have no performance rating). In addition, I randomly deleted three of the well-being scores in order to mimic a missing completely at random (MCAR) mechanism (e.g., the human resources department inadvertently loses an applicant's well-being questionnaire). This data set is far too small for a serious application of multiple imputation, but it is useful for illustrating the basic mechanics of the imputation phase.

**TABLE 7.1. Employee Selection Data Set**

| IQ | Psychological well-being | Job performance |
|----|--------------------------|-----------------|
| 78 | 13 | — |
| 84 | 9 | — |
| 84 | 10 | — |
| 85 | 10 | — |
| 87 | — | — |
| 91 | 3 | — |
| 92 | 12 | — |
| 94 | 3 | — |
| 94 | 13 | — |
| 96 | — | — |
| 99 | 6 | 7 |
| 105 | 12 | 10 |
| 105 | 14 | 11 |
| 106 | 10 | 15 |
| 108 | — | 10 |
| 112 | 10 | 10 |
| 113 | 14 | 12 |
| 115 | 14 | 14 |
| 118 | 12 | 16 |
| 134 | 11 | 12 |

## 7.2 A CONCEPTUAL DESCRIPTION OF THE IMPUTATION PHASE

Rubin (1987) developed multiple imputation in the Bayesian framework, and data augmentation relies heavily on Bayesian methodology. The imputation phase has relatively intuitive logic (e.g., repeatedly impute the data and update the parameters), but its reliance on Bayesian principles can make it difficult to grasp. This section gives a conceptual description of data augmentation that does not rely on Bayesian statistics. The goal of this section is to lay the foundation for the more precise explanation that I give in the next section, but also to provide an overview of data augmentation for researchers who want to use multiple imputation without necessarily mastering its mathematical underpinnings. I use the IQ and job performance scores from Table 7.1 to illustrate the imputation phase. A bivariate analysis with a single incomplete variable is a very basic application of data augmentation, but the ideas in this section readily generalize to multivariate analyses.

### The I-Step

The data augmentation algorithm is a two-step procedure that consists of an imputation step (I-step) and a posterior step (P-step). Procedurally, the **I-step** is identical to the stochastic regression procedure from Chapter 2. Specifically, the I-step uses an estimate of the mean vector and the covariance matrix to build a set of regression equations that predict the incomplete variables from the observed variables. The bivariate analysis example is straightforward because there is only one pattern with missing data (the subset of cases with missing job performance scores), and thus only one regression equation. The imputation equation is

$$JP_i^* = [\hat{\beta}_0 + \hat{\beta}_1(IQ_i)] + z_i \tag{7.1}$$

where $JP_i^*$ is the imputed job performance rating for case $i$, the brackets contain the regression coefficients that generate the predicted job performance rating for that individual, and $z_i$ is a random residual from a normal distribution. The normal curve that generates the residuals has a mean of zero and a variance equal to the residual variance from the regression of job performance on IQ (i.e., $\sigma_{JP|IQ}^2$). Consistent with stochastic regression imputation, substituting an IQ score into the bracketed terms yields a predicted job performance rating. The predicted scores fall directly on a regression line (or a regression surface, in the multivariate case), so adding a normally distributed residual term to each predicted value restores variability to the imputed data.

### The P-Step

The ultimate goal of the imputation phase is to generate $m$ complete data sets, each of which contains unique estimates of the missing values. Creating unique imputations requires different estimates of the regression coefficients at each I-step, and the purpose of the **P-step** is to generate alternate estimates of the mean vector and the covariance matrix (the building blocks of the I-step regression equations). Although this process relies heavily on Bayesian estimation principles, it is straightforward to understand at a conceptual level. Specifically, the P-step begins by using the filled-in data from the preceding I-step to estimate the mean vector and the covariance matrix. Next, the algorithm generates a new set of parameter values by adding a random residual term to each element in $\hat{\boldsymbol{\mu}}$ and $\hat{\boldsymbol{\Sigma}}$. Randomly perturbing the parameter values is akin to drawing a new set of plausible estimates from a sampling distribution (or alternatively, a posterior distribution).

To illustrate the P-step in more detail, suppose that the mean and the variance of the filled-in job performance scores from a particular I-step are $\hat{\mu}_{JP} = 10$ and $\hat{\sigma}^2_{JP} = 9$, respectively. The sampling distribution (or in the Bayesian context, the posterior distribution) of the mean is a normal curve with a standard deviation of $\hat{\sigma}/\sqrt{N}$, so a new sample of 20 job performance scores should produce a mean that deviates from the current estimate by $3/\sqrt{20} = 0.67$ points, on average. To generate an alternate estimate of the mean, the P-step uses Monte Carlo simulation to draw a random residual term from a normal distribution with a mean of zero and a standard deviation of 0.67. Adding this residual to $\hat{\mu}_{JP} = 10$ gives a new estimate of the job performance mean that randomly differs from that of the filled-in data. The same process generates new covariance matrix elements, but these parameters require a different residual distribution (the inverse Wishart distribution from Chapter 6).

Adding residual terms to the elements in the mean vector and the covariance matrix produces parameter values that randomly differ from those that produced the regression coefficients at the preceding I-step. Carrying the updated estimates forward to the next I-step yields a new set of regression coefficients and a different set of imputations. The new imputations carry forward to the next P-step, where the algorithm generates another set of plausible parameter estimates. Repeating this two-step procedure a large number of times creates multiple copies of the data, each of which contains unique estimates of the missing values.

## 7.3 A BAYESIAN DESCRIPTION OF THE IMPUTATION PHASE

The previous description of the data augmentation algorithm is conceptual in nature and omits many of the mathematical details. This section expands the previous ideas and gives a more precise explanation of the I-step and the P-step. In particular, I illustrate how the Bayesian estimation principles from Chapter 6 apply to the imputation phase. In doing so, I continue to use the IQ and job performance scores from Table 7.1. Again, a bivariate analysis with a single incomplete variable is a very basic example, but surprisingly few changes occur when applying data augmentation to multivariate data.

### The I-Step

As I explained in the previous section, the computational details of the I-step are identical to stochastic regression (i.e., use regression equations to predict the incomplete variables from the observed variables and add random residuals to the predicted scores). To illustrate the imputation process graphically, the top panel of Figure 7.2 shows a scatterplot of a set of imputed job performance ratings. The solid regression line corresponds to the predicted job performance scores (i.e., the values generated by the bracketed terms in Equation 7.1), and the dashed lines represent the random residuals (i.e., the $z_i$ values).

From a Bayesian perspective, the imputed values are random draws from a **conditional distribution** that depends on the observed data and the estimates of the mean vector and the covariance matrix at a particular I-step. (Bayesian texts sometimes refer to this distribution as the **posterior predictive distribution**.) The bottom panel of Figure 7.2 imposes normal residual distributions over the regression line at IQ values of 80, 90, and 100. Each of the normal curves represents the conditional distribution of job performance ratings, given the particular IQ score on the horizontal axis (i.e., the distribution of performance ratings for a hypothetical subsample of cases that share the same IQ). The regression line intersects each distribution at its mean, so the predicted job performance ratings (i.e., the bracketed terms in Equation 7.1) are **conditional means** (i.e., the expected performance rating for a hypothetical subsample of cases that share the same IQ). The normal curves represent the distri-

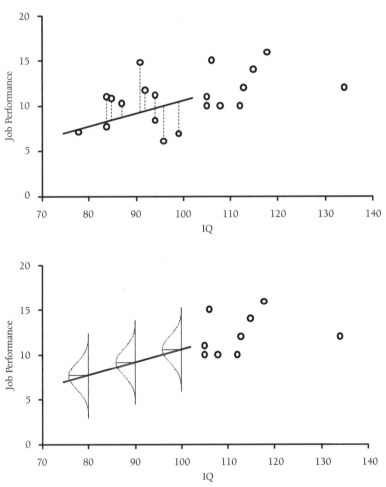

**FIGURE 7.2.** The top panel shows a hypothetical imputed data set. The solid regression line denotes the predicted job performance scores, and the dashed lines represent the random residuals. The bottom panel shows normal curves imposed over the regression line at IQ values of 80, 90, and 100. These curves represent the conditional distribution of job performance ratings at three different IQ scores (i.e., the distribution of performance ratings for a hypothetical subsample of cases that share the same IQ). The imputed values are random draws from the conditional distributions.

bution of the residuals, so adding a $z_i$ value to each predicted score effectively simulates a random draw from a distribution of plausible replacement values that is contingent on the observed IQ data.

More formally, the following equation summarizes the I-step

$$Y_t^* \sim p(Y_{\mathrm{mis}} \mid Y_{\mathrm{obs}}, \theta_{t-1}^*) \tag{7.2}$$

where $Y_t^*$ represents the imputed values at I-step $t$, $Y_{\mathrm{mis}}$ is the missing portion of the data (e.g., the missing job performance ratings), $Y_{\mathrm{obs}}$ is the observed portion of data (e.g., the observed IQ scores), and $\theta_{t-1}^*$ denotes the mean vector and the covariance matrix from the preceding P-step (i.e., the parameter values that generate the imputation regression equations). In words, Equation 7.2 says that the imputed values at a particular I-step are random draws from a distribution (the $\sim$ symbol means "distributed as") of plausible replacement values that depends on the observed data and the current parameter estimates. Regardless of how you conceptualize the I-step, the computational details amount to stochastic regression imputation.

## The P-Step

The P-step is essentially a standalone Bayesian analysis that describes the posterior distributions of the mean vector and the covariance matrix. Recall that a Bayesian analysis consists of three steps: specify a prior distribution, estimate a likelihood function, and define the posterior distribution. This section presents the relevant posterior distributions but provides no background on their derivations. Chapter 6 describes the Bayesian analytic steps in some detail, so it may be useful to review Sections 6.8 through 6.10 before proceeding.

Creating multiple sets of imputed values requires different estimates of the mean vector and the covariance matrix at each I-step, and the purpose of the P-step is to generate alternate parameter values. The Bayesian framework is ideally suited for this task because it views a parameter as a random variable that has a distribution of values. In the previous section, I stated that the P-step generates new parameter estimates by adding a random residual term to each element in $\hat{\boldsymbol{\mu}}$ and $\hat{\boldsymbol{\Sigma}}$. This description is conceptually accurate, but mathematically imprecise. More accurately, the P-step randomly draws a new mean vector and a new covariance matrix from their respective posterior distributions. Throughout the chapter, I refer to these new estimates as **simulated parameters** because Monte Carlo computer simulation techniques generate their values.

To begin, the P-step uses the filled-in data from the preceding I-step to compute the sample means and the sample sum of squares and cross products matrix (i.e., $\hat{\boldsymbol{\mu}}$ and $\hat{\boldsymbol{\Lambda}}$, respectively). Having obtained these quantities, note that the posterior distribution of the covariance matrix is

$$p(\boldsymbol{\Sigma} \mid \hat{\boldsymbol{\mu}}, \mathbf{Y}) \sim W^{-1}(N-1, \hat{\boldsymbol{\Lambda}}) \tag{7.3}$$

where $p(\boldsymbol{\Sigma} \mid \hat{\boldsymbol{\mu}}, Y)$ denotes the posterior, $\hat{\boldsymbol{\mu}}$ is the vector of sample means, $\mathbf{Y}$ is the filled-in data matrix from the preceding I-step, $\sim W^{-1}$ represents the inverse Wishart distribution, $N-1$ is the degrees of freedom (i.e., the distribution's expected value), and $\hat{\Lambda}$ is the sample sum of squares and cross products matrix (i.e., the matrix that defines the spread of the distribution). Notice that this posterior distribution has the same form as the one from Chapter 6 (see Equation 6.20). Having defined the shape of the posterior distribution, the data augmentation algorithm uses Monte Carlo simulation techniques to "draw" a new covariance matrix from the posterior. Procedurally, this amounts to using a computer to generate a matrix of random numbers from the distribution in Equation 7.3. To avoid confusion with the sample estimates, I denote the simulated covariance matrix as $\Sigma^*$.

The algorithm uses a similar procedure to create a new set of means. Specifically, the sample means and the simulated covariance matrix define the posterior distribution of the mean vector, as follows:

$$p(\hat{\mu}|Y, \Sigma) \sim MN(\hat{\mu}, N^{-1}\Sigma^*) \tag{7.4}$$

where $p(\hat{\mu}|Y, \Sigma)$ is the posterior, $\sim MN$ denotes a multivariate normal distribution, $\hat{\mu}$ is the vector of sample means, and $\Sigma^*$ is the simulated covariance matrix. Again, this posterior distribution is the same as the one described in Chapter 6 (see Equation 6.9). Finally, Monte Carlo computer simulation techniques generate a new set of means from the distribution in Equation 7.4. I denote the resulting estimates as $\hat{\mu}^*$.

After drawing new parameter values from the posterior distributions, the subsequent I-step uses the updated estimates to construct a new set of regression coefficients and a different set of imputations. The new imputations carry forward to the next P-step, where the algorithm draws another set of plausible parameter estimates. Repeating the two-step procedure a number of times generates multiple copies of the data, each of which contains unique estimates of the missing values.

More formally, the following equation summarizes the P-step

$$\theta_t^* \sim p(\theta|Y_{obs}, Y_t^*) \tag{7.5}$$

where $\theta_t^*$ denotes the simulated parameter values from P-step $t$ (i.e., $\mu^*$ and $\Sigma^*$), $Y_{obs}$ is the observed data (e.g., the observed IQ scores), and $Y_t^*$ contains the imputed values from the preceding I-step. In words, Equation 7.5 says that the simulated parameter values from P-step $t$ are random draws from a distribution that depends on the observed data and the filled-in values from the preceding I-step. A lack of familiarity with Bayesian estimation can make it difficult to grasp the nuances of the P-step, but the process described above is conceptually straightforward: use the filled-in data to estimate the mean vector and the covariance matrix and generate a new set of plausible parameter values by adding a random residual to each element in $\hat{\mu}$ and $\hat{\Sigma}$.

## 7.4 A BIVARIATE ANALYSIS EXAMPLE

Having outlined data augmentation in more detail, I use the IQ and job performance scores in Table 7.1 to illustrate a worked example. Multiple imputation software programs fully automate the data augmentation procedure, so there is no need to perform the computational steps manually. Nevertheless, examining what happens at each step of the process is instructive and gives some insight into the inner workings of the "black box."

Consistent with a maximum likelihood analysis, data augmentation requires an initial estimate of the mean vector and the covariance matrix to get started. For reasons discussed later, maximum likelihood parameter estimates make good starting values, so I use the estimates from Chapter 4 for this purpose.

$$\hat{\boldsymbol{\mu}}_0 = \begin{bmatrix} \hat{\mu}_{IQ} \\ \hat{\mu}_{JP} \end{bmatrix} = \begin{bmatrix} 100.000 \\ 10.281 \end{bmatrix}$$

$$\hat{\boldsymbol{\Sigma}}_0 = \begin{bmatrix} \hat{\sigma}^2_{IQ} & \hat{\sigma}_{IQ,JP} \\ \hat{\sigma}_{JP,IQ} & \hat{\sigma}^2_{JP} \end{bmatrix} = \begin{bmatrix} 189.600 & 23.392 \\ 23.392 & 8.206 \end{bmatrix}$$

Throughout this section, I use a numeric subscript to index each data augmentation cycle, and the value of zero indicates that these parameter estimates are starting values that precede the first I-step.

The initial I-step uses the elements in $\hat{\boldsymbol{\mu}}_0$ and $\hat{\boldsymbol{\Sigma}}_0$ to derive the regression equation that fills in the missing data. The necessary estimates are

$$\hat{\beta}_1 = \frac{\hat{\sigma}_{IQ,JP}}{\hat{\sigma}^2_{IQ}} \tag{7.6}$$

$$\hat{\beta}_0 = \hat{\mu}_{JP} - \hat{\beta}_1 \hat{\mu}_{IQ} \tag{7.7}$$

$$\hat{\sigma}^2_{JP|IQ} = \hat{\sigma}^2_{JP} - \hat{\beta}^2_1 \hat{\sigma}^2_{IQ} \tag{7.8}$$

where $\hat{\beta}_0$ and $\hat{\beta}_1$ are the intercept and slope coefficients, respectively, and $\hat{\sigma}^2_{JP|IQ}$ is the residual variance from the regression of job performance on IQ. The means, variances, and covariances that appear on the right side of the equations are elements from the mean vector and the covariance matrix.

To begin, substituting the appropriate elements of $\hat{\boldsymbol{\mu}}_0$ and $\hat{\boldsymbol{\Sigma}}_0$ into Equations 7.6 through 7.8 produces the following regression estimates: $\hat{\beta}_0 = -.057$, $\hat{\beta}_1 = 0.123$, and $\hat{\sigma}^2_{JP|IQ} = 5.320$. Next, substituting the regression coefficients and the observed IQ scores into the bracketed terms in Equation 7.1 generates predicted job performance ratings for the 10 incomplete cases. The predicted scores fall directly on a regression line, so adding normally distributed residual terms restores variability to the imputed data. I used Monte Carlo simulation methods to generate these residuals from a normal distribution with a mean of zero and a variance equal to 5.320 (the previous residual variance estimate), and I subsequently added these terms to each predicted job performance rating. Table 7.2 summarizes the imputation steps and shows the predicted scores, residual terms, and the imputed values. Again, each imputed value is a random draw from a distribution of plausible job performance ratings that is conditional on a particular IQ score.

The P-step is a standalone Bayesian analysis, the goal of which is to describe the posterior distributions of the mean vector and the covariance matrix. To begin, the P-step uses the

**TABLE 7.2. Imputed Values from the Initial I-Step of the Bivariate Example**

| IQ | Job performance | Predicted score | Random residual | Imputed value |
|---|---|---|---|---|
| 78 | — | 7.567 | 1.247 | 8.814 |
| 84 | — | 8.307 | 1.023 | 9.330 |
| 84 | — | 8.307 | −1.586 | 6.721 |
| 85 | — | 8.430 | 1.285 | 9.716 |
| 87 | — | 8.677 | −0.228 | 8.449 |
| 91 | — | 9.171 | 0.469 | 9.640 |
| 92 | — | 9.294 | −3.663 | 5.631 |
| 94 | — | 9.541 | −2.389 | 7.152 |
| 94 | — | 9.541 | −0.329 | 9.212 |
| 96 | — | 9.787 | −0.189 | 9.598 |
| 99 | 7 | — | — | — |
| 105 | 10 | — | — | — |
| 105 | 11 | — | — | — |
| 106 | 15 | — | — | — |
| 108 | 10 | — | — | — |
| 112 | 10 | — | — | — |
| 113 | 12 | — | — | — |
| 115 | 14 | — | — | — |
| 118 | 16 | — | — | — |
| 134 | 12 | — | — | — |

complete data set from the preceding I-step to estimate the mean vector and the covariance matrix. The data in Table 7.2 yield the following estimates.

$$\hat{\boldsymbol{\mu}}_1 = \begin{bmatrix} 100.000 \\ 10.063 \end{bmatrix}$$

$$\hat{\boldsymbol{\Sigma}}_1 = \begin{bmatrix} 199.579 & 25.081 \\ 25.081 & 7.270 \end{bmatrix}$$

Again, the numeric subscript denotes the fact that $\hat{\boldsymbol{\mu}}_1$ and $\hat{\boldsymbol{\Sigma}}_1$ are estimates from the first data augmentation cycle.

The ultimate goal of the P-step is to sample new estimates of the mean vector and the covariance matrix from their respective posterior distributions, so that the next I-step can use these updated parameter values to construct a different set of regression coefficients. The posterior distribution of the covariance matrix depends on the sample size, the sample means, and the sum of squares and cross products matrix, $\hat{\boldsymbol{\Lambda}}_1 = (N - 1)\hat{\boldsymbol{\Sigma}}_1$. Substituting $\hat{\boldsymbol{\Lambda}}_1$ into Equation 7.3 gives the following posterior distribution.

$$p(\boldsymbol{\Sigma} \mid \hat{\boldsymbol{\mu}}_1, \mathbf{Y}) \sim W^{-1}(N - 1, \hat{\boldsymbol{\Lambda}}_1)$$

Next, I used Monte Carlo simulation to draw a new covariance matrix from this posterior. Procedurally, this amounts to programming a computer to generate a matrix of random numbers from an inverse Wishart distribution with 19 degrees of freedom and a sum of squares and cross products matrix equal to $\hat{\Lambda}_1$. Interested readers can consult Schafer (1997, p. 184) for specific programming instructions. Monte Carlo simulation generated the following covariance matrix.

$$\Sigma_1^* = \begin{bmatrix} 488.873 & 36.663 \\ 36.663 & 7.493 \end{bmatrix}$$

Consistent with the previous section, the asterisk denotes the fact that the covariance matrix is a simulated estimate.

The sample means and the simulated covariance matrix define the posterior distribution of the mean vector, as follows:

$$p(\mu \,|\, Y, \Sigma) \sim MN(\hat{\mu}_1, N^{-1}\Sigma_1^*)$$

To draw a new estimate of the mean vector from its posterior, I used Monte Carlo simulation to generate two data points from a multivariate normal distribution with a mean vector of $\hat{\mu}_1$ and a covariance matrix equal to $N^{-1}\Sigma_1^*$. This gave the following estimates.

$$\mu_1^* = \begin{bmatrix} 87.929 \\ 8.162 \end{bmatrix}$$

Conceptually, using computer simulation procedures to generate $\mu_1^*$ and $\Sigma_1^*$ is akin to adding a random residual term to each element in $\hat{\mu}_1$ and $\hat{\Sigma}_1$. Regardless of how you think about it, this process yields new parameter values that randomly differ from the estimates that generated the regression coefficients at the initial I-step.

Having completed the first cycle, data augmentation returns to the I-step and uses the simulated parameter values to generate a new set of imputations. To illustrate, I estimated the regression parameters for the second I-step by substituting the appropriate elements of $\mu_1^*$ and $\Sigma_1^*$ into Equations 7.6 through 7.8. Doing so produced the following estimates: $\hat{\beta}_0 = 2.564$, $\hat{\beta}_1 = 0.075$, and $\hat{\sigma}_{JP|IQ}^2 = 4.743$. Table 7.3 shows the predicted scores, residual terms, and imputed values from the second I-step. As before, the bracketed terms in Equation 7.1 generate the predicted job performance ratings for the 10 incomplete cases, and I augmented each predicted score with a random residual term from a normal distribution with a mean of zero and a variance equal to 4.743. The regression coefficients from the second I-step are randomly different from those at the previous I-step, so it follows that the imputations in Table 7.3 are different from those in Table 7.2.

The second P-step is procedurally identical to the first. As before, the P-step uses the filled-in data to estimate the mean vector and the covariance matrix. The data in Table 7.3 yield the following estimates.

$$\hat{\mu}_2 = \begin{bmatrix} 100.000 \\ 10.767 \end{bmatrix}$$

$$\hat{\Sigma}_2 = \begin{bmatrix} 199.579 & 18.624 \\ 18.624 & 5.818 \end{bmatrix}$$

**TABLE 7.3. Imputed Values from the Second I-Step of the Bivariate Example**

| IQ | Job performance | Predicted score | Random residual | Imputed value |
|---|---|---|---|---|
| 78 | — | 8.413 | 0.261 | 8.675 |
| 84 | — | 8.863 | 1.358 | 10.221 |
| 84 | — | 8.863 | −1.576 | 7.287 |
| 85 | — | 8.938 | 1.914 | 10.852 |
| 87 | — | 9.088 | −0.297 | 8.791 |
| 91 | — | 9.388 | 2.725 | 12.113 |
| 92 | — | 9.463 | −0.510 | 8.953 |
| 94 | — | 9.613 | 3.000 | 12.613 |
| 94 | — | 9.613 | −1.399 | 8.214 |
| 96 | — | 9.763 | 0.865 | 10.628 |
| 99 | 7 | — | — | — |
| 105 | 10 | — | — | — |
| 105 | 11 | — | — | — |
| 106 | 15 | — | — | — |
| 108 | 10 | — | — | — |
| 112 | 10 | — | — | — |
| 113 | 12 | — | — | — |
| 115 | 14 | — | — | — |
| 118 | 16 | — | — | — |
| 134 | 12 | — | — | — |

The sample size, the sample means, and the sum of squares and cross products matrix define the posterior distribution of the covariance matrix

$$p(\Sigma \,|\, \hat{\mu}_2, Y) \sim W^{-1}(N - 1, \hat{\Lambda}_2)$$

and using Monte Carlo simulation to generate a random draw from this distribution produced the following estimates:

$$\Sigma_2^* = \begin{bmatrix} 258.754 & 26.418 \\ 26.418 & 7.929 \end{bmatrix}$$

The sample means and the simulated covariance matrix define the posterior distribution of the mean vector

$$p(\mu \,|\, Y, \Sigma) \sim MN(\hat{\mu}_2, N^{-1}\Sigma_2^*)$$

and I again used Monte Carlo procedures to draw a new pair of means from this distribution.

$$\mu_2^* = \begin{bmatrix} 101.277 \\ 10.339 \end{bmatrix}$$

**TABLE 7.4. Simulated Parameters from the First 20 P-Steps of the Bivariate Example**

| P-Step | $\mu_{IQ}^*$ | $\mu_{JP}^*$ | $\sigma_{IQ}^{2*}$ | $\sigma_{JP,IQ}^*$ | $\sigma_{JP}^{2*}$ |
|--------|----------|----------|-----------|-----------|-----------|
| 1  | 87.929  | 8.162  | 488.873 | 36.663  | 7.493  |
| 2  | 101.277 | 10.339 | 258.754 | 26.418  | 7.929  |
| 3  | 105.008 | 11.088 | 234.612 | 35.607  | 9.631  |
| 4  | 104.608 | 11.414 | 186.003 | 31.542  | 10.205 |
| 5  | 100.621 | 11.080 | 311.717 | 38.136  | 9.161  |
| 6  | 99.774  | 9.929  | 191.862 | 19.771  | 6.655  |
| 7  | 95.161  | 9.959  | 316.123 | 34.109  | 7.641  |
| 8  | 106.298 | 11.451 | 308.825 | 26.468  | 10.873 |
| 9  | 99.470  | 9.862  | 218.068 | 18.509  | 10.136 |
| 10 | 102.117 | 11.976 | 349.522 | 27.239  | 13.159 |
| 11 | 99.774  | 10.797 | 221.643 | −0.813  | 7.077  |
| 12 | 97.273  | 11.903 | 261.294 | 0.813   | 4.329  |
| 13 | 92.820  | 10.882 | 234.744 | 19.840  | 12.870 |
| 14 | 99.974  | 10.424 | 256.293 | 4.937   | 4.881  |
| 15 | 98.452  | 10.573 | 327.198 | 3.915   | 4.365  |
| 16 | 103.664 | 11.705 | 216.647 | 10.612  | 5.964  |
| 17 | 103.860 | 11.306 | 202.434 | 21.347  | 12.383 |
| 18 | 97.445  | 11.595 | 384.950 | 3.103   | 3.795  |
| 19 | 99.501  | 11.560 | 218.074 | 11.698  | 5.258  |
| 20 | 93.604  | 11.099 | 127.753 | 10.401  | 7.271  |

As you might have guessed, the next I-step constructs a new regression equation from $\mu_2^*$ and $\Sigma_2^*$ and uses this equation to generate another set of imputations. The subsequent P-step uses the parameter estimates from filled-in data (i.e., $\hat{\mu}_3$ and $\hat{\Sigma}_3$) to define the posterior distributions, from which it draws yet another set of plausible parameter values.

Data augmentation repeatedly cycles between the I-step and the P-step, often for several thousand iterations. Unlike maximum likelihood estimation, the algorithm generates parameter estimates that randomly vary across successive P-steps, so the elements in $\mu^*$ and $\Sigma^*$ never converge to a single value. For example, Table 7.4 shows the simulated parameters from the first 20 P-steps of the bivariate analysis. Notice that the estimates randomly bounce around from one cycle to the next and never land on a stationary value. This is true for every parameter, including those associated with the complete IQ variable (i.e., $\mu_{IQ}$ and $\sigma_{IQ}^2$). The random behavior of the parameter estimates across the P-steps leads to a very different definition of convergence and adds a layer of complexity that was not present with maximum likelihood estimation. I discuss the issue of convergence in considerable detail later in the chapter.

## 7.5 DATA AUGMENTATION WITH MULTIVARIATE DATA

The previous bivariate illustration is relatively straightforward because the missing values are isolated to a single variable. Applying data augmentation to multivariate data is typically more complex because each missing data pattern requires a unique regression equation (or set of equations). Despite this complication, the basic procedure is the same and only requires a slight modification to the I-step. To illustrate the changes to the I-step, I use the full data set in Table 7.1. Data augmentation with three variables is still relatively straightforward, but the logic of this example generalizes to data sets with any number of variables. Finally, note that the procedural details of the P-step are unaffected by the shift from bivariate to multivariate data, so there is no need for further discussion of this aspect of the procedure.

Not including the complete cases, there are three missing data patterns in Table 7.1: cases that are missing (1) job performance ratings only, (2) well-being scores only, and (3) both job performance and well-being scores. The presence of multiple missing data patterns complicates the imputation process somewhat because each missing data pattern requires a unique regression equation. To illustrate, Table 7.5 shows the regression equations for the three missing data patterns. Consistent with the bivariate example, the I-step uses the mean vector and the covariance matrix from the preceding P-step to estimate the regression coefficients and the corresponding residual variances. After constructing the regression equations, the algorithm generates predicted values by substituting the observed data into the relevant regression equation, and it augments each predicted score with a normally distributed residual term. Each regression equation now requires its own residual distribution, but the basic idea is the same as before. Finally, whenever two or more variables are missing, the residual distribution is multivariate normal with a mean vector of zero and a covariance matrix equal to the residual covariance matrix from the multivariate regression of the incomplete variables on the complete variables. For example, the third missing data pattern (i.e., the subset of cases with missing job performance and well-being scores) requires residuals from a multivariate normal distribution with a covariance matrix equal to the residual covariance matrix from the multivariate regression of job performance and well-being on IQ.

Estimating unique regression equations for each missing data pattern is the only procedural change associated with multivariate data. The number of missing data patterns can often be quite large, but a computational algorithm called the sweep operator simplifies the imputation process. The sweep operator repeatedly applies a series of transformations to $\mu$ and $\Sigma$ and yields new matrices that contain the desired regression coefficients and residual variances. A number of detailed descriptions of the sweep operator are available to readers who are interested in additional details (e.g., Dempster, 1969; Goodnight, 1979; Little & Rubin, 2002). The changes to the I-step have no bearing on the P-step, and the process of simulating new parameter values is identical to the earlier bivariate example.

**TABLE 7.5. I-Step Regression Equations for a Multivariate Analysis**

| Missing variables | Regression equation | Residual distribution |
|---|---|---|
| Job performance | $JP_i^* = \hat{\beta}_0 + \hat{\beta}_1(IQ_i) + \hat{\beta}_2(WB_i) + z_i$ | $z_i \sim N(0, \hat{\sigma}^2_{JP|IQ,WB})$ |
| Well-being | $WB_i^* = \hat{\beta}_0 + \hat{\beta}_1(IQ_i) + \hat{\beta}_2(JP_i) + z_i$ | $z_i \sim N(0, \hat{\sigma}^2_{WB|IQ,JP})$ |
| Job performance and well-being | $JP_i^* = \hat{\beta}_0 + \hat{\beta}_1(IQ_i) + z_i$ $WB_i^* = \hat{\beta}_0 + \hat{\beta}_1(IQ_i) + z_i$ | $Z_i \sim MN(0, \hat{\Sigma}_{JP,WB|IQ})$ |

## 7.6 SELECTING VARIABLES FOR IMPUTATION

Deciding which variables to include in the imputation phase is an important aspect of a multiple imputation analysis. At a minimum, the imputation process should include any variable that you intend to use in a subsequent statistical analysis. Excluding an analysis model variable will attenuate its associations with other variables, even if the data are MCAR or MAR. This underscores the importance of variable selection because an inadequate imputation model can introduce biases that would not occur in a maximum likelihood analysis. Fortunately, including too many variables in the imputation process is unlikely to produce bias, so adopting a liberal approach to variable selection is usually a good strategy. The primary downside of including too many variables is the possibility of convergence problems (as an upper limit, the number of variables cannot exceed the number of cases).

In addition to including analysis model variables, the imputation phase should preserve any higher-order effects that are of interest in the analysis phase as well as any other special features of the data. In particular, researchers in the behavioral and the social sciences are often interested in estimating interaction (i.e., moderation) effects where the magnitude of the association between two variables depends on a third variable (e.g., a regression model where gender moderates the association between psychological well-being and job performance). In addition, many common statistical analyses address implicit interaction effects. For example, multiple group structural equation models and multilevel models do not necessarily contain interaction terms, but they do posit group differences in the mean structure, the covariance structure, or both. Regardless of whether the higher-order effect is an explicit part of the statistical analysis or a hidden feature of the data, it is necessary to specify an imputation model that preserves any complex associations among the variables. Again, failing to do so can bias the subsequent analysis results, regardless of the missing data mechanism. I address this topic in detail in Chapter 9, but for now, it is important to raise awareness of the issue.

Chapter 5 introduced the idea of an inclusive analysis strategy that incorporates a number of auxiliary variables into the missing data handling procedure (Collins, Schafer, & Kam, 2001). Recall that an auxiliary variable is one that is ancillary to the substantive research questions but is a potential correlate of missingness or a correlate of an incomplete analysis model variable. Methodologists have long recommended the use of auxiliary variables in a multiple-imputation analysis. For example, Rubin (1996, p. 479) stated that "the advice has always been to include as many variables as possible when doing multiple imputation." Using auxiliary variables in a multiple imputation analysis is particularly straightforward because the variables only play a role in the imputation phase. Including auxiliary variables in the imputation process infuses the filled-in values with the auxiliary information, so there is no need to include the extra variables in the subsequent analysis phase. This is in contrast to maximum likelihood estimation, which incorporates auxiliary variables via the slightly awkward saturated correlates approach. As an aside, multiple imputation can generally handle a larger set of auxiliary variables than a maximum likelihood analysis, so there is usually no reason to limit the number of auxiliary variables. Chapter 5 describes the process of identifying auxiliary variables, so that information need not be reiterated here.

Finally, although it is important to include all analysis variables in the imputation phase, it makes no difference whether a particular variable will ultimately serve as an explanatory variable or an outcome variable. For example, Chapter 8 illustrates a multiple regression analysis in which psychological well-being and job satisfaction predict job performance. Both predictor variables have missing data, but the imputation model uses the observed job performance scores to impute the missing values. At first glance, using an outcome variable to impute an incomplete independent variable may seem incorrect and somewhat circular. However, the addition of a random residual term to each imputed value eliminates any bias that might result from doing so (Little & Rubin, 2002). In fact, multiple imputation programs make no distinction between independent and dependent variables and only require you to specify a set of input variables.

## 7.7 THE MEANING OF CONVERGENCE

The data augmentation algorithm belongs to a family of **Markov Chain Monte Carlo** (i.e., MCMC) procedures (Jackman, 2000). The goal of a Markov chain Monte Carlo algorithm is to simulate random draws from a distribution (e.g., random draws from the posterior distribution or from the distribution of missing values). Repeatedly cycling between the I- and P-steps creates a so-called data augmentation chain, as follows:

$$Y_1^*, \theta_1^*, Y_2^*, \theta_2^*, Y_3^*, \theta_3^*, Y_4^*, \theta_4^*, \ldots, Y_t^*, \theta_t^*$$

where $Y_t^*$ represents the imputed values at I-step $t$ and $\theta_t^*$ contains the simulated parameter values at P-step $t$. Over the course of a long enough chain, the I-step generates imputations from a large array of plausible parameter values, so the $Y_t^*$ values are effectively drawn from a distribution that averages over the entire range of the posterior distribution. Similarly, the P-step generates parameters from a large number of plausible $Y_t^*$ values, so the simulated parameters form a posterior distribution that averages over all possible values of the missing data.

Simulating random draws from a distribution requires a new definition of convergence. Whereas maximum likelihood converges when the parameter estimates no longer change across successive iterations, data augmentation converges when the *distributions* become stable and no longer change in a systematic fashion (i.e., the distributions become **stationary**). The complicated aspect of this definition is that each step in the data augmentation chain is dependent on the previous step. That is, the simulated parameters at P-step $t$ depend on the imputed values at the preceding I-step, the imputations at I-step $t + 1$ depend on the simulated parameters from P-step $t$, the simulated parameters at P-step $t + 1$ depend on the imputed values at I-step $t + 1$, and so on. Although the behavior of the data augmentation algorithm is seemingly random from one cycle to the next, the mutual dependence of the I- and P-steps induces a correlation between the simulated parameters from successive P-steps. By extension, analyzing data sets from successive I-steps is inappropriate because the resulting imputations are also dependent (i.e., imputations from adjacent I-steps do not originate from a stable distribution).

Researchers often assess convergence by determining the number of data augmentation cycles that need to lapse before the imputations at iteration $t + k$ are independent of those at iteration $t$. Monitoring the behavior of the simulated parameter values across a large number of P-steps is one way to do this. For example, suppose that 10 data augmentation cycles separate two sets of simulated parameter values, $\theta_t^*$ and $\theta_{t+10}^*$. A correlation between $\theta_t^*$ and $\theta_{t+10}^*$ suggests that the posterior distribution is systematically changing after 10 cycles. Consequently, analyzing data sets that are separated by only 10 data augmentation cycles is inappropriate because the imputed values are also dependent. In contrast, suppose that $\theta_t^*$ is uncorrelated with the simulated parameters from 50 cycles later in the chain. The lack of correlation suggests that $\theta_t^*$ and $\theta_{t+50}^*$ originate from a stable posterior distribution, so the two sets of parameter values should produce independent imputations. From a practical perspective, this implies that at least 50 data augmentation cycles need to separate the data sets that you analyze in the subsequent analysis phase.

## 7.8 CONVERGENCE DIAGNOSTICS

Methodologists have proposed dozens of techniques for assessing the convergence of data augmentation, the majority of which are computationally complex and difficult to implement (e.g., Gelman & Rubin, 1992; Geweke, 1992; Geyer, 1992; Johnson, 1996; Mykland, Tierney, & Yu, 1995; Ritter & Tanner, 1992; Roberts, 1992; Zellner & Min, 1995). A comprehensive review of convergence diagnostics is beyond the scope of this chapter, but interested readers can consult Cowles and Carlin (1996) for an overview of some of these procedures. I focus primarily on the use of graphical displays (time-series plots and autocorrelation function plots) because these methods are readily available in multiple imputation software packages. Graphical techniques are certainly not foolproof, but they are straightforward to implement and are relatively easy to understand.

Assessing convergence requires an exploratory data augmentation chain. The purpose of the exploratory analysis is to gather the simulated parameter values from a large number of P-steps and use graphical displays to examine their behavior (the literature sometimes refers to this as an **output analysis**). Establishing guidelines for the length of the exploratory chain is difficult because a number of factors influence convergence speed (e.g., the missing data rate, the choice of starting values for the mean vector and the covariance matrix). Running the data augmentation algorithm for several thousand cycles is probably sufficient in most situations, but data sets with a large proportion of missing values may require longer chains. In this section, I use the small data set in Table 7.1 to illustrate graphical diagnostic techniques. I generated an exploratory data augmentation chain of 5,000 cycles and saved the simulated parameters from each P-step to a file for further analysis. As you will see, the information from this exploratory analysis is important for planning the final data augmentation chain that generates the imputed data sets.

### What Does EM Tell You about Convergence?

Using the EM algorithm (an algorithm that generates maximum likelihood estimates of the mean vector and the covariance matrix; see Chapter 4) to estimate the mean vector and the covariance matrix is a useful precursor to a multiple imputation analysis. EM estimates make good starting values for data augmentation because they tend to be representative of the posterior distribution. Consequently, data augmentation will generally converge more rapidly from a set of EM starting values. In addition, the number of EM iterations is a useful diagnostic for assessing convergence. Schafer and colleagues (Schafer, 1997; Schafer & Olsen, 1998) suggest that EM converges more slowly than data augmentation, so researchers often estimate convergence speed by doubling the number of EM iterations. This approach is far from ideal, and blindly relying on the "two times the number of EM iterations" rule of thumb is not a good way to assess convergence. Nevertheless, the EM algorithm is a good starting point. Returning to the data in Table 7.1, note that the EM algorithm converged in 60 iterations, so data augmentation may require even fewer cycles to converge. However, doubling the number of EM iterations can provide a more conservative initial guess about convergence speed.

## 7.9 TIME-SERIES PLOTS

A **time-series plot** displays the simulated parameter values from the P-step on the vertical axis and the data augmentation cycles along the horizontal axis. To illustrate, consider the exploratory data augmentation chain that I generated from the small job performance data set. Figure 7.3 shows time-series plots for the job performance and the psychological well-being means. I arbitrarily chose to plot the parameter values from the first 200 data augmentation cycles, but did so after inspecting the plots over the entire chain. The top panel of Figure 7.3 suggests that the well-being means bounce around in a seemingly random fashion with no discernible long-term trends. The absence of trend is an ideal situation and suggests that this parameter quickly converges to a stable distribution. In contrast, the bottom panel of the figure shows a time-series plot that is somewhat less ideal (though not bad). Specifically, notice that the job performance means exhibit systematic upward and downward trends that last for 40 iterations or more. These systematic trends suggest that this parameter's posterior distribution requires at least 40 P-steps to converge (i.e., 40 data augmentation cycles need to lapse before the simulated parameters become independent). I examined the time-series plots for all of the means and covariance matrix elements, and they were largely consistent with those in Figure 7.3.

Figure 7.3 emphasizes that the simulated parameters can converge at different rates. For example, the job performance mean systematically wandered up and down while the well-being mean settled into a random pattern almost immediately. Perhaps not surprisingly, the missing data rate—or more accurately, the fraction of missing information—is responsible for these differences. The **fraction of missing information** quantifies the proportion of a parameter's sampling error that is due to missing data. I describe this concept in more detail in Chapter 8, but you can think of missing information as a measure that combines the missing data rate and the magnitude of the correlations among the variables. For example, the fraction of missing information and the proportion of missing data are roughly equal when variables are uncorrelated, but the missing information is typically less than the missing data rate when variables are correlated because the shared variability among the variables mitigates the loss of information.

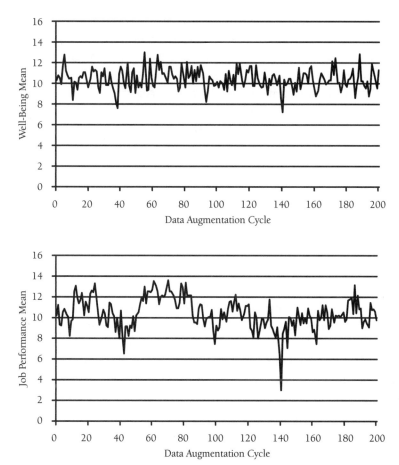

**FIGURE 7.3.** Time-series plots for the simulated well-being and job performance means. The top panel shows a time-series plot that exhibits no systematic trends. The bottom panel shows systematic trends that last for 40 iterations or more.

Because the fraction of missing information tends to vary across the elements in the mean vector and the covariance matrix, you should attempt to examine time-series plots for every parameter that is affected by missing data. Paying particularly close attention to parameters with high rates of missing information (i.e., high missing data rates) is a good idea because these parameters tend to converge most slowly. Multivariate data sets often have a prohibitively large number of covariance matrix elements, so the fraction of missing information can serve as a screening device for identifying the most important time-series plots (multiple imputation programs typically report these values). As shown in the next chapter, the fraction of missing information influences the magnitude of the multiple-imputation standard errors, so inspecting these values is often useful in and of itself.

## Worst Linear Function

In addition to inspecting the behavior of individual parameters, it is useful to examine a summary measure that Schafer (1997) terms the worst linear function of the parameters. The

**worst linear function** combines the simulated parameters from each P-step into a single composite that weights each parameter according to its convergence speed. The idea behind the worst linear function is to create a summary measure that converges more slowly than the individual parameters, so the time series plot of the worst linear function should provide a conservative gauge of convergence speed. However, Schafer (1997) cautions that the worst linear function is not a definitive diagnostic tool, because other combinations of the simulated parameters may converge at an even slower rate.

The worst linear function is a weighted sum of the simulated parameters at P-step $t$

$$\text{WLF}_t = \mathbf{v}^T \boldsymbol{\theta}_t^* \tag{7.9}$$

where $\boldsymbol{\theta}_t^*$ is a column vector that contains the simulated parameter values and $\mathbf{v}$ is a weight vector that quantifies the change in the corresponding maximum likelihood estimates at the final EM iteration. Parameters that converge slowly exhibit the greatest change at the final iteration, so $\mathbf{v}$ assigns larger weights to parameters that converge slowly. The complete-data parameters do not change at the final EM iteration, so they do not contribute to the function (the weights are zero for these parameters). Finally, note that the worst linear function can take on positive or negative values because it centers the parameters in $\boldsymbol{\theta}_t^*$ at their maximum likelihood estimates.

With regard to the exploratory data chain from the small job performance data set, Figure 7.4 shows the time-series plot of the worst linear function. Notice that the function exhibits systematic upward and downward trends that last for approximately 50 iterations. Taken together, Figures 7.3 and 7.4 suggest that the joint posterior distribution is stable (i.e., the simulated parameter values are no longer dependent) after about 50 data augmentation cycles, although certain parameters (e.g., the well-being mean) converge far more rapidly. From a practical perspective, this implies that at least 50 data augmentation cycles need to separate the data sets that you analyze in the subsequent analysis phase. Doubling or tripling this number provides an extra margin of safety.

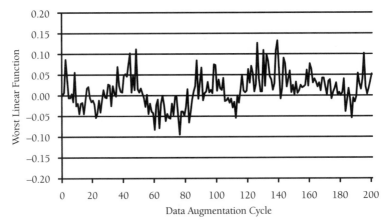

**FIGURE 7.4.** Time-series plot for the worst linear function of the parameters. The worst linear function shows systematic trends that last for approximately 60 iterations.

## 7.10 AUTOCORRELATION FUNCTION PLOTS

The systematic trends in the previous time-series plots suggest that certain parameters are serially dependent across successive data augmentation cycles. The **autocorrelation** quantifies the magnitude and duration of this dependency and is an important diagnostic tool for assessing convergence. The lag-$k$ autocorrelation is the Pearson correlation between sets of parameter values separated by $k$ iterations in the data augmentation chain. To illustrate, reconsider the exploratory chain of 5,000 data augmentation cycles that I generated from the data in Table 7.1. The Lag-1 columns of Table 7.6 show the simulated job performance means from P-steps 1 through 10 and 4,991 through 5,000. Notice that the one row (i.e., one data augmentation cycle) offsets the parameter values, such that the mean at P-step 2 is coupled to the mean at P-step 1, the mean at P-step 3 is linked to the mean at P-step 2, and so on. Computing the Pearson correlation between the 4,999 pairs of parameter values gives the lag-1 autocorrelation, $r_1 = 0.61$. This correlation indicates that the job performance mean at P-step $t$ is highly dependent on the mean at the preceding iteration. Computing additional lag-$k$ correlations can help determine the duration of this dependency. For example, Table 7.6 also shows data excerpts for the lag-2 and the lag-3 autocorrelations. The lag-2 autocorrelation quantifies the dependency between estimates separated by two iterations (e.g., the mean from P-step 3 is linked to the estimate from P-step 1, the mean at P-step 4 is coupled with the mean from P-step 2, and so on), and the lag-3 autocorrelation separates the simulated

**TABLE 7.6. Data for the Lag–1, Lag–2, and Lag–3 Autocorrelations**

| Simulated values | | Parameter values for autocorrelation computations | | | | | |
|---|---|---|---|---|---|---|---|
| P-step | $\mu_{jP}^*$ | Lag-1 | | Lag-2 | | Lag-3 | |
| 1 | 8.16 | 8.16 | — | 8.16 | — | 8.16 | — |
| 2 | 10.34 | 10.34 | 8.16 | 10.34 | — | 10.34 | — |
| 3 | 11.09 | 11.09 | 10.34 | 11.09 | 8.16 | 11.09 | — |
| 4 | 11.41 | 11.41 | 11.09 | 11.41 | 10.34 | 11.41 | 8.16 |
| 5 | 11.08 | 11.08 | 11.41 | 11.08 | 11.09 | 11.08 | 10.34 |
| 6 | 9.93 | 9.93 | 11.08 | 9.93 | 11.41 | 9.93 | 11.09 |
| 7 | 9.96 | 9.96 | 9.93 | 9.96 | 11.08 | 9.96 | 11.41 |
| 8 | 11.45 | 11.45 | 9.96 | 11.45 | 9.93 | 11.45 | 11.08 |
| 9 | 9.86 | 9.86 | 11.45 | 9.86 | 9.96 | 9.86 | 9.93 |
| 10 | 11.98 | 11.98 | 9.86 | 11.98 | 11.45 | 11.98 | 9.96 |
| ... | ... | ... | ... | ... | ... | ... | ... |
| 4991 | 10.66 | 10.66 | 11.29 | 10.66 | 10.88 | 10.66 | 9.53 |
| 4992 | 11.11 | 11.11 | 10.66 | 11.11 | 11.29 | 11.11 | 10.88 |
| 4993 | 12.13 | 12.13 | 11.11 | 12.13 | 10.66 | 12.13 | 11.29 |
| 4994 | 10.54 | 10.54 | 12.13 | 10.54 | 11.11 | 10.54 | 10.66 |
| 4995 | 11.22 | 11.22 | 10.54 | 11.22 | 12.13 | 11.22 | 11.11 |
| 4996 | 10.63 | 10.63 | 11.22 | 10.63 | 10.54 | 10.63 | 12.13 |
| 4997 | 9.94 | 9.94 | 10.63 | 9.94 | 11.22 | 9.94 | 10.54 |
| 4998 | 12.17 | 12.17 | 9.94 | 12.17 | 10.63 | 12.17 | 11.22 |
| 4999 | 11.79 | 11.79 | 12.17 | 11.79 | 9.94 | 11.79 | 10.63 |
| 5000 | 11.34 | 11.34 | 11.79 | 11.34 | 12.17 | 11.34 | 9.94 |

parameter values by three iterations. The estimates of the lag-2 and lag-3 correlations are $r_2$ = 0.52 and $r_3$ = 0.46, respectively.

An **autocorrelation function plot** (also known as a **correlogram**) is a graphical summary that displays the autocorrelation values on the vertical axis and the lag values on the horizontal axis. For example, Figure 7.5 shows the autocorrelation function plots for the job performance and the well-being means. The horizontal dashed lines represent the two-tailed critical values for an alpha level of 0.05 (Bartlett, 1946). The top panel of Figure 7.5 shows that autocorrelation in the well-being means drops to within sampling error of zero almost immediately. This suggests that the parameter's distribution becomes stable after a very small number of data augmentation cycles. In contrast, the bottom panel of the figure shows autocorrelations that exceed chance levels (i.e., fall outside the critical values) for nearly 60 data augmentation cycles. This suggests that the posterior distribution of the job performance

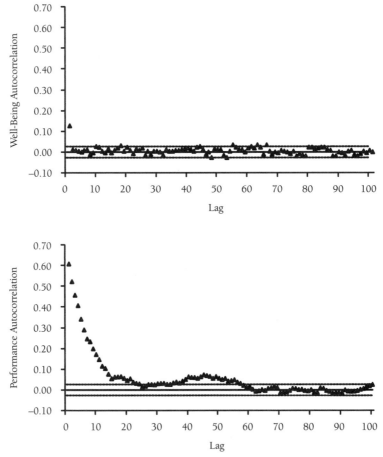

**FIGURE 7.5.** Autocorrelation function plots (correlograms) for the simulated well-being and job performance means. The top plot shows autocorrelations (denoted by a triangle symbol) that drop to within sampling error of zero almost immediately. The bottom plot shows nonzero autocorrelations that persist for nearly 60 iterations.

mean requires approximately 60 data augmentation cycles to become stationary. As an aside, autocorrelations are subject to considerable sampling fluctuation, so data augmentation chains that are several thousand cycles in length will provide the best assessment of serial dependencies.

Figures 7.3 and 7.5 are largely consistent with one another. For example, the time-series plot indicates that the job performance mean has systematic trends lasting for at least 40 data augmentation cycles, and the corresponding autocorrelation plot indicates serial dependencies that last for approximately 60 iterations. In contrast, both plots suggest that distribution of the well-being mean stabilizes almost immediately. Taken together, the diagnostic information suggests that the slowest parameters are stationary (i.e., become independent) after about 60 iterations, although some distributions are stable well before that. Again, multiplying this value by a factor of two or three is a conservative strategy for planning the final data augmentation run.

## 7.11 ASSESSING CONVERGENCE FROM ALTERNATE STARTING VALUES

Thus far, I have only considered using EM estimates as starting values for data augmentation. EM estimates are ideal in the sense that they are often located near the center of the posterior distribution. However, methodologists disagree on whether a single set of starting values is sufficient for assessing convergence (Gelman & Rubin, 1992; Geyer, 1992; Raftery & Lewis, 1992). For example, Raftery and Lewis (1992) argue that a single exploratory data augmentation chain is usually sufficient, whereas Gelman and Rubin (1992) recommend using multiple exploratory data augmentation chains, each of which uses starting values for $\mu$ and $\Sigma$ that are far from the center of their respective posterior distributions.

Multiple exploratory chains are useful for assessing whether idiosyncratic features of the data influence convergence and can yield a more conservative gauge of convergence speed. However, generating alternate starting values can be computationally complex and difficult to implement (Gelman & Rubin, 1992). One straightforward approach is to use the bootstrap to generate starting values for each exploratory data augmentation chain (Schafer, 1997). The bootstrap treats the data as a miniature population from which it draws samples of size $N$ with replacement (see Chapter 5 for additional information on the bootstrap). The bootstrap procedure can generate a small number of alternate estimates of the mean vector and the covariance matrix. Because the ultimate goal is to start data augmentation with parameter values that are far from the center of their posterior distributions, the bootstrap estimates should be somewhat noisy and unrepresentative of their true values. To accomplish this, Schafer (1997) recommends drawing bootstrap samples with half as many cases as the original data set because the additional sampling error is likely to yield estimates from the tails of the posterior distribution. After generating a small number of alternative starting values, you can run multiple exploratory data augmentation chains and use graphical diagnostic techniques to examine the convergence of each chain. Some multiple imputation programs generate bootstrap starting values, so implementing this approach is relatively straightforward.

## 7.12 CONVERGENCE PROBLEMS

You may occasionally encounter situations in which data augmentation fails to converge. For example, Figure 7.6 shows what the time-series and autocorrelation function plots would look like when data augmentation fails to converge. The times-series plot indicates the presence of systematic trends lasting for several hundred iterations, and the autocorrelation function plot shows serial dependencies that persist for an extended period (e.g., the lag-200 correlation is approximately $r_{200} = 0.70$).

Convergence problems can occur because some of the parameters are inestimable or because the number of variables is close to the number of cases. Eliminating the problematic variables is one way to solve convergence problems, but this solution may not be ideal, particularly if it alters the substantive research goals. An alternate strategy is to use a so-called

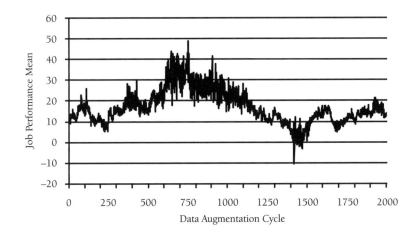

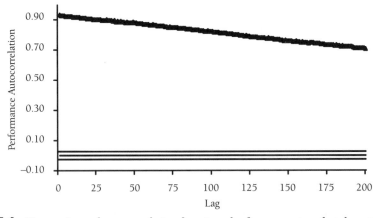

**FIGURE 7.6.** Time-series and autocorrelation function plot for parameters that do not converge. The top panel shows a time-series plot that exhibits systematic trends that last for hundreds of iterations and simulated parameter values that are outside of the plausible score range of 1 to 20. The bottom panel shows autocorrelations (denoted by a triangle symbol) that are close to $r = 0.70$ at lag-200.

**ridge prior distribution** for the covariance matrix. The basic idea behind the ridge prior is to add a small number of imaginary data records from a hypothetical population where the variables are uncorrelated. Adding these extra cases can stabilize estimation and eliminate convergence problems. Chapter 9 describes the ridge prior in more detail.

## 7.13 GENERATING THE FINAL SET OF IMPUTATIONS

After assessing convergence, you can begin planning the data augmentation run that will generate the imputed data sets for the subsequent analysis phase. As I explained previously, an important objective of the imputation phase is to generate data sets that mimic independent draws from the distribution of the missing values. There are two strategies for generating independent imputations: sample imputed data sets at regular intervals in the data augmentation chain (e.g., save and analyze the imputed data set from every 200$^{th}$ I-step), or generate several data augmentation chains and save the imputed data at the final I-step in each chain. The multiple imputation literature refers to these two approaches as sequential and parallel data augmentation chains, respectively.

### Sequential Data Augmentation Chains

One way to generate independent imputations is to sample imputed data sets at regular intervals in a single data augmentation chain (e.g., save and analyze the data from every 200th I-step). The literature sometimes refers to this approach as **sequential data augmentation**. The difficulty with sequential data augmentation is determining the number of iterations that need to lapse between each saved file (i.e., the number of **between-imputation iterations**). Choosing too large an interval is not a problem, but specifying too few between-imputation iterations can result in correlated imputations and negatively biased standard errors. Fortunately, the time-series and autocorrelation function plots provide the necessary information to specify the number of between-imputation iterations. For example, if the longest serial dependency lasts for 20 data augmentation cycles, then the between-imputation interval should be at least 20 iterations. Again, the graphical diagnostics are far from perfect, so doubling or tripling that value is probably a safe strategy.

To illustrate sequential data augmentation, reconsider the data in Table 7.1. Suppose that the goal is to generate $m = 20$ complete data sets for the subsequent analysis phase. The graphical diagnostics from the earlier example suggest that the slowest parameters converged (i.e., became independent) after about 60 iterations, so between-imputation interval should be at least 60 cycles, if not longer. Specifying 200 between-imputations is probably sufficient because this interval is more than three times larger than the slowest convergence rate. Consequently, the final data augmentation chain consists of 4,000 cycles. Specifically, an initial **burn-in period** of 200 cycles precedes the first data set, and 200 between-imputation cycles separate each of the remaining data sets. The burn-in iterations give the parameter distributions time to stabilize, and the between-imputation iterations ensure that the resulting imputations are independent.

## Parallel Data Augmentation Chains

**Parallel data augmentation** is a second method for generating independent imputations. Rather than saving data sets at specified intervals in the chain, this approach generates several chains and saves the imputed data at the final I-step in each chain. For example, generating 20 imputations from the data in Table 7.1 would require 20 separate data augmentation chains, each of which is comprised of 200 iterations. The $m$ chains can originate from a common set of starting values or from different estimates of the mean vector and the covariance matrix. The primary consideration is to generate chains that are long enough to ensure that the distribution of missing values has stabilized and that the imputations are independent of the starting values. As with sequential approach, graphical diagnostics can determine the length of the data augmentation chains.

Methodologists have debated on whether to use sequential or parallel data augmentation chains. Much of this discussion centers on the detection of convergence problems (e.g., Gelman & Rubin, 1992; Geyer, 1992; Raftery & Lewis, 1992), but computational efficiency is also a consideration (e.g., Schafer, 1997, pp. 137–138; Smith & Roberts, 1993). If the parameter distributions converge properly, it probably makes little difference whether a single chain or multiple chains generate the final imputations. Because sequential chains are somewhat easier to implement in existing software packages, the final decision may be one of convenience. My advice is to explore convergence using a relatively small number of parallel chains that originate from a diverse set of starting values. If you are comfortable that the algorithm is converging properly, choose a conservative number of burn-in and between-imputation iterations and generate the final set of imputations from a single data augmentation chain.

## 7.14 HOW MANY DATA SETS ARE NEEDED?

Choosing the number of imputed data sets to save and analyze is one of the most basic decisions in a multiple imputation analysis. Conventional wisdom suggests that multiple imputation analyses require relatively few imputations, and the literature historically recommends between three and five imputed data sets (e.g., Rubin, 1987, 1996; Schafer, 1997; Schafer & Olsen, 1998). However, there are good reasons to use many more imputations. In the next chapter, I show that multiple imputation standard errors decrease as the number of imputations increases, and analyzing an infinite number of imputed data sets yields the lowest possible standard error. Obviously, it is not feasible to analyze an infinite number of data sets, but this property suggests that using a large number of imputations can improve power. Power issues aside, some of the multiparameter significance tests outlined in Chapter 8 become more accurate as $m$ increases, so analyzing a large number of data sets can improve the validity of these tests.

## Relative Efficiency

The recommendation to use between three and five data sets follows from the fact that the resulting standard errors are not appreciably larger than their hypothetical minimum values. **Relative efficiency** quantifies the magnitude of a multiple imputation standard error (or more precisely the sampling variance, or squared standard error) relative to its theoretical minimum

$$RE = \left(1 + \frac{FMI}{m}\right)^{-1} \tag{7.10}$$

where $m$ is the number of imputed data sets and FMI is the fraction of missing information (Rubin, 1987). I describe the fraction of missing information in Chapter 8, but for now, you can think of it as being roughly equal to the proportion of missing data. To illustrate, suppose that $m = 5$ and the fraction of missing information for a particular parameter is 0.20 (e.g., there is a 20% missing data rate). Equation 7.10 suggests that the sampling variance (i.e., squared standard error) based on an infinite number of imputations is 96% as large as the sampling variance based on only $m = 5$ imputations. From a practical standpoint, this means that analyzing five imputed data sets should produce a standard error that is only $\sqrt{1 + (0.20/5)} = 1.02$ times larger than its hypothetical minimum value.

Table 7.7 shows the relative efficiency and proportional increase in the standard error for different fractions of missing information and different numbers of imputations. The table shows two noticeable trends. First, the largest gains in efficiency (or alternatively, largest reductions in the standard error) occur between 3 and 10 imputations, and using more than 10 data sets has little additional benefit. Second, using a large number of imputations is most beneficial when the fraction of missing information is large. Researchers have traditionally relied on relative efficiency estimates such as those in Table 7.6 when choosing the number of imputations. Doing so has led to the common recommendation to analyze between three and five imputed data sets. Interestingly, this common rule of thumb does not necessarily maximize power.

## The Number of Imputations and Power

Graham, Olchowski, and Gilreath (2007) used computer simulation studies to show that the number of imputations has a more dramatic impact on power than it does on relative

**TABLE 7.7. Relative Efficiency and Proportional Increase in Standard Error for Different Fractions of Missing Information and Numbers of Imputations**

| FMI | $m = 3$ | | $m = 5$ | | $m = 10$ | | $m = 20$ | |
| --- | --- | --- | --- | --- | --- | --- | --- | --- |
| | R.E. | P.S.E. | R.E. | P.S.E. | R.E. | P.S.E. | R.E. | P.S.E. |
| 0.10 | 0.97 | 1.02 | 0.98 | 1.01 | 0.99 | 1.00 | 1.00 | 1.00 |
| 0.20 | 0.94 | 1.03 | 0.96 | 1.02 | 0.98 | 1.01 | 0.99 | 1.00 |
| 0.30 | 0.91 | 1.05 | 0.94 | 1.03 | 0.97 | 1.01 | 0.99 | 1.01 |
| 0.40 | 0.88 | 1.06 | 0.93 | 1.04 | 0.96 | 1.02 | 0.98 | 1.01 |
| 0.50 | 0.86 | 1.08 | 0.91 | 1.05 | 0.95 | 1.02 | 0.98 | 1.01 |
| 0.60 | 0.83 | 1.10 | 0.89 | 1.06 | 0.94 | 1.03 | 0.97 | 1.01 |
| 0.70 | 0.81 | 1.11 | 0.88 | 1.07 | 0.93 | 1.03 | 0.97 | 1.02 |

Note. R.E. = relative efficiency; P.S.E. = proportional increase in standard error; $m$ = number of imputations; FMI = fraction of missing information.

efficiency. For example, returning to Table 7.7, the combination of $m = 5$ and FMI = .50 yields a relative efficiency value of .91. In contrast, Graham et al. show that the power for this set of conditions is 13% below its ideal value. Decreasing the number of imputations to $m = 3$ reduces relative efficiency to .86, but reduces power to 75% of its optimal level.

Contrary to conventional wisdom, the Graham et al. study indicates that using more than 10 imputations has a beneficial impact on statistical power. Considered as a whole, their simulations suggest that 20 imputations are sufficient for many realistic situations, and increasing the number of imputations beyond 20 will only affect power if the fraction of missing information is very high (e.g., FMI > 0.50). The Graham et al. study also shows that an analysis based on 20 imputations yields comparable power to a maximum likelihood analysis, so generating a *minimum* of 20 imputed data sets seems to be a good rule of thumb for many situations.

## Other Considerations

Power issues aside, there are other good reasons to use a large number of imputations. As I mentioned previously, analyzing a large number of data sets can improve the validity of the multiparameter significance tests in the next chapter. In addition, the estimates of missing information that most imputation programs report can be very noisy when the number of imputations is small (Graham et al., 2007; Harel, 2007; Schafer, 1997), and stable estimates require between 50 and 100 imputations (Harel, 2007). Obtaining accurate estimates of the missing information is usually not an important analytic goal, but these estimates are useful for assessing the impact of missing data on standard errors. Taken as a whole, there are many issues to consider when deciding on the number of imputed data sets to save and analyze. Although $m = 20$ appears to be a good rule of thumb, increasing the number of imputations beyond this point is a good idea and often adds very little to the total processing time.

## 7.15 SUMMARY

Multiple imputation is an alternative to maximum likelihood estimation and is the other state-of-the-art missing data technique that methodologists currently recommend. The imputation approach outlined in this chapter makes the same assumptions as maximum likelihood estimation—MAR data and multivariate normality—but takes the very different tack of filling in the missing values prior to the analysis. A multiple imputation analysis consists of three distinct steps: the imputation phase, the analysis phase, and the pooling phase. The imputation phase creates multiple copies of the data set (e.g., $m = 20$), each of which contains different estimates of the missing values. The purpose of the analysis phase is to analyze the filled-in data sets. This step applies the same statistical procedures that you would have used had the data been complete. Procedurally, the only difference is that you perform each analysis $m$ times, once for each imputed data set. Finally, the pooling phase uses Rubin's (1987) rules to combine the $m$ sets of parameter estimates and standard errors into a single set of results. Because of its complexity, the imputation phase was the primary focus of this chapter.

The imputation phase uses an iterative data augmentation algorithm that consists of an I-step and a P-step. The I-step uses an estimate of the mean vector and the covariance matrix to build a set of regression equations where the complete variables for a given missing data pattern predict the incomplete variables for that pattern. Substituting the observed data into these equations generates predicted scores for the missing variables. The predicted scores fall directly on a regression surface, so the imputation procedure restores variability to the data by adding a normally distributed residual term to each predicted value. From a Bayesian perspective, each imputed value is a random draw from the conditional distribution of the missing values, given the observed data (i.e., draws from the posterior predictive distribution). However, from a procedural standpoint, the I-step amounts to stochastic regression imputation.

The ultimate goal of the imputation phase is to generate $m$ complete data sets, each of which contains different estimates of the missing values. Creating unique sets of imputations requires different estimates of the mean vector and the covariance matrix at each I-step, and the purpose of the P-step is to generate these estimates. The P-step begins by using the filled-in data from the preceding I-step to estimate the mean vector and the covariance matrix, after which it generates alternative parameter estimates by randomly drawing new values from their respective posterior distributions. Conceptually, the algorithm generates new parameter values by adding a random residual term to each element in the complete-data mean vector and covariance matrix. The subsequent I-step uses these simulated parameter values to construct a new set of regression coefficients, and the process begins anew. Repeating the two-step procedure a number of times generates multiple copies of the data, each of which contains unique estimates of the missing values.

Unlike maximum likelihood estimation, data augmentation generates parameter values that constantly vary across successive P-steps. Although the behavior of the data augmentation algorithm is seemingly random from one cycle to the next, the parameter values and the imputations from successive iterations are correlated. Because the ultimate goal is to simulate independent draws from a distribution of plausible values, it is inappropriate to save and analyze the filled-in data sets from successive I-steps. One way to simulate independent draws from the distribution of missing data is to sample imputed data sets at regular intervals in the data augmentation chain (e.g., save and analyze the data from every 200th I-step). Time-series and autocorrelation function plots can help determine if the number of between-imputation iterations is large enough to produce independent sets of imputed values.

The convergence diagnostics play an important role in planning the final data augmentation run that generates the complete data sets. Choosing the number of imputed data sets to save and analyze is one of the most basic decisions in a multiple imputation analysis. Conventional wisdom suggests that multiple imputation analyses require relatively few imputations, and the literature historically recommends between three and five imputed data sets. However, contemporary research suggests that analyzing 20 data sets will maximize power in most situations. Although $m = 20$ appears to be a good rule of thumb, there is no downside (other than computer processing time) to using far more imputations (e.g., $m = 50$ or $m = 100$).

The next chapter describes the analysis and pooling phases. The purpose of the analysis phase is to analyze the filled-in data sets from the preceding imputation phase. This step consists of $m$ statistical analyses, one for each imputed data set. The analysis phase yields several sets of parameter estimates and standard errors, so the goal of the pooling phase is to combine everything into a single set of results. Rubin (1987) outlined relatively straightforward formulas for pooling parameter estimates and standard errors. Because the analysis phase is relatively straightforward, most of Chapter 8 is devoted to the pooling phase and related inferential procedures. At the end of Chapter 8, I revisit some of the data analysis examples from Chapter 4 and illustrate how to analyze the data using multiple imputation.

## 7.16 RECOMMENDED READINGS

Allison, P. D. (2002). *Missing data*. Newbury Park, CA: Sage.

Graham, J. W. (2009). Missing data analysis: Making it work in the real world. *Annual Review of Psychology, 60*, 549–576.

Graham, J. W., Olchowski, A E., Gilreath, T. D. (2007). How many imputations are really needed? Some practical clarifications of multiple imputation theory. *Prevention Science, 8*, 206–213.

Rubin, D. B. (1987). *Multiple imputation for nonresponse in surveys*. New York: Wiley.

Rubin, D. B. (1996). Multiple imputation after 18+ years. *Journal of the American Statistical Association, 91*, 473–489.

Schafer, J. L. (1997). *Analysis of incomplete multivariate data*. New York: Chapman.

Schafer, J. L., & Graham, J. W. (2002). Missing data: Our view of the state of the art. *Psychological Methods, 7*, 147–177.

Schafer, J. L., & Olsen, M. K. (1998). Multiple imputation for multivariate missing-data problems: A data analyst's perspective. *Multivariate Behavioral Research, 33*, 545–571.

Sinharay, S., Stern, H. S., & Russell, D. (2001). The use of multiple imputation for the analysis of missing data. *Psychological Methods, 6*, 317–329.

# 8

# The Analysis and Pooling Phases of Multiple Imputation

## 8.1 CHAPTER OVERVIEW

A multiple imputation analysis consists of three distinct steps: the imputation phase, the analysis phase, and the pooling phase. Chapter 7 described the mechanics of the imputation phase, and the purpose of this chapter is to outline the analysis and pooling phases. The purpose of the analysis phase is to analyze the filled-in data sets from the preceding imputation phase. This step consists of $m$ statistical analyses, one for each imputed data set. The analysis phase yields several sets of parameter estimates and standard errors, so the goal of the pooling phase is to combine everything into a single set of results. Rubin (1987) outlined relatively straightforward formulas for pooling parameter estimates and standard errors. For example, the pooled parameter estimate is simply the arithmetic average of the estimates from the analysis phase. Combining the standard errors is slightly more complex but follows the same logic. The analysis phase is probably the easiest aspect of multiple imputation and requires very little explanation. Consequently, the majority of this chapter is devoted to the pooling phase, including the various significance testing procedures that are available at this step.

As an advance warning, this chapter is relatively dense with equations, largely due to the complexity of the multiple imputation significance tests. Not all of these formulas are equally important. For example, understanding Rubin's (1987) equations for combining parameter estimates and standard errors is probably far more important than trying to digest the different test statistics and their degrees of freedom. Software packages implement the majority of the significance testing procedures that I outline in this chapter, so there is usually no need to compute the formulas by hand. Nevertheless, I felt that it was important for this chapter to serve as a comprehensive reference, so I included more equations than usual. The abundance of equations should not hinder readers who are interested primarily in applying multiple imputation to their own research because the majority of the text does not require an in-depth understanding of the formulas.

**TABLE 8.1. Employee Selection Data Set**

| IQ | Psychological well-being | Job performance |
|----|--------------------------|-----------------|
| 78 | 13 | — |
| 84 | 9 | — |
| 84 | 10 | — |
| 85 | 10 | — |
| 87 | — | — |
| 91 | 3 | — |
| 92 | 12 | — |
| 94 | 3 | — |
| 94 | 13 | — |
| 96 | — | — |
| 99 | 6 | 7 |
| 105 | 12 | 10 |
| 105 | 14 | 11 |
| 106 | 10 | 15 |
| 108 | — | 10 |
| 112 | 10 | 10 |
| 113 | 14 | 12 |
| 115 | 14 | 14 |
| 118 | 12 | 16 |
| 134 | 11 | 12 |

I use the small data set in Table 8.1 to illustrate ideas throughout this chapter. I designed these data to mimic an employee selection scenario in which prospective employees complete an IQ test and a psychological well-being questionnaire during their interview. The company subsequently hires the applicants that score in the upper half of the IQ distribution, and a supervisor rates their job performance following a 6-month probationary period. Note that the job performance scores are missing at random (MAR) because they are systematically missing as a function of IQ (i.e., individuals in the lower half of the IQ distribution were never hired, and thus have no performance rating). In addition, I randomly deleted three of the well-being scores in order to mimic a situation where the applicant's well-being questionnaire is inadvertently lost.

## 8.2 THE ANALYSIS PHASE

The analysis phase is probably the easiest aspect of a multiple imputation analysis. The imputation phase generates $m$ imputed data sets, each of which contains different estimates of the missing values. The purpose of the analysis phase, as noted earlier, is to analyze the filled-in data sets. This step consists of $m$ statistical analyses, one for each imputed data set. For example, suppose that a researcher had previously generated 20 imputations and is now interested in estimating a multiple regression equation. In the analysis phase, she would simply repeat the regression analysis 20 times, once for each data set. The researcher can employ the same analysis procedures and the same software package that she would have used had the data been complete. Of course, repeating the analysis 20 times sounds incredibly tedious, but an increasing number of software packages have built-in routines that automate this process.

As an important aside, auxiliary variables play no role in the analysis phase. Multiple imputation can readily accommodate auxiliary variables, but this is handled in the imputation phase. The imputation process infuses the imputed values with the information from the auxiliary variables, so there is no need to include the additional variables in the subsequent analysis step. This is in contrast to maximum likelihood estimation, which uses the somewhat awkward saturated correlates approach to incorporate auxiliary variables. Although multiple imputation is arguably more difficult to implement, it holds a clear advantage over maximum likelihood when it comes to dealing with auxiliary variables.

## 8.3 COMBINING PARAMETER ESTIMATES IN THE POOLING PHASE

The analysis phase yields $m$ different estimates of each parameter, any one of which is unbiased if the data are MAR. Rather than rely on the results from any single data set, a multiple imputation analysis pools the $m$ parameter values into a single point estimate. Rubin (1987) defined the **multiple imputation point estimate** as the arithmetic average of the $m$ estimates

$$\bar{\theta} = \frac{1}{m} \sum_{t=1}^{m} \hat{\theta}_t \qquad (8.1)$$

where $\hat{\theta}_t$ is the parameter estimate from data set $t$ and $\bar{\theta}$ is the pooled estimate. Notice that Equation 8.1 is the usual formula for the sample mean, where the parameter estimates serve as data points. Although Rubin (1987) developed multiple imputation in the Bayesian framework, the pooled point estimate is meaningful from either a Bayesian or a frequentist perspective. From the frequentist standpoint, $\bar{\theta}$ is a point estimate of the fixed population parameter, whereas the Bayesian paradigm views $\bar{\theta}$ as the mean of the observed-data posterior distribution (Little & Rubin, 2002, pp. 210–211; Rubin, 1987).

### A Bivariate Analysis Example

To illustrate the pooling process, suppose that it is of interest to use the data in Table 8.1 to estimate the regression of job performance on IQ. After generating 20 imputed data sets, I fit an ordinary least squares regression model to each data set and saved the estimates and the standard errors to a file for further analysis. Table 8.2 shows the regression slopes from the analysis phase. As seen in the table, the regression coefficients ranged between –0.025 and 0.239. Substituting the 20 estimates into Equation 8.1 yields a pooled point estimate of $\bar{\theta} =$ 0.105. The fact that the pooled estimate is an average of 20 different values has no bearing on its interpretation. Consistent with a complete-data regression analysis, 0.105 is the expected change in job performance for a one-point increase in IQ.

**TABLE 8.2. Regression Coefficients and Sampling Variances from the Bivariate Analysis Example**

| Imputation | $\hat{\theta}_t$ | $SE_t$ | $SE_t^2$ |
|---|---|---|---|
| 1 | 0.12630 | 0.03639 | 0.00132 |
| 2 | 0.09499 | 0.04978 | 0.00248 |
| 3 | 0.05515 | 0.08348 | 0.00697 |
| 4 | 0.06942 | 0.03509 | 0.00123 |
| 5 | 0.16699 | 0.03901 | 0.00152 |
| 6 | 0.02960 | 0.06283 | 0.00395 |
| 7 | 0.20581 | 0.04523 | 0.00205 |
| 8 | 0.02627 | 0.03739 | 0.00140 |
| 9 | 0.05293 | 0.03456 | 0.00119 |
| 10 | 0.15939 | 0.05294 | 0.00280 |
| 11 | 0.18642 | 0.03604 | 0.00130 |
| 12 | 0.14726 | 0.03933 | 0.00155 |
| 13 | 0.23944 | 0.03601 | 0.00130 |
| 14 | 0.04638 | 0.04718 | 0.00223 |
| 15 | 0.10295 | 0.05341 | 0.00285 |
| 16 | 0.07162 | 0.04275 | 0.00183 |
| 17 | 0.20742 | 0.03783 | 0.00143 |
| 18 | −0.02501 | 0.04752 | 0.00226 |
| 19 | 0.09447 | 0.03839 | 0.00147 |
| 20 | 0.04705 | 0.04372 | 0.00191 |

## 8.4 TRANSFORMING PARAMETER ESTIMATES PRIOR TO COMBINING

The pooling formula in Equation 8.1 assumes that the parameter estimates are asymptotically (i.e., in very large samples) normally distributed. However, some parameters meet this requirement better than others do, particularly in small and moderate samples. For example, the sampling distribution of Pearson's correlation is normal when the population correlation equals zero but becomes increasingly skewed as $\rho$ approaches plus or minus one. Many common variance estimates (e.g., $R^2$ statistics, standard deviations, estimates of variances, and covariances) also have skewed sampling distributions (or from the Bayesian framework, skewed posterior distributions). These distributions eventually normalize as the sample size gets very large, but they can be markedly non-normal in small and moderate samples. Averaging $m$ parameter values into a single estimate is asymptotically valid for any parameter, but applying normalizing transformations prior to the pooling phase may improve the accuracy of certain estimates (Schafer, 1997).

To illustrate the use of normalizing transformations, consider Pearson's correlation coefficient. Fisher's (1915) $z$ transformation is a natural choice for pooling correlations because it places the estimates on a metric that more closely approximates a normal distribution. The transformation is

$$z_t = \frac{1}{2} \log\left(\frac{r_t + 1}{r_t - 1}\right) \tag{8.2}$$

where $r_t$ is the correlation coefficient from data set $t$ and $z_t$ is the corresponding transformed coefficient. Substituting the transformed correlations into Equation 8.1 expresses the average correlation on the $z$ score metric, and the equation below transforms the pooled estimate back to the correlation metric.

$$\bar{r} = \left( \frac{e^{2\bar{\theta}} - 1}{e^{2\bar{\theta}} + 1} \right) \tag{8.3}$$

Applying normalizing transformations to variances and covariances is more complex because the appropriate transformation may not be immediately obvious. For example, a logarithmic transformation may work best for a distribution with substantial positive skewness, whereas a square root transformation may be more appropriate for a moderately skewed distribution. When transforming raw data, methodologists often recommend experimenting with different transformations to identify the one that best normalizes the data, but this exploratory approach is unlikely to work well in the pooling phase. Given the potential difficulties associated with specifying an appropriate transformation, it is reasonable to ask whether the use of transformations makes any practical difference. Because parameter distributions tend to normalize as $N$ increases, it is also important to determine whether there is a sample size at which transformations are no longer necessary. I am unaware of any studies that have systematically evaluated the use of transformations at the pooling phase, so I performed some computer simulations to examine this issue.

Briefly, the computer simulations generated 1,000 samples of bivariate normal data from a population with a correlation of $\rho = .50$. I subsequently imposed missing completely at random (MCAR) data by randomly deleting 25% of the values from one of the variables. Because the sample size plays an important role, I examined six different sample size conditions ($N = 50, 100, 200, 300, 500,$ and $1,000$). Finally, I created $m = 10$ imputations for each sample and applied logarithmic and square root transformations prior to pooling variances, covariances, and $R^2$ statistics. Although my simulations were very limited in scope, they do suggest that normalizing transformations tend to make very little difference, particularly when the sample size exceeds $N = 200$. Averaging the transformed estimates did reduce bias, but the mean squared errors of the transformed estimates were virtually identical to those of the raw estimates (the mean squared error is an overall measure of accuracy that combines bias and sampling error). The mean squared error results are interesting because they suggest that normalizing transformations increase sampling error to a degree that effectively negates the reduction in bias. Consequently, there may be little or no practical advantage to transforming estimates prior to combining them. (Fisher's transformation is a notable exception because it provides a convenient mechanism for significance testing.) As a caveat, my simulations were very limited in scope, so it is a good idea to view the results with some caution. Further methodological research should attempt to clarify this issue.

## 8.5 POOLING STANDARD ERRORS

The analysis phase also yields $m$ estimates of each standard error. Pooling standard errors is not as simple as computing an arithmetic average, but Rubin's (1987) combining rules are still relatively straightforward. Multiple imputation standard errors combine two sources of sampling fluctuation: the sampling error that would have resulted had the data been complete, and the additional sampling error that results from missing data. As an aside, Rubin's pooling formulas operate on the sampling variance metric rather than on the standard error metric. However, the sampling variance is simply the squared standard error, so switching to the standard error metric is an easy conversion.

## Within-Imputation Variance

A multiple imputation standard error consists of two sources of sampling fluctuation: within-imputation variance and between-imputation variance. The **within-imputation variance** is the arithmetic average of the $m$ sampling variances

$$V_W = \frac{1}{m} \sum_{t=1}^{m} SE_t^2 \tag{8.4}$$

where $V_W$ denotes the within-imputation variance, and $SE_t^2$ is the squared standard error (i.e., sampling variance) from data set $t$. Notice that Equation 8.4 is the usual formula for the sample mean, where the sampling variances serve as data points. Equation 8.4 averages complete-data sampling variances, so the within-imputation variance effectively estimates the sampling variability that would have resulted had there been no missing data.

## Between-Imputation Variance

At an intuitive level, missing values should increase standard errors because they add an additional layer of noise to the parameter estimates. Single imputation techniques fail to address this issue because they treat the filled-in values as real data. Consequently, even the best single imputation technique (e.g., stochastic regression imputation) will underestimate standard errors. Analyzing multiply imputed data sets solves this problem because it provides a mechanism for estimating the additional source of sampling error. As an illustration, reconsider the regression coefficients in Table 8.2. The variation in the regression coefficients from one data set to the next (the estimates range between –0.025 and 0.239) is solely due to the use of different imputed values. Consequently, the variability of the parameter values across the $m$ data sets estimates the additional sampling fluctuation that results from the missing data.

More formally, the **between-imputation variance** quantifies the variability of a parameter estimate across the $m$ data sets, as follows:

$$V_B = \frac{1}{m-1} \sum_{t=1}^{m} (\hat{\theta}_t - \bar{\theta})^2 \tag{8.5}$$

where $V_B$ denotes the between-imputation variance, $\hat{\theta}_t$ is the parameter estimate from data set $t$, and $\bar{\theta}$ is the average point estimate from Equation 8.1. Notice that Equation 8.5 is the usual formula for the sample variance, where the parameter estimates serve as data points. Again, the between-imputation variance represents the additional sampling error that results from the missing data because the fluctuation of the $\hat{\theta}_t$ values from one data set to the next is solely due to the use of different imputed values.

## Total Sampling Variance

Equations 8.4 and 8.5 decompose sampling error into two components: the sampling fluctuation that would have resulted had the data been complete (i.e., the within-imputation variance) and the additional sampling error that results from the missing data (i.e., the between-imputation variance). The **total sampling variance** combines these two components into a single quantity, as follows:

$$V_T = V_W + V_B + \frac{V_B}{m} \tag{8.6}$$

You might have anticipated that the total sampling variance is just the sum of the within- and between-imputation components, but the equation has an additional term, $V_B / m$. The between-imputation variance in Equation 8.5 requires the average parameter estimate (i.e., $\bar{\theta}$), and this mean is also subject to sampling error. The right-most term in Equation 8.6 quantifies the sampling variance (i.e., squared standard error) of the mean and essentially serves as a correction factor for using a finite number of imputations. (As $m$ goes to infinity, this term vanishes and the total variance becomes the sum of $V_W$ and $V_B$.)

Researchers are generally accustomed to reporting their results on the standard error metric rather than on the variance metric. Therefore, taking the square root of the total variance gives the multiple imputation standard error, as follows:

$$SE = \sqrt{V_T} \tag{8.7}$$

Throughout this section, I have been referring to various quantities as sampling variances, which implies repeated sampling (i.e., a frequentist interpretation). However, the total variance is meaningful from either a Bayesian or a frequentist perspective. From a frequentist perspective, the total variance estimates the variability of a parameter estimate across repeated samples. In contrast, the Bayesian paradigm views $V_T$ as the variance of the observed-data posterior distribution. The difference in terminology is not just semantics and represents an important philosophical difference between the two paradigms (see Chapter 6). Because the standard error is a familiar concept, I use this term throughout the remainder of the book (much of the multiple imputation literature follows the same convention).

## An ANOVA Analogy

Partitioning a parameter's sampling variance into within- and between-imputation components is very similar to what happens in an analysis of variance (ANOVA). ANOVA partitions score variation into two orthogonal sources: explained variability that is attributable to an explanatory variable (i.e., between-group variability) and residual variation that remains after accounting for the explanatory variable (i.e., within-group variability). The pooling phase partitions variance in a manner that closely resembles an ANOVA analysis, but it does so using the variation in a *parameter* distribution rather than a score distribution.

To align the previous concepts with an ANOVA analysis, you can think of missingness as an explanatory variable and the total sampling variance as the variability in the outcome variable. In this analogy, the between-imputation variance quantifies the portion of the parameter's variance that is due to the explanatory variable (i.e., the missing data) and is akin to the between-group mean square from an ANOVA analysis. The within-imputation variance is the residual variation that remains after subtracting out the explanatory variable's influence (i.e., the sampling variation that would result had there been no missing data) and is analogous to the mean square error in an ANOVA. Thinking about $V_W$ and $V_B$ in ANOVA terms puts Rubin's (1987) combining rules in a familiar context, but it also leads to an intuitive interpretation of some important quantities that I define later in the chapter.

## A Bivariate Analysis Example

To illustrate the process of combining standard errors, reconsider the regression of job performance on IQ. Table 8.2 also shows the standard errors and the sampling variances from the 20 regression analyses. Averaging the squared standard errors in the right-most column of the table yields a within-imputation variance of $V_W = 0.00215$. Again, this is an estimate of the sampling variability that would have resulted had the data been complete. Next, using Equation 8.5 to compute the variance of the regression coefficients across the 20 imputations gives a between-imputation variance of $V_B = 0.00515$. As I explained previously, the between-imputation variance represents the additional uncertainty that results from the missing data. Finally, substituting $V_W$ and $V_B$ into Equation 8.6 yields the total variance, $V_T = 0.00756$, and taking the square root of this value gives the multiple imputation standard error, $SE = 0.087$. Notice that the pooled standard error is considerably larger than most of the individual standard errors in Table 8.2. (The average complete-data standard error is 0.045.) This makes intuitive sense because multiple imputation explicitly incorporates the additional sampling error that accrues from the missing data.

## 8.6 THE FRACTION OF MISSING INFORMATION AND THE RELATIVE INCREASE IN VARIANCE

The within-imputation variance, between-imputation variance, and the total variance define two useful diagnostic measures, the fraction of missing information and the relative increase in variance due to nonresponse. These measures are important because they (1) quantify the influence of missing data on the standard errors, (2) dictate the convergence speed of the data augmentation algorithm, and (3) help define the significance tests outlined later in the chapter.

## The Fraction of Missing Information

I briefly introduced the fraction of missing information in Chapter 7, where I described it as a diagnostic measure that adjusts the missing data rate by the correlations among the variables. More specifically, the **fraction of missing information** quantifies the missing data's influence on the sampling variance of a parameter estimate. An intuitive expression for the fraction of missing information is as follows.

$$\text{FMI} = \frac{V_B + V_B/m}{V_T} \tag{8.8}$$

Equation 8.8 assumes that the number of imputations is very large; thus, an alternate expression that adjusts for a finite number of imputations is

$$\text{FMI}_1 = \frac{V_B + V_B/m + 2/(v + 3)}{V_T} \tag{8.9}$$

where $v$ is a degrees of freedom value that is defined later in Equation 8.12. The value of $v$ increases to infinity as $m$ goes to infinity, so the additional terms in the numerator essentially vanish with a very large number of imputations. The result is the more straightforward expression in Equation 8.8.

Focusing on Equation 8.8, the fraction of missing information has an intuitive interpretation. The denominator is the total sampling variance (i.e., squared standard error), and the numerator quantifies the additional sampling variation that accrues from the missing data. Consequently, the fraction of missing information is the proportion of the total sampling variance that is due to the missing data. If you think of between- and within-imputation variance as being similar to the between- and within-group variation from ANOVA, then the fraction of missing information is analogous to an $R^2$ statistic. In the context of multiple imputation, the pooling phase partitions the variation in a parameter distribution rather than a score distribution, but the $R^2$ analogy is useful for understanding the equation.

With regard to the previous regression example, substituting $V_B = 0.00515$ and $V_T = 0.00755$ into Equation 8.8 yields FMI = 0.715. This value indicates that 71.5% of the regression coefficient's sampling variance is attributable to the missing data. Using the more complex expression in Equation 8.9 gives an estimate that is more appropriate for a finite number of imputations, but the interpretation remains the same (i.e., $\text{FMI}_1 = 0.729$, so approximately 73% of the sampling variance is due to the missing data). I previously described missing information as a summary measure that combines the missing data rate and the correlations among the variables. The missing information is typically lower than the missing data rate, particularly when the variables in the imputation model are predictive of the missing values. In this situation, the correlations among the variables mitigate the information loss, such that the increase in sampling error is not completely commensurate with the overall reduction in the sample size. The regression analysis produced a fraction of missing information that exceeds the missing data rate, but this is likely an artifact of the sample size and the number of imputations (accurate FMI estimates require far more than 20 data sets).

The fraction of missing information is also a useful diagnostic tool because it influences the convergence of the data augmentation algorithm. (Parameters with high rates of missing information tend to converge slowly.) Consequently, paying especially close attention to parameters with large fractions of missing information is a good strategy when examining the graphical diagnostics from the imputation phase. Because some multiple imputation software packages report the fraction of missing information as a by-product of the imputation phase, usually these estimates are readily available. As an aside, methodologists have noted that the fraction of missing information tends to be noisy and somewhat untrustworthy (Harel, 2007; Schafer, 1997), particularly with fewer than 100 imputations (Harel, 2007). However, estimating the fraction of missing information is usually not the primary analytic goal, so approximate estimates are often acceptable.

## Relative Increase in Variance

Like the fraction of missing information, the relative increase in variance quantifies the missing data's influence on the sampling variance of a parameter estimate, but it does so in a slightly different fashion. A standard formulation of the **relative increase in variance** is

$$\text{RIV} = \frac{V_B + V_B/m}{V_W} = \frac{\text{FMI}}{1 - \text{FMI}} \tag{8.10}$$

To understand the relative increase in variance, consider the meaning of its component parts. The denominator of Equation 8.10 estimates the sampling variance that would have resulted had there been no missing data, and the numerator of the equation quantifies the additional sampling variation that accrues from the missing data. Consequently, the relative increase in variance gives proportional increase in the sampling variance that is due to the missing data. For example, if the missing data have no influence on the sampling error of a particular parameter, the between-imputation variance is zero, as is the relative increase in variance. In contrast, if the between-imputation variance is equal to the within-imputation variance, then the relative increase in variance equals one. Returning to the previous regression analysis, note that the between- and the within-imputation variance estimates are $V_B = 0.00515$ and $V_W = 0.00215$, respectively. Substituting these values into Equation 8.10 yields RIV = 2.51. This means that the sampling fluctuation due to the missing data is two and a half times larger than the sampling variance of a complete-data analysis.

Like the fraction of missing information, the relative increase in variance dictates the convergence speed of the data augmentation algorithm. Equation 8.10 shows that FMI and RIV are one-to-one transformations, so it makes little difference which measure you choose to examine. Several of the significance tests outlined in subsequent sections rely on the relative increase in variance (or equivalently, the fractional missing information), so these concepts will resurface throughout the remainder of the chapter.

## 8.7 WHEN IS MULTIPLE IMPUTATION COMPARABLE TO MAXIMUM LIKELIHOOD?

Having gained an understanding of all three phases in a multiple imputation analysis, it is useful to consider the comparability of maximum likelihood and multiple imputation. Maximum likelihood and multiple imputation are equivalent techniques in the sense that they both assume multivariate normality and MAR data. Despite making the same assumptions, the two approaches may or may not yield similar parameter estimates and standard errors. Assuming that the sample size and the number of imputations are both large enough to eliminate idiosyncratic performance differences, the set of input variables and the relative complexity of the imputation model and the analysis model largely determine whether the two procedures produce similar results (Collins, Schafer, & Kam, 2001; Schafer, 2003).

When comparing multiple imputation and maximum likelihood, the first thing to consider is whether the imputation phase uses the same set of variables as the analysis phase. To illustrate, consider an analysis model that involves three variables, $X$, $M$, and $Y$. A researcher could use maximum likelihood to directly estimate the analysis model, or she could impute the data and analyze the $m$ complete data sets. If the imputation phase includes additional variables that are not part of maximum likelihood analysis (e.g., a set of auxiliary variables), then the two procedures can yield different estimates, standard errors, or both. If the imputation phase includes only $X$, $M$, and $Y$, then multiple imputation and maximum likelihood are seemingly on an equal footing because they make the same assumptions and use the same set of input variables. However, the comparability of the two procedures still depends on the relative complexity of the imputation and the analysis models.

Recall from Chapter 7 that the imputation phase of a multiple imputation analysis uses a multiple regression model to fill in the missing values. A multiple regression model is known as a **saturated model** because the number of parameters in the model exactly equals the number of elements in the mean vector and the covariance matrix (i.e., there is a one-to-one transformation that links the regression model parameters to the elements in $\hat{\mu}$ and $\hat{\Sigma}$). In practical terms, this means that the imputation phase uses the most complex model possible to impute the missing values (i.e., estimating the regression model expends all of the information present in the mean vector and the covariance matrix). The subsequent analysis model may or may not be as complex as the imputation regression model, and the relative parsimony of these two models has a bearing on the comparability of multiple imputation and maximum likelihood.

To illustrate the parsimony issue, consider a mediation analysis in which $X$ predicts $M$, $M$ predicts $Y$, and $X$ also has a direct influence on $Y$. The top panel of Figure 8.1 shows a path diagram of this model. To begin, notice that the mediation model is saturated because it, too, estimates every possible association among the variables. Assuming that the imputation phase includes only three variables, then a maximum likelihood analysis of the mediation model estimates the same number of parameters as the imputation phase (i.e., the number of parameters in the mediation model equals the number of elements in $\hat{\mu}$ and $\hat{\Sigma}$). When the imputation and analysis models use the same set of input variables and estimate the same number of parameters, the two models are said to be **congenial** (Meng, 1994). In this situation, multiple imputation and maximum likelihood should produce very similar estimates

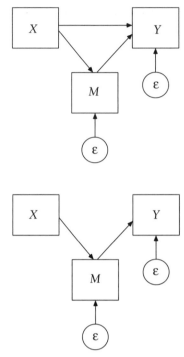

**FIGURE 8.1.** Path diagram of a mediation analysis model. The top panel shows a model where $X$ has a direct relationship with $Y$ and is also related to $Y$ via a mediating variable, $M$. The bottom panel shows a model where $X$ and $Y$ are only related via their mutual association with $M$.

and standard errors (Collins et al., 2001; Schafer, 2003). All things being equal, Bayesian estimation is asymptotically (i.e., in large samples) equivalent to maximum likelihood (Gelman, Carlin, Stern, & Rubin, 1995), so there is no theoretical reason for the procedures to produce different results.

Next, consider an analysis model that restricts the association between $X$ and $Y$ to zero during estimation, such that the relationship between $X$ and $Y$ is completely mediated by $M$. The bottom panel of Figure 8.1 shows a path diagram of this model. Unlike the previous example, the imputation and analysis models are now **uncongenial** because they differ in complexity. That is, the analysis model restricts the association between $X$ and $Y$, whereas the imputation regression model does not. When the imputation and analysis models are uncongenial but use the same set of input variables, multiple imputation and maximum likelihood should produce very similar parameter estimates, but multiple imputation standard errors may be slightly larger (Collins et al., 2001; Schafer, 2003). In effect, the imputation phase uses an unnecessarily complex model to deal with the missing data, and this additional complexity can add a small amount of noise to the resulting estimates. However, the difference between the two sets of standard errors is usually trivial, so uncongeniality is not necessarily a reason to favor maximum likelihood estimation.

The previous example might suggest that uncongeniality is detrimental to a multiple imputation analysis. However, uncongeniality can be beneficial when it results from an inclusive analysis strategy that incorporates auxiliary variables that are correlates of missingness or correlates of the incomplete analysis model variables. Because a single set of imputations can serve as input data for a variety of different analyses, it is natural for the imputation phase to include a much larger set of variables than would appear in any single analysis model. Returning to the analysis models in Figure 8.1, note that an ideal imputation model would include the mediation model variables, variables from other analyses, and a set of auxiliary variables. When the imputation phase includes additional variables that are not part of the analysis model, multiple imputation and maximum likelihood can yield different parameter estimates, standard errors, or both. Idiosyncratic features of the data influence these discrepancies, so it is difficult to make predictions about the pattern and the magnitude of the differences (e.g., some estimates may be similar, others may be different; one procedure may produce smaller standard errors for some parameters but not others).

A final situation in which multiple imputation and maximum likelihood can differ occurs when the imputation model is more restrictive than the analysis model. Returning to the mediation example, suppose that it is of interest to determine whether the regression coefficient between $X$ and $M$ is different for males and females (e.g., using a multiple group path analysis model or a regression model with interaction terms). Furthermore, suppose that the imputation phase includes $X$, $M$, $Y$, and a gender dummy code. In this situation, including the dummy code in the imputation phase accounts for mean differences between males and females, but omitting the gender by $X$ product term effectively assumes that the gender groups have the same covariance between $X$ and $M$. This is a potentially harmful form of uncongeniality because the subsequent analyses can attenuate the interaction effect. Maximum likelihood estimation would not suffer from this problem, so it is possible for the two approaches to produce very different estimates and standard errors. This example underscores the well-established but important point that omitting analysis variables from the imputation phase can produce biased parameter estimates, regardless of the missing data mechanism (Meng, 1994; Rubin, 1996).

## 8.8 AN ILLUSTRATIVE COMPUTER SIMULATION STUDY

In Chapter 4, I illustrated the accuracy of maximum likelihood analyses using computer simulations. Having outlined the analysis and pooling phases, I repeated these simulations, this time using multiple imputation to deal with missing data. The simulation programs generated 1,000 samples of $N = 250$ from a population model that mimicked the IQ and job performance data in Table 8.1. The first simulation created MCAR data by randomly deleting 50% of the job performance ratings. The second simulation modeled MAR data and eliminated job performance scores for the cases in the lower half of the IQ distribution. The final simulation generated missing not at random (MNAR) data by deleting the job performance scores for the cases in the lower half of the job performance distribution. After generating each data set, I used the data augmentation algorithm from Chapter 7 to create $m = 10$ imputed data sets for each sample. Next, I estimated the mean vector and the covariance matrix from each imputed data set and used Equation 8.1 to pool the resulting estimates. Table 8.3 shows the average multiple-imputation estimates from the simulations and uses **bold** typeface to

**TABLE 8.3. Average Parameter Estimates from the
Illustrative Computer Simulation**

| Parameter | Population value | Multiple imputation | Maximum likelihood |
|---|---|---|---|
| | MCAR simulation | | |
| $\mu_{IQ}$ | 100.00 | 99.98 | 100.02 |
| $\mu_{JP}$ | 12.00 | 11.99 | 11.99 |
| $\sigma^2_{IQ}$ | 169.00 | 169.34 | 168.25 |
| $\sigma^2_{JP}$ | 9.00 | 9.08 | 8.96 |
| $\sigma_{IQ,JP}$ | 19.50 | 19.51 | 19.48 |
| | MAR simulation | | |
| $\mu_{IQ}$ | 100.00 | 100.00 | 100.01 |
| $\mu_{JP}$ | 12.00 | 12.00 | 12.01 |
| $\sigma^2_{IQ}$ | 169.00 | 168.46 | 168.50 |
| $\sigma^2_{JP}$ | 9.00 | 9.23 | 8.96 |
| $\sigma_{IQ,JP}$ | 19.50 | 19.43 | 19.15 |
| | MNAR simulation | | |
| $\mu_{IQ}$ | 100.00 | 100.02 | 100.00 |
| $\mu_{JP}$ | 12.00 | 14.13 | 14.12 |
| $\sigma^2_{IQ}$ | 169.00 | 170.37 | 169.11 |
| $\sigma^2_{JP}$ | 9.00 | 3.42 | 3.33 |
| $\sigma_{IQ,JP}$ | 19.50 | 8.51 | 8.55 |

highlight severely biased estimates. For comparison purposes, the table also shows the corresponding maximum likelihood estimates.

As seen in the table, the multiple imputation and maximum likelihood parameter estimates are virtually indistinguishable in all three simulations, which is not surprising given that the imputation and analysis models are congenial (i.e., they include the same variables and estimate the same number of parameters). Consistent with maximum likelihood estimation, multiple imputation produced unbiased estimates in the MCAR and MAR simulations but gave biased estimates in the MNAR simulation. However, it is important to point out that the MNAR bias was confined to the parameters that were affected by missing data. Although these simulations were limited in scope, the results are consistent with missing data theory (Rubin, 1976; Schafer, 1997) and with previous simulation studies (e.g., Allison, 2000; Collins et al., 2001; Graham & Schafer, 1999; Newman, 2003).

## 8.9 SIGNIFICANCE TESTING USING THE *t* STATISTIC

The next few sections outline a number of multiple imputation significance tests. Again, the subsequent sections are relatively dense with equations, but not all of these formulas are equally important (e.g., the degrees of freedom equations are complex and not very intuitive). The abundance of equations should not hinder readers who are primarily interested in applying multiple imputation to their own research because the majority of the text does not require an in-depth understanding of the formulas.

In the context of a maximum likelihood analysis, the Wald $z$ test provides a mechanism for assessing whether a parameter estimate is statistically different from some hypothesized value. Multiple imputation analyses use an analogous $t$ statistic. Like the Wald test, the numerator of the $t$ statistic compares the point estimate to some hypothesized value, and the denominator contains the standard error, as follows:

$$t = \frac{\bar{\theta} - \theta_0}{\sqrt{V_T}} \tag{8.11}$$

where $\bar{\theta}$ is the pooled point estimate, and $\theta_0$ is the hypothesized parameter value. Researchers typically test whether a parameter is significantly different from zero, in which case the $t$ statistic reduces to the ratio of the point estimate to its standard error.

Many complete-data statistical procedures employ a $t$ statistic similar to that in Equation 8.11, but the multiple imputation test statistic uses a complex expression for the degrees of freedom (Rubin, 1987; Rubin & Schenker, 1986).

$$v = (m - 1)\left(1 + \frac{V_W}{V_B + V_B/m}\right)^2 = (m - 1)\left(\frac{1}{FMI^2}\right) \tag{8.12}$$

With complete data, the $t$ sampling distribution converges to a normal curve as the sample size becomes very large (i.e., the degrees of freedom approach infinity). Interestingly, the sample size does not directly influence the value of $v$. Instead, the degrees of freedom increase as the number of imputations increase or as the fraction of missing information decreases. For example, substituting $m = 20$ and FMI = .25 (e.g., a 25% missing data rate) into Equation 8.12 yields $v = 304$, whereas $m = 20$ and FMI = .05 gives a degrees of freedom value of $v = 7600$.

In small to moderate samples, $v$ can substantially exceed the degrees of freedom that would have resulted had the data been complete. Returning to the previous regression example, observe that the complete-data regression of job performance on IQ would have $N - k - 1 = 18$ degrees of freedom, where $k$ is the number of predictor variables. In contrast, Equation 8.12 yields a value of $v = 37.148$. To correct this problem, Barnard and Rubin (1999) proposed the following adjusted degrees of freedom value

$$v_1 = \left(\frac{1}{v} + \frac{1}{\tilde{v}}\right)^{-1} \tag{8.13}$$

where

$$\tilde{v} = (1 - FMI)\left(\frac{df_{com} + 1}{df_{com} + 3}\right)df_{com} \tag{8.14}$$

and $df_{com}$ is the degrees of freedom that would have resulted had the data been complete. Unlike $v$, the adjusted degrees of freedom value increases as the sample size increases and never exceeds the complete-data degrees of freedom. For example, the adjusted degrees of freedom for the previous regression example is $v_1 = 4.124$ as opposed to $v = 37.148$. Barnard and Rubin's (1999) computer simulations suggest that $v_1$ improves the accuracy of confidence intervals in small samples, so you should use the adjusted degrees of freedom whenever possible.

## Confidence Intervals

Establishing a confidence interval around a multiple imputation point estimate requires the appropriate critical values from a $t$ distribution with $v_1$ degrees of freedom. To get the upper and lower confidence interval limits, you multiply the standard error by the appropriate critical value and add the resulting product to the pooled point estimate, as follows:

$$\bar{\theta} + (t_{v_1, 1-\alpha/2})\left(\sqrt{V_T}\right) \tag{8.15}$$

where $t_{v_1, 1-\alpha/2}$ is the $t$ critical value that separates the desired proportion of the distribution. For example, the 95% confidence interval requires the $t$ critical value that separates the upper and the lower 2.5% of a $t$ sampling distribution with $v_1$ degrees of freedom. Multiple imputation software programs generally report confidence intervals, but you can obtain the $t$ critical values from other software programs (e.g., Excel), if need be.

## A Bivariate Analysis Example

Returning to the previous bivariate analysis, note that the regression of job performance on IQ produced a slope estimate of $\bar{\theta} = 0.105$ and a standard error of $SE = 0.087$. The test statistic for the regression coefficient is $t = 1.207$, and referencing the statistic to a $t$ distribution with $v_1 = 4.124$ degrees of freedom returns a probability value of $p = .29$. With an alpha level of 0.05, the two-tailed critical value for a $t$ distribution with 4.124 degrees of freedom is 2.776, therefore, substituting the appropriate values into Equation 8.15 gives upper and lower confidence limits of 0.347 and −0.137, respectively. Aside from using a fractional degrees of freedom value, the significance testing procedure is virtually identical to that of a complete-data analysis.

## Revisiting the Number of Imputations

Recall from Chapter 7 that the number of imputations has an impact on the power of multiple imputation significance tests, such that power improves as $m$ increases. The equations in this section illustrate that increasing the number of imputations can improve power in two ways. First, reconsider the expression for the total sampling variance (i.e., squared standard error) in Equation 8.6. The formula includes a correction factor (i.e., $V_B / m$) that quantifies the sampling error of the pooled point estimate. Increasing the number of imputations decreases the value of the correction factor and thus decreases the standard error. Increasing the number of imputations also improves power in a more subtle fashion. Equations 8.12 and 8.13 show that the degrees of freedom value increases as the number of imputations increases. As the degrees of freedom increase, the $t$ critical value decreases, making it easier to reject the null hypothesis. Consequently, all things being equal, analyses with a large number of imputations will produce more powerful significance tests than analyses with a small number of imputations. Computer simulation studies suggest that $m = 20$ is a good rule of thumb for many situations (Graham, Olchowski, & Gilreath, 2007), but increasing the number of imputations beyond this point is certainly a good idea, if processing time permits. Using a large number of imputations will also improve the performance of the multiple-parameter significance tests that are described next, although much less is known about the impact of $m$ on these tests.

## 8.10 AN OVERVIEW OF MULTIPARAMETER SIGNIFICANCE TESTS

In many situations it is of interest to determine whether a set of parameters is significantly different from zero. For example, in a multiple regression analysis, researchers are often interested in testing whether two or more regression slopes are different from zero. In an ordinary least squares analysis with complete data, it is standard practice to use an omnibus $F$ test for this purpose. In the context of maximum likelihood estimation, the multivariate Wald test and the likelihood ratio statistic are analogous procedures. Multiple imputation also offers different mechanisms for testing a set of parameter estimates (the literature sometimes refers to these procedures as **multiparameter inference** or **multivariate inference**), although relatively little is known about the performance of these tests.

The subsequent sections describe three different multiparameter significance tests. Following Schafer (1997), I refer to these tests as $D_1$, $D_2$, and $D_3$. The $D_1$ statistic uses the pooled parameter estimates and the pooled sampling variances to construct a test that closely resembles the multivariate Wald statistic from Chapter 3. In contrast, $D_2$ and $D_3$ pool significance tests from the analysis phase; the $D_2$ statistic pools Wald tests, and the $D_3$ statistic pools likelihood ratio tests. Although these procedures accomplish the same task, they are not equally trustworthy, nor are they equally easy to implement. The $D_1$ and $D_3$ statistics are asymptotically equivalent, but $D_1$ is easier to implement because it is readily available in multiple imputation software programs. (At the time of this writing, relatively few programs compute $D_3$.) Computing $D_2$ is straightforward, but it appears to be the least trustworthy of the three test statistics.

## 8.11 TESTING MULTIPLE PARAMETERS USING THE $D_1$ STATISTIC

The $D_1$ statistic uses the pooled parameter estimates and the pooled sampling variances to construct a test that closely resembles the multivariate Wald statistic. Recall from Chapter 3 that the Wald test is

$$\omega = (\hat{\boldsymbol{\theta}} - \boldsymbol{\theta}_0)^T \text{var}(\hat{\boldsymbol{\theta}})^{-1} (\hat{\boldsymbol{\theta}} - \boldsymbol{\theta}_0) \qquad (8.16)$$

where $\hat{\boldsymbol{\theta}}$ is a vector of parameter estimates, $\boldsymbol{\theta}_0$ is a vector of hypothesized values (typically zeros), and $\text{var}(\hat{\boldsymbol{\theta}})$ contains the appropriate elements from the parameter covariance matrix. In order to construct an analogous test for a multiple imputation analysis, it is first necessary to extend Rubin's (1987) pooling equations to multiple parameters and parameter covariance matrices.

## Pooling Multiple Parameter Estimates

Because Rubin's (1987) procedure for combining parameter estimates is unaffected by the shift to multiple parameters, the multiple imputation point estimate is still the arithmetic average of the $m$ sets of estimates (see Equation 8.1). Constructing a test that resembles the Wald statistic requires matrix computations, so a column vector $\boldsymbol{\theta}_t$ contains the set of estimates from data set $t$, and the vector $\bar{\boldsymbol{\theta}}$ holds the pooled point estimates.

## Pooling Parameter Covariance Matrices

The Wald test in Equation 8.16 uses elements from the parameter covariance matrix to standardize the deviations between the parameter estimates and the hypothesized values. The $D_1$ statistic uses the same procedure, so it is necessary to extend Rubin's (1987) variance partitioning formulas to multiple parameters. The basic logic of the pooling process remains the same, but covariance matrices quantify the within- and between-imputation variability.

With a single parameter, the within-imputation variance is the arithmetic average of the $m$ sampling variances. In the multivariate context, the **within-imputation covariance matrix** is the average of the $m$ parameter covariance matrices, as follows:

$$\mathbf{V}_W = \frac{1}{m} \sum_{t=1}^{m} \text{var}(\hat{\boldsymbol{\theta}}_t) \qquad (8.17)$$

where $\mathbf{V}_W$ is the average within-imputation covariance matrix, and $\text{var}(\hat{\boldsymbol{\theta}}_t)$ is the parameter covariance matrix from data set $t$. Consistent with the single parameter case, $\mathbf{V}_W$ estimates the parameter covariance matrix that would have resulted had the data been complete.

Filling in the data with different sets of imputed values causes the parameter estimates to vary across the $m$ analyses, and this between-imputation variability is an important component of the total sampling error. The **between-imputation covariance matrix** quantifies this variation, as follows:

$$\mathbf{V}_B = \frac{1}{m-1} \sum_{t=1}^{m} (\hat{\boldsymbol{\theta}}_t - \bar{\boldsymbol{\theta}})(\hat{\boldsymbol{\theta}}_t - \bar{\boldsymbol{\theta}})^T \qquad (8.18)$$

where $\mathbf{V}_B$ is the between-imputation covariance matrix, $\hat{\boldsymbol{\theta}}_t$ contains the parameter estimates from data set $t$, and $\bar{\boldsymbol{\theta}}$ is the vector of pooled point estimates (i.e., the arithmetic average of the $\hat{\boldsymbol{\theta}}_t$ vectors). The diagonal elements of $\mathbf{V}_B$ contain the between-imputation variance estimates for individual parameters, and the off-diagonal elements quantify the extent to which the between-imputation fluctuation in one parameter is related to the between-imputation fluctuation in another parameter. Considered as a whole, the between-imputation covariance matrix represents the additional sampling fluctuation that results from the missing data.

Finally, the **total parameter covariance matrix** combines the within- and between-imputation covariance matrices, as follow:

$$V_T = V_W + V_B + \frac{1}{m}V_B \tag{8.19}$$

The matrix $V_T$ reflects the total sampling fluctuation in a set of parameter estimates. Like the parameter covariance matrix from a maximum likelihood analysis, the diagonal elements of $V_T$ contain sampling variances, and the off-diagonals contain covariances between pairs of estimates.

## An Alternate Estimate of the Total Covariance Matrix

The between-imputation covariance matrix in Equation 8.18 is prone to a great deal of sampling error when the number of imputations is small, and this results in a poor estimate of the total parameter covariance matrix. Consequently, using the total covariance matrix in Equation 8.19 to construct a Wald-like test statistic can produce inaccurate inferences. Li, Raghunathan, and Rubin (1991) proposed a solution to this problem that requires an alternate expression for the total covariance matrix.

$$\tilde{V}_T = (1 + \text{ARIV})V_W \tag{8.20}$$

Earlier in the chapter, I introduced the relative increase in variance due to nonresponse. The ARIV term in the equation above estimates the **average relative increase in variance** across the $k$ parameter estimates in $\bar{\theta}$ and is defined by

$$\text{ARIV} = \frac{(1 + m^{-1})\text{tr}(V_B V_W^{-1})}{k} \tag{8.21}$$

where tr denotes the trace operator (i.e., the sum of the diagonal elements).

To better understand $\tilde{V}_T$, reconsider the total sampling variance for a single parameter. Applying some algebra to Equation 8.6 gives

$$V_T = (1 + \text{RIV})V_W \tag{8.22}$$

where RIV is the relative increase in variance from Equation 8.10. Defining the total variance in this way makes it clear that $\tilde{V}_T$ is a matrix analog of $V_T$, where the average relative increase in variance replaces RIV. Because ARIV condenses the information in the between-imputation covariance matrix into a single numeric value (i.e., ARIV), $\tilde{V}_T$ can provide a more stable estimate of the total parameter covariance matrix.

## The $D_1$ Statistic

Li, Raghunathan, et al. (1991) proposed the following test statistic:

$$D_1 = \frac{1}{k} (\bar{\boldsymbol{\theta}} - \boldsymbol{\theta}_0)^T (\tilde{\mathbf{V}}_T)^{-1} (\bar{\boldsymbol{\theta}} - \boldsymbol{\theta}_0) \qquad (8.23)$$

where $k$ is the number of parameters in $\bar{\boldsymbol{\theta}}$. Although $D_1$ closely resembles the Wald test in Equation 8.16, its sampling distribution is far more complex. Li, Raghunathan, et al. suggest using an $F$ distribution with $k$ numerator degrees of freedom and $v_2$ denominator degrees of freedom to obtain a probability value, where

$$v_2 = 4 + (km - k - 4)\left[1 + \left(1 - \frac{2}{km - k}\right)\frac{1}{\text{ARIV}}\right]^2 \qquad (8.24)$$

In a situation where $km - k$ is less than or equal to 4, they recommend an alternate expression for $v_2$, as follows.

$$v_2 = \frac{(km - k)\left(1 + \frac{1}{k}\right)\left(1 + \frac{1}{\text{ARIV}}\right)^2}{2} \qquad (8.25)$$

The $D_1$ statistic uses a total parameter covariance matrix based on the average relative increase in variance. This formulation of the test statistics assumes that the relative increase in variance (or equivalently, the fraction of missing information) is the same for all parameters (i.e., ARIV is representative of each parameter's RIV value). This assumption is unlikely to hold in practice because it essentially requires that the analysis variables have the same missing data rates and the same correlations. Li, Raghunathan, et al. (1991) used Monte Carlo simulations to study the performance of the $D_1$ statistic under a variety of different conditions. Their simulation results suggest that $D_1$ has type I error rates close to the nominal 0.05 level, but it lacks power when the number of parameters is large or the number of imputations is small. For example, they show that an analysis that uses $m = 4$ imputations has approximately 10% less power than a hypothetical analysis based on an infinite number of imputations. The authors only report power levels for $m = 4$ imputations, but it is reasonable to expect power to improve as the number of imputations increases. As a final note, the derivation of $D_1$ assumes a very large sample size, but no research to date has investigated its performance in small to moderate samples. Consequently, it is difficult to assess the trustworthiness of the $D_1$ statistic in realistic research scenarios.

## An Analysis Example

To illustrate the $D_1$ statistic, suppose that it is of interest to use the data in Table 8.1 to estimate the regression of job performance on IQ and psychological well-being. After generating

20 imputations, I fit an ordinary least squares regression model to each data set and saved the estimates and parameter covariance matrices to a file for further analysis. In a multiple regression analysis, researchers typically use an omnibus $F$ test to determine whether two or more coefficients are significantly different from zero, and the $D_1$ statistic can serve a similar role in a multiple imputation analysis. Table 8.4 shows the parameter estimates and the parameter covariance matrices from the 20 analyses. Note that I excluded the regression intercept and its covariance matrix elements from the table because the intercept is not part of the usual omnibus test. Consequently, the diagonal elements of each parameter covariance matrix contain the sampling variances (i.e., squared standard errors), and the off-diagonal is the covariance between the two regression slopes.

To begin, averaging the 20 sets of regression coefficients gives the following vector of point estimates.

$$\bar{\theta} = \begin{bmatrix} \bar{\beta}_{IQ} \\ \bar{\beta}_{WB} \end{bmatrix} = \begin{bmatrix} .083 \\ .365 \end{bmatrix}$$

The interpretation of the regression coefficients is identical to that of a complete-data analysis. For example, holding psychological well-being constant, a one-point increase in IQ is associated with a 0.083 increase in job performance ratings, on average.

Next, I computed the pooled parameter covariance matrix. Averaging the covariance matrices in Table 8.4 yields the pooled within-imputation covariance matrix.

$$V_W = \begin{bmatrix} .00159 & -.00176 \\ -.00176 & .02708 \end{bmatrix}$$

Again, $V_W$ estimates the parameter covariance matrix that would have resulted had there been no missing data. Next, I used the $m$ sets of regression coefficients and the corresponding pooled values to compute the between-imputation covariance matrix that quantifies the additional sampling fluctuation that accrues from the missing data.

$$V_B = \begin{bmatrix} .00689 & -.01723 \\ -.01723 & .11446 \end{bmatrix}$$

Computing the total covariance matrix requires the average relative increase in variance. Substituting the previous estimates of $V_W$ and $V_B$ into Equation 8.21 gives ARIV = 4.042. This value suggests that the sampling variance due to the missing data is, on average, four times larger than the sampling variance that would have resulted had the data been complete. Next, substituting ARIV and $V_W$ into Equation 8.20 gives the total parameter covariance matrix as follows:

$$\tilde{V}_T = \begin{bmatrix} .00802 & -.00889 \\ -.00889 & .13654 \end{bmatrix}$$

**TABLE 8.4. Coefficients and Parameter Covariance Matrices from the Multiple Regression Example**

| Imputation | Estimate | | Covariance matrix | | Imputation | Estimate | | Covariance matrix | |
|---|---|---|---|---|---|---|---|---|---|
| 1 | $\hat{\beta}_{IQ}$ | 0.12714 | 0.00153 | −0.00183 | 11 | $\hat{\beta}_{IQ}$ | 0.16918 | 0.00137 | −0.00164 |
| | $\hat{\beta}_{WB}$ | −0.01162 | −0.00183 | 0.02521 | | $\hat{\beta}_{WB}$ | 0.19610 | −0.00164 | 0.01861 |
| 2 | $\hat{\beta}_{IQ}$ | 0.06811 | 0.00105 | −0.00067 | 12 | $\hat{\beta}_{IQ}$ | 0.13184 | 0.00137 | −0.00119 |
| | $\hat{\beta}_{WB}$ | 0.66786 | −0.00067 | 0.01670 | | $\hat{\beta}_{WB}$ | 0.32367 | −0.00119 | 0.02498 |
| 3 | $\hat{\beta}_{IQ}$ | −0.02464 | 0.00383 | −0.00448 | 13 | $\hat{\beta}_{IQ}$ | 0.23750 | 0.00152 | −0.00200 |
| | $\hat{\beta}_{WB}$ | 1.06036 | −0.00448 | 0.05952 | | $\hat{\beta}_{WB}$ | 0.02645 | −0.00200 | 0.02741 |
| 4 | $\hat{\beta}_{IQ}$ | 0.06189 | 0.00126 | −0.00099 | 14 | $\hat{\beta}_{IQ}$ | 0.02960 | 0.00226 | −0.00250 |
| | $\hat{\beta}_{WB}$ | 0.16877 | −0.00099 | 0.02218 | | $\hat{\beta}_{WB}$ | 0.29091 | −0.00250 | 0.04341 |
| 5 | $\hat{\beta}_{IQ}$ | 0.16090 | 0.00172 | −0.00206 | 15 | $\hat{\beta}_{IQ}$ | 0.04459 | 0.00121 | −0.00149 |
| | $\hat{\beta}_{WB}$ | 0.09261 | −0.00206 | 0.03131 | | $\hat{\beta}_{WB}$ | 0.76175 | −0.00149 | 0.01943 |
| 6 | $\hat{\beta}_{IQ}$ | −0.00272 | 0.00183 | −0.00118 | 16 | $\hat{\beta}_{IQ}$ | 0.04217 | 0.00161 | −0.00210 |
| | $\hat{\beta}_{WB}$ | 0.82762 | −0.00118 | 0.03015 | | $\hat{\beta}_{WB}$ | 0.39766 | −0.00210 | 0.02830 |
| 7 | $\hat{\beta}_{IQ}$ | 0.22419 | 0.00220 | −0.00296 | 17 | $\hat{\beta}_{IQ}$ | 0.18720 | 0.00112 | −0.00097 |
| | $\hat{\beta}_{WB}$ | −0.24891 | −0.00296 | 0.04012 | | $\hat{\beta}_{WB}$ | 0.34958 | −0.00097 | 0.01684 |
| 8 | $\hat{\beta}_{IQ}$ | 0.03216 | 0.00159 | −0.00199 | 18 | $\hat{\beta}_{IQ}$ | −0.07194 | 0.00163 | −0.00234 |
| | $\hat{\beta}_{WB}$ | −0.08738 | −0.00199 | 0.02956 | | $\hat{\beta}_{WB}$ | 0.56429 | −0.00234 | 0.02812 |
| 9 | $\hat{\beta}_{IQ}$ | 0.03843 | 0.00112 | −0.00114 | 19 | $\hat{\beta}_{IQ}$ | 0.07507 | 0.00109 | −0.00086 |
| | $\hat{\beta}_{WB}$ | 0.26239 | −0.00114 | 0.02068 | | $\hat{\beta}_{WB}$ | 0.37283 | −0.00086 | 0.01653 |
| 10 | $\hat{\beta}_{IQ}$ | 0.09957 | 0.00139 | −0.00197 | 20 | $\hat{\beta}_{IQ}$ | 0.02076 | 0.00113 | −0.00089 |
| | $\hat{\beta}_{WB}$ | 0.77943 | −0.00197 | 0.02568 | | $\hat{\beta}_{WB}$ | 0.50011 | −0.00089 | 0.01690 |

Finally, substituting the parameter estimates and the total covariance matrix into Equation 8.23 yields $D_1 = 1.245$, as follows:

$$D_1 = \frac{1}{2}\left(\begin{bmatrix} .083 \\ .365 \end{bmatrix} - \begin{bmatrix} 0 \\ 0 \end{bmatrix}\right)^T \begin{bmatrix} .00802 & -.00889 \\ -.00889 & .13654 \end{bmatrix}^{-1} \left(\begin{bmatrix} .083 \\ .365 \end{bmatrix} - \begin{bmatrix} 0 \\ 0 \end{bmatrix}\right) = 1.45$$

Referencing $D_1$ against an $F$ distribution with $k = 2$ and $v_2 = 55.806$ degrees of freedom returns a probability value of $p = .30$. $D_1$ is analogous to an omnibus $F$ statistic, so the lack of significance suggests that the pair of regression coefficients is not statistically different from zero (i.e., considered as a set, the explanatory variables do not predict job performance). Fortunately, the $D_1$ statistic is available in a number of software programs, so performing the tedious matrix computations is rarely necessary.

## 8.12 TESTING MULTIPLE PARAMETERS BY COMBINING WALD TESTS

A second approach for conducting multiparameter significance tests is to pool significance tests from the analysis phase. Li, Meng, Raghunathan, and Rubin (1991) outlined a procedure for pooling Wald tests, which I henceforth refer to as the $D_2$ statistic. To begin, $D_2$ requires the arithmetic average of the $m$ Wald tests, as follows:

$$\bar{\omega} = \frac{1}{m} \sum_{t=1}^{m} \omega_t \tag{8.26}$$

where $\omega_t$ is the Wald statistic from data set $t$ and $\bar{\omega}$ is the mean test statistic. Similar to the $D_1$ statistic, $D_2$ also requires an estimate of the average relative increase in variance. Li, Meng, et al. (1991) provide an expression that relies only on the $m$ Wald statistics

$$\text{ARIV}_1 = (1 + m^{-1})\left[\frac{1}{m-1} \sum_{t=1}^{m} \left(\sqrt{\omega_t} - \overline{\sqrt{\omega}}\right)^2\right] \tag{8.27}$$

where $\sqrt{\omega_t}$ is the square root of the Wald statistic from data set $t$, and $\overline{\sqrt{\omega}}$ is the average of the $\sqrt{\omega_t}$ values. (Collectively, the terms in brackets quantify the variance of the square root of the Wald statistics.) Although it does not resemble its previous counterpart, $\text{ARIV}_1$ has the same interpretation as ARIV. Finally, the $D_2$ statistic is as follows:

$$D_2 = \frac{\bar{\omega}k^{-1} - (m+1)(m-1)^{-1}\text{ARIV}_1}{1 + \text{ARIV}_1} \tag{8.28}$$

To generate a probability value, Li, Meng, et al. recommend an $F$ reference distribution with $k$ numerator degrees of freedom and $v_3$ denominator degrees of freedom, where

$$v_3 = k^{-3/m}(m-1)\left(1 + \frac{1}{\text{ARIV}_1}\right)^2 \tag{8.29}$$

The interpretation of $D_2$ is similar to that of a complete-data Wald statistic. That is, a statistically significant test statistic indicates that the parameter estimates differ from their hypothesized values.

Li, Meng, et al. (1991) used Monte Carlo simulations to study the performance of $D_2$ statistic under a variety of conditions. Their results suggest that type I error rates can either be too high or too low, depending on the fraction of missing information (e.g., when the fraction of missing information was less than 20%, type I errors dropped below the nominal 0.05 level). Their simulations also indicate that $D_2$ has lower power than $D_1$. Considered as a whole, these simulation results suggest that $D_2$ does not yield accurate inferences, and the authors recommend using the procedure "primarily as a screening test statistic" (p. 83). You should use the $D_1$ statistic whenever possible, but a custom program for computing $D_2$ is available on the companion website, if necessary.

## 8.13 TESTING MULTIPLE PARAMETERS BY COMBINING LIKELIHOOD RATIO STATISTICS

A final option for conducting multiparameter significance tests is to combine likelihood ratio test statistics from the analysis phase. Meng and Rubin (1992) outline such a procedure, and I subsequently refer to their test statistic as $D_3$. As a brief reminder, recall that the likelihood ratio statistic uses the log-likelihood value to compare the relative fit of two nested models, as follows:

$$\text{LR} = -2(\log L_{\text{Restricted}} - \log L_{\text{Full}}) \tag{8.30}$$

where $\log L_{\text{Full}}$ and $\log L_{\text{Restricted}}$ are the log-likelihood values from the full and the restricted models, respectively. The restricted model may include a subset of the parameters from the full model (e.g., a regression model where the slopes are constrained to zero during estimation), or it can differ from the full model by a set of complex parameter constraints (e.g., a confirmatory factor analysis model is a restricted model that expresses the population covariance matrix as a function of the factor model parameters).

To begin, the $D_3$ requires the average likelihood ratio test from the analysis phase, as follows:

$$\overline{\text{LR}} = \frac{1}{m} \sum_{t=1}^{m} \text{LR}_t \tag{8.31}$$

where $\overline{\text{LR}}$ is the arithmetic average of the $m$ likelihood ratio statistics, and $\text{LR}_t$ is the likelihood ratio test from data set $t$. The computations also require the pooled parameter estimates from both models. I denote these parameter vectors as $\bar{\boldsymbol{\theta}}_F$ and $\bar{\boldsymbol{\theta}}_R$ for the full and the restricted models, respectively.

After pooling the test statistics and the parameter estimates, the next step is to re-estimate the full and the restricted models, this time constraining the model parameters to their pooled values (i.e., estimate the full model $m$ times, each time fixing the model parameters to the values in $\bar{\boldsymbol{\theta}}_F$). Estimating the models with parameter constraints yields a second set of $m$ likelihood ratio tests that compare the relative fit of the constrained models. The purpose of this step is to obtain the arithmetic average of these likelihood ratio tests (e.g., by substituting the LR values into Equation 8.31). I denote this average as $\overline{\text{LR}}_{\text{Constrained}}$ in order to differentiate it from $\overline{\text{LR}}$.

Finally, the $D_3$ test statistic is as follows:

$$D_3 = \frac{\overline{\text{LR}}_{\text{Constrained}}}{k(1 + \text{ARIV}_2)} \tag{8.32}$$

where $\text{ARIV}_2$ is yet another estimate of the average relative increase in variance.

$$\text{ARIV}_2 = \frac{m+1}{k(m-1)}(\overline{\text{LR}} - \overline{\text{LR}}_{\text{Constrained}}) \tag{8.33}$$

To obtain a probability value for $D_3$, Meng and Rubin recommend an $F$ reference distribution with $k$ numerator degrees of freedom and $v_4$ denominator degrees of freedom. In this context, $k$ is the number of parameter constraints (i.e., the degrees of freedom for the complete-data likelihood ratio test), and $v_4$ is

$$v_4 = 4 + (km - k - 4)\left[1 + \left(1 - \frac{2}{km - k}\right)\frac{1}{\text{ARIV}_2}\right]^2 \tag{8.34}$$

In the situation where $km - k$ is less than or equal to four, Meng and Rubin recommend an alternate expression for $v_4$, as follows.

$$v_4 = \frac{(km - k)(1 + k^{-1})\left(1 + \frac{1}{\text{ARIV}_3}\right)^2}{2} \tag{8.35}$$

Meng and Rubin show that $D_3$ is asymptotically equivalent to $D_1$, so the two tests should yield similar conclusions in large samples. However, because virtually no research studies have compared the two test statistics, it is difficult to assess their relative performance in realistic research scenarios. All things being equal, $D_1$ is more convenient because it is readily available in a number of popular software programs. However, $D_3$ is potentially useful in structural equation modeling analyses because it provides a mechanism for assessing model fit (e.g., by pooling the chi-square tests of model fit). In the structural equation modeling context, the full model is a saturated model (e.g., a model that estimates the sample covariance matrix), and the restricted model is the hypothesized model (e.g., a confirmatory factor analysis model that expresses the population covariance matrix as a function of the factor model parameters). The so-called chi-square test of model fit is a likelihood ratio test that compares the relative fit of these two models. Methodologists have yet to develop procedures for pooling structural equation modeling fit indices (e.g., the CFI, RMSEA), so the $D_3$ statistic is currently the only formal option for assessing fit. I illustrate the use of $D_3$ for this purpose in one of the subsequent data analysis examples.

## 8.14 DATA ANALYSIS EXAMPLE 1

In the remainder of the chapter, I use three data analysis examples to illustrate various aspects of a multiple imputation analysis. Chapter 7 did not include data analysis examples, so the subsequent examples illustrate all three phases of a multiple imputation analysis. To facilitate comparisons between maximum likelihood estimation and multiple imputation, the analysis examples are identical to those from Chapter 4.

The first analysis example illustrates the use of multiple imputation to estimate a mean vector, covariance matrix, and a correlation matrix.* The data for this analysis are made up of scores from 480 employees on eight work-related variables: gender, age, job tenure, IQ, psychological well-being, job satisfaction, job performance, and turnover intentions. I generated these data to mimic the correlation structure of published research articles in the management and psychology literature (e.g., Wright & Bonett, 2007; Wright, Cropanzano, & Bonett, 2007). The data have three missing data patterns, each of which is comprised of one- third of the sample. The first pattern consists of cases with complete data, and the remaining two patterns have missing data on either well-being or job satisfaction. These patterns mimic a situation in which the data are missing by design (e.g., to reduce the cost of data collection).

### The Imputation Phase

First, I used the EM algorithm to estimate the mean vector and the covariance matrix. EM converged in only 20 iterations, which suggests that the data augmentation algorithm should also converge very quickly. Next, I generated an exploratory chain of 5,000 data augmentation cycles and saved the simulated parameter values from each P-step. The purpose of this initial analysis was to assess the convergence of the data augmentation algorithm, and I did so by examining time-series and autocorrelation function plots for each element in the mean vector and the covariance matrix.

To illustrate the convergence diagnostics, Figure 8.2 shows the times-series and autocorrelation function plots for the simulated covariance between well-being and job satisfaction. I paid particularly close attention to the convergence behavior of this parameter because it has the highest percentage of missing data, and thus one of the highest fractions of missing information (only 33% of the cases have data on both variables). The time-series plot in the top panel of Figure 8.2 suggests that the covariances randomly vary, with no discernible long-term trends. In fact, the upward and downward trends in the plot typically last for fewer than 20 iterations. The autocorrelation plot in the bottom panel of the figure also shows very fast convergence, as the autocorrelations drop to chance levels by lag 10 (i.e., the correlation between parameter values separated by 10 iterations is not significantly different from zero). I examined the plots for the remaining parameters, and they were largely consistent with

---

*Analysis syntax and data are available on the companion website, *www.appliedmissingdata.com*.

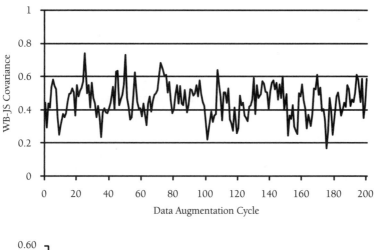

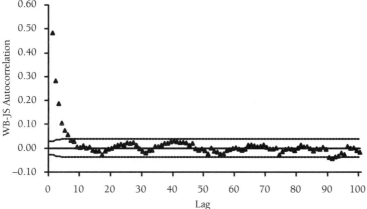

**FIGURE 8.2.** Time-series plots for the covariance between psychological well-being (WB) and job satisfaction (JS). The top panel shows a time-series plot with no long-term trends. The bottom panel shows autocorrelations that drop to within sampling error of zero after 10 data augmentation cycles.

those in Figure 8.2. Taken together, the graphical diagnostics suggest that the data augmentation algorithm converges very quickly, perhaps in fewer than 20 iterations. The fast convergence may seem somewhat surprising given that such a large proportion of the well-being and job satisfaction scores were missing. However, this example is an ideal situation because the data are MCAR by design.

As a general rule, it is a good idea to assess convergence using a small number of alternate starting values (e.g., bootstrap estimates of $\mu$ and $\Sigma$). However, the graphical displays were so ideal that this additional step did not seem necessary. Consequently, I generated the final imputations using a single data augmentation chain. The graphical diagnostics suggest that the data augmentation algorithm converges in fewer than 20 iterations, but I took a conservative tack of specifying 100 burn-in and 100 between-imputation iterations (i.e., I saved the first imputed data set after an initial burn-in period of 100 cycles and saved subsequent data sets at every 100th I-step thereafter). The exploratory data augmentation chain took just a few seconds to run, so I opted to generate $m = 50$ imputations for the analysis phase. Estimating means and correlations from 50 data sets takes very little time, so using a large number of imputations posed no practical problems.

## The Analysis Phase

I analyzed each of the 50 data sets in the analysis phase. This step produced an estimate of the mean vector, the covariance matrix, and the correlation matrix from each of the 50 filled-in data sets. Although it sounds tedious to repeat the analysis that many times, many software programs automate the process. As an aside, programs that automate the analysis phase have different formatting requirements for the imputed data files. For example, some software packages make it very easy to analyze a data set where the imputations are stacked in a single file, whereas other programs require separate data sets. The companion website has software examples that illustrate both approaches.

## The Pooling Phase

In the pooling phase, I used Rubin's (1987) formulas to combine the parameter estimates. Although some of the parameters are unlikely to satisfy the normality requirement (e.g., variances and covariances), I averaged the variable means and the covariance matrix elements without applying any transformations. Fisher's (1915) $z$ transformation is a natural choice for the pooling correlations because it transforms the estimates to a metric that more closely approximates a normal distribution, and it provides a straightforward mechanism for performing significance tests. Equation 8.2 gives the transformation, and the corresponding standard error is as follows:

$$SE_t = \frac{1}{\sqrt{N-3}} \tag{8.36}$$

After pooling the transformed estimates and their standard errors, I used Equation 8.3 to back-transform the average coefficients to the correlation metric.

Table 8.5 shows the pooled point estimates along with the corresponding maximum likelihood estimates from Chapter 4. As seen in the table, the multiple imputation and maximum likelihood estimates are quite similar. The close correspondence of the two sets of estimates is not surprising given that both techniques make the same assumptions (MAR data and multivariate normality) and use the same set of input variables. You might have noticed that maximum likelihood estimates of variances and covariances are slightly smaller than those of multiple imputation, even for the variables that have complete data (e.g., the age variance estimates are 29.968 and 28.908 for multiple imputation and maximum likelihood, respectively). These systematic (albeit small) differences result from the fact that maximum likelihood estimates use $N$ in the denominator rather than $N - 1$.

**TABLE 8.5. Mean, Covariance, and Correlation Estimates from Data Analysis Example 1**

| Variable | 1 | 2 | 3 | 4 | 5 | 6 | 7 | 8 |
|---|---|---|---|---|---|---|---|---|
| | | | | Multiple imputation | | | | |
| 1: Age | 28.968 | 0.504 | −0.010 | .181 | 0.139 | −0.049 | −0.150 | 0.015 |
| 2: Tenure | 8.477 | 9.755 | −0.034 | .156 | 0.153 | 0.016 | 0.011 | 0.001 |
| 3: Female | −0.028 | −0.052 | 0.249 | .113 | 0.038 | −0.015 | 0.005 | 0.068 |
| 4: Well-being | 1.147 | 0.576 | 0.066 | 1.395 | 0.321 | 0.456 | −0.255 | 0.293 |
| 5: Satisfaction | 0.888 | 0.567 | 0.023 | 0.449 | 1.406 | 0.184 | −0.234 | 0.407 |
| 6: Performance | −0.331 | 0.061 | −0.009 | 0.675 | 0.274 | 1.574 | −.346 | 0.426 |
| 7: Turnover | −0.378 | 0.016 | 0.001 | −0.141 | −0.129 | −0.203 | 0.218 | −0.180 |
| 8: IQ | 0.675 | 0.026 | 0.285 | 2.912 | 4.063 | 4.505 | −0.707 | 71.040 |
| Means | 37.948 | 10.054 | 0.542 | 6.291 | 5.946 | 6.021 | 0.321 | 100.102 |
| | | | | Maximum likelihood | | | | |
| 1: Age | 28.908 | 0.504 | −0.010 | 0.182 | 0.136 | −0.049 | −0.150 | 0.015 |
| 2: Tenure | 8.459 | 9.735 | −0.034 | 0.155 | 0.154 | 0.016 | 0.011 | 0.001 |
| 3: Female | −0.028 | −0.052 | 0.248 | 0.115 | 0.047 | −0.015 | 0.005 | 0.068 |
| 4: Well-being | 1.148 | 0.569 | 0.067 | 1.382 | 0.322 | 0.456 | −0.257 | 0.291 |
| 5: Satisfaction | 0.861 | 0.565 | 0.028 | 0.446 | 1.386 | 0.184 | −0.234 | 0.411 |
| 6: Performance | −0.330 | 0.061 | −0.009 | 0.671 | 0.271 | 1.570 | −0.346 | 0.426 |
| 7: Turnover | −0.377 | 0.016 | 0.001 | −0.141 | −0.129 | −0.203 | 0.218 | −0.180 |
| 8: IQ | 0.674 | 0.026 | 0.284 | 2.876 | 4.074 | 4.496 | −0.706 | 70.892 |
| Means | 37.948 | 10.054 | 0.542 | 6.288 | 5.950 | 6.021 | 0.321 | 100.102 |

*Note.* Correlations are shown in the upper diagonal in **bold** typeface. Elements affected by missing data are enclosed in the shaded box.

## 8.15 DATA ANALYSIS EXAMPLE 2

The second analysis example applies multiple imputation to a multiple regression model.* The analysis uses the same employee data set as the first example and involves the regression of job performance ratings on psychological well-being and job satisfaction, as follows:

$$JP_i = \beta_0 + \beta_1(WB_i) + \beta_2(SAT_i) + \varepsilon$$

I reused the 50 imputations from the previous example for this analysis. Carefully planning the imputation model allows you to use the same imputed data sets for many (if not all) of the subsequent analyses. At a minimum, the imputation phase must include all of the associations that are of interest in the subsequent analysis phase. I imputed the data using all eight variables in the data set, so I can perform any analysis that involves the zero-order associations among the variables. I would only need to generate a new set of imputations if my analysis model included higher-order terms (e.g., interactions) or other variables that I excluded from the imputation phase.

---

* Analysis syntax and data are available on the companion website, *www.appliedmissingdata.com.*

## The Analysis and Pooling Phases

In the analysis phase, I estimated the regression model parameters separately for each of the 50 filled-in data sets. The imputation phase incorporated a number of extra variables that were not part of the regression analysis (i.e., age, job tenure, gender, IQ), so these additional variables effectively served as auxiliary variables. It is important to reiterate that auxiliary variables play no role in the analysis phase (the filled-in values already contain the auxiliary information), so I did not include the extra variables in the regression model.

In a multiple regression analysis, researchers typically use an omnibus $F$ test to determine whether two or more coefficients are statistically different from zero. Of the three multiparameter significance tests outlined previously in the chapter, the $D_1$ statistic is particularly convenient because it is readily available in multiple imputation software programs. Consequently, I used $D_1$ to assess whether the two regression slopes were different from zero. This procedure produced a test statistic of $D_1 = 42.87$, and referencing this value against an $F$ distribution with $k = 2$ and $v_2 = 899.07$ degrees of freedom returned a probability value of $p < .001$. The substantive interpretation of $D_1$ is identical to that of an omnibus $F$ statistic, so rejecting the null hypothesis implies that at least one of the regression coefficients is significantly different from zero.

As an aside, the $D_1$ statistic assumes that the fractions of missing information are identical across parameters. Multiple imputation software programs generally report these quantities, and the estimates from this analysis are 0.27 and 0.39 for the well-being and job satisfaction slopes, respectively. Recall that missing information is akin to an $R^2$ statistic, such that a value of 0.27 indicates that 27% of the well-being slope's sampling variance (i.e., squared standard error) is attributable to missing data. Although the fractions of missing information are not identical, the magnitude of this difference is probably not large enough to seriously distort the $D_1$ statistic (Li, Raghunathan, et al., 1991). I could have also used the $D_2$ or $D_3$ statistics to test the regression coefficients, but $D_1$ is far easier to implement.

Researchers typically follow up a significant omnibus test by examining the partial regression coefficients. Table 8.6 gives the regression model estimates along with the saturated correlates model estimates from Chapter 5. As seen in the table, psychological well-being was a significant predictor of job performance, $\hat{\beta}_1 = 0.470$, $t(231.01) = 8.79$, $p < .001$, but job satisfaction was not, $\hat{\beta}_2 = 0.045$, $t(154.84) = 0.77$, $p = .44$. The interpretation of these regression coefficients is the same as an ordinary least squares analysis. For example, holding job satisfaction constant, a one-point increase in psychological well-being yields a .470 increase in job performance ratings, on average. Note that I used Barnard and Rubin's (1999) degrees of freedom for the $t$ tests. This degrees of freedom expression relies, in part, on the degrees of freedom for a complete-data test statistic (e.g., $df_{com} = N - k - 1 = 477$, where $k$ is the number of predictors). I point this out because some multiple imputation software programs require the user to specify the complete-data degrees of freedom value when requesting Barnard and Rubin's formula.

Finally, notice that multiple imputation and maximum likelihood produced very similar parameter estimates and standard errors. In this particular example, the two missing data handling approaches are not exactly comparable because the saturated correlates model in Chapter 5 included only IQ and turnover intentions as auxiliary variables. Nevertheless, the

**TABLE 8.6. Regression Model Estimates from Data Analysis Example 2**

| Parameter | Estimate | SE | t |
|---|---|---|---|
| | Multiple imputation | | |
| $\beta_0$ (intercept) | 6.021 | 0.060 | 118.096 |
| $\beta_1$ (well-being) | 0.470 | 0.053 | 8.791 |
| $\beta_2$ (satisfaction) | 0.045 | 0.058 | 0.772 |
| $R^2$ | .208 | | |
| | Maximum likelihood | | |
| $\beta_0$ (intercept) | 6.020 | 0.053 | 114.642 |
| $\beta_1$ (well-being) | 0.475 | 0.054 | 8.798 |
| $\beta_2$ (satisfaction) | 0.035 | 0.058 | 0.605 |
| $R^2$ | .208 | | |

*Note.* Predictors were centered at the maximum likelihood estimates of the mean.

estimates are quite similar, even though the multiple imputation analysis used a larger set of auxiliary variables.

## 8.16 DATA ANALYSIS EXAMPLE 3

The final data analysis example applies multiple imputation to a confirmatory factor analysis model.* The analyses use artificial data from a questionnaire on eating disorder risk. Briefly, the data contain the responses from 400 college-age women on 10 questions from the Eating Attitudes Test (EAT; Garner, Olmsted, Bohr, & Garfinkel, 1982), a widely used measure of eating disorder risk. The 10 questions measure two constructs: Drive for Thinness (e.g., "I avoid eating when I'm hungry") and Food Preoccupation (e.g., "I find myself preoccupied with food"), and mimic the two-factor structure proposed by Doninger, Enders, and Burnett (2005). The 10 questionnaire items combine to measure two constructs. The Drive for Thinness scale consists of seven items ($EAT_1$, $EAT_2$, $EAT_{10}$, $EAT_{11}$, $EAT_{12}$, $EAT_{14}$, and $EAT_{24}$), and the Food Preoccupation scale has three items ($EAT_3$, $EAT_{18}$, and $EAT_{21}$). Figure 4.2 shows a graphic of the EAT factor structure and abbreviated descriptions of the item stems. The data set also contains an anxiety scale score, a variable that measures beliefs about Western standards of beauty (e.g., high scores indicate that respondents internalize a thin ideal of beauty), and body mass index (BMI) values.

Variables in the EAT data set are missing for a variety of reasons. I simulated MCAR data by randomly deleting scores from the anxiety variable, the Western standards of beauty scale, and two of the EAT questions ($EAT_2$ and $EAT_{21}$). It seems reasonable to expect a relationship between body weight and missingness, so I created MAR data on five variables ($EAT_1$, $EAT_{10}$,

---

*Analysis syntax and data are available on the companion website, *www.appliedmissingdata.com*.

$EAT_{12}$, $EAT_{18}$, and $EAT_{24}$) by deleting the EAT scores for a subset of cases in both tails of the BMI distribution. These same EAT questions were also missing for individuals with elevated anxiety scores. Finally, I introduced a small amount of MNAR data by deleting a number of the high body mass index scores (e.g., to mimic a situation where females with high BMI values refuse to be weighed). The deletion process typically produced a missing data rate of 5 to 10% on each variable.

## The Imputation Phase

To get a rough gauge of convergence speed, I first used the EM algorithm to estimate the mean vector and the covariance matrix for the entire set of 13 variables (the 10 EAT items, body mass index, anxiety, and Western standard of beauty). EM converged in only nine iterations, which suggests that data augmentation should also converge very quickly. Next, I generated an exploratory chain of 5,000 data augmentation cycles and saved the simulated parameter estimates from each P-step. The purpose of this initial analysis was to assess the convergence of the data augmentation algorithm, and I did so by examining time-series and autocorrelation function plots for each simulated parameter value in the mean vector and the covariance matrix. For the sake of brevity, I illustrate these plots using the covariance between $EAT_1$ and $EAT_{18}$. I chose this parameter because it has one of the highest fractions of missing information (i.e., this pair of variables has one of the highest missing data rates and the lowest correlations). The fraction of missing information largely dictates convergence speed, so this parameter should be among the slowest to converge.

Figure 8.3 shows the time-series and autocorrelation function plots for the covariance between $EAT_1$ and $EAT_{18}$. The time-series plot in the top panel of Figure 8.3 suggests that the simulated covariance values randomly vary with no discernible trends whatsoever. The autocorrelation plot in the bottom panel shows that the autocorrelations drop to chance levels by the second lag (i.e., the correlation between parameter values separated by two iterations is not significantly different from zero). Thus, this parameter appears to converge almost immediately. I examined the plots for the remaining parameters, and they were largely consistent with those in Figure 8.3. Taken together, the graphical diagnostics indicate that the data augmentation algorithm converges very quickly, perhaps in fewer than 10 iterations. The rather fast convergence follows from the fact that the fractions of missing information were generally rather low (e.g., values between 2 and 10% were common).

Having established the convergence of the data augmentation algorithm, I used a single data augmentation chain to generate the imputations. Although the data augmentation algorithm appears to converge in fewer than 10 iterations, I took a conservative approach and specified 100 burn-in iterations and 100 between-imputation iterations (i.e., i.e., I saved the first imputed data set after an initial burn-in period of 100 cycles and saved subsequent data sets at every 100th I-step thereafter). For this analysis, I created $m = 100$ imputations for the analysis phase. Because a confirmatory factor analysis model takes very little time to estimate, using a large number of imputations does not pose a computational burden. Analyzing a large number of data sets is also useful for assessing model fit (more on this later). Finally, note that I used the entire set of 13 variables in the imputation phase. The factor analysis model includes the 10 questionnaire items, so the additional variables (body mass index,

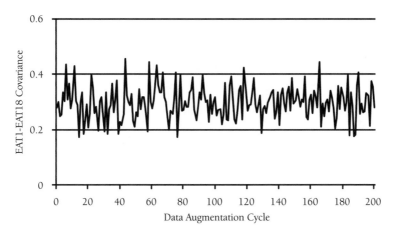

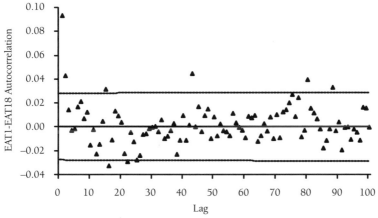

**FIGURE 8.3.** Time-series plots for the covariance between questions 1 and 18 from the EAT questionnaire ($EAT_1$ and $EAT_{18}$, respectively). The top panel shows a time-series plot with no long-term trends. The bottom panel shows autocorrelations that drop to within sampling error of zero by the second data augmentation cycle.

anxiety, and Western standards of beauty) effectively served as auxiliary variables. Again, there is no need to use the auxiliary variables in the subsequent analysis phase.

## The Analysis and Pooling Phases

In the analysis phase, I estimated the factor model parameters separately for each of the 100 filled-in data sets. The discrete nature of the questionnaire items violates the multivariate normality assumption, so I used robust (i.e., sandwich estimator) standard errors for each analysis (see Chapter 5). The analysis step produced 100 sets of results, and I subsequently used Rubin's (1987) formulas to combine the parameter estimates and the standard errors (pooling robust standard errors is no different from pooling normal-theory standard errors). Although some of the parameters are unlikely to satisfy the normality requirement (e.g., factor variances, residual variances), I averaged the estimates without applying any transformations.

**TABLE 8.7. Confirmatory Factor Analysis Estimates from Data Analysis Example 3**

| Variable | Loadings | | Intercepts | | Residuals | |
|---|---|---|---|---|---|---|
| | Estimate | SE | Estimate | SE | Estimate | SE |
| | | | Multiple imputation | | | |
| $EAT_1$ | 0.743 | 0.049 | 4.006 | 0.055 | 0.606 | 0.067 |
| $EAT_2$ | 0.651 | 0.050 | 3.937 | 0.050 | 0.536 | 0.053 |
| $EAT_{10}$ | 0.808 | 0.052 | 3.955 | 0.050 | 0.331 | 0.038 |
| $EAT_{11}$ | 0.765 | 0.049 | 3.937 | 0.047 | 0.299 | 0.027 |
| $EAT_{12}$ | 0.665 | 0.054 | 3.929 | 0.051 | 0.540 | 0.057 |
| $EAT_{14}$ | 0.900 | 0.048 | 3.962 | 0.051 | 0.237 | 0.028 |
| $EAT_{24}$ | 0.625 | 0.053 | 3.985 | 0.051 | 0.604 | 0.050 |
| $EAT_3$ | 0.774 | 0.052 | 3.967 | 0.050 | 0.413 | 0.043 |
| $EAT_{18}$ | 0.749 | 0.055 | 3.982 | 0.052 | 0.456 | 0.049 |
| $EAT_{21}$ | 0.859 | 0.052 | 3.950 | 0.051 | 0.270 | 0.043 |
| | | | Maximum likelihood | | | |
| $EAT_1$ | 0.741 | 0.049 | 4.004 | 0.055 | 0.604 | 0.069 |
| $EAT_2$ | 0.649 | 0.050 | 3.937 | 0.050 | 0.535 | 0.054 |
| $EAT_{10}$ | 0.808 | 0.052 | 3.953 | 0.050 | 0.328 | 0.039 |
| $EAT_{11}$ | 0.764 | 0.049 | 3.938 | 0.047 | 0.300 | 0.027 |
| $EAT_{12}$ | 0.662 | 0.055 | 3.929 | 0.051 | 0.538 | 0.058 |
| $EAT_{14}$ | 0.901 | 0.047 | 3.963 | 0.051 | 0.234 | 0.028 |
| $EAT_{24}$ | 0.622 | 0.053 | 3.986 | 0.051 | 0.599 | 0.049 |
| $EAT_3$ | 0.772 | 0.052 | 3.967 | 0.050 | 0.415 | 0.042 |
| $EAT_{18}$ | 0.751 | 0.056 | 3.982 | 0.052 | 0.451 | 0.050 |
| $EAT_{21}$ | 0.862 | 0.053 | 3.952 | 0.051 | 0.264 | 0.043 |

Repeating the factor analysis 100 times sounds incredibly tedious, but some structural equation modeling software programs can fully automate the analysis and pooling phases. In fact, estimating the models and combining the results took less than 10 seconds on a laptop computer.

Table 8.7 shows selected parameter estimates and standard errors, along with the corresponding maximum likelihood estimates. To maximize the comparability of the two sets of results, the table gives the saturated correlates estimates from Chapter 5. As seen in the table, multiple imputation and maximum likelihood produced nearly identical estimates and standard errors. Again, this is not a surprise because the two procedures used the same set of variables (i.e., the saturated correlates model included the same 13 variables that I used in the imputation phase). Consistent with the previous analyses, the interpretation of the model parameters is unaffected by the missing data handling procedure. For example, the factor loadings estimate the expected change in the questionnaire items for a one-standard-deviation increase in the latent construct. This interpretation follows from the fact that I fixed the variances of the latent variables to unity in order to identify the model.

Assessing model fit is an important part of a structural equation modeling analysis. Earlier in the chapter, I outlined a $D_3$ statistic that combines likelihood ratio tests from a multiple imputation analysis (Meng & Rubin, 1992). This procedure is potentially useful for structural equation modeling analyses because it provides a mechanism for assessing model fit (e.g., by pooling the chi-square test of model fit). In the context of a confirmatory factor analysis, the saturated model serves as the full model, and the hypothesized factor model is the restricted model. The so-called chi-square test of model fit is a likelihood ratio test that compares the relative fit of these two models.

To illustrate the $D_3$ statistic, I fit the confirmatory factor model and the saturated model to each imputed data set and saved the resulting likelihood ratio tests. This step is straightforward because structural equation modeling programs report the likelihood ratio (i.e., chi-square) test as standard output. Averaging the likelihood ratio tests produced $\overline{LR} = 61.94$. In the next step, I re-estimated the two models after constraining the parameters to their pooled values. For example, I estimated the two-factor model on each imputed data set, but did so by constraining the factor model parameters to the pooled estimates in Table 8.7. I applied the same procedure to the saturated model. Estimating the constrained models produced another set of 100 likelihood ratio tests, the average of which was $\overline{LR}_{Constrained} = 56.93$. The $D_3$ statistic requires the average relative increase in variance, and substituting the appropriate quantities into Equation 8.33 gives $ARIV_2 = 0.15$. (The factor model has 34 fewer parameters than the saturated model, so $k = 34$.) Finally, substituting the appropriate values into Equation 8.32, a test statistic of $D_3 = 1.456$, and referencing this value to an $F$ distribution with $k = 34$ and $v_4 = 197,410.74$ degrees of freedom gives a probability value of $p = .04$. Because the substantive interpretation of $D_3$ is identical to that of the likelihood ratio test, rejecting the null hypothesis implies that the factor model does not fit the data as well as the saturated model. For comparison purposes, the saturated correlates model from Chapter 5 produced a likelihood ratio test of $\chi^2(34) = 49.04$, $p = .05$. Although the two analyses produced very similar conclusions about model fit in this particular example, no studies have examined the performance of $D_3$ in structural equation modeling applications. Until more research accumulates, it seems prudent to interpret $D_3$ with some caution.

Researchers generally augment the likelihood ratio test with a number of other fit indices. The methodological literature currently favors the CFI, RMSEA, and the SRMR (Hu & Bentler, 1998, 1999), but there is no established method for pooling these indices. In order to get some sense about model fit, I used the 100 estimates of each index to construct an empirical distribution. The distributions were approximately normal and had means of 0.987 (CFI), 0.041 (RMSEA), and 0.031 (SRMR). I arbitrarily examined the 5th and the 95th percentiles of each index, and these values were as follows: CFI ($P_5 = 0.981$, $P_{95} = 0.993$), RMSEA ($P_5 = 0.032$, $P_{95} = 0.050$), and SRMR ($P_5 = 0.028$, $P_{95} = 0.034$). High CFI values are indicative of good model fit, so the CFI value at the 5th percentile of the distribution should provide a conservative assessment of fit. In contrast, lower values of the RMSEA and SRMR are indicative of good fit, so the values at the 95th percentile of these distributions would be conservative. Considered as a whole, the means and the percentiles of the distributions suggest that the two-factor model fits the data adequately (e.g., the values at the mean and the 5th percentile of the CFI distribution exceed the conventional cutoff of 0.95). The approach outlined here is purely ad hoc and has no theoretical rationale. Until methodologists develop formal pooling rules for popular fit indices, this is probably the best you can do.

## 8.17 SUMMARY

A multiple imputation analysis consists of three distinct steps: the imputation phase, the analysis phase, and the pooling phase. The product of the imputation phase is a set of filled-in data sets, each of which contains different estimates of the missing values. The purpose of the analysis phase is to analyze the filled-in data sets from the preceding imputation phase. This step consists of $m$ statistical analyses, one for each imputed data set. The analysis phase yields several sets of parameter estimates and standard errors, so the goal of the pooling phase is to combine everything into a single set of results. Rubin (1987) outlined relatively straightforward formulas for pooling parameter estimates and standard errors. The pooled parameter estimate is simply the arithmetic average of the estimates from the analysis phase. Combining standard errors is somewhat more complex because it involves two sources of sampling variation. The within-imputation variance is the arithmetic average of the $m$ sampling variances (i.e., squared standard errors), and the between-imputation variance quantifies the variability of an estimate across the $m$ imputations. The within-imputation variance estimates the sampling fluctuation that would have resulted had there been no missing data, and the between-imputation variance captures the increase in sampling error due to missing data. Together, these two sources of variation combine to form the total sampling variance, the square root of which is the standard error.

The chapter outlined four significance testing procedures. The familiar $t$ statistic (the pooled estimate divided by its standard errors) is useful for testing whether a single estimate is different from some hypothesized value. Multiple imputation also offers different mechanisms for testing a set of parameter estimates. The $D_1$ statistic uses pooled parameter estimates and pooled parameter covariance matrices to construct a test that closely resembles the multivariate Wald statistic. A second approach is to compute a significance test for each imputed data set and pool the resulting test statistics. The $D_2$ statistic pools Wald tests from the analysis phase, and the $D_3$ statistic pools likelihood ratio tests. Although these procedures accomplish the same task, they are not equally trustworthy, nor are they equally easy to implement. Relatively little is known about the performance of the multiparameter significance tests, but it is clear that $D_1$ and $D_3$ are preferable to $D_2$.

Chapter 9 outlines a number of practical issues that arise during the imputation phase of a multiple imputation analysis. Specifically, the chapter offers advice on dealing with convergence problems, non-normal data (including nominal and ordinal variables), interaction effects, and large multiple-item questionnaire data sets. The chapter also provides a brief overview of some alternative imputation algorithms that are appropriate for special types of data structures (e.g., mixtures of categorical and continuous variables, multilevel data).

## 8.18 RECOMMENDED READINGS

Allison, P. D. (2002). *Missing data*. Newbury Park, CA: Sage.

Rubin, D. B. (1987). *Multiple imputation for nonresponse in surveys*. Hoboken, NJ: Wiley.

√Rubin, D. B. (1996). Multiple imputation after 18+ years. *Journal of the American Statistical Association, 91*, 473–489.

Schafer, J. L. (1997). *Analysis of incomplete multivariate data*. New York: Chapman.

Schafer, J. L., & Olsen, M. K. (1998). Multiple imputation for multivariate missing-data problems: A data analyst's perspective. *Multivariate Behavioral Research, 33*, 545–571.

Sinharay, S., Stern, H. S., & Russell, D. (2001). The use of multiple imputation for the analysis of missing data. *Psychological Methods, 6*, 317–329

# Practical Issues in Multiple Imputation

## 9.1 CHAPTER OVERVIEW

Having outlined the technical and the procedural details of multiple imputation in Chapters 7 and 8, I now address a number of practical issues that can arise in a multiple imputation analysis. Chapter 7 outlined a few such practical problems (e.g., assessing convergence, choosing the number of between-imputation iterations, deciding which variables to include in the imputation model), but several others need to be considered. Specifically, this chapter offers advice on dealing with convergence problems, non-normal data (including nominal and ordinal variables), interactive effects, and large multiple-item questionnaire data sets. The chapter also gives a brief overview of some alternative imputation algorithms that are appropriate for special types of data structures (e.g., mixtures of categorical and continuous variables, multilevel data). As you will see, this chapter is relatively applied in nature and is geared toward practical recommendations rather than toward technical issues. As an aside, many of the issues in this chapter have not been well studied in the methodological literature, so the practical guidelines that I offer are likely to change as additional methodological research accumulates.

## 9.2 DEALING WITH CONVERGENCE PROBLEMS

The data augmentation algorithm occasionally fails to converge, and it is useful to have some strategies for dealing with the problem. To illustrate a convergence problem, reconsider the small employee data set that I have been using throughout the book. First, I computed a binary employment status variable that denotes whether the company hired each applicant. Table 9.1 shows the resulting data. Next, I used the four variables in the table to generate 5,000 cycles of data augmentation. The fact that a preliminary EM analysis converged in only 25 iterations suggests that data augmentation should also converge very quickly, but graphical diagnostics suggested otherwise.

**TABLE 9.1. Employee Selection Data Set**

| IQ | Psychological well-being | Job performance | Employment status |
|----|--------------------------|-----------------|-------------------|
| 78 | 13 | — | 0 |
| 84 | 9 | — | 0 |
| 84 | 10 | — | 0 |
| 85 | 10 | — | 0 |
| 87 | — | — | 0 |
| 91 | 3 | — | 0 |
| 92 | 12 | — | 0 |
| 94 | 3 | — | 0 |
| 94 | 13 | — | 0 |
| 96 | — | — | 0 |
| 99 | 6 | 7 | 1 |
| 105 | 12 | 10 | 1 |
| 105 | 14 | 11 | 1 |
| 106 | 10 | 15 | 1 |
| 108 | — | 10 | 1 |
| 112 | 10 | 10 | 1 |
| 113 | 14 | 12 | 1 |
| 115 | 14 | 14 | 1 |
| 118 | 12 | 16 | 1 |
| 134 | 11 | 12 | 1 |

Figure 9.1 shows the time-series and autocorrelation function plots for the job performance mean. Two problems are apparent in the time-series plot: systematic trends that last for hundreds of iterations, and implausible parameter values (e.g., many of the simulated means fall outside the 1 to 20 score range). The autocorrelation function plot in the bottom panel of Figure 9.1 is also problematic and shows strong serial dependencies that persist for many cycles. In this example, data augmentation fails to converge because job performance scores are completely missing for the subsample of applicants that the company did not hire. Consequently, there is insufficient data to estimate the association between job performance ratings and the binary employment status variable. At first glance, this seems at odds with the fact that EM converged after only 25 iterations. However, EM's behavior is deceptive because alternate starting values produce a completely different solution. In reality, there is no way to identify a single set of parameter values that are most likely to have produced the observed data.

Convergence problems such as those in Figure 9.1 often occur because there is insufficient data to estimate certain parameters. In some situations, the lack of data results from including too many variables in the imputation phase. For example, when the number of variables exceeds the number of cases, the data contain linear dependencies that cause mathematical difficulties for regression-based imputation. Because missing values reduce the amount of information in a data set, convergence problems can occur even when the number of variables is much smaller than the number of cases. A peculiar missing data pattern can also lead to estimation difficulties and convergence failures. For example, the cohort-sequential

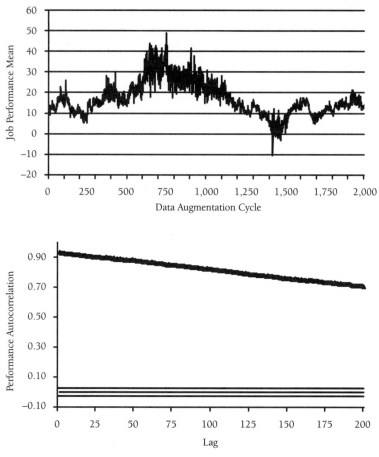

**FIGURE 9.1.** Time-series and autocorrelation function plot for parameters that do not converge. The top panel shows a time-series plot that exhibits systematic trends that last for hundreds of iterations and simulated parameter values that are outside of the plausible score range of 1 to 20. The bottom panel shows autocorrelations (denoted by a triangle symbol) that are close to $r = 0.70$ at lag-200.

design from Chapter 1 has variable pairs that are concurrently missing, making it impossible to estimate certain elements of the covariance matrix. The same is true for the data in Table 9.1.

## The Ridge Prior Distribution

In some situations, reducing the number of variables or eliminating problematic variables is the only way to eliminate convergence problems. An alternate strategy is to use a so-called **ridge prior distribution** for the covariance matrix. The standard practice in a multiple imputation analysis is to adopt a noninformative prior distribution that carries no information about the mean vector and the covariance matrix. Consequently, the data alone define the posterior distributions of $\boldsymbol{\mu}$ and $\boldsymbol{\Sigma}$ at each P-step. The ridge prior is a semi-informative distribution that contributes additional information about the covariance matrix. Conceptually, the ridge prior adds a small number of imaginary data records from a hypothetical population where the variables are uncorrelated. These additional data points can stabilize estimation and eliminate convergence problems, but they do so at the cost of introducing a slight bias to the simulated parameter values (and thus the imputations).

To illustrate the ridge prior, consider a hypothetical imputation model that consists of two variables and $N = 100$ cases. Furthermore, suppose the filled-in data from a particular I-step yields the following sample covariance matrix and sum of squares and cross products matrix.

$$\hat{\Sigma}_t = \begin{bmatrix} 1.00 & .50 \\ .50 & 1.00 \end{bmatrix}$$

$$\hat{\Lambda}_t = (N-1)\hat{\Sigma}_t = \begin{bmatrix} 99.00 & 49.50 \\ 49.50 & 99.00 \end{bmatrix}$$

Recall from Chapter 7 that each P-step is a standalone Bayesian analysis that describes the posterior distributions and subsequently draws a new set of estimates of the mean vector and the covariance matrix from their distributions. With the standard noninformative prior, the posterior distribution of the covariance matrix is an inverse Wishart distribution, the shape of which depends on the filled-in data from the preceding I-step (i.e., the sample size and $\hat{\Lambda}_t$).

The ridge prior is also an inverse Wishart distribution, but its shape depends on a degrees of freedom value and an estimate of the sum of squares and cross products matrix. (Collectively, these two parameters are the distribution's hyperparameters.) The sum of squares and cross products matrix for the prior is straightforward because it comes from a population covariance matrix with off-diagonal elements of zero and variances equal to those of the filled-in data. For example, the ridge covariance matrix for the previous bivariate example is as follows.

$$\Sigma_t = \begin{bmatrix} 1 & 0 \\ 0 & 1 \end{bmatrix}$$

Notice that the variances are identical to those of the filled-in data, but the covariance is zero. Generating the sum of squares and cross products matrix for the prior requires a degrees of freedom value. The degrees of freedom value quantifies the number of "imaginary data points" that you assign to the prior and effectively determines the amount of influence that the prior exerts on the simulated parameter values. For example, assigning two degrees of freedom to the prior is akin to saying that an imaginary sample of two cases generated the previous covariance matrix. Doing so leads to the following sum of squares and cross products matrix:

$$\Lambda_t = (df_p)\Sigma_t = 2\begin{bmatrix} 1 & 0 \\ 0 & 1 \end{bmatrix} = \begin{bmatrix} 2 & 0 \\ 0 & 2 \end{bmatrix}$$

where $df_p$ is the degrees of freedom value for the prior.

After implementing a ridge prior, the pooled degrees of freedom (i.e., the degrees of freedom from the data plus the number of imaginary cases that you assign to the prior) and the pooled sum of squares and cross products matrix (i.e., the sum of $\mathbf{\Lambda}_t$ and $\hat{\mathbf{\Lambda}}_t$) define the shape of the posterior distribution, as follows.

$$p(\mathbf{\Sigma} \mid \hat{\mathbf{\mu}}, \mathbf{Y}) \sim W^{-1}(df_p + N - 1, [\mathbf{\Lambda}_t + \hat{\mathbf{\Lambda}}_t]) \tag{9.1}$$

Notice that the shape of the posterior distribution depends on the data and the additional information from the prior (e.g., the usual posterior distribution has $N - 1$ and $\hat{\mathbf{\Lambda}}_t$ as its parameter values). Conceptually, the ridge prior adds $df_p$ imaginary data points from a population with uncorrelated variables. Altering the shape of the posterior distribution is the only change that occurs from implementing a ridge prior. Consistent with the description of data augmentation in Chapter 7, the P-step uses Monte Carlo simulation techniques to draw a new covariance matrix from the posterior, and the subsequent I-step uses these simulated parameters to construct a set of imputation regression equations.

The ridge prior eliminates convergence problems by increasing the effective sample size, but it attenuates the associations among the variables in the process. For example, pooling the degrees of freedom values and the sum of squares and cross products matrices from the bivariate example yields the following covariance matrix.

$$\hat{\mathbf{\Sigma}}_t = (df_p + N - 1)^{-1}(\mathbf{\Lambda}_t + \hat{\mathbf{\Lambda}}_t) = \frac{1}{2 + 99}\left(\begin{bmatrix} 2 & 0 \\ 1 & 2 \end{bmatrix} + \begin{bmatrix} 99.00 & 49.50 \\ 49.50 & 99.00 \end{bmatrix}\right) = \begin{bmatrix} 1.00 & .49 \\ .49 & 1.00 \end{bmatrix}$$

Notice that the covariance matrix has the same diagonal elements (i.e., variances) as the sample covariance matrix, but its off-diagonal elements are slightly smaller in magnitude. This follows from the fact that the prior distribution contributes two cases from a hypothetical population with uncorrelated variables. The imputation regression equations at the subsequent I-step depend on the parameter values from the P-step, so it makes intuitive sense that the imputations will also contain some bias. The magnitude of this bias depends on the number of data points that you assign to the prior, so you should try to minimize the prior distribution's degrees of freedom value. It is impossible to establish good rules of thumb, and identifying an appropriate degrees of freedom value usually requires some experimentation.

To illustrate the effect of the ridge prior, I performed data augmentation on the small employee data set, this time using a ridge prior with two degrees of freedom. The top panel of Figure 9.2 shows the time-series plot for the simulated job performance means. Notice that the long-term trends are gone and that the means stay within a plausible range of values. The bottom panel of the figure shows the time-series plot for the covariance between employment status and job performance ratings. This parameter was previously inestimable, but the simulated parameters now vary around zero (the value specified by the prior). Both plots still display systematic trends, but the ridge prior dramatically reduces the problems that were evident in Figure 9.1.

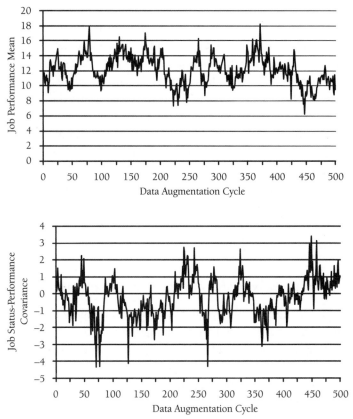

**FIGURE 9.2.** Time-series plot after specifying a ridge prior with $v = 2$ degrees of freedom. The top panel shows a time-series plot of the job performance mean. The ridge prior eliminated the long-term dependencies, and the simulated parameters take on plausible values. The bottom panel shows the covariance between job status and job performance. This parameter was not estimable without the ridge prior, but now varies around a value of zero (the covariance specified by the prior).

## 9.3 DEALING WITH NON-NORMAL DATA

The data augmentation algorithm assumes multivariate normality, both at the I-step and at the P-step (e.g., the I-step draws residuals from a normal distribution, and the P-step distributions follow from assuming a normal distribution for the population data). However, Schafer and colleagues suggest that normality-based imputation can work for a variety of different distribution types (Bernaards, Belin, & Schafer, 2007; Graham & Schafer, 1999; Schafer, 1997; Schafer & Olsen, 1998). This is an important practical issue because normality is often the exception rather than the rule (Micceri, 1989). The next section describes special issues that arise with discrete data (e.g., nominal and ordinal variables), but for now it is useful to address normality violations in more general terms.

Empirical studies suggest that normality violations may not pose a serious threat to the accuracy of multiple imputation parameter estimates (Demirtas, Freels, & Yucel, 2008; Graham & Schafer, 1999; Leite & Beretvas, 2004; Rubin & Schenker, 1986; Schafer, 1997).

Perhaps not surprisingly, the magnitude of the bias depends on the sample size and the missing data rate. For example, Demirtas et al. (2008) found that the parameter estimates and standard errors from a bivariate data analysis were relatively accurate with a sample size of $N = 400$ but were quite distorted with a sample size of $N = 40$. Other simulation studies have reported accurate estimates and confidence intervals with sample sizes as low as $N = 100$ (Graham & Schafer, 1999; Schafer, 1997). The percentage of missing data also plays a role, such that bias increases as the missing data rate increases. Although it is difficult to establish rules of thumb about the percentage of missing data, Demirtas et al. (2008) reported accurate parameter estimates with missingness rates as high as 25%. Finally, the impact of normality violations varies across different parameter estimates. For example, variance estimates are sensitive to scores in the tails of a distribution, so they are likely to exhibit more bias than means and regression coefficients. Other parameters that depend on the tails of a distribution (e.g., extreme quantiles such as the 90th percentile) can also be quite sensitive to normality violations (Demirtas et al., 2008; Schafer, 1997).

## Applying Normalizing Transformations at the Imputation Phase

One way to mitigate the impact of normality violations is to apply normalizing transformations at the imputation phase. Researchers sometimes object to transformations because the metric of the resulting scores is unfamiliar. However, variables can have different scales during the imputation and pooling phases, so it is possible to impute the variable on a transformed metric (e.g., a logarithmic scale) and analyze it on its original metric. Popular multiple-imputation software programs offer a variety of common data transformations, and these programs can automatically back-transform variables to their original metric when outputting the imputed data sets. Analyzing non-normal variables can still cause problems in the subsequent analysis phase, but applying data transformations at the imputation phase can improve the validity of data augmentation.

Despite their intuitive appeal, data transformations pose two potential problems. First, choosing an appropriate transformation is not necessarily straightforward. For example, logarithmic or square root transformations can work well for positively skewed variables, but the magnitude of the skewness and the kurtosis dictates the choice of transformation. Methodologists sometimes recommend experimenting with different transformations until you identify the one that best normalizes the data (Tabachnick & Fidell, 2007). This approach is difficult to implement, however, because there are currently no software programs that estimate skewness and kurtosis with missing data. Unfortunately, using deletion methods to assess the utility of different transformations can produce wildly inaccurate estimates of skewness and kurtosis, particularly if data are systematically missing from a distribution's tails. Data transformations are also problematic because they can alter the covariate structure of the data. Regression-based imputation relies heavily on the associations among the variables, so imputing variables on a transformed metric and back-transforming the scores to the original metric can potentially affect the accuracy of the imputations and the resulting parameter values. This has prompted some methodologists to raise strong concerns over the appropriate use of transformations in the context of multiple imputation (Demirtas et al., 2008, pp. 82–83). Further methodological research is needed to clarify this issue.

## Applying Corrective Procedures at the Analysis Phase

Non-normal data can also cause problems at the analysis phase. The methodological literature suggests that normality violations have a limited impact on parameter estimates but can bias standard errors and distort the likelihood ratio test (Finney & DiStefano, 2006; West, Finch, & Curran, 1995). The corrective procedures described in Chapter 5 (e.g., robust standard errors and rescaled test statistics) have long been available for complete-data analyses, and some of these procedures are readily applicable to multiple imputation. For example, it is perfectly appropriate to apply Rubin's (1987) pooling formulas to robust (i.e., sandwich estimator) standard errors. Similarly, the sandwich estimator can generate the within-imputation covariance matrices for the $D_1$ test statistic from Chapter 8. Unfortunately, it is unclear how to implement corrective procedures for the likelihood ratio test. For example, the methodological literature offers no guidance on whether it is appropriate to use rescaled likelihood ratio tests to compute the $D_3$ statistic. This is a fruitful area for future methodological research.

## 9.4 TO ROUND OR NOT TO ROUND?

Discrete measurement scales are exceedingly common in the behavioral and the social sciences, and researchers often incorporate nominal and ordinal variables into the imputation phase. Methodologists have developed specialized imputation algorithms for mixtures of categorical and continuous variables (e.g., the general location model—Schafer, 1997; sequential regression imputation—Raghunathan, Lepkowski, Van Hoewyk, & Solenberger, 2001), some of which I describe later in the chapter. However, these more complex categorical data models do not necessarily produce accurate parameter estimates (Belin, Hu, Young, & Grusky, 1999), so data augmentation may be the best option.

One consequence of applying an imputation model for normal data to discrete variables is that the resulting imputations will have decimals. The traditional advice is to round the imputed values to the nearest integer or to the nearest plausible value (Schafer, 1997; Schafer & Olsen, 1998; Sinharay, Stern, & Russell, 2001). For example, Schafer (1997, p. 148) suggests that "the continuous imputes should be rounded off to the nearest category to preserve the distributional properties as fully as possible and to make them intelligible to the analyst." At an intuitive level, rounding is appealing because it eliminates implausible values and yields imputations that are aesthetically consistent with the observed data. However, recent research suggests that rounding may not be necessary and can actually lead to biased parameter estimates.

Much of the empirical work on rounding has focused on binary variables (Allison, 2005; Bernaards et al., 2007; Horton, Lipsitz, & Parzen, 2003; Yucel, He, & Zaslavsky, 2008). These studies clearly suggest that rounding is something to avoid. At an intuitive level, it is reasonable to expect the effects of rounding to diminish as the number of ordinal response options increases. To date, relatively few studies have systematically examined the impact of rounding multiple-category ordinal variables (e.g., 5-point Likert scales). Computer simulation studies provide some indirect evidence that rounding is not as problematic with 5-category ordinal variables (Van Ginkel, Van der Ark, & Sijtsma, 2007a, 2007b), but analyzing the fractional imputations still appears to be the best option, at least for now (Wu & Enders, 2009). In some situations the analysis model requires rounding (e.g., a binary outcome in a logistic regression, a set of dummy variables). The remainder of this section describes some strategies for dealing with this issue.

## Rounding Binary Variables

The impact of rounding seems to be most pronounced with binary variables. Including an incomplete binary variable (e.g., a dummy variable with codes of zero and one) in the imputation phase will produce a range of imputed values, including fractional values between zero and one, values greater than one, and even negative values. One strategy for converting fractional imputations to binary values is to apply a 0.50 rounding threshold to the imputed values (i.e., round imputed values that exceed 0.50 to one, and round imputed values that are less than 0.50 to zero). However, recent research suggests that this so-called **naïve rounding** scheme introduces bias, whereas analyzing the fractional imputations does not (Allison, 2005; Bernaards et al., 2007; Horton et al., 2003; Yucel et al., 2008). Although these studies clearly suggest that rounding a binary variable is a bad idea, some analysis models require a binary outcome variable (e.g., a logistic regression that predicts membership in one of two categories). For these situations, methodologists have proposed rounding rules that appear to work somewhat better than a simple 0.50 threshold. I describe two such strategies next.

Bernaards et al. (2007) describe a so-called **adaptive rounding** procedure that relies on the normal approximation to a binomial distribution. For each imputed data set, adaptive rounding applies the following threshold:

$$c = \hat{\mu}_{UR} - \Phi^{-1}(\hat{\mu}_{UR})\sqrt{\hat{\mu}_{UR}(1 - \hat{\mu}_{UR})} \qquad (9.2)$$

where c is the rounding threshold, $\hat{\mu}_{UR}$ is the mean of the imputed (i.e., unrounded) binary variable, and $\Phi^{-1}(\hat{\mu}_{UR})$ is the z value from a standard normal distribution, below which the $\hat{\mu}_{UR}$ proportion of the distribution falls (i.e., the inverse of the standard normal cumulative distribution). To illustrate the adaptive rounding procedure, suppose that the mean of a binary variable is $\hat{\mu}_{UR} = 0.67$ in a particular imputed data set. In a standard normal distribution, a z value of 0.44 separates the lowest 67% of the curve from the rest of the distribution. Consequently, substituting $\hat{\mu}_{UR} = 0.67$ and $\Phi^{-1}(\hat{\mu}_{UR}) = 0.44$ into Equation 9.2 yields a rounding threshold of 0.463. Consistent with naïve rounding, imputed values that exceed the threshold are rounded to one, and values that fall below the threshold get rounded to zero.

Yucel et al. (2008) describe an alternate rounding strategy that they refer to as **calibration**. The first step of the calibration procedure is to create a copy of the raw data and delete the observed values of the incomplete binary variable from this file (i.e., make the binary variable completely missing). The second step is to vertically concatenate the original data and the copied data into a single stacked file. The final step is to impute the missing values in the concatenated file. Imputing the stacked data file yields filled-in values for the subsample of cases that actually have complete data on the binary variable. The idea behind calibration is to use these values to identify a rounding threshold that reproduces the frequency of ones and zero in the raw data.

**TABLE 9.2. Illustration of Calibration Rounding for a Binary Variable**

| Stacked data | | | Imputed data | | | Rounded data | | |
|---|---|---|---|---|---|---|---|---|
| ID | X | Y | ID | X | Y | ID | X | Y |
| | | | | | Original data | | | |
| 1 | 7 | 0 | 1 | 7 | 0 | 1 | 7 | 0 |
| 2 | 10 | 1 | 2 | 10 | 1 | 2 | 10 | 1 |
| 3 | 3 | 1 | 3 | 3 | 1 | 3 | 3 | 1 |
| 4 | 5 | 0 | 4 | 5 | 0 | 4 | 5 | 0 |
| 5 | 5 | 1 | 5 | 5 | 1 | 5 | 5 | 1 |
| 6 | 8 | 0 | 6 | 8 | 0 | 6 | 8 | 0 |
| 7 | 1 | — | 7 | 1 | 0.596 | 7 | 1 | 1 |
| 8 | 2 | — | 8 | 2 | 0.172 | 8 | 2 | 0 |
| 9 | 4 | — | 9 | 4 | 0.857 | 9 | 4 | 1 |
| 10 | 8 | — | 10 | 8 | 0.961 | 10 | 8 | 1 |
| | | | | | Duplicate data | | | |
| 1 | 7 | — | 6 | 8 | 0.270 | N/A | N/A | N/A |
| 2 | 10 | — | 4 | 5 | 0.311 | N/A | N/A | N/A |
| 3 | 3 | — | 5 | 5 | 0.315 | N/A | N/A | N/A |
| 4 | 5 | — | 1 | 7 | 0.500 | N/A | N/A | N/A |
| 5 | 5 | — | 3 | 3 | 0.733 | N/A | N/A | N/A |
| 6 | 8 | — | 2 | 10 | 0.737 | N/A | N/A | N/A |
| 7 | 1 | — | 7 | 1 | 0.451 | N/A | N/A | N/A |
| 8 | 2 | — | 8 | 2 | 0.421 | N/A | N/A | N/A |
| 9 | 4 | — | 9 | 4 | 0.535 | N/A | N/A | N/A |
| 10 | 8 | — | 10 | 8 | 0.953 | N/A | N/A | N/A |

To illustrate the calibration procedure, Table 9.2 shows a hypothetical sample of $N = 10$ cases, 60% of which have data on a binary variable, Y. Furthermore, among the subsample of cases that have data, 50% have a code of one. The left-most set of columns shows the original data and the duplicate data file where Y is completely missing. The middle set of columns shows the data that result from imputing the entire set of $N = 20$ data records. Notice that the subsample of complete cases (i.e., the calibration subsample) has imputed values that range between 0.270 and 0.737. The goal of calibration is to use this subset of imputations to identify a rounding threshold that reproduces the frequency of ones and zeros in the observed data (i.e., a 50/50 split). For clarity, Table 9.2 orders the calibration subsample (shown in a shaded box) by their imputed values. As you can see, applying a rounding threshold of 0.32 to the calibration subsample yields a 50/50 split of ones and zeros. I applied this threshold to the four incomplete cases from the original sample, and the right-most column of the table shows the resulting Y values.

To date, no research has compared adaptive rounding to calibration, but both approaches appear to be superior to naïve rounding (Bernaards et al., 2007; Yucel et al., 2008). Calibration is likely to exhibit some bias with missing at random (MAR) data (Yucel et al., 2008), but simulation studies suggest that adaptive rounding does not suffer from this problem

(Bernaards et al., 2007). Adaptive rounding also has the advantage of being easier to implement, so until more research accumulates, it seems prudent to recommend this approach over calibration and naïve rounding.

## Rounding a Set of Dummy Variables

A second situation in which rounding may be necessary occurs with incomplete nominal variables that have more than two categories. The appropriate way to impute a nominal variable is to recast it as a set of $g - 1$ dummy variables prior to imputation. With complete data, cases that belong to the reference group (e.g., a control group or some other normative group) have a value of zero on the entire set of dummy variables, and the remaining cases have zeros on all but one of the code variables (Cohen, Cohen, West, & Aiken, 2003). However, applying naive rounding to a set of imputed dummy variables can produce illogical values where a case has a code of one on multiple dummy variables. Consequently, it is necessary to apply rounding rules that produce a logical set of dummy codes.

Allison (2002) proposed straightforward rules for rounding a set of dummy variables. The cases with missing data on the nominal variable have imputed values for each of the $g - 1$ dummy codes. The first step of Allison's procedure is to compute a new variable that subtracts the sum of the imputed values from a value of one. This new variable serves as a pseudo-imputation for membership in the reference category (i.e., the group coded all zeros). Next, if the pseudo-imputation variable has the highest numeric value, you round the $g - 1$ dummy codes to zero, thereby assigning the case to the reference group. Otherwise, if the highest imputed value corresponds to one of the $g - 1$ dummy variables, you assign a value of one to the appropriate code variable and set the remaining dummy codes to zero. To illustrate Allison's rounding rules, Table 9.3 shows a small set of hypothetical imputations for a set of two dummy codes, $D_1$ and $D_2$ (i.e., a nominal variable with three categories). The first two columns contain the imputed values for $D_1$ and $D_2$ and the middle column is the pseudo-imputation for membership in the reference category (i.e., $1 - D_1 - D_2$). As you can see, the highest value in the first three columns determines each case's group membership. It is important to note that Allison's rounding rules have not been evaluated in the literature. Nevertheless, his rules provide a convenient solution for an imputation model that includes a number of multiple-category nominal variables.

## TABLE 9.3. Illustration of Dummy Code Rounding Rules

| Imputed codes | | | Rounded codes | |
|---|---|---|---|---|
| $D_1$ | $D_2$ | $1 - D_1 - D_2$ | $D_1$ | $D_2$ |
| 0.65 | 0.23 | 0.12 | 1 | 0 |
| −0.12 | 0.55 | 0.57 | 0 | 0 |
| 0.77 | −0.02 | 0.25 | 1 | 0 |
| 0.37 | 0.82 | −0.19 | 0 | 1 |
| 0.05 | 1.08 | −0.13 | 0 | 1 |
| 0.42 | −0.02 | 0.60 | 0 | 0 |

## Out-of-Range Imputations

In addition to producing fractional values, data augmentation will often produce imputations that fall outside of the plausible score range (e.g., a 5-point Likert variable that has an imputed value of 5.23). There are essentially three options for dealing with out-of-range values: (1) analyze the imputed values as they are, (2) round to the nearest plausible score value, or (3) generate new imputations for cases that have out-of-range values (e.g., by adding a new random residual to each predicted score). Multiple-imputation software packages make the latter two options easy to implement, but analyzing the out-of-range values may be a fine option, particularly if they are relatively few in number. At an intuitive level, out-of-range imputations can inflate variance estimates, but this bias is probably trivial if the number of implausible values is relatively small.

A large proportion of out-of-range imputations can be symptomatic of a normality violation, so transforming the data at the imputation phase may reduce or eliminate out-of-range values. However, transformations are unlikely to eliminate implausible imputations that occur when an ordinal variable has an asymmetric distribution (e.g., responses are isolated to small number of categories). Rounding the imputed values to the nearest plausible value is one solution, but an alternate strategy is to recast the ordinal variable as a set of dummy codes and apply Allison's (2001) rounding rules following imputation.

## 9.5 PRESERVING INTERACTION EFFECTS

Researchers in the behavioral and the social sciences are often interested in estimating interaction (i.e., moderation) effects where the magnitude of the association between two variables depends on a third variable. In some situations, the interaction effect appears as an explicit term in the analysis model. For example, if it was of interest to determine whether the association between psychological well-being and job performance is different for males and females, including a product term in a multiple regression model could address this question (i.e., moderated multiple regression; Aiken & West, 1991). Many other analyses model implicit interaction effects. For example, multiple-group structural equation models do not contain explicit interaction terms, yet they allow for group differences in the mean structure, the covariance structure, or both. A multilevel model with random intercepts and slopes is another analysis that involves implicit interaction effects.

When using multiple imputation to treat missing data, it is important to specify an imputation model that preserves any interaction effects that are of interest in the subsequent analysis model because failing to do so will attenuate the magnitude of these effects, even if the data are missing completely at random (MCAR). For example, if gender moderates the association between psychological well-being and job performance, failing to build this complex association into the imputation model is likely to produce an analysis that masks the gender difference. Similarly, an imputation model that fails to preserve group differences in the mean or the covariance structure could lead to the conclusion that the parameters of a multiple group structural equation model are invariant (i.e., the same) across groups when they are truly different in the population. This section outlines different imputation strategies for dealing with interactive effects. The appropriate strategy depends largely on whether the interaction involves a categorical or a continuous moderator variable.

## Interactions That Involve Quantitative Variables

If the analysis model includes an interaction effect between two quantitative variables, then the imputation phase should include a variable that is the product of the two interacting variables. This is effectively the only way to preserve the interaction. For example, suppose that it is of interest to determine whether the number of years on the job moderates the relationship between psychological well-being and job performance. A standard approach for addressing this question is to estimate a multiple regression model that includes main effects and a product term as predictor variables (e.g., years on the job, psychological well-being, and the product of years on the job and well-being). The imputation phase also employs a multiple regression model, so it too should include the same set of variables. The product variable is particularly important because it preserves the complex associations among the variables. It is important to point out that including a product variable in the imputation phase does not create an interaction effect where none exists. Rather, it simply preserves the natural structure of the data. Finally, note that the product term strategy also applies to nonlinear associations. For example, if the analysis model includes a quadratic effect, then the imputation phase should include main effects and a squared term.

When an analysis model includes an interaction effect between two or more quantitative variables, it is important to center predictor variables at their means (i.e., subtract the mean from each score) prior to analyzing the data (Aiken & West, 1991). However, centering becomes difficult when one of the variables in the product term has missing data. One option is to center the variables prior to imputation, compute the necessary product term, and fill in the missing variables (including the product term) on their centered metrics. This approach requires estimates of the variable means, so maximum likelihood estimates (e.g., from an initial EM analysis) are a logical choice. A second strategy is to fill in the missing variables (including the product term) on their original metrics and subsequently perform the centering procedure on each of the complete data sets. Because the product of two uncentered variables has a larger mean and a larger variance than the product of two centered variables (Bohrnstedt & Goldberger, 1969), this method requires a complete rescaling of the imputed product variable. Neither of these approaches has been evaluated in the literature, but centering the variables prior to imputation is far easier and tends to yield estimates that are similar to those of a maximum likelihood analysis. Until further research suggests otherwise, this is probably the best strategy.

## Interactions That Involve a Categorical Variable

When it is of interest to examine an interaction effect that involves a categorical variable, imputing the data separately for each subgroup is often more accurate than including product terms in the imputation model (Enders & Gottschall, in press). To understand why, suppose that it is of interest to determine whether a binary categorical variable $D$ moderates the association between $X$ and $Y$ (e.g., gender moderates the association between psychological well-being and job performance). Furthermore, suppose that some individuals have missing $Y$ values. Using a product term to preserve the interaction effect yields the following imputation model:

$$y_i^* = \hat{\beta}_0 + \hat{\beta}_1(X_i) + \hat{\beta}_2(D_i) + \hat{\beta}_2(X_i)(D_i) + z_i \tag{9.3}$$

where $y_i^*$ is the imputed value for case $i$, $X_i$ and $D_i$ are the observed scores for that case, and $z_i$ is a normally distributed residual term. Including the dummy code variable in the imputation model preserves group mean differences on $Y$, and the product term preserves group differences in the covariance between $X$ and $Y$. It may not be immediately obvious, but using a single normal distribution to generate the residual terms effectively assumes that both groups have the same $Y$ variance (i.e., data augmentation generates imputations that are **homoscedastic**). This subtle assumption may have a relatively minor impact on many analyses, but in a number of situations the substantive goal is to determine whether the covariance structure is the same across qualitatively different subpopulations (e.g., measurement invariance analyses, multiple-group structural equation models). If the subgroups have different population variances, then the product term approach will generate imputations that mask these group differences (Enders & Gottschall, in press).

A simple solution to the previous problem is to impute the data separately for each subgroup (i.e., **separate-group imputation**). Because this approach uses a unique imputation equation and a unique residual distribution for each subpopulation, every element in the mean vector and the covariance matrix will freely vary across groups. The downsides of separate-group imputation are that it (1) is limited to situations that involve categorical moderator variables, (2) requires adequate group sizes, and (3) necessitates additional effort to assess convergence (e.g., by examining the time-series and autocorrelation function plots for each subgroup). Despite these potential limitations, the approach is very easy to implement in multiple imputation software programs and has performed well in computer simulation studies, even with a smple size as low as $n = 50$ per group (Enders & Gottschall, in press).

## Models with Implicit Interaction Effects

Many common statistical analyses involve implicit interaction effects. Multiple-group structural equation models are one such example. To illustrate, consider a measurement invariance analysis in which it is of interest to determine whether the factor model parameters (e.g., the loadings, measurement intercepts) are the same across qualitatively different subpopulations (e.g., males and females, Caucasians, and Hispanics). A typical measurement invariance analysis begins with separate factor models for each subgroup. Subsequent analysis steps constrain sets of parameter estimates (e.g., the factor loadings) to be equal across groups. If the constrained model fits the data as well as the unconstrained model, then there is evidence that the subgroups have the same population mean vector or covariance matrix. In contrast, a constrained model that shows worse fit suggests that the subgroups have a different mean vector or covariance matrix.

Multiple-group structural equation models do not contain explicit interaction effects, but they allow for group differences in the mean structure, covariance structure, or both.

Consequently, it is necessary to specify an imputation model that preserves these group differences. Incorporating product terms into the imputation phase is problematic because it generates imputations from a model that assumes equal variances across groups. As a result, the subsequent analyses are likely to suggest that certain parameters are invariant (i.e., the same) across groups, when they are actually different in the population. In contrast, separate-group imputation naturally preserves group differences in the mean vector and the covariance matrix and will lead to more accurate assessments of subgroup differences. Computer simulations suggest that the separate-group imputation approach produces accurate parameter estimates in a variety of multiple-group structural equation models (e.g., moderated mediation, multiple-group confirmatory factor analysis, multiple-group growth curves), with sample sizes as low as $n = 50$ per group (Enders & Gottschall, in press).

A multilevel model with random intercepts and slopes is another analysis that contains implicit interaction effects. To illustrate, consider an educational study in which students (i.e., level-1 units) are nested within schools (i.e., level-2 units). Furthermore, suppose that it is of interest to examine the influence of student socioeconomic status on academic achievement. A random intercept model is one in which the mean achievement level differs across schools, and a random slope model allows the association between socioeconomic status and achievement to vary across schools. These group differences in the mean and the covariance structure show up as variance estimates rather than as regression coefficients, but they are interaction effects, nevertheless.

The data augmentation algorithm from Chapter 7 is not designed for multilevel data structures where the associations among variables potentially vary across clusters. In principle, separate-group imputation is appropriate for imputing missing values at the lowest level of the data hierarchy (e.g., by imputing individual-level variables separately for each cluster), but this approach requires a relatively large number of cases within each cluster. Many (if not most) common applications of multilevel modeling (e.g., dyadic data, longitudinal data, children nested within classrooms) do not have adequate group sizes to support this method. A better strategy is to use a specialized imputation algorithm for multilevel data (Schafer, 2001; Schafer & Yucel, 2002; Yucel, 2008). I describe one such algorithm later in the chapter.

## A Cautionary Note on Latent Categorical Variables

A number of popular statistical models treat group membership as a latent categorical variable. Finite mixture models (McLachlan & Peel, 2000; Muthén, 2001, 2004) and latent class models (McCutcheon, 1987) are two common examples. Consistent with a multiple group structural equation model, it is often of interest to determine whether the latent classes have different mean and covariance structures. For example, a growth mixture model is characterized by a number of latent subgroups, each of which can have a different growth trajectory (i.e., different mean structures) and varying degrees of individual heterogeneity in the growth trajectories (i.e., different covariance structures). These models are important to consider because they are becoming increasingly common in the social sciences.

Because group membership is inferred from the data during the analysis, there is no way to use product terms or separate-group imputation to preserve the implicit interaction effects that are present in the data. Consequently, multiple imputation can produce biased estimates of the model parameters, even when the data are MCAR (Enders & Gottschall, in press). Fortunately, maximum likelihood missing data routines are readily available for many popular latent class models (e.g., growth mixture models, factor mixture models), so there is no need to rely on multiple imputation. Methodologists are also beginning to develop imputation algorithms for latent categorical variables (Vermunt, Van Ginkel, Van der Ark, & Sijtsma, 2008). As a result, these procedures are likely to become increasingly common in the near future.

## 9.6 IMPUTING MULTIPLE-ITEM QUESTIONNAIRES

Researchers in the behavioral and the social sciences routinely use multiple-item questionnaires to measure complex constructs. For example, psychologists typically use several questionnaire items to measure depression, each of which taps into a different depressive symptom (e.g., sadness, lack of energy, sleep difficulties, feelings of hopelessness). With multiple-item questionnaires, respondents often omit one or more of the items within a given scale. Multiple imputation is advantageous because it provides a mechanism for dealing with item-level missingness (maximum likelihood can be less flexible in this regard). However, imputation can be challenging or even impossible when the data contain a large number of questionnaire items. This is an important practical issue because it is not uncommon for researchers to administer a dozen or more questionnaires in a single study, each of which may contain 20 or more items. The number of variables can quickly multiply in a longitudinal study that has several questionnaires administered on multiple occasions.

Ideally, the imputation phase should include all of the individual questionnaire items because this maximizes the information that goes into creating the imputations. However, item-level imputation may not be feasible when the number of questionnaire items is very large. As an upper limit, the number of variables in the imputation model cannot exceed the number of cases because the input data contain linear dependencies that cause mathematical difficulties for regression-based imputation. Because missing data exacerbate these mathematical difficulties, the allowable number of variables tends to be much lower than the number of cases. One possible solution for imputing large data sets is to use a ridge prior described earlier in the chapter. Conceptually, the ridge prior adds a number of imaginary data records (i.e., degrees of freedom) to the estimation process, but it does so at the cost of attenuating the associations among the variables. A complex imputation model can require a relatively large number of additional degrees of freedom, in which case the ridge prior might be a poor solution. An alternative approach is to perform separate data augmentation runs for different subsets of variables. However, this strategy effectively assumes that variables from different subsets are uncorrelated, and it is viable only if variables from different subsets are not part of the same analysis model. This section outlines three alternative approaches for imputing large questionnaire data sets: scale-level, duplicate scale, and a three-step imputation approach.

### Scale-Level Imputation

When collecting data with multiple-item questionnaires, researchers are often interested in analyzing scale scores based on a sum or an average of the item responses. When the analysis

**TABLE 9.4. Input Data for Item-Level, Scale-Level, and Duplicate-Scale Imputation**

| | | | | | | | Scale-level imputation | | | Duplicate-scale imputation | | | | |
|---|---|---|---|---|---|---|---|---|---|---|---|---|---|---|
| | | Item-level imputation | | | | | | | | | | | | |
| $X_1$ | $X_2$ | $X_3$ | $Y_1$ | $Y_2$ | $Y_3$ | $Z$ | $S_X$ | $S_Y$ | $Z$ | $S_X$ | $S_Y$ | $Z$ | $A_X$ | $A_Y$ |
| 5 | 4 | 5 | 3 | — | 4 | 20 | 4.67 | — | 20 | 4.67 | — | 20 | 4.67 | 3.50 |
| 2 | — | 1 | 3 | 2 | 3 | 17 | — | 2.67 | 17 | — | 2.67 | 17 | 1.50 | 2.67 |
| 4 | 3 | 5 | 5 | 5 | 4 | 24 | 4.00 | 4.67 | 24 | 4.00 | 4.67 | 24 | 4.00 | 4.67 |
| — | 3 | 2 | — | — | 4 | 13 | — | — | 13 | — | — | 13 | 2.50 | 4.00 |
| 1 | 1 | 3 | 2 | 2 | 1 | 9 | 1.67 | 1.67 | 9 | 1.67 | 1.67 | 9 | 1.67 | 1.67 |

*Note.* $S_X$ and $S_Y$ are scale scores that average the individual questionnaire items ($X_1 - X_3$ and $Y_1 - Y_3$). The scale scores are missing if one or more of the items are missing. $A_X$ and $A_Y$ are averages of the available items within each scale, and $Z$ is an auxiliary variable.

model involves scale scores, ignoring the item-level data and imputing the scale scores themselves can dramatically reduce the number of imputation model variables (Graham, 2009). Under this **scale-level imputation** approach, the cases that have complete data on a particular subset of items (e.g., a set of depression items) also have complete data on the scale score, whereas the individuals who fail to answer one or more of the questionnaire items have missing data. To illustrate, Table 9.4 shows a small data set with a single auxiliary variable and six questionnaire items ($X_1$ to $X_3$ and $Y_1$ to $Y_3$) that combine to form two subscales, $S_X$ and $S_Y$. The scale-level imputation procedure for these data would include just three variables: $S_X$, $S_Y$, and the auxiliary variable, $Z$.

Scale-level imputation can dramatically reduce the number of variables in the imputation model and can eliminate the mathematical difficulties associated with imputing a large number of individual items. However, it does so at the cost of reducing statistical power. In my experience, scale-level imputation can increase standard errors by up to 10% relative to an ideal analysis that uses scale scores from an item-level imputation procedure. This decrease in statistical power becomes increasingly evident as the number of items within a scale increases. The failure of scale-level imputation stems from the fact that questionnaire items within a scale tend to have stronger correlations than items from different scales. Consequently, the imputation phase effectively discards the strongest predictors of the missing scale scores (i.e., the items within the scale) in favor of weaker correlates (i.e., items from different scales).

One way to mitigate the power loss from scale-level imputation is to incorporate the item-level information back into the imputation model. A simple way to do this is to compute a second set of scale scores by averaging the available items within each questionnaire. For example, if a respondent answered 8 out of 10 items on a particular questionnaire, the scale score for that individual would be the average of the eight observed items. Incorporating these additional scales into the imputation phase as auxiliary variables can recapture much of the item-level information that scale-level imputation ignores. For lack of a better term, I henceforth refer to this approach as **duplicate-scale imputation**. The right-most section of Table 9.4 illustrates the input data for this method. Notice that the complete cases have identical scores on both sets of scales (e.g., $S_X$ and $A_X$ are the same), whereas the incomplete cases only have data on the duplicate scales. The duplicate-scale imputation approach requires twice as many variables as scale-level imputation, but it can dramatically reduce the complexity of the imputation model. For example, suppose that the two questionnaires in Table 9.4 had 20 items each. Duplicate-scale imputation would still only require five variables: $S_X$, $S_Y$, $A_X$, $A_Y$, and $Z$.

In my experience, duplicate-scale imputation tends to yield parameter estimates and standard errors that are nearly identical to those of an ideal analysis that uses scale scores from an item-level imputation procedure. However, getting duplicate-scale imputation to work properly requires an additional nuance. Because the cases with complete data have identical scores on both sets of scales, the data contain linear dependencies that cause estimation problems for data augmentation. Using a ridge prior distribution to add imaginary data records to the imputation process can solve this problem. Fortunately, adding a small number of additional degrees of freedom usually eliminates the linear dependencies, so any bias that results from use of a ridge prior is negligible. For example, later in the chapter I present an analysis example in which adding a single imaginary data record (i.e., a ridge prior with a single degree of freedom) eliminates the linear dependencies in the imputation model and produces parameter estimates and standard errors that are virtually identical to those of item-level imputation.

## A Three-Step Approach for Item-Level Imputation

The duplicate-scale approach can work well for analyses that involve scale scores, but many analysis models require item-level data (e.g., internal consistency reliability analyses, confirmatory factor analyses). In situations where the number of items is prohibitively large, Little, McConnell, Howard, and Stump (2008) outline a three-step approach for item-level imputation. The idea behind their procedure is to separately impute different subsets of questionnaire items. This strategy is usually undesirable because it assumes that variables from different item subsets are uncorrelated. However, Little et al. solve this problem by using scale scores to preserve the between-subset associations.

The Little et al. procedure requires a complete set of scale scores. The authors use scale-level imputation to generate these scores, but averaging the available items within a scale is another option. These initial scale scores are simply temporary auxiliary variables, so the method that you use to generate them probably makes little difference. The second step involves an iterative imputation process that repeatedly fills in the item scores from one subset while using the scale scores from the remaining subsets as auxiliary variables. As an example, consider a study that collects data on 10 multiple-item questionnaires (i.e., $Q_1$ to $Q_{10}$), each of which has 20 items. The first imputation phase might consist of the 20 items from $Q_1$ and the scale scores for $Q_2$ through $Q_{10}$. Similarly, the second imputation model could include the $Q_2$ items and the scale scores for the nine remaining questionnaires (i.e., $Q_1$, $Q_3$ through $Q_{10}$). Depending on the sample size, it may be possible to perform fewer data augmentation runs with larger item subsets (e.g., impute the items from $Q_1$ through $Q_5$ while using the scale scores for $Q_6$ through $Q_{10}$ as auxiliary variables). After completing the imputation process for each item subset, the temporary placeholder scales from the first step are no longer necessary. Consequently, the final step is to discard the initial scales and compute a new set of composite scores from the filled-in item responses.

To date, no studies have evaluated the duplicate-scale approach or the three-step imputation approach. Because a single scale score preserves the between-subset associations, these procedures probably work best when the items within one subset have relatively uniform correlations with the items from another subset. Fortunately, this is a fairly realistic condition for many scales in the behavioral and the social sciences, so these procedures probably work well in a variety of settings. The imputation of large item-level data sets is an important practical topic that warrants future methodological research.

## 9.7 ALTERNATE IMPUTATION ALGORITHMS

Although the data augmentation algorithm in Chapter 7 is probably the most popular imputation strategy, methodologists have developed a number of alternative imputation routines. Some of these algorithms are applicable to specialized situations that are relatively uncommon in the behavioral and the social sciences (e.g., data comprised entirely of categorical variables; Schafer, 1997; randomized trials with monotone missing data patterns; Lavori, Dawson, & Shera, 1995), while others are suitable replacements for data augmentation (King, Honaker, Joseph, & Scheve, 2001). A thorough review of different imputation options is beyond the scope of this chapter, but it is useful to briefly describe some of these alternative models. This section begins with a description of an EM-based imputation algorithm that is statistically equivalent to data augmentation. Next, the section outlines two algorithms for imputing data sets that contain a mixture of categorical and continuous variables. The final section describes an imputation algorithm for multilevel data structures. Note that the algorithms in this section simply replace data augmentation in the imputation phase and do not require changes to the analysis and pooling phases.

### EM-Based Algorithms for Multivariate Normal Data

Generating unique sets of imputations from multivariate normal data requires several alternate estimates of the mean vector and the covariance matrix. The P-step of data augmentation generates these estimates by simulating random draws from a posterior distribution. King et al. (2001) describe two approaches that use the EM algorithm from Chapter 4 to generate alternate estimates of the mean vector and the covariance matrix. These EM-based approaches also simulate random draws from a posterior distribution, but they do so in a very different fashion. The EM with an importance sampling algorithm is particularly interesting because it is statistically equivalent to data augmentation, yet it does not require the same complicated definition of convergence.

**EM with sampling** (EMS) begins by using the EM algorithm to estimate the mean vector and the covariance matrix. These maximum likelihood estimates describe the central tendency of the posterior distributions from which the algorithm will draw alternate parameter estimates. Next, the algorithm computes the parameter covariance matrix for the EM estimates and uses this matrix to define the spread of the posterior distributions. Having characterized the shape of the posterior distribution, the EMS algorithm uses Monte Carlo simulation techniques to draw $m$ new estimates of the mean vector and the covariance matrix from their respective posteriors. This process does not require a long iterative chain. Rather, the algorithm simply generates the desired number of alternate estimates. Finally, EMS uses each set of parameter values to construct regression equations that impute the missing values. The final imputation stage is identical to stochastic regression imputation (or alternatively, the I-step of data augmentation).

Using the parameter covariance matrix to estimate the spread of the posterior distribution is only appropriate in very large samples and can produce biased parameter estimates in small to moderate samples (King et al., 2001). To correct this problem, King et al. proposed a modified algorithm that they call **EM with importance sampling** (EMIS). EMIS also uses maximum likelihood estimates and the parameter covariance matrix to approximate the posterior distributions, but it uses the likelihood function to fine-tune the shape of the distributions. Rather than retaining every set of simulated the parameter values, the algorithm selectively discards the estimates that are inconsistent with the data (i.e., estimates that have a low likelihood of producing the sample data).

More specifically, the EMIS algorithm works as follows. First, the algorithm uses Monte Carlo simulation techniques to draw a set of alternate parameter values from a multivariate normal posterior distribution, the shape of which is defined by the EM estimates and the corresponding parameter covariance matrix. With small to moderate samples, the true posterior distribution may quite skewed, in which case the simulated parameters are not always accurate. Then, to remedy this problem, EMIS uses the likelihood function to weed out implausible parameter values. (Assuming a noninformative prior distribution, the likelihood function has the same shape as the correct posterior distribution.) Specifically, the algorithm generates an **importance ratio** by substituting the simulated parameters into the likelihood function and converting the resulting likelihood value into a probability. Simulated parameter values that have a high likelihood of producing the sample data also have a high importance ratio (i.e., probability), whereas parameters that are unlikely to have produced the sample data have a low importance ratio. To decide whether to retain a particular set of parameters, the algorithm generates a uniform random number between zero and one and compares this number to the importance ratio. EMIS retains the estimates if the uniform random number is less than the importance ratio. Otherwise, the algorithm discards the estimates and generates a new set. This so-called **acceptance-rejection algorithm** repeatedly screens simulated parameter values until it retains $m$ sets of plausible estimates. The resulting estimates more closely approximate random draws from the true posterior distribution, the shape of which may not resemble a normal distribution. Finally, EMIS uses the retained parameter values to construct regression equations that impute the missing values. The final imputation stage is identical to stochastic regression imputation.

The EMIS algorithm is statistically equivalent to data augmentation (i.e., it will yield the same analysis results, on average) but offers some potential advantages. One advantage is that EMIS can be easier to implement. Because the simulated parameter values do not depend on the imputed values from a preceding iteration, the $m$ sets of imputations are automatically independent samples from the distribution of missing values. This simplifies the imputation process considerably because it eliminates the need for graphical convergence diagnostics. By extension, there is no need to worry about the number of between-imputation iterations or other convergence-related issues that make data augmentation challenging to implement. Speed is a second advantage. Data augmentation often requires thousands of iterations to generate a relatively small number of data sets. With large data files, this can take a considerable amount of time. Because EMIS does not continually iterate between draws, it can generate the same number of data sets in a much shorter period (e.g., problems that take data augmentation several minutes to run take EMIS just a few seconds). Although data augmentation is the predominant method for generating imputations with multivariate normal data, the EMIS algorithm is certainly worth considering. At the time of this writing, Amelia is the only software program that implements EMIS.

## Algorithms for Categorical and Continuous Variables

One shortcoming of the data augmentation is that it assumes a common distribution for every variable in the data set (i.e., the multivariate normal distribution). This is an unrealistic assumption because data sets often contain a mixture of categorical and continuous variables. Schafer (1997) and colleagues suggest that normality-based imputation can often work well with categorical (e.g., nominal and ordinal) variables, but it is worth considering imputation algorithms that do not assume a common distribution. This section describes two such approaches: the general location model and sequential regression imputation. These methods are similar in the sense that they apply different imputation models to categorical and continuous variables, but their procedural details are quite different. Of the two, sequential regression is particularly promising because it is conceptually straightforward and has performed well in empirical studies.

Schafer (1997, Chapter 9) describes an imputation approach for categorical and continuous variables based on the so-called **general location model** (Little & Schluchter, 1985; Olkin & Tate, 1961). The general location model uses a fully crossed contingency table to represent the categorical variables, and it assumes that the continuous variables follow a normal distribution within each cell of the table. The model for the continuous variables resembles a factorial multivariate analysis of variance (MANOVA) in the sense that the cells share a common covariance matrix but can have different means. To illustrate the general location model, consider a data set with two continuous variables and two categorical variables, both of which have three levels. (The categories can be ordered, but the model treats them as nominal.) The saturated general location model for this example has 29 parameters. The contingency table is comprised of nine cells, so the categorical variables contribute eight parameters to the model (if the sample size is fixed, the frequency for the ninth cell is determined by the other eight). The continuous variable means vary across cells, adding another 18 parameters, and the covariance matrix of the continuous variables has three unique elements.

Schafer (1997) outlined a data augmentation algorithm for the general location model that consists of an I-step and a P-step. The procedure follows the same basic logic as data augmentation for multivariate normal data, but it uses different distribution families (e.g., the categorical variables follow a multinomial distribution, and the continuous variables are normally distributed within cells of the contingency table). The I-step imputes the incomplete categorical variables by assigning each missing observation to a cell in the contingency table, and it then uses a stochastic regression procedure to impute the missing continuous variables. The continuous variables inform the categorical imputations and vice versa. Conditional on the imputations from the preceding I-step, the P-step draws new cell probabilities for the contingency table and subsequently generates a new covariance matrix and a new set of cell means. Schafer describes the data augmentation algorithm in considerable detail, and both Schafer and Belin et al. (1999) illustrate applications of the general location model.

The general location model is seemingly well-suited for many realistic missing data problems, but it may not be the best option for imputing mixtures of categorical and continuous variables. One problem is that the model becomes exceedingly complex as the number of variables increases. For example, Belin et al. (1999) applied the general location model to a data set with 16 binary variables and 18 continuous variables. Although this data set is not unusually large, the saturated model has more than one million parameters! The staggering number of parameters is attributable to the fact that the model includes main effects as well as every possible higher-order interaction among the categorical variables. In practice, it is usually necessary to perform a series of preliminary analyses to simplify the model prior to data augmentation, but doing so adds a layer of complexity to the imputation process. Complexity issues aside, Belin et al. (1999) raise concerns about the accuracy of the general location model, particularly for categorical imputations. Until further research is done, it may be best to view the general location model with some caution.

**Sequential regression imputation** is a second approach for imputing data sets that contain mixtures of categorical and continuous variables. (The literature also refers to this method as **chained equations** and **fully conditional specification**.) Unlike the general location model, sequential regression imputation fills in the data on a variable-by-variable basis, each time matching the imputation model to a variable's distributional form. For example, the algorithm can use a linear regression to impute continuous variables, a logistic regression to impute binary variables, a Poisson regression to impute count variables, and so on. The remainder of this section gives a brief overview of the algorithm, and a number of sources provide more detailed descriptions of this approach (Raghunathan et al., 2001; van Buuren, 2007; van Buuren, Brand, Groothuis-Oudshoorn, & Rubin, 2006).

Like data augmentation, the sequential regression approach uses regression equations to generate draws from the conditional distribution of the missing values, given the observed data. However, the mechanics of imputation are quite different. For one, the algorithm imputes variables in a sequence, one at a time. The imputation order is determined by the rates of missingness, where the variable with the fewest missing values gets imputed first, the variable with the next lowest missing data rate gets imputed second, and so on. Each step in the imputation sequence can apply a regression model that is appropriate for the scale of the incomplete variable (e.g., a logistic regression imputes incomplete binary variables, a linear regression imputes normally distributed variables, and so on). Unlike data augmentation, each regression model uses the filled-in values from one sequence to generate imputations for subsequent sequences. For example, suppose that $Y_3$ gets imputed in the first regression sequence, $Y_1$ gets imputed in the second sequence, and $Y_4$ in the final sequence. After the initial sequence, the algorithm treats $Y_3$ as a complete variable and uses the observed and the imputed values as predictors of the missing $Y_1$ scores. Similarly, the next sequence uses the filled-in values of $Y_3$ and $Y_1$ to impute $Y_4$.

After filling in the entire data set, the algorithm uses a Bayesian procedure that is akin to the P-step of data augmentation to sample a new set of regression parameters, and the process begins anew. The second and subsequent rounds of imputation also fill in the data on a variable-by-variable basis, but they do so using all variables in the imputation model, including the filled-in variables from the preceding iteration. For example, the filled-in values of $Y_1$ and $Y_4$ from the first imputation cycle serve as predictors of $Y_3$ in the first sequence of the second imputation cycle. The sequential regression algorithm iterates for a specified number of cycles, and the imputed values from the final iteration serve as data for a subsequent analysis. Repeating the imputation chain $m$ times generates unique sets of imputed values.

The sequential regression approach has a number of advantages over data augmentation. Most importantly, it is unnecessary to assume that the variables share a common distribution because the algorithm tailors the imputation model to each incomplete variable. In addition, formulating a separate imputation model for each variable makes it easy to specify constraints that preserve special characteristics of the data. For example, to avoid logical inconsistencies between two variables, the range of imputed values for one variable can depend on the responses to another variable. Similarly, it is straightforward to accommodate survey skip patterns by restricting imputation to the subsample of cases that endorse a screener question. Despite its advantages, using separate regression models for imputation also introduces difficulties. For one, implementing the procedure is more cumbersome because it requires additional programming that is not necessary with data augmentation. Second, the use of diverse regression models can produce a situation where the algorithm fails to converge to a stable distribution (Raghunathan et al., 2001). In addition, assessing convergence is typically more difficult with sequential regression than it is with data augmentation (see Van Buuuren, 2007, for an illustration). Despite these potentially serious difficulties, simulation studies suggest that sequential regression performs well and can produce unbiased parameter estimates and standard errors (Raguhunathan et al., 2001; van Buuren et al., 2006). Although additional methodological research is needed, the sequential regression method may become a viable alternative to data augmentation when the data contain mixtures of categorical and continuous variables. A number of specialized software packages implement the sequential regression approach (e.g., MICE, ICE, IVEWARE), and the SPSS Missing Values add-on (available in version 17 and higher) also offers this imputation option.

## An Algorithm for Multilevel Data

Multilevel data structures are characterized by observations that are nested within higher-level units or clusters (e.g., children nested within schools, employees nested within workgroups, repeated measures nested within individuals). Multilevel analysis techniques are well-suited for these data structures because they appropriately account for the nesting and allow researchers to investigate associations at different levels of the data hierarchy (Raudenbush & Bryk, 2002). The data augmentation algorithm from Chapter 7 is inappropriate for multilevel data sets because it fails to preserve between-cluster differences in the mean structure and the covariance structure. For example, in an education study, the association between socioeconomic status and student achievement might differ across schools, but data augmentation imputes missing values from a model where this association is constant for all schools in the sample. Not surprisingly, this can seriously distort the subsequent parameter estimates.

Methodologists have developed specialized imputation algorithms for multilevel data (Schafer, 2001; Schafer & Yucel, 2002; Yucel, 2008). These routines may require software packages that you are not familiar with (e.g., the PAN library for the S-Plus program), but taking the time to learn one of these programs can provide an advantage over using maximum likelihood to estimate a multilevel model with missing data. At this time, multilevel software packages generally allow for missing data on outcome variables, but they eliminate cases with missing predictor variables. Although there is often little reason to prefer multiple imputation over maximum likelihood (or vice versa), the ability to retain cases with missing predictor variables gives multiple imputation a clear advantage in this situation. Analyzing multiply imputed data sets is also very straightforward because a number of multilevel software packages have facilities for automating the analysis and pooling phases.

Before describing the multilevel imputation algorithm, it is useful to review the multilevel model. As an illustration, consider a study of school achievement where children (i.e., level-1 units) are nested within a number of different schools (i.e., level-2 units). Furthermore, suppose that it is of interest to predict student achievement based on socioeconomic status and school size. The multilevel regression model for this analysis is

$$Y_{ij} = \gamma_{00} + \gamma_{10}(SES_{ij}) + \gamma_{01}(Size_j) + \gamma_{11}(SES_{ij})(Size_j) + u_{oj} + u_{1j}(SES_{ij}) + r_{ij} \qquad (9.4)$$

where $Y_{ij}$ is the achievement score for child $i$ in school $j$, the $\gamma$ terms are regression coefficients, $u_{0j}$ is a level-2 residual that allows the achievement means to differ across schools, $u_{1j}$ is a level-2 residual that allows the association between socioeconomic status and achievement to vary across schools, and $r_{ij}$ is a level-1 residual that captures individual differences within a particular school. The level-2 residuals (i.e., the $u$ terms) in the equation are essentially latent variables, the values of which differ across clusters (e.g., schools). Finally, it is worth noting that the multilevel model estimates a level-1 and a level-2 covariance matrix as opposed to the residuals themselves.

Multilevel imputation uses an iterative algorithm called the **Gibbs sampler** (Casella & George, 1992; Gelfand & Smith, 1990), which closely resembles data augmentation. The Gibbs sampler consists of a series of steps where the values at one step depend on the quantities from the previous step. In the context of multiple imputation, each iteration of the Gibbs sampler consists of three steps: (1) draw level-2 residuals from a distribution of plausible values, (2) draw new parameter values (i.e., regression coefficients, the level-2 covariance matrix, and the level-1 covariance matrix) from their respective posterior distributions, and (3) impute the missing values. I give a brief sketch of the imputation algorithm in the remainder of this section; interested readers can find additional details in Schafer (2001) and Schafer and Yucel (2002).

To begin, the Gibbs sampler draws a set of level-2 residuals from a normal distribution. The exact shape of this distribution depends on the filled-in data and the parameter values (i.e., the regression coefficients and the covariance matrices) from the previous iteration. The level-2 residuals are an important starting point because they define the shape of the posterior distributions in the second step and because they facilitate the computation of the multilevel model parameters. Next, the Gibbs sampler uses Monte Carlo simulation to draw new parameter values from their respective posterior distributions. Similar to the P-step of data augmentation, the algorithm draws the level-1 and level-2 covariance matrices from an inverse Wishart distribution, and it uses a multivariate normal distribution to generate a new set of regression coefficients. The exact shape of these distributions depends on the level-2 residuals from the first step and on the imputed values from the preceding iteration. The final step of the Gibbs sampler generates predicted scores for each case by substituting the observed variables and the level-2 residuals into a multilevel regression model similar to that in Equation 9.5. Consistent with the I-step of data augmentation, the algorithm restores variability to the imputed data by augmenting each predicted score with a normally distributed residual term.

Implementing a multilevel imputation model involves additional nuances that are not relevant to standard data augmentation. For example, deciding what to include in the imputation model becomes more complex. Following standard procedure, the imputation phase should include analysis model variables and auxiliary variables. However, you also need to decide which level-2 residual terms (i.e., random effects) to include in the imputation regression model. These residuals determine whether the association between two variables varies across clusters, so omitting an important residual term can bias the subsequent parameter estimates. Although it may seem like a good idea to include every possible residual term, doing so can lead to estimation problems and convergence failures. In addition to specifying which residual terms get included in the model, it is necessary to specify a covariance structure for the residuals. For example, a saturated covariance matrix allows the residuals for different variables to freely correlate, but it is also possible to specify a matrix that restricts the between-variable associations to zero. The first option will better preserve the associations among the variables, but the complexity of the resulting imputation model can cause estimation problems. Schafer (2001) and Schafer and Yucel (2002) describe model specification issues in more detail and give an analysis example that applies a multilevel imputation model.

## 9.8 MULTIPLE-IMPUTATION SOFTWARE OPTIONS

A number of software packages generate multiply imputed data sets, some of which are commercially available, while others are freely available on the Internet. Software programs tend to change at a rapid pace, so a detailed description of these packages would quickly become out of date. Rather, this section provides a very general overview of multiple imputation computing options, and I discuss a small handful of software options in more detail in Chapter 11. A variety of resources are available for readers interested in the details of specific software programs (e.g., Allison, 2000; Honaker, King, & Blackwell, 2009; Horton & Lipsitz, 2001; Raghunathan, Solenberger, & Van Hoewyk, 2002; Royston, 2005; Schafer & Olsen, 1998; Yuan, 2000), and there are also useful websites that provide information about individual software packages (e.g., *www.multiple-imputation.com*).

Multiple-imputation software packages generally fall into one of three categories: programs that (1) generate multiply imputed data sets, (2) analyze multiply imputed data sets created by other programs, and (3) generate and analyze multiply imputed data sets. The programs that generate multiple imputations tend to offer the same set of features, some of which are described earlier in this chapter and in previous chapters (e.g., data transformations, rounding options, ridge prior distributions). Although there is considerable overlap in features, software programs differ in the type and the number of algorithms that they implement. For example, the SAS MI procedure implements the data augmentation algorithm, whereas SPSS offers the sequential regression approach (also known as chained equations and fully conditional specification) in its Missing Values add-on. SAS and SPSS are arguably the most popular statistical software packages in the social and the behavioral sciences, but a number of specialized imputation programs are also available (e.g., NORM, Amelia, MICE), as are open-source programs that offer a variety of user-written modules (e.g., the S-Plus and R statistical packages). Finally, software programs differ in their overall ease of use; some programs have point-and-click interfaces (e.g., the NORM program), but most are syntax driven (e.g., the SAS MI procedure and various R modules).

Regardless of which program you use to generate the multiple imputations, you have a number of options for analyzing the data and combining the resulting estimates. For example, many popular software packages offer built-in routines for analyzing multiply imputed data sets (e.g., SAS, Mplus, HLM, to name just a few). Some of these programs require considerable programming to combine the $m$ sets of estimates and standard errors, whereas others are so easy to use that the pooling process is virtually transparent to the user. Software programs also differ in the amount of summary information that they provide, so this is an additional consideration when choosing an analysis platform. For example, some programs output detailed diagnostic information (e.g., fraction of missing information, relative increase in variance, between- and within-imputation variance), whereas others simply report the pooled estimates and standard errors. In my experience, it is often convenient to use one program to generate the imputations and use a different program to analyze the data, but this choice is largely one of personal preference.

## 9.9 DATA ANALYSIS EXAMPLE 1

The first analysis example uses multiple imputation to estimate a regression model with an interaction term.* The data for this analysis consist of scores from 480 employees on eight work-related variables: gender, age, job tenure, IQ, psychological well-being, job satisfaction, job performance, and turnover intentions. I generated these data to mimic the correlation structure of published research articles in the management and psychology literature (e.g., Wright & Bonett, 2007; Wright, Cropanzano, & Bonett, 2007). The data have three missing data patterns, each of which accounts for one-third of the sample. The first pattern consists of cases with complete data, and the remaining two patterns have missing data on either well-being or job satisfaction. These patterns mimic a situation in which the data are missing by design (e.g., to reduce the cost of data collection).

The goal of the analysis is to determine whether gender moderates the association between psychological well-being and job performance. The multiple regression equation is as follows:

$$JP_i = \beta_0 + \beta_1(WB_i) + \beta_2(FEMALE_i) + \beta_3(WB_i)(FEMALE_i) + \varepsilon$$

*Analysis syntax and data are available on the companion website, *www.appliedmissingdata.com*.

Using maximum likelihood to estimate a model with an interaction term is straightforward and follows the same procedure as any multiple regression analysis (e.g., see the analysis example in Chapter 4). However, dealing with interactive effects is more complex in a multiple imputation analysis because the imputation phase must account for group differences in the mean and the covariance structure. With a nominal moderator variable such as gender, the best way to preserve an interactive effect is to impute the data separately for each group.

## The Imputation Phase

To implement separate-group imputation, I sorted the data by gender and performed data augmentation separately for males and females. Note that the imputation model included every variable except gender, which was constant in each group. As I explained previously, separate-group imputation naturally preserves interaction effects because it allows the mean and the covariance structure to freely vary across subpopulations. The graphical diagnostics for males and females suggested fast convergence, so I specified 100 burn-in and 100 between-imputation iterations (i.e., I saved the first imputed data set after an initial burn-in period of 100 cycles and saved subsequent data sets at every 100th I-step thereafter). Consistent with the analysis example from Chapter 8, I opted to use $m = 50$ imputations for the analysis phase.

## The Analysis and Pooling Phases

The standard advice in the regression literature is to center continuous predictor variables at the grand mean (Aiken & West, 1991; Cohen et al., 2003). To do so, I merged the male and female files and computed the mean well-being score within each of the 50 imputed data sets. Next, I centered the psychological well-being scores by subtracting the appropriate mean from each score, and I then computed a product variable (i.e., interaction term) by multiplying gender and the centered well-being scores. Finally, I estimated a multiple regression model with job performance scores as the outcome variable and gender, psychological well-being, and the product term as predictors. The analysis phase produced 50 sets of regression coefficients and standard errors that I subsequently pooled into a single set of results.

Researchers often begin a regression analysis with an omnibus $F$ test, and the $D_1$ statistic from Chapter 8 is ideally suited for this purpose. This analysis produced a test statistic of $D_1 = 40.34$. Referencing this value to an $F$ distribution with 3 numerator and 3802.40 denominator degrees of freedom returned a probability value of $p < .001$. Consistent with the omnibus $F$ test from an ordinary least squares regression analysis, a significant test statistic indicates that at least one of the regression slopes is statistically different from zero.

Table 9.5 shows the pooled estimates and standard errors, along with the corresponding maximum likelihood estimates from Chapter 4. Although the imputation and analysis models are not congenial (the imputation model is more complex than the analysis model), the two analysis procedure produced nearly identical parameter estimates and standard errors. Turning to the individual parameter estimates note that, males and females do not differ with respect to their mean job performance ratings, $\hat{\beta}_2 = -0.175$, $t = -1.66$, $p = .10$, but the interaction term indicates that the association between well-being and performance is differ-

**TABLE 9.5. Regression Model Estimates from Data Analysis Example 1**

| Parameter | Estimate | SE | t |
|---|---|---|---|
| | Multiple imputation | | |
| $\beta_0$ (intercept) | 6.092 | 0.076 | 79.828 |
| $\beta_1$ (well-being) | 0.332 | 0.065 | 5.107 |
| $\beta_2$ (gender) | −0.173 | 0.105 | −1.644 |
| $\beta_3$ (interaction) | 0.355 | 0.100 | 3.566 |
| $\hat{\sigma}_e^2$ (Residual) | 1.193 | 0.083 | 14.403 |
| $R^2$ | 0.240 | | |
| | Maximum likelihood estimation | | |
| $\beta_0$ (intercept) | 6.091 | 0.076 | 79.755 |
| $\beta_1$ (well-being) | 0.337 | 0.071 | 4.723 |
| $\beta_2$ (gender) | −0.167 | 0.105 | −1.587 |
| $\beta_3$ (interaction) | 0.362 | 0.106 | 3.426 |
| $\hat{\sigma}_e^2$ (residual) | 1.234 | 0.084 | 14.650 |
| $R^2$ | 0.214 | | |

*Note.* Predictors were centered at the maximum likelihood estimates of the mean.

ent for males and females, $\hat{\beta}_3 = 0.355$, $t = 3.57$, $p < .001$. Because the gender variable is coded such that female = 1 and male = 0, the sign of the interaction coefficient indicates that the relationship is stronger for females. Notice that the interpretation of the regression coefficients is identical to what it would have been had the data been complete. In addition, the computation of simple slopes is identical to that of a complete-data analysis. For example, the regression equation for the subsample of males (the group coded 0) is $\hat{Y}_M = \hat{\beta}_0 + \hat{\beta}_1(WB)$, and the corresponding equation for females (the group coded 1) is $\hat{Y}_F = (\hat{\beta}_0 + \hat{\beta}_2) + (\hat{\beta}_1 + \hat{\beta}_3)(WB)$.

## 9.10 DATA ANALYSIS EXAMPLE 2

The second data analysis example illustrates the difference between scale-level imputation and duplicate-scale imputation.* The analyses use artificial data from a questionnaire on eating disorder risk. Briefly, the data contain the responses from 400 college-aged women on 10 questions from the Eating Attitudes Test (EAT; Garner, Olmsted, Bohr, & Garfinkel, 1982), a widely used measure of eating disorder risk. The 10 questions measure two constructs, Drive for Thinness (e.g., "I avoid eating when I'm hungry") and Food Preoccupation (e.g., "I find myself preoccupied with food"), and mimic the two-factor structure proposed by Doninger, Enders, and Burnett (2005). The data set also contains an anxiety scale score, a variable that

---

* Analysis syntax and data are available on the companion website, *www.appliedmissingdata.com.*

measures beliefs about Western standards of beauty (e.g., high scores indicate that respondents internalize a thin ideal of beauty), and body mass index (BMI) values.

Variables in the EAT data set are missing for a variety of reasons. I simulated MCAR data by randomly deleting scores from the anxiety variable, the Western standards of beauty scale, and two of the EAT questions ($EAT_2$ and $EAT_{21}$). Expecting a relationship between body weight and missingness, I created MAR data on five variables ($EAT_1$, $EAT_{10}$, $EAT_{12}$, $EAT_{18}$, and $EAT_{24}$) by deleting the EAT scores for a subset of cases in both tails of the BMI distribution. These same EAT questions were also missing for individuals with elevated anxiety scores. Finally, I introduced a small amount of MNAR data by deleting a number of the high body mass index scores (e.g., to mimic a situation where females with high BMI values refuse to be weighed). The deletion process typically produced a missing data rate of 5 to 10% on each variable.

## The Imputation Phase

For the imputation phase, I generated three sets of $m = 20$ imputations by (1) imputing the individual questionnaire items (i.e., item-level imputation), (2) imputing the scale scores directly (i.e., scale-level imputation), and (3) imputing the scale scores using averages of the available items as auxiliary variables (i.e., duplicate-scale imputation). The number of variables in this data set is not nearly large enough to pose a problem for item-level imputation (the ideal procedure). Nevertheless, imputing the data using three approaches is useful for illustrating the differences that can result from using scale-level and duplicate-scale imputation. For each strategy, I used a single sequential data augmentation chain with 100 burn-in and 100 between-imputation iterations. The data augmentation algorithm converged very quickly and without problems, so there is no need to present the graphical diagnostics from the exploratory data augmentation chain.

The item-level imputation model included all 13 variables in the data set (i.e., the 10 EAT questionnaire items, anxiety scores, Western standards of beauty scores, and body mass index values). For scale imputation, I began by computing scale scores by averaging the two sets of questionnaire items. The Drive for Thinness scale consists of seven items ($EAT_1$, $EAT_2$, $EAT_{10}$, $EAT_{11}$, $EAT_{12}$, $EAT_{14}$, and $EAT_{24}$), and the Food Preoccupation scale has three items ($EAT_3$, $EAT_{18}$, and $EAT_{21}$). Consequently, the Drive for Thinness scale score was an average of seven Likert items, and the Food Preoccupation scale was an average of three items. I restricted the scale score computations to the cases with complete data, so respondents who were missing one or more of the item responses within a particular scale were also missing the scale score. This produced 291 cases with Drive for Thinness scores, 352 cases with Food Preoccupation scores, and 276 individuals with complete data on both scale scores. The subsequent scale-level imputation model had five variables: the two EAT scale scores, anxiety scores, Western standards of beauty scores, and body mass index values.

The duplicate-scale imputation procedure was identical to that of scale imputation, but it also included two additional variables that I computed by averaging the available items within each scale. Again, the purpose of the duplicate scales is to recapture the important item-level information that scale imputation discards. An important nuance of the duplicate-score approach is that the input data contain linear dependencies. Although the graphical diagnostics looked ideal, the software package issued a warning message that the initial covariance matrix (i.e., the Bayesian estimate of $\Sigma$ that generates the regressions for the first I-step) was singular. I eliminated this problem by specifying a ridge prior distribution with a single degree of freedom. This effectively added one imaginary data record to the data augmentation procedure.

## The Analysis and Pooling Phases

To keep the analysis model simple, I estimated the mean vector and the covariance matrix for five variables: the Drive for Thinness and Food Preoccupation scale scores, the anxiety scores, the Western standards of beauty scores, and the body mass index values. The analysis phase produced a mean vector and a covariance matrix for each of the 20 imputed data sets. I subsequently used the pooling formulas from Chapter 8 to combine the estimates and the standard errors; Table 9.6 shows the results for three imputation approaches. Even when the ultimate goal is to analyze scale scores, imputing the individual questionnaire items and computing scale scores from the filled-in item responses should provide better results than imputing the scale scores directly. Consequently, the item-level imputation is the "gold standard" against which to compare the other methods. Focusing on the covariance matrix elements for the EAT scale scores, notice that scale-level imputation produced larger standard errors than item-level imputation. Also, notice that the standard error inflation tends to be somewhat larger for the seven-item Drive for Thinness scale. This suggests that the power loss may increase as the number of scale items increases. In contrast, duplicate-scale imputation produced estimates and standard errors that are quite similar to those of item-level imputation. Scale-level imputation performed poorly because questionnaire items within a scale tend to have stronger correlations than items from different scales. Consequently, the imputation phase effectively discards the strongest predictors of the missing scale scores (i.e., the items within the scale) in favor of weaker correlates (i.e., items from different scales). Although it is not possible to draw firm conclusions from a single artificial data set, the standard error differences in Table 9.6 are consistent with what you might expect to see in real data sets.

## 9.11 SUMMARY

This chapter addressed a number of practical issues that arise during the imputation phase. The chapter began with a discussion of convergence problems. Convergence issues often occur because there is insufficient data to estimate certain parameters. This lack of data can result from including too many variables in the imputation phase or from a peculiar missing data pattern. In some situations, reducing the number of variables or eliminating the problematic variables can solve convergence problems. An alternate strategy is to specify a ridge prior distribution for the covariance matrix. Conceptually, the ridge prior adds a small number of imaginary data records (i.e., degrees of freedom) from a hypothetical population where the variables are uncorrelated. These additional data points can stabilize estimation and eliminate convergence problems, but they do so at the cost of introducing a slight bias to the simulated parameter values (and thus the imputations). The biasing effect of the ridge prior

**TABLE 9.6. Mean Vector and Covariance Matrix Estimates from Data Analysis Example 2**

| Variable | 1 | 2 | 3 | 4 | 5 |
|---|---|---|---|---|---|
| | | | Item-level imputation | | |
| 1: DFT | 0.612 (0.044) | | | | |
| 2: FP | 0.349 (0.039) | 0.759 (0.054) | | | |
| 3: ANX | 1.227 (0.135) | 1.254 (0.149) | 9.078 (0.655) | | |
| 4: WSB | 0.549 (0.084) | 0.462 (0.089) | 0.997 (0.307) | 3.667 (0.270) | |
| 5: BMI | 0.846 (0.115) | 0.664 (0.125) | 1.164 (0.422) | 1.109 (0.275) | 7.343 (0.521) |
| Means | 3.959 (0.039) | 3.966 (0.044) | 11.979 (0.152) | 8.964 (0.099) | 22.405 (0.136) |
| | | | Scale-level imputation | | |
| 1: DFT | 0.599 (0.047) | | | | |
| 2: FP | 0.349 (0.042) | 0.739 (0.521) | | | |
| 3: ANX | 1.213 (0.151) | 1.236 (0.151) | 9.035 (0.663) | | |
| 4: WSB | 0.577 (0.083) | 0.443 (0.093) | 1.007 (0.306) | 8.964 (0.097) | |
| 5: BMI | 0.815 (0.126) | 0.617 (0.129) | 1.137 (0.418) | 1.087 (0.274) | 7.347 (0.521) |
| Means | 3.957 (0.047) | 3.971 (0.044) | 11.979 (0.153) | 8.964 (0.097) | 22.401 (0.136) |
| | | | Duplicate-scale imputation | | |
| 1: DFT | 0.616 (0.044) | | | | |
| 2: FP | 0.353 (0.039) | 0.768 (0.054) | | | |
| 3: ANX | 1.223 (0.135) | 1.227 (0.149) | 9.009 (0.649) | | |
| 4: WSB | 0.547 (0.082) | 0.452 (0.089) | 1.050 (0.308) | 3.637 (0.266) | |
| 5: BMI | 0.838 (0.115) | 0.668 (0.125) | 1.134 (0.419) | 1.111 (0.278) | 7.369 (0.524) |
| Means | 3.959 (0.039) | 3.967 (0.044) | 11.965 (0.152) | 8.968 (0.098) | 22.402 (0.137) |

*Note.* DFT = drive for thinness; FP = food preoccupation; ANX = anxiety; WSB = Western standards of beauty; BMI = body mass index. Values in parentheses are standard errors.

depends on the number of degrees of freedom that you assign to the prior, so it is generally a good idea to select a value that is as small as possible.

Like maximum likelihood estimation, the data augmentation algorithm in Chapter 7 assumes multivariate normality, both at the I-step and at the P-step. However, methodologists suggest that normality-based imputation can work for a variety of different distribution types. Empirical studies suggest that normality violations may not pose a serious threat to the accuracy of multiple imputation parameter estimates, particularly if the sample size is not too small and the missing data rate is not too large. One way to mitigate the impact of normality violations is to apply normalizing transformations to the data prior to performing data augmentation. Variables can have different scales during the imputation and pooling phases, so you can impute a variable on a transformed metric (e.g., a logarithmic scale) and subsequently analyze it on its original metric.

Nominal and ordinal variables are a special case of non-normal data that arises frequently in the behavioral and the social sciences. One consequence of applying an imputation model for normal data to discrete variables is that the resulting imputations will have decimals. The traditional advice is to round imputed values to the nearest integer or to the nearest plausible value in order to produce imputations that are aesthetically consistent with the observed data. However, recent research suggests that rounding may not be necessary and can actually lead to biased parameter estimates. Aesthetics aside, there appear to be no negative consequences associated with analyzing fractional imputations, so analyzing the data without rounding seems to be the safest strategy, at least for now. However, in some cases the analysis model requires rounding (e.g., a binary outcome in a logistic regression, a set of dummy variables), and the chapter described some rounding strategies for these situations.

Researchers in the behavioral and the social sciences are often interested in estimating interaction (i.e., moderation) effects where the magnitude of the association between two variables depends on a third variable. When using multiple imputation to treat missing data, it is important to specify an imputation model that preserves any interaction effects that are of interest in the subsequent analysis model. Failing to do so will attenuate the magnitude of these effects, even if the data are MCAR or MAR. The best strategy for preserving interaction effects depends largely on whether the interaction involves a continuous or a categorical moderator variable. If the analysis model includes an interaction effect between two quantitative variables, the only way to preserve the interaction effect is to include a product variable in the imputation phase. The downside of this approach is that the imputation regression model generates filled-in values that are homoscedastic. This subtlety may have a relatively minor impact on many analyses, but in a number of situations the substantive goal is to determine whether the covariance structure is the same across qualitatively different subpopulations (e.g., measurement invariance analyses, multiple-group structural equation models). If the subgroups have different population variances, then the product term approach will generate imputations that mask these group differences. Consequently, when an interactive effect involves a categorical moderator variable, imputing the data separately for each subgroup is often more accurate than including product terms in the imputation model.

Researchers in the behavioral and social sciences routinely use multiple-item questionnaires to measure complex constructs. Multiple imputation is advantageous for dealing with item-level missingness, but imputation can be challenging when a data set contains a large number of variables. Ideally, the imputation phase should include all of the individual questionnaire items in order to maximize the information that goes into creating the imputations. However, this may not be feasible when the number of questionnaire items is very large. When the analysis model involves scale scores, ignoring the item-level data and imputing the scale scores themselves can dramatically reduce the number of imputation model variables. This approach tends to lack power, but using the average of the available items as auxiliary variables (i.e., duplicate-scale imputation) can yield estimates and standard errors that are quite similar to those of an item-level imputation procedure. For situations that require item-level data, I outlined a three-step approach for item-level imputation. The basic idea behind this procedure is to separately impute different subsets of questionnaire items, each time using scale scores to preserve the between-subset associations among the items.

The chapter concluded with a description of some alternate imputation algorithms. Although the data augmentation algorithm in Chapter 7 is probably the most popular imputation strategy, methodologists have developed a number of alternative imputation algorithms. The chapter described an EM-based imputation algorithm that is statistically equivalent to data augmentation. This EMIS algorithm is appealing because it automatically yields independent imputations and does so more quickly than data augmentation. The chapter also described two algorithms (the general location model and sequential regression) appropriate for data sets that contain a mixture of categorical and continuous variables. Of these two, the sequential regression approach appears particularly promising. Unlike data augmentation, which assumes a common distribution for every variable in the data set, sequential regression imputation fills in the data on a variable-by-variable basis, each time matching the imputation model to a variable's distributional form. Preliminary simulation studies suggest that this procedure works well. Finally, I described an imputation algorithm for multilevel data structures. This algorithm is important because standard data augmentation fails to preserve any differences in the mean and the covariance structure that might exist across clusters.

The majority of this book is devoted to two so-called modern missing data techniques: maximum likelihood and multiple imputation. These methods use quite different approaches, but both assume MAR data. Although MAR-based methods are a substantial improvement over traditional methods that require the MCAR mechanism, they will produce bias when the data are missing not at random (MNAR). Chapter 10 outlines models that are designed specifically for MNAR data. As you will see, these MNAR methods are far from perfect and require assumptions that can be just as tenuous as MAR. In fact, when the model assumptions are violated, MNAR approaches can yield estimates that are worse than what you would have obtained from an MAR analysis. Nevertheless, MNAR models are useful for sensitivity analysis and are an important area of ongoing methodological research.

## 9.12 RECOMMENDED READINGS

Allison, P. D. (2002). *Missing data*. Newbury Park, CA: Sage.

Graham, J. W. (2009). Missing data analysis: Making it work in the real world. *Annual Review of Psychology*, *60*, 549–576.

Graham, J. W., & Schafer, J. L. (1999). On the performance of multiple imputation for multivariate data with small sample size. In R. Hoyle (Ed.), *Statistical strategies for small sample research* (pp. 1–29). Thousand Oaks, CA: Sage.

Horton, N. J., & Lipsitz, S. R. (2001). Multiple imputation in practice: Comparison of software packages for regression models with missing data. *The American Statistician*, *55*, 244–254.

Schafer, J. L. (1997). *Analysis of incomplete multivariate data*. New York: Chapman.

Schafer, J. L., & Olsen, M. K. (1998). Multiple imputation for multivariate missing-data problems: A data analyst's perspective. *Multivariate Behavioral Research*, *33*, 545–571.

# 10

# Models for Missing
# Not at Random Data

## 10.1 CHAPTER OVERVIEW

Until now, this book has focused primarily on analysis methods that assume missing at random (MAR) data. Although MAR-based approaches represent the current state of the art (Schafer & Graham, 2002), a considerable amount of methodological research is devoted models for missing not at random (MNAR) data. This chapter outlines two classes of MNAR models: the selection model and the pattern mixture model. Both models attempt to describe the joint distribution of the data and the probability of missingness, but they do so in a very different manner. For example, the selection model is a two-part model that combines the substantive analysis with an additional regression equation that predicts response probabilities. In contrast, the pattern mixture model forms subgroups of cases that share the same missing data pattern and estimates the substantive analysis model within each pattern. In both frameworks, the model that describes the incidence of missing data is essentially a nuisance, but incorporating this additional component into the estimation process can potentially reduce or eliminate bias that results from MAR violations.

The intuitive appeal of an MNAR analysis may have you wondering why these models are relegated to a single chapter. As you will see, MNAR models require assumptions that are every bit as tenuous as the MAR mechanism (and probably more so). For example, selection models rely heavily on untestable distributional assumptions, and pattern mixture models generally require researchers to specify assumed values for one or more inestimable parameters. Ultimately, there is no way to verify that these requirements are met, and assumption violations can produce estimates that are even worse than those from an MAR-based analysis. The fact that MNAR models rely so heavily on narrow, untestable assumptions has led some methodologists to caution against their routine use (Allison, 2002; Demirtas & Schafer, 2003; Schafer & Graham, 2002). A common view is that MNAR models are most appropriate for sensitivity analyses that apply different models (and thus different assumptions) to the same data. Despite their inherent limitations, MNAR analysis models are likely to gain in popularity, so it is important to become familiar with these approaches.

**TABLE 10.1. Job Performance Data Set**

| IQ | Psychological well-being | Job performance Hypothetical | Job performance Observed |
|---|---|---|---|
| 78 | 13 | 9 | 9 |
| 84 | 9 | 13 | 13 |
| 84 | 10 | 10 | 10 |
| 85 | 10 | 8 | — |
| 87 | 7 | 7 | — |
| 91 | 3 | 7 | — |
| 92 | 12 | 9 | 9 |
| 94 | 3 | 9 | 9 |
| 94 | 13 | 11 | 11 |
| 96 | 7 | 7 | — |
| 99 | 6 | 7 | — |
| 105 | 12 | 10 | 10 |
| 105 | 14 | 11 | 11 |
| 106 | 10 | 15 | 15 |
| 108 | 7 | 10 | 10 |
| 112 | 10 | 10 | 10 |
| 113 | 14 | 12 | 12 |
| 115 | 14 | 14 | 14 |
| 118 | 12 | 16 | 16 |
| 134 | 11 | 12 | 12 |

As an aside, there is a substantial literature on the application of MNAR models to longitudinal data analyses. In particular, these models have received a great deal of attention in the clinical trials literature, perhaps because the MNAR mechanism is plausible in medical studies where attrition often results from death or deteriorating health (Pauler, McCoy, & Moinpour, 2003). In line with this emphasis, much of this chapter describes MNAR models for longitudinal growth curve analyses. To keep things manageable, I confine the examples to a linear growth model, but the basic modeling ideas readily extend to quadratic growth curves (Demirtas & Schafer, 2003; Enders, 2010; Verbeke & Molenberghs, 2000). I give a relatively brief overview of the linear growth model in this chapter, and a number of excellent resources are available to readers interested in additional details (Bollen & Curran, 2006; Bryk & Raudenbush, 1987; Hancock & Lawrence, 2006; Raudenbush & Bryk, 2002; Singer & Willett, 2003).

In the first half of the chapter, I use the small data set in Table 10.1 to illustrate the selection model and the pattern mixture model. I designed these data to mimic an employee selection scenario in which prospective employees complete an IQ test during their job interview and a supervisor subsequently evaluates their job performance following a 6-month probationary period. Furthermore, suppose that a group of employees quits just before their 6-month evaluation because they anticipate a negative performance review. The table shows the hypothetically complete job performance scores along with the observed performance ratings. As you can see, job performance ratings are MNAR because employees with the lowest hypothetical values have higher rates of missingness (i.e., the probability of missing data is directly related to the rating that the employee would have received at their 6-month review). If the company's goal is to estimate the mean job performance rating for the entire population of new employees, MAR missing data handling procedures will produce distorted estimates because they fail to account for the systematic missingness at the low end of the job performance distribution.

## 10.2 AN AD HOC APPROACH TO DEALING WITH MNAR DATA

The need to apply MNAR models stems from a concern that maximum likelihood and multiple imputation parameter estimates are not robust to departures from an MAR mechanism. The selection model and pattern mixture model formally address this concern by incorporating an additional model that describes the propensity for missing data. Until recently, a lack of software options has limited the application of these models, so researchers have relied on ad hoc approaches for testing the sensitivity of MAR-based estimates. Rubin (1987) and others (Allison, 2002; Graham, Hofer, Donaldson, MacKinnon, & Schafer, 1997) outline a simple approach that you can readily implement within a multiple imputation analysis. Because this method is so straightforward, it warrants a brief discussion.

Rubin's (1987) idea for an ad hoc sensitivity analysis is simple: generate multiple imputations under an MAR mechanism, then add a constant to the imputed values to compensate for the possibility that the MAR-based imputations may be too high or too low. As an illustration, consider the small job performance data set in Table 10.1. Suppose that the company has reason to believe that an MNAR mechanism is plausible, such that the employees who quit prior to their 6-month evaluation have systematically lower job performance ratings than the general population. If this is true, then MAR-based analyses are likely to overestimate the mean performance rating. To explore whether the mean estimate is sensitive to this distortion, the company could use a standard multiple imputation routine to generate imputed job performance ratings and lower each imputation by some arbitrary constant. Analyzing the imputed data sets with and without the constant values may help assess whether the mean is sensitive to departures from an MAR mechanism.

Rubin (1987, p. 203) recommends a constant value that increases or decreases MAR-based imputations by 20%, but this suggestion is arbitrary. An alternate approach is to use Cohen's (1988) effect size guidelines for a standardized mean difference. For example, the maximum likelihood estimate of the job performance standard deviation is $SD = 2.24$. Cohen's benchmark for a medium effect size is $d = 0.50$, so subtracting a constant value of 1.12 from each imputed value imposes a downward adjustment of one-half of a standard deviation unit. Expressing the constant as a percentage or as a standardized mean difference is an arbitrary choice, but Cohen's guidelines have the advantage of providing a familiar metric.

Rubin (1987) gives a number of other suggestions for ad hoc sensitivity analyses. For example, if there is reason to believe that more than one mechanism might be at play, then applying the constant to a subset of the imputed values might be appropriate. Rubin recommends adding or subtracting a constant value to 50% of the imputed scores, but this suggestion is also arbitrary. The purpose of a sensitivity analysis is to explore the variability of the parameter estimates across a variety of models and assumptions, so there is no need to choose a single set of conditions. The simplicity of Rubin's ad hoc approach makes it easy to impute and analyze the data under a number of different scenarios. Readers who are interested in additional details can consult. Graham et al. (1997, pp. 354–358), which provides a thorough description of a sensitivity analysis that uses this ad hoc approach.

## 10.3 THE THEORETICAL RATIONALE FOR MNAR MODELS

Recall from Chapter 1 that Rubin's (1976) missing data theory views individuals as having a pair of observations on each variable: a score value that may or may not be observed (i.e., $Y_{obs}$ or $Y_{mis}$), and a corresponding code on a binary missing data indicator, $R$ (i.e., $r = 1$ if the score is observed, and $r = 0$ if the value is missing). Defining the propensity for missing data as a variable implies that some unknown population model (e.g., a logistic regression) governs whether $R$ takes on a value of zero or one. Because researchers rarely know why the data are missing, estimating a model that explains the probability of missingness is difficult, if not impossible. Fortunately, Rubin showed that the parameters that describe the missing data distribution carry no unique information about the substantive model parameters, provided that the data are MAR. For this reason, the missing data literature often describes the MAR mechanism as ignorable missingness because there is no need to consider the parameters of the missing data distribution when performing likelihood-based analyses (this includes both maximum likelihood estimation and multiple imputation).

An MNAR mechanism implies that the parameters of the missing data model carry important information about the substantive model parameters, and vice versa. Consequently, an MAR-based analysis that ignores the missing data model will produce biased parameter estimates because it does not fully adjust for the "cause" of missingness. The MNAR models in this chapter attempt to mitigate this bias by incorporating a model that describes the propensity for missing data, although they do so in different ways. For example, the selection model incorporates a regression equation that predicts the response probabilities, whereas the pattern mixture model stratifies the sample by missing data pattern and estimates the model separately within each pattern. The joint distribution of the data and the probability of missingness is the key to understanding the rationale behind these two approaches.

The joint distribution of the data and the probability of missingness is

$$p(Y, R) \tag{10.1}$$

where $p$ is a generic symbol for a probability distribution, $Y$ represents the sample data, and $R$ is the corresponding missing data indicator. In words, Equation 10.1 states that there is a distribution (and thus a set of unknown parameter values) that describes the mutual occurrence of different score values and missing data. The two classes of MNAR models differ in how they define the unknown parameters of this distribution.

The selection model factors the joint distribution into the product of two component distributions, as follows:

$$p(Y, R) = p(R \mid Y)p(Y) \tag{10.2}$$

where $p(R|Y)$ is the conditional distribution of missingness, given $Y$, and $p(Y)$ is the marginal distribution of the data. In words, the conditional distribution defines the probability that an individual with a particular score value has missing data, and the marginal distribution describes the probability of obtaining different scores. In practice, the marginal distribution is the substantive analysis model (i.e., the model that you would have estimated had there been no missing data), and the conditional distribution is a regression model that describes the response probabilities.

The pattern mixture model uses an alternative factorization of the joint distribution

$$p(Y, R) = p(Y|R)p(R) \tag{10.3}$$

where $p(Y|R)$ is the conditional distribution of the data, given a particular value of $R$, and $p(R)$ is the marginal distribution of missingness. This factorization also describes the mutual occurrence of different $Y$ values and missing data, but it does so by switching the roles of $Y$ and $R$. Specifically, the conditional distribution now governs the probability of obtaining different $Y$ values within a subgroup of cases that share the same missing data pattern, and the marginal distribution describes the incidence of different missing data patterns. The factorization in Equation 10.3 provides the rationale for stratifying the sample by missing data pattern and estimating the substantive model separately within each pattern.

The selection model and the pattern mixture model are exchangeable in the sense that they attempt to explain the same phenomena and rely on alternative factorizations of the same joint distribution. However, the two factorizations lead to very different assumptions, so the models may or may not produce the same point estimates. In fact, it is possible for two MNAR analyses to produce very different sets of parameter estimates. Some methodologists favor the pattern mixture model because it requires more transparent assumptions than the selection model (Little & Rubin, 2002). However, a common viewpoint is that both procedures can play a role in a sensitivity analysis that applies different models (and thus different assumptions) to the same data. I illustrate a sensitivity analysis at the end of the chapter.

## 10.4 THE CLASSIC SELECTION MODEL

Heckman (1976, 1979) proposed the **selection model** as a method for correcting bias in a regression model with MNAR data on the outcome variable. (Note that Heckman uses the terms **truncation** and **sample selection** to describe MNAR data.) Heckman's work spawned a great deal of interest in the econometrics literature, and there is now a considerable body of methodological research devoted to the selection model. This section illustrates the classic selection model, and I later describe variations of the model for longitudinal analyses. Econometricians and methodologists have extended the selection model in a variety of ways, but a thorough review of this literature is well beyond the scope of this chapter. A number of resources are available to readers who want additional details on the selection model and its extensions (e.g., Puhani, 2000; Winship & Mare, 1992).

Heckman's (1976, 1979) selection model is a two-part model that combines the substantive regression model with an additional regression equation that predicts response probabilities. To illustrate, reconsider the small data set in Table 10.1. First, suppose that the substantive regression model (i.e., the regression that the company would have estimated had there been no missing data) is as follows:

$$JP = \beta_0 + \beta_1(IQ) + \varepsilon \tag{10.4}$$

where $\beta_0$ and $\beta_1$ are the intercept and slope coefficients, respectively, from the regression of job performance on IQ. Second, assume that the IQ scores are centered at the grand mean, such that $\beta_0$ is the job performance mean. Returning to the factorization in Equation 10.2, note that the regression model above corresponds to the marginal distribution, $p(Y)$.

The second part of the selection model is a regression equation that predicts response probabilities. The classic selection model defines the propensity for missing data on the outcome variable as a normally distributed latent variable. Cases that fall above some threshold on this latent variable have data, whereas the cases that fall below the threshold have missing values. Throughout the remainder of this section, I denote this latent variable as $R^*$ in order to differentiate it from the binary missing data indicator, $R$. Returning to the job performance example, suppose that the company uses psychological well-being scores to predict missingness, as follows:

$$R^* = \gamma_0 + \gamma_1(WB) + \zeta \tag{10.5}$$

where $R^*$ is an individual's latent propensity for missing data (e.g., an employee's anticipated job performance rating), $\gamma_0$ and $\gamma_1$ denote the regression intercept and slope, respectively, and $\zeta$ is a residual term. Note that the previous regression equations can share the same predictor variables, but it is good to have at least one predictor in the missing data model that does not appear in the substantive regression equation. Returning to the factorization in Equation 10.2, note that the regression model above corresponds to the conditional distribution of the missing data, $p(R|Y)$.

Figure 10.1 shows the previous selection model as a path diagram. Following standard conventions, rectangles denote manifest variables, ellipses represent latent variables, and single-headed straight arrows are regression coefficients. The double-headed curved arrow that connects $\varepsilon$ and $\zeta$ is a correlation between the residuals from the two regression equations. As I explain later, this correlation is very important because it is the mechanism by which the missing data model adjusts for bias in substantive model regression coefficients.

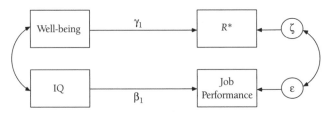

**FIGURE 10.1.** Path diagram of the classic Heckman selection model. $R^*$ represents the latent response probabilities, $\beta_1$ is the regression slope from the substantive model, and $\gamma_1$ is the slope from the missing data model. The double-headed curved arrow that connects $\varepsilon$ and $\zeta$ is a correlation between the residuals from the two regression equations.

## How Does the Selection Model Reduce Bias?

An MNAR mechanism implies that the data and the probability of missingness have a joint distribution, such that the data values carry information about the probability of missingness, and vice versa. The selection model incorporates this dependency via a bivariate normal distribution for the residual terms, as follows:

$$\begin{bmatrix} \varepsilon \\ \zeta \end{bmatrix} \sim \mathrm{BN}\left( \begin{bmatrix} 0 \\ 0 \end{bmatrix}, \begin{bmatrix} \sigma_\varepsilon^2 & \sigma_{\varepsilon,\zeta} \\ \sigma_{\zeta,\varepsilon} & \sigma_\zeta^2 \end{bmatrix} \right)$$

where ~ means "distributed as," the vector of zeros denotes the fact that the residuals have means of zero, $\sigma_\varepsilon^2$ and $\sigma_\zeta^2$ are the residual variances from Equations 10.4 and 10.5, respectively, and $\sigma_{\zeta,\varepsilon}$ is the covariance between the residual terms. Again, the covariance between $\varepsilon$ and $\zeta$ is particularly important because it is the mechanism by which the missing data model adjusts for bias in the substantive model.

To illustrate how the selection model works, reconsider the previous job performance example. An MAR analysis assumes that the explanatory variables in the substantive regression model (e.g., IQ) fully explain the probability of missingness, so any adjustment to the parameter estimates is due solely to the predictors. For example, suppose that the company used IQ scores to impute the missing job performance ratings. The positive correlation between IQ and job performance suggests that an employee with a low IQ score would have a low imputed value, and vice versa. However, with MNAR data, estimating the missing job performance scores based on IQ alone does not eliminate bias because a residual correlation exists between job ratings and the probability of missingness, even after controlling for IQ (i.e., the latent response probabilities contribute information about the missing score values, above and beyond IQ). Conceptually, simultaneously estimating the two selection model regression equations is akin to using both IQ and $R^*$ to impute the missing job performance ratings. Although the estimation process does not actually fill in the missing values, it does identify parameter estimates (i.e., the $\beta$ and $\gamma$ coefficients in Equations 10.4 and 10.5) that are consistent with a normally distributed population where job performance and $R^*$ (or equivalently, $\varepsilon$ and $\zeta$) are positively correlated. Consequently, the presence of the $R^*$ regression equation adjusts the substantive model parameter estimates in a manner that is analogous to an imputation procedure based on IQ and $R^*$. To the extent that $R^*$ and the outcome variable are related, this leads to different estimates than an MAR-based analysis that relies solely on the predictors in the substantive model to adjust for missingness.

Although it may not be immediately obvious, the correlation between $\varepsilon$ and $\zeta$ also quantifies the magnitude of the MAR violation. Specifically, a correlation of zero implies that the data are MAR because is no residual relationship exists between the outcome variable and the probability of missing data after controlling for the explanatory variables in the substantive regression model. Conversely, a nonzero correlation suggests that the data are MNAR because missingness is related to the outcome, even after accounting for other variables. At first glance, the residual correlation appears to provide a method for empirically testing the MAR mechanism (e.g., if the residual correlation is significantly different from zero, the data are inconsistent with an MAR mechanism). However, the selection model is highly sensitive to the bivariate normality assumption, and relatively minor violations of this assumption can dramatically alter the resulting parameter estimates, including the residual correlation. Consequently, using the residual correlation to test the MAR mechanism has virtually no practical utility and should be avoided.

## The Probit Regression Model

The preceding description of the selection model is somewhat vague because I have yet to explain how to estimate the two regression models. In particular, the regression model in Equation 10.5 requires some clarification because the latent $R*$ values are themselves completely missing. In practice, there is no way of knowing an individual's true propensity for missing data, so it is necessary to use the binary missing data indicator $R$ as the dependent variable. In effect, $R$ serves as a manifest indicator for $R*$, such that the cases that score above some threshold on $R*$ have complete data (i.e., $r = 1$), and cases that fall below the threshold have missing values (i.e., $r = 0$). Although logistic regression is a common approach for analyzing binary outcomes, the classic selection model uses **probit regression** to predict $R$. Because probit regression is relatively uncommon in many areas of the social and the behavioral sciences, a brief overview of the probit model is warranted before proceeding. Readers interested in additional details on probit regression can consult Pampel (2000) and Agresti (2002), among others.

Probit regression is actually quite similar to logistic regression and tends to yield the same substantive conclusions. Like the logistic model, probit regression uses an S-shaped function to describe the association between a predictor variable and the probability of an event (in this context, the probability of complete data, or $r = 1$). However, the probit model uses the **cumulative standard normal distribution** transformation to generate predicted probabilities. For readers who are unfamiliar with this distribution, the cumulative standard normal distribution is an S-shaped function, the height of which corresponds to the proportion of the standard normal curve that falls below a particular $z$ value.

Returning to job performance example, the probit model expresses the predicted probability of a complete response as

$$p(R = 1 \mid WB) = \Phi[\gamma_0 + \gamma_1(WB)] \tag{10.6}$$

where $p(R = 1 \mid WB)$ is the probability that an individual with a particular well-being score has a job performance rating, $\gamma_0$ and $\gamma_1$ denote the regression intercept and slope, respectively, and $\Phi$ is the cumulative normal distribution function. Substituting a well-being score into the bracketed portion of Equation 10.6 yields a predicted $z$ score, and the cumulative standard normal distribution function transforms the $z$ score into a predicted probability.

To further illustrate probit regression, I used the small data set in Table 10.1 to estimate a probit model that predicts missingness from psychological well-being. The intercept and slope estimates from this analysis are $\hat{\gamma}_0 = -1.884$ and $\hat{\gamma}_1 = 0.290$, respectively. Substituting the regression coefficients into Equation 10.6 gives the following expression.

$$p(R = 1 \mid WB) = \Phi\left[\hat{\gamma}_0 + \hat{\gamma}_1(WB)\right] = \Phi[-1.884 + .290(WB)]$$

Collectively, the bracketed terms produce a predicted value on the $z$ score metric. For example, the predicted value for an employee with a well-being score of 10 is $[-1.884 + 0.290(10)]$ = 1.016. Substituting this value into the cumulative normal distribution function (i.e., $\Phi$) converts the $z$ score into a probability. For example, $\Phi[1.016] = 0.845$ is the predicted probability that an employee with a well-being score of 10 has a job performance rating (i.e., 0.845 is the proportion of the standard normal curve that falls below a $z$ value of 1.016).

## 10.5 ESTIMATING THE SELECTION MODEL

The two principal approaches for estimating the classic selection model are maximum likelihood and a two-step method based on ordinary least squares regression. Both methods have advantages and disadvantages, and a substantial body of literature has examined the performance of these estimators (e.g., see Puhani, 2000). This section presents a brief overview of these two approaches, and additional technical details are available elsewhere in the literature (Amemiya, 1985; Heckman, 1976, 1979; Puhani, 2000; Stolzenberg & Relles, 1997). As an aside, methodologists have proposed a number of estimators that differ from those in this section. A thorough review of these procedures is beyond the scope of this chapter, but Puhani (2000) and Winship and Mare (1992) discuss a few of these alternatives.

Maximum likelihood estimates the multivariate regression model parameters (e.g., the path model in Figure 10.1) in a single analytic step. The basic logic of the estimation process is identical to what I describe in Chapters 3 and 4. That is, an iterative algorithm "auditions" different combinations of parameter values until it identifies the estimates that produce the highest likelihood of producing the sample data, assuming that $R^*$ and the outcome variable have a bivariate normal distribution in the population. Maximum likelihood estimators are available in a number of statistical software packages; readers who are interested in the technical details of the selection model likelihood function can consult Amemiya (1985, pp. 385–387).

At the time of his original work, maximum likelihood estimation routines were not yet widely available, so Heckman (1976, 1979) outlined a two-step estimator based on ordinary least squares regression (the literature also refers to this method as the **limited information maximum likelihood** estimator). The first step of Heckman's procedure uses a probit model to regress the missing data indicator $R$ on one or more covariates. The purpose of this step is to obtain the predicted probabilities of response. The second step of the procedure uses ordinary least squares with listwise deletion to estimate the substantive regression model. Heckman showed that including the predicted probabilities (or more accurately, a transformation of the probabilities called the **Mill's ratio**) as an additional explanatory variable can correct the bias in the ordinary least squares regression coefficients. As an aside, the two-step procedure underestimates standard errors, so additional computational procedures (e.g., the bootstrap, asymptotic approximations) are required to obtain accurate significance tests (Heckman, 1979).

## 10.6 LIMITATIONS OF THE SELECTION MODEL

A relatively large number of empirical studies have examined the performance of the selection model (e.g., Hartman, 1991; Leung & Yu, 1996; Manning, Duan, & Rogers, 1987; Nawata, 1993, 1994; Nelson, 1984; Paarsch, 1984; Stolzenberg & Relles, 1990). These studies suggest that the selection model can reduce or eliminate bias when its assumptions are met. However, in many realistic scenarios, the model can produce estimates that are even worse than those of MAR-based missing data handling methods. Unfortunately, these assumptions are largely untestable, so there is no practical way to judge the model's performance in a real data analysis.

The regression equation that describes the propensity to respond is the mechanism by which the selection model mitigates bias, but it is also an Achilles' heel. For one, this regression model needs to be correctly specified. As an example, one of the data analyses at the end of the chapter illustrates a situation in which missingness depends on an interactive effect, such that low-scoring cases in the treatment condition and high-scoring cases in the control condition have higher rates of missingness. The selection model that I apply to this example omits this interaction term from the regression model that predicts missingness, which ends up biasing the substantive model parameters. (This may not be the only source of bias, but it is almost certainly a contributing factor.) Unfortunately, researchers rarely know why the data are missing, so generating an appropriate set of predictors can be a challenge.

Related to the issue of model specification, empirical studies show that the selection model is highly dependent on the degree of collinearity among the predictor variables. In particular, problems arise when the predictor variables in the probit regression are correlated with those from the substantive regression model. The reason collinearity is detrimental is relatively technical (Puhani, 2000; Stolzenberg and Relles, 1997), but the problem is fairly intuitive if you consider the two-step estimator. Recall that the two-step estimator includes the predicted probabilities from the probit regression as an explanatory variable in the substantive regression model. Because the predicted probabilities are a composite of the explanatory variables in the probit model, they will be highly correlated with any variables that appear in both equations. This collinearity can introduce a substantial amount of sampling error into the estimates, and this influx of noise can be so great that it essentially negates any reduction in bias. Collinearity problems are most pronounced when the regression equations share a common set of explanatory variables. Thus, the usual recommendation is to include at least one predictor in the probit model that does not appear in the substantive regression model. However, this strategy does not necessarily solve the collinearity problem, and the selection model can produce inaccurate estimates even when the two equations contain unique sets of predictor variables.

Finally, selection model parameter estimates are highly dependent on the bivariate normality assumption for the residuals. This assumption is particularly problematic because it is largely untestable. For example, a sample of scores from a normally distributed population can appear skewed because values are systematically missing from one tail of the score distribution or because the sample accurately reflects the true shape of the population data. To make matters worse, the latent $R^*$ values are completely missing, so there is ultimately no way to verify that the joint distribution of the residuals is bivariate normal, even if the distribution of the outcome is normal. As you will see in the next section, even slight departures from normality can produce substantial bias.

## 10.7 AN ILLUSTRATIVE ANALYSIS

The MNAR models in this chapter address an important shortcoming of the MAR-based missing data-handling approaches. However, the performance of these models also depends on untestable assumptions that are unlikely to hold in real data sets. To illustrate the sensitivity of the selection model to collinearity and nonnormality, I generated three artificial data sets of $N = 2000$ cases and used maximum likelihood to estimate the selection model.* To keep things simple, I used bivariate regression models similar to those in Equations 10.4 and 10.5. To correctly model the underlying selection process, I generated a standard normal $R^*$ variable that had a population correlation of $\rho = .70$ with the outcome variable from the substantive regression model. Next, I imposed MNAR missing data by eliminating the outcome variable for cases that fell in the lowest quartile of the $R^*$ distribution. For the probit portion of the model, I generated a single explanatory variable that had a population correlation of $\rho = .40$ with $R^*$. The first artificial data set mimicked an ideal set of conditions where the predictor variables from the two regression models are uncorrelated and the entire set of variables is multivariate normal. The second data set was identical to the first, except that the explanatory variables had a modest population correlation of $\rho = .30$. In the final data set, the predictor variables were uncorrelated, but the population distribution of the outcome variable was somewhat nonnormal (skewness = 1.10 and kurtosis = 2.50).

Table 10.2 shows the intercept and slope estimates from the substantive regression model. For comparison purposes, the table also gives the estimates from a complete-data analysis and a maximum likelihood analysis that assumes an MAR mechanism. To begin, consider the estimates from the section labeled Analysis 1. These estimates represent an ideal situation in which the selection model assumptions are met. As expected, the selection model accurately adjusts for the MNAR missingness and yields estimates that are quite similar to those of the complete data. In contrast, the systematic missing data in the lower tail of the $Y$ distribution causes maximum likelihood to overestimate the regression intercept. (The explanatory variable is centered at the grand mean, so the intercept is an estimate of the outcome variable mean.)

The estimates from the section labeled Analysis 2 reflect a situation wherein the predictor variables in the two regression equations have a modest correlation. Notice that the selection model intercept estimate is approximately two standard error units below the complete-data intercept, and the slope coefficient is too high. In fact, the maximum likelihood slope estimate is far more accurate than that of the selection model. Finally, the section labeled Analysis 3 gives the estimates from a data set with a skewed outcome variable. Consistent with Analysis 2, the selection model yields biased estimates of the intercept and slope. Although the selection model intercept is somewhat more accurate than that of maximum likelihood, its slope coefficient is severely distorted.

---

*Analysis syntax and data are available on the companion website, *www.appliedmissingdata.com*.

**TABLE 10.2. Estimates from Selection Model Illustration**

| Analysis method | Intercept | | Slope | |
|---|---|---|---|---|
| | Estimate | SE | Estimate | SE |
| Analysis 1: Assumptions satisfied | | | | |
| Complete data | 100.100 | 0.205 | 0.385 | 0.021 |
| Maximum likelihood | 102.991 | 0.202 | 0.393 | 0.021 |
| Selection model | 100.325 | 0.333 | 0.384 | 0.020 |
| Analysis 2: Correlated predictors | | | | |
| Complete data | 100.080 | 0.204 | 0.393 | 0.021 |
| Maximum likelihood | 102.970 | 0.202 | 0.393 | 0.021 |
| Selection model | 99.617 | 0.249 | 0.454 | 0.018 |
| Analysis 3: Non-normal outcome variable | | | | |
| Complete data | 100.056 | 0.205 | 0.371 | 0.021 |
| Maximum likelihood | 102.609 | 0.225 | 0.409 | 0.023 |
| Selection model | 98.434 | 0.275 | 0.303 | 0.020 |

Considered as a whole, the estimates in Table 10.2 illustrate two important points. First, when its assumptions are satisfied, the selection model can virtually eliminate the bias that results from MNAR data on an outcome variable. Second, modest correlations among the predictor variables and moderate departures from normality can produce severely biased estimates. In fact, the selection model estimates may be far worse than those of maximum likelihood and multiple imputation. From a practical perspective, the estimates in Table 10.2 suggest that the selection model may be of limited utility because the conditions in Analysis 2 and Analysis 3 are probably representative of many—if not most—realistic data sets. Of course, caution is warranted in drawing firm conclusions from a single artificial data set, but the analysis results are consistent with those from published Monte Carlo studies.

## 10.8 THE PATTERN MIXTURE MODEL

The **pattern mixture model** provides an alternate framework for MNAR data (Glynn, Laird, & Rubin, 1986; Little, 1993; Rubin, 1987). Like the selection model, the pattern mixture model integrates the distribution of missingness into the analysis, but it does so in a very different fashion. Specifically, the pattern mixture approach forms subgroups of cases that share the same missing data pattern and estimates the substantive model within each pattern. Returning to the factorization in Equation 10.3, note that the pattern-specific analysis models correspond to the conditional distribution, $p(Y|R)$, and the missing data pattern proportions align with the marginal distribution, $p(R)$. The pattern-specific estimates that result from a pattern mixture model analysis are usually not of substantive interest, so averaging the estimates across the missing data patterns yields a single set of estimates that account for MNAR data. This section uses the small data set from Table 10.1 to illustrate the pattern mixture model, and I later describe variations of the model for longitudinal analyses.

Suppose that the substantive goal is to estimate the mean job performance rating. The first step of the procedure forms subgroups of cases that share the same missing data pattern. The data set in Table 10.1 has only two missing data patterns: cases with complete data on both IQ and job performance, and cases with IQ scores only. For the complete cases, it is possible to estimate the means and the variances of both variables as well as the covariance between IQ and job performance. However, the employees who quit prior to their 6-month review have no job performance ratings, so it is only possible to estimate the mean and the variance of the IQ scores. Consequently, the subgroup of cases with missing data has three inestimable parameters (i.e., the mean and the variance of the job performance ratings and the covariance between IQ and job performance).

The bivariate example illustrates an important practical problem with pattern mixture models, namely, that the patterns with missing data typically have one or more inestimable parameters. For this reason, pattern mixture models are said to be **underidentified**. In practice, estimating a pattern mixture model requires assumptions about the inestimable parameter values. To solve this problem, methodologists have proposed a number of so-called **identifying restrictions** that essentially equate the inestimable parameters from one missing data pattern to the estimable parameters from one or more of the other patterns. I describe several of these approaches later in the chapter, but for now, I focus on the complete case missing variable restriction (Little, 1993). Like its name implies, the **complete case missing variable restriction** equates the inestimable parameters from one missing data pattern to the estimable parameters of the complete cases. I illustrate how to use this approach to estimate the mean, and Little (1993, p. 128) gives the equations for estimating variances and covariances.

To illustrate the complete case missing variable restriction, reconsider the job performance data in Table 10.1. The first step is to express the job performance mean (one of the inestimable parameters) as a function of the IQ scores, as follows:

$$\mu_{JP} = \beta_0 + \beta_1(\mu_{IQ}) \tag{10.7}$$

where $\beta_0$ and $\beta_1$ are the intercept and slope coefficients, respectively, from the regression of job performance on IQ. Equation 10.7 follows from standard linear regression, where substituting the mean of an explanatory variable into the regression equation returns the outcome variable mean as a predicted score. Of course, Equation 10.7 does not solve the estimation problem because the intercept and slope coefficients are also inestimable. The complete case missing variable restriction replaces the inestimable regression coefficients with the intercept and slope from the subset of complete cases.

Returning to the data in Table 10.1, the regression coefficients for the subset of complete cases are $\hat{\beta}_0^{(C)} = 4.287$ and $\hat{\beta}_1^{(C)} = 0.069$. (Throughout the remainder of the chapter I use a superscript in parentheses to denote a specific missing data pattern.) The job performance mean for the incomplete cases is now estimable because all of the terms on the right side of Equation 10.7 have values. Specifically, substituting the regression coefficients for the complete cases and the IQ mean for the incomplete cases (i.e., $\hat{\mu}_{IQ}^{(M)} = 91.600$) into Equation 10.7 yields the following estimate of the job performance mean

$$\hat{\mu}_{JP}^{(M)} = \hat{\beta}_0^{(C)} + \hat{\beta}_1^{(C)}(\hat{\mu}_{IQ}^{(M)}) = 4.287 + 0.069(91.600) = 10.607$$

where the M and C superscripts denote the missing and complete cases, respectively. Note that the corresponding estimate for the complete cases is $\hat{\mu}_{JP}^{(C)} = 11.400$.

## Averaging across Missing Data Patterns

The pattern-specific mean estimates (i.e., $\hat{\mu}_{JP}^{(C)} = 11.400$ and $\hat{\mu}_{JP}^{(M)} = 10.607$) suggest that the employees that quit prior to their 6-month evaluation have somewhat lower job performance ratings than the employees who stay on the job. While this information is interesting and useful, the company is probably more interested in estimating the mean job performance rating for the entire population of employees. Averaging the pattern-specific estimates yields a single estimate that accounts for MNAR data. (The literature sometimes refers to this as a **marginal parameter estimate**.) More specifically, this marginal estimate is the weighted average of the pattern-specific estimates, where the weight for a given pattern is simply the proportion of cases in that pattern. Returning to the job performance example, note that the pattern proportions are $\hat{\pi}_C = 0.75$ and $\hat{\pi}_M = 0.25$ for the complete and incomplete cases, respectively. The final estimate of the job performance mean is the weighted average of the pattern-specific means, as follows.

$$\hat{\mu}_{JP} = \hat{\pi}_C\hat{\mu}_{JP}^{(C)} + \hat{\pi}_M\hat{\mu}_{JP}^{(M)} = 0.75(11.400) + 0.25(10.607) = 11.201 \qquad (10.8)$$

The previous bivariate example is far less complex than most real-world analysis problems. Nevertheless, the basic logic of the pattern mixture model (i.e., obtain pattern-specific estimates and average over the missing data patterns) applies to virtually any analysis.

As an important aside, a pattern mixture model analysis does not yield standard errors for the averaged estimates. Notice from Equation 10.8 that the final estimate of the mean is a linear combination of four estimates (i.e., the pattern-specific means and the pattern proportions), each of which is affected by sampling error. Computing the standard error for an estimate that is a function of other estimates requires a computational approach known as the delta method. I describe how to compute these standard errors later in the chapter.

## 10.9 LIMITATIONS OF THE PATTERN MIXTURE MODEL

Like the selection model, the pattern mixture model's reliance on untestable assumptions is its weakness. Although the model does not rely explicitly on distributional assumptions, it does require the user to specify values for the inestimable parameters. To the extent that these assumed values are correct, the model can reduce or eliminate bias. However, specifying the wrong values can produce substantial bias, even when the data are MAR (Demirtas & Schafer, 2003). Specifying values for the inestimable parameters is an unavoidable—and perhaps troubling—aspect of pattern mixture modeling. However, some methodologists argue that this is actually an advantage of the model because it forces researchers to make their assumptions explicit. This is in contrast to the selection model, which is only estimable because of implicit distributional assumptions (i.e., the bivariate normality of the residual terms). Like every other missing data handling method in this book, the pattern mixture model is prone to substantial bias when its assumptions are incorrect, and there is no way to test these assumptions. However, the possibility of using different approaches to generate values for the inestimable parameters makes the pattern mixture model an ideal tool for sensitivity analyses because you can examine the stability of the resulting estimates across a variety of scenarios.

## 10.10 AN OVERVIEW OF THE LONGITUDINAL GROWTH MODEL

Much of the recent methodological work on MNAR models has focused on longitudinal data analyses. In particular, methodologists have put considerable effort into the development of selection models and pattern mixture models for growth curve analyses (also known as multilevel models, linear mixed models, hierarchical linear models, and latent growth models). Because the growth model is integral to much of the remaining material in this chapter, a brief overview is warranted. Researchers in the social and the behavioral sciences routinely use the multilevel modeling framework or the structural equation modeling framework to estimate these models. This section gives a brief description of both modeling frameworks, and a number of excellent resources are available to readers who are interested in additional details (Bollen & Curran, 2006; Bryk & Raudenbush, 1987; Hancock & Lawrence, 2006; Raudenbush & Bryk, 2002; Singer & Willett, 2003).

### The Multilevel Growth Model

The multilevel growth model expresses the outcome variable as a function of a temporal predictor variable that captures the passage of time. The basic linear growth model is

$$Y_{ti} = \gamma_{00} + \gamma_{10}(TIME_{ti}) + u_{0i} + u_{1i}(TIME_{ti}) + r_{ti} \tag{10.9}$$

where $Y_{ti}$ is the outcome score for case $i$ at time $t$, $TIME_{ti}$ is the value of the temporal predictor for case $i$ at time $t$ (e.g., elapsed time, age, data collection wave), $\gamma_{00}$ is the intercept, $\gamma_{10}$ is the expected change in the outcome variable for a one-unit increment in the $TIME$ variable, $u_{0i}$ and $u_{1i}$ are residuals that allow the intercepts and the slopes to vary across individuals, and $r_{ti}$ is a time-specific residual.

To put the growth model in a substantive context, consider a longitudinal study that examines the change in depressive symptoms during the course of a two-month intervention. Furthermore, suppose that the researchers administer a depression questionnaire at the beginning of the intervention, one month after the start of the intervention, and two months after entry into treatment. In this scenario, the $TIME$ variable quantifies the number of months since the start of the intervention (i.e., 0 = the baseline assessment, 1 = the one-month follow-up, and 2 = the two-month follow-up). This coding scheme facilitates the interpretation of the model parameters, such that $\gamma_{00}$ represents the baseline mean (i.e., the expected value when the *TIME* variable equals zero) and $\gamma_{10}$ is the average change per month. The $u_{0j}$ and $u_{1j}$ terms are residuals that allow for individual differences in baseline scores and change rates, respectively. The growth model does not estimate the residuals themselves, but rather the variance of the residuals. For example, the variance of $u_{0j}$ quantifies individual differences in depression at the baseline assessment, and the variance of $u_{1j}$ captures the degree to which the change rates vary across individuals.

## The Latent Growth Curve Model

The structural equation modeling framework views the linear growth model as a two-factor confirmatory factor analysis model with a mean structure. To illustrate, Figure 10.2 shows a path diagram of the growth model from the hypothetical depression study. Consistent with standard path diagram conventions, ellipses represent latent variables, rectangles denote manifest (i.e., measured) variables, single-headed straight arrows symbolize regression coefficients, and double-headed curved arrows are correlations. For consistency, the figure uses the same notation system as Equation 10.9.

To begin, the path diagram shows the repeated measures variables (i.e., the $Y_{ti}$ values in Equation 10.9) as three rectangles. The Intercept and Slope ellipses are latent variables that represent the idealized linear growth trajectory (i.e., a latent growth curve) for a particular individual (i.e., the $u_{0i}$ and $u_{1i}$ terms in Equation 10.9, respectively). The unit factor loadings (i.e., the arrows that connect the latent variables to the manifest depression scores) for the Intercept latent variable reflect the fact that the intercept is a constant component of an individual's score at any given point in time, and the loadings for the Slope latent variable represent the amount of elapsed time between assessments (i.e., the values of the *TIME* vari-

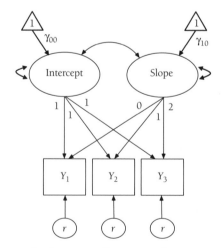

**FIGURE 10.2.** Path diagram of a three-wave linear growth curve model. The Intercept and Slope ellipses are latent variables that represent the individual growth trajectories. The primary parameters of interest are the latent variable means and the latent variable variances. The diagram denotes the means as the single-headed straight arrows linking the triangles (a column vector of ones) to the latent variables, and the variances are the double-headed curved arrows between each latent variable and itself.

able in Equation 10.9). The primary parameters of interest are the latent variable means (i.e., the $\gamma$ coefficients in Equation 10.9) and the latent variable variances. The path diagram denotes the means as single-headed straight arrows that connect the triangles (column vectors of ones) to the latent variables, and the variances are the double-headed curved arrows that link the latent variables to themselves.

Although the two modeling frameworks appear to be different from one another, the multilevel model and the structural equation model are quite similar. In fact, in many situations the two frameworks produce identical parameter estimates (Mehta & West, 2000; Raudenbush, 2001). Despite their similarity, the software programs that implement the two modeling frameworks tend to differ (sometimes dramatically) in their capabilities. Multilevel modeling software packages can estimate some of the models that I describe in this chapter, but structural equation modeling is a more flexible tool for estimating MNAR models for longitudinal data. The remainder of this chapter is devoted to selection models and pattern mixture models for longitudinal data analyses; I use structural equation modeling software to estimate several of these MNAR models later in the chapter.

## 10.11 A LONGITUDINAL SELECTION MODEL

Diggle and Kenward (1994) outline a selection model for longitudinal analyses where participants permanently drop out of a study at some point after the initial data collection wave (i.e., a monotone missing data pattern). Following the logic of the classic selection model, the **Diggle and Kenward selection model** is a two-part model that combines the growth curve analysis with an additional set of regression equations that predict response probabilities. Diggle and Kenward use a growth model similar to that in Equation 10.9 to describe the change in the repeated measures variables, and they use a logistic, rather than a probit, model for the binary missing data indicators. In the logistic portion of the model, the probability of missingness at wave $t$ depends on the outcome variable at time $t$ and the outcome variable from the previous data collection wave. The logistic model can also include any predictors from the growth portion of the model. Because logistic regression analyses are relatively common in the behavioral and the social sciences, I do not outline the model here. A number of resources are available to readers interested in additional information on logistic regression (Agresti, 2002; Cohen, Cohen, West, & Aiken, 2003; Pampel, 2000).

To illustrate the selection model, reconsider the longitudinal depression study from the previous section. Figure 10.3 shows a path diagram of the model. The rectangles labeled $R_2$ and $R_3$ are binary missing data indicators for the one- and two-month follow-up assessments, respectively. The missing data indicators take on a value of 0 at any assessment where $Y_t$ is observed, a value of 1 at the assessment immediately following dropout, and a missing value at all subsequent assessments. For example, a participant that drops out of the study after the initial data collection wave would have indicator values of $R_2 = 1$ and $R_3 = $ missing. This coding is consistent with that of a discrete-time survival model, but other schemes can be used to represent both intermittent missingness and permanent dropout (e.g., multinomial logistic codes). Note that the baseline assessment does not require a missing data indicator because the model assumes that every case has data at the beginning of the study. Although it is not

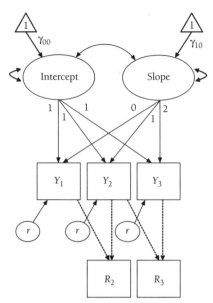

**FIGURE 10.3.** Path diagram of a three-wave selection model. The Intercept and Slope ellipses are latent variables that represent the individual growth trajectories. The primary parameters of interest are the latent variable means and the latent variable variances. The diagram denotes the means as the single-headed straight arrows linking the triangles (a column vector of ones) to the latent variables, and the variances are the double-headed curved arrows between each latent variable and itself. The dashed lines are logistic regressions that predict the binary missing data indicators (i.e., response probabilities).

immediately obvious from the diagram, the model contains a mixture of linear and logistic regression coefficients. To differentiate these two sets of coefficients, I use solid lines to denote linear regressions and dashed lines to represent logistic regressions.

In principle, the logistic regression coefficients in Figure 10.3 carry information about the missing data mechanism. For example, a significant path between $Y_2$ and $R_2$ or between $Y_3$ and $R_3$ implies an MNAR mechanism (i.e., dropout at time $t$ is related to the underlying values of $Y$ at time $t$). Similarly, a significant relationship between $Y_1$ and $R_2$ or between $Y_2$ and $R_3$ suggests that the data are MAR (i.e., dropout at time $t$ is related to the scores from a previous assessment). If the entire set of logistic regression coefficients is nonsignificant, this suggests that the data are MCAR (i.e., dropout is unrelated to variables in the model). Hypothetically, it is possible to test the MAR mechanism by comparing the fit of the model in Figure 10.3 to that of a nested model that constrains the MNAR coefficients (e.g., the regression of $R_3$ on $Y_3$) to zero. However, I previously illustrated that the selection model parameter estimates are highly sensitive to slight departures from normality, so the validity of any significance tests is highly suspect. The Diggle and Kenward model assumes that the repeated measures variables are multivariate normal, so it too is subject to substantial bias when the normality assumption is violated. The volatile nature of the selection model parameter estimates makes any test of the MAR assumption practically worthless.

A number of sources are available to readers who are interested in a more detailed description of the Diggle and Kenward selection model (Diggle & Kenward, 1994; Little, 1995; Molenberghs & Kenward, 2007; Verbeke & Molenberghs, 2000). Later in the chapter, I estimate a model that is similar to the one in Figure 10.3, and a number of practical applications of the model are available elsewhere in the literature (e.g., Foster & Fang, 2004; Kenward, 1998; Michiels, Molenberghs, Bijnens, Vangeneugden, & Thijs, 2002).

## 10.12 RANDOM COEFFICIENT SELECTION MODELS

The so-called **random coefficient selection model** (the literature also refers to this as the **shared parameter model**) is another selection-type model for longitudinal data analyses (De Gruttola & Tu, 1994; Little, 1995; Schluchter, 1992; Shih, Quan, & Chang, 1994; Wu & Carroll, 1988). Unlike the Diggle and Kenward (1994) model, the random coefficient selection model uses the individual growth curves (e.g., the latent variables in Figure 10.2, or the $u_{0i}$ and $u_{1i}$ values in Equation 10.9) to predict the probability of missing data. As an example, Figure 10.4 shows a variant of the random coefficient selection model for the earlier depression example. Consistent with the Diggle and Kenward model, the straight arrows that connect the Intercept and Slope latent variables to the missing data indicators represent logistic regression coefficients. By linking the indicator variables to the individual growth trajectories, the random effect selection model effectively allows the probability of dropout at time $t$ to depend on the entire set of repeated measures variables, including the hypothetical scores from future data collection waves (Little, 1995).

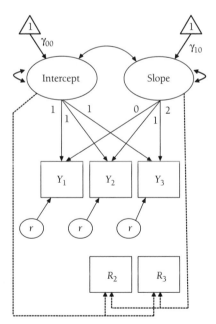

**FIGURE 10.4.** Path diagram of a three-wave random coefficient selection model. The Intercept and Slope ellipses are latent variables that represent the individual growth trajectories. The primary parameters of interest are the latent variable means and the latent variable variances. The diagram denotes the means as the single-headed straight arrows linking the triangles (a column vector of ones) to the latent variables, and the variances are the double-headed curved arrows between each latent variable and itself. The dashed lines are logistic regressions that predict the binary missing data indicators (i.e., response probabilities).

The model in Figure 10.4 is similar to that of Wu and Carroll (1988), but methodologists have proposed variations of the selection model that do not involve binary missing data indicators. For example, Schluchter (1992) and De Gruttola and Tu (1994) describe a model that replaces the binary missing data indicators with a continuous variable that quantifies the assessment at which dropout occurs. Little (1995) gives a brief description of some of these alternatives.

## 10.13 PATTERN MIXTURE MODELS FOR LONGITUDINAL ANALYSES

Applying the pattern mixture model to a longitudinal analysis follows the same basic logic as the earlier bivariate analysis example (i.e., estimate the growth model separately for each missing data pattern and compute a single set of estimates by averaging the pattern-specific regression coefficients). To illustrate the model, reconsider the longitudinal depression study from the previous section. Assuming that there is no intermittent missing data, there are three missing data patterns: cases that permanently drop out after the baseline assessment, cases that drop out after the one-month follow-up, and cases that complete the study. The pattern mixture approach estimates the linear growth curve model in Equation 10.9 separately within each missing data pattern. However, like the bivariate example, some of the model parameters are inestimable. For example, it is possible to estimate a linear function for the cases with two depression scores, but there is insufficient data to estimate the full set of variance and covariance parameters for this subgroup. The estimation problem is more obvious for the cases that drop out after the baseline assessment because there is no way to estimate a trend.

In practice, pattern mixture models require explicit assumptions about the trajectory shapes that would have resulted had the data been complete. These assumptions often take the form of extrapolation techniques that extend the pattern-specific growth trajectories beyond the range of the complete data or identifying restrictions that equate the inestimable parameters from one pattern to the estimable parameters from one or more of the other patterns. To illustrate, consider the cases that leave the depression study following the baseline assessment. The intercept coefficient (i.e., the $\gamma_{00}$ term in Equation 10.9) is estimable, but the linear trend (i.e., $\gamma_{10}$) is not. One option is to assume that the linear coefficient for the dropouts is identical to that of the complete cases; this is the complete case missing variable restriction described in the previous section. An alternative option is to assume that the inestimable linear trend is identical to the growth rate for the cases that go missing after the one-month follow-up. These are just two options for specifying the inestimable coefficients, and I describe others in the next section.

The pattern-specific growth curves are an intermediate step toward the ultimate goal, which is to estimate the population growth trajectory. Consistent with the earlier bivariate example, the population estimate is the weighted average of the pattern-specific estimates. For example, the final intercept estimate from the depression study is

$$\hat{\hat{\gamma}}_{00} = \hat{\pi}_1 \hat{\gamma}_{00}^{(1)} + \hat{\pi}_2 \hat{\gamma}_{00}^{(2)} + \hat{\pi}_3 \hat{\gamma}_{00}^{(3)} \tag{10.10}$$

where $\hat{\bar{\gamma}}_{00}$ is the average intercept, the $\hat{\pi}$ terms are the pattern proportions, and the $\hat{\gamma}_{00}^{(P)}$ co-efficients are the pattern-specific estimates. As before, the superscripts denote the missing data patterns. The average slope coefficient follows the same logic, but one of the pattern-specific estimates will appear twice in the equation. For example, the complete case missing variable restriction replaces the inestimable linear trend for Pattern 1 (the cases that drop out after baseline) with the linear coefficient from Pattern 3 (the complete cases). This identifying restriction leads to the following weighted average.

$$\hat{\bar{\gamma}}_{10} = \hat{\pi}_1\hat{\gamma}_{10}^{(3)} + \hat{\pi}_2\hat{\gamma}_{10}^{(2)} + \hat{\pi}_3\hat{\gamma}_{10}^{(3)} \tag{10.11}$$

As explained previously, special computational procedures are needed to obtain standard errors for the average estimates. These computations are explained in a later section.

## 10.14 IDENTIFICATION STRATEGIES FOR LONGITUDINAL PATTERN MIXTURE MODELS

The inherent difficulty with pattern mixture models is that the observed data do not contain enough information to estimate the pattern-specific parameters. To get around this, method-ologists have proposed a number of identification strategies that essentially augment the ob-served data with assumptions about the inestimable parameter values (Demirtas & Schafer, 2003; Fitzmaurice, Laird, & Shneyer, 2001; Hedeker & Gibbons, 1997; Little, 1993; Molen-berghs, Michiels, Kenward, & Diggle, 1998; Thijs, Molenberghs, Michiels, & Curran, 2002; Verbeke & Molenberghs, 2000). The approaches described in this section achieve identifi-cation by simplifying the model (e.g., combining missing data patterns) or by equating the inestimable parameters from one missing data pattern to the estimable parameters from an-other pattern. The literature describes other estimation strategies, but the methods described here have received the most attention. Demirtas and Schafer (2003) provide an overview of several alternatives.

### Combining Missing Data Patterns

Returning to the depression example, one way to sidestep the identification issue is to com-bine missing patterns. Specifically, combining the cases with missing values into a single pattern yields enough data to estimate a linear trend and thus eliminates the need for param-eter substitution methods. Hedeker and Gibbons (1997) describe this approach in some detail, so I henceforth refer to this method as the **Hedeker and Gibbons model**. In their analysis of psychiatric drug trial data, Hedeker and Gibbons pooled patterns with missing data into a single subgroup and used a binary variable to denote completers (i.e., the cases with complete data at every wave) and dropouts (i.e., the cases with one or more missing values). They then used the missing data indicator and a number of interaction terms as predictor variables in a linear growth model.

Returning to the depression example, the cases that leave the study prior to the two-month follow-up combine to form a single group of dropouts, and the cases that finish the study form the group of completers. Including the missing data pattern as a predictor in the growth model gives

$$
\begin{aligned}
Y_{ti} = \beta_{00} + \beta_{10}(TIME_{ti}) + \beta_{01}(DROPOUT_i) + \beta_{11}(DROPOUT_i)(TIME_{ti}) \\
+ u_{0i} + u_{1i}(TIME_{ti}) + r_{ti}
\end{aligned}
\tag{10.12}
$$

where $DROPOUT$ denotes the missing data pattern (0 = completers, 1 = dropouts). Representing the missing data patterns as a dummy variable leads to the following interpretation of the regression coefficients: $\beta_{00}$ is the baseline mean for the completers, $\beta_{10}$ is the monthly growth rate for the completers, $\beta_{01}$ is the baseline mean difference between the completers and the dropouts, and $\beta_{11}$ is the growth rate difference between the two patterns. Consequently, $\beta_{00} + \beta_{01}$ gives the baseline mean for the dropouts and $\beta_{10} + \beta_{11}$ yields the dropout growth rate. It may not be immediately obvious, but the Hedeker and Gibbons model assumes that the variance and covariance parameters are the same for both groups.

The Hedeker and Gibbons model yields pattern-specific estimates for the completers and the dropouts, and averaging the estimates follows the same procedure as before. For example, the final intercept estimate is

$$
\hat{\gamma}_{00} = \hat{\pi}_C\hat{\beta}_{00} + \hat{\pi}_D(\hat{\beta}_{00} + \hat{\beta}_{01}) = \hat{\pi}_C\hat{\gamma}_{00}^{(C)} + \hat{\pi}_D\hat{\gamma}_{00}^{(D)}
\tag{10.13}
$$

and the final slope estimate is

$$
\hat{\gamma}_{10} = \hat{\pi}_C\hat{\beta}_{10} + \hat{\pi}_D(\hat{\beta}_{10} + \hat{\beta}_{11}) = \hat{\pi}_C\hat{\gamma}_{10}^{(C)} + \hat{\pi}_D\hat{\gamma}_{10}^{(D)}
\tag{10.14}
$$

Later in the chapter I illustrate a more complex analysis example that incorporates a binary treatment variable into the model.

Perhaps the biggest advantage of the Hedeker and Gibbons model is that it does not require special software. In addition, the model is useful in studies with a large number of repeated measurements and in studies that employ individually varying assessment schedules. With a large number of repeated measurements, the number of missing data patterns is likely to be large and the number of cases within each pattern is likely to be small. When individuals have different assessment schedules, it is possible that no two cases quit the study at exactly the same time, leaving a single case per pattern. In both situations, combining missing data patterns can improve the reliability of the pattern-specific estimates. The downside of the Hedeker and Gibbons model is that it treats all incomplete cases alike. In reality, individuals that go missing at the beginning of a study may be quite different from cases that drop out near the end of a study, in which case the model can produce biased parameter estimates.

## Identifying Restrictions

A second identification strategy is to impose so-called identifying restrictions that replace the inestimable parameters from one missing data pattern with the estimates from another pattern (Demirtas & Schafer, 2003; Little, 1993; Molenberghs et al., 1998; Verbeke & Molenberghs, 2000). Methodologists have proposed a number of possible restrictions, one of which is the complete case missing variable restriction that I described previously. At an intuitive level, borrowing information from the complete cases may be undesirable, particularly if you suspect that the dropouts follow a different growth trajectory than the completers. As an alternative, the **neighboring case missing variable restriction** borrows parameter estimates from a similar group of incomplete cases. Applied to the depression study, the neighboring case restriction replaces the inestimable linear trend from Pattern 1 (the cases that drop out after the baseline assessment) with the linear coefficient from Pattern 2 (the cases that quit after the one-month follow-up). As a final option, the **available case missing variable restriction** replaces an inestimable growth coefficient with the weighted average of the estimates from other patterns. For example, in the depression study, the weighted average of the two estimable linear terms replaces the inestimable coefficient for Pattern 1, where the relative sample sizes of the two donor patterns determine the weights. I illustrate the identifying restrictions in the analysis examples at the end of the chapter.

## 10.15 DELTA METHOD STANDARD ERRORS

The final estimates from a pattern mixture model are weighted averages of the pattern-specific estimates. Because these marginal estimates are not an explicit part of the estimation routine, additional computational steps are required to obtain their standard errors. The **delta method** is a widely used technique for deriving an approximate standard error for an estimate that is a function of other model parameters and is the predominant method for generating pattern mixture model standard errors (Hedeker & Gibbons, 1997; Hogan & Laird, 1997; Molenberghs & Kenward, 2007). In this section, I use the average intercept parameter from the depression study to sketch the procedural details of the delta method, and the analysis examples in the subsequent sections provide additional details.

Applying the delta method to a pattern mixture model involves five steps: (1) obtain the first derivatives of the weighted average, (2) obtain the parameter covariance matrix for the pattern-specific growth model coefficients, (3) obtain the parameter covariance matrix for the pattern proportions, (4) combine the parameter covariance matrices into a single matrix, and (5) use the quantities from the previous steps to compute the standard error. Describing the mathematical rationale behind the computational steps is beyond the scope of this chapter, but interested readers can find accessible descriptions of the delta method elsewhere in the literature (MacKinnon, 2008, pp. 91–94; Raykov & Marcoulides, 2004).

Begin by reconsidering the average intercept estimate from the depression study.

$$\hat{\bar{\gamma}}_{00} = \hat{\pi}_1 \hat{\gamma}_{00}^{(1)} + \hat{\pi}_2 \hat{\gamma}_{00}^{(2)} + \hat{\pi}_3 \hat{\gamma}_{00}^{(3)} \tag{10.15}$$

The first step of the delta method uses differential calculus to obtain the first derivatives of the weighted average equation. You might recall from Chapter 3 that a first derivative quantifies the slope of a function at a particular value of a variable that appears in the function. The right side of the equation shows that $\hat{\bar{\gamma}}_{00}$ varies as a function of six estimates (the three pattern-specific intercept coefficients and the three pattern proportions), so there are six first derivatives. Differentiation involves a series of steps, each of which treats one of the estimates in the function as a variable while holding all other estimates constant.

To illustrate the differentiation process, consider the first derivative of the weighted average with respect to $\hat{\gamma}_{00}^{(1)}$. Differentiation treats $\hat{\gamma}_{00}^{(1)}$ as a variable and sets all other estimates constant, as follows:

$$\hat{\bar{\gamma}}_{00} = \hat{\pi}_1 \hat{\gamma}_{00}^{(1)} + (\text{constants}) \tag{10.16}$$

The derivative (i.e., slope) of a constant is zero, so the terms that do not involve $\hat{\gamma}_{00}^{(1)}$ disappear from the equation, leaving only $\hat{\pi}_1 \hat{\gamma}_{00}^{(1)}$. This remaining term is a simple linear equation that describes the influence of $\hat{\gamma}_{00}^{(1)}$ on $\hat{\bar{\gamma}}_{00}$, holding all other estimates in Equation 10.15 constant. Because $\hat{\pi}_1$ is a multiplicative constant that describes the relationship between $\hat{\gamma}_{00}^{(1)}$ and $\hat{\bar{\gamma}}_{00}$, it is the first derivative of the weighted average with respect to $\hat{\gamma}_{00}^{(1)}$. Repeating the differentiation process yields the first derivatives for the remaining parameters in Equation 10.15. For example, the first derivative with respect to $\hat{\gamma}_{00}^{(2)}$ is $\hat{\pi}_2$, the first derivative with respect to $\hat{\gamma}_{00}^{(3)}$ is $\hat{\pi}_3$, the first derivative with respect to $\hat{\pi}_1$ is $\hat{\gamma}_{00}^{(1)}$, and so on. Collecting the derivatives in a vector yields

$$\mathbf{D}^T = \begin{bmatrix} \hat{\pi}_1 & \hat{\pi}_2 & \hat{\pi}_3 & \hat{\gamma}_{00}^{(1)} & \hat{\gamma}_{00}^{(2)} & \hat{\gamma}_{00}^{(3)} \end{bmatrix} \tag{10.17}$$

Note that the order of the derivatives is important. The matrix in Equation 10.17 lists the derivatives for the pattern-specific growth model coefficients first, followed by the derivatives for the pattern proportions. The derivative vector will come up again in the final computational step.

Perhaps not surprisingly, the standard errors (or more accurately, the sampling variances) of the six estimates in Equation 10.15 play an important role in the defining the standard error of the average intercept estimate. Consequently, the next two steps of the delta method obtain parameter covariance matrices for the estimates in the weighted average. For simplicity, I temporarily separate the matrices for the regression coefficients and the pattern proportions. Recall from previous chapters that the parameter covariance matrix is a symmetric matrix that contains sampling variances (i.e., squared standard errors) on the main diagonal and has the covariances between pairs of estimates in the off-diagonal. The parameter covariance matrix for the pattern-specific intercept estimates is a 3 by 3 matrix that takes the following form.

$$\text{var}(\hat{\boldsymbol{\gamma}}) = \begin{bmatrix} \text{var}(\hat{\gamma}_{00}^{(1)}) & \text{cov}(\hat{\gamma}_{00}^{(1)}, \hat{\gamma}_{00}^{(2)}) & \text{cov}(\hat{\gamma}_{00}^{(1)}, \hat{\gamma}_{00}^{(3)}) \\ \text{cov}(\hat{\gamma}_{00}^{(2)}, \hat{\gamma}_{00}^{(1)}) & \text{var}(\hat{\gamma}_{00}^{(2)}) & \text{cov}(\hat{\gamma}_{00}^{(2)}, \hat{\gamma}_{00}^{(3)}) \\ \text{cov}(\hat{\gamma}_{00}^{(3)}, \hat{\gamma}_{00}^{(1)}) & \text{cov}(\hat{\gamma}_{00}^{(3)}, \hat{\gamma}_{00}^{(2)}) & \text{var}(\hat{\gamma}_{00}^{(3)}) \end{bmatrix} \tag{10.18}$$

Because software programs routinely report the parameter covariance matrix, obtaining $\text{var}(\hat{\boldsymbol{\gamma}})$ is simply a matter of extracting the appropriate elements from the full covariance matrix. Note that the full parameter covariance matrix will be much larger than the matrix above because it contains the variances and covariances for all model parameters, not just the intercept coefficients.

It is also necessary to obtain the parameter covariance matrix for the pattern proportions because these too are fallible estimates from the data. The pattern proportions are not explicit parameters in the pattern mixture model, so software programs do not typically report the parameter covariance matrix for these estimates. However, the necessary matrix is given by

$$\text{var}(\hat{\boldsymbol{\pi}}) = \frac{1}{N}[\text{diag}(\hat{\boldsymbol{\pi}}) - \hat{\boldsymbol{\pi}}\hat{\boldsymbol{\pi}}^T] \qquad (10.19)$$

where $\hat{\pi}$ is a column vector that contains the pattern proportions, and $\text{diag}(\hat{\pi})$ is a so-called diagonal matrix that contains the pattern proportions on the main diagonal and zero values in the off-diagonal. Continuing with the depression example, the parameter covariance matrix for the pattern proportions is as follows:

$$\text{var}(\hat{\boldsymbol{\pi}}) = N^{-1}\left(\begin{bmatrix} \hat{\pi}_1 & 0 & 0 \\ 0 & \hat{\pi}_2 & 0 \\ 0 & 0 & \hat{\pi}_3 \end{bmatrix} - \begin{bmatrix} \hat{\pi}_1 \\ \hat{\pi}_2 \\ \hat{\pi}_3 \end{bmatrix}\begin{bmatrix} \hat{\pi}_1 & \hat{\pi}_2 & \hat{\pi}_3 \end{bmatrix}\right)$$

$$= \begin{bmatrix} \text{var}(\hat{\pi}_1) & \text{cov}(\hat{\pi}_1, \hat{\pi}_3) & \text{cov}(\hat{\pi}_1, \hat{\pi}_3) \\ \text{cov}(\hat{\pi}_2, \hat{\pi}_1) & \text{var}(\hat{\pi}_2) & \text{cov}(\hat{\pi}_2, \hat{\pi}_3) \\ \text{cov}(\hat{\pi}_3, \hat{\pi}_1) & \text{cov}(\hat{\pi}_3, \hat{\pi}_2) & \text{var}(\hat{\pi}_3) \end{bmatrix} \qquad (10.20)$$

As before, the diagonal elements of $\text{var}(\hat{\pi})$ are sampling variances (i.e., squared standard errors) and the off-diagonal elements are covariances.

Having obtained separate covariance matrices for the growth model coefficients and the pattern proportions, the next step is to combine these matrices into a single parameter covariance matrix. The form of this matrix is

$$\text{var}(\hat{\boldsymbol{\gamma}}, \hat{\boldsymbol{\pi}}) = \begin{bmatrix} \text{var}(\hat{\boldsymbol{\gamma}}) & 0 \\ 0 & \text{var}(\hat{\boldsymbol{\pi}}) \end{bmatrix} \qquad (10.21)$$

where each element of the matrix is actually a standalone submatrix. For example, $\text{var}(\hat{\gamma})$ is the 3 by 3 matrix in Equation 10.18, $\text{var}(\hat{\pi})$ is the 3 by 3 matrix in Equation 10.20, and 0 is a 3 by 3 matrix containing all zeros. Combining the three submatrices yields a 6 by 6 parameter covariance matrix. The parameter order in the combined matrix corresponds to the order of the elements in the first derivative vector (i.e., the order of the rows and the columns corresponds to $\hat{\gamma}_{00}^{(1)}, \hat{\gamma}_{00}^{(2)}, \hat{\gamma}_{00}^{(3)}, \hat{\pi}_1, \hat{\pi}_2,$ and $\hat{\pi}_3$).

The final step of the delta method is to compute the standard error. The approximate sampling variance of the average intercept coefficient is as follows:

$$\text{var}(\hat{\gamma}_{00}) = D^T\text{var}(\hat{\boldsymbol{\gamma}}, \hat{\boldsymbol{\pi}})D \qquad (10.22)$$

where the outer vectors contain the first derivatives from Equation 10.17, and the inner matrix is the combined parameter covariance matrix from Equation 10.21. Note that Equation 10.22 has the same basic form as the sandwich estimator (i.e., robust) standard errors from

Chapter 5. Equation 10.22 yields a single value that is the approximate sampling variance of the average intercept coefficient, and the square root of this value is the delta method standard error. The size of the matrices in the right side of the equation will change depending on the number of missing data patterns and the specific details of the analysis, but the general form of the equation remains the same. The analysis examples in the subsequent sections provide additional details on the standard error computations.

## 10.16 OVERVIEW OF THE DATA ANALYSIS EXAMPLES

Methodologists often recommend sensitivity analyses that fit a number of different MNAR models to the same data set (Demirtas & Schafer, 2003; Michiels et al., 2002; Rubin, 1987; Verbeke & Molenberghs, 2000). In line with this recommendation, the remainder of the chapter describes several analysis examples that apply a variety of missing data models to a linear growth curve analysis. The data for the analyses consist of depression scores from 280 patients measured on three different occasions (baseline, one-month follow-up, and two-month follow-up). I generated the data to mimic a randomized trial where a researcher assigns individuals to either a treatment or a control condition. Furthermore, there are three missing data patterns within each of the two treatment arms: cases that permanently drop out after the initial wave, cases that drop out after the second wave, and cases that complete the study. Figure 10.5 shows the variable means broken down by the missing data pattern and by the treatment group.

The missing values in the longitudinal data set represent a mixture of MAR and MNAR mechanisms. Specifically, the data are MAR (i.e., missingness is dependent on baseline scores) for roughly half of the 38 cases that drop out after the baseline assessment, and the

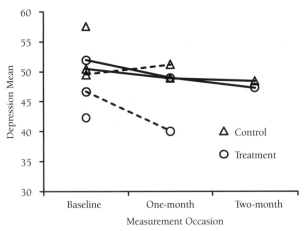

**FIGURE 10.5.** Line graph of the depression means broken down by missing data pattern and by treatment group. Within the treatment group, cases with lower scores have a higher probability of missingness, while higher scores are associated with missingness in the control group. This mechanism mimics a situation where the treatment cases that experience rapid decreases in depressive symptoms have a tendency to leave the study, whereas the control cases with the highest depression scores are more likely to drop out.

data are MNAR for all cases that drop out after the one-month follow-up. Within the treatment group, cases with lower scores have a higher probability of missingness, while higher scores are associated with missingness in the control group. This mechanism mimics a situation in which the treatment cases that experience the greatest improvement (i.e., rapid decreases in depressive symptoms) have a tendency to leave the study because they are no longer feeling depressed, whereas the control cases with the highest depression scores are more likely to drop out because their symptoms are not improving.

The substantive goal of this analysis is to determine whether the average change rates differ by treatment condition (i.e., determine whether there is treatment group by time interaction). The substantive analysis is a linear growth curve model where a binary treatment indicator (0 = control, 1 = treatment) predicts the intercepts and slopes, as follows:

$$Y_{ti} = \gamma_{00} + \gamma_{10}(TIME_{ti}) + \gamma_{01}(TXGROUP_i) + \gamma_{11}(TXGROUP_i)(TIME_{ti})$$
$$+ u_{0i} + u_{1i}(TIME_{ti}) + r_{ti} \qquad (10.23)$$

In the model above, the *TIME* variable is a temporal predictor that takes on a value of 0 at baseline, a value of 1 at the one-month follow-up, and a value of 2 at the two-month follow-up. This coding scheme facilitates the interpretation of the model parameters, such that $\gamma_{00}$ represents the control group mean at the baseline assessment and $\gamma_{10}$ is the average change per month for the control group. Because a dummy variable represents treatment group membership, the $\gamma_{01}$ coefficient gives the baseline mean difference between the treatment and the control group, and $\gamma_{11}$ quantifies the growth rate difference between the two conditions (i.e., the treatment group by time interaction). Finally, the $u_{0j}$ and $u_{1j}$ terms are residuals that allow for individual differences in initial status and change rates, respectively, and $r_{ij}$ is a residual that captures the remaining within-person variation that exists after accounting for the passage of time. The growth model does not estimate the residuals themselves, but rather the variance of the residuals (e.g., the variance of $u_{0j}$ quantifies individual score differences at the first wave, the variance of $u_{1j}$ captures heterogeneity in the individual growth trajectories). Figure 10.6 shows a path diagram of the model.

## Complete-Data Analysis Results

As a reference point, I estimated the growth model in Equation 10.23 prior to deleting any values from the data set. The control group had a baseline mean of $\hat{\gamma}_{00} = 51.109$ and a nonsignificant monthly change rate, $\hat{\gamma}_{10} = -0.543$, $z = -1.16$, $p = .24$. The treatment group did not differ from the control group at baseline, $\hat{\gamma}_{01} = -1.498$, $z = -1.25$, $p = .21$, which is to be expected in a randomized study. Finally, the key parameter of interest—the treatment group by time interaction—was statistically significant and indicated that the treatment cases declined more rapidly than the control cases, $\hat{\gamma}_{11} = -1.680$, $z = -2.56$, $p = .01$ (the treatment group slope was $\hat{\gamma}_{10} + \hat{\gamma}_{11} = -2.223$). Although the preceding estimates are not identical to the true population values, they can serve as a useful benchmark for comparing the performance of the missing data models.

The presence of a significant interaction effect suggests that the intervention produced a mean difference at the end of the study. The growth model parameter estimates can generate

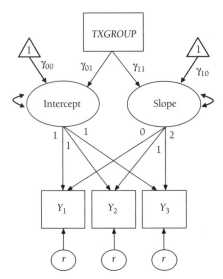

**FIGURE 10.6.** Path diagram of a three-wave linear growth curve model with a binary predictor variable. The Intercept and Slope ellipses are latent variables that represent the individual growth trajectories. The diagram denotes the control group baseline mean and slope (i.e., $\gamma_{00}$ and $\gamma_{10}$, respectively) as the single-headed straight arrows linking the triangles (a column vector of ones) to the latent variables. The arrows connecting the binary predictor variable to the latent variables are the treatment group differences in the baseline mean and growth rate (i.e., $\gamma_{01}$ and $\gamma_{11}$, respectively). The latent variable variances are the double-headed curved arrows between each latent variable and itself.

model-predicted means for each group at the two-month follow-up. For example, the expected value for the control group is

$$\hat{Y}_C = \hat{\gamma}_{00} + \hat{\gamma}_{10}(TIME_{ti}) = 51.109 - 0.543(2) = 50.023 \tag{10.24}$$

and the corresponding estimate for the treatment group is

$$\hat{Y}_T = \left(\hat{\gamma}_{00} + \hat{\gamma}_{01}\right) + \left(\hat{\gamma}_{10} + \hat{\gamma}_{11}\right)(TIME_{ti}) = 49.611 - 2.223(2) = 45.165 \tag{10.25}$$

Subtracting the two means and expressing the absolute difference relative to the pooled baseline standard deviation ($SD = 10.44$) gives a standardized mean difference of $d = 0.47$, which is just shy of Cohen's (1988) benchmark for a medium effect size (i.e., $d > 0.50$). I use this effect size as a baseline for comparing the relative performance of the subsequent missing data models.

## 10.17 DATA ANALYSIS EXAMPLE 1

The first analysis example uses MAR-based maximum likelihood missing data handling to estimate the growth model in Equation 10.23.* Table 10.3 gives the parameter estimates and

---

*Analysis syntax and data are available on the companion website, *www.appliedmissingdata.com.*

**TABLE 10.3 Maximum Likelihood Estimates from Analysis Example 1**

| Parameter | Estimate | SE | z | p |
|---|---|---|---|---|
| Control baseline mean ($\gamma_{00}$) | 51.260 | 0.862 | 59.482 | < .001 |
| Control growth rate ($\gamma_{10}$) | –1.188 | 0.516 | –2.304 | 0.021 |
| Baseline difference ($\gamma_{01}$) | –1.559 | 1.241 | –1.284 | 0.199 |
| Growth rate difference ($\gamma_{11}$) | –0.836 | 0.726 | –1.151 | 0.250 |
| Wave 3 mean difference ($d$) | 0.310 | | | |

*Note.* For comparison purposes, the complete-data estimates are $\gamma_{00} = 51.109$, $\gamma_{10} = -0.543$, $\gamma_{01} = -1.498$, and $\gamma_{11} = -1.680$. The effect size at the two-month follow-up is $d = 0.466$.

standard errors from this analysis. As seen in the table, maximum likelihood produced a nonsignificant baseline mean difference that was quite similar to that of complete-data analysis ($\hat{\gamma}_{01} = -1.559$ versus $\hat{\gamma}_{01} = -1.498$, respectively). The similarity of these two estimates is probably not surprising given that the baseline scores were complete. However, the MAR-based analysis produced a very different substantive conclusion about the treatment effect. Specifically, the control group showed a significant decrease in depressive symptoms over time, $\hat{\gamma}_{10} = -1.188$, $z = -2.30$, $p = .02$, and the treatment group by time interaction was non-significant, $\hat{\gamma}_{11} = -0.836$, $z = -1.15$, $p = .25$, suggesting that the two groups effectively changed at the same rate.

Substituting the maximum likelihood parameter estimates into Equations 10.24 and 10.25 gives model-predicted means of $\hat{Y}_T = 45.653$ and $\hat{Y}_C = 48.884$ for the treatment and the control group, respectively. Expressing the absolute difference in these means relative to the pooled baseline standard deviation ($SD = 10.44$) yields a standardized mean difference of $d = 0.31$, a value that is noticeably lower than the $d = 0.47$ effect size from the complete-data analysis. The fact that the maximum likelihood attenuates the treatment effect makes intuitive sense given that values are systematically missing from the upper tail of the control group distribution and the lower tail of the treatment group distribution.

## 10.18 DATA ANALYSIS EXAMPLE 2

The second analysis example applies the Diggle and Kenward (1994) selection model to depression data.* Recall that the selection model augments the growth model with a logistic model that predicts the response probabilities. Applying the selection model to the depression data requires a binary missing data indicator (1 = missing, 0 = complete) for both the one-month and the two-month follow-up assessments. (The baseline measurement does not require an indicator because the data are complete.) In the logistic portion of the model, the probability of missingness at the one-month follow-up depends on the depression scores at baseline, the depression scores at the one-month follow-up, and the treatment group dummy variable. Similarly, the probability of missing data at the two-month follow-up depends on scores from the one-month follow-up, scores from the two-month follow-up, and the dummy variable. Figure 10.7 shows a path model diagram of the selection model. To differentiate the

---

*Analysis syntax and data are available on the companion website, *www.appliedmissingdata.com*.

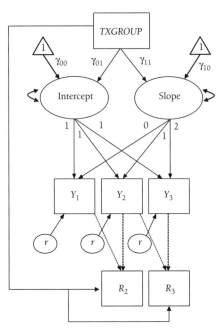

**FIGURE 10.7.** Path diagram of a three-wave selection model with a binary predictor variable. The Intercept and Slope ellipses are latent variables that represent the individual growth trajectories. The diagram denotes the control group baseline mean and slope (i.e., $\gamma_{00}$ and $\gamma_{10}$, respectively) as the single-headed straight arrows linking the triangles (a column vector of ones) to the latent variables. The arrows connecting the binary predictor variable to the latent variables are the treatment group differences in the baseline mean and growth rate (i.e., $\gamma_{01}$ and $\gamma_{11}$, respectively). The dashed lines are logistic regressions that predict the binary missing data indicators (i.e., response probabilities).

growth model from the logistic model, the figure uses solid lines to denote linear regressions and uses dashed lines to represent logistic regressions. For consistency, I continue to use the multilevel modeling notation from the previous analyses.

Table 10.4 shows the parameter estimates and standard errors from the selection model analysis. The top portion of the table contains the growth model parameter estimates, and the bottom portion of the table gives the estimates from the logistic model. As seen in the table, the control group had a baseline mean of $\hat{\gamma}_{00} = 51.231$, and the initial mean difference between the two groups was non-significant, $\hat{\gamma}_{01} = -1.506$, $z = -1.24$, $p = .21$. The control group showed no significant decrease in depressive symptoms over time, $\hat{\gamma}_{10} = -1.383$, $z = -.832$, $p = .40$, and the treatment group by time interaction was nonsignificant, $\hat{\gamma}_{11} = -.805$, $z = -1.08$, $p = .28$.

Substituting the growth model estimates into Equations 10.24 and 10.25 gives model-predicted means of $\hat{Y}_T = 45.397$ and $\hat{Y}_C = 48.465$ for the treatment and the control group, respectively. Expressing the absolute difference in the means relative to the pooled baseline standard deviation ($SD = 10.44$) yields a standardized mean difference of $d = .29$, which is slightly less than a medium effect size by Cohen's (1988) standards. Notice that the selection model produced the same substantive conclusion as the maximum likelihood analysis (i.e.,

**Table 10.4. Selection Model Estimates from Analysis Example 2**

| Parameter | Estimate | SE | $z$ | $p$ |
|---|---|---|---|---|
| | Growth model | | | |
| Control baseline mean ($\gamma_{00}$) | 51.231 | 0.862 | 59.419 | < 0.001 |
| Control growth rate ($\gamma_{10}$) | −1.383 | 1.663 | −0.832 | 0.405 |
| Baseline difference ($\gamma_{01}$) | −1.506 | 1.212 | −1.242 | 0.214 |
| Growth rate difference ($\gamma_{11}$) | −0.781 | 0.783 | −0.998 | 0.318 |
| Wave 3 mean difference ($d$) | 0.290 | | | |
| | Logistic model | | | |
| $\beta_1$ ($Y_{t-1} \rightarrow R_t$) | −0.007 | 0.097 | −0.072 | 0.943 |
| $\beta_2$ ($Y_t \rightarrow R_t$) | −0.022 | 0.185 | −0.119 | 0.906 |
| $\beta_3$ (*TXGROUP* $\rightarrow R_t$) | −0.215 | 0.392 | −0.549 | 0.583 |

*Note:* For comparison purposes, the complete-data estimates are $\gamma_{00} = 51.109$, $\gamma_{10} = -0.543$, $\gamma_{01} = -1.498$, and $\gamma_{11} = -1.680$. The effect size at the 2-month follow-up is $d = 0.466$.

the control group improved at roughly the same rate as the treatment group), and underestimated the complete-data effect size by about the same amount.

Although the regression coefficients from the selection portion of the model are not of substantive interest, they warrant a brief discussion. It is important to reiterate that the estimates in the bottom portion of Table 10.4 are logistic regression coefficients. For example, consider the regression of the missing data indicators (1 = missing, 0 = complete) on treatment group membership, $\hat{\beta}_3 = -.215$. This coefficient indicates that treatment group membership decreases the log odds of missing data by −.215, holding other predictor variables constant. The fact that the logistic coefficients are not significant may owe to the fact that the selection portion of the model is misspecified. Recall that the relationship between depression scores and missingness is in the opposite direction for the two intervention groups. Returning to the path diagram in Figure 10.7, there is no interaction term in the model that captures the moderating influence of treatment group membership on the relationship between depression scores and missingness, and this misspecification likely explains at least part of the bias in the growth model estimates. Of course, in any real-world data analysis, there is no way of knowing whether the logistic regressions accurately depict the underlying missing data mechanism, so it is impossible to judge the accuracy of the selection model parameter estimates. The results of this analysis underscore the important conclusion that the accuracy of any missing data analysis—not just an MAR-based analysis—depends on the veracity of its assumptions.

## 10.19 DATA ANALYSIS EXAMPLE 3

The third data analysis example applies the Hedeker and Gibbons (1997) pattern mixture model to the depression data.* Recall from a previous section that Hedeker and Gibbons

---

*Analysis syntax and data are available on the companion website, *www.appliedmissingdata.com.*

generate pattern-specific parameter estimates by incorporating a binary missing data indicator as an explanatory variable in the growth model. To apply their model to the depression data, I classified cases as completers (i.e., the individuals with complete data at the two-month follow-up) or dropouts (i.e., the cases with one or more missing values) and estimated the following growth model.

$$
\begin{aligned}
Y_{ti} = {}& \beta_{00} + \beta_{01}(TXGROUP_i) + \beta_{02}(DROPOUT_i) + \beta_{03}(TXGROUP_i)(DROPOUT_i) \\
& + \beta_{10}(TIME_{ti}) + \beta_{11}(TXGROUP_i)(TIME_{ti}) + \beta_{12}(DROPOUT_i)(TIME_{ti}) \qquad (10.26) \\
& + \beta_{13}(DROPOUT_i)(TXGROUP_i)(TIME_{ti}) + u_{0i} + u_{1i}(TIME_{ti}) + r_{ti}
\end{aligned}
$$

Because the regression coefficients in this equation ultimately combine to produce pattern-specific estimates of the four coefficients in Equation 10.23 (i.e., $\gamma_{00}$, $\gamma_{01}$, $\gamma_{10}$, and $\gamma_{11}$), I use $\beta$ in order to avoid any confusion that might result from using two sets of $\gamma$ coefficients.

In Equation 10.26, $DROPOUT$ is a binary variable that denotes the two missing data patterns (0 = completers, 1 = dropouts). Substituting $DROPOUT = 0$ into the equation eliminates several terms, leaving only the coefficients for the complete cases. Within the subsample of completers, $\beta_{00}$ and $\beta_{10}$ quantify the mean initial status and the mean growth rate for the control group, respectively, $\beta_{01}$ is the baseline mean difference between the treatment and the control group, and $\beta_{11}$ is the growth rate difference between the groups. These coefficients alone define the growth model parameters for the completers, as follows:

$$
\begin{aligned}
\hat{Y}_{ti}^{(C)} &= \hat{\beta}_{00} + \hat{\beta}_{10}(TIME_{ti}) + \hat{\beta}_{01}(TXGROUP_i) + \hat{\beta}_{11}(TXGROUP_i)(TIME_{ti}) \\
&= \hat{\gamma}_{00}^{(C)} + \hat{\gamma}_{10}^{(C)}(TIME_{ti}) + \hat{\gamma}_{01}^{(C)}(TXGROUP_i) + \hat{\gamma}_{11}^{(C)}(TXGROUP_i)(TIME_{ti})
\end{aligned} \qquad (10.27)
$$

Substituting $DROPOUT = 1$ into Equation 10.26 activates four coefficients that quantify differences between the two missing data patterns. Specifically, $\beta_{02}$ is the amount by which the baseline control group mean differs between the completers and the dropouts and $\beta_{12}$ is the amount by which the control group growth rate differs between missing data patterns. Similarly, $\beta_{03}$ and $\beta_{13}$ quantify the extent to which the treatment group regression coefficients (i.e., the baseline mean difference and slope difference, respectively) differ between the completers and the dropouts. Consequently, the regression coefficients from Equation 10.26 model combine to produce the growth model parameters for the dropouts, as follows:

$$
\begin{aligned}
\hat{Y}_{ti}^{(D)} &= \left(\hat{\beta}_{00} + \hat{\beta}_{02}\right) + \left(\hat{\beta}_{10} + \hat{\beta}_{12}\right)(TIME_{ti}) + \left(\hat{\beta}_{01} + \hat{\beta}_{03}\right)(TXGROUP_i) \\
&\quad + \left(\hat{\beta}_{11} + \hat{\beta}_{13}\right)(TXGROUP_i)(TIME_{ti}) \\
&= \hat{\gamma}_{00}^{(D)} + \hat{\gamma}_{10}^{(D)}(TIME_{ti}) + \hat{\gamma}_{01}^{(D)}(TXGROUP_i) \\
&\quad + \hat{\gamma}_{11}^{(D)}(TXGROUP_i)(TIME_{ti})
\end{aligned} \qquad (10.28)
$$

Table 10.5 gives the parameter estimates and standard errors from the Hedeker and Gibbons model. Substituting the regression coefficients into Equations 10.27 and 10.28 gives the pattern-specific estimates in Table 10.6. Notice that the baseline mean difference between the treatment and the control cases is substantially larger in the dropout group than in the completer group ($\hat{\gamma}_{01}^{(D)} = -8.701$ versus $\hat{\gamma}_{01}^{(C)} = 1.467$, respectively), and the treat-

**TABLE 10.5. Hedeker and Gibbons Model Estimates from Analysis Example 3**

| Parameter | Estimate | SE | z | p |
|---|---|---|---|---|
| | *Completer estimates* | | | |
| Control baseline mean ($\beta_{00}$) | 50.298 | 0.993 | 50.642 | < .001 |
| Control growth rate ($\beta_{10}$) | −1.015 | 0.547 | −1.855 | 0.064 |
| Baseline difference ($\beta_{01}$) | 1.467 | 1.384 | 1.060 | 0.289 |
| Growth rate difference ($\beta_{11}$) | −1.320 | 0.763 | −1.730 | 0.084 |
| | *Difference between dropout and completer estimates* | | | |
| Control baseline mean ($\beta_{02}$) | 3.034 | 1.848 | 1.641 | 0.101 |
| Control growth rate ($\beta_{12}$) | 0.777 | 1.929 | 0.403 | 0.687 |
| Baseline difference ($\beta_{03}$) | −10.168 | 2.652 | −3.834 | < .001 |
| Growth rate difference ($\beta_{13}$) | −4.059 | 2.790 | −1.455 | 0.146 |

ment group by time interaction is also more pronounced for the dropouts ($\hat{\gamma}_{11}^{(D)} = -5.378$ versus $\hat{\gamma}_{11}^{(C)} = 1.320$, respectively).

The product of a pattern mixture model is a set of estimates that averages over the missing data patterns. To illustrate, consider the treatment group by time interaction (i.e., the $\gamma_{11}$ coefficient in Equation 10.23). The proportion of completers and dropouts is $\hat{\pi}_C = 0.714$ and $\hat{\pi}_D = 0.286$, respectively, so the weighted average is

$$\hat{\bar{\gamma}}_{11} = \hat{\pi}_C \hat{\gamma}_{11}^{(C)} + \hat{\pi}_D \hat{\gamma}_{11}^{(D)} = 0.714(-1.320) + 0.286(-5.378) = -2.479 \qquad (10.29)$$

Note that Hedeker and Gibbons (1997, p. 74) describe an alternate weighting scheme that stratifies the pattern proportions by treatment group. The depression data set has very similar completion rates in the two treatment conditions (approximately 70% in the treatment group and 73% in the control), so using the overall pattern proportions is appropriate. However, in situations where the completion rates are significantly different, stratifying the proportions is likely to improve the resulting estimates.

Table 10.7 shows the average parameter estimates and the delta method standard errors from the pattern mixture model analysis. As seen in the table, the control group had a baseline mean of $\hat{\bar{\gamma}}_{00} = 51.165$, and the baseline mean difference between the two groups was

**TABLE 10.6. Pattern-Specific Estimates from Analysis Example 3**

| Parameter | Completers ($\hat{\pi}_C = 0.714$) | Dropouts ($\hat{\pi}_D = 0.286$) |
|---|---|---|
| Control baseline mean ($\gamma_{00}$) | 50.298 | 53.332 |
| Control growth rate ($\gamma_{10}$) | −1.015 | −0.238 |
| Baseline difference ($\gamma_{01}$) | 1.467 | −8.701 |
| Growth rate difference ($\gamma_{11}$) | −1.320 | −5.378 |

**TABLE 10.7. Average Pattern Mixture Model Estimates from Analysis Example 3**

| Parameter | Estimate | SE | $z$ | $p$ |
|---|---|---|---|---|
| Control baseline mean ($\gamma_{00}$) | 51.165 | 0.842 | 60.775 | < .001 |
| Control growth rate ($\gamma_{10}$) | –0.793 | 0.658 | –1.206 | 0.228 |
| Baseline difference ($\gamma_{01}$) | –1.438 | 1.213 | –1.185 | 0.236 |
| Growth rate difference ($\gamma_{11}$) | –2.479 | 0.947 | –2.617 | 0.009 |
| Wave 3 mean difference ($d$) | 0.613 | | | |

*Note.* For comparison purposes, the complete-data estimates are $\gamma_{00} = 51.109$, $\gamma_{10} = -.543$, $\gamma_{01} = -1.498$, and $\gamma_{11} = -1.680$. The effect size at the 2-month follow-up is $d = 0.466$.

nonsignificant, $\hat{\gamma}_{01} = -1.438$, $z = -1.19$, $p = .24$. Consistent with the complete-data analysis, the monthly change rate for the control group was nonsignificant, $\hat{\gamma}_{10} = -0.793$, $z = -1.21$, $p = .23$, and the treatment group by time interaction was significant, $\hat{\gamma}_{11} = -2.479$, $z = -2.62$, $p = .01$, such that the treatment group showed a more rapid decrease in symptoms.

Substituting the growth model estimates into Equations 10.24 and 10.25 gives model-predicted means of $\hat{Y}_T = 43.183$ and $\hat{Y}_C = 49.579$ for the treatment and the control group, respectively. Expressing the absolute difference in the means relative to the pooled baseline standard deviation ($SD = 10.44$) yields a standardized mean difference of $d = 0.61$, which exceeds Cohen's (1988) benchmark for a medium effect size (i.e., $d > 0.50$). Thus far, the pattern mixture model is the only missing data analysis to produce the same substantive conclusion as the complete-data analysis (i.e., the treatment group improved at a more rapid pace than the control group). However, the accuracy of the final point estimates was comparable to that of the MAR-based analysis, such that the pattern mixture model overestimated the complete-data effect size ($d = 0.47$) by roughly the same amount that maximum likelihood underestimated the effect size.

## Standard Error Computations

Because the estimates in Table 10.7 are weighted averages of other model parameters, it is necessary to use the delta method to compute their standard errors. In this section, I briefly sketch the computational steps for the treatment group by time interaction (i.e., the $\hat{\gamma}_{11}$ coefficient), but the process is largely the same for the remaining parameters. A SAS program that automates these computations is available on the companion website, so readers who are not interested in the technical details can skip to the next analysis example.

It is useful to express the average estimate as a function of its component estimates, as follows:

$$\hat{\gamma}_{11} = \hat{\pi}_C\hat{\beta}_{11} + \hat{\pi}_D\left(\hat{\beta}_{11} + \hat{\beta}_{13}\right) \tag{10.30}$$

The first step of the delta method is to obtain the first derivatives for each estimate in the weighted average. The interaction coefficient is a function of four unique estimates (two pattern-specific regression coefficients and two pattern proportions), so there are four first derivatives. Differentiating the right side of Equation 10.30 with respect to each estimate gives the following derivative vector:

$$D = \begin{bmatrix} (\hat{\pi}_C + \hat{\pi}_D) \\ \hat{\pi}_D \\ \hat{\beta}_{11} \\ (\hat{\beta}_{11} + \hat{\beta}_{13}) \end{bmatrix}$$

where $\hat{\pi}_C + \hat{\pi}_D$ is the first derivative with respect to $\hat{\beta}_{11}$, $\hat{\pi}_D$ is the first derivative with respect to $\hat{\beta}_{13}$, $\hat{\beta}_{11}$ is the first derivative with respect to $\hat{\pi}_C$, and $\hat{\beta}_{11} + \hat{\beta}_{13}$ is the derivative for $\hat{\pi}_D$.

The next two steps of the delta method construct a parameter covariance matrix for the estimates in the weighted average. The covariance matrix for the regression coefficients is a 2 by 2 matrix that has sampling variances (i.e., squared standard errors) on the diagonal and the covariance between $\hat{\beta}_{11}$ and $\hat{\beta}_{13}$ on the off-diagonals. To obtain this matrix, you simply extract the appropriate elements from the full parameter covariance matrix that appears on the computer output. The covariance matrix for the pattern proportions is not a direct by-product of the pattern mixture model, but it is relatively easy to compute from Equation 10.19. The final parameter covariance matrix is a block diagonal matrix that combines the two previous matrices. The form of this matrix is as follows:

$$\mathrm{var}(\hat{\boldsymbol{\beta}}, \hat{\boldsymbol{\pi}}) = \begin{bmatrix} \mathrm{var}(\hat{\boldsymbol{\beta}}) & 0 \\ 0 & \mathrm{var}(\hat{\boldsymbol{\pi}}) \end{bmatrix}$$

$$= \begin{bmatrix} \mathrm{var}(\hat{\beta}_{11}) & \mathrm{cov}(\hat{\beta}_{11}, \hat{\beta}_{13}) & 0 & 0 \\ \mathrm{cov}(\hat{\beta}_{13}, \hat{\beta}_{11}) & \mathrm{var}(\hat{\beta}_{13}) & 0 & 0 \\ 0 & 0 & \mathrm{var}(\hat{\pi}_C) & \mathrm{cov}(\hat{\pi}_C, \hat{\pi}_D) \\ 0 & 0 & \mathrm{cov}(\hat{\pi}_D, \hat{\pi}_C) & \mathrm{var}(\hat{\pi}_D) \end{bmatrix}$$

The final step of the delta method is to compute the standard error. Pre- and postmultiplying the parameter covariance matrix by the previous derivative vector (see Equation 10.22) yields the sampling variance for the interaction coefficient, and taking the square root of this value gives its standard error.

## 10.20 DATA ANALYSIS EXAMPLE 4

The Hedeker and Gibbons (1997) model uses a binary missing data indicator and a number of product terms to generate pattern-specific growth model estimates. Another option is to estimate the growth model in Equation 10.23 separately within each missing data pattern. The difficulty with this approach is that some patterns may not have enough data to support estimation. For example, in the depression data, the cases that drop out after the baseline assessment have two inestimable parameters: the control group slope (i.e., the $\gamma_{10}$ coefficient) and the treatment group by time interaction (i.e., the $\gamma_{11}$ coefficient). A solution to this problem is to impose identifying restrictions that replace the inestimable parameters from one missing data pattern with the estimates from another pattern. The data analyses in this section illustrate two such strategies—the complete case missing variable restriction and the neighboring case missing variable restriction.

Traditionally, methodologists have used multilevel multiple imputation routines to fill in the data in a manner consistent with a particular identifying restriction (Demirtas & Schafer, 2003; Thijs et al., 2002; Verbeke & Molenberghs, 2000). The need for imputation largely arose from a lack of maximum likelihood estimation options, but it is now possible to use certain structural equation modeling programs (e.g., Mplus; Muthén & Muthén, 1998–2009) to estimate pattern mixture models with identifying restrictions. The structural equation modeling approach treats the missing data patterns as known latent classes. That is, unlike traditional latent class analyses, the model assigns cases to classes with a probability of either one or zero (probabilities that are usually estimated from the data). For example, the depression data set has three missing data patterns and thus three latent classes. The cases that drop out after the baseline assessment define one of the latent classes, and these cases have a zero probability of belonging to one of the other two classes. The structural equation modeling approach allows each missing data pattern to have a unique set of parameter estimates, and between-class equality constraints provide a way to implement the identifying restrictions (e.g., by fixing the inestimable parameters from one pattern equal to the estimable parameters from another pattern).

Turning to the depression data, I used structural equation modeling software to estimate a pattern mixture model with three known latent classes (i.e., missing data patterns).* Within each pattern, I estimated the growth model from Equation 10.23. As I explained previously, the cases that drop out after the baseline assessment (i.e., Pattern 1) have two inestimable parameters—the control group slope and the growth rate difference (i.e., the treatment group by time interaction). The complete case missing variable restriction equates these inestimable parameters to the estimates from the complete cases (i.e., Pattern 3). Consequently, the Pattern 1 growth model is

$$\hat{Y}_{ti}^{(1)} = \hat{\gamma}_{00}^{(1)} + \hat{\gamma}_{10}^{(3)}(TIME_{ti}) + \hat{\gamma}_{01}^{(1)}(TXGROUP_i) + \hat{\gamma}_{11}^{(3)}(TXGROUP_i)(TIME_{ti}) \quad (10.31)$$

where the numeric superscript denotes the missing data pattern. In a similar vein, the neighboring case missing variable restriction equates the inestimable parameters with the estimates from the cases that drop out after the one-month follow-up (i.e., Pattern 2). The result is the following model.

$$\hat{Y}_{ti}^{(1)} = \hat{\gamma}_{00}^{(1)} + \hat{\gamma}_{10}^{(2)}(TIME_{ti}) + \hat{\gamma}_{01}^{(1)}(TXGROUP_i) + \hat{\gamma}_{11}^{(2)}(TXGROUP_i)(TIME_{ti}) \quad (10.32)$$

Procedurally, I implemented the identifying restrictions by constraining pairs of parameters to be equal during estimation. For example, I implemented the complete case missing variable restriction by specifying an equality constraint on the control group slope for Pat-

* Analysis syntax and data are available on the companion website, *www.appliedmissingdata.com*.

terns 1 and 3. Specifying these equality constraints is straightforward in structural equation modeling software packages. As an important aside, the missing data make it difficult or impossible to estimate pattern-specific variance estimates. To get around this problem, I estimated a model that assumes a common covariance matrix across patterns. Although it is not necessarily obvious, the Hedeker and Gibbons (1997) model makes the same assumption.

Table 10.8 gives the pattern-specific growth model estimates for both identifying restrictions. Notice that the growth rate parameters (i.e., the $\gamma_{10}$ and $\gamma_{11}$ coefficients) for Pattern 1 are identical to those of either Pattern 2 or Pattern 3, which is a consequence of implementing the identifying restrictions. The product of a pattern mixture model is a set of estimates that averages over the missing data patterns. To illustrate, consider the baseline mean difference between the treatment and the control group (i.e., the $\gamma_{01}$ coefficient in Equation 10.23). The missing data pattern proportions are $\hat{\pi}_1 = 0.136$, $\hat{\pi}_2 = 0.150$, and $\hat{\pi}_3 = 0.714$, so the average estimate is

$$
\begin{aligned}
\hat{\bar{\gamma}}_{01} &= \hat{\pi}_1\hat{\gamma}_{01}^{(1)} + \hat{\pi}_2\hat{\gamma}_{01}^{(2)} + \hat{\pi}_3\hat{\gamma}_{01}^{(3)} \\
&= 0.136(-15.218) + 0.150(-2.801) + 0.714(1.468) = -1.437
\end{aligned}
\tag{10.33}
$$

Because this parameter is estimable in each pattern, the complete case and the neighboring case missing variable restrictions produce the same average estimate. As a second example, consider the treatment group by time interaction (i.e., the $\gamma_{11}$ coefficient in Equation 10.23). The average estimate from the complete case missing variable restriction model is

$$
\begin{aligned}
\hat{\bar{\gamma}}_{11} &= \hat{\pi}_1\hat{\gamma}_{11}^{(3)} + \hat{\pi}_2\hat{\gamma}_{11}^{(2)} + \hat{\pi}_3\hat{\gamma}_{11}^{(3)} \\
&= 0.136(-1.319) + 0.150(-8.331) + 0.714(-1.319) = -2.371
\end{aligned}
\tag{10.34}
$$

**TABLE 10.8. Pattern-Specific Estimates from Analysis Example 4**

| Parameter | Pattern 1 ($\hat{\pi}_1 = 0.136$) | Pattern 2 ($\hat{\pi}_2 = 0.150$) | Pattern 3 ($\hat{\pi}_3 = 0.714$) |
|---|---|---|---|
| Complete case missing variable restriction | | | |
| Control baseline mean ($\gamma_{00}$) | 57.551 | 49.500 | 50.297 |
| Control growth rate ($\gamma_{10}$) | −1.015 | 1.681 | −1.015 |
| Baseline difference ($\gamma_{01}$) | −15.218 | −2.801 | 1.468 |
| Growth rate difference ($\gamma_{11}$) | −1.319 | −8.331 | −1.319 |
| Neighboring case missing variable restriction | | | |
| Control baseline mean ($\gamma_{00}$) | 57.551 | 49.500 | 50.297 |
| Control growth rate ($\gamma_{10}$) | 1.681 | 1.681 | −1.015 |
| Baseline difference ($\gamma_{01}$) | −15.218 | −2.801 | 1.468 |
| Growth rate difference ($\gamma_{11}$) | −8.331 | −8.331 | −1.319 |

*Note.* Pattern 1 = cases that drop out after baseline; Pattern 2 = cases that drop out after one-month follow-up; Pattern 3 = complete cases.

**TABLE 10.9. Average Pattern Mixture Model Estimates from Analysis Example 4**

| Parameter | Estimate | SE | z | p |
|---|---|---|---|---|
| *Complete case missing variable restriction* | | | | |
| Control baseline mean ($\gamma_{00}$) | 51.162 | 0.803 | 63.752 | < .001 |
| Control growth rate ($\gamma_{10}$) | −0.611 | 0.616 | −0.992 | 0.321 |
| Baseline difference ($\gamma_{01}$) | −1.437 | 1.209 | −1.189 | 0.235 |
| Growth rate difference ($\gamma_{11}$) | −2.371 | 0.804 | −2.948 | 0.003 |
| Wave 3 mean difference (*d*) | 0.592 | | | |
| *Neighboring case missing variable restriction* | | | | |
| Control baseline mean ($\gamma_{00}$) | 51.162 | 0.803 | 63.752 | < .001 |
| Control growth rate ($\gamma_{10}$) | −0.245 | 0.797 | −0.307 | 0.759 |
| Baseline difference ($\gamma_{01}$) | −1.437 | 1.209 | −1.189 | 0.235 |
| Growth rate difference ($\gamma_{11}$) | −3.323 | 1.028 | −3.231 | 0.001 |
| Wave 3 mean difference (*d*) | 0.775 | | | |

*Note.* For comparison purposes, the complete-data estimates are $\gamma_{00} = 51.109$, $\gamma_{10} = -0.543$, $\gamma_{01} = -1.498$, and $\gamma_{11} = -1.680$. The effect size at the 2-month follow-up is $d = 0.466$.

and the corresponding estimate from the neighboring case missing variable restriction is

$$\hat{\bar{\gamma}}_{11} = \hat{\pi}_1 \hat{\gamma}_{11}^{(2)} + \hat{\pi}_2 \hat{\gamma}_{11}^{(2)} + \hat{\pi}_3 \hat{\gamma}_{11}^{(3)}$$
$$= 0.136(-8.331) + 0.150(-8.331) + 0.714(-1.319) = -3.323 \tag{10.35}$$

Because the two identifying restrictions make different assumptions about the inestimable parameters, it should come as no surprise that they produce different point estimates.

Table 10.9 shows the average parameter estimates and the delta method standard errors from the pattern mixture model analyses. As seen in the table, both identifying restrictions produced the same substantive conclusion, albeit with different point estimates. Specifically, both analyses produced a nonsignificant change rate for the control group (i.e., the $\hat{\bar{\gamma}}_{10}$ coefficient) and a significant treatment group by time interaction (i.e., $\hat{\bar{\gamma}}_{11}$), such that the treatment group showed a more rapid decrease in depressive symptoms. Substituting the growth model estimates into Equations 10.24 and 10.25 gives model-predicted means of $\hat{Y}_T = 43.761$ and $\hat{Y}_C = 49.940$ for the complete case missing variable restriction and means of $\hat{Y}_T = 42.589$ and $\hat{Y}_C = 50.672$ for the neighboring case missing variable restriction. Expressing the absolute difference in the means relative to the pooled baseline standard deviation ($SD = 10.44$) yields standardized mean difference values of $d = 0.59$ and $d = 0.78$ for the complete case and neighboring case missing variable restrictions, respectively. Consistent with the Hedeker and Gibbons (1997) analysis, both pattern mixture models overestimated the complete-data effect size.

## Standard Error Computations

The pattern mixture estimates in Table 10.9 are weighted averages of the pattern-specific estimates, so it is again necessary to use the delta method to compute their standard errors. In
this section, I briefly sketch the computational steps for the treatment group by time interaction (i.e., the $\hat{\gamma}_{11}$ coefficient) because the identifying restrictions influence the computations for this parameter. A SAS program that automates these computations is available on
the companion website; readers who are not interested in the technical details can therefore
skip to the next section.

The first step of the delta method is to obtain the first derivatives for each unique estimate in the weighted average. For example, reconsider the weighted averages in Equations
10.34 and 10.35. The interaction coefficient is a function of five unique estimates (i.e., $\hat{\gamma}_{11}^{(2)}$,
$\hat{\gamma}_{11}^{(3)}$, $\hat{\pi}_1$, $\hat{\pi}_2$, and $\hat{\pi}_3$), so there are five first derivatives. Differentiating the right side of Equation
10.34 with respect to each estimate gives the derivative vector for the complete case missing
variable restriction.

$$\mathbf{D}_{\mathrm{CCMV}} = \begin{bmatrix} \hat{\pi}_2 \\ (\hat{\pi}_1 + \hat{\pi}_3) \\ \hat{\gamma}_{11}^{(3)} \\ \hat{\gamma}_{11}^{(2)} \\ \hat{\gamma}_{11}^{(3)} \end{bmatrix}$$

In a similar vein, differentiating the right side of Equation 10.35 gives the derivative vector
for the neighboring case missing variable restriction.

$$\mathbf{D}_{\mathrm{NCMV}} = \begin{bmatrix} (\hat{\pi}_1 + \hat{\pi}_2) \\ \hat{\pi}_3 \\ \hat{\gamma}_{11}^{(2)} \\ \hat{\gamma}_{11}^{(2)} \\ \hat{\gamma}_{11}^{(3)} \end{bmatrix}$$

Note that the order of the elements is the same in both vectors, such that the first element is
the first derivative with respect to $\hat{\gamma}_{11}^{(2)}$, the second element is the first derivative with respect
to $\hat{\gamma}_{11}^{(3)}$, the third element is the derivative for $\hat{\pi}_1$, the fourth element is the derivative for $\hat{\pi}_2$,
and final element is the derivative for $\hat{\pi}_3$.

The next two steps of the delta method construct a parameter covariance matrix for
the estimates in the weighted average. The covariance matrix for the regression coefficients is
a 2 by 2 matrix that has sampling variances (i.e., squared standard errors) on the diagonal
and the covariance between $\hat{\gamma}_{11}^{(2)}$ and $\hat{\gamma}_{11}^{(3)}$ on the off-diagonals. Again, these values are part of
the parameter covariance matrix from the full model. Equation 10.19 generates the covari-
ance matrix for the pattern proportions, which in this example is a 3 by 3 matrix. The final
parameter covariance matrix is a block diagonal matrix that combines the two previous
matrices, as follows.

$$\mathrm{var}(\hat{\gamma}, \hat{\pi}) = \begin{bmatrix} \mathrm{var}(\hat{\gamma}) & 0 \\ 0 & \mathrm{var}(\hat{\pi}) \end{bmatrix}$$

$$= \begin{bmatrix} \mathrm{var}(\hat{\gamma}_{11}^{(2)}) & \mathrm{cov}(\hat{\gamma}_{11}^{(2)}, \hat{\gamma}_{11}^{(3)}) & 0 & 0 & 0 \\ \mathrm{cov}(\hat{\gamma}_{11}^{(3)}, \hat{\gamma}_{11}^{(2)}) & \mathrm{var}(\hat{\gamma}_{11}^{(3)}) & 0 & 0 & 0 \\ 0 & 0 & \mathrm{var}(\hat{\pi}_1) & \mathrm{cov}(\hat{\pi}_1, \hat{\pi}_2) & \mathrm{cov}(\hat{\pi}_1, \hat{\pi}_3) \\ 0 & 0 & \mathrm{cov}(\hat{\pi}_2, \hat{\pi}_1) & \mathrm{var}(\hat{\pi}_2) & \mathrm{cov}(\hat{\pi}_2, \hat{\pi}_3) \\ 0 & 0 & \mathrm{cov}(\hat{\pi}_3, \hat{\pi}_1) & \mathrm{cov}(\hat{\pi}_3, \hat{\pi}_2) & \mathrm{var}(\hat{\pi}_3) \end{bmatrix}$$

Note that two identifying restrictions share the same parameter covariance matrix because their respective weighted averages depend on the same set of estimates. Finally, substituting the appropriate matrices into Equation 10.22 yields the sampling variance (i.e., the squared standard error) for the treatment group by time interaction, and taking the square root of this value gives the standard error.

The delta method computations for the remaining parameter estimates follow the same steps that have been outlined. In fact, the computations for the control group slope (i.e., the $\hat{\gamma}_{10}$ coefficient) are identical, except that $\hat{\gamma}_{10}^{(2)}$ and $\hat{\gamma}_{10}^{(3)}$ replace $\hat{\gamma}_{11}^{(2)}$ and $\hat{\gamma}_{11}^{(3)}$ in previous matrices. Because the standard errors for the estimable parameters (i.e., $\hat{\gamma}_{00}$ and $\hat{\gamma}_{01}$) are a function of six unique estimates (e.g., see Equation 10.33), the derivative matrices have six elements and the final parameter covariance matrix is a 6 by 6 matrix. Again, a SAS program that automates the delta method computations is available on the companion website.

## Sensitivity Analysis Summary

The preceding analysis examples used five different missing data-handling techniques to estimate the linear growth model. The results of this sensitivity analysis are somewhat disconcerting because no single model accurately reproduced the complete-data analysis results. Specifically, MAR-based maximum likelihood estimation and the selection model underestimated the true effect size, while the pattern mixture models overestimated the complete-data effect size by about the same amount. One the one hand, the five models apply very different assumptions, so it should come as no surprise that the resulting estimates are different. Nevertheless, it is disturbing that the models failed to reach a consensus about the nature of the treatment effect. Unfortunately, it is relatively common for sensitivity analyses to produce different sets of estimates (e.g., Demirtas & Schafer, 2003; Foster & Fang, 2003). Thus, choosing among a set of competing models is really a matter of adopting the set of assumptions that you are most comfortable with.

## 10.21 SUMMARY

Although MAR-based approaches represent the current state of the art, a considerable amount of methodological research is devoted to models for MNAR data. This chapter outlines two such classes of MNAR models: the selection model and the pattern mixture model. Both models attempt to describe the joint distribution of the data and the probability of missingness, but they do so in a very different way.

The classic selection model was designed for a regression model with MNAR data on the outcome variable. The selection model is a two-part model that combines the substantive regression equation with an additional regression equation that predicts response probabilities. The two parts of the model are linked via correlated residuals, and this linkage is essentially the mechanism by which the missing data model corrects for bias in the substantive model. To achieve identification, the model assumes that the underlying response probabilities and the incomplete outcome variable (or more accurately, the residuals from the two regression equations) follow a bivariate normal distribution. This assumption is not trivial because even slight departures from normality can produce substantial bias. Methodologists have adapted the selection model for longitudinal data analyses. In this context, the selection model combines a growth curve analysis with a set of logistic regressions that describe the probability of response at each measurement occasion. In the logistic portion of the model, each incomplete outcome variable has a corresponding binary missing data indicator, and the probability of response at wave $t$ depends on the outcome variable at time $t$ and the outcome variable from the previous data collection wave.

The pattern mixture model uses a different strategy to describe the joint distribution of the data and the probability of missingness. The pattern mixture approach forms subgroups of cases that share the same missing data pattern and estimates the substantive model within each pattern. Doing so yields a set of parameter estimates for each missing data pattern, and computing the weighted average of the pattern-specific estimates gives a single set of estimates. Because the average estimates are linear combinations of other model parameters, additional computational steps are required to obtain their standard errors. The delta method is the predominant approach for generating pattern mixture model standard errors.

An inherent difficulty with pattern mixture models is that the observed data do not contain enough information to estimate certain pattern-specific parameters. This problem is readily apparent in longitudinal models where it becomes impossible to estimate developmental trends for the cases that drop out early in a study. To address this problem, methodologists have proposed a number of identification strategies that essentially augment the observed data with assumptions about the inestimable parameter values. Simplifying the model by aggregating missing patterns is one potential solution, and replacing the inestimable parameters from one missing data pattern with the estimates from another pattern is a second solution. The flexibility of using different approaches to generate values for the inestimable parameters makes the pattern mixture model an ideal tool for sensitivity analyses because you can examine the stability of the resulting estimates across a variety of assumptions.

Despite their intuitive appeal, MNAR models require assumptions that are every bit as tenuous as the MAR mechanism. Among other things, the selection model relies heavily on the normality assumption, and pattern mixture models require researchers to accurately specify the values of one or more inestimable parameters. Ultimately, there is no way to verify that these requirements are met, and assumption violations can produce severely biased estimates. The fact that MNAR models rely so heavily on narrow, untestable assumptions has led some methodologists to caution against their routine use. A common opinion is that MNAR models are most appropriate for sensitivity analyses that apply different models to the same data. However, sensitivity analyses are often disconcerting because alternate models can produce very different point estimates. The analysis examples at the end of the chapter clearly illustrate this point.

Despite their inherent limitations, MNAR models are likely to gain in popularity, so researchers will increasingly have to choose between MAR and MNAR analyses. Missing data handling techniques are only as good as the veracity of the assumptions they rely on, so thoughtfully applying these models is always important. In the end, choosing among a set of competing models is a matter of adopting the set of assumptions with which you are most at ease.

## 10.22 RECOMMENDED READINGS

Allison, P. D. (2002). *Missing data*. Newbury Park, CA: Sage.

Demirtas, H., & Schafer, J. L. (2003). On the performance of random-coefficient pattern-mixture models for non-ignorable drop-out. *Statistics in Medicine*, 22, 2553–2575.

Graham, J. W., Hofer, S. M., Donaldson, S. I., MacKinnon, D. P., & Schafer, J. L. (1997). Analysis with missing data in prevention research. In K. J. Bryant, M. Windle, & S. G. West (Eds.), *The science of prevention: Methodological advances from alcohol and substance abuse research* (pp. 325–366). Washington, DC: American Psychological Association.

Heckman, J. T. (1976). The common structure of statistical models of truncation, sample selection and limited dependent variables and a simple estimator for such models. *The Annals of Economic and Social Measurement*, 5, 475–492.

Hedeker, D., & Gibbons, R. D. (1997). Application of random-effects pattern-mixture models for missing data in longitudinal studies. *Psychological Methods*, 2, 64–78.

Little, R. J. A. (1993). Pattern-mixture models for multivariate incomplete data. *Journal of the American Statistical Association*, 88, 125–134.

Schafer, J. L., & Graham, J. W. (2002). Missing data: Our view of the state of the art. *Psychological Methods*, 7, 147–177.

# Wrapping Things Up
## Some Final Practical Considerations

## 11.1 CHAPTER OVERVIEW

This final chapter addresses a small number of remaining practical considerations that arise when dealing with missing data. Specifically, the first two sections of the chapter describe the missing data-handling options of several popular software programs. The analysis examples in previous chapters were program-independent in the sense that they rarely mentioned specific software packages by name. Because missing data-handling options vary widely from one program to the next, it is important to have some sense of the options that are currently available. To this end, I provide an overview of the analysis options in several popular programs that implement maximum likelihood estimation and multiple imputation. The next section of the chapter provides some practical advice on choosing between maximum likelihood and multiple imputation. All things being equal, the two methods are likely to produce very similar estimates and standard errors, so the choice of technique is often one of personal preference. However, certain analysis-specific factors make maximum likelihood preferable to multiple imputation or vice versa. This chapter describes several of these scenarios. The final section of the chapter focuses on missing data reporting practices. Despite recommendations from the methodological literature, reviews of published studies suggest that researchers often fail to report information about missing data and the procedures that they used to deal with the problem (Peugh & Enders, 2004). To this end, I give specific suggestions for improving reporting practices and provide templates for conveying the results of a missing data analysis.

## 11.2 MAXIMUM LIKELIHOOD SOFTWARE OPTIONS

A relatively large number of statistical software packages offer maximum likelihood analysis options. A thorough review of these options is made difficult by the fact that programs tend

329

to implement maximum likelihood solutions on an analysis-by-analysis basis. For example, SAS implements maximum likelihood estimation with certain procedures (e.g., a longitudinal growth model in the MIXED procedure; a classic Heckman selection model in the QLIM procedure) but defaults to traditional missing data handling techniques in most cases. The same is true for other general-use statistical software programs. Both SAS and SPSS implement the EM algorithm. In SAS, the EM algorithm is part of the PROC MI, and SPSS offers EM estimation as part of its Missing Values Analysis package. However, both programs are limited to estimating a mean vector and covariance matrix, so this analysis option has limited utility.

Many of the recent software innovations have occurred within the latent variable modeling framework, and every commercially available structural equation modeling software package now implements maximum likelihood missing data handling. (This approach is often referred to as full information maximum likelihood estimation, or simply FIML.) The latent variable modeling framework encompasses a vast number of analytic methods that researchers use on a routine basis (e.g., correlation, regression, ANOVA, factor analysis, path analysis, structural equation models, mixture models, multilevel models). Structural equation modeling software is therefore an ideal tool for many missing data estimation problems. Because of their flexibility and breadth, I rely exclusively on structural equation programs to generate the analysis examples throughout the book and restrict the software review to these packages. Providing specific programming instructions for structural equation modeling software is beyond the scope of this chapter, but a number of resources are available to readers interested in learning one or more of these programs (e.g., Arbuckle, 2007; Bentler & Wu, 2002; Blunch, 2008; Byrne, 1998, 2006, 2009; Hancock & Mueller, 2006; Jöreskog & Sörbom, 2006; Muthén & Muthén, 1998–2009).

Structural equation modeling programs have undergone dramatic improvements in the number of and type of missing data analyses they can perform. With these packages continuing to evolve at a rapid pace, I use a website to maintain an up-to-date set of program files for the analysis examples in the book. Nevertheless, it is useful to document the current capabilities of the commercially available software programs. Table 11.1 shows a checklist of analysis options for AMOS 16.0, EQS 6.1, LISREL 8.8, and Mplus 5.2. The checklist reflects the analysis features of each software package at the time of this writing, although many of the options are also available in previous releases. Note that the checklist is not exhaustive, and some packages provide additional missing data handling options that do not appear in the table (e.g., tables that list the frequency of each missing data pattern; functions that create binary missing data indicators; matrices that report the missing data rates for individual variables or pairs of variables). Nevertheless, the checklist does reflect most of the major analysis options from previous chapters.

## AMOS

AMOS (Arbuckle, 2007) was the first commercial structural equation modeling software program to implement maximum likelihood missing data handling. The missing data handling options in AMOS are well-suited for normally distributed variables, but the program currently lacks several of the desirable options that are available in other packages (e.g., corrective procedures for non-normal missing data). One of the unique strengths of AMOS is its

**TABLE 11.1. Missing Data Handling Capabilities of Commercial Structural Equation Modeling Programs**

| Technique | AMOS | EQS | LISREL | Mplus |
|---|---|---|---|---|
| Maximum likelihood options | | | | |
| Maximum likelihood with continuous outcomes | ✓ | ✓ | ✓ | ✓ |
| Maximum likelihood with binary outcomes | | | | ✓ |
| Incomplete explanatory variables | ✓ | ✓ | ✓ | ✓ |
| Standard errors based on observed information | ✓ | ✓ | | ✓ |
| Robust standard errors | | ✓ | ✓ | ✓ |
| Naïve bootstrap | | ✓ | | ✓ |
| Bollen–Stine bootstrap | | ✓ | | ✓ |
| Rescaled likelihood ratio test | | ✓ | ✓ | ✓ |
| Automated auxiliary variable models | | | | ✓ |
| Selection and pattern mixture models | | | | ✓ |
| Multiple imputation options | | | | |
| Generate multiply imputed data sets | ✓ | | ✓ | |
| Analyze and combine estimates | | | | ✓ |
| Multiparameter significance tests | | | | ✓ |
| Miscellaneous options | | | | |
| MCAR tests | | ✓ | | |
| Tests of multivariate normality | | ✓ | ✓ | |
| Monte Carlo simulation with missing data | | ✓ | | ✓ |

ability to generate multiply imputed data sets. (The program also performs regression imputation and stochastic regression imputation.) AMOS implements the same basic data augmentation algorithm from Chapter 7, but it offers the option of generating imputations under different hypothesized models. For example, AMOS can generate imputations that are consistent with a particular factor analysis model (e.g., a two-factor confirmatory factor analysis model) in addition to the usual saturated model (i.e., a model based on the mean vector and the covariance matrix). If the hypothesized model that generates the imputations is correct (e.g., a two-factor model describes the structure of the population data), then the subsequent estimates should have somewhat lower standard errors than the corresponding estimates from a saturated imputation model. The downside using a parsimonious model to generate the imputations is that the resulting estimates may be biased if the hypothesized imputation model is incorrect. Finally, AMOS does not currently implement facilities for analyzing multiply imputed data sets and combining the resulting estimates and standard errors.

## EQS

EQS (Bentler & Wu, 2002) has a rather extensive list of missing data handling capabilities. Like AMOS, EQS is well-suited for analyzing normally distributed variables, but it also offers a number of corrective procedures for non-normal data, including rescaled test statistics, robust standard errors, and the bootstrap. Although EQS has no options for generating or analyzing multiply imputed data sets, it does provide tests of the missing completely at random (MCAR) mechanism, an estimate of Mardia's multivariate kurtosis (Yuan, Lambert, & Fouladi, 2004), and built-in computer simulation routines for generating artificial data sets with missing values (e.g., for estimating power in a planned missingness design).

## LISREL

LISREL's (Jöreskog & Sörbom, 2006) missing data handling options are somewhere between those of AMOS and EQS. LISREL is also well-suited for analyzing normally distributed variables, and it does offer some corrective procedures for non-normal data (robust standard errors and rescaled test statistics). LISREL currently estimates standard errors based on the expected, rather than the observed, information matrix. Like AMOS, LISREL can generate multiply imputed data sets via the data augmentation algorithm, but it strictly relies on a saturated model to do so. (This is consistent with the imputation procedure from Chapter 7.) LISREL also performs similar response pattern imputation and regression imputation. The LISREL documentation is somewhat confusing because it describes regression imputation as an EM-based procedure. The program does use an EM estimate of the mean vector and the covariance matrix to generate the imputation regression equations, but this approach is still prone to the same biases as standard regression imputation. Finally, LISREL does not currently implement routines for analyzing multiply imputed data sets and combining the resulting estimates and standard errors. However, second-party programs to pool estimates are available (e.g., see *www.Quant.ku.edu*).

## Mplus

Mplus (Muthén & Muthén, 1998–2009) currently offers the most diverse set of missing data handling options. In particular, Mplus is the only package that (1) performs maximum likelihood missing data handling with binary outcomes (e.g., estimates a logistic regression with missing data), (2) automates the inclusion of auxiliary variables via Graham's (2003) saturated correlates model, (3) estimates missing not at random (MNAR) models, and (4) analyzes multiply imputed data sets and pools the resulting estimates and standard errors. With regard to its MNAR modeling capabilities, Mplus has a number of useful features that are ideal for estimating selection models and pattern mixture models. For example, Mplus can accommodate models that include mixtures of continuous and binary outcomes, so it is relatively straightforward to estimate the longitudinal selection models from Chapter 10. (The program also has a feature for creating binary missing data indicators.) Mplus offers extensive mixture modeling capabilities, so it is also straightforward to estimate a variety of pattern mixture models for longitudinal data, including models that implement the complete case and neighboring case missing variable restrictions. I exclusively used Mplus to estimate the MNAR models in Chapter 10. Related to its multiple-imputation analysis options, Mplus fully automates the analysis and pooling phase. Thus, the process of analyzing multiply imputed data sets is virtually transparent to the user (though the program does not generate imputations).

The program features single-parameter and multiparameter significance tests, including the $D_1$ and $D_3$ test statistics. Mplus uses somewhat different reference distributions from those described in Chapter 8 (e.g., a standard normal distribution generates the probability value for the single parameter test statistic, and a chi-square distribution generates the probability value for the $D_3$ statistic).

## 11.3 MULTIPLE-IMPUTATION SOFTWARE OPTIONS

A number of software packages generate and analyze multiply imputed data sets, some of which are commercially available, whereas others are freely available on the Internet. A detailed review of the many different imputation programs could easily fill an entire chapter, so I focus on three popular programs: NORM, SAS, and SPSS. These programs are flexible because they can generate multiply imputed data sets and can pool the estimates and standard errors from a multiple imputation analysis. (Many programs can do one or the other, but not both.) Because SAS and SPSS are arguably the most popular statistical software packages in the social and the behavioral sciences, it is particularly important to outline features of these programs. A variety of resources are available for readers interested in other software options (e.g., Allison, 2000; Honaker, King, & Blackwell, 2009; Horton & Lipsitz, 2001; Raghunathan, Solenberger, & Van Hoewyk, 2002; Royston, 2005), and there are also useful websites that provide information about imputation software programs (e.g., *www.multiple-imputation.com*).

Table 11.2 shows a checklist of analysis options for NORM 2.03, SAS 9.2, and SPSS 18.0. The checklist reflects the analysis features at the time of this writing, although some of the options are also available in previous releases. Note that the checklist is not exhaustive, and some packages provide additional options that do not appear in the table. (SAS, in particular, offers the user a variety of options.) However, the checklist does reflect most of the major analysis options from previous chapters. Consistent with the maximum likelihood analysis examples, I maintain an up-to-date set of multiple imputation program files for the analysis examples on the companion website.

## NORM

NORM (Schafer, 1999) is a freeware package that implements the data augmentation algorithm from Chapter 7. The program is available as standalone software for Windows or as an S-Plus library. I give a brief overview of the Windows version of NORM here; interested readers can consult Schafer and Olsen (1998) for a more detailed description of the program. In addition, the companion website has step-by-step instructions for using NORM, including screenshots that illustrate the major analysis features.

The Windows version of NORM is very easy to use because all of the analysis options are accessible via a point-and-click interface. The program readily imports text data files that are saved in a space-delimited free format. NORM offers a number of useful imputation options, including a variety of data transformations, automatic dummy coding of categorical variables, rounding, and graphical convergence diagnostics (autocorrelation function plots and time-series plots), to name a few. Although the program does not perform statistical

**TABLE 11.2. Analysis Options for Selected Multiple Imputation Software Programs**

| Technique | NORM | SAS | SPSS* |
|---|---|---|---|
| *Imputation phase options* | | | |
| Bootstrap starting values | | ✓ | |
| Ridge prior distribution | ✓ | ✓ | |
| Variable transformations | ✓ | ✓ | |
| Constraints on minimum and maximum values | | ✓ | ✓ |
| Rounding for imputed values | ✓ | ✓ | ✓ |
| Graphical convergence diagnostics | ✓ | ✓ | * |
| *Pooling phase options* | | | |
| Combine estimates and standard errors | ✓ | ✓ | ✓ |
| Bernard and Rubin degrees of freedom | | ✓ | |
| Missing data diagnostics (e.g., FMI, RIV) | ✓ | ✓ | ✓ |
| $D_1$ multiparameter test statistic | ✓ | ✓ | |
| $D_2$ multiparameter test statistic | | | |
| $D_3$ multiparameter test statistic | | | |

*Note.* FMI = fraction of missing information; RIV = relative increase in variance. *SPSS does not automate this option, but it produces the information necessary to construct graphical diagnostics.

analyses, it does generate maximum likelihood estimates of the mean vector and the covariance matrix via the EM algorithm. The EM option is useful for monitoring convergence speed and for generating an initial set of parameter values for data augmentation. Unlike SAS and SPSS, NORM saves each imputed data set to a separate text file. Some programs that analyze multiply imputed data sets require this file format (e.g., Mplus), whereas others require the imputed data sets to be stacked in a single file (e.g., SAS and SPSS).

NORM is not an analysis program, but it can pool the estimates and standard errors from other software packages. To conduct single-parameter significance tests, the estimates and their standard errors need to be assembled in a single text file. NORM subsequently imports this file and performs the *t* tests from Chapter 8. Multiparameter significance tests follow a similar procedure, but the input text file must contain the estimates and the parameter covariance matrix from each imputed data set. (The Help menu shows how to arrange the contents of the text files.) Copying and pasting the estimates and standard errors into a text file can be inconvenient, particularly when the number of imputations is very large. However, the advantage of NORM is that it can pool the analysis results from any program and offers a straightforward graphical interface for doing so.

## SAS

A multiple imputation procedure (PROC MI) has been available in SAS for several years. The MI procedure implements specialized algorithms for monotone missing data patterns, but its primary imputation method is the data augmentation algorithm from Chapter 7. As seen in

Table 11.2, PROC MI offers a comprehensive set of options for customizing the imputation process that includes virtually every procedure described in Chapters 7 through 9 (as well as several others that I omit). Unlike NORM, the MI procedure stacks the imputations in a single file and assigns an identification variable to each data set. The stacked file format is particularly convenient for the analysis phase because most SAS procedures have a BY subcommand that produces separate analyses for subgroups of cases defined by one or more variables in the data set. Listing the imputation identifier on the BY subcommand instructs SAS to perform an analysis separately for each imputed data set.

The MIANALYZE procedure pools the estimates and standard errors from a set of analyses. With the exception of the $D_2$ and $D_3$ test statistics, MIANALYZE offers all of the options from Chapter 8. The procedure is flexible in the sense that it can pool the results from virtually any analysis, but getting the estimates and standard errors in the correct format may require considerable effort. Some analysis procedures (e.g., PROC REG, PROC MIXED) can save parameter estimates and standard errors to a file that is compatible with the MIANALYZE procedure. However, for many analyses, SAS either does not output the necessary information to a file or does not output the information in a format that MIANALYZE can use. Even when SAS does save the analysis results in an appropriate format, it may not save all of the estimates that are of interest. In these situations, it is necessary to use the Output Delivery System (ODS) to create a custom file compatible with MIANALYZE. This may not be a trivial task, particularly for users who are not facile with the SAS programming language. Considered together, the MI and MIANALYZE procedures are powerful tools that offer a rich set of features. However, for users unfamiliar with the SAS programming environment, NORM and SPSS offer interfaces that are far more user-friendly.

## SPSS

SPSS implemented a multiple imputation procedure beginning in version 17. The imputation routine in SPSS is not as feature-rich as that of SAS, but it does have some unique features. Most notably, SPSS uses sequential regression imputation as opposed to data augmentation. (The SPSS documentation refers to this method as fully conditional specification.) Recall from Chapter 9 that the sequential regression approach fills in the data on a variable-by-variable basis, each time matching the imputation model to a variable's distributional form. Currently, SPSS uses logistic regression to impute incomplete nominal and ordinal variables, and it uses linear regression to impute continuous variables. (The scale of each variable is defined in the Variable View tab of the graphical interface.) Defining all incomplete variables as continuous (SPSS refers to this variable type as a "scale" variable) effectively implements normality-based imputation that resembles the data augmentation algorithm. However, the sequential nature of the imputation process is quite different from data augmentation because variables are imputed in a sequence, where the order is determined by the rates of missingness.

The SPSS imputation facility lacks several useful options that are available in SAS (e.g., a ridge prior distribution, variable transformations), although it does allow the user to round the imputed values and constrain minimum and maximum values. The program does not automatically produce graphical convergence diagnostics. However, SPSS can save the variable means and standard deviations from each iteration to a data file; it is therefore relatively straightforward to construct time-series plots and estimate autocorrelations. Other useful diagnostic measures such as the worst linear function are not available.

One of the major advantages of using SPSS is that the pooling phase is completely automated and is virtually transparent to the user. Like SAS, the SPSS imputation procedure stacks the imputations in a single file and assigns an identification variable to each data set. SPSS has a SPLIT FILE command that divides a data set into subgroups defined by one or more variables in the file. Entering the imputation identifier into the SPLIT FILE command invokes an algorithm that automatically pools the estimates and standard errors from all subsequent analyses. Performing an analysis after invoking the SPLIT FILE command (available from the Data pull-down menu) produces an output file that contains the estimates and standard errors for each imputed data set as well as the pooled results. Again, the pooling procedure is completely transparent and requires no effort on the part of the user. The pooling algorithm does not interface with all SPSS procedures, but it does work for many common analyses. When the pooling algorithm is not available, the SPSS output file lists the analysis results separately for each imputed data set.

## 11.4 CHOOSING BETWEEN MAXIMUM LIKELIHOOD AND MULTIPLE IMPUTATION

Chapter 8 described the situations in which maximum likelihood and multiple imputation are likely to produce similar analysis results. The comparability of the two procedures is largely determined by the relative complexity of the imputation regression model and the subsequent analysis model (i.e., congeniality). For example, if the imputation model contains the same variables as the subsequent analysis model, then maximum likelihood and multiple imputation are likely to produce similar results. In contrast, if the imputation regression model includes additional variables that are not part of the subsequent analysis, the two approaches may produce different estimates, standard errors, or both (Collins, Schafer, & Kam, 2001). Given that the two procedures frequently produce very similar results, the choice of technique is often one of personal preference. However, there are analysis-specific factors that make maximum likelihood preferable to multiple imputation or vice versa. This section describes a few of these factors. The subsequent discussion, though not exhaustive, provides an overview of the practical issues that arise in real data analyses. As you will see, the factors that influence the decision to use one technique over another can vary from one analysis to the next and may also depend on the availability of certain software programs.

### Advantage: Multiple Imputation

One situation in which multiple imputation potentially holds an advantage over maximum likelihood estimation is in the use of auxiliary variables (i.e., variables that are potential correlates of missingness or correlates of the incomplete analysis model variables). Currently, Graham's (2003) saturated correlates model is the easiest approach for incorporating auxiliary variables into a maximum likelihood analysis. Recall from Chapter 5 that the saturated correlates model borrows information from the auxiliary variables via a series of correlations between the auxiliary variables and the analysis model variables (or their residual terms). Mplus is currently the only structural equation modeling program that has built-in facilities for incorporating auxiliary variables. Other packages require the user to manually specify the model. Depending on the software package, this approach can be a bit cumbersome.

In contrast, multiple imputation readily accommodates auxiliary variables as additional predictors in the imputation phase. Because the imputation process infuses the imputed values with the information from the auxiliary variables, there is no need to include the additional variables in the subsequent analyses. When performing a large number of analyses, it is convenient to deal with the auxiliary variables in a single preliminary step as opposed to an analysis-by-analysis basis. In addition, multiple imputation can often accommodate a larger set of auxiliary variables than a maximum likelihood analysis. (Using a large number of auxiliary variables can lead to estimation problems for maximum likelihood.) Although multiple imputation generally has a practical edge when it comes to auxiliary variables, this advantage may be trivial if you have access to Mplus.

A second situation in which multiple imputation potentially holds an advantage over maximum likelihood is in the treatment of incomplete explanatory variables. In the context of multiple imputation, it makes no difference whether a particular variable serves as an independent variable or an outcome variable in the subsequent analysis. The primary concern is that all of the analysis variables appear in the imputation regression model, regardless of their subsequent role. In contrast, maximum likelihood integrates the missing data handling into the estimation process, so a variable's role in the analysis is potentially important. For some analysis models, there is no reason to prefer multiple imputation to maximum likelihood. For example, commercially available structural equation modeling programs allow the predictor variables in a multiple regression model to have missing data. However, in some situations implementing maximum likelihood estimation will result in a loss of cases. For example, multilevel modeling software programs (including structural equation modeling programs that estimate multilevel models) uniformly exclude cases with missing data on one or more of the predictor variables. In this situation, multiple imputation is the only missing data handling strategy that will retain the entire sample. However, it is important to reiterate that single-level imputation algorithms (e.g., data augmentation, sequential regression) are not appropriate for multilevel data. Methodologists have developed specialized imputation algorithms for multilevel data (Schafer, 2001; Schafer & Yucel, 2002; Yucel, 2008), but these routines may require software packages that you are not familiar with (e.g., the PAN library for the S-Plus program). Taking the time to learn one of these programs is clearly advantageous when estimating multilevel models with missing data.

As a final example, the problem of item-level missing data is one where multiple imputation has a solid advantage over maximum likelihood estimation. Researchers in the behavioral and the social sciences routinely use multiple-item questionnaires to measure complex constructs (e.g., psychologists typically use several questionnaire items to measure depression, each of which taps into a different depressive symptom). With multiple-item questionnaires, respondents often omit one or more of the items within a given scale. With few exceptions, multiple imputation is a more flexible method for dealing with item nonresponse. For example, suppose that a psychologist is interested in computing a depression scale score by summing the responses to 20 individual questionnaire items. Furthermore, suppose that the ultimate goal is to use the resulting scale scores as the outcome variable in a multiple regression analysis. Applying multiple imputation to this scenario is relatively straightforward because the researcher would simply impute the missing questionnaire items and compute a scale score for each imputed data set. Armed with a collection of complete data sets, the researcher could perform the regression analysis along with any ancillary analyses that require the item-level responses (e.g., factor analyses, reliability analyses).

Because maximum likelihood estimation does not fill in the data, there is no way to compute a single scale score that incorporates the partial information at the item level. One option would be to compute the scale score for the cases that have complete data and treat the resulting composite as missing for any respondent that failed to answer one or more of the questionnaire items. Failing to utilize the item-level data from incomplete data records may not bias the resulting regression coefficients, but it would likely cause a reduction in power relative to multiple imputation. A second option would be to treat the scale score as a latent variable in the regression model and use the individual questionnaire items as manifest indicators of the latent factor. This strategy incorporates the partial item responses in a manner that is comparable to multiple imputation, but it adds a layer of complexity to an otherwise straightforward analysis.

## Advantage: Maximum Likelihood

Researchers in the behavioral and the social sciences are often interested in estimating interaction (i.e., moderation) effects where the magnitude of the association between two variables depends on a third variable. (For example, the magnitude of the association between psychological well-being and job performance depends on a third variable such as gender or years of experience on the job.) Maximum likelihood estimation usually holds an advantage over multiple imputation when it comes to estimating interaction effects. The standard approach for assessing interactions is to include a product term in a multiple regression model (i.e., moderated multiple regression; Aiken & West, 1991). Estimating interaction effects is straightforward in the context of maximum likelihood missing data handling because the product term is no different from any other variable. Furthermore, centering the two variables that form the product term follows the same logic as a complete-data analysis (e.g., center the variables at the maximum likelihood mean estimates, then compute the product term). Of course, the product variable would have missing values if one of the variables involved in the product is incomplete, but this is not a problem, provided that the software program allows for missing data on predictor variables.

The difficulty with multiple imputation and interaction effects occurs during the imputation phase, where it is necessary to specify an imputation model that appropriately preserves any interaction effects that might be present in the data. When an interaction effect involves a categorical moderator variable such as gender, imputing the data separately for each subgroup will adequately preserve the interaction effect in the imputed data sets. The situation becomes more difficult with a quantitative moderator variable because the methodological literature has yet to establish the best approach for centering the predictor variables. One option is to center the variables prior to imputation (e.g., using the maximum likelihood mean estimates), compute the necessary product term, and fill in the missing variables (including the product term) on their centered metrics. A second strategy is to fill in the missing variables (including the product term) on their original metrics and subsequently perform the centering procedure on each of the complete data sets. Because the product of two uncentered variables has a different mean and variance than the product of two centered variables (Bohrnstedt & Goldberger, 1969), this method requires a complete rescaling of the imputed product variable. The ambiguity in the centering process makes maximum likelihood estimation a clear winner when it comes to dealing with interaction effects.

Structural equation models represent another class of analyses where maximum likelihood estimation is generally preferable to multiple imputation. For one, every commercially available structural equation program offers maximum likelihood missing data handling, so implementing the procedure is very easy. Multiple imputation is also relatively easy to implement because some structural equation modeling programs (e.g., Mplus) have built-in facilities for automating the analysis and pooling phases. Although it is currently possible to use the $D_3$ statistic from Chapter 8 to pool likelihood ratio tests (e.g., the chi-square test of model fit) from a structural equation modeling analysis, methodologists have yet to develop principled approaches for pooling popular fit indices such as the RMSEA, CFI, and SRMR. Given the important role that fit assessments play in structural equation modeling analyses, the lack of pooling rules is a serious drawback of multiple imputation. Maximum likelihood does not suffer from this problem because most popular fit indices are available in a missing data analysis.

As an aside, the recommendation to use maximum likelihood in conjunction with structural equation models partially depends on the scaling of the analysis model variables. For example, most structural equation modeling programs offer a weighted least squares estimator for ordered categorical variables. However, this estimator uses a pairwise deletion approach for dealing with missing values and thus requires stricter assumptions about the missing data mechanism. In situations where the complete-data analysis would have relied on weighted least squares estimation, multiple imputation may provide a better option than maximum likelihood estimation. Nevertheless, imputation is not a perfect solution because it is still necessary to generate discrete imputed values. One option is to use normality-based imputation in conjunction with rounding. A second possibility is to implement an imputation algorithm that accommodates mixtures of categorical and continuous variables (e.g., sequential regression imputation).

When reading some of the previous chapters, you might have noticed that the methodological literature offers relatively little guidance on a number of practical issues that arise during a multiple imputation analysis (e.g., rounding imputed values, transforming parameter estimates prior to pooling, imputing large item-level data sets, correcting test statistics for non-normality, pooling fit indices from a structural equation model). Multiple imputation requires a number of nuanced steps and decisions that are not relevant to maximum likelihood estimation. Therefore it probably comes as no surprise that some of the procedural details are a bit underdeveloped. Although maximum likelihood may lack flexibility in certain situations (e.g., analyses that involve summed scale scores), it tends to have fewer procedural ambiguities. On a related point, implementing maximum likelihood is nearly always easier than implementing multiple imputation. For researchers who are already familiar with structural equation modeling programs, invoking maximum likelihood estimation is as simple as adding another keyword or another line of code. In fact, the missing data handling is so transparent that users can readily implement procedure without knowing anything about the inner workings of the "black box." (Some would argue that this is not necessarily a good thing.) Multiple imputation arguably has a much steeper learning curve, so the time required to effectively implement the procedure tends to be much greater. All things being equal, maximum likelihood estimation has a clear advantage with regard to ease of use. Consequently, when a maximum likelihood solution is available for a particular analysis, it probably makes good sense to choose it over multiple imputation.

## 11.5 REPORTING THE RESULTS FROM A MISSING DATA ANALYSIS

A 1999 report by the American Psychological Association's (APA) Task Force on Statistical Inference stated that, "Before presenting results, report complications, protocol violations, and other unanticipated events in data collection. These include missing data, attrition, and nonresponse" (Wilkinson & Task Force on Statistical Inference, 1999, p. 597). Recommendations such as this can be found throughout the research methods literature, yet reviews of published studies suggest that researchers often fail to report information about missing data and the procedures they used to deal with the problem (Peugh & Enders, 2004). Accordingly, this section gives suggestions for improving reporting practices and provides templates for conveying the results of a missing data analysis.

Beyond simply increasing the level of detail in published research studies, improving missing data reporting practices can have the added benefit of reassuring reviewers and editors that modern missing data techniques are methodologically sound. In my experience, substantive researchers are often concerned about implementing sophisticated missing data techniques because they feel that reviewers or editors will view their study in a negative light, presumably because they are unfamiliar with or suspicious of these newer approaches. Although this concern is understandable, resorting to flawed procedures in order to avoid criticism from an uninformed reviewer or editor is a poor reason for avoiding sophisticated missing data methodology. Until researchers, editors, and journal reviewers become familiar with modern missing data handling techniques, it is probably a good idea to be a bit "teachy" when preparing a manuscript for publication. The templates that I give in this section reflect this approach.

As a basic starting point, published research reports should always acknowledge the presence of missing data. Although this recommendation seems obvious, many published research studies fail to report any information about missing data. For example, Peugh and Enders (2004) reviewed hundreds of published articles in the 1999 and 2003 volumes of several education and psychology journals. In 1999, roughly one-third of the research reports with detectable missing data (e.g., studies where the degrees of freedom values changed across a set of ANOVAs) explicitly acknowledged the problem. Fortunately, reporting practices improved in the 2003 review, such that three-quarters of the studies with detectable missing data disclosed the problem. Although reporting practices are getting better in this regard, it is reasonable to expect that *every* study with missing data should explicitly acknowledge the problem. This recommendation is consistent with that of the APA Task Force, among others. Ideally, published studies should also describe the extent of the missing data problem. For unintentional missing data, a minimally sufficient description should include the range of missing data rates across the analysis variables. This description could consist of a sentence or two and possibly a small table, as follows: "Across the 13 variables that we used in the analyses, the missing data proportions ranged between 2 and 11%. Table 2 gives the missing data rates for each of the analysis variables."

Beyond acknowledging the presence of and describing the amount of missing data, a more detailed report might include comparisons of the missing and the complete cases. Published research studies occasionally report these comparisons, but the purpose is usually to justify a complete-case analysis (e.g., if no significant differences are found, researchers often perform their analyses after eliminating the incomplete cases). Because there is rarely a good reason to eliminate incomplete data records, examining mean differences across missing data patterns is most useful when the goal is to identify potential correlates of missingness that can serve as auxiliary variables in subsequent analyses. To conserve journal space, the mean comparisons could be part of a broader description of auxiliary variables. To illustrate, consider a hypothetical study of eating disorder risk in high-school-age females. A brief description of the auxiliary variables might look like this:

> Mean comparisons revealed that the participants with incomplete data had higher body mass index values and higher levels of peer pressure, on average. To correct for any systematic bias that might be related to these differences, we used body mass index and peer pressure as auxiliary variables in all analyses that didn't already include these variables. We also used parental reports of food preoccupation as an auxiliary variable because of its high correlation with the incomplete self-reports. The methodological literature currently recommends an inclusive analysis strategy that incorporates auxiliary variables into the missing data handling procedure because this approach can make the missing at random assumption more plausible and can improve statistical power (Collins, Schafer, & Kam, 2001).

Notice that the template includes a sentence that essentially instructs the reader about the use of auxiliary variables. Again, taking a didactic approach can help reduce or eliminate concerns about an unfamiliar technique. (Published examples of auxiliary variable models are still relatively rare.)

In the case of a planned missing data, a minimally sufficient report would necessarily include a more detailed description of the missing data. Although the specifics of the description would probably vary from study to study, a good rule of thumb is to provide the same level of detail as you would for any other procedural aspect of a study. In this situation, comparisons of the incomplete and complete cases are unnecessary because the data are missing at random by definition, although a description of auxiliary variables may still be warranted (e.g., correlates of the incomplete variables could still appear in the analyses). To illustrate a written template for a planned missing data design, consider a hypothetical longitudinal study with six data collection waves, where each respondent has intentional missing data at one or more of the measurement occasions.

> To reduce the burden on the study participants and to improve the logistics of data collection, we implemented a planned missing data design (Graham, Taylor, and Cumsille, 2001; Graham, Taylor, Olchowski, & Cumsille, 2006). Briefly, we divided the sample into six random subgroups, such that the members of each subgroup provided data at four or five of the six data collection waves. Table 3 shows the 6 missing data patterns and the proportion of the sample in each pattern. We used a series of computer simulation studies to identify a configuration of missing values that would minimize the loss of power relative to a complete-data design. Depending on the effect size values that we used in the simulations, the design in the table produced power values that were between 87 and 94% as large as the corresponding complete-data analyses. It is important to note that planned missing data designs such as the one that we implemented produce missing completely at random data (i.e., missingness is unrelated to the study variables). Consequently, the missing data are benign and cannot introduce bias into the parameter estimates. Furthermore, analyzing the data with maximum likelihood missing data handling resulted in a minimal loss of power because it is unnecessary to exclude cases from the analyses. We judged that the relatively small drop in power was an acceptable trade-off for reducing respondent burden and streamlining the logistics of data collection.

The preceding description would be appropriate for one of the longitudinal designs in Graham, Taylor, and Cumsille (2001), but the write-up could easily be adapted to other types of planned missingness designs. Again, notice that the template is relatively didactic in nature.

Because the use of maximum likelihood estimation and multiple imputation has steadily increased in recent years, it is relatively easy to find published studies that have employed these methods. Nevertheless, it is useful to have templates for describing these procedures because modern missing data methods are still widely misunderstood. To illustrate, reconsider the hypothetical study of eating disorder risk from one of the previous examples. A description of maximum likelihood missing data handling might look like this:

> We used the maximum likelihood estimation option in the Mplus 5.2 software program to deal with the missing data in the multiple regression model and used the robust standard error option to correct for nonnormality. Furthermore, we used Graham's (2003) saturated correlates approach to incorporate three auxiliary variables (body mass index, peer pressure, parental ratings of food preoccupation) into the analysis. It is important to point out that the auxiliary variables can potentially reduce bias and improve power, but they do so without altering the substantive interpretation of the parameters (i.e., the regression coefficients have the same interpretation as they would have had there been no missing data). Because the auxiliary variable correlations are not of substantive interest, we do not report these parameters here. Finally, note that methodologists currently regard maximum likelihood estimation as a state-of-the-art missing data technique because it improves the accuracy and the power of the analyses relative to other missing data handling methods (Schafer & Graham, 2002).

From a procedural standpoint, multiple imputation is far more involved than maximum likelihood because it requires multiple steps and many decisions. Ideally, the description of the imputation phase should convey information about convergence diagnostics, the number of burn-in and between-imputation iterations, the number of imputations, and the variables that were used in the imputation phase. Fully describing the nuances of the imputation phase alone could easily consume a full manuscript page, so the difficulty becomes finding the right balance of detail and brevity. With regard to the hypothetical study of eating disorder risk, a description of multiple imputation could be as follows:

> Prior to performing the analyses, we used multiple imputation to deal with the missing data. Briefly, multiple imputation uses a regression-based procedure to generate multiple copies of the data set, each of which contains different estimates of the missing values. We used the data augmentation algorithm in the SAS MI procedure to generate 50 imputed data sets (Graham, Olchowski, & Gilreath, 2007, recommend at least 20 for most situations). Graphical diagnostics from an exploratory analysis suggested that the data sets should be separated by at least 50 iterations of the imputation algorithm, so we took the conservative tack of saving the first data set at the 300th iteration and saved additional data sets every 300th iteration thereafter. The imputation process included the 13 variables that appeared in one or more of the subsequent regression analyses as well as three auxiliary variables (body mass index, peer pressure, and parental ratings of food preoccupation). After creating the complete data sets, we estimated the multiple regression models on each filled-in data set and subsequently used Rubin's (1987) formulas to combine the parameter estimates and standard errors into a single set of results. Note that methodologists currently regard multiple imputation as a "state of the art" missing data technique because it improves the accuracy and the power of the analyses relative to other missing data handling methods (Schafer & Graham, 2002).

The previous description is far from comprehensive and omits many of the small details that arise during the imputation process (e.g., rounding, applying transformations). Certain analyses may require additional information (e.g., analyses that involve interactive effects, categorical and continuous variables, multilevel data, etc.), but the template above includes much of the core information. When implementing multiple imputation, it may be a good idea to offer the reader additional details about the imputation process upon request or to place a full description of the imputation procedure in an appendix that could appear in the electronic version of the manuscript.

The previous templates are just ideas for reporting various aspects of a missing data analysis. Obviously, these passages can be expanded or shortened to fit the specifics of a given study. By providing templates, it is my hope that missing data reporting practices can improve, but also that consumers of research will become increasingly familiar with the techniques in this book.

## 11.6 FINAL THOUGHTS

Modern missing data handling techniques are beginning to take hold in some areas of the behavioral and the social sciences, and researchers are becoming increasingly aware that traditional approaches for dealing with missing data are fundamentally flawed. A previous section in this chapter highlighted the pros and cons of maximum likelihood and multiple imputation, but it is useful to think about analysis options more broadly. Eliminating traditional techniques (e.g., deletion methods and single imputation) from consideration leaves two alternatives: an analysis that assumes a missing at random (MAR) mechanism (maximum likelihood estimation or multiple imputation), or an analysis that assumes an MNAR mechanism (selection models or a pattern mixture models). Because the data provide little or no evidence in favor of one approach or another, MAR and MNAR analysis models ultimately represent a choice between competing assumptions. A missing data handling techniques is only as good as the veracity of its assumptions, so adopting a defensible analysis (or alternatively, adopting an analysis that minimizes the risk of violating key assumptions) is important.

In my experience, researchers (including journal editors and reviewers) are sometimes quick to assume that a sinister attrition mechanism is at play, such that MAR-based analyses are automatically invalid. Even if the missing values do follow an MNAR mechanism (and there is no way to tell), selection models and pattern mixture models are not necessarily the best solution. These MNAR models rely on assumptions that are probably far more tenuous than the MAR mechanism. In truth, the range of conditions that satisfies the assumptions for an MNAR analysis is much narrower than the range of conditions that satisfies the MAR mechanism. This being the case, a well-executed MAR analysis may be preferable to an MNAR analysis, even if there is reason to believe that missingness is systematically related to the outcome variable. Other methodologists have voiced a similar opinion. For example, in discussing the trade-offs between MAR and MNAR analyses, Schafer (2003, p. 30) stated, "Rather than rely heavily on poorly estimated MNAR models, I would prefer to examine auxiliary variables that may be related to missingness … and include them in a richer imputation model under assumption of MAR."

Missing data analyses are difficult because there is no inherently correct methodological procedure. In many (if not most) situations, blindly applying maximum likelihood estimation or multiple imputation will likely lead to a more accurate set of estimates than using one of the traditional missing data handling techniques. In that sense, a thoughtless MAR analysis is probably better than the best traditional missing data approach. However, Schafer's (2003, p. 30) point is that a good MAR model may be better than a bad MNAR model. While simply increasing the frequency with which researchers use MAR-based analysis techniques is a good short-term goal, elevating the sophistication level of MAR analyses may prove to be the best long-term solution for missing data. Of course, achieving this goal requires time and effort at every stage of the research process, and implementing a sophisticated MAR analysis requires researchers to be proactive about missing data. Among other things, this includes planning for missing data, anticipating the possible reasons for attrition, collecting data on possible correlates of missingness, documenting the reasons behind attrition, exploring potential auxiliary variables, and generally establishing a reasoned argument that supports a particular set of assumptions. Until more robust MNAR analysis models become available (and that may never happen), increasing the sophistication level of MAR analysis may be the best that we can do.

## 11.7 RECOMMENDED READINGS

Byrne, B. M. (1998). *Structural equation modeling with LISREL: Basic concepts, applications, and programming.* Mahwah, NJ: Erlbaum.

Byrne, B. M. (2006). *Structural equation modeling with EQS: Basic concepts, applications, and programming.* Mahwah, NJ: Erlbaum.

Byrne, B. M. (2009). *Structural equation modeling with AMOS: Basic concepts, applications, and programming.* New York: Routledge.

Enders, C. K. (2006). Analyzing structural equation models with missing data. In G. R. Hancock & R. O. Mueller (Eds.), *A Second course in structural equation modeling* (pp. 313-344). Greenwich, CT: Information Age.

Hancock, G. R., & Mueller, R. O. (Eds.). (2006). *Structural equation modeling: A second course.* Greenwich, CT: Information Age.

Horton, N. J., & Lipsitz, S. R. (2001). Multiple imputation in practice. Comparison of software packages for regression models with missing data. *The American Statistician, 55,* 244–254.

Muthén, L. K., & Muthén, B. O. (2004). *Mplus: The comprehensive modeling program for applied researchers— Users guide.* Los Angeles, CA: Muthén & Muthén.

Schafer, J. L., & Olsen, M. K. (1998). Multiple imputation for multivariate missing-data problems: A data analyst's perspective. *Multivariate Behavioral Research, 33,* 545–571.

# References

Agresti, A. (2002). *Categorical data analysis* (2nd ed.). Hoboken, NJ: Wiley.

Aiken, L. S., & West, S. G. (1991). *Multiple regression: Testing and interpreting interactions.* Newbury Park, CA: Sage.

Allison, P. D. (1987). Estimation of linear models with incomplete data. In C. C. Clogg (Ed.), *Sociological methodology, 1987* (pp. 71–103). San Francisco: Jossey-Bass.

Allison, P. D. (2000). Multiple imputation for missing data: A cautionary tale. *Sociological Methods and Research, 28,* 301–309.

Allison, P. D. (2002). *Missing data.* Newbury Park, CA: Sage.

Allison, P. D. (2005). *Imputation of categorical variables with PROC MI.* Paper presented at the 2005 SAS Users Group International conference. Retrieved January 30, 2009, from www2.sas.com/proceedings/sugi30/toc.html.

Amemiya, T. (1985). *Advanced econometrics.* Cambridge, MA: Harvard University Press.

Anderson, T. W. (1957). Maximum likelihood estimates for a multivariate normal distribution when some observations are missing. *Journal of the American Statistical Association, 52,* 200–203.

Arbuckle, J. L. (1996). Full information estimation in the presence of incomplete data. In G. A. Marcoulides & R. E. Schumacker (Eds.), *Advanced structural equation modeling* (pp. 243–277). Mahwah, NJ: Erlbaum.

Arbuckle, J. L. (2007). *Amos 16 user's guide.* Chicago: SPSS.

Arminger, G., & Sobel, M. E. (1990). Pseudo-maximum likelihood estimation of mean and covariance structures with missing data. *Journal of the American Statistical Association, 85,* 195–203.

Azar, B. (2002). Finding a solution for missing data. *Monitor on Psychology, 33,* 70.

Azen, S. P., Van Guilder, M., & Hill, M. A. (1989). Estimation of parameters and missing values under a regression model with non-normally distribution and non-randomly incomplete data. *Statistics in Medicine, 8,* 217–228.

Barnard, J., & Rubin, D. B. (1999). Small-sample degrees of freedom with multiple imputation. *Biometrika, 86,* 948–955.

Bartlett, M. S. (1946). On the theoretical specification of sampling properties of autocorrelated time series. *Journal of the Royal Statistical Society, Series B, 8,* 27–41.

Beale, E. M. L., & Little, R. J. A. (1975). Missing values in multivariate analysis. *Journal of the Royal Statistical Society, Series B, 37,* 129–145.

Belin, T. R., Hu, M-Y., Young, A. S., & Grusky, O. (1999). Performance of a general location model with an ignorable missing-data assumption in a multivariate mental health services study. *Statistics in Medicine, 18,* 3123–3135.

Bentler, P. M. (1983). Some contributions to efficient statistics in structural models: Specification and estimation of moment structures. *Psychometrika, 48,* 493–517.

Bentler, P. M. (1990). Comparative fit indexes in structural models. *Psychological Bulletin, 107,* 238–246.

Bentler, P. M., & Wu, E. J. C. (2002). *EQS 6 for Windows user's guide* [Computer software and manual]. Encino, CA: Multivariate Software.

Beran, R., & Srivastava, M. S. (1985). Bootstrap tests and confidence regions for functions of a covariance matrix. *Annals of Statistics, 13*, 95–115.

Bernaards, C. A., Belin, T. R., & Schafer, J. L. (2007). Robustness of a multivariate normal approximation for imputation of incomplete binary data. *Statistics in Medicine, 26*, 1368–1382.

Blunch, N. J. (2008). *Introduction to structural equation modeling using SPSS and AMOS*. Thousand Oaks, CA: Sage.

Bodner, T. E. (2006). Missing data: Prevalence and reporting practices. *Psychological Reports, 99*, 675–680.

Bohrnstedt, G. W., & Goldberger, A. S. (1969). On the exact covariance of products of random variables. *Journal of the American Statistical Association, 64*, 1439–1442.

Bollen, K. A. (1989). *Structural equations with latent variables*. New York: Wiley.

Bollen, K. A., & Curran, P. J. (2006). *Latent curve models: A structural equation approach*. Hoboken, NJ: Wiley.

Bollen, K. A. & Stine, R. A. (1992). Bootstrapping goodness-of-fit measures in structural equation models. *Sociological Methods and Research, 21*, 205–229.

Bolstad, W. M. (2007). *Introduction to Bayesian statistics* (2nd ed.). New York: Wiley.

Brown, R. L. (1994). Efficacy of the indirect approach for estimating structural equation models with missing data: A comparison of five methods. *Structural Equation Modeling: A Multidisciplinary Journal, 1*, 287–316.

Browne, M. W. (1984). Asymptotic distribution-free methods for the analysis of covariance structures. *British Journal of Mathematical and Statistical Psychology, 37*, 62–83.

Bryk, A. S., & Raudenbush, S. W. (1987). Application of hierarchical linear models to assessing change. *Psychological Bulletin, 101*, 147–158.

Buck, S. F. (1960). A method of estimation of missing values in multivariate data suitable for use with an electronic computer. *Journal of the Royal Statistical Society, Series B, 22*, 302–306.

Buse, A. (1982). The likelihood ratio, Wald, and Lagrange multiplier tests: An expository note. *The American Statistician, 36*, 153–157.

Byrne, B. M. (1998). *Structural equation modeling with LISREL: Basic concepts, applications, and programming*. Mahwah, NJ: Erlbaum.

Byrne, B. M. (2006). *Structural equation modeling with EQS: Basic concepts, applications, and programming*. Mahwah, NJ: Erlbaum.

Byrne, B. M. (2009). *Structural equation modeling with AMOS: Basic concepts, applications, and programming*. New York: Routledge.

Casella, G., & George, E. I. (1992). Explaining the Gibbs Sampler. *The American Statistician, 46*, 167–174.

Chen, H. Y., & Little, R. (1999). A test of missing completely at random for generalised estimating equations with missing data. *Biometrika, 86*, 1–13.

Chou, C. P., & Bentler, P.M. (1995). Estimates and tests in structural equation modeling. In R. H. Hoyle (Ed.), *Structural equation modeling: Issues and applications* (pp. 37–55). Newbury Park, CA: Sage.

Chou, C. P., Bentler, P. M., & Satorra, A. (1991). Scaled test statistics and robust standard errors for nonnormal data in covariance structure analysis: A Monte Carlo study. *British Journal of Mathematical and Statistical Psychology, 44*, 347–357.

Cohen, J. (1988). *Statistical power analysis for the behavioral sciences* (2nd ed.). Hillsdale, NJ: Erlbaum.

Cohen, J., Cohen, P., West, S. G., & Aiken, L. S. (2003). *Applied multiple regression/correlation analysis for the behavioral sciences* (3rd ed.). Mahwah, NJ: Erlbaum.

Collins, L. M., Schafer, J. L., & Kam, C-M. (2001). A comparison of inclusive and restrictive strategies in modern missing data procedures. *Psychological Methods, 6*, 330–351.

Cook, R. J., Zeng, L., & Yi, G. Y. (2004). Marginal analysis of incomplete longitudinal binary data: A cautionary note on LOCF imputation. *Biometrics, 60*, 820–828.

Cowles, M. K., & Carlin, B. P. (1996). Markov chain Monte Carlo convergence diagnostics: A comparative review. *Journal of the American Statistical Association, 91*, 883–904.

Curran, P. J., West, S. G., & Finch, J. F. (1996). The robustness of test statistics to nonnormality and specification error in confirmatory factor analysis. *Psychological Methods, 1*, 16–29.

De Gruttola, V., & Tu, X. M. (1994). Modelling progression of CD4–lymphocyte count at its relationship to survival time. *Biometrics, 50,* 1003–1014.

Demirtas, H., & Schafer, J. L. (2003). On the performance of random-coefficient pattern-mixture models for non-ignorable drop-out. *Statistics in Medicine, 22,* 2553–2575.

Demirtas, H., Freels, S. A., & Yucel, R. M. (2008). Plausibility of multivariate normality assumption when multiple imputing non-Gaussian continuous outcomes: A simulation assessment. *Journal of Statistical Computation and Simulation, 78,* 69–84.

Dempster, A. P. (1969). *Elements of continuous multivariate analysis.* Reading, MA: Addison-Wesley.

Dempster, A. P., Laird, N. M., & Rubin, D. B. (1977). Maximum likelihood from incomplete data via the EM algorithm. *Journal of the Royal Statistical Society, Series B, 39,* 1–38.

Diggle, P. J. (1989). Testing for random dropouts in repeated measurement data. *Biometrics, 45,* 1255–1258.

Diggle, P., & Kenward, M. G. (1994). Informative dropout in longitudinal data analysis. *Applied Statistics, 43,* 49–94.

DiStefano, C. (2002). The impact of categorization with confirmatory factor analysis. *Structural Equation Modeling: A Multidisciplinary Journal, 9,* 327–346.

Dixon, W. J. (1988). *BMDP statistical software.* Los Angeles: University of California Press.

Doninger, G. L., Enders, C. K., & Burnett, K. F. (2005). Validity evidence for Eating Attitudes Test scores in a sample of female college athletes. *Measurement in Physical Education and Exercise Science, 9,* 35–49.

Downey, R. G., & King, C. V. (1998). Missing data in Likert ratings: A comparison of replacement methods. *Journal of General Psychology, 125,* 175–191.

Duncan, S. C., Duncan, T. E., & Hops, H. (1996). Analysis of longitudinal data within accelerated longitudinal designs. *Psychological Methods, 1,* 236–248.

Edgett, G. L. (1956). Multiple regression with missing observations among the independent variables. *Journal of the American Statistical Association, 51,* 122–131.

Efron, B., & Hinkley, D. V. (1978). Assessing the accuracy of the maximum likelihood estimator: Observed versus expected Fisher information. *Biometrika, 65,* 457–487.

Efron, B., & Tibshirani, R. J. (1993). *An introduction to the bootstrap.* New York: Chapman & Hall.

Eliason, S. R. (1993). *Maximum likelihood estimation: Logic and practice.* Newbury Park, CA: Sage.

Enders, C. K. (2001). The impact of nonnormality on full information maximum likelihood estimation for structural equation models with missing data. *Psychological Methods, 6,* 352–370.

Enders, C. K. (2002). Applying the Bollen–Stine bootstrap for goodness-of-fit measures to structural equation models with missing data. *Multivariate Behavioral Research, 37,* 359–377.

Enders, C. K. (2003). Using the expectation maximization algorithm to estimate coefficient alpha for scales with item-level missing data. *Psychological Methods, 8,* 322–337.

Enders, C. K. (2004). The impact of missing data on sample reliability estimates: Implications for reliability reporting practices. *Educational and Psychological Measurement, 64,* 419–436.

Enders, C. K. (2005). A SAS macro for implementing the modified Bollen-Stine bootstrap for missing data: Implementing the bootstrap using existing structural equation modeling software. *Structural Equation Modeling: A Multidisciplinary Journal, 12,* 620–641.

Enders, C. K. (2006). Analyzing structural equation models with missing data. In G. R. Hancock & R. O. Mueller (Eds.), *A Second course in structural equation modeling* (pp. 313–344). Greenwich, CT: Information Age.

Enders, C. K. (2008). A note on the use of missing auxiliary variables in full information maximum likelihood-based structural equation models. *Structural Equation Modeling: A Multidisciplinary Journal, 15,* 434–448.

Enders, C. K. (2010). *Missing not at random models for latent curve analyses.* Manuscript submitted for publication.

Enders, C. K., & Bandalos, D. L. (2001). The relative performance of full information maximum likelihood estimation for missing data in structural equation models. *Structural Equation Modeling: A Multidisciplinary Journal, 8,* 430–457.

Enders, C. K., & Gottschall, A. C. (in press). Multiple imputation strategies for multiple group structural equation models. *Structural Equation Modeling: A Multidisciplinary Journal.*

Enders, C. K., & Peugh, J. L. (2004). Using an EM covariance matrix to estimate structural equation models with missing data. Choosing an adjusted sample size to improve the accuracy of inferences. *Structural Equation Modeling: An Interdisciplinary Journal, 11,* 1–19.

Enders, C., Dietz, S., Montague, M., & Dixon, J. (2006). Modern alternatives for dealing with missing data in special education research. In T. E. Scruggs & M. A. Mastropieri (Eds.), *Advances in learning and behavioral disorders* (Vol. 19, pp. 101–130). New York: Elsevier.

Fears, T. R., Benichou, J., & Gail, M. H. (1996). A reminder of the fallibility of the Wald statistic. *The American Statistician, 50,* 226–227.

Finch, J. F., West, S. G., & MacKinnon, D. P. (1997). Effects of sample size and nonnormality on the estimation of mediated effects in latent variable models. *Structural Equation Modeling: A Multidisciplinary Journal, 4,* 87–107.

Finkbeiner, C. (1979). Estimation for the multiple factor model when data are missing. *Psychometrika, 44,* 409–420.

Finney, S. J., & DiStefano, C. (2006). Nonnormal and categorical data in structural equation models. In G. R. Hancock & R. O. Mueller (Eds.). *A second course in structural equation modeling* (pp. 269–314). Greenwich, CT: Information Age.

Fisher, R. A. (1915). Frequency distribution of the values of the correlation coefficient in samples of an indefinitely large population. *Biometrika, 10,* 507–521.

Fitzmaurice, G. M., Laird, N. M., & Shneyer, L. (2001). An alternative parameterization of the general linear mixture model for longitudinal data with non-ignorable drop-outs. *Statistics in Medicine, 20,* 1009–1021.

Ford, B. L. (1983). An overview of hot-deck procedures. In W. G. Madow, I. Olkin, & D. B Rubin (Eds.), *Incomplete data in sample surveys* (pp. 185–207). New York: Academic Press.

Foster, E. M., & Fang, G. Y. (2004). Alternative methods for handling attrition: An illustration using data from the Fast Track evaluation. *Evaluation Review, 28,* 434–464.

Freedman, D. A. (2006). One the so-called "Huber sandwich estimator" and "robust standard errors." *The American Statistician, 60,* 299–302.

Garner, D. M., Olmsted, M. P., Bohr, Y., & Garfinkel, P. E. (1982). The Eating Attitudes Test: Psychometric features and clinical correlates. *Psychological Medicine, 12,* 871–878.

Gelfand, A. E., & Smith, A. F. M. (1990). Sampling-based approaches to calculating marginal densities. *Journal of the American Statistical Association, 85,* 398–409.

Gelman, A., & Rubin, D. B. (1992). Inference from iterative simulation using multiple sequences. *Statistical Science, 7,* 457–472.

Gelman, A., Carlin, J. B., Stern, H. S., & Rubin, D. B. (1995). *Bayesian data analysis.* Boca Raton, FL: Chapman & Hall.

Geweke, J. (1992). Evaluating the accuracy of sampling-based approaches to the calculation of posterior moments. In J. O. Berger, J. M. Bernardo, A. P. Dawid, & A. F. M. Smith (Eds.), *Bayesian statistics 4* (pp. 164–193). Oxford, UK: Oxford University Press.

Geyer, C. J. (1992). Practical Markov chain Monte Carlo. *Statistical Science, 7,* 473–483.

Glasser, M. (1964). Linear regression analysis with missing observations among the independent variables. *Journal of the American Statistical Association, 59,* 834–844.

Gleason, T. C., & Staelin, R. (1975). A proposal for handling missing data. *Psychometrika, 40,* 229–252.

Glynn, R. J., Laird, N. M., & Rubin, D. B. (1986). Selection modeling versus mixture modeling with non-ignorable nonresponse. In H. Wainer (Ed.), *Drawing inferences from self-selected samples* (pp. 115–142). New York: Springer-Verlag.

Gold, M. S., & Bentler, P. M. (2000). Treatments of missing data: A Monte Carlo comparison of RBHDI, iterative stochastic regression imputation, and expectation-maximization. *Structural Equation Modeling: A Multidisciplinary Journal, 7,* 319–355.

Gonzalez, R., & Griffin, D. (2001). Testing parameters in structural equation modeling: Every "one" matters. *Psychological Methods, 6,* 258–269.

Goodnight, J. H. (1979). A tutorial on the SWEEP operator. *The American Statistician, 33,* 149–158.

Graham, J. W. (2003). Adding missing-data relevant variables to FIML-based structural equation models. *Structural Equation Modeling: A Multidisciplinary Journal, 10,* 80–100.

Graham, J. W. (2009). Missing data analysis: Making it work in the real world. *Annual Review of Psychology*, *60*, 549–576.

Graham, J. W., & Schafer, J. L. (1999). On the performance of multiple imputation for multivariate data with small sample size. In R. Hoyle (Ed.), *Statistical strategies for small sample research* (pp. 1–29). Thousand Oaks, CA: Sage.

Graham, J. W., Hofer, S. M., & MacKinnon, D. P. (1996). Maximizing the usefulness of data obtained with planned missing value patterns: An application of maximum likelihood procedures. *Multivariate Behavioral Research*, *31*, 197–218.

Graham, J. W., Hofer, S. M., Donaldson, S. I., MacKinnon, D. P., & Schafer, J. L. (1997). Analysis with missing data in prevention research. In K. J. Bryant, M. Windle, & S. G. West (Eds.), *The science of prevention: Methodological advances from alcohol and substance abuse research* (pp. 325–366). Washington, DC: American Psychological Association.

Graham, J. W., Olchowski, A. E., & Gilreath, T. D. (2007). How many imputations are really needed? Some practical clarifications of multiple imputation theory. *Prevention Science*, *8*, 206–213.

Graham, J. W., Taylor, B. J., & Cumsille, P. E. (2001). Planned missing data designs in the analysis of change. In L. M. Collins & A. G. Sayer (Eds.), *New methods for the analysis of change* (pp. 335–353). Washington, DC: American Psychological Association.

Graham, J. W., Taylor, B. J., Olchowski, A. E., & Cumsille, P. E. (2006). Planned missing data designs in psychological research. *Psychological Methods*, *11*, 323–343.

Haitovsky, Y. (1968). Missing data in regression analysis. *Journal of the Royal Statistical Society, Series B*, *30*, 67–82.

Hancock, G. R., & Lawrence, F. R. (2006). Using latent growth models to evaluate longitudinal change. In G. R. Hancock & R. O. Mueller (Eds.), *Structural equation modeling: A second course* (pp. 171–196). Greenwood, CT: Information Age Publishing.

Hancock, G. R., & Mueller, R. O. (Eds.). (2006). *Structural equation modeling: A second course*. Greenwich, CT: Information Age.

Harel, O. (2007). Inferences on missing information under multiple imputation and two-stage multiple imputation. *Statistical Methodology*, *4*, 75–89.

Hartley, H. O. (1958). Maximum likelihood estimation from incomplete data. *Biometrics*, *14*, 174–194.

Hartley, H. O., & Hocking, R. R. (1971). The analysis of incomplete data. *Biometrics*, *27*, 783–808.

Hartman, R. S. (1991). A Monte Carlo analysis of alternative estimators in models involving selectivity. *Journal of Business and Economic Statistics*, *9*, 41–49.

Heckman, J. T. (1976). The common structure of statistical models of truncation, sample selection and limited dependent variables and a simple estimator for such models. *The Annals of Economic and Social Measurement*, *5*, 475–492.

Heckman, J. T. (1979). Sample selection bias as a specification error. *Econometrica*, *47*, 153–161.

Hedeker, D., & Gibbons, R. D. (1997). Application of random-effects pattern-mixture models for missing data in longitudinal studies. *Psychological Methods*, *2*, 64–78.

Hedeker, D., Gibbons, R. D., & Waternaux, C. (1999). Sample size estimation for longitudinal designs with attrition: Comparing time-related contrasts between two groups. *Journal of Educational and Behavioral Statistics*, *24*, 70–93.

Hogan, J. W., & Laird, N. M. (1997). Mixture models for the joint distribution of repeated measures and event times. *Statistics in Medicine*, *16*, 239–257.

Honaker, J., King, G., & Blackwell, M. (2009). Amelia II: A program for missing data [Computer software and manual]. Retrieved February 4, 2009, from gking.harvard.edu.

Horton, N. J., & Lipsitz, S. R. (2001). Multiple imputation in practice. Comparison of software packages for regression models with missing data. *The American Statistician*, *55*, 244–254.

Horton, N. J., Lipsitz, S. R., & Parzen, M. (2003). A potential for bias when rounding in multiple imputation. *The American Statistician*, *57*, 229–232.

Hu, L-T., & Bentler, P. M. (1998). Fit indices in covariance structure modeling: Sensitivity to underparameterized model misspecification. *Psychological Methods*, *3*, 424–453.

Hu, L-T., & Bentler, P. M. (1999). Cutoff criteria for fit indexes in covariance structure analysis: Conventional criteria versus new alternatives. *Structural Equation Modeling: A Multidisciplinary Journal*, *6*, 1–55.

Hu, L-T., Bentler, P. M., & Kano, Y. (1992). Can test statistics in covariance structure analysis be trusted? *Psychological Bulletin, 112,* 351–362.

Huber, P. (1967). The behavior of maximum likelihood estimates under nonstandard conditions. *Proceedings of the 5th Berkeley Symposium on Mathematical Statistics and Probability, 1,* 221–233.

Ioannidis, J. P. A., Haidich, A. B., Pappa, M., Pantazis, N., Kokori, S. I., Tektonidou, M. G., et al. (2001). Comparison of evidence of treatment effects in randomized and nonrandomized studies. *Journal of the American Medical Association, 286,* 821–830.

Jackman, S. (2000). Estimation and inference via Bayesian simulation: An introduction to Markov chain Monte Carlo. *American Journal of Political Science, 44,* 375–404.

Jamshidian, M., & Bentler, P. M. (1999). ML estimation of mean and covariance structures with missing data using complete data routines. *Journal of Educational and Behavioral Statistics, 24,* 21–41.

Jeffreys, H. (1946). An invariant form of the prior probability in estimation problems. *Proceedings of the Royal Society of London, Series A, 186,* 453–461.

Jeffreys, H. (1961). *Theory of probability* (3rd ed.). London: Oxford University Press.

Johnson, E. G. (1992). The design of the National Assessment of Educational Progress. *Journal of Educational Measurement, 29,* 95–110.

Johnson, R. A., & Wichern, D. W. (2007). *Applied multivariate statistical analysis* (6th ed.). Englewood Cliffs, NJ: Prentice Hall.

Johnson, V. E. (1996). Studying convergence of Markov chain Monte Carlo algorithms using coupled sample paths. *Journal of the American Statistical Association, 91,* 154–166.

Jöreskog, K. G., & Sörbom, D. (1993). *PRELIS 2 user's reference guide* [Computer software]. Chicago: Scientific Software.

Jöreskog, K. G., & Sörbom, D. (2006). *LISREL 8. 8 for Windows* [Computer software and manual]. Lincolnwood, IL: Scientific Software International.

Kaplan, D. (2000). *Structural equation modeling: Foundations and extensions.* Thousand Oaks, CA: Sage.

Kass, R. E., & Wasserman, L. (1996). The selection of prior distributions by formal rules. *Journal of the American Statistical Association, 91,* 1343–1370.

Keel, P. K., Mitchell, J. E., Davis, T. L., & Crow, S. J. (2002). Long-term impact of treatment in women diagnosed with bulimia nervosa. *International Journal of Eating Disorders, 31,* 151–158.

Kenward, M. G. (1998). Selection models for repeated measurements with non-random dropout: An illustration of sensitivity. *Statistics in Medicine, 17,* 2723–2732.

Kenward, M. G., & Molenberghs, G. (1998). Likelihood based frequentist inference when data are missing at random. *Statistical Science, 13,* 236–247.

Kim, J., & Curry, J. (1977). The treatment of missing data in multivariate analyses. *Sociological Methods and Research, 6,* 215–240.

Kim, K. H., & Bentler, P. M. (2002). Tests of homogeneity of means and covariance matrices for multivariate incomplete data. *Psychometrika, 67,* 609–624.

King, G., Honaker, J., Joseph, A., & Scheve, K. (2001). Analyzing incomplete political science data: An alternative algorithm for multiple imputation. *American Political Science Review, 95,* 49–69.

Kline, R. B. (2005). *Principles and practice of structural equation modeling* (2nd ed.). New York: Guilford.

Kromrey, J. D., & Hines, C. V. (1994). Nonrandomly missing data in multiple regression: An empirical comparison of common missing-data treatments. *Educational and Psychological Measurement, 54,* 573–593.

Laird, N. M. (1988). Missing data in longitudinal studies. *Statistics in Medicine, 7,* 305–315.

Lavori, P. W., Dawson, R., & Shera, D. (1995). A multiple imputation strategy for clinical trials with truncation of patient data. *Statistics in Medicine, 14,* 1913–1925.

Lee, M. D., & Wagenmakers, E-J. (2005). Bayesian statistical inference in psychology: Comment on Trafimow (2003). *Psychological Review, 112,* 662–668.

Leite, W. L., & Beretvas, N. (2004, April). *The performance of multiple imputation for Likert-type items with missing data.* Paper presented at the Annual Meeting of the American Educational Research Association.

Leung, S. F., & Yu, S. (1996). On the choice between sample selection and two-part models. *Journal of Econometrics, 72,* 197–229.

Li, K. H., Meng, X. L., Raghunathan, T. E., & Rubin, D. B. (1991). Significance levels from repeated p-values with multiply-imputed data. *Statistica Sinica, 1,* 65–92.

Li, K. H., Raghunathan, T. E., & Rubin, D. B. (1991). Large sample significance levels from multiply imputed data using moment-based statistics and an F reference distribution. *Journal of the American Statistical Association, 86*, 1065–1073.

Liang, J., & Bentler, P. M. (2004). An EM algorithm for fitting two-level structural equation models. *Psychometrika, 69*, 101–122.

Lipsey, M. W., & Wilson, D. B. (1993). The efficacy of psychological, educational, and behavioral treatment: Confirmation from meta-analysis. *The American Psychologist, 48*, 1181–1209.

Little, R. J. A. (1976). Comments on a paper by D. B. Rubin. *Biometrika, 63*, 590–591.

Little, R. J. A. (1988). A test of missing completely at random for multivariate data with missing values. *Journal of the American Statistical Association, 83*, 1198–1202.

Little, R. J. A. (1992. Regression with missing X's: A review. *Journal of the American Statistical Association, 87*, 1227–1237.

Little, R. J. A. (1993). Pattern-mixture models for multivariate incomplete data. *Journal of the American Statistical Association, 88*, 125–134.

Little, R. J. A. (1995). Modeling the drop-out mechanism in repeated-measures studies. *Journal of the American Statistical Association, 90*, 1112–1121.

Little, R. J. A., & Rubin, D. B. (2002). *Statistical analysis with missing data* (2nd ed.). Hoboken, NJ: Wiley.

Little, R. J. A., & Schluchter, M. D. (1985). Maximum likelihood estimation for mixed continuous and categorical data with missing values. *Biometrika, 72*, 497–512.

Little, T. D., McConnell, E. K., Howard, W. J., & Stump, K. N. (2008). *Missing data in large data projects: Two methods of missing data imputation when working with large data projects*. Retrieved January 30, 2009, from *www.quant.ku.edu/resources/guides.html*.

Liu, G., & Gould, A. L. (2002). Comparison of alternative strategies for analysis of longitudinal trials. *Journal of Biopharmaceutical Statistics, 12*, 207–226.

Lord, F. M. (1955). Estimation of parameters from incomplete data. *Journal of the American Statistical Association, 50*, 870–876.

Lord, F. M. (1962). Estimating norms by item sampling. *Educational and Psychological Measurement, 22*, 259–267.

MacKinnon, D. P. (2008). *Introduction to statistical mediation analysis*. Mahwah, NJ: Erlbaum.

Mallinckrodt, C. H., Clark, W. S., & David, S. R. (2001). Accounting for dropout bias using mixed effects models. *Journal of Biopharmaceutical Statistics, 11*, 9–21.

Manning, W. G., Duan, N., & Rogers, W. H. (1987). Monte Carlo evidence on the choice between sample selection and two-part models. *Journal of Econometrics, 35*, 197–229.

Marsh, H. W. (1998). Pairwise deletion for missing data in structural equation models: Nonpositive definite matrices, parameter estimates, goodness of fit, and adjusted sample sizes. *Structural Equation Modeling: A Multidisciplinary Journal, 5*, 22–36.

McCutcheon, A. L. (1987). *Latent class analysis*. Newbury Park, CA: Sage.

McLachlan, G. J., & Krishnan, T. (1997). *The EM algorithm and extensions*. New York: Wiley.

McLachlan, G. J., & Peel, D. (2000). *Finite mixture models*. New York: Wiley.

Mehta, P. D., & West, S. G. (2000). Putting the individual back into individual growth curves. *Psychological Methods, 5*, 23–43.

Meng, X-L. (1994). Multiple-imputation inferences with uncongenial sources of input. *Statistical Science, 9*, 538–558.

Meng, X-L., & Rubin, D. B. (1991). Using EM to obtain asymptotic variance-covariance matrices: The SEM algorithm. *Journal of the American Statistical Association, 86*, 899–909.

Meng, X-L. & Rubin, D. B. (1992). Performing likelihood ratio tests with multiply-imputed data sets. *Biometrika, 79*, 103–111.

Micceri, T. (1989). The unicorn, the normal curve, and other improbable creatures. *Psychological Bulletin, 105*, 156–166.

Michiels, B., Molenberghs, G., Bijnens, L., Vangeneugden, T., & Thijs, H. (2002). Selection models and pattern-mixture models to analyse longitudinal quality of life data subject to drop-out. *Statistics in Medicine, 21*, 1023–1041.

Molenberghs, G., & Kenward, M. G. (2007). *Missing data in clinical studies*. West Sussex, UK: Wiley.

Molenberghs, G., Michiels, B., Kenward, M. G., & Diggle, P. J. (1998). Monotone missing data and pattern-mixture models. *Statistica Neerlandica, 52*, 153–161.

Molenberghs, G., Thijs, H., Jansen, I., & Beunckens, C., Kenward, M. G., Mallinckrodt, C., et al. (2004). Analyzing incomplete longitudinal clinical trial data. *Biostatistics, 5*, 445–464.

Montgomery, D. C. (1997). *Design and analysis of experiments* (4th ed.). New York: Wiley.

Muthén, B. (2001). Latent variable mixture modeling. In G. A. Marcoulides & R. E. Schumacker (Eds.), *New developments and techniques in structural equation modeling* (pp. 1–33). Mahwah, NJ: Erlbaum.

Muthén, B. (2004). Latent variable analysis: Growth mixture modeling and related techniques for longitudinal data. In D. Kaplan (Ed.), *Handbook of quantitative methodology for the social sciences* (pp. 345–368). Newbury Park, CA: Sage.

Muthén, B., Kaplan, D., & Hollis, M. (1987). On structural equation modeling with data that are not missing completely at random. *Psychometrika, 52*, 431–462.

Muthén, L. K., & Muthén, B. O. (2002). How to use a Monte Carlo study to decide on sample size and determine power. *Structural Equation Modeling: A Multidisciplinary Journal, 9*, 599–620.

Muthén, L. K., & Muthén, B. O. (1998–2009). *Mplus user's guide* (5th ed.). Los Angeles: Muthén & Muthén.

Muthén, B., & Shedden, K. (1999). Finite mixture modeling with mixture outcomes using the EM algorithm. *Biometrics, 55*, 463–469.

Mykland, P., Tierney, L., & Yu, B. (1995). Regeneration in Markov chain samplers. *Journal of the American Statistical Association, 90*, 233–241.

Nawata, K. (1993). A note on the estimation of models with sample-selection biases. *Economics Letters, 42*, 15–24.

Nawata, K. (1994). Estimation of sample selection bias models by the maximum likelihood estimator and Heckman's two-step estimator. *Economics Letters, 45*, 33–40.

Nelson, F. D. (1984). Efficiency of the two-step estimator for models with endogenous sample selection. *Journal of Econometrics, 24*, 181–196.

Nesselroade, J. R., & Baltes, P. B. (1979). *Longitudinal research in the study of behavior and development*. New York: Academic Press.

Newman, D. A. (2003). Longitudinal modeling with randomly and systematically missing data: A simulation of ad hoc, maximum likelihood, and multiple imputation techniques. *Organizational Research Methods, 6*, 328–362.

Olinsky, A., Chen, S., & Harlow, L. (2003). The comparative efficacy of imputation methods for missing data in structural equation modeling. *European Journal of Operational Research, 151*, 53–79.

Olkin, I., & Tate, R. F. (1961). Multivariate correlation models with mixed discrete and continuous variables. *Annuals of Mathematical Statistics, 32*, 448–465.

Orchard, T., & Woodbury, M. A. (1972). A missing information principle: Theory and applications. *Proceedings of the 6th Berkeley Symposium on Mathematical Statistics and Probability, 1*, 697–715.

Paarsch, H. J. (1984). A Monte Carlo comparison of estimators for censored regression models. *Journal of Econometrics, 24*, 197–213.

Pampel, F. C. (2000). *Logistic regression: A primer*. Thousand Oaks, CA: Sage.

Park, T., & Lee, S-Y. (1997). A test of missing completely at random for longitudinal data with missing observations. *Statistics in Medicine, 16*, 1859–1871.

Pauler, D. K., McCoy, S., & Moinpour, C. (2003). Pattern mixture models for longitudinal quality of life students in advanced stage disease. *Statistics in Medicine, 22*, 795–809.

Pawitan, Y. (2000). A reminder of the fallibility of the Wald statistic: Likelihood explanation. *The American Statistician, 54*, 54–56.

Paxton, P., Curran, P. J., Bollen, K. A., Kirby, J., & Chen, F. (2001). Monte Carlo experiments: Design and implementation. *Structural Equation Modeling: A Multidisciplinary Journal, 8*, 287–312.

Pearson, K. (1903). Mathematical contributions to the theory of evolution—XI. On the influence of natural selection on the variability and correlation of organs. *Philosophical Transactions of the Royal Society of London, Series A, 321*, 1–66.

Peugh, J. L., & Enders, C. K. (2004). Missing data in educational research: A review of reporting practices and suggestions for improvement. *Review of Educational Research, 74*, 525–556.

Pruzek, R. M. (1997). An introduction to Bayesian inference and its applications. In L. L. Harlow, S. A. Mulaik, & J. H. Steiger (Eds.), *What if there were no significance tests?* (pp. 287–318). Mahwah, NJ: Erlbaum.

Puhani, P. A. (2000). The Heckman correction for sample selection and its critique. *Journal of Economic Surveys, 14*, 53–67.

Raftery, A. E., & Lewis, S. M. (1992). One long run with diagnostics: Implementation strategies for Markov chain Monte Carlo. *Statistical Science, 7*, 493–497.

Raghunathan, T. E., & Grizzle, J. E. (1995). A split questionnaire survey design. *Journal of the American Statistical Association, 90*, 54–63.

Raghunathan, T. E., Lepkowski, J. M., Van Hoewyk, J., & Solenberger, P. (2001). A multivariate technique for multiply imputing missing values using a sequence of regression models. *Survey Methodology, 27*, 85–95.

Raghunathan, T. E., Solenberger, P. W., & Van Hoewyk, J. (2002). IVEware: Imputation and variance estimation software [Computer software and manual]. Retrieved February 4, 2009, from www.isr.umich.edu/src/smp.ive.

Raudenbush, S. W. (2001). Toward a coherent framework for comparing trajectories of individual change. In L. M. Collins & A. G. Sayer (Eds.), *New methods for the analysis of change* (pp. 35–64). Washington, DC: American Psychological Association.

Raudenbush, S. W., & Bryk, A. S. (2002). *Hierarchical linear models: Applications and data analysis methods* (2nd ed.). Thousand Oaks, CA: Sage.

Raykov, T., & Marcoulides, G. A. (2004). Using the delta method for approximate interval estimation of parameter functions in SEM. *Structural Equation Modeling: A Multidisciplinary Journal, 11*, 621–637.

Raymond, M. R., & Roberts, D. M. (1987). A comparison of methods for treating incomplete data in selection research. *Educational and Psychological Measurement, 47*, 13–26.

Ritter, C., & Tanner, M. A. (1992). Facilitating the Gibbs sampler: The Gibbs stopper and the Griddy-Gibbs sampler. *Journal of the American Statistical Association, 87*, 861–868.

Roberts, G. O. (1992). Convergence diagnostics of the Gibbs sampler. In J. O. Berger, J. M. Bernardo, A. P. Dawid, & A. F. M. Smith (Eds.), *Bayesian statistics 4* (pp. 164–193). Oxford, UK: Oxford University Press.

Royston, P. (2005). Multiple imputation of missing values: Update. *The Stata Journal, 5*, 1–14.

Rubin, D. B. (1974). Estimating causal effects of treatment in randomized and non-randomized studies. *Journal of Educational Psychology, 66*, 688–701.

Rubin, D. B. (1976). Inference and missing data. *Biometrika, 63*, 581–592.

Rubin, D. B. (1978a). Bayesian inference for causal effects: The role of randomization. *Annals of Statistics, 6*, 34–58.

Rubin, D. B. (1978b). Multiple imputations in sample surveys—A phenomenological Bayesian approach to nonresponse. *Proceedings of the Survey Research Methods Section of the American Statistical Association*, 30–34.

Rubin, D. B. (1987). *Multiple imputation for nonresponse in surveys*. Hoboken, NJ: Wiley.

Rubin, D. B. (1992). Meta-analysis: Literature synthesis or effect-size surface estimation? *Journal of Educational Statistics, 17*, 363–374.

Rubin, D. B. (1996). Multiple imputation after 18+ years. *Journal of the American Statistical Association, 91*, 473–489.

Rubin, D. B., & Schenker, N. (1986). Multiple imputation for interval estimation from simple random samples with ignorable response. *Journal of the American Statistical Association, 81*, 366–374.

Rupp, A. A., Dey, D. K., & Zumbo, B. D. (2004). To Bayes or not to Bayes, from whether to when: Applications of Bayesian methodology to modeling. *Structural Equation Modeling: An Interdisciplinary Journal, 11*, 424–451.

Sackett, P. R., & Yang, H. (2000). Correction for range restriction: An expanded typology. *Journal of Applied Psychology, 85*, 112–118.

Satorra, A., & Bentler, P. M. (1988). Scaling corrections for chi-square statistics in covariance structure analysis. *Proceedings of Business and Economics Sections* (pp. 308–313). Alexandria, VA: American Statistical Association.

Satorra, A., & Bentler, P. M. (1994). Corrections to test statistics and standard errors in covariance structure analysis. In A. Von Eye & C. C. Clogg (Eds.), Latent variables analysis: *Applications for developmental research* (pp. 399–419). Newbury Park, CA: Sage.

Satorra, A., & Bentler, P. M. (2001). A scaled difference chi-square test statistic for moment structure analysis. *Psychometrika, 66,* 507–514.

Savalei, V. (2008). Is the ML chi-square ever robust to nonnormality? A cautionary note with missing data. *Structural Equation Modeling: An Interdisciplinary Journal, 15,* 1–22.

Savalei, V., & Bentler, P. M. (2005). A statistically justified pairwise ML method for incomplete nonnormal data: A comparison with direct ML and pairwise ADF. *Structural Equation Modeling: An Interdisciplinary Journal, 12,* 183–214.

Savalei, V., & Bentler, P. M. (2007). *A two-stage approach to missing data: Theory and application to auxiliary variables.* Retrieved September 18, 2008, from *preprints.stat.ucla.edu.*

Schafer, J. L. (1997). *Analysis of incomplete multivariate data.* Boca Raton, FL: Chapman & Hall.

Schafer, J. L. (1999). *NORM: Multiple imputation of incomplete multivariate data under a normal model* [Computer software]. University Park: Department of Statistics, Pennsylvania State University.

Schafer, J. L. (2001). Multiple imputation with PAN. In A. G. Sayer & L. M. Collins (Eds.), *New methods for the analysis of change* (pp. 355–377). Washington, DC: American Psychological Association.

Schafer, J. L. (2003). Multiple imputation in multivariate problems when the imputation and analysis models differ. *Statistica Neerlandica, 57,* 19–35.

Schafer, J. L., & Graham, J. W. (2002). Missing data: Our view of the state of the art. *Psychological Methods, 7,* 147–177.

Schafer, J. L., & Olsen, M. K. (1998). Multiple imputation for multivariate missing-data problems: A data analyst's perspective. *Multivariate Behavioral Research, 33,* 545–571.

Schafer, J. L., & Yucel, R. M. (2002). Computational strategies for multivariate linear mixed-effects models with missing data. *Journal of Computational and Graphical Statistics, 11,* 437–457.

Scheuren, F. (2005). Multiple imputation: How it began and continues. *The American Statistician, 59,* 315–319.

Schluchter, M. D. (1992). Methods for the analysis of informatively censored longitudinal data. *Statistics in Medicine, 11,* 1861–1870.

Shao, J., & Zhong, B. (2004). Last observation carry-forward and last observation analysis. *Statistics in Medicine, 22,* 2429–2441.

Share, D., McCrady, B., & Epstein, E. (2002). Stage of change and decisional balance for women seeking alcohol treatment. *Addictive Behaviors, 29,* 525–535.

Shih, W. J., Quan, H., & Chang, M. N. (1994). Estimation of the mean when data contain non-ignorable missing values from a random effects model. *Statistics and Probability Letters, 19,* 249–257.

Shoemaker, D. M. (1973). *Principles and procedures of multiple matrix sampling.* Cambridge, MA: Ballinger.

Singer, J. D., & Willett, J. B. (2003). *Applied longitudinal data analysis: Modeling change and event occurrence.* New York: Oxford University Press.

Sinharay, S., Stern, H. S., & Russell, D. (2001). The use of multiple imputation for the analysis of missing data. *Psychological Methods, 6,* 317–329.

Smith, A. F. M., & Roberts, G. O. (1993). Bayesian computation via the Gibbs sampler and related Markov chain Monte Carlo methods. *Journal of the Royal Statistical Society, Series B, 55,* 3–23.

Stephenson, B. & Stern, H. S. (1998). A primer on the Bayesian approach to statistical inference. *Stats, 23,* 3–9.

Stine, R. (1989). An introduction to bootstrap methods: Examples and ideas. *Sociological Methods and Research, 18,* 243–291.

Stolzenberg, R. M., & Relles, D. A. (1990). Theory testing in a world of constrained research design. *Sociological Methods and Research, 18,* 395–415.

Stolzenberg, R. M., & Relles, D. A. (1997). Tools for intuition about sample selection bias and its correction. *American Sociological Review, 62,* 494–507.

Tabachnick, B. G., & Fidell, L. S. (2007). *Using multivariate statistics* (5th ed.). Boston: Allyn & Bacon.

Tanner, M. A., & Wong, W. H. (1987). The calculation of posterior distributions by data augmentation. *Journal of the American Statistical Association, 82,* 528–540.

Thijs, H., Molenberghs, G., Michiels, B., & Curran, D. (2002). Strategies to fit pattern-mixture models. *Biostatistics, 3*, 245–265.

Thoemmes, F., & Enders, C. K. (2007, April). *A structural equation model for testing whether data are missing completely at random*. Paper presented at the annual meeting of the American Educational Research Association, Chicago, IL.

Timm, N. H. (1970). The estimation of variance-covariance and correlation matrices from incomplete data. *Psychometrika, 35*, 417–437.

Trawinksi, I. M., & Bargmann, R. E. (1964). Maximum likelihood estimation with incomplete multivariate data. *The Annals of Mathematical Statistics, 35*, 647–657.

Tu, X. M., Zhang, J., Kowalski, J., Shults, J., Feng, C., Sun, W., et al. (2007). Power analysis for longitudinal study designs with missing data. *Statistics in Medicine, 26*, 2958–2981.

van Buuren, S. (2007). Multiple imputation of discrete and continuous data by fully conditional specification. *Statistical Methods in Medical Research, 16*, 219–242.

van Buuren, S., Brand, J. P. L., Groothuis-Oudshoorn, C. G. M., & Rubin, D. B. (2006). Fully conditional specification in multivariate imputation. *Journal of Statistical Computation and Simulation, 76*, 1049–1064.

Van Ginkel, J. R., Van der Ark, L. A., & Sijtsma, K. (2007a). Multiple imputation for item scores when test data are factorially complex. *British Journal of Mathematical and Statistical Psychology, 60*, 315–337.

Van Ginkel, J. R., Van der Ark, L. A., & Sijtsma, K. (2007b). Multiple imputation of item scores in test and questionnaire data, and influence on psychometric results. *Multivariate Behavioral Research, 42*, 387–414.

Verbeke, G., & Molenberghs, G. (2000). *Linear mixed models for longitudinal data*. New York: Springer-Verlag.

Vermunt, J. K., Van Ginkel, J. R., Van der Ark, L. A., & Sijtsma, K. (2008). Multiple imputation of categorical data using latent class analysis. *Sociological Methodology, 33*, 369–397.

von Hippel, P. T. (2004). Biases in SPSS 12. 0 Missing Values Analysis. *The American Statistician, 58*, 160–164.

West, S., & Thoemmes, F. (in press). Campbell's and Rubin's perspectives on causal inference and generalization: An introduction. *Psychological Methods*.

West, S. G., Finch, J. F., & Curran, P. J. (1995). Structural equation models with nonnormal variables: Problems and remedies. In R. H. Hoyle (Ed.), *Structural equation modeling: Concepts, issues, and applications* (pp. 56–75). Newbury Park, CA: Sage.

White, H. (1982). Maximum likelihood estimation of misspecified models. *Econometrica, 50*, 1–26.

Widaman, K. F., & Thompson, J. S. (2003). On specifying the null model for incremental fit indices in structural equation modeling. *Psychological Methods, 8*, 16–37.

Wilkinson, L., & Task Force on Statistical Inference (1999). Statistical methods in psychology journals: Guidelines and explanations. *American Psychologist, 54*, 594–604.

Wilks, S. S. (1932). Moments and distributions of estimates of population parameters from fragmentary samples. *The Annals of Mathematical Statistics, 3*, 163–195.

Winship, C., & Mare, R. D. (1992). Models for sample selection bias. *Annual Review of Sociology, 18*, 327–350.

Wood, A. M., White, I. R., & Thompson, S. G. (2004). Are missing outcome data adequately handled? A review of published randomized controlled trials in major medical journals. *Clinical Trials, 1*, 368–376.

Wothke, W. (1993). Nonpositive definite matrices in structural equation modeling. In K. A. Bollen & J. S. Long (Eds.), *Testing structural equation models* (pp. 256–293). Newbury Park, CA: Sage.

Wothke, W. (2000). Longitudinal and multigroup modeling with missing data. In T. D. Little, K. U. Schnabel, & J. Baumert (Eds.), *Modeling longitudinal and multilevel data: Practical issues, applied approaches, and specific examples* (pp. 219–240). Mahwah, NJ: Erlbaum.

Wright, T. A., & Bonett, D. G. (2007). Job satisfaction and psychological well-being as nonadditive predictors of workplace turnover. *Journal of Management, 33*, 141–160.

Wright, T. A., Cropanzano, R., & Bonett, D. G. (2007). The moderating role of employee positive well being on the relation between job satisfaction and job performance. *Occupational Health Psychology, 12*, 93–104.

Wu, M. C., & Carroll, R. J. (1988). Estimation and comparison of changes in the presence of informative right censoring by modeling the censoring process. *Biometrics, 44*, 175–188.

Wu, W., & Enders, C. K. (2009). *The impact of rounding imputed values in a multiple imputation analysis.* Manuscript in preparation.

Yuan, K-H. (2007). *Normal theory ML for missing data with violation of distribution assumptions.* Manuscript submitted for publication.

Yuan, K-H., & Bentler, P. M. (1997). Improving parameter tests in covariance structure analysis. *Computational Statistics and Data Analysis, 26*, 177–198.

Yuan, K-H., & Bentler, P. M. (2000). Three likelihood-based methods for mean and covariance structure analysis with nonnormal missing data. *Sociological Methodology, 30*, 165–200.

Yuan, K-H., & Hayashi, K. (2003). Bootstrap approach to inference and power analysis based on three test statistics for covariance structure models. *British Journal of Mathematical and Statistical Psychology, 56*, 93–110.

Yuan, K-H., Bentler, P. M., & Zhang, W. (2005). The effect of skewness and kurtosis on mean and covariance structure analysis: The univariate case and its multivariate implication. *Sociological Methods and Research, 24*, 240–258.

Yuan, K-H., Lambert, P. L., & Fouladi, R. T. (2004). Mardia's multivariate kurtosis with missing data. *Multivariate Behavioral Research, 39*, 413–437.

Yuan, Y. C. (2000). *Multiple imputation for missing data: Concepts and new development.* Paper presented at the 2000 SAS Users Group International conference. Retrieved February 4, 2009, from *www2.sas.com/proceedings/sugi25/25/25p267.pdf.*

Yucel, R. M. (2008). Multiple imputation inference for multivariate multilevel continuous data with ignorable non-response. *Philosophical Transactions of the Royal Society, Series A*, 1–16.

Yucel, R. M., He, Y., & Zaslavsky, A. M. (2008). Using calibration to improve rounding in imputation. *The American Statistician, 62*, 1–5.

Yung, Y. F., & Bentler, P. M. (1996). Bootstrapping techniques in analysis of mean and covariance structures. In G. A. Marcoulides & R. E. Schumacker (Eds.), *Advanced structural equation modeling: Techniques and issues* (pp. 195–226). Hillsdale, NJ: Erlbaum.

Zellner, A., & Min, C-K. (1995). Gibbs sampler convergence criteria. *Journal of the American Statistical Association, 90*, 921–927.

# Author Index

Agresti, 294, 303
Aiken, L. S., 264, 265, 266, 280, 303, 338
Allison, P. D., 113, 164, 216, 230, 252, 261, 262, 264, 265, 278, 286, 287, 289, 328, 333
Amemiya, T., 295
Anderson, T. W., 86
Arbuckle, J. L., 39, 96, 126, 330
Arminger, G., 140, 145
Azen, S. P., 39

## B

Baltes, P. B., 29
Bandalos, D. L., 39, 43, 50, 55, 96, 126
Bargmann, R. E., 110
Barnard, J., 231, 232, 246
Bartlett, M. S., 208
Beale, E. M. L., 1, 46, 86, 103
Belin, T. R., 259, 261, 275
Benichou, J., 79, 80
Bentler, P. M., 18, 47, 50, 96, 104, 123, 133, 134, 138, 139, 140, 145, 148, 149, 157, 163, 251, 330, 331
Beran, R., 150
Beretvas, N., 259
Bernaards, C. A., 259, 261, 262, 263, 264
Bijnens, L., 305
Blackwell, M., 278, 333
Blunch, N. J., 330
Bodner, T. E., 1
Bohr, Y., 32, 119, 157, 247, 281
Bohrnstedt, G. W., 266, 339
Bollen, K. A., 30, 76, 81, 92, 123, 134, 137, 140, 145, 150, 151, 163, 288, 301

Bolstad, W. M., 164, 186
Bonett, D. G., 80, 114, 154, 242, 279
Brand, J. P. L., 275
Brown, R. L., 39, 43, 49, 50, 55
Browne, M. W., 140
Bryk, A. S., 5, 80, 104, 276, 288, 301
Buck, S. F., 44, 46
Burnett, K. F., 32, 120, 157, 247, 281
Buse, A., 79, 85
Byrne, B. M., 330, 344, 345

## C

Carlin, B. P., 203
Carlin, J. B., 164, 186, 228
Carroll, R. J., 305, 306
Casella, G., 277
Chang, M. N., 305
Chen, F., 30
Chen, H. Y., 18
Chen, S., 43, 96
Chou, C. P., 140, 145
Clark, W. S., 52
Cohen, J., 19, 24, 31, 32, 33, 264, 280, 289, 303, 314, 316, 320
Cohen, P., 264, 303
Collins, L. M., 14, 16, 17, 19, 33, 121, 124, 128, 129, 130, 131, 133, 163, 201, 227, 228, 230, 336, 341
Cook, R. J., 52
Cowles, M. K., 203
Cropanzano, R., 80, 114, 154, 242, 279
Crow, S. J., 51
Cumsille, P. E., 15, 22, 36, 132, 342

359

Curran, D., 307
Curran, P. J., 30, 80, 124, 140, 261, 288, 301
Curry, J., 39, 43

**D**

David, S. R., 52
Davis, T. L., 51
Dawson, R., 188, 272
De Gruttola, V., 305, 306
Demirtas, H., 259, 260, 287, 288, 300, 307, 308,
    312, 322, 326, 328
Dempster, A. P., 1, 44, 86, 103, 105, 112, 126, 200
Dey, D. K., 164, 186
Dietz, S., 16, 132
Diggle, P., 6, 18, 303, 304, 305, 307, 315
DiStefano, C., 80, 124, 140, 145, 163, 261
Dixon, J., 16, 132
Dixon, W. J., 18, 33
Donaldson, S. I., 16, 132, 289, 328
Doninger, G. L., 32, 120, 157, 247, 281
Downey, R. G., 51
Duan, N., 296
Duncan, S. C., 29
Duncan, T. E., 29

**E**

Edgett, G. L., 86
Efron, B., 98, 145
Eliason, S. R., 76, 85
Enders, C. K., 1, 16, 18, 21, 32, 37, 39, 41, 43, 50,
    51, 55, 85, 96, 104, 120, 122, 124, 126, 132,
    134, 137, 140, 145, 146, 148, 153, 154, 157,
    161, 164, 247, 262, 266, 267, 268, 269, 281,
    288, 329, 340, 345
Epstein, E., 51

**F**

Fang, G. Y., 15, 305, 326
Fears, T. R., 79, 80
Fidell, L. S., 71, 260
Finch, J. F., 80, 124, 140, 261
Finkbeiner, C., 86
Finney, S. J., 80, 124, 140, 163, 261
Fisher, R. A., 220, 221, 244
Fitzmaurice, G. M., 307
Ford, B. L., 49
Foster, E. M., 15, 305, 326
Fouladi, R. T., 332
Freedman, D. A., 143, 163
Freels, S. A., 259

**G**

Gail, M. H., 79, 80
Garfinkel, P. E., 32, 119, 157, 247, 281
Garner, D. M., 32, 119, 157, 247, 281
Gelfand, A. E., 277
Gelman, A., 164, 186, 203, 209, 212, 228
George, E. I., 277
Geweke, J., 203
Geyer, C. J., 203, 209
Gibbons, R. D., 15, 30, 307, 308, 309, 317, 318,
    319, 321, 323, 324, 328
Gilreath, T. D., 213, 216, 233, 343
Glasser, M., 41
Gleason, T. C., 43, 46
Glynn, R. J., 298
Gold, M. S., 47, 50, 96, 140
Goldberger, A. S., 266, 339
Gonzalez, R., 80
Goodnight, J. H., 44, 112, 200
Gottschall, A., 266, 267, 268, 269
Gould, A. L., 52
Graham, J. W., 1, 5, 9, 11, 15, 16, 17, 22, 23, 24,
    27, 28, 29, 31, 36, 49, 51, 55, 56, 83, 87,
    127, 128, 132, 133, 134, 135, 137, 140,
    156, 163, 164, 187, 213, 214, 216, 230,
    233, 259, 260, 270, 286, 287, 289, 290,
    328, 332, 336, 342, 343
Griffin, D., 80
Grizzle, J. E., 22
Groothuis-Oudshoorn, C. G. M., 275
Grusky, O., 261

**H**

Haitovsky, Y., 39
Hancock, G. R., 288, 301, 330, 345
Harel, O., 214, 226
Harlow, L., 43, 96
Hartley, H. O., 86, 110
Hartman, R. S., 296
Hayashi, K., 148
He, Y., 261
Heckman, J. T., 291, 292, 295, 328
Hedeker, D., 15, 30, 307, 308, 309, 317, 318,
    319, 321, 323, 324, 328
Hill, M. A., 39
Hines, C. V., 39, 43, 46
Hinkley, D. V., 98
Hocking, R. R., 86, 110
Hofer, S. M., 5, 16, 132, 140, 289, 328
Hogan, J. W., 309
Hollis, M., 18, 113

Honaker, J., 188, 272, 278, 333
Hops, H., 29
Horton, N. J., 261, 262, 278, 286, 333, 345
Howard, W. J., 271
Hu, L-T., 123, 140, 157, 251
Hu, M-Y., 261
Huber, P., 143

**I**

Ioannidis, J. P. A., 169

**J**

Jackman, S., 202
Jamshidian, M., 104
Jeffreys, H., 176
Johnson, E. G., 22
Johnson, R. A., 71
Johnson, V. E., 203
Jöreskog, K. G., 49, 50, 330, 332
Joseph, A., 188, 272

**K**

Kam, C-M., 14, 16, 121, 128, 163, 201, 227,
    336, 341
Kano, Y., 140
Kaplan, D., 18, 113, 123
Kass, R. E., 175
Keel, P. K., 51
Kenward, M. G., 6, 97, 99, 102, 126, 145, 303,
    304, 305, 307, 309, 315
Kim, J., 39, 43
Kim, K. H., 18
King, C. V., 51
King, G., 188, 272, 273, 278, 333
Kirby, J., 30
Kline, R. B., 81, 117, 123, 134, 137
Krishnan, T., 104
Kromrey, J. D., 39, 43, 46

**L**

Laird, N. M., 1, 86, 102, 126, 298, 307, 309
Lambert, P. L., 332
Lavori, P. W., 188, 272
Lawrence, F. R., 288, 301
Lee, M. D., 164, 186
Lee, S-Y., 18
Leite, W. L., 259
Lepkowski, J. M., 188, 261
Leung, S. F., 296

Lewis, S. M., 209, 212
Li, K. H., 235, 236, 239, 240, 246
Liang, J., 104
Lipsey, M. W., 169
Lipsitz, S. R., 261, 278, 286, 333, 345
Little, R. J. A., 1, 2, 5, 6, 9, 18, 19, 20, 21, 32,
    35, 36, 37, 40, 41, 42, 43, 44, 46, 47, 48,
    49, 53, 55, 86, 97, 99, 102, 103, 106,
    110, 112, 147, 164, 185, 200, 202, 219,
    274, 291, 298, 299, 304, 305, 306, 307,
    308, 328
Little, T. D., 271
Liu, G., 52
Lord, F. M., 22, 86

**M**

MacKinnon, D. P., 5, 16, 132, 140, 289, 309,
    328
Mallinckrodt, C. H., 52
Manning, W. G., 296
Marcoulides, G. A., 309
Mare, R. D., 291, 295
Marsh, H. W., 41, 42
McConnell, E. K., 271
McCoy, S., 288
McCrady, B., 51
McCutcheon, A. L., 268
McLachlan, G. J., 104, 268
Mehta, P. D., 303
Meng, X-L., 110, 227, 229, 239, 240, 241, 251
Micceri, T., 140, 259
Michiels, B., 305, 307, 312
Min, C-K., 203
Mitchell, J. E., 51
Moinpour, C., 288
Molenberghs, G., 52, 97, 99, 102, 126,
    145, 288, 304, 305, 307, 308, 309,
    312, 322
Montague, M., 16, 132
Montgomery, D. C., 21
Mueller, R. O., 330, 345
Muthén, B., 18, 96, 104, 113, 268
Muthén, B. O., 30, 322, 330, 332, 345
Muthén, L. K., 30, 322, 330, 332, 345
Mykland, P., 203

**N**

Nawata, K., 296
Nelson, F. D., 296
Nesselroade, J. R., 29
Newman, D. A., 47, 230

**O**

Olchowski, A. E., 15, 36, 132, 213, 216, 233, 342, 343
Olinsky, A., 43, 46, 96
Olkin, I., 274
Olmsted, M. P., 32, 119, 157, 247, 281
Olsen, M. K., 164, 204, 212, 216, 253, 259, 261, 278, 333, 345
Orchard, T., 86, 103

**P**

Paarsch, H. J., 296
Pampel, F. C., 294, 303
Park, T., 18
Parzen, M., 261
Pauler, D. K., 288
Pawitan, Y., 79
Paxton, P., 30
Pearson, K., 21
Peel, D., 268
Peugh, J. L., 1, 37, 39, 41, 55, 104, 120, 134, 329, 340
Pruzek, R. M., 164, 186
Puhani, P. A., 291, 295, 296

**Q**

Quan, H., 305

**R**

Raftery, A. E., 209, 212
Raghunathan, T. E., 22, 188, 235, 236, 239, 246, 261, 275, 276, 278, 333
Raudenbush, S. W., 5, 80, 104, 276, 288, 301, 303
Raykov, T., 309
Raymond, M. R., 43, 46
Relles, D. A., 295, 296
Ritter, C., 203
Roberts, D. M., 43, 46
Roberts, G. O., 203, 212
Rogers, W. H., 296
Royston, P., 188, 278, 333
Rubin, D. B., 1, 2, 3, 5, 6, 9, 10, 11, 12, 13, 14, 17, 18, 21, 35, 36, 37, 43, 44, 47, 49, 53, 55, 86, 93, 96, 97, 99, 102, 106, 110, 112, 126, 128, 133, 147, 164, 169, 185, 186, 187, 190, 200, 201, 202, 203, 209, 212, 213, 214, 216, 217, 219, 221, 222, 224, 228, 229, 230, 231, 232, 234, 235, 239, 240, 241, 244, 246, 249, 251, 252, 259, 261, 275, 289, 290, 291, 298, 312, 343
Rupp, A. A., 164, 186
Russell, D., 164, 216, 253, 261

**S**

Sackett, P. R., 21
Satorra, A., 140, 148, 149
Savalei, V., 133, 134, 139, 140, 148
Schafer, J. L., 1, 4, 9, 11, 14, 15, 16, 17, 36, 49, 51, 55, 56, 83, 87, 121, 127, 128, 131, 132, 163, 164, 185, 186, 187, 188, 201, 204, 205, 206, 209, 212, 214, 216, 220, 226, 227, 228, 230, 233, 253, 259, 260, 261, 268, 272, 274, 275, 277, 278, 286, 287, 288, 289, 300, 307, 308, 312, 322, 326, 328, 333, 336, 337, 341, 342, 343, 344, 345
Schenker, N., 231, 259
Scheuren, F., 5, 49
Scheve, K., 188, 272
Schluchter, M. D., 274, 305, 306
Shao, J., 52
Share, D., 51
Shedden, K., 104
Shera, D., 188, 272
Shih, W. J., 305
Shneyer, L., 307
Shoemaker, D. M., 22
Sijtsma, K., 261, 269
Singer, J. D., 288, 301
Sinharay, S., 164, 216, 253, 261
Smith, A. F. M., 212, 277
Sobel, M. E., 140, 145
Solenberger, P., 188, 261
Solenberger, P. W., 278, 333
Sörbom, D., 49, 50, 330, 332
Srivastava, M. S., 150
Staelin, R., 43, 46
Stephenson, B., 164
Stern, H. S., 164, 186, 216, 228, 253, 261
Stine, R. A., 140, 145, 150, 151, 163
Stolzenberg, R. M., 295, 296
Stump, K. N., 271

**T**

Tabachnick, B. G., 71, 260
Tanner, M. A., 186, 188, 203
Tate, R. F., 274
Taylor, B. J., 15, 22, 36, 132, 342
Thijs, H., 305, 307, 322
Thoemmes, F., 18, 21

Thompson, J. S., 138
Thompson, S. G., 52, 55
Tibshirani, R. J., 145
Tierney, L., 203
Timm, N. H., 43, 46
Trawinksi, I. M., 110
Tu, X. M., 30, 305, 306

**V**

van Buuren, S., 188, 275, 276
Van der Ark, L. A., 261, 269
Van Ginkel, J. R., 261, 269
Van Guilder, M., 39
Van Hoewyk, J., 188, 261, 278, 333
Vangeneugden, T., 305
Verbeke, G., 288, 304, 307, 308, 312, 322
Vermunt, J. K., 269
von Hippel, P. T., 113

**W**

Wagenmakers, E-J., 164, 186
Wasserman, L., 175
Waternaux, C., 30
West, S., 21, 80, 124, 140, 261, 264, 265, 266,
    280, 303, 338
White, H., 141, 143, 145
White, I. R., 52, 55
Wichern, D. W., 71
Widaman, K. F., 138
Wilkinson, L., 1, 13, 37, 39, 340
Wilks, S. S., 42

Willett, J. B., 288, 301
Wilson, D. B., 169
Winship, C., 291, 295
Wong, W. H., 186, 188
Wood, A. M., 52, 55
Woodbury, M. A., 86, 103
Wothke, W., 39, 41, 43, 96
Wright, T. A., 80, 114, 154, 242, 279
Wu, E. J. C., 330, 331
Wu, M. C., 305, 306
Wu, W., 262

**Y**

Yang, H., 21
Yi, G. Y., 52
Young, A. S., 261
Yu, B., 203
Yu, S., 296
Yuan, K-H., 104, 133, 134, 140, 141, 143, 145,
    148, 149, 163, 278, 332
Yucel, R. M., 259, 261, 262, 263, 268, 277, 278,
    337
Yung, Y. F., 148

**Z**

Zaslavsky, A. M., 261
Zellner, A., 203
Zeng, L., 52
Zhang, W., 140, 163
Zhong, B., 52
Zumbo, B. D., 164, 186

# Subject Index

*Note.* "f" following a page number indicates a figure; "t" following a page number indicates a table.

Acceptance-rejection algorithm, 273
Accuracy of a maximum likelihood analysis. *see also* Maximum likelihood estimation
    auxiliary variables, 128–134, 130*t*, 131*f*
    example of a data analysis, 154–161, 155*t*, 156*t*, 158*f*, 159*f*, 161*t*
    inclusive analysis strategy and, 127–129
    non-normal data and, 140
    overview, 127, 161–163
    rescaled likelihood ratio test, 148–149
    saturated correlates model, 134–140, 135*f*, 136*f*, 139*f*
    standard errors, 141–145, 144*t*, 145–148, 146*t*
Adaptive rounding, 262
Alternate imputation algorithms, 272–278. *see also* EM algorithm
AMOS software, 330–331, 331*t*
Analysis phase. *see also* Multiple imputation
    corrective procedures, 261
    examples of, 242–251, 243*f*, 245*t*, 247*t*, 249*f*, 250*t*, 280–281, 281*t*, 283, 284*t*
    overview, 215–216, 217–219, 218*t*, 252
    *t*-test approach and, 231–232
Analytic techniques
    example of, 32–35, 34*t*
    inclusive analysis strategy, 16–17, 17*f*
    missing data mechanism and, 13–14
    overview, 35
    power analyses for planned missing data and, 30–32
ANOVA analysis, 223–224

Arithmetic mean imputation, 42–43, 43*f*, 53, 54*t*. *see also* Single imputation methods
Augmentation algorithm, 188
Autocorrelation function plots, 207–209, 207*t*, 208*f*
Auxiliary variables
    accuracy of a maximum likelihood analysis, 161–163
    computer simulation, 129–131, 130*t*, 131*f*, 332–333
    example of a data analysis, 155–156, 156*t*, 157–161, 158*f*, 159*f*, 161*t*
    identifying a set of, 131–133
    inclusive analysis strategy and, 16–17, 128–129
    reporting results from a data analysis and, 341
    saturated correlates model, 134–140, 135*f*, 136*f*, 139*f*
Available case missing variable restriction, 309
Available-case analysis. *see* Pairwise deletion
Average relative increase in variance, 235
Averaging the available items technique, 50–51

**B**

Bayes' theorem, 170–171, 177–179, 178*f*
Bayesian estimation
    Bayes' theorem, 170–171
    data analysis example, 171–175, 172*t*
    imputation phase and, 191–194, 192*f*
    multiple imputation and, 175–176, 275–276
    overview, 163, 164–170, 166*f*, 167*f*, 168*f*, 185–186

Bayesian estimation (*continued*)
  posterior distribution of the mean and, 176–185, 177*f*, 178*f*, 180*f*, 181*f*, 182*f*, 184*f*
  P-step and, 190–191, 195–196, 257
Beta distribution, 171
Between-imputation variance, 211, 222–224, 234–235
Bias, 43, 48, 137, 293–294
Biased parameter estimates, 53, 54*t*
Binary variables, 172–173, 261–264, 263*t*
Binomial density function, 172–173
Bivariate analysis
  analysis and pooling phase and, 224
  Bollen–Stine bootstrap, 151–153, 152*t*, 153*f*
  bootstrap standard errors, 147
  EM algorithm and, 105–110, 108*t*, 109*t*, 110*t*
  example of, 73–75, 74*t*, 106–110, 108*t*, 109*t*, 110*t*
  maximum likelihood missing data handling and, 99–102, 101*t*
  multiple imputation and, 194–199, 196*t*, 198*t*, 199*t*
  pooling process and, 219, 220*t*, 221
  robust standard errors and, 144–145, 144*t*
  *t*-test approach and, 232
Bivariate normal distribution, 69, 70*f*, 71, 71*f*
Bollen–Stine bootstrap. *see also* Bootstrap resampling approach
  example of a data analysis, 157–161, 158*f*, 159*f*, 161*t*
  overview, 150–154, 152*t*, 153*f*, 162
Bootstrap resampling approach
  likelihood ratio test statistic, 150–154, 152*t*, 153*f*
  overview, 145–146, 162
  stochastic regression imputation and, 48
Bootstrap standard errors, 145–148, 146*t*, 154–155, 155*t*
Burn-in period, 211

**C**

Calibration, 262–264, 263*t*
Categorical variable, 266–267, 274–276
Central chi-square distribution, 157–159, 159*f*. *see also* Chi-square distribution
Chained equations, 275–276
Chi-square distribution
  Bayesian estimation, 180
  Bollen–Stine bootstrap, 153*f*
  example of a data analysis, 157–159, 159*f*
  likelihood estimation, 82–83, 148–149

Chi-square of model fit, 78–79, 241–242
Classic selection model, 291–295, 292*f*, 327
Cohen's approach, 31
Cohort-sequential design, 29–30, 30*t*
Collinearity problems, 296–298, 298*t*
Comparative Fit Index (CFI), 138, 139*f*
Complete case missing variable restriction, 299, 323–324
Complete data, 9–10, 10*t*, 38–39, 38*f*, 104, 123–124, 124*t*
Complete-case analysis. *see* Listwise deletion
Complete-case regression, 47
Computer simulation
  auxiliary variables, 129–131, 130*t*, 131*f*
  example of, 52–54, 54*t*
  maximum likelihood missing data handling and, 95–97, 96*t*, 102–103, 103*t*
  Monte Carlo power simulations, 30–32, 52–54, 54*t*
  multiple imputation and, 197, 213–214, 229–230, 230*t*, 261–262
  stochastic regression imputation and, 47
Computer software
  bivariate analysis, 73–75, 74*t*
  Bollen–Stine bootstrap, 154
  delta method, 310–311
  example of a data analysis that uses the EM algorithm, 117, 120–121
  LISREL software package, 49–50
  maximum likelihood estimation and, 80, 81–82, 112–113, 329–333, 331*t*
  multiple imputation and, 278–279, 333–336, 334*t*
  pairwise deletion, 41–42
  similar response pattern imputation and, 49–50
Conditional distribution, 192
Conditional expectations, 106
Conditional mean imputation. *see* Regression imputation
Conditional means, 192–193, 192*f*
Confidence interval coverage rates
  bootstrap standard errors, 147
  example of a computer simulation, 53–54
  maximum likelihood missing data handling and, 96–97, 102–103, 103*t*
Confidence intervals, 232
Confirmatory factor analysis
  example of a data analysis, 123–124, 124*t*, 157–161, 158*f*, 159*f*, 161*t*
  iterative optimization algorithms and, 75–76
  multiple imputation and, 247–251, 249*f*, 250*t*, 251

Congenial models, 227

Continuous variables, 274–276

Convergence
   assessing from alternate starting values, 209
   multiple imputation and, 202–204, 215,
      242–243, 243*f*, 254–258, 255*t*, 256*f*,
      259*f*
   problems in, 210–211, 210*f*

Convergence criterion, 104

Correlation coefficient, 41

Correlation matrix
   example of a data analysis that uses the EM
      algorithm, 113–114, 114*t*
   maximum likelihood estimation and, 80, 81*t*
   multiple imputation and, 242–244, 243*f*,
      245*t*

Correlation power estimates, 25–26, 26*t*. *see also*
   Power

Correlogram. *see* Autocorrelation function plots

Covariance matrix
   auxiliary variables, 133–134
   Bayesian estimation, 186
   bivariate analysis and, 196, 198
   Bollen–Stine bootstrap, 152, 152*t*
   EM algorithm and, 104–106
   example of, 52–54, 54*t*, 82–83, 113–114, 114*t*,
      119–122, 120*t*, 121*f*, 122–124, 122*t*, 123*t*,
      124*t*
   I-step, 215
   iterative optimization algorithms and, 76
   maximum likelihood estimation and, 80, 81*t*
   multiple imputation and, 242–244, 243*f*, 245*t*,
      284*t*
   pairwise deletion and, 41
   pooling process and, 234–235
   posterior distribution of, 183–184, 184*f*
   ridge prior distribution for, 210–211
   three-form design and, 24–25, 25*t*

Covariances, 18

Cumulative standard normal distribution, 294


**D**

$D_1$ statistic, 233–239, 238*t*, 252

$D_2$ statistic, 239–240, 252

$D_3$ statistic, 240–242, 250–251, 252

Data analysis. *see also* Analytic techniques
   example of, 32–35, 34*t*, 80–83, 81*t*, 82*f*, 83*t*
   maximum likelihood estimation and, 56
   overview, 35
   power analyses for planned missing data and,
      30–32

Data augmentation
   bivariate analysis and, 194–199, 196*t*, 198*t*,
      199*t*
   computer software options and, 334–335
   convergence and, 202, 202–203, 209, 210–211,
      210*f*
   EMIS algorithm and, 273–274
   general location model, 274–275
   generating the final set of imputations, 211–212
   multiple imputation and, 282, 284–285
   multivariate data and, 199–200, 200*t*
   non-normal data and, 259
   overview, 190
   ridge prior distribution and, 258

Deletion methods, 39–42, 40*f*, 120–121

Delta method, 309–312, 320–321, 326

Density function, 57. *see also* Probability density
   function

Derivative values, 74–75, 310

Diggle and Kenward selection model
   examples of, 315–317, 316*f*, 317*t*
   overview, 303–304, 304*f*

Direct maximum likelihood, 86

Distribution of missing data, 9–10, 10*t*, 11–12,
   12*f*

Dummy variables, 264, 264*t*

Duplicate-scale imputation, 270–271, 281–283


**E**

Eating Attitudes Test (EAT)
   data analysis example, 32–35, 34*t*, 119–122,
      120*t*, 121*f*, 122*t*, 123*t*, 157–161, 158*f*,
      159*f*, 161*t*
   multiple imputation and, 247–251, 249*f*, 250*t*,
      281–283

EM algorithm
   bootstrap resampling approach, 154–155, 155*t*
   computer software options and, 332, 334
   convergence and, 203–204
   example of, 106–110, 108*t*, 109*t*, 110*t*,
      113–124, 114*t*, 116*f*, 117*t*, 119*f*, 120*t*,
      121*f*, 122*t*, 123*t*, 124*t*
   multiple imputation and, 242, 254–255,
      272–274
   multivariate data and, 110–112, 111*t*
   overview, 103–106, 125–126
   software options for, 113
   worst linear function of the parameters, 206

EM with importance sampling (EMIS), 273–274.
   *see also* EM algorithm

EM with sampling (EMS), 272–273

Empirical sampling distribution, 31
EQS software, 154, 331–332, 331*t*
E-step
  example of, 107–110, 108*t*, 109*t*
  multivariate data and, 110–112
  overview, 104–106, 125–126
Estimating unknown parameters, 60–62, 61*t*, 62*f*,
    63*f*. *see also* Maximum likelihood estimation
Estimation, 92–94, 92*t*, 95*t*, 97
Expectation maximization (EM) algorithm, 86
Expected information matrix, 98–99, 102–103,
    103*t*
Exploratory factor analysis, 121–122, 122*t*, 123*t*
Extra dependent variable model, 133–134

**F**

Factor analysis, 121–122, 122*t*, 123*t*
Finite mixtures, 104
First derivative, 63–65, 64*f*, 73–74, 141–142
Fisher's information matrix. *see* Information
    matrix
Fraction of missing information, 204–205,
    224–226
Fractional factorial design, 21–22
Frequentist paradigm, 165
Full information maximum likelihood, 86, 113
Full model, 78–79
Fully conditional specification, 275–276

**G**

General location model, 274–275
General missing data pattern, 4–5, 4*f*
Gibbs sampler, 277–278
Graham's rules, 134–135, 135*f*, 332–333

**H**

Hedeker and Gibbons model, 307–308, 317–321,
    319*t*, 320*t*
Hessian matrix, 74–75, 74*f*, 97, 99
Homogeneity of means and covariances, 18
Hot-deck imputation, 49. *see also* Single imputation
    methods

**I**

Identifying restrictions, 299
Ignorable missingness, 13
Implicit interaction effects, 267–268. *see also*
    Interaction effects

Imputation, 42, 113, 201–202. *see also* Multiple
    imputation; Single imputation methods
Imputation phase. *see also* Multiple imputation
  Bayesian description of, 191–194, 192*f*
  example of, 280, 282–283
  multiple imputation and, 242–244, 243*f*
  normalizing transformations, 260
  overview, 187–191, 188*f*, 189*t*
  quantitative variables and, 266–269
  reporting results from a data analysis and,
      342–343
  selecting variables for, 201–202
Imputation step (I-step). *see* I-step
Inclusive analysis strategy. *see also* Analytic
    techniques
  accuracy of a maximum likelihood analysis,
      127–129, 161–162
  example of a data analysis that uses the EM
      algorithm, 121–122, 122*t*, 123*t*
  inclusive analysis strategy and, 128–129
  multiple imputation and, 201–202
  overview, 16–17, 17*f*
Incremental fit indices, 137–138
Independence model, 137–138
Information matrix
  estimating standard errors and, 97
  maximum likelihood missing data handling
      and, 101*t*, 102–103, 103*t*
  overview, 74*f*, 75, 100–101
  robust standard errors, 142–143
Interaction effects
  maximum likelihood estimation and,
      338–339
  multiple imputation and, 265–269, 279–281,
      281*t*
  three-form design and, 27–28, 28*t*
Intercept, 302–303, 302*f*
Inverse chi-square distribution, 180
Inverse Wishart distribution, 183–184
I-step
  autocorrelation function plots, 207–209,
      207*t*, 208*f*
  Bayesian estimation and, 191–193, 192*f*
  bivariate analysis and, 197, 198*t*
  convergence and, 209, 210–211, 210*f*
  general location model and, 274–275
  generating the final set of imputations,
      211–212
  multivariate data and, 200, 200*t*
  non-normal data and, 259–261
  overview, 190, 214–215
  time-series plots and, 204–206, 205*f*, 206*f*

Item-level imputation, 271–272
Iterative optimization algorithms, 75–76

**J**

Jeffreys' prior, 176, 181, 181*f*, 184, 185, 186

**L**

Last observation carried forward technique,
    51–52, 52*t*. *see also* Single imputation
    methods
Latent categorical variables, 268–269
Latent growth curve model, 302–303, 302*f*
Latent variable pattern, 4*f*, 5, 113, 135–137, 330
Latent variable regression analysis, 135–137
Likelihood function
    Bayesian estimation and, 166–167, 167*f*,
        170–171, 179–181, 180*f*
    data analysis example, 172–173, 172*t*
    posterior distribution of the mean and,
        176–177, 177*t*, 179–181, 180*f*, 183–184,
        184*f*
Likelihood ratio test statistic. *see also* Maximum
        likelihood estimation
    bootstrap resampling approach, 150–154, 152*t*,
        153*f*
    chi-square test of model fit and, 241–242
    choosing between the Wald statistic and, 79–80
    example of a data analysis, 158–159
    multiparameter significance tests and, 240–242
    multiple imputation and, 250–251
    non-normal data and, 150–154, 152*t*, 158–159,
        159*f*, 162
    overview, 78–79, 84–85
Likelihood value. *see also* Maximum likelihood
        estimation
    example of a data analysis that uses the EM
        algorithm, 113–114, 114*t*
    overview, 58, 58*f*, 70–71
    rescaled likelihood ratio test, 148–149
Limited information maximum likelihood, 295
LISREL software package, 49–50, 113, 331*t*, 332
Listwise deletion. *see also* Deletion methods
    computer simulation, 54*t*, 95–97, 96*t*
    maximum likelihood missing data handling and,
        92–93
    overview, 39–40, 40*f*, 55
Little's MCAR test, 19–21, 32–33
Log likelihood. *see also* Maximum likelihood
        estimation
    bivariate analysis and, 74–75

EM algorithm and, 109–110, 110*t*
estimating standard errors and, 65–69, 65*f*, 66*f*,
    67*f*
estimating unknown parameters, 61–62, 62*f*,
    63*f*
example of a data analysis, 115–118, 116*f*, 117*t*,
    118, 122–124, 124*t*, 158–159
identifying maximum likelihood estimates,
    72–73, 73*f*
iterative optimization algorithms and, 76
maximum likelihood missing data handling and,
    88–92, 91*t*, 93–94, 95*t*
multivariate normal log-likelihood, 71–72, 73*f*
overview, 60, 84–85
robust standard errors and, 141–142
sample likelihood and, 59*t*
second derivative and, 68–69
Log-likelihood function for the mean
    estimating unknown parameters, 61–62, 62*f*,
        63*f*
    first derivative and, 63–65, 64*f*
    second derivative and, 68–69
Longitudinal designs
    last observation carried forward technique,
        51–52, 52*t*
    missing not at random (MNAR) data and,
        312–314, 312*f*, 314*f*
    patterns mixture model, 306–309
    planned missing data and, 28–30, 28*t*, 29*t*, 30*t*
    reporting results from a data analysis and, 342
Longitudinal growth model, 301–303, 302*f*

**M**

*m* sampling variances, 218, 221–223
*m* statistical analyses, 215–216, 232–233
Mahalanobis distance, 57, 58, 71, 123
Manifest variable models, 134–135, 135*f*
Marginal distribution, 174–175
Marginal parameter estimate, 300
Markov chain Monte Carlo algorithm, 202–203
Maximum likelihood estimation. *see also* Accuracy
        of a maximum likelihood analysis; Maximum
        likelihood missing data handling
    auxiliary variables, 133–134, 161–162
    bivariate analysis, 73–75, 74*t*
    bootstrap resampling approach, 155–156,
        156*t*
    choosing between multiple imputation and,
        336–340
    computer software options for, 329–333, 331*t*
    convergence and, 203–204

Maximum likelihood estimation (*continued*)
  data augmentation and, 195
  EM algorithm, 115–118, 116*f*, 117*t*, 118–119,
      119*f*, 120*t*, 121–122, 122*t*, 123–124, 123*t*,
      124*t*
  estimating standard errors and, 65–69, 65*f*, 66*f*,
      67*f*
  estimating unknown parameters, 60–62, 61*t*,
      62*f*, 63*f*
  example of, 33, 80–83, 81*t*, 82*f*, 83*t*, 115–118,
      116*f*, 117*t*, 118–119, 119*f*, 120*t*, 121–122,
      122*t*, 123–124, 123*t*, 124*t*
  first derivative and, 63–65, 64*f*
  identifying, 72–73
  iterative optimization algorithms, 75–76
  likelihood ratio test statistic, 78–79
  log-likelihood, 60
  maximum likelihood missing data handling and,
      92–94, 92*t*, 95*t*, 125–126
  missing not at random (MNAR) data and,
      314–315, 315*t*
  Monte Carlo power simulations and, 31
  multiple imputation and, 214, 227–229, 228*f*,
      284
  with multivariate normal data, 69–73, 70*f*, 71*f*,
      73*f*
  overview, 1–2, 35, 56, 83–85, 125–126
  probability density function and, 57–58
  reporting results from, 340–343
  sample likelihood, 59–60
  selection model and, 297
  significance testing using the Wald statistic,
      77–78
  software options for, 112–113
  univariate normal distribution, 56–58, 57*t*, 58*f*
Maximum likelihood missing data handling. *see
    also* Maximum likelihood estimation
  bivariate analysis, 99–102, 101*t*
  computer simulation, 95–97, 96*t*, 102–103,
      103*t*
  EM algorithm and, 103–110, 108*t*, 109*t*, 110*t*,
      113–124, 114*t*, 116*f*, 117*t*, 119*f*, 120*t*,
      121*f*, 122*t*, 123*t*, 124*t*
  estimating standard errors and, 97
  estimation and, 92–94, 92*t*, 95*t*
  examples of, 113–124, 114*t*, 116*f*, 117*t*, 119*f*,
      120*t*, 121*f*, 122*t*, 123*t*, 124*t*
  log-likelihood, 88–92, 91*t*
  observed vs. expected information and, 98–99
  overview, 86–88, 87*t*, 125–126
  rationale for, 127
  software options for, 112–113

Mean vector
  auxiliary variables, 133–134
  Bayesian estimation, 178–179, 186
  bivariate analysis and, 196, 198
  Bollen–Stine bootstrap, 152*t*
  EM algorithm and, 104–106
  example of a data analysis that uses the EM
      algorithm, 113–114, 114*t*
  I-step, 215
  maximum likelihood estimation and, 80, 81*t*
  multiple imputation and, 242–244, 243*f*, 245*t*,
      284*t*
Mediation analysis model, 227–229, 228*f*
Mill's ratio, 295
Missing at random (MAR) data
  auxiliary variables, 132, 137
  computer simulation, 95–97, 96*t*
  data analysis example, 32–35, 34*t*
  distribution of missing data, 9–10, 10*t*
  example of, 52–54, 54*t*, 160
  inclusive analysis strategy and, 16–17, 17*f*,
      128
  maximum likelihood missing data handling
      and, 87, 125–126
  missing data mechanism and, 13–14
  multiple imputation and, 229–230, 230*t*
  overview, 6, 7*t*, 37–39, 38*f*, 343–344
  planned missing data and, 21–23
  plausibility of, 14–16, 15*f*
  stochastic regression imputation and, 46
Missing completely at random (MCAR) data
  auxiliary variables, 130, 132, 137
  computer simulation, 95–97, 96*t*
  data analysis example, 32–35, 34*t*
  deletion methods and, 39
  estimating standard errors and, 97
  example of a computer simulation, 52–54, 54*t*
  inclusive analysis strategy and, 16–17, 17*f*
  interaction effects and, 265–266
  listwise deletion and, 39–40, 40*f*
  maximum likelihood estimation and, 87,
      125–126
  missing data mechanism and, 13–14
  multiple imputation and, 229–230, 230*t*
  overview, 7–8, 7*t*, 37
  planned missing data and, 21–23
  regression imputation and, 45–46
  testing, 17–21
Missing data patterns, 2–5, 3*f*, 4*f*. *see also* Pattern
    mixture model
Missing data theory
  mathematical details of, 9–12, 10*t*, 12*f*

overview, 2, 5–8, 7t, 9–12, 10t, 12f, 35
    parameters of, 13–14
Missing not at random (MNAR) data
    computer simulation, 95–97, 96t
    computer software options and, 332–333
    data analysis and, 312–314, 312f, 314f
    delta method, 309–312
    examples of, 52–54, 54t, 314–326, 315t, 316f,
        317t, 319t, 320t, 323t, 324t
    inclusive analysis strategy and, 16–17, 17f, 128
    longitudinal designs and, 301–303, 302f,
        303–305, 304f, 306–309
    maximum likelihood estimation and, 87
    missing data mechanism and, 13–14, 14–16,
        15f
    multiple imputation and, 229–230, 230t
    overview, 7t, 8, 287–289, 288t, 326–328,
        343–344
    patterns mixture model, 298–301, 306–309
    random coefficient selection model, 305–306,
        305f
    selection model, 291–297, 292f, 297–298,
        298t
    theoretical rationale for, 290–291
Monotone missing data pattern, 4, 4f, 334–335
Monte Carlo power simulations
    auxiliary variables, 137
    bivariate analysis and, 196–197, 198–199
    bootstrap resampling approach, 162
    example of, 52–54, 54t
    Gibbs sampler, 277–278
    maximum likelihood missing data handling
        and, 102–103, 103t
    multiple imputation and, 272–273
    planned missing data and, 30–32
    ridge prior distribution and, 258
    stochastic regression imputation and, 47
Mplus software, 154, 331t, 332–333
M-step, 104–111, 125–126
Multilevel data, 276–278
Multilevel growth model, 301–302
Multilevel models, 104, 276–278
Multiparameter inference, 233
Multiparameter significance tests, 233, 239–240,
    240–242
Multiple explorator chains, 209
Multiple imputation. see also Analysis phase;
    Imputation; Imputation phase; Pooling phase
    alternate imputation algorithms, 272–278
    autocorrelation function plots, 207–209, 207t,
        208f
    Bayesian estimation and, 175–176

bivariate analysis and, 194–199, 196t, 198t,
    199t
choosing between maximum likelihood and,
    336–340
computer simulation and, 229–230, 230t,
    331–332, 331t, 333–336, 334t
convergence and, 209, 210–211, 210f, 254–258,
    255t, 256f, 259f
data augmentation and, 199–200, 200t
examples of, 118–119, 119f, 120t, 242–251,
    243f, 245t, 247t, 249f, 250t, 279–283,
    281t, 284t
generating the final set of imputations,
    211–212
interaction effects, 265–269
maximum likelihood estimation and, 227–229,
    228f
multiple-item questionnaires and, 269–272,
    270t
non-normal data and, 259–261
number of data sets needed, 212–214, 213t
overview, 1–2, 164, 185, 186, 187–188,
    214–216, 252, 254, 283–286
quantitative variables, 266–269
reporting results from, 340–343
rounding and, 261–265, 263t, 264t
selecting variables for, 201–202
software options for, 278–279
time-series plots and, 204–206, 205f, 206f
t-test approach, 230–233
Multiple imputation point estimate, 219
Multiple regression analysis
    auxiliary variables, 155–156, 156t
    example of a data analysis that uses the EM
        algorithm, 115–118, 116f, 117t, 118–119,
        119f, 120t
    iterative optimization algorithms and, 75–76
    maximum likelihood estimation and, 81–83,
        82f, 83t
    multiple imputation and, 245–247, 247t,
        279–281, 281t
Multiple-item questionnaires, 269–272, 270t,
    337–338
Multivariate analyses, 94, 199–200, 200t, 233
Multivariate normal data
    Bayesian estimation, 178–179
    EM algorithm and, 110–112, 111t
    maximum likelihood estimation and, 69–73,
        70f, 71f, 73f, 140
    multiple imputation and, 259
Multivariate normal log-likelihood, 71–72
Multivariate Wald test, 78

**N**

Naïve bootstrap, 145, 150, 152, 159f. *see also*
    Bootstrap standard errors
Naïve rounding, 262, 263
Neighboring case missing variable restriction, 309
Nested models, 78–79
Nominal variables, 284–285
Noninformative prior distribution, 166
Non-normal data
    Bollen–Stine bootstrap, 150–151
    example of a data analysis, 157–161, 158f, 159f,
        161t
    maximum likelihood estimation and, 140, 162
    multiple imputation and, 259–261
Nonpositive definite matrices, 41
NORM software, 333–334, 334t
Normalizing transformations, 260
Null hypothesis, 152
Null model, 137–138, 150


**O**

Observed data, 9
Observed information, 98–99, 100–101, 101t,
    102–103, 103t
Omnibus $F$ test, 156
Ordinal variables, 284–285
Out-of-range imputations, 265
Output analysis, 203


**P**

Pairwise deletion, 40–42, 55, 106–107. *see also*
    Deletion methods
Parallel data augmentation chains, 212
Parameter covariance matrix
    computer software options and, 334
    maximum likelihood missing data handling and,
        100–101, 101t
    missing not at random (MNAR) data and,
        325–326
    overview, 75, 75f
    robust standard errors and, 144–145, 144t
Parameter estimates
    example of a computer simulation, 53, 54t
    pooling process and, 220–221, 234
    selection model and, 296–297
Pattern mixture model
    examples of, 317–321, 319t, 320t, 321–326,
        323t, 324t
    limitations of, 300–301

longitudinal analyses and, 306–307
    missing not at random (MNAR) data and, 290,
        298–301
Patterns, missing data. *see* Missing data patterns
Pearson's correlation coefficient, 220–221
Person mean imputation, 51. *see also* Single
        imputation methods
Planned missing data
    for longitudinal designs, 28–30, 28t, 29t, 30t
    overview, 2, 21–23, 35–36
    power analyses for, 30–32
    reporting results from a data analysis and,
        341–342
Planned missing data pattern, 4f, 5
Pooling phase. *see also* Multiple imputation
    $D_1$ statistic and, 233–239, 238t
    $D_2$ statistic and, 239–240
    $D_3$ statistic and, 240–242
    examples of, 242–251, 243f, 245t, 247t, 249f,
        250t, 280–281, 281t, 283, 284t
    overview, 187–188, 214, 215–216, 252
    parameter estimates and, 219, 220–221, 220t
    standard errors, 221–224
    $t$-test approach and, 231–232
    Wald tests and, 239–240
Population mean, 177–178, 178f
Population regression coefficient, 150, 152
Posterior distribution
    Bayesian estimation and, 170–171, 173–174,
        177–185, 178f, 180f, 181–182, 181f, 182f,
        184f, 185
    bivariate analysis and, 196, 198
    data analysis example, 172t
    marginal distribution and, 174–175
    overview, 167–169, 168f
    ridge prior distribution and, 258
Posterior distribution of the mean, 176–179, 177t,
        178f
Posterior predictive distribution, 192, 192f
Posterior step (P-step). *see* P-step
Power
    multiple imputation and, 213–214
    planned missing data and, 30–32
    scale-level imputation and, 270
    three-form design and, 24–27, 24t, 25t, 26t
Power analyses, 30–32
Power simulation, 30–32
Prior distribution. *see also* Bayesian estimation
    Bayes' theorem, 170–171
    Bayesian estimation and, 181, 184
    data analysis example, 171–175, 172t
    overview, 166, 169–170

Probability density function, 56–58, 57t, 58f
Probability theory, 59
Probit regression model, 294–295
Prorated scale score. *see* Person mean
    imputation
P-step
    Bayesian estimation, 193–194, 257
    bivariate analysis and, 195–196
    convergence and, 202–203
    general location model and, 274–275
    multiple imputation and, 242, 248
    non-normal data and, 259–261
    overview, 190–191, 215
    time-series plots and, 204–206, 205f, 206f

**Q**

Quantitative variables, 266–269
Questionnaire data
    averaging the available items, 51
    data analysis example, 32–35, 34t
    longitudinal designs and, 28–30, 28t, 29t, 30t
    multiple imputation and, 269–272, 270t,
        337–338
    planned missing data and, 22, 28–30, 28t, 29t,
        30t, 35
    three-form design and, 23–28, 23t, 24t, 25t,
        26t, 28t

**R**

Regression analysis
    example of a data analysis, 115–118, 116f,
        117t, 155–156, 156t
    iterative optimization algorithms and, 75–76
    latent variable models, 135–137
    maximum likelihood estimation and, 81–83,
        82f, 83t
Regression imputation. *see also* Single imputation
    methods
    EM algorithm and, 113
    example of a computer simulation, 52–54, 54t
    overview, 44–46, 45t, 46f
    software options for, 113
    stochastic regression imputation, 46–48, 48f
Regression model
    bootstrap resampling approach, 150
    inclusive analysis strategy and, 128
    multiple imputation and, 246, 279–281, 281t
Relative efficiency, 212–213, 213t
Relative increase in variance, 226
Reliability analysis, 121–122, 122t, 123t

Reporting results from a missing data analysis,
    340–343
Rescaling procedure, 148–149, 158–159
Restricted maximum likelihood, 80, 81t
Restricted model, 78–79
Ridge prior distribution, 210–211, 256–258,
    259f
Robust standard errors, 141–145, 144t. *see also*
    Standard errors
Rounding, 261–265, 263t, 264t
Rubin's Causal Model
    inclusive analysis strategy and, 128
    missing not at random (MNAR) data and, 290
    multiple imputation and, 185
    overview, 214
    planned missing data and, 21–22
    standard errors and, 221–222

**S**

Sample covariance, 41
Sample likelihood, 59–60, 59t. *see also* Maximum
    likelihood estimation
Sample log-likelihood, 60. *see also* Log likelihood
Sampling distribution, 31, 150
Sampling variance, 67–68
Sandwich estimator, 143–144
SAS software, 333, 334–335, 334t
Satorra–Bentler chi-square, 148–149
Saturated correlates model
    accuracy of a maximum likelihood analysis and,
        161–162
    limitations of, 138–140
    overview, 133–134, 134–140, 135f, 136f, 139f
Saturated model, 227
Scale score, 51
Scale-level imputation, 269–271, 270t, 271–272,
    281–283
Scaling factor, 170–171, 174
Scatter-plot, 38f
Second derivative
    maximum likelihood estimation and, 73–74,
        100
    negative value of, 68–69
    role of, 66–67, 66t
    standard errors and, 74–75, 97, 141–142
Selection model
    estimating, 295
    examples of, 297–298, 298t, 315–317, 316f,
        317t
    limitations of, 296–297
    overview, 291–295, 292f

Sensitivity analysis, 326
Separate-group imputation, 267
Sequential data augmentation chains, 211
Sequential regression imputation, 275–276
Significance testing, 77–78, 152–153
Similar response pattern imputation, 49–50. *see also* Single imputation methods
Simulation process, 30–32. *see also* Computer simulation
Single imputation methods. *see also* Imputation
    arithmetic mean imputation, 42–43, 43*f*
    example of a computer simulation, 52–54, 54*t*
    hot-deck imputation, 49
    last observation carried forward technique, 51–52, 52*t*
    overview, 42, 55
    person mean imputation, 50–51
    regression imputation, 44–46, 45*t*, 46*f*
    similar response pattern imputation, 49–50
    stochastic regression imputation, 46–48, 48*f*
Slope, 302–303, 302*f*
SPSS software package, 113, 333, 334*t*, 335–336
Squared standard error, 75
Standard deviation, 102
Standard error of the mean, 67–68
Standard errors
    accuracy of a maximum likelihood analysis, 141–145, 144*t*
    analysis and pooling phase and, 252
    computer software options and, 334
    EM algorithm, 154–155, 155*t*
    estimating, 65–69, 65*f*, 66*f*, 67*f*
    examples of, 63–65, 64*f*, 73–74, 97, 102–103, 103*t*, 120–121, 160–161, 320–321
    missing not at random (MNAR) data and, 325–326
    pairwise deletion and, 41–42
    parameter covariance matrix, 75
    pooling process and, 221–224
    scale-level imputation and, 270
    significance testing using the Wald statistic, 77–78
Starting values, 76
Stationary distributions, 202
Statistical power. *see* Power
Stochastic regression imputation. *see also* Imputation; Regression imputation; Single imputation methods

example of a computer simulation, 53–54, 54*t*
    I-step and, 190
    maximum likelihood missing data handling and, 96–97
    multiple imputation and, 164
    overview, 46–48, 48*f*
Structural equation modeling
    Bollen–Stine bootstrap, 154
    computer software options and, 330, 330–331, 331*t*
    EM algorithm and, 104
    example of a data analysis that uses the EM algorithm, 117, 122–124, 124*t*
    implicit interaction effects and, 267–268
    interaction effects and, 265
    maximum likelihood estimation and, 81–82, 339
    multiple imputation and, 250–251
    Satorra–Bentler chi-square, 149
    saturated correlates model, 139–140
    similar response pattern imputation and, 49–50
    software options for, 113
Substantive analysis, 313
Substantive regression model, 291–292
Sufficient statistics, 105
Sweep operator, 112

**T**

Three-form design, 23–28, 23*t*, 24*t*, 25*t*, 26*t*, 28*t*
Three-step approach for item-level imputation, 271–272
Three-wave selection model, 304, 304*f*
Time-series plots, 204–206, 205*f*, 206*f*
Total covariance matrix, 235–236, 237
Total parameter covariance matrix, 235
Total sampling variance, 223
*t*-test approach
    auxiliary variables, 132
    data analysis example, 33, 35
    multiple imputation and, 230–233, 246
    overview, 252
    testing MCAR data mechanism and, 18–19
Two-factor model
    example of a data analysis, 123–124, 124*t*, 157, 158–159
    selection model, 291–295, 292*f*
Two-stage approach, 133–134, 161–162
Two-step estimator, 296–297

## U

Uncongenial models, 228
Underidentified pattern mixture models, 299
Unit nonresponse pattern, 3, 4*f*
Univariate density function, 69–70
Univariate normal distribution, 56–58, 57*t*, 58*f*,
    141
Univariate pattern, 3, 4*f*
Univariate *t*-test comparisons, 18–19, 132. *see also*
    *t*-test approach
Univariate Wald test, 77
Unknown mean, 182–183

## W

Wald statistic
    choosing between the likelihood ratio test
        statistic and, 79–80
    example of, 82–83
    multiple parameters and, 239–240
    overview, 77–78, 233
Wishart distribution, 257
Within-imputation covariance matrix, 234
Within-imputation variance, 222, 223–224, 252
Worst linear function of the parameters, 205–206,
    206*f*

# About the Author

**Craig K. Enders, PhD**, is Associate Professor in the Quantitative Psychology concentration in the Department of Psychology at Arizona State University. The majority of his research focuses on analytic issues related to missing data analyses. He also does research in the area of structural equation modeling and multilevel modeling. Dr. Enders is a member of the American Psychological Association and is also active in the American Educational Research Association.